SUDAN
ANCIENT TREASURES

SUDA

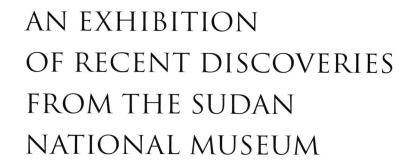

ANCIENT TREASURES

AN EXHIBITION OF RECENT DISCOVERIES FROM THE SUDAN NATIONAL MUSEUM

EDITED BY DEREK A. WELSBY AND JULIE R. ANDERSON

THE BRITISH MUSEUM PRESS

CONTRIBUTORS

CONTENTS

PREFACE

The British Museum has long been involved in the archaeology of Sudan and is proud to have played a part in the foundation, a century ago, of Sudan's first museum, an event fittingly celebrated in this magnificent loan exhibition, *Sudan: Ancient Treasures*.

Offering a unique window on Sudan's remarkable history and the origins of its rich cultural diversity, the exhibition – a selection of representative pieces from the National Museum in Khartoum – covers an extraordinarily long period of time: the earliest objects are 200,000 years old, the most recent date to the nineteenth century AD. The exhibition contains many beautiful things but its aims are not primarily aesthetic. Exploring key places and themes, it illustrates development and change but also impressive continuity. Admirably complementing the larger, universal purpose of the British Museum's permanent collections, *Sudan: Ancient Treasures* adds materially to our understanding of the country's place in the world across thousands of years.

The exhibition forms an integral part of the continuing scholarly collaboration between the British Museum and Sudan's National Corporation for Antiquities and Museums. In bringing the project to fruition, we acknowledge the generous co-operation of HE Mr Abdel Jaleel Al-Basha, Minister of Tourism and National Heritage, and Mr Hassan Hussein Idris Ahmed, Director-General of NCAM. For further encouragement and support, we are much indebted to HE Dr Hasan Abdin, the Sudanese Ambassador to the United Kingdom, and his colleagues, as we are also to HE Mr William Patey, the British Ambassador to Sudan, and members of his staff.

NEIL MacGREGOR
Director, The British Museum

FOREWORD

Cultural relations between Sudan and Britain in the field of archaeology began in AD 1820, when British explorers George Waddington and Barnard Hanbury conducted the first archaeological documentation and excavations at Nuri and Jebel Barkal. Later, in 1897, the Trustees of the British Museum sent Sir E.A.Wallis Budge on an archaeological expedition to Sudan to acquire objects for the British Museum and for the new Museum of Khartoum, which opened in 1904. Between 1910 and 1913, and 1929 and 1936, the Oxford University Mission directed by Professor F.Ll. Griffith and later by L. Kirwan excavated at Faras, Sanam Abu Dom, Kawa and Firka. A second British mission from the Liverpool University Institute of Archaeology led by Professor J. Garstang conducted archaeological work at the Royal City of Meroe, the capital of the Kushite kingdom at Begrawiya. Sudan has stirred the interest of archaeologists from many different countries, and numerous expeditions have since joined the British missions in conducting scientific research for the benefit of the international community.

The exhibition theme, *Sudan: Ancient Treasures, An exhibition of recent discoveries*, was agreed following discussions between British Museum representatives and the Minister of Tourism and National Heritage, as well as with the Director General of the National Corporation for Antiquities and Museums (NCAM), in Khartoum in October 2003. This project is a collaborative effort between NCAM and the British Museum to commemorate the one hundredth anniversary of the first museum in Sudan (1904–2004). The main objectives of the exhibition and catalogue are to show the interconnections between Sudan's ancient cultures and those of its neighbours, to expand scientific research, and to promote the history of Sudan to a worldwide audience. The exhibition is site-orientated and presented in chronological order from the prehistoric period through to Islamic civilization. The objects displayed illustrate the period and site in which they were discovered.

It is hoped that the exhibition will create a greater international public awareness of the cultural heritage of Sudan and increase the public's desire to visit these sites. Increasingly, cultural tourism within Sudan is becoming recognized as offering new and more varied experiences to both Sudanese and foreign tourists. Sudan's ethno-cultural diversity presents a unique cultural context.

The spirit of partnership and cooperation between Sudan and Britain over the last hundred years in the field of archaeology and museums will be furthered by this exhibition to the benefit of both nations and the international community as a whole. I would like to thank the British Embassy in Khartoum, the Sudanese Embassy in London and especially the British Museum staff, in particular Mr Vivian Davies, Keeper of the Department of Ancient Egypt and Sudan, and Dr Derek Welsby, Assistant Keeper in the same department and Honorary Secretary of the Sudan Archaeological Research Society, for the effort they have made in presenting Sudan's cultural heritage in Europe.

HASSAN HUSSEIN IDRIS AHMED
Director General, The National Corporation
for Antiquities and Museums, Sudan

تمهيد

حسن حسين ادريس احمد
مدير عام الهيئة القومية للآثار والمتاحف

ترجع العلاقات الثقافية بين السودان وبريطانيا فى حقل الآثار الى عام 1820 م، عندما قام اثنان من الرحالة البريطانيين هما جورج ودنجتون وبرنارد هنبرى باجراء أول عمليات التسجيل الآثرى والحفائر فى موقعى نورى وجبل البركل. وفيما بعد أرسل أمناء المتحف الريطانى السير والاس بدج الى السودان عام 1897 فى بعثة أثرية بغرض جمع الآثار لحساب المتحف البريطانى و المتحف الجديد فى الخرطوم والذى تم افتتاحه عام 1904.

وفيما بين الأعوام 1910– 1913 و 1929– 1936 قامت بعثة جامعة أكسفورد تحت ادارة ف. جريفث والذى حل محله فبما بعد السير ل. كيروان بالتنقيب فى مناطق فرص، صنم أبو دوم، كوة، وفركة. وقامت بعثة بريطانية ثانية من معهد الآثار فى جامعة ليفربول بقيادة ج. جارستانج بالتنقيب فى المدينة الملكية بمروى، عاصمة مملكة كوش بالبجراوية. ومنذئذ أثارت السودان اهتمام علماء الآثار من بلدان شتى، و انضمت الأن بعثات عديدة الى البعثة البريطانية فى القيام بالبحث العلمى من أجل المجتمع الدولى.

وقد تم الاتفاق على موضوع المعرض "السودان: كنوز عريقة. معرض اكتشافات حديثة"، عقب الحوارات التى دارت فى الخرطوم فى اكتوبر 2003 بين وفد المتحف البريطانى وبين السيد وزير السياحة والتراث القومى والمدير العام للهيئة القومية للآثار والمتاحف (NCAM). ويأتى هذا المشروع كثمرة للتعاون المشترك بين الهيئة القومية للآثار والمتاحف وبين المتحف البريطانى احتفالا بمرور مائة عام على افتتاح أول متحف فى السودان (1904–2004). وتتمثل الأهداف الرئيسية للمعرض والدليل فى توضيح العلاقات المترابطة بين الحضارات القديمة فى السودان وبين حضارات جيرانه، وتوسيع مجال البحث العلمى، وتطوير السياحة فى أنحاء البلاد. وقد تم تنظيم المعرض طبقا للمواقع الأثرية والتى جرى تقديمها في سياق التسلسل التاريخى منذ عصر ماقبل التاريخ حتى الحضارة الاسلامية. وتمثل الآثار المعروضة الفترة الزمنية وموقع العثور عليها خير تمثيل.

ونأمل أن يؤدى المعرض الى زيادة الوعى العام للأسرة الدولية بالتراث الحضارى للسودان واثارة رغبة الجمهور لزيارة هذه المواقع الأثرية. وهناك اعتراف متزايد بأهمية ماتقدمه السياحة الثقافية فى السودان من تجارب جديدة ومتنوعة للسياح السودانين والأجانب على السواء.

يعتبر هذا المعرض خطوة هامة لتطوير آفاق التعاون وروح المشاركة التى سادت بين السودان وبريطانيا عبر قرن من الزمان فى مجال البحث الأثرى والعرض المتحفى وذلك من أجل خير الشعبين والمجتمع الدولى عامة.

وأود هنا التعبير عن شكرى للسفارة البريطانية فى الخرطوم، والسفارة السودانية فى لندن، وتقديرى العميق للعاملين بالمتحف البريطانى وخاصة السيد فيڤيان ديڤيز، أمين قسم الآثار المصرية والسودانية، والدكتور ديريك ويلسبى، الأمين المساعد بنفس القسم والأمين الشرفى لجمعية بحوث الآثار السودانية، وذلك لمابذلوه من جهد مشكور لعرض التراث الحضارى للسودان فى أوروبا.

FOREWORD

Sudan, the largest country in Africa, has a hugely impressive archaeological heritage, but one that is still relatively unrecognized, especially as compared with that of its neighbour, Egypt. For millennia the bridge between the Mediterranean world and sub-Saharan Africa, and once the home of the powerful Kingdom of Kush – Pharaonic Egypt's formidable adversary and sometime conqueror – Sudan contains thousands of ancient sites including several great urban and religious centres, products of a long and fascinating history, the uncovering of which continues apace through the process of archaeological discovery. The result of a joint initiative between the British Museum and the National Corporation for Antiquities and Museums of Sudan, this special exhibition, *Sudan: Ancient Treasures*, is designed to introduce Sudan's history and archaeology to a wider audience, with emphasis on a number of key sites, which have been the subject of systematic investigation in recent years and have yielded especially exciting new information.

The exhibition, containing over 300 antiquities, is unique in that its contents, ranging in date from the Palaeolithic to the early Islamic period, are drawn entirely from Sudan itself – from the rich collections of the National Museum, Khartoum, and its satellite institutions. The majority of the pieces are recent discoveries and most have never previously been seen abroad. Appropriately, the exhibition celebrates an important anniversary, the centenary of Sudan's first museum (the forerunner of the current National Museum), which was opened in 1904. It also marks the British Museum's renewed commitment to the study and promotion of Sudan's indigenous cultures, reflected already in an extensive programme of fieldwork and publication (undertaken with the Sudan Archaeological Research Society), and in a significant change of departmental name: the Museum's Department of Egyptian Antiquities has recently become the Department of Ancient Egypt and Sudan.

The organization of the exhibition has been in the hands of Derek Welsby and Julie Anderson of the Department of Ancient Egypt and Sudan, who have received every co-operation from the staff of NCAM, especially the Director General, Hassan Hussein Idris Ahmed, and his senior colleagues, Siddiq Mohamed Gasm Elseed, Abdel Rahman Ali Mohamed, Salah eldin Mohamed Ahmed and Hyder Hamid Mukhtar. In its preparation, Philippa Pierce, Barbara Wills and staff of the British Museum's Department of Conservation and Scientific Research have played a major role, while its design has been the responsibility of Jon Ould of the Department of Presentation. Additional graphic design for the catalogue was undertaken by Claire Thorne of the Department of Ancient Egypt and Sudan. Drs Welsby and Anderson are also the editors of this accompanying volume, the final production of which has been managed by Laura Brockbank of British Museum Press, proofread by Johanna Stephenson and designed by Harry Green. A collective work, with photographs by Rocco Ricci and the staff of the British Museum's Photographic Department, particularly Sandra Marshall, it draws on the scholarly authority of a large number of colleagues from all over the world for whose contributions we are very grateful. The volume represents not only a comprehensive record of this unique project but a substantial contribution to new knowledge and, we trust, will be of lasting value.

W. V. DAVIES
Keeper, Department of Ancient Egypt and Sudan,
The British Museum

SUDAN NATIONAL MUSEUM, PAST AND PRESENT

SIDDIQ MOHAMED
GASM ELSEED

THE NATIONAL CORPORATION
FOR ANTIQUITIES AND
MUSEUMS, SUDAN

Under Turco–Egyptian rule in Sudan (1821–81), numerous travellers and scholars visited the country and most paid special attention to the archaeological sites. Their pioneering studies and documentation generated interest and formed a foundation for archaeological work in the country which, in turn, ultimately resulted in the creation of a museum to house this material. The beginning of condominium rule by the British and Egyptians (1899), and the creation of Gordon Memorial College in 1902 in Khartoum, marked a new era in the history of Sudan. The first museum in Sudan, the Khartoum Museum, was founded there shortly afterwards, and although small, was a sound beginning.

J.W. Crowfoot was nominated to look after the museum. However, his primary job as Inspector of Education did not allow him to devote much time to archaeological and museum work. Peter Drummond succeeded Crowfoot and he paid great attention to archaeological work, which resulted in an increase in the museum's collections. He states clearly in one of his reports that it was 'high time' to start looking for an adequate area to build a museum to house these collections. Despite Drummond's report, little progress was made towards the development of the museum, although archaeological excavations continued. The outbreak of the First World War halted all work related to the museum, and Drummond was transferred to another job. F. Addison took over and was the first to issue a museum guide and rearrange the displays in new showcases. In 1931 G.W. Grabham succeeded Addison. Although there had been little change in the buildings and collections themselves, the museum was very active and gaining increasing attention from the public to whom it was opened in 1932.

The turning point in the history of the museum and for Sudanese antiquities came in 1939, when a permanent post for antiquities was created under the name 'Commissioner for Archaeology', and a separate budget granted. A.J. Arkell was the first to fill this post full-time. Arkell concentrated his efforts on the development of the museum and its role within the community. He was supported in this endeavour by L.P. Kirwan, another British archaeologist. Unfortunately the outbreak of the Second World War halted this work, particularly when the Gordon College buildings were occupied by the military. Arkell left government service in 1948, after the establishment of the Flinders Petrie Library and the creation of a plan for a permanent museum in a more suitable place. P.L. Shinnie succeeded Arkell as the Commissioner for Archaeology.

An important amendment to the Antiquities Service Ordinance was made in 1952, giving the museum board legal status. An organizational structure was created to administer the museum and the various departments of the Khartoum Museum were incorporated into a single museum renamed the Sudan Museum. H.N. Chittick was nominated to fill the post of Curator. The most important feature of the Chittick era was the establishment of photographic documentation, although at this time much of this work was carried out by the Commissioner due to a lack of trained staff in this field.

The long-awaited dream of a permanent museum came to life in 1959, when the decision to build the Aswan High Dam was taken. The area along the Nile, from Aswan to south of the Second Cataract, was thoroughly documented prior to the rise in water level that permanently flooded the region. Many institutions from

1 Sudan National Museum, Khartoum.
Façade of the main building.

different parts of the world participated in this rescue campaign of documentation and excavation. The Sudanese Antiquities Service staff (now the National Corporation for Antiquities and Museums), headed by Thabit Hassan Thabit as Commissioner and Nigm Ed Din Mohammed Sharif as Field Inspector, played a very important role in helping to make this campaign a success. Large numbers of objects were excavated and many monuments were dismantled and transported to Khartoum.

The transfer of this new large collection and vast number of archeological monuments to Khartoum increased the need for and encouraged the creation of a permanent museum, and the museum's present location was chosen. When the construction of the museum buildings was complete, temples, statues and other monuments were re-erected and an artificial lake representing the Nile Valley was dug. The temples and monuments were positioned in relation to one another, according to their original geographical locations.

The Sudan National Museum was inaugurated in 1971. It is primarily an archaeological museum, consisting of a main building which houses two permanent exhibition spaces on two floors connected by an inclined ramp. The ground floor displays ancient Sudanese civilizations dating to the prehistoric era, the early culture of Kerma, the period of influence of the Egyptian kingdoms and the Kushite kingdoms of Napata and Meroe. The upper floor exhibits Christian and medieval Islamic antiquities. The creation of the Sudan National Museum has been the result of much hard work. The museum has the purpose of protecting, conserving, and displaying Sudan's rich cultural heritage for the benefit not only of Sudan but also the global community.

THE ARCHAEOLOGY
AND HISTORY OF SUDAN

DEREK A. WELSBY

Our knowledge of the archaeology of Sudan is almost totally confined to the northern third of the country: that is, to the desert and semi-desert regions (fig. 2). Initially interest was focused principally on the Nile Valley and the large upstanding monuments of the Kerma culture, the Pharaonic Egyptians, the Kushites and the medieval Christian kingdoms. The work of Henry Wellcome in the Sennar region on the Upper Blue Nile in 1910–14 marked the advent of a much wider archaeological interest and showed an appreciation of the value of excavating sites which were not of themselves visually impressive. After the First World War men such as W. Shaw and D. Newbold ranged far and wide outside the Nile Valley recording the presence of abundant remains of prehistoric occupation in what is now barren desert. They were followed by A.J. Arkell who, with the publication of his excavations at Khartoum Hospital (1944–5) and esh-Shaheinab (1949), set the foundations on which the archaeology of prehistoric Sudan is based. Today there is a much more holistic approach to the archaeology of the region with teams working at the major historic sites in the Nile Valley, and over the Eastern and Western Deserts from the borders of Chad and Libya to the Red Sea coast.

Many of the cultures which flourished in Sudan, both along the Nile and in the regions to the east and west, are identical to, or closely connected with, those known from Egypt. The modern border between the two countries at latitude 22°N serves to arbitrarily divide these cultures, at least in terms of archaeologists working on the ground. Many of the earliest archaeologists to work in Sudan were trained as Egyptologists and saw their work as an adjunct to their activities in Egypt. The situation today is very different, with archaeologists working in Sudan having backgrounds in many different fields. This has led to a much greater focus on the indigenous roots of Sudanese cultures, and the influences from Egypt during the Pharaonic and subsequent periods are now seen in their correct perspective as foreign elements.

Although interaction between the cultures of Egypt and Sudan has been of immense significance in the Nile Valley, other areas of Sudan were little if at all affected by Egyptian or indeed by other Nile Valley cultures. To the west of the valley there are strong cultural links with the Chad Basin, although similar strong links between the cultures of eastern Sudan and the Ethiopian plateau remain elusive. The relationship between the northern and southern Sudan is almost entirely unknown as

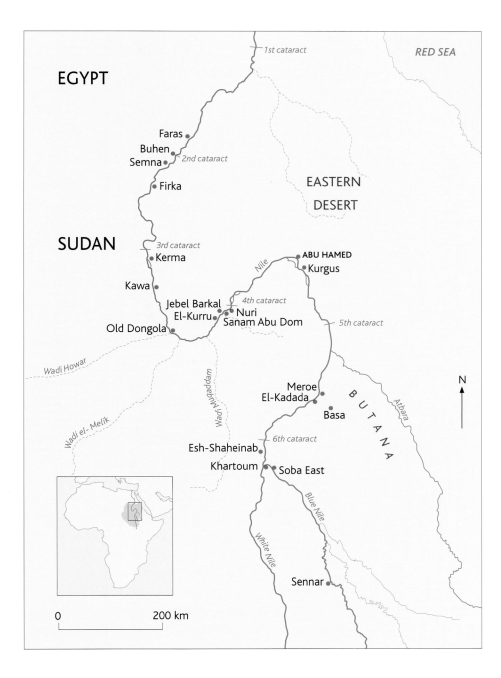

2 Map of the Middle Nile Basin.

virtually no archaeology has been undertaken in the south, initially through a lack of interest and latterly as a result of the poor security situation.

The conquest of the Sudan by the Ottoman armies of Mohammed Ali Pasha in the 1820s opened up the country to European antiquarians. The publications of such works as Waddington and Hanbury's *Journal of a Visit to Some Parts of Ethiopia* (1822), Cailliaud's *Voyage à Meroé* (1826–7) and the twelve monumental volumes of *Denkmaeler aus Aegypten und Aethiopien* by Lepsius (1849–53) focused attention on Sudan's ancient heritage. The work of these scholars was mainly that of recording upstanding monuments. On the conquest of the country by the Anglo-Egyptian forces between 1896 and 1898, a new phase in the study of the Sudan's ancient cultures began. As early as 1897 Wallis Budge was sent by the Trustees of the British Museum, with the approval of the Anglo-Egyptian authorities, to undertake work at Jebel

Barkal. This brought about the advent in the Sudanese Nile Valley of excavation as a major tool for expanding our knowledge of the past.[1]

One of the driving forces behind archaeology in the Sudan has been the need to react to rescue situations. The heightenings of the Aswan Dam, although not directly affecting Sudanese territory, brought to light a vast amount of material relevant to its cultures. Archaeologists involved in those rescue activities, G. Reisner in particular, but also many others, then moved their activities south of the border. There were contemporary threats in Sudan, and Arkell's work on the Khartoum Hospital site prior to the building's construction was the first rescue archaeology project. However, it was the construction of the Aswan High Dam that really made an impact on Sudanese archaeology, destroying forever a vast tract of the river valley while at the same time offering unprecedented opportunities for archaeological research.

Sudan is now a rapidly developing country and increasingly archaeology is focused on rescue activities prior to the expansion of agriculture and housing, to the construction of roads, and again prior to the building of dams: that currently under construction at the Fourth Cataract will inundate 170 km of the valley.

Whilst being mindful of the limitations placed on our knowledge of Sudan's ancient cultures by the dearth of work south of latitude 12°N, there is a considerable and ever-growing body of evidence which provides an understanding of human activity in Sudan over the last 200,000 years or more. This study also has a wider significance in that man's adaptation to his environment provides a sensitive indicator of climatic and environmental change, particularly in the regions where phases of hyper-aridity have fluctuated with pluvial periods – the expansion and retraction of the Sahara Desert is not a phenomenon confined to the later twentieth century.

The earliest artefactual evidence for the presence of humans in Sudan comes from the Early Palaeolithic, about 300,000 years ago. Middle Palaeolithic occupation, from about 70,000 years ago, is widespread, represented in the archaeological record by a developed stone toolkit. By the later Palaeolithic, about 50–40,000 years ago, a number of different cultural groups can be identified which, owing to the hyper-arid phase, are principally in the Nile Valley. The early Holocene, around the eighth millennium BC, saw the onset of more clement conditions with the spread of people across much of what is now the Sahara Desert. It was at this time that one of the most ubiquitous of human inventions – pottery – appears, along with the domestication of animals. Agriculture followed thereafter, offering considerable advantages for human development, but with it a greater reliance on a stable, predictable climatic cycle. By the sixth millennium BC the early Holocene pluvial period was coming to an end and, at least in northern Sudan, there was a gradual shift of population and/or change in subsistence strategy as the increasingly dry conditions prevailed. The river began to assume a pre-eminence, becoming the longest oasis in the world.

Contemporary with the creation of a complex state in Egypt, a process completed by around 3200 BC, the development of a more complex society can be observed in northern Sudan with the rise to prominence of certain individuals, visible in the archaeological record through their rich graves. Already these developments had been observed during the Neolithic (fifth–fourth millennia BC) and can be documented at Kadruka, for example (see pp. 42–8). To the south of the ancient Egyptian border, in an area known to the Egyptians as *Wawat*, the rich culture of what is known as the A-Group can be recognized in the archaeological record from about 3700 BC. The A-Group people, situated between the First and Second Cataracts, were distinguished by the presence of numerous imported Egyptian goods, settlements containing storage pits and small huts of wooden construction, and distinctive burial customs. Among the products of the A-Group is very fine eggshell pottery; thereafter pottery remained one of the finest products of the northern and central Sudanese Nile Valley (Nubia) up to the end of the medieval period over 4,000 years later.

Around 3000 BC the Egyptians were drawn into the region, lured by their quest for raw materials and their desire to access the riches of sub-Saharan Africa. An Early Dynastic king (3100–2686 BC) left an inscription by the Second Cataract, and under the Old Kingdom (2686–2181 BC) a settlement was established nearby at Buhen. This was broadly contemporary with the growth further upstream of an indigenous culture, christened by archaeologists the 'Kerma culture' (*c.* 2500–1500 BC), which developed out of the pre-existing Late Neolithic cultures. First attested at the eponymous site Kerma in the Northern Dongola Reach, the cultural assemblage is found over a vast area, at least from Sai to a little above the Fourth Cataract. During the Middle Kingdom (2055–1650 BC) the Egyptians pushed south, advancing their frontier at least as far upstream as Semna, 60 km beyond the Second Cataract, with perhaps, an outpost on the northern tip of Sai Island. A series of imposing forts was built which testifies to the respect the Egyptians felt for their southern neighbours in the Kingdom of Kush. By this time Kerma had developed into a massive metropolis, the first in sub-Saharan Africa, with elaborate defences enclosing a dense agglomeration of dwellings, palaces, storehouses and temples.

With the withdrawal of the Egyptians at the end of the Middle Kingdom the kings of Kush rapidly filled the power vacuum and, allied with the Hyksos in the Nile Delta, posed a formidable threat to the small Egyptian state centred on Thebes. At that time the kings of Kush ruled a state extending at least from the First Cataract perhaps as far upstream as the Fifth Cataract. Their wealth is indicated by the impressive remains of their capital, while their power is highlighted by their burials, where up to 400 individuals were sacrificed on their deaths. The resurgence of Egyptian power, begun by Kamose (1555–1550 BC) and confirmed by Ahmose (1550–1525 BC), led to a power struggle between Egypt and Kush culminating in the conquest of the latter by Thutmose I (1504–1492 BC) and the establishment of the border of the empire at Kurgus, south of Abu Hamed. Further to the south the Neolithic cultures appear to have remained, while those to the west, far beyond the writ of the Nile Valley's rulers, looked to the Chad Basin for their cultural contacts.

The Egyptian conquest had an important impact on the Nile Valley but, on their withdrawal in the early eleventh century BC, many of the indigenous cultural traits, particularly with regard to pottery manufacture and funerary customs, reasserted themselves. By the ninth century BC a new regime had emerged, known to us initially from the burials of the earliest rulers at el-Kurru. Development appears to have been rapid; by the mid-eighth century BC King Kashta, as the champion of the Egyptian god Amun who had been adopted by the rulers of this second Kingdom of Kush, extended his control to Thebes and his successor Piankhi (Piye) went on to conquer the whole of the Egyptian Nile valley. Under Piankhi and his immediate successors, known in Egyptian history as the pharaohs of the 25th Dynasty, the Kushites ruled an empire stretching from the borders of Palestine possibly as far upstream as the Blue and White Niles. Kushite control of Egypt was short-lived but after they were ousted from Egypt Kush still remained a major power for over a thousand years. Kushite culture is a rich amalgam of that of Egypt, whether Pharaonic, Persian, Hellenistic or Roman, and indigenous African traditions.

The Kushite empire broke up during the fourth century AD, leading to the abandonment of much of the society's Egyptian veneer. Once again we see the emergence of royal burials under tumuli, and human sacrifice again becomes prominent. By the mid-sixth century AD the political situation had stabilized and three kingdoms controlled the Nile Valley from the First Cataract to the Blue and White Niles: Nobadia in the north with its capital at Faras, Makuria in the centre based at Old Dongola and Alwa in the south with its capital at Soba East. It was at this time that the most fundamental of cultural changes, at least since the arrival of the pharaonic Egyptians, made itself felt – the conversion of these kingdoms to Christianity. Within a short period of time the worship of the old pharaonic/Kushite gods disappeared, along with temples and grandiose burials accompanied by rich and abundant grave goods. Instead we see the arrival of the church, humble burials – even of the rulers – and what appears to be a dramatic increase in literacy in Greek, Coptic, Old Nubian and later Arabic. After a spirited resistance against the armies of Islam during the seventh century AD the Christian kingdoms developed a rich and varied culture before dynastic strife, along with Ayyubid and Mameluke aggression from the north and the expansion of the Funj from the south, brought about their collapse and the Islamization of the country by around AD 1500. Thereafter the north and the Red Sea littoral fell under Ottoman control, and central Sudan was ruled by the sultans of the Funj based at Sennar on the Blue Nile.

The modern state of Sudan owes its present territorial boundaries largely to the conquests initiated by Mohammed Ali, who dispatched his armies up the Nile in AD 1819–20. The Turqiya, as this period is known, was brought to an end by the nationalist movement of the Mahdi, whose triumphant capture of Khartoum in January AD 1885 was to lead to Anglo-Egyptian involvement in Sudan a decade later and the birth of the present Republic of the Sudan.

This exhibition charts the development of human culture within Sudan from its earliest manifestations in the Palaeolithic until the late nineteenth century AD. Principally following a chronological progression, leading experts in the field have contributed general introductions to each period, which are illustrated by a number of type sites. Descriptions of the type sites have, wherever possible, been written by those archaeologists who have excavated them or continue to do so. As many of the sites featured are still under excavation, this exhibition and catalogue are only an interim statement reflecting the present state of our knowledge. With over thirty archaeological missions currently active in Sudan, new and often important discoveries relating to many different periods and issues are made every year. Another facet of the exhibition focuses on themes, highlighting continuity and change in pottery production and funerary culture, the importance of Sudan as a source of gold, and the nature of Kushite religion.

Sudan has an extremely rich and varied cultural history illustrated by a wealth of fine artefacts and dramatic archaeological sites. Ancient civilization on the Nile did not cease at the First Cataract, nor did it derive solely from those cultures which flourished in Ancient Egypt. It is hoped that *Sudan: Ancient Treasures* will serve to highlight Sudan's past glories, its great archaeological potential, and the superb collections of the National Museum in Khartoum.

1 For general accounts of the history and archaeology of Sudan see Adams 1977; Edwards 2004; Shinnie 1967; 1996; Udal 1998; Welsby 1996; 2002.

1 Statue of a lion

Ferruginous sandstone

Basa

Kushite (Meroitic), mid-first century BC

Lion: H 1.575 m, W (at haunches) 520 mm,
Th 1.1 m; base: H 135 mm, W 510 mm, Th 1.1 m

SNM 24393

A lion carved from hard ferruginous sandstone sits on its haunches with its tail neatly wrapped around its left side and over its left thigh, facing forward on a rectangular base. The mane, which is indicated in low relief, terminates at the back in a knot, and between this and the ears is carved a large scarab with triple wings. There is a prominent collar around and below the face. A rectangular 'apron' covers the chest and upper front legs, decorated with a pectoral of seven strands of pendant beads. Above these are two cartouches 190 mm high containing text in Meroitic hieroglyphs: 'The Lord of the Two Lands, the king ever-living Amanikhabale'.

This lion, one of several found at Basa (see also cat. 2), came from the west side of the *hafir* where it was set on a pedestal made from two courses of red brick covered in plaster. The lion was a potent symbol of the might of the Kushite state, and is frequently associated with the ruler who sits on a lion throne and is accompanied by a lion mauling prisoners – as on the pylons of the Lion Temple at Naqa. The lion is also associated with one of the chief gods of the Kushite state, Apedemak, who is frequently shown as a lion-headed human figure. Apedemak was the Kushite god of war and also of fertility. In this guise his presence at a *hafir* is very appropriate. *Hafirs* were presumably constructed by the Kushite state to provide water for the transhuming and nomadic populations of the Keraba and Butana. After the wet season, when surface water became scarce, these people would have been forced to congregate with their animals at the *hafirs*. The lion statues and the nearby temple will have demonstrated to them the power and might of the state, and presumably the state would have taken the opportunity to tax them at this point.   DAW

Crowfoot 1911, 14–17, pl. VI, 9; Griffith 1911, 70, pls XXVI, 46, XXVII, 46

1

2 Statue of a lion and prisoner

Ferruginous sandstone

Basa

Kushite (Meroitic), mid-first century BC

Lion: H 1.65 m, W (at haunches) *c.* 570 mm,
Th 1.172 m; base: H 150 mm, W 550 mm, Th 1.172 m

SNM 441

A lion carved from hard ferruginous sand-stone rears up on its haunches, resting its front paws on the shoulders of a hapless kneeling prisoner with his elbows bound behind his back and to his ankles. The lion has the prisoner's head firmly grasped in its jaws. The tail is neatly wrapped around its left side and over its left thigh. The mane is shown in low relief framing the lion's face. The prisoner is depicted wearing a short loincloth or kilt tied at the waist, the ties extending downward over the thighs. The lion and prisoner stand on a rectangular base.

This is one of two lion statues which flanked the entrance into the *temenos* of the temple at Basa. The statue graphically portrays the power and might of the Kushite state.   DAW

Crowfoot 1911, 14–17, pls VII, 16, 17, VIII, 18

3 Statue of King Anlamani

Grey granitic gneiss

Jebel Barkal, fragments found divided between (trench) B 500 A and (temple room) B 801 B

Kushite (Napatan), last quarter of seventh century BC

Statue: H 2.04 m, W (across chest) 585 mm,
Th 690 mm; base: H 115 mm, W 410 mm, Th 700 mm

SNM 1845

Anlamani was the fourth successor of Taharqo. He is represented by two statues in the Barkal cache: this one and a colossal (3.81 m high) second now in Boston. He appears in a third statue from Kerma (Bonnet and Valbelle 2003, in press; Valbelle 2003a, 295–7, fig. 8). Here his flesh parts have been polished, while his crown, kilt, cord necklace and other ornaments have been left rough for plastering and gilding. The text on the back pillar reads: 'King of Upper and Lower Egypt, Lord of the Two Lands, accomplisher of deeds, Ankh-ka-Ra, son of Ra, of his body, whom he loves, Anlamani, beloved of Amun of Napata, who dwells in Pure Mountain [i.e. Jebel Barkal], given life [forever].'

During his first excavating season (1916) at the Jebel Barkal temples G.A. Reisner and his Harvard University–Museum of Fine Arts Boston Expedition discovered two separate caches of fragments comprising ten complete or nearly complete granite royal statues. These represented, sometimes in multiple image, Taharqo and four of his five Kushite successors up to the early sixth century BC. They had stood in the first court of the Great Temple of Amun (B 501). Seven of the statues, like this one, were lifesize or nearly so; three others were of colossal scale; and one represented a queen. Buried in pits outside the temple with debris from a fire, they all appeared to have been deliberately broken in conjunction with a conflagration and subsequently buried. It is now generally supposed that they were destroyed in a sudden attack on the Barkal sanctuary by the invading army of the Egyptian king Psammetik II in 593 BC, during which the temples and royal palace were also torched (Kendall 1996a). A second cache of statues, representing the same rulers and possibly destroyed in the same campaign, was found in 2003 at Kerma by Charles Bonnet and his team from the University of Geneva (Bonnet 2003, 260–70; Bonnet and Valbelle 2003, in press; Radja 2003, 27; Zäid 2003, 44–9).   TK

Dunham 1970, 23, fig. 14, pl. XX; Kendall 1996c, 468–76; Reisner 1917, 215–17, pl. 41; 1920, 251–3; 1931, 82, no. 48

4 Wall painting of a Nubian queen protected by the holy Virgin and Child

Mud plaster, paint

Faras Cathedral, north aisle, west face of the first pilaster, 1.30 m above floor level (field no. 21)

Second half of twelfth century AD

Virgin Mary figure: H 1.75 m, W 590 mm; child: H 370 mm; queen: H 1.16 m, W 372 mm

SNM 24362

Legend: Greek text on both sides of the Virgin's head written in black paint:
'Saint Mary, Virgin, Mother of Christ' on the left;
'Jesus Christ' on the right.

Both figures are shown standing *en face*. The Virgin with the Child on her left arm holds with both hands, in a gesture of protection, the smaller figure of the dark-faced Nubian queen. The Christ, his right hand around Mary's neck, *rotulus* in his left hand, is

2

3

depicted face on above the waist, but the legs with bent knees are shown in profile. The queen looks straight ahead, but because of the crossed gazes of the Virgin and Child and the slight bend of their heads, the spiritual contact between all three figures is clearly visible. The Virgin is clad in a long-sleeved *chiton* decorated with *potamoi*, on which she wears the *maphorion* draped on the shawl tightly covering the hair. Her head is encircled with a halo. The queen is depicted in full court splendour which is manifested by her rich attire: the crown, veil, cloak, necklace and earrings. The long sleeves of her *chiton* are decorated with a wide band creating the attribute of majesty and prestige. She wears shoes with a covered instep. The purse in the queen's hand explicitly indicates her role as a donor or founder. The little cross on her forehead distinctly shows her faith. The painting is a typical votive representation, painted in the church in order to obtain grace and salvation for a given person.

The figure protected by the Virgin is here conventionally called the 'queen'. She undoubtedly is a high-ranking person within the court hierarchy, as is confirmed by her attire. The iconography and the way in which the figures are represented, their attributes, the decorative elements on the robes and the colouring of the painting clearly indicate that it was made during the late period of Nubian painting (end of the eleventh–fourteenth centuries AD). It is one of the many created by the same workshop, active in the Faras Cathedral during the late period. The latest research may indicate that the formerly established dating, the end of the eleventh to the beginning of the twelfth century AD, should be shifted to the end of the twelfth century AD.   MM-C

Godlewski 1995, 59; Martens 1972, 211–12, 221–2, figs 49, 50; Martens-Czarnecka 1982, 92–4, 96, 100, 103, figs 135, 143; 1992, 307–16; Michałowski 1964, 92, figs 44, 46; 1966, 23, pl. XIX, 2; 1967, 167–8, pls 94, 95a; 1972, 380, fig. 5; Rassart-Debergh 1972, 269, fig. 11; Rostkowska 1972, 200, fig. 4

4

1

THE PALAEOLITHIC AND MESOLITHIC

ELENA A.A. GARCEA

THE PALAEOLITHIC (EARLIEST TIME TO 8000 BC)

The earliest settlers in Nubia date back to at least 300,000 years ago, possibly even 1 million years ago. They originated from East Africa and belonged to the species of *Homo erectus* (or *Homo ergaster*), who gradually colonized the entire African continent and dispersed out of Africa into south-western Asia and eventually into Europe. They produced stone tools flaked on both sides; the most characteristic are teardrop-shaped handaxes and bifacial foliates, which typify the Acheulian period, a late Lower Palaeolithic technological complex. Acheulian groups were hunter-gatherers and used stone tools not only for hunting but also for digging, woodworking, hide-working, and many other purposes. The Levallois technique of core preparation[1] appeared during the Acheulian and continued later. This knapping technique allowed one to predetermine the size and shape of flakes and blades.

Until recently Khor Abu Anga, near Omdurman, was the most representative Palaeolithic site (fig. 5), having a stratigraphic sequence with Lower and Middle Palaeolithic artefact assemblages.[2] Numerous Acheulian and Middle Palaeolithic sites were located around Wadi Halfa, Jebel Brinikol, Abu Simbel and Arkin during surveys preceding the construction of the Aswan High Dam.[3] Lower and Middle Palaeolithic artefacts were recorded in the Dongola Reach, near ed-Debba,[4] and at Khashm el-Girba.[5] The salvage programme in the Multaga-Abu Dom resettlement area for the Merowe Dam found evidence of early Middle Palaeolithic occupation below Aterian cultural levels.[6] The latter tool industry is widespread in the Sahara and the Maghreb, but is scarcely known in Nubia.

The Middle Palaeolithic presents a distinct appearance. According to the Guichards,[7] who mostly surveyed stone workshops and quarries, the Nubian Middle Palaeolithic I (beginning about 70,000 years ago), with heavy-duty biface tools, is older and resembles the contemporary Eastern African Sangoan industry. The Middle Palaeolithic II is later, exhibiting refined bifacial foliate tools, and is similar to the contemporary North African Aterian and the sub-Saharan Lupemban tool industries. Marks suggested a different classification, noting that bifacial foliates are often missing from habitation sites.[8] He distinguished between a Denticulate Mousterian and two types of Nubian Mousterian, with and without bifaces.[9]

The latest excavations at Site B-8-11, on Sai Island (fig. 3),[10] have provided

3 Excavation of Site 8-B-11 on Sai Island.

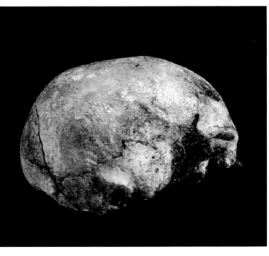

4 Archaic modern human skull discovered at Singa on the Blue Nile.

comprehensive information about the early Nubian populations. The site was occupied from the Acheulian to the Middle Palaeolithic (see below). The transition from the Lower to the Middle Palaeolithic not only represents a technological and chronological shift, between 300,000 and 200,000 years ago, but also documents the replacement of the last groups of *Homo erectus* by the earliest modern *Homo sapiens*. For example, an archaic modern human skull was discovered at Singa, on the Blue Nile (fig. 4).[11] Its morphological features[12] and an associated Levallois flake[13] suggested its attribution to the Middle Palaeolithic, which was confirmed by artefacts collected nearby at Abu Hugar.[14] Other modern human remains were recovered at Soleb, together with Levallois flakes and bones of fish, turtle, crocodile, giraffe, gazelle, warthog, hippopotamus and rhinoceros.[15] Some extinct species, including porcupine, giraffoid, antilopine, and long-horned buffalo, were discovered at Singa and Abu Hugar.[16] Elephant bones from Khashm el-Girba[17] complete the Middle Palaeolithic animal repertoire, suggesting an environment of open wooded grasslands with local rainfall.

The advent of modern humans brought about a number of innovations indispensable to the flourishing of subsequent civilizations; of these, language was the most important. New technological skills were developed which enabled humans to flake different types of rocks and to make a variety of tools, including more efficient hafted tools. Modern behaviour developed with the ability to adapt to various environments

5 Map showing Palaeolithic and Mesolithic sites mentioned in the text.

and climates, facilitating movement over larger territories, and the practice of new subsistence activities such as fishing and fowling, in addition to hunting and gathering.

The Upper Palaeolithic was only found in Lower Nubia due to shifts and floods of the river. The Khormusan tool industry, named for the site of Khor Musa, dating from 36,000 years ago, continued the Levallois toolmaking tradition, but with decreased tool sizes.[18] The subsequent Halfan industry discovered near Wadi Halfa featured numerous microblades. This culture dated from 19,000 years ago and partly overlapped with the Khormusan. Halfan sites were more permanently occupied than those earlier.[19]

The Qadan, from the site of Qada, dating to 15,000–9,000 years ago, anticipated some technological features of the Mesolithic industry, such as microliths, grind-stones, and occasionally pottery. Excavations at Jebel Sahaba unearthed the earliest

6 Burial with associated flakes from Jebel Sahaba.

cemetery in Nubia, comprising fifty-nine skeletons buried in oval pits, most of which were covered with stone slabs. Burials were single, double or multiple, and contained various configurations of adults and children, reaching a maximum of six individuals. Stone flakes, up to twenty-seven in one case, were associated with some bodies and are thought to have pierced the soft tissue, thereby causing death; occasionally small lithics were even embedded in the bone (fig. 6). It was suggested that these late Palaeolithic populations had developed a strong sense of territoriality, leading to warfare and mass violence.[20] However, a re-analysis of the skeletons indicates a healthy population[21] that did not die during a single episode, but at different times and in varying numbers.

THE MESOLITHIC (8000–5000 BC)

In Upper Nubia a gap separates the Middle Palaeolithic occupations from the following culture, which was first identified near Khartoum Hospital and there subsequently named Khartoum Mesolithic,[22] while in Lower Nubia it was called the Khartoum Variant.[23] These were semi-sedentary populations with a food collecting economy, producing pottery, microlithic tools, grindstones and bone tools, including harpoons (fig. 7). They settled along the Nile and its tributaries (see fig. 5), and practised intensive exploitation of riverine resources, particularly fishing and mollusc-gathering, and buried their dead inside their settlements. Grindstones were used for grinding wild seeds and dry meat or fish, powdering colouring substances, refining bone tools, and pounding clay for pottery manufacturing.

The Mesolithic revealed two main horizons or periods, an early and a late, dated 8600–6500 BC and 6500–5500 BC, respectively. The earliest sites are located at Abu Darbein and ed-Damer.[24] They are earlier than those near Khartoum, where other sites were excavated around Saggai.[25] On the White Nile, Shabona is the most important site.[26] Jebel Moya is located further south between the White and the Blue Nile.[27] Mesolithic sites extended west of the Nile along the

7 Mesolithic microlithic tools.

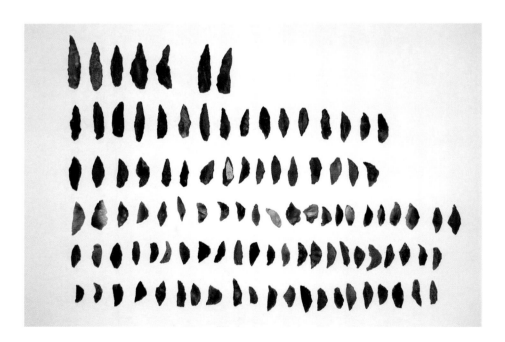

Wadi Howar,[28] and to the east, at Shaqadud,[29] in the Gash Delta,[30] and at Khashm el-Girba.[31]

Early Mesolithic ceramics were decorated with incised wavy lines and impressed zigzags using combs that were applied on the soft clay before drying. Around 7,000 years ago the climate in the eastern Sahara deteriorated and some groups moved toward the Nile, entering into contact with local populations. They brought with them their ceramic traditions, typically represented by impressed dotted wavy lines, which replaced incised wavy lines. Islang,[32] el-Qoz,[33] Kabbashi[34] and Shaqadud[35] yielded stratigraphic sequences with late Mesolithic material following that of the early Mesolithic.

1 In the Levallois core preparation, a suitable stone was selected and first prepared through the careful removal of flakes in order to produce a shape from which a specific stone tool could be created.
2 Arkell 1949b; Carlson and Sigsted 1967/8.
3 Chmielewski 1968; Guichard and Guichard 1968; Marks 1968c.
4 Marks et al. 1971.
5 Shiner 1971b.
6 Garcea 2003.
7 Guichard and Guichard 1968.
8 Marks 1968c.
9 Marks recognized cultural affinities with the Middle Paleolithic Mousterian industry of Europe through the various toolmaking techniques.
10 See van Peer, this volume, pp. 25–8.
11 Wells 1951.
12 Stringer 1979.
13 Arkell 1949b.
14 Lacaille 1951.
15 Sausse 1975.
16 Bate 1951.
17 Shiner 1971b.
18 Marks 1968b.
19 Marks 1968a.
20 Wendorf et al. 1966.
21 Judd 2003.
22 Arkell 1949a.
23 Shiner 1968; Nordström 1972.
24 Haaland and Magid 1995.
25 See Caneva, this volume, pp. 29–30; Caneva 1983.
26 Clark 1989.
27 Addison 1949; Caneva 1991.
28 Kuper 1981; Keding 1997a; 1998; Jesse 2003.
29 Marks and Mohammed-Ali 1991.
30 Fattovich 1989.
31 Fattovich et al. 1984.
32 Mohammed-Ali 1982.
33 Arkell 1953.
34 Caneva et al. 1993.
35 Caneva and Marks 1990.

SAI

PHILIP VAN PEER

Palaeolithic sites on Sai Island were first noticed by A.J. Arkell in the 1940s.[1] In particular, he mentioned a locality at the southern foot of Jebel Adou, the Nubian sandstone inselberg that dominates the island. In an almost visionary description, he emphasized the potential for this place to reveal important information about the origin of North African Middle Stone Age populations. In later years, this site received the formal code 8-B-11, but no fieldwork was performed. It was essentially forgotten until its rediscovery in 1996 by a Belgian team from the University of Leuven that had joined the French Archaeological Mission at Sai.[2]

The extraordinary geomorphological conditions of the area were immediately realized. A large depression cut by ancient Nile river channels into the Nubian sandstone bedrock appeared to be filled with fine sediments. The latter were protected from the severe erosional forces of the last 80,000 years by a sandstone ridge on the southern edge of the site. This rare situation is sometimes called a 'sediment trap' and is extremely favourable for archaeological research. In the sediments, deposited by low-energy streams or by

wind activity, the remains of temporary visits by human groups have a good chance of being preserved in excellent condition, with minimal disturbance to their spatial contexts (fig. 8).

Since 1996 six field seasons have been undertaken here and the results have largely exceeded the initial expectations. Remains of at least eight human occupations during the Palaeolithic period have been identified, ranging in time between perhaps half a million and 100,000 years ago. No other Middle Nile Valley site excavated in modern times presents comparably detailed evidence for the early human presence in the region. Unfortunately, the sediments are not suited to the preservation of materials other than stone or mineral materials such as bone.

Occupation levels predating 130,000 years ago are related to a small stream, a tributary to the River Nile of the time. The oldest occupation debris, transported from the original position upstream, is within the basal fill of this gully. Lithic tools include so-called choppers and chopping tools. There is no clue as to their precise age but it is likely that they are much older than 200,000 years. Around this time the climate seems to have been relatively humid and there was an Acheulian settlement on the northern bank of the stream. Large pointed handaxes were typical tool forms. They were probably used for a variety of tasks, in particular butchering activities.

Shortly afterwards the climate became arid, as evidenced by the deposition of wind-blown sands on top of the Acheulian debris. During this period, the first phase of the Middle Palaeolithic, human groups known as Sangoan, manufacturing a lithic industry (cat. 6), arrived in this part of the Nile Valley. The artefacts of the first Sangoan occupation were eroded out of the upper part of the sands during a short phase of gully activity. This indicates that the lapse of time between the Acheulian and the Sangoan cannot have been very long.

Evidence of unprecedented behaviour is documented from this lowermost Sangoan level onwards (fig. 9). Numerous lumps of red and yellow iron-oxide were found (cat. 10). These must have been exploited somewhere in the vicinity of the site and carried there. Some lumps show evidence of rubbing, and tools such as grinding stones and pecked pebbles may have been used in pigment-producing activities (cats 7, 9, 11).

8 View of Site 8-B-11 from the top of Jebel Adou, looking south. In the background, the sandstone rim can be seen protecting the sediments within from erosion.

9 The 2002 field season, excavations in progress. In the large trench in the foreground, the lowermost Sangoan level is being exposed. The section shows the superposition of Nile silts (upper part) on top of the gully sediments (lower part).

Dated to between 180,000 and 200,000 years ago, this is one of the earliest sites in the world with such evidence. The grinding equipment may also have been used to process plant foods, in particular during the next Sangoan occupation level. Here, fine quartzitic cobbles were found with microscopic traces of plants, probably grasses, on them. Core-axes, typical Sangoan heavy-duty tools made of quartz, may have served in plant-harvesting activities. It is possible that these Sangoan assemblages represent the first presence of anatomically modern humans in this part of Africa.

The third, uppermost Sangoan level is dated to 150,000 years ago. Its lithic industry shows transitional features towards a new facies of the Middle Palaeolithic called the Nubian Complex. This was a local development in this part of Africa whereby the heavy-duty tools were gradually replaced by thin foliate points. This change seems to be connected with an increased amount of hunting in daily subsistence activities. After the Nubian Complex was established, the site became submerged beneath a large Nile floodplain. It is in the silty sediments of this plain that three Nubian Complex settlements were found. No direct dates are available as yet, but on geomorphological grounds they are likely to be around 100,000 years old or slightly older. During the next millennia, the climate became extremely arid and no more human occupation is attested until the beginning of the Holocene.

1 Arkell 1949b.
2 Van Peer *et al.* 2003.

5

5 Handaxe

Sandstone

Sai Island, Site 8-B-11, Level 5, no. S02/39/149

Early to Middle Palaeolithic Transition, *c.* 200,000 years ago

L 189 mm, W 97 mm, Th 42 mm

SNM 31191

This handaxe is of a type common in the Late Acheulian, a Palaeolithic tool industry as defined by archaeologists. Its general shape is lanceolate; the thick base was shaped by the removal of a few large flakes whereas the tip was carefully trimmed by alternating secondary retouch. It is made from locally available Nubian sandstone. This object was found on a land surface dating to the late Middle Pleistocene, amongst a small scatter of artefacts containing one other handaxe and numerous production flakes from a third. The latter handaxe itself was not present.

The small Acheulian cluster overlies a wider distribution of Early/Middle Palaeolithic, Sangoan artefacts. The latter are always made out of quartz and are radically different in terms of typology. This evidence indicates that these are the remains of two separate occupation events by humans with very different behaviour patterns, who were roaming in the same landscape.

Evidence of other Early/Middle Palaeolithic and Late Acheulian occupations were found below the present one, suggesting that the Early to Middle Palaeolithic transition was a rapid phenomenon caused by population replacement.

The handaxe is covered with a calcitic crust as a result of pedogenetic processes occurring in the early Late Pleistocene. PvP

Van Peer *et al.* 2003

6 Axe

Quartz

Sai Island, Site 8-B-11, Level 5, no. S00/18

Early to Middle Palaeolithic Transition, *c.* 200,000 years ago

L 94 mm, W 60 mm, Th 34 mm

SNM 31190

This is a core-axe of the so-called Khor Abu Anga type. The outline of the object is oval and it presents a well-developed longitudinal symmetry. The edges are characteristically shaped as a result of the particular production technique: using a hard hammer for direct percussion. This core-axe was made from a thick quartz flake. On the upper part, a large negative of an 'adze-blow' is visible. This was intended to sharpen the edge for use. Pebbles of fine quartz are locally available in ancient Nile terraces. This particular object was probably prepared at the spot where the quartz was exploited, and brought to Site 8-B-11 in a more or less prepared state. At this site it received its final preparation: its insertion into a haft.

Core-axes are characteristic tools for an Early/Middle Palaeolithic tool industry called

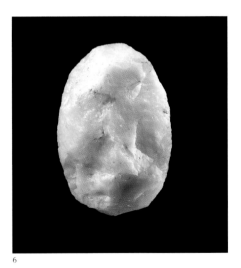

6

the Sangoan. Until recently, the latter was believed to be a sub-Saharan phenomenon. The discovery of three well-defined Sangoan levels at Sai provides the first firm evidence for a much larger distribution of the Sangoan throughout Africa. PvP

Van Peer *et al.* 2003

7 Grinding stone

Sandstone

Sai Island, Site 8-B-11, Level 6, no. S02/148

Early to Middle Palaeolithic Transition, *c.* 200,000 years ago

L 550 mm, W 255 mm, Th 100 mm

SNM 31189

This is an exceptional object made of local Nubian sandstone. A natural slab was shaped into a roughly rectangular form by removing large flakes from the sides. Then one face of the slab was made flat by pecking it with a stone hammer, except for two areas where the natural surface of the slab was preserved. A large depression was cut out, surrounded by a series of small holes that seem to have originated as a result of a rotating movement. It may have served as a grinding stone or mortar. After a fracture along the edge, in the area of the depression, the object was reshaped by means of obverse flakes. Two of these were recovered nearby and were refitted at the right edge of the object. Its present shape, therefore, is the result of a reworking of the grinding stone, perhaps an opportunistic adaptation to a new function.

This is one of the earliest examples in the world of an intensively shaped grinding stone. In fact, such objects are extremely rare throughout the Palaeolithic period. It testifies to complex behaviour in the Early/Middle Palaeolithic. PvP

Van Peer *et al.* 2003

7

8 Grinding stone

Sandstone

Sai Island, Site 8-B-11, Level 6

Early to Middle Palaeolithic Transition, *c.* 200,000 years ago

L 141 mm, W 63 mm, Th 34 mm

SNM 31188

Fragment of a grinding stone made of local Nubian sandstone and deliberately shaped into a circular form. It was found lying on one of its flat faces. The exposed face was stained with particles of manganese and calcite as a result of later soil formation. Sediment can be observed adhering to this face as the object has not been cleaned since its recovery during the excavations. The grinding stone will be analysed microscopically in order to detect specific wear patterns and, eventually, organic or mineral traces of the substances that were ground with this tool.

Besides grinding stones, other tools relating to grinding activities have been found in the Sangoan levels at Site 8-B-11. There are several examples of rubbing stones with smoothly polished surfaces that were hand-held and used to grind vegetal substances. On one of them, the polish was found to include mineral particles of different grass species. There are also spherical objects, known as bolas, which may have been used as pecking tools for the grinding stones.   PvP

Van Peer *et al.* 2003

9 Pebble with streaks of pigment

Chert

Sai Island, Site 8-B-11, Level 6

Early to Middle Palaeolithic Transition, *c.* 200,000 years ago

L 58 mm, W 31 mm, Th 19 mm

SNM 31185

This pebble was found amongst a dense concentration of raw ochre lumps. It is the only example from Site 8-B-11 so far on which both yellow and red pigment appear to have been smeared. The flat face of the pebble shows the presence of a central, discontinuous patch of red and a large patch of yellow is present in the upper left part. It is impossible to tell if these colour patches result from pigment processing activities or if they were consciously applied here. In the latter case, this object may have to be considered as a 'work of art'. Hence, except for the heavily debated Berekhat Ram figurine from Israel, this would be the earliest evidence of artistic expression preceding a

8

recently reported engraved ochre stick from Blombos Cave, South Africa, by about 130,000 years.   PvP

Van Peer *et al.* 2003

10 Red and yellow pigments

Iron oxide

Sai Island, Site 8-B-11, Level 6

Early to Middle Palaeolithic Transition, *c.* 200,000 years ago

SNM 31187

The earliest Sangoan level at Site 8-B-11 exhibits some of the world's earliest clear evidence for the exploitation of red and yellow iron oxides, and black manganese oxide and their processing into pigments. Numerous lumps were found in this level. The iron oxides were exploited from the Nubian sandstone bedrock in the site's vicinity and transported to it as lumps of variable dimensions.

Here, four lumps are exhibited representing various stages of the manufacturing process. These include an unworked piece of yellow iron oxide, a fragment of yellow ochre showing chipping on its sides and rubbing striations on one of its faces, a red ochre with

rubbing striations and a completely smoothed red ochre fragment, created as a result of intensive rubbing.

It is unknown what the pigments were used for, but it seems likely that it was, at least on occasion, in the context of symbolic activities. As in other African Middle Palaeolithic sites, yellow pigment lumps are by far the most numerous which seems to indicate a preference for yellow colours.   PvP

Van Peer *et al.* 2003

11 Pebble with wear polish

Chert

Sai Island, Site 8-B-11, Level 6

Early to Middle Palaeolithic Transition, *c.* 200,000 years ago

L 60 mm, W 32 mm, Th 21 mm

SNM 31186

This small chert pebble was found underneath the large grinding stone (cat. 7) in Level 6. On top of its natural gloss, resulting from its transportation in the Nile river bed, one of its faces shows a very intensive polish. This polish, with parallel striations, is undoubtedly the result of the pebble's use by humans.

Chert pebbles showing an association of clearly contrasting colours, such as red and black in this case, are extremely rare in the natural gravel deposits which were exposed at the site during the early Middle Palaeolithic occupation. Nevertheless they occur quite frequently in Level 6 and it is, therefore, likely that they were deliberately selected from the wider environment. As some of them show adhering particles of ochre, their use seems to be related to pigment processing. This, in turn, suggests that pigment processing may have had ritual connotations.   PvP

Van Peer *et al.* 2003

9, 10, 11

THE SAGGAI REGION

ISABELLA CANEVA

The site of Saggai was excavated between 1979 and 1981, and again in 1990.[1] One of the prehistoric settlements which line the right bank of the Nile, about 40 km north of Khartoum, it was the first such site to be excavated after A.J. Arkell's archaeological discoveries in the area. It revealed a culture similar to that of the Khartoum Hospital site[2] and was carbon-14 dated to *c.* 5700 BC.

The site consisted of an extensive dwelling area, with abundant settlement remains such as artefacts and food residues, scattered in a 600 mm-thick archaeological deposit. Human burials were found in all test pits, as in all other such sites, which suggests that burials in these cultures were commonly associated with the dwellings.

Chronologically on the borderline between the Palaeolithic and Neolithic, this culture is characterized by peculiar technological achievements, which include its pottery production and a complex settlement and territorial occupation. The earliest pottery is, quite unexpectedly, of very high technical quality (thin-walled, well fired) and aesthetic appearance (intensively and finely decorated with impressed motifs). The decoration covers the whole surface, from the rim to the round bottom, on most of the pots. The motifs, which vary according to the technique and tool used, are either widely spaced or packed, or arranged in bands, with different designs sometimes alternated. Implements include a wide range of bone artefacts (harpoons, perforators and handles), grinding stones and a large number of geometric microliths to be hafted into composite tools. Hunting and fishing were the main strategies for food procurement, as is attested by the tools and bone waste. Human bone pathology and chemistry suggest that the Saggai people consumed fish, molluscs and meat.

Sedentariness and pottery-making in non-food producing societies are among the most notable peculiarities of African prehistory. The combined presence at Saggai of pottery and grinding equipment, which are quite common throughout the Sahara and Sudan well before the adoption of any form of food production, should not be taken as an argument for the presence of agriculture. The absence of botanical evidence and low ecological probability speak against it. The earliest post-Palaeolithic hunter-gatherers were defined in Sudan as Mesolithic because of their sedentary sites which lay close to the river, and because of their heavy dependence on riverine resources, as shown by food residues. These cultures, dated in this area to between *c.* 6000 and 4100 BC, were basically settled along the Nile but used the hinterland as a complementary hunting territory as well as a supply area for raw material for their grinding equipment. Besides this rather ordinary site catchment, however, these groups were recently discovered to have established an exceptionally complex settlement pattern in the area. This system comprised functionally specialized settlements distributed over a vast territory, which extended from the Nile to at least 40 km inland. The characteristics of these sites differed, with permanent sites along the river being used in the winter, the dry season, and long-term camp-sites in the hinterland in the summer, the rainy season. Both settlement areas were complemented by a number of hunting locations, on top of the small jebels scattered throughout the area.

These cultures are characterized by peculiar technological achievements, such as their production of pottery and grinding equipment, and a complex site and territorial organization, with permanent settlements, containing graves, seasonal transhumance and functionally specialized sites. Pottery is not itself an element of social complexity, but may be considered to reflect such complexity. Seasonal sedentariness and territorial organization are other aspects which point to the presence of well-defined roles within the social group. All these elements emphasize the differences in corresponding cultural developments between Sudan (and the rest of Saharan Africa) on the one hand, and the Near East and Europe on the other. The late hunter-gatherers of Sudan, therefore, do not fit into the ordinary organizational model of hunter-gatherers but are, rather, the direct precursors of the first food-producers, i.e. the herders who have characterized Sudan ever since.

1 Caneva 1983; 1988; Caneva *et al.* 1993.
2 Arkell 1949a.

12

14

12 Beads

Ostrich eggshell

Saggai, no. KAH.L4c/3

Mesolithic, *c.* 5500 BC

D 6–9 mm, Th 1 mm

SNM 31259

The earliest necklaces uncovered in Sudan are composed of these thin, disc-shaped beads. Most were carved out of ostrich eggshell fragments which were perforated with a lithic borer and strung together before being shaped into discs. Some, which are not, however, distinguishable with the naked eye, were made of fine-grained limestone. Such beads were frequently found in Mesolithic deposits, though never in specific funerary contexts, which suggests that they were used in daily life.   IC

Zarattini 1983, 244

13 Harpoon

Bone

Geili, no. GE1.D4.4

Mesolithic, *c.* 5500 BC

L 130 mm, W 23 mm, Th 10 mm

SNM 31258

This almost complete bone harpoon was found in the deposits of the Neolithic site of Geili, but is probably to be ascribed to a Mesolithic occupation of the site. This type of weapon was one of the most characteristic elements of the hunting toolkit of the early riverine sites. Though fragments are frequently found,

complete harpoons are extremely rare as they easily broke while being used to catch big fish or other game. This example has a long butt. Harpoons, with up to four barbs on one side only, have been found at other Mesolithic sites, such as Khartoum Hospital (Arkell 1949a, 75). The notch was probably designed to prevent the rope from slipping off the harpoon.   IC

Caneva 1988, 138

14 Lunate lithics

Quartz

Kabbashi, no. TAM.CSW.2a

Mesolithic, *c.* 5500 BC

L 20–30 mm, W 8–12 mm, Th 2–4 mm

SNM 31257

Crescent-shaped microliths were the most typical lithic elements produced during the Mesolithic. They were struck from small, round pebbles, usually of rolled quartz, which were found scattered on the surface of the desert, and retouched into different geometric shapes. Microlithic lunates, triangles and trapezes were inserted into wooden or bone shafts in various serial combinations to obtain composite tools, most of which consisted of hunting weapons such as arrows or harpoons.   IC

Caneva *et al.* 1993

15 Potsherds

Ceramic

Kabbashi, nos SAG.E(16); TAM.M2; A1.E2; KAB S2

Mesolithic, *c.* 5500 BC

L *c.* 43 mm, W *c.* 55 mm

SNM 31256

Sudanese Mesolithic pottery is one of the earliest instances of pottery in the world, and is one of the rare examples produced in a hunter-gatherer context. It is characterized by a high quality of shaping, firing and decoration, with thin walls and fine-grained ware with inclusions of small grains of quartz. This early pottery displays a wide variety of decorative techniques made with a range of different motifs and tools. The decoration covered the whole surface on most of the pots, from the rim to the round base. The motifs vary according to the technique and tool used – they are either widely spaced or packed, or arranged in bands, with different designs sometimes alternating. A study of the earliest decorative techniques has shown that independent pottery-making traditions existed in the Nile Valley and the Sahara.   IC

13

15

EL-BARGA

MATTHIEU HONEGGER

In the Nile Valley the Mesolithic period corresponds to the last hunter-gatherer societies (*c.* 8500–5500 BC).[1] The communities of that time did not yet practise agriculture and do not seem to have possessed domesticated animals; however, they did make pottery[2] and used querns to grind the wild grains that they gathered. Subsistence was generally orientated towards the exploitation of the Nile (molluscs, fish and other aquatic animals), but hunting terrestrial mammals and the collection of plants may have also played an important role. Mesolithic sites often yield a high density of artefacts and are frequently accompanied by a few burials. These remains argue for a certain degree of sedentariness, even if we have to envisage that members of the group moved seasonally to carry out certain activities (such as fishing and hunting).

It is from the central Sudan that the Mesolithic period of the Nile Valley is best known, beginning with the work of A.J. Arkell in the 1940s.[3] Several excavations carried out in the Khartoum area, around Shendi and in the Butana, allow for the reconstruction of the *modus vivendi* of the time with some precision.[4] Further north research is less advanced and, despite the presence of several sites, it is only at the latitude of the Second Cataract, in the Western Desert, that more in-depth studies have been carried out.[5] Along the Nile in Egypt, information on the Mesolithic is almost non-existent.

In the area around Kerma, the recent excavation of a Mesolithic settlement has provided new information on this little-known period in Upper Nubia. A survey conducted in 2001 led to the discovery of several settlements and cemeteries. One of these, threatened with destruction, has been the object of excavation for two years. Called el-Barga, this site is located on an elevation formed by a rise of the rocky substratum, at a little less than 15 km from the Nile.[6] It consists of a habitation area and of several dozen burials divided into two sectors: one to the north, the other to the south (fig. 10).

The northern sector is the oldest; it dates to *c.* 7500–7000 BC and contains traces of a settlement, as well as eleven burials. The remains of domestic activities are represented by an abundant microlithic industry, animal bones, of which the majority are of fish, shells, querns and grinders, some ostrich eggshell beads and a few bone tools including a double-pointed harpoon.

The clearing of an area of more than 200 m² has allowed us to find the floor of a hut dug into the sandstone substratum. It is a sub-circular cavity a little less than 5 m in diameter, whose depth is over 500 mm. To the south a nearby depression can be made out; located

10 Site plan of el-Barga, located on a hill by the alluvial plain. To the north is the Mesolithic settlement with burials, and to the south is a second more recent burial area. Contours at 100 mm intervals.

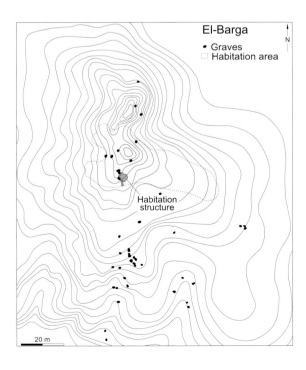

11 Plan of a dwelling with three inhumed individuals inside or nearby. Contours at 100 mm intervals.

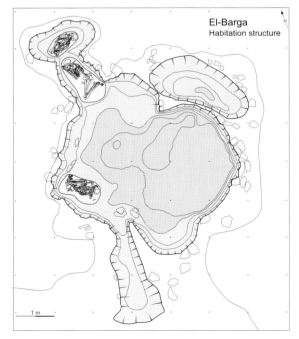

12, 13 Graves of males, discovered in or near the settlement in the northern sector. The individuals were placed inside a leather sack which has now vanished. The unusual position of some of the arms and legs is the result of the bodies having been buried in forced positions.

on the side opposite to the direction of the prevailing winds, it probably corresponds to the entrance of the hut. The dwelling was probably covered by a conical roof made of an armature in wood directly anchored on the edge of the pit, somewhat like the huts at Nabta Playa in the Egyptian desert.[7]

Three male burials were associated with the hut. One was set in the interior, while the other two were located around the edge (fig. 11). There are another eight inhumations in the northern sector. The majority are of adult men, of a notable size and robust build. The bodies were generally placed in a pit and were not accompanied by grave goods, with the exception of one grave that contained a shell. Three burials present an unusual situation: the bones of the legs and sometimes those of the arms seem to have been dislocated, as if the bodies had been forced into a small space, probably a sack (figs 12, 13).

The graves of the southern sector are later in date, c. 6000 BC, a time that may correspond to the beginning of the Neolithic in the area. Some thirty inhumations have been excavated (fig. 15), containing mostly women and children. The grave goods are fairly abundant, generally consisting of shells, necklaces of ostrich eggshell beads (cat. 19) and bracelets of hippopotamus ivory (fig. 14, cat. 18). Stone beads and ceramics are rare. The pots discovered in the tombs are generally complete. They sometimes have a flat bottom and their surface can be decorated entirely. The most surprising objects come from the adult burials. These are flat stones, partially polished, that appear to be the prototypes of cosmetic tablets (cat. 17). In two burials they were accompanied by small stone rubbers. Cosmetic tablets are common in the Neolithic and protohistoric burials where they can be highly sophisticated. In comparison, the examples of el-Barga are still rustic, but are some of the oldest found in the Nile Valley.

The other category of funerary goods discovered in the adult burials is a series of stone lip plugs (cat. 16). These have been consistently found in the vicinity of the mouths of the individuals, which confirms that they were inserted in their upper or lower lips. The lip plugs are particularly rare in Egyptian prehistory and protohistory. On the other hand, they occur more commonly in Sudan, notably in late contexts, from the last millennium BC onwards. They are still used today by some African populations.[8] The examples from el-Barga represent, as far as we know, the earliest examples from north-east Africa.

14 Grave in the southern sector containing a child of approximately six years of age, accompanied by two bracelets of hippopotamus ivory.

15 Field season 2004. Excavating graves in the southern sector.

1 The proposed dates are approximate. They can vary according to the region under consideration and still depend on ongoing research.
2 Cf. Mohamed-Ali and Khabir 2003.
3 The excavation of a site in the city of Khartoum in 1944–5 revealed the existence of the Mesolithic horizon called 'Early Khartoum'. This is characterized by the presence of pottery and by an economy orientated towards the exploitation of water resources (Arkell 1949a).
4 Cf. Caneva et al. 1993; Haaland and Magid 1995.
5 Notably at Nabta Playa (Wendorf and Schild 2001).
6 Honegger 2003, 284–90.
7 These huts are globally dated between 7000 and 6000 BC (Wendorf and Schild 2001).
8 Cf. Fischer 1998.

16 Lip plugs

Ivory, carnelian, amazonite, mesolite

El-Barga, southern sector, Graves 9, 12, 14, 22, 26

Mesolithic or early Neolithic

a L 11 mm, D 3–7 mm, amazonite

b L 10.5 mm, D 1.5–3 mm, amazonite

c L 24 mm, D 1–3 mm, ivory

d L 14 mm, D 1.5–4 mm, carnelian

e L 9 mm, D 1.5–5 mm, mesolite

SNM 31136a–e respectively

Five small bilobed objects were found in the graves of adults near the mouths of the individuals. They are lip plugs that were inserted in a perforation made at the level of the lower or upper lip. They have been carefully made of

16a–e, clockwise from top left

different coloured stones, or in ivory in the case of the longest example. Lip plugs are particularly rare in Egyptian pre- and proto-history, although some have been found in a Badarian context (Hendrickx *et al.* 2001, 87–8). They are more commonly found in the Sudan, especially in contexts of the last millennium BC. At Jebel Moya several lip plugs were discovered, especially in female burials (Gerharz 1994, 89–92). They were attached to the lips or nostril of the individuals. Today people in East Africa still use this type of ornament (Fischer 1998).   MH

17 Palette and grinder

Stone

El-Barga, southern sector, Grave 8

Mesolithic or early Neolithic

L 72 mm, W 54 mm, Th 5 mm

L 28 mm, W 38 mm, Th 20 mm

SNM 31139A–B respectively

Some of the adult graves of el-Barga have yielded partially polished flat pebbles with slightly concave centres. These correspond to the prototypes of make-up palettes, a similar example having been discovered in a domestic context with traces of haematite. Sometimes the palettes are found together with small spherical grinders. Their extremities

17

often show traces of polishing or percussion similar to the finish found on more recent examples such as Pre-Kerma palettes (cat. 47). Make-up palettes, which can attain a high degree of sophistication, are common in Neolithic and protohistoric graves (Reinold 2000a, 58, 64; Nordström 1972, pl. 54). In comparison, the examples of el-Barga, which are usually placed near the stomach of the bodies or by their sides, are still rustic, but are some of the oldest examples found in the Nile Valley.   MH

18 Bracelets

Ivory

El-Barga, southern sector, Graves 18 and 22

Mesolithic or early Neolithic

L 65 mm, W 58 mm, Th 12 mm

L 62 mm, W 61 mm, Th *c.* 12 mm

SNM 31128A–B respectively

The two bracelets presented here are of hippopotamus ivory; their dimensions and other characteristics are similar. Relatively thick, one of their facets still presents the surface of the original canine, which is of an impressive size, and must have belonged to a very large hippopotamus. The bracelets have been made from the tooth cut longitudinally rather than being cut as a cross section. They were then perforated and partially polished. This type of bracelet is found both in adult and infant graves. These thick examples were found by the wrists of the skeleton, but the finer pieces could also be worn at the biceps. Ivory bracelets are common in burials along the Nile Valley. Amongst others, they have been found in the Neolithic graves at Kadruka (Reinold 2000a, 79), in Neolithic or Predynastic burials in Upper Egypt (Brunton and Caton-Thompson 1928), in A-Group contexts (Nordström 1972, 127) and at Kerma (Bonnet 1990a, 180).   MH

18

19 Beads

Ostrich eggshell

El-Barga, southern sector, Grave 9

Mesolithic or early Neolithic

4 strands: L approx. 400 mm; bead: D 5 mm,
Th 1.5 mm

SNM 31129

Ostrich eggshell beads are found fairly frequently among Mesolithic or early Neolithic
grave goods. This assemblage, made up of
nearly one thousand beads, was found in a
female grave near the head. It seems that it
was not a necklace, but a type of hairnet. In
one infant burial of the same period, a string
of ostrich eggshell beads was tied around the
waist. In Nubian pre- and protohistory these
beads are consistently found. Some examples
have been discovered in the Mesolithic
dwelling in the northern sector of el-Barga
(7500–7000 BC). Some are finished while
others are in the process of manufacture,
with unpolished edges, or without the perforation made with the aid of a piercing tool.
Beads of this type are also known in Neolithic
and A-Group contexts, as well as in a Kerma
context (Nordström 1972, 124).   MH

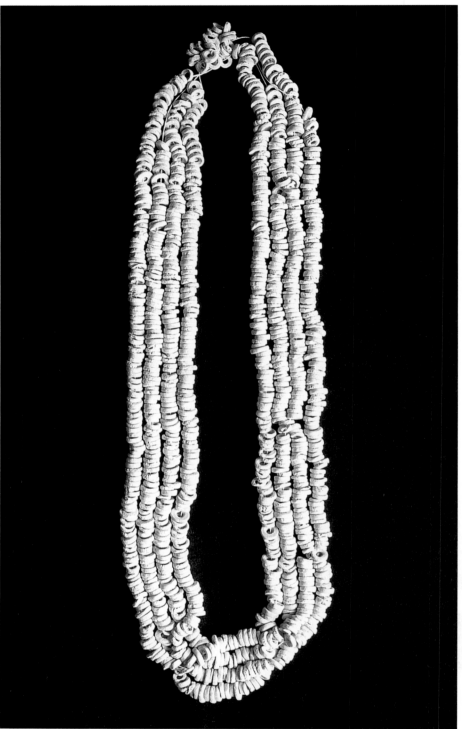

19

2

THE NEOLITHIC

FRIEDERIKE JESSE

16 Excavations at esh-Shaheinab. *Left*: the site from the south-west. *Right*: the site during excavation, looking north.

17 *Below* Pottery and stone tools from esh-Shaheinab: 1 pottery with impressed zigzag decoration; 2 borers; 3 lunates; 4 gouge.

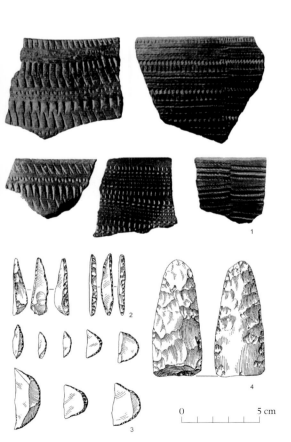

The Neolithic, with its different regional adaptations, is today well known in the Sudan (fig. 18). It lasts from *c.* 4900 BC to *c.* 3000 BC. Two phases can be distinguished: the Early Neolithic, also called Khartoum Neolithic or esh-Shaheinab Complex, dates from 4900 to 3800 BC; the Late Neolithic from thereon to 3000 BC.[1]

A HISTORY OF RESEARCH

More than fifty years ago the pioneering work of A.J. Arkell at sites in Khartoum province provided the first outline of the prehistoric development in Sudan: the hunting-gathering way of life of Early Khartoum was followed by the food-producing economy of the settlers of esh-Shaheinab.[2] The excavation at esh-Shaheinab in 1949 (fig. 16) and the description of the archaeological material became the point of reference for what Arkell proposed calling 'Khartoum Neolithic'. The traces of herding of cattle, sheep and goat found at that site[3] made him favour that term instead of the first proposed name 'Gouge Culture' from the characteristic stone tools, the gouges (fig. 17, 4).[4]

It was only in the 1960s that archaeological research started to intensify. During the Aswan High Dam campaign intensive international archaeological work around the Second Cataract in Nubia was undertaken.[5] The Abkan was identified as a cultural group and considered comparable to the Khartoum Neolithic.[6] A research team of the Southern Methodist University in Dallas, working in the Dongola Reach, defined the Tergis Group and the Karat Group,[7] both with affinities to the Khartoum Neolithic, the latter also with the Abkan.[8]

From the 1970s onwards, the central Sudan was again the focus of research.

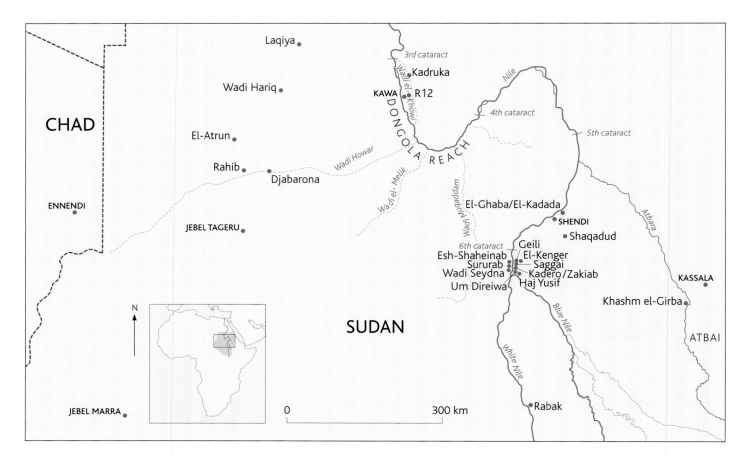

18 Map of Neolithic sites mentioned in the text.

Excavations at Kadero (fig. 19), Geili, Zakiab, Um Direiwa and Haj Yusif – just to name a few – by Italian, Polish, Norwegian and Spanish researchers provided a wealth of new information.[9] Emphasis was no longer laid on the simple collection of data but on providing models and ideas concerning cultural processes, especially the origins of food production. On the west bank of the Nile investigations were made in the middle of the 1970s by the University of Khartoum between Wadi Seydna and Sururab.[10] Rescue operations near Shendi by the French Archaeological Research Unit (SFDAS) of the National Corporation for Antiquities and Museums started in 1976 and expanded Arkell's chronological framework with new information concerning the latest periods of the Neolithic.[11]

The 1980s and the following decades saw not only an extension of the research areas within the Nile Valley itself, but also to areas east and west of the river. The

19 The site of Kadero during excavation in 2001.

excavation of the 'Joint University of Khartoum/Southern Methodist University Butana Project' at Shaqadud in the Butana provided the longest stratigraphic sequence known so far in the Sudan, indicating use of the site from the sixth to the second millennium BC.[12] The Butana Archaeological Project worked at Shaqadud and also in the Khashm el-Girba region, soon combining their efforts with the Italian Archaeological Mission to the Sudan (Kassala) of the Istituto Universitario Orientale, Naples.[13] A team from the University of Bergen performed fieldwork at Rabak, about 230 km south of Khartoum.[14] Work by the SFDAS in the area of the Third Cataract led to the discovery of important sites, especially the cemetery of Kadruka.[15] The Northern Dongola Reach Survey by the Sudan Archaeological Research Society (SARS) showed extensive Neolithic presence around Kawa (fig. 20).[16] In 1980 multi-disciplinary research projects of the University of Cologne started working in the desert areas west of the Nile: the BOS project (Besiedlungsgeschichte der Ost-Sahara), followed by the ACACIA project (Arid Climate, Adaptation and Cultural Innovation in Africa).[17]

Crucial questions that now lead research concern the introduction of domesticated stock, especially cattle, and the adoption of a food-producing way of life, the evolution of social complexity and the obvious gaps in the story, especially between the end of the Neolithic period and the beginning of historic times. In the Wadi Howar region west of the Nile the interaction between the prehistoric groups and the environment through times of increasing aridity is of major interest.

20 Northern Dongola Reach: the Neolithic cemetery at Site E4. Severe wind erosion has uncovered many of the bodies, the bones from which are strewn across the ground.

THE ECOLOGICAL CONTEXT

The Neolithic period started in the fifth millennium BC, at a time when the climate, in what is now the Sahara, was still warm and humid, although it was becoming more and more arid.[18] The shift of the Nile to its westernmost channel around 4300 BC was a decisive ecological change.[19] In the desert east and west of the river, increasing aridity led to a concentration of human settlements in geographically favoured areas such as the different wadi systems in the eastern Sahara.[20] The ecological changes were, however, gradual, affecting the prehistoric dwellers less than cultural or socio-economic changes such as the adoption of food production.[21]

THE ARCHAEOLOGICAL MATERIAL

All sites of the Neolithic period are marked by a more or less dense scatter of potsherds, lithics, grinding material and bones (fig. 21). The graves offer better conditions of preservation than habitation sites: finds of leather in the cemeteries of Kadruka are proof of that.[22] Pottery and lithics have been used by archaeologists to define the Neolithic and to differentiate regional groups. The pottery displays a large variety of decorative patterns.[23] Typical for the period of esh-Shaheinab are different forms of impressed zigzag decoration (fig. 17, 1), especially a zigzag pattern consisting of 'V's and dots.[24] Incised decoration, black-topped pottery and rippled ware are also present. The pottery is well-made, tempered with fine quartz grains, well-smoothed and often polished.[25] Vessel forms are simple in general and consist of bowls or pots with narrow mouths and a hemispherical or ovoid shape. Vessels with a flat base and ladle pots also

21 A dense scatter of archaeological finds on the surface of Abu Tabari S02/1 in the Lower Wadi Howar.

22 A caliciform beaker found at the settlement of Abu Tabari S02/1 in the Lower Wadi Howar.

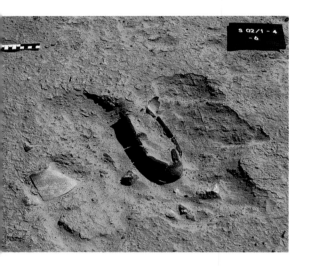

occur. For the Late Neolithic vessel shapes are more diverse and include numerous caliciform beakers (fig. 22).[26] Rocker stamp is still used as a decorative technique, but now finely incised decoration appears and rippled ware occurs.

The lithic industry is characterized by the production of stone flake tools. Quartz is the dominant raw material[27] but chert and agate are also used. The spectrum of tools is small; lunates, groovers and borers are the most prominent forms (fig. 17, 2–3).[28] Composite tools[29] and polished tools such as axes and maceheads of different shapes appear. Typical for sites in the Khartoum area are the gouges, mostly made of rhyolite (fig. 17, 4).[30] Portable art is attested in the graves at several sites, for example at el-Kadada and Kadruka where human female figurines made of burnt clay or occasionally sandstone have been found.[31] Personal adornments include different kinds of beads, bracelets and pendants.[32] Ostrich eggshell was used as a raw material for bead production but ostrich eggs were also used as containers.[33]

THE SUBSISTENCE REGIME

The adoption of food production was not an abrupt change in the way of subsistence. It was well prepared by the already rather sedentary way of life of the preceding Early Khartoum period, the people engaging in storage and more complex systems of food procuring. Domesticated stock, cattle, sheep and goat fitted well into the already structured society. Internal social factors may have been the driving spirit behind the motivation for the shift to pastoralism, not necessarily ecological changes.[34] The diet consisted of meat, milk and probably the blood of cattle, supplemented by fish, molluscs and vegetable food.[35] Cultivation of plants is difficult to discern. The presence of grinding material is inconclusive as wild grains could have been processed. Barley is attested in the graves of Kadruka from the fifth millennium BC.[36] Analysis of plant impressions on pottery from Kadero, Zakiab, Um Direiwa and el-Kadada clearly shows that sorghum was exploited.[37] People probably tended and harvested wild cereal grains such as sorghum but had not yet domesticated them.[38]

Domestic livestock was present from about 4900 BC onwards in the Nile Valley.[39] Its introduction was rapid but patchy and the amount of domestic stock differed enormously from area to area. At esh-Shaheinab, Geili and el-Kenger about 16 per cent of the mammalian assemblages belonged to domestic species, while at sites such as Kadero or Zakiab it was about 80 per cent.[40] In Lower Nubia only a few

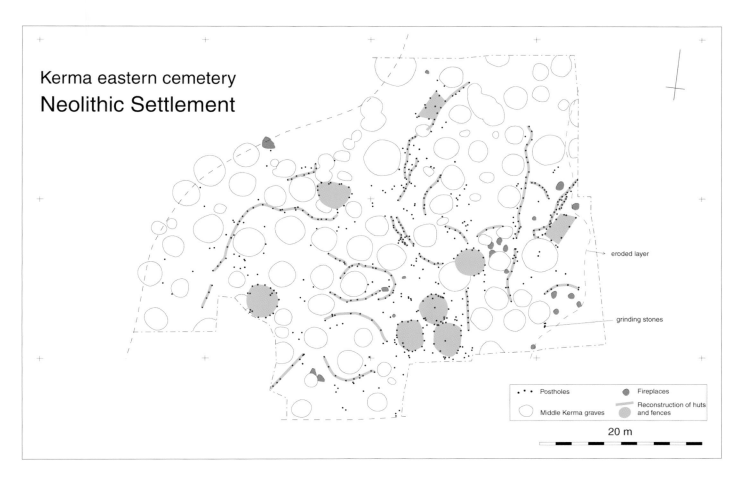

Kerma eastern cemetery
Neolithic Settlement

eroded layer

grinding stones

	Postholes	●	Fireplaces
◯	Middle Kerma graves	●	Reconstruction of huts and fences

20 m

23 The Neolithic settlement at Kerma.

bones of cattle and goat are known at sites of the Abkan.[41] In the Wadi Howar region evidence of cattle appears around 4200 BC, and during the Leiterband Horizon, starting at 4000 BC, cattle herding became the main way of life.[42] Cattle bones represent 90 to 99 per cent of the identifiable mammalian bones on the sites. In the Atbai region south-east of Khartoum domestic livestock was introduced only at the end of the fourth millennium BC.[43]

A wide range of subsistence methods can be seen for the Khartoum Neolithic. Intensive use of livestock, mainly cattle, is attested in the central Sudan and for the Leiterband Horizon in the Wadi Howar region, whereas domestic stock only played a minor role in Nubia or in the areas east of the Nile. People obviously experimented with different strategies of subsistence. These coexisted probably as a symbiotic relationship between different groups who specialized in certain subsistence strategies and then exchanged food supplies and commodities.[44] The large amount of small livestock (sheep and goat) at the Late Neolithic site of el-Kadada,[45] however, may point to an environment already affected by increasing aridity and represent a human response to that change.

SETTLEMENT PATTERNS

Evidence for settlement structures is scarce. At esh-Shaheinab a great number of hearths and some areas paved with small lumps of sandstone, probably used for cooking meat, have been found. No traces of post-holes were noted: the dwellings of the Neolithic settlers may just have been of grass or grass mats.[46] Recent discoveries by the team of the University of Geneva in the Eastern Cemetery at Kerma shed new light on the nature of settlement (fig. 23). Post-holes and fire-places, dating to *c*. 4500 BC, were found covering an area of about 1500 m². Mapping of the post-holes allowed for the reconstruction of roughly circular huts with a diameter of about 4 m, and two rectangular buildings. Palisades existed, partly forming enclosures related to the huts.[47]

A model of seasonal adaptation can be envisioned for sites of the Neolithic period and may be described in greater detail for central Sudan (fig. 24).[48] Large base camps, used more or less the whole year round, coexist with seasonal camps for herding. Fishing was practised in dry season camps close to the river. The dead were buried in cemeteries, which are sometimes closely associated with the settlement areas.[49] In the Wadi Howar region, the dead were, however, buried within the settlement areas.[50] In the areas east and west of the Nile, seasonal movement can also be seen.

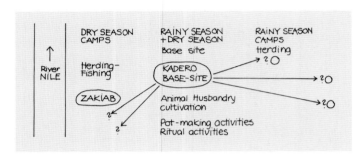

24 A model of seasonal adaptation for the area of Kadero.

SOCIAL COMPLEXITY

Food-producing societies are considered more complex than hunter-gatherer societies. The notion of storage, property and wealth connected with a food-producing way of life leads to social differentiation.[51] Gender was certainly still the basic principle for the division of labour. In modern societies, gathering is mainly a female activity, and women thus have a preponderant role in plant-tending. Herding as well as hunting and fishing are typical male activities. Women also tend to be responsible for pottery-making, collection of firewood and activities related to food preparation.[52] Craft specialization started at this time: at Kadero, an eighteen- to twenty-five-year-old man was buried with a complete set of tools for knapping stone.[53]

Most information concerning social complexity comes from the analysis of the large number of cemeteries in the Nile Valley. Already the Early Neolithic cemeteries, such as Kadero or Kadruka, indicate the existence of a social elite.[54] Richly furnished graves, mostly of men, can clearly be distinguished. Chiefdoms with a well-established elite and based on a concept of hereditary inequality can be postulated. However, the central grave of the Kadruka 18 Cemetery is that of a woman,[55] indicating that women could also have a powerful place in society.

The process of social differentiation continued during the Late Neolithic[56] and finally opened the way for the establishment of well-structured societies such as the Kerma state. The layout of several graves in Cemetery C at el-Kadada indicates that human sacrifice was practised.[57] Evidence for violence is also seen at the Late Neolithic Cemetery R12 in the Northern Dongola Reach: a lumbar vertebra with a flint-backed piece or a lunate still embedded in it has been found.[58]

Cattle played an important role in ideology and ritual during the Neolithic period. Bucrania were placed as grave-offerings with the dead and appear in the cemeteries of el-Ghaba, Kadruka and el-Kadada.[59] The idea of pastoral people stressing the role of cattle beyond their actual role of subsistence – cattle culture – is already evident.[60]

TOWARDS HISTORIC TIMES

Continuous development can be seen during the Neolithic period, though regional components are always visible. The end of the Neolithic differs considerably in different areas. In the north the formation of the A-Group, Pre-Kerma and later the Kerma state is observed.[61] In the central Sudan there is an obvious gap in the settlement history,[62] while in the southern Atbai the formation of the Gash Group of the third millennium BC may also be a powerful entity.[63] In the west the pastoral way of life continued, showing new networks of contact.[64] The central Sudan at this time was probably a periphery between two centres, one in Nubia, the other in the southern Atbai, used by nomadic people leaving only scant traces.[65] This could explain the still-existing gap in the history of the central Nile Valley before the beginning of the Kushite period.

1 Krzyżaniak 1995, 119.
2 Arkell 1949a; 1953.
3 Gautier 1989, tab. 1.
4 Arkell 1953, 102.
5 Geus 1992b.
6 Nordström 1972, 12–17.
7 Shiner 1971a.
8 Marks *et al.* 1968, 321–2; Nordström 1972, 16.
9 Caneva 1988; 1996; Haaland 1987; Kobusiewicz 1996; Krzyżaniak 1984; 1991; 1992a; 1992b; 1995; Fernandez *et al.* 1989; Stemler 1990.
10 Mohammed-Ali 1982.
11 Geus 1984; 1986; 1992a, 255–6; Lecointe 1987; Reinold 1987, 17–43; 2000, 60–61.
12 Marks and Mohammed-Ali 1991.
13 Fattovich *et al.* 1984; Marks and Sadr 1988; Marks 1993.
14 Haaland 1987.
15 Reinold 1987, 44–54; 1991; 2000a, 75–82.
16 Welsby 2001d.
17 Kuper 1981; 1988; 1995; Schuck 1989; Keding 1998; 2000; Hoelzmann *et al.* 2001.
18 Reinold 2001, 58.
19 Caneva 1988, 364.
20 Neumann 1989.
21 Shiner 1971a.
22 Reinold 2000a, 82.
23 Arkell 1953, 68–77; Chłodnicki 1984; Caneva 1988, 79–114; Haaland 1987, 144–79; Marks and Mohammed-Ali 1991, 65–93; Reinold 2002.
24 Arkell 1953, 71.
25 For example, Caneva 1988, 72.
26 Reinold 2002.
27 Marks and Mohammed-Ali 1991, 251.
28 For example, Arkell 1953, 26; Caneva 1988, 121–34; Haaland 1987, 102, tab. 9.
29 Krzyżaniak 1992b, 246.
30 Arkell 1953, 31–2.
31 Reinold 2002, 213–17.
32 For example, Arkell 1953; Caneva 1988; Reinold 2000a.
33 Reinold 2002, 208.
34 Caneva 1985, 428.
35 Caneva 1988, 365.
36 Reinold 2000a, 58.
37 Stemler 1990.
38 Haaland 1987, 204–6.
39 Krzyżaniak 1992a, 269.
40 Gautier 1989.
41 Nordström 1972, 16.
42 Keding 1997b; Van Neer and Uerpmann 1989, 332.
43 Marks and Sadr 1988, 78.
44 Clark 1984, 125.
45 Gautier 1986.
46 Arkell 1953, 79–80, 102.
47 Honegger 2001, 18–19.
48 Haaland 1987.
49 Caneva 1988.
50 Jesse and Keding 2002.
51 Caneva 1988, 368.
52 Haaland 1987.
53 Kobusiewicz 1996, 354.
54 For example, Krzyżaniak 1992a, 270; Reinold 2000a.
55 Reinold 2000a, 77.
56 Krzyżaniak 1992a, 271.
57 Reinold 2000a, 70–71.
58 Salvatori and Usai 2002.
59 Reinold 2000a.
60 Caneva 1988, 366–7.
61 Reinold 2000a.
62 Caneva 1988, 361.
63 Fattovich 1993.
64 Keding 1998.
65 Caneva 1988, 371.

KADRUKA

JACQUES REINOLD

Wadi el-Khowi is an ancient palaeochannel of the Nile on the eastern border of the Seleim and Kerma Basins. It was colonized primarily during the Neolithic. The spread of modern farming to these lands during the 1980s led the French Section of the Sudan Antiquities Service[1] to undertake a programme of survey and rescue excavation.

The present study area is 25 km in length. For the Neolithic period some fifty sites were discovered, of which twenty were cemeteries. The settlements are always found on flat ground. More varied in the distant past, the terrain has gradually been levelled by wind erosion and by deposits of sand that have filled in the depressions. A conservative estimate puts the land deflation since the Neolithic at half a metre.[2] The sites thus present themselves as scatters of objects, occupation levels and structures having disappeared. Excavation only yields the material necessary to prepare typologies, not to analyse the use of space. It is different with the cemeteries, which were always dug into hillocks, the depth of the tomb pits allowing for their preservation. The main interest of these prehistoric cemeteries[3] is that they hold the key that allows us to study the systems of organization of the people. In fact, in a Neolithic context, the location of the tomb within the funerary space can be translated into the social position of the dead person within the community. Following is a brief review of the principal results from the study of these cemeteries.

Cemetery KDK21 is the oldest,[4] and though still undergoing excavation (fig. 25), has already yielded some important results. The funerary mound was man-made, and thus testifies to a social cohesion necessary for such an enterprise. Individual burials of dogs, arranged on the perimeter of the cemetery at each of the four cardinal points, suggest sophisticated rituals (fig. 26). Stelae border some of the grave pits, the first examples of a practice that one finds in other, later Nubian civilizations (fig. 27). Hearths near the grave cuts and at different levels suggest the practice of specific rites. A rectangular area without graves to the east of the mound may correspond to a structure of which only the negative remains. The main tomb is that of a woman for whom a man has undoubtedly been sacrificed (fig. 28).

25 Cemetery KDK21: general view with Wadi el-Khowi in the background. The area in the foreground corresponds to the location of a building and was free of burials.

a woman had a dozen individuals placed in a circle around her burial in the centre of the mound.

Cemetery KDK1, the most recent,[7] presents a completely different arrangement. In this case it was at the time of death of the principal person in the group (fig. 29), a man of over forty, that the decision was made to use a new cemetery. The variety and the richness of the funerary goods that accompany the burial (cats 22, 273) mark him as the chief of this community of agriculturalists and stock-raisers, during the fifth millennium BC. The spatial organization of the burials presents a division into two groups (fig. 30). The one located at the summit develops in concentric circles around Tomb 131 and includes the individuals (all ages and sexes mixed) with the greatest number of grave goods. The further from the centre of the circle, the poorer the grave goods. The other group, which is located on the slope, presents a higher percentage of females. The grave goods are poorer than those of the first group and certain prestige objects are completely absent. The preferential spread of certain types of objects, as well as the arrangement of the grave cuts,

26 Cemetery KDK21/190–91: pit with two dogs bordering the cemetery to the north.

Cemetery KDK13 is contemporary with KDK21,[5] from which it is 2 km distant. Very degraded, it has not been possible to study the social structure of the group buried here. It yielded ceramic material different from that found at KDK21, and therefore shows contemporary occupation in the area by different human groups. It should be mentioned that the conical-shaped containers recovered here give us the first examples of the decoration called 'rippled ware' that only appear elsewhere in Nubia with the A-Group and Pre-Kerma cultures.

Cemetery KDK18, a little later in date,[6] shows the use of the funerary space around an 'alley' left free of burials. In the final phase of its use, the main burial of

27 *Left* Cemetery KDK21: view of the stelae in the north-west area.

28 *Above* Cemetery KDK21: graves 240–41. The main burial is of a female with a sacrificed male placed in the same grave to the north.

29 Cemetery KDK1:
main burial
(KDK1/131).

indicates a difference in status between the inhumations and suggests a very class-conscious society. With
the change in the sex of the principal burial comes also
a change in the distribution of some of the objects.
Here the caliciform beakers linked to funerary libations, present in Cemeteries KDK21 and KDK18 in the
female burials, are, in the case of Cemetery KDK1, the
appanage of the males (cats 22, 271).

To conclude this brief description, the first point
to be noted is the impossibility of making palaeo-
demographic evaluations for these communities. In
fact, these cemeteries never contained all members of
the group. A proportion of them were always buried in
very large cemeteries (with over a thousand inhumations) used over long periods. The reason for this
practice remains unknown. The homogeneity of the
archaeological material suggests that the small cemeteries were used by the same group over a short period
of time (probably no more than a century). If these
cemeteries present several similarities and suggest a
common root, especially on the level of material culture, conversely they also indicate customs that vary
from one cemetery to another within the same geographical area. At this stage of our research, the
constants and the variants seem to show both the
homogeneity of these populations and a rapid evolution of their social fabric. The absolute dates at our disposal are not always sufficient to be able to determine
precisely if these customs are specific to a particular
period of time, which would allow us to trace their
evolution, or if they correspond to the existence in the
same period of several societies organized according to
different models. However, considering the homogeneity of the ceramic material collected at each site,
there seems to be one population whose social structure is undergoing a period of change or evolution. The
material culture, which shows close relations with
that of later periods, also demonstrates a cultural
continuity within this area near the Third Cataract.
Having reached a certain stage of social hierarchy, the
basic character of these societies did not continue to
evolve except to accommodate an increasing population. Thus they served as the prelude to the appearance
of kingdoms, which fits well with the concept that
Neolithic communities were organized as chiefdoms.[8]

30 Plan of Cemetery
KDK1, showing the
spread in concentric
circles around burial
no. 131.

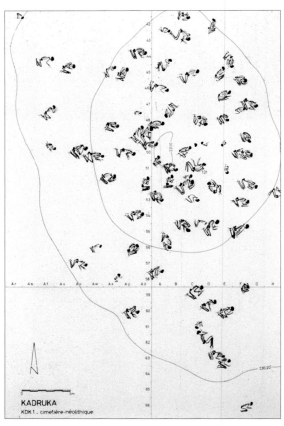

KADRUKA
KDK1 . cimetière-néolithique

1 The French Section of the Sudan Antiquities Service
(Section Française de la Direction des Antiquités du Soudan) is a
permanent mission at the disposal of the National Corporation for
Antiquities and Museums, answering to the French Ministry of
Foreign Affairs. For a general bibliography of the sites studied
here, see Reinold 1997. For studies of the individual sites see
Reinold 1993a; 1997; 1998; 2000a; 2001; 2002; 2003a.

2 Cf. Reinold 1992. To the south of the Seleim Basin, research
has shown an even greater degradation (Welsby 2001d, 608–10),
but to the north in the Kerma Basin the situation is different.
There the Neolithic horizons are preserved and allow for a
stratigraphic study (Honegger 2001) of the settlement levels.
3 Of a total of seventeen cemeteries, three were completely
excavated (KDK1, 13 and 18), sondages were carried out at five
(KDK4, 15, 19, 22 and 33), and three are in the course of
excavation (KDK2, 21, 22). This has allowed for the excavation
of a little over 600 tombs. These cemeteries thus permit us to
study the funerary practices over more than a millennium, from
4620+/−80 BC (for KDK33) to 3340+/−60 BC (for KDK1). Cf. Geus,
this volume, p. 276.
4 It has furnished four dates ranging between 3900+/−70 BC and
3960+/−60 BC.

5 It has furnished three dates ranging between 3860+/–60 BC and 4040+/–60 BC.

6 It has furnished five dates ranging between 3520+/–70 BC and 3630+/–70 BC.

7 It has furnished three dates ranging between 3340+/–60 BC and 3640+/–60 BC, although this last date seems too high. The two others, between 3340+/–60 BC and 3410+/–70 BC, conform better to the homogeneity of the artefacts that cannot have ranged over three centuries.

8 To conclude, it is necessary to point out that the research on the Seleim and Kerma Basins benefits from cooperation between the Section Française de la Direction des Antiquités du Soudan, the University of Geneva with Charles Bonnet and Matthieu Honegger, and the Sudan Archaeological Research Society with Derek Welsby, Donatella Usai and Sandro Salvatori (Salvatori and Usai 2001; 2002). One of the most fortuitous results of this cooperation is to have demonstrated the development of cultures since prehistory, without hiatus. The enduring settlement in this region is the basis for a study of settlement through time and our contribution to the history of the Sudan.

20

20 Female anthropomorphic figurine

Terracotta

El-Kadada, Cemetery C, Grave 95, KDD 85/95/1

Neolithic, middle of fourth millennium BC

H 68 mm, W 23 mm, Th 22 mm

SNM 26970

With one exception, these Neolithic female figurines are always stylized representations of the human body (cf. cats 272–3). The limbs are not depicted and the 'base' of the body is flattened. Always of small size, these figurines were conceived according to the principle of a curvilinear arabesque composition of joining ovals. The heads are small and the hair, here represented by a pecked cap, is always shown. The navel is always depicted, although the reason for this is unknown. Incised grooves around the neck undoubtedly represent necklaces (one example also shows two small holes, by the location of the arms that were intended to hold in place a string of ostrich eggshell beads); those at the level of the pelvis seem to correspond to tattoos or to decorated clothes.

Figurines of this form are the most frequent type found at el-Kadada, although they are not found elsewhere in Nubia. The closest stylistic comparisons are in Saharan rock art, particularly at Messak. The female representations there show the same kind of hairstyle and the robes they wear have the same flattened cylindrical appearance.   JR

Reinold 2000a, 80, 138, no. 37; 2000b, 17, no. 37; 2003b, 247, no. 214; Wildung 1997, 18, no. 3; 1999, fig. 13

21 Comb

Elephant ivory

Kadruka, Cemetery KDK 1, Grave 104, KDK 1/104/1

Neolithic, first quarter of fifth millennium BC

L 91+ mm, W 41 mm, Th 12.4 mm

SNM 26870

This comb was probably made from an elephant tusk that was sawn off and then polished. The distal side is broken but originally had seven tines of which only the bases remain. They were slightly oblique in relation to the longitudinal axis of the piece. Elephant

21

or hippopotamus ivory is mainly used to make personal ornaments, combs, needles, bracelets and make-up boxes. The latter chiefly contain green powders, resulting from the grinding of malachite. Blocks of ivory, fashioned from elephant tusks, sometimes in the process of being carved, are found in some grave deposits.

The example presented here comes from the fill of a disturbed grave that contained the bones of two individuals, an adult male and female, and it was the only remaining object. While they are common in later periods, these objects are rare in the Neolithic, perhaps because of problems connected with their preservation, and are all of the same type. The grave of the primary person (KDK1/131) exceptionally contained two that were placed by the edge of the grave cut, next to a quern. They were used for grooming or decoration. In connection with grooming, it is interesting to note the elegant coiffures depicted on some Neolithic figurines (cat. 20).   JR

Reinold 1994b, 80, no. 81; 1998, fig. 6; 2000a, 78, fig. 137, no. 12; 2000b, 13, no. 12; 2003b, 195, no. 118

22 Caliciform beaker

Terracotta with gypsum infill
Kadruka, Cemetery 1, Grave 131, KDK1/131/18
Neolithic, 4228 BC (calibrated) (5360 BP +/−70)
H 374 mm, max. D 219 mm, min. D 62 mm
SNM 26883

This vessel belongs morphologically to the group of medium-sized (ER-M) pots with composite form, and to the category of vessels known as 'caliciform' (cf. cat. 271). It has been made using the coil technique. The surfaces are polished. The decoration has been produced by means of a rocker stamp: the teeth of the comb are pressed into the clay by a pivoting movement which uses the last point obtained as a pivot to continue in the opposite direction. The wide mouth is

decorated with a seven-pointed star motif. The body is divided into three registers, the middle one having merely been burnished. The two others are separated into panels (three for the lower and five for the upper) by thin spiral bands starting from the base of the vessel. The panels are filled in with dotted lines that by the change of axis of the comb produce an angular motif quite close to the chevron motif. To highlight the decorative nature of the dots they have been infilled with gypsum. While fairly rare, this shape is found in different periods of the Neolithic, lasting over a thousand years, both in the central Sudan as well as in Nubia. It was

discovered in the grave of the 'chieftain' that also contained a figurine, cat. 273, and was used for funerary libations.   JR

Reinold 1991, 25, no. 6; 1994a, 86, no. 86; 1998, fig. 1; 2000a, 61, fig. 138, no. 35; 2000b, 16; 2002, 107, fig. 4; 2003b, 220, no. 166; Wildung 1997, 22, no. 9

23 Female anthropomorphic figurine

Terracotta
El-Kadada, Cemetery C, Grave 9, KDD76/9/2
Neolithic, middle of fourth millennium BC
H 89.8 mm, max. D 40.7 mm
SNM 26895

Figurines such as this, designed along the principle of the circle, are a recurring theme

22

23

24

from the Palaeolithic onwards. There are examples from Nubia and the central Sudan. The most characteristic is the statue shown here. Nearly 90 mm tall, it is made of clay and represents a stylized female. The body is made up of three spheres of decreasing size that are connected by concave elements at the neck and waist. The head is a mere continuation of the neck with two oblique incisions to indicate the eyes and a braid. The body itself gives an indication of the shoulders, breasts, and pelvis. The moulded body has been incised to show the eyes, the hair, and a necklace. The motifs incised on the breasts and the pelvis may be tattoos or representations of clothes.

The figurine comes from the disturbed grave of a child aged between five and seven years. It was placed by the neck of the child.

JR

Reinold 1987, 34, fig. 7; 1994a, 56, fig. p. 55; 2000a, 68, fig. 138, no. 39; 2000b, 17, no. 39; 2002, 214, fig. 15; 2003b, 247, no. 213; Welsby 1995, 104, no. I.73; Wildung 1997, 18, no. 2

24 Basin

Terracotta and yellow ochre

Kadruka, Cemetery 1, Grave 39, KDK1/39/1

Neolithic, first quarter of fifth millennium BC

H 90 mm, max. D 198 mm; rim interior D 181 mm

SNM 26877 (wrongly inscribed on the vessel as SNM 26892)

Like all pottery of the period this vessel is hand-made, using the so-called coil technique. Morphologically it belongs to the group of pots with not very wide mouths and of

25

medium size (PEM).[1] During the earliest phases of the Neolithic it is the predominant form, but it remains common in the later phases. Of black colour, it is covered in a yellow slip; the exterior is burnished, while the interior has been smoothed. The rim is decorated with short incisions that cut each other at right angles, forming a net motif. The body has painted decoration, or rather a layer

of coloured slip (obtained from Nubian sandstone) applied as angular ribbons, like the nets used to suspend the vessels. Painted decoration is often used in later periods but is unusual in the Neolithic: only this cemetery contains some examples. The unpainted pottery from this site, with the exception of the caliciform beakers, does not have decoration on the actual body of the vessels. The decoration is limited to the rim and consists of incisions arranged in various motifs. This vessel was found behind the pelvis of a female body; her grave had been disturbed and no longer contained anything but a bucranium above (over) the legs.   JR

1 For a discussion of ceramic morphology see Reinold 1987, 29–30.

Reinold 1994b, 83, no. 87; 2000a, 47; 2000b, 15, no. 33; 2002, 213, fig. 13

25 Female anthropomorphic figurine

Terracotta

Kadruka, Cemetery 18, Grave 5, KDK18/5/1

Neolithic, second quarter of fifth millennium BC

H 80 mm, W 61 mm, Th 42 mm

SNM 28680

This is the only example of a figurine fashioned from a small ball of clay and simply left to dry. It was shaped by attaching round balls of decreasing size together by means of a concave object, and is prolonged by a kind of cylinder, forming the neck and ending with a small excrescence that represents the head. A simple swelling denotes the chest, while the breasts are not indicated.

The significance of these female figurines and their presence in the graves has given rise to several theories. However, in the absence of any written sources or specific information about the religious beliefs of these cultures, one has to be very cautious in interpreting them. Whilst always in a funerary environment, they have been found in different contexts – in graves of children, women and men, some rich in grave goods, though occasionally they were the only such object in the grave. The only certainty is that the schematization of the human body is not due to a lack of skill of the artist (one figurine is made in such a realistic fashion that it has formed the basis of an anatomic-physiological lecture), but to the desire to produce a symbolic representation of it.   JR

Reinold 2000a, 78, fig. 138, no. 40; 2000b, 17, no. 40

26 Bowl/strainer

Terracotta

Kadruka, Cemetery 1, Grave 120, KDK 1/120/3

Neolithic, first quarter of fifth millennium BC

H 61 mm; max. D 87 mm; rim interior D 780 mm;
avg D of perforations 2.2 mm

SNM 26882

This receptacle morphologically belongs to the
category of small-sized (PE-P) receptacles with

26

not very wide mouth – the category of bowls.
As its body is covered by small perforations,
made from the interior towards the exterior,
undoubtedly with a stick, it is clear that it was
used as a strainer. Of grey colour, its walls have
been smoothed. Decoration is limited to the
rim and just below it on the exterior, and consists of a series of angular lines deeply incised,
of which one branch runs along the lip of the
rim and just below it on the exterior.

Once again, this type of vessel is characteristic of Cemetery KDK1 at Kadruka. In the
context of the European Neolithic it would be
seen as a strainer used in the production of
cheese. The fact that it was found filled with
chaff does not permit us to formulate any
hypothesis about its function. It comes from
the rich burial of a child of about ten years of
age, which also yielded four pots including a
caliciform beaker, a bucranium, a cosmetic
container containing a very long and thin
needle as well as malachite powder and a
composite tool with microliths. This last
object, certainly not used by a child of ten,
shows that the goods placed in the graves were
chosen by the living and testified to the rank of
the dead and their position within society.   JR

Reinold 1994b, 86, no. 94; Wildung 1997, 27,
no. 15

27 Beaker

Terracotta, red and yellow ochre

Kadruka, Cemetery 1, Grave 142

Neolithic, first quarter of fifth millennium BC

H 131 mm; max. D 122 mm; rim interior D 109 mm

SNM 28732

This vessel morphologically belongs to the
category of small-sized (PR-P) pots with
slightly inward leaning sides – the category of
beakers. It presents the unusual characteristic of having a flat base.

Unusual in the central Sudan, pots with
flat bases are not found in Upper Nubia except
in Cemetery KDK1 at Kadruka, which has
furnished numerous examples. This cemetery
is also the only one to have yielded bowls and
jars with carinated profiles. This pot, whose
rim was broken, has been repaired by making
a double line of perforations (fifteen in total)
to allow the introduction of a ligature. The
painted decoration is unusual: this beaker is
the only example that exhibits rectangular
decoration motifs. The vessel is divided into
three horizontal bands: the uppermost is of
yellow slip, the middle one does not include
decoration, and the lower and the base are
covered in red colour. It was found in the
grave of a man with two other painted pots
and several bucrania.   JR

Reinold 2000a, 66, fig. 138, no. 34; 2000b, 15,
no. 34

28 Beads and pendants

Green veined stone and agate

Kadruka, Cemetery 21, Grave 107, KDK21/107/4-6

Neolithic, second half of fifth millennium BC

H 12–22 mm, W 6.5–13 mm, Th 3–6 mm,
D of perforations 2–3 mm

SNM 28799

Beads are very common in the Neolithic.
They are made of different materials ranging
from types of stone (sandstone, agate, amazonite, quartz and green stone), to ivory, bone
and ostrich eggshell. The term 'bead' is
intended for disc, ring or spherical beads that
are usually given a final polish. The term
'pendant' refers to all other shapes, the most
common being the 'teardrop'. In the present
case we have three examples for which the
craftsman has used small pebbles that he has
simply perforated working from both facets, a
process that limits the risk of the piece
shattering during the drilling. Beads and
pendants may be found isolated or in groups
to form bracelets and necklaces. In rare
instances the latter include different types of

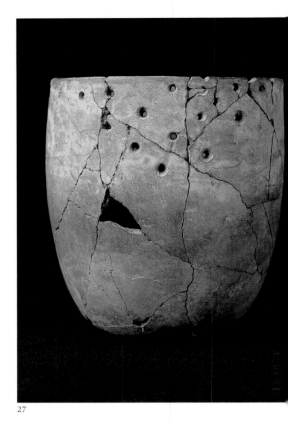

27

bead. The beads were worn by men, women
and children. Cemetery KDK1 at Kadruka
yielded an infant burial of a child under five
years of age, with a sheep placed in the grave.
The animal had around its neck a necklace of
amazonite beads. Isolated pendants are often
found by the necks of children.   JR

Reinold 2000a, 59, fig. 137, no. 19; 2000b, 14,
no. 19

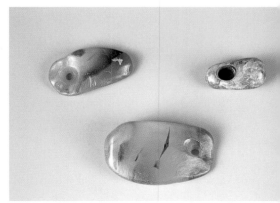

28

KADERO

LECH KRZYŻANIAK

This site is situated some 20 km north of the centre of Khartoum and 6 km to the east of the Nile, in an area which increasingly is becoming the edge of greater Khartoum. The site consists of a low mound approximately 4 ha in surface area. Geological research carried out recently on and near the site demonstrated that the mound was in existence long before the first human settlement was established on its surface during the Early Khartoum period; it was

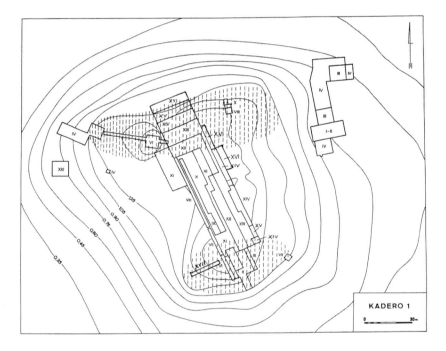

31 Plan of Kadero.

apparently created at the end of the Pleistocene out of Blue Nile sands and eroded low desert sediments.[1]

The site is covered almost entirely with the remains of a Khartoum Neolithic occupation. Some potsherds of the Early Khartoum tradition have been also found at the site and may be the remains of a seasonal camp of this fishing-hunting-gathering group. The Neolithic remains are composed of two settlement middens and a cemetery. There is no doubt that these remains belong to the same human group. The site was initially tested in 1972 and excavations have been undertaken in alternate years ever since (figs 31, 32).

A series of radiocarbon determinations date Kadero to the fifth millennium BC. Excavations on both middens have resulted in the discovery of a large amount of typical settlement material: potsherds, different lithics including grinding stones, bone implements, isolated personal adornments, and animal and plant remains. Particularly striking is the exceptionally large number of fragments of lower and upper grindstones, indicating intensive use of these tools (cat. 29). Animal remains consisted of both game and domestic animals. Of the mammals, a large majority of remains – some 82 per cent – belonged to domestic stock: cattle, sheep and goat. However, the Kadero Neolithic faunal remains are dominated by cattle, which represent some 80 per cent of all domestic skeletal material in the sample. In some cases it was possible for an archaeozoologist to find fragments of the heavy, long horns of these cattle. The game species were represented by fauna that lived in the seasonally flooded riverain savannah.

Despite the use of various sampling methods, little has been learnt about the plant material from Kadero. With the exception of an African hackberry tree, *Celtis integrifolia*, and the dom palm *Hyphaena thebaica*, no other plant seeds have been found in the middens or graves. The remaining botanical finds consist of typical savannah bushes and trees, so the question regarding the kind of plant material being processed on the numerous grindstones discovered at Kadero still remains unanswered.

The lithic material from the Kadero middens is dominated by different quartz artefacts: tools, debitage and raw pieces that originated from the low desert. Quartz was supplemented by a high-quality rhyolite stone that originated from the volcanic rocks of the Sixth Cataract. This rhyolite was used to manufacture gouges, amongst other tools, which are diagnostic of the Khartoum Neolithic (esh-Shaheinab Neolithic). It is thought that these gouges and axeheads, also made of rhyolite, could have been used for woodworking. Excavation on both middens has also yielded a large sample of pottery. It has been possible to find potsherds with adjoining edges only in a very few instances. This indicates a heavy mixing of the midden material, which in turn seems to suggest that these middens were formed by the systematic sweeping of the habitation areas – situated on other parts of the mound – by the Neolithic Kaderans. The forms, technology and decoration of this pottery are typical for the Khartoum Neolithic. The best examples come from the furnishings of the Kadero inhumations. Bone artefacts from the Kadero middens

32 Excavations at
Kadero in 1991.

33 Tomb 113: a richly
furnished Neolithic
grave.

are represented by a few examples of cutting tools (axe-heads) and piercing tools (awls). Among the personal adornments, which occur rather infrequently, are beads made of ostrich eggshell, bone and carnelian.

While the information yielded from the settlement middens focuses on the ecology, subsistence, pottery, lithic and bone toolkit and their respective technologies, excavation of the local burial ground sheds interesting and much-needed light on the demography and skeletal morphology of the Kaderan individuals, as well as on the social structure of this Neolithic group.

Thus far some 200 Neolithic graves have been excavated at Kadero. It seems that they are distributed on the central and eastern part of the mound rather than on its western portion. Adults of both sexes, juveniles and babies were interred in these graves, although the latter are clearly under-represented, a situation typical of prehistoric cemeteries. Two different groups of graves can be seen at this site, as determined by the variation in the quantity and quality of tomb furnishings. The large majority of inhumations were found without any, or with few, goods, for example, a pottery vessel of utility ware. The same gender and age composition of individuals occurs in the other, but much smaller, group of richly furnished graves which comprised 8–10 per cent of the whole sample. These rich graves tend to occur in clusters. They are interpreted as burials of the Kadero Neolithic social elite (fig. 33). Their grave pits were excavated deeper than those of the poor class of graves, and their furnishings display the full spectrum of the Khartoum Neolithic inventory. It is worth mentioning several kinds of grave goods:

amongst the pottery, often painted red, all types previously known from esh-Shaheinab and other Neolithic sites are represented, and vessels belonging to the finest class of prehistoric African pottery are included. Imports include Red Sea shells used as beads, beads made of amazonite and lumps of malachite. Anklets and bracelets made of elephant ivory (fig. 34), bracelets

34 Tomb 162: an individual with ivory bracelets.

made of hippopotamus ivory, toiletry kits composed of stone palettes and grinders, and personal decorations such as necklaces composed of carnelian beads are particularly impressive. Stone maceheads occur only in the graves of adult men. The Kadero graveyard also yielded unusual finds such as regular rows of quartz lunates with remains of mastic adhering to their backs. These have been interpreted as the remains of cutting tools composed originally of a wooden or bone handle, and with a cutting edge made of these microliths.

The Kadero site has yielded finds that have enriched the archaeological inventory of the Khartoum Neolithic culture, but it seems that the real importance of this site stems from its unique character: it has a settlement and burial ground that belonged to the same human group, thus shedding light on a broad spectrum of all aspects of life. Considering the wider implication for the later prehistory of north-eastern Africa, the information concerning the structure of this early pastoral society is of particular importance.

1 For bibliographic references to Kadero, see Krzyżaniak and Krzyżaniak *et al.* in the Bibliography of this volume.

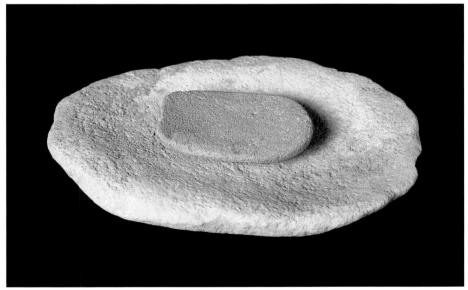

29

29 Grindstone

Sandstone

Kadero, Grave 202, no. 202/3

Neolithic

Quern (lower grindstone): L 320 mm, W 230 mm, Th 60 mm: small (upper ?) grinding stone or palette: L 131 mm, W 87 mm, Th 26 mm

SNM 31149A–B

This is the only example of a lower grindstone found intact at Kadero thus far. It has a regular shape and its working surface bears traces of delicate pecking, undoubtedly to make it grind better. The upper grinding stone or palette seems to have two working surfaces, which may indicate that this object served two functions. As its upper surface is finer than the lower one, this seems to point to its use as a palette.   LK

30

31

30 Cup

Ceramic

Kadero, Grave 203, no. 203/1

Neolithic

H 130 mm; rim: max. D 107 mm; base: max.
D 87 mm

SNM 31147

This is a flat-bottomed cup without a handle.
The rim is decorated with incised lines and
the outer surface with four horizontal rows of
incised triangles. The underside of the base is
decorated with three 'bow'-like lines. Outer
and inner surfaces are light brown with dark
patches. The pot was originally found in
fragments. This is an atypical form for the
Khartoum Neolithic. So far, only two such
pots, almost identical to each other in form
and decoration, have been found in the
Neolithic cemetery at Kadero. This pot should
perhaps be dated to the beginning of the Late
Khartoum Neolithic.   LK

31 Bowl

Ceramic

Kadero, Grave 220

Neolithic

H 140 mm, max. D 126 mm; rim: D 120 mm

SNM 31148

A deep bowl with a rounded base, the entire
outer surface, including the base, is decorated
with a design consisting of small impressed
dots and short triangles. The outer and inner
surfaces are light brown with darker patches.
The pot was originally found in fragments
and is a typical form both in shape and decoration for the Khartoum Neolithic.   LK

THE WADI HOWAR

FRIEDERICKE JESSE

To sum up, there appears to have been living along the wadi, and in the neighbouring oases, a considerable population, practising agriculture, pasturing cattle, making good pottery with very varied incised designs, using ostrich-shell beads and occasionally beads of turquoise ... and burying their dead in a contracted position. (Shaw 1936)

The Wadi Howar, today a large dry river system at the southern margin of the Sahara, was once the most important western tributary of the Nile and a significant link with the inner parts of Africa (fig. 35). It originates in the mountainous region between the Ennedi and Jebel Marra, and joins the Nile between the Third and Fourth cataracts, opposite Old Dongola.[1] Together with the surrounding areas, including Jebel Tageru, a large sandstone plateau, and the Ennedi Erg, a former swamp and lake region, this part of the Southern Libyan Desert offers great potential for the study of prehistoric settlements.[2]

The whole region is now barren desert. Monsoonal rains coming from the south turned the area from around 8300 BC onwards into an environment perfectly suited for human settlement: the wadi then was a chain of lakes and temporary water pools. Savannah vegetation bordered the stretches of water and large mammals thrived.[3] Due to the intense research started by the University of Cologne in 1980, more than 2,000 archaeological sites of different periods are now known in the Southern Libyan Desert indicating prehistoric settlement from the sixth to the second millennium BC.[4] Through analyses of the various pottery types, three main cultural horizons can be distinguished (fig. 36).

The first settlers arrived in the sixth millennium BC and found perfect ecological conditions: permanent surface water, savannah-type vegetation, large mammals and fish. Well-made pottery characterizes this period; distinctive are the Dotted Wavy Line and the Laqiya type patterns (*c.* 5200–4000 BC) (fig. 37, 1–2).[5] The latter is an indicator of regional diversification as this pattern is known neither in the Nile Valley nor further west.[6]

Traces of this early pottery horizon have been found throughout the region. The large sites are situated in

35 The Middle Wadi Howar as seen from Jebel Rahib.

36 The cultural
sequence of Wadi
Howar.

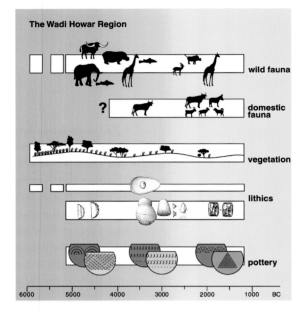

The Wadi Howar Region

wild fauna

domestic fauna

?

vegetation

lithics

pottery

6000   5000   4000   3000   2000   1000   BC

37 Some
archaeological
material from the
Wadi Howar:
1 Dotted Wavy Line,
Abu Tabari 84/50;
2 Laqiya type pattern,
Conical Hill S95/4;
3 Leiterband pattern,
Djabarona 80/86;
4 Handessi A,
Djabarona 84/1;
5 Darfur axe,
Djabarona 84/13;
6 Handessi B,
Djabarona S96/119.

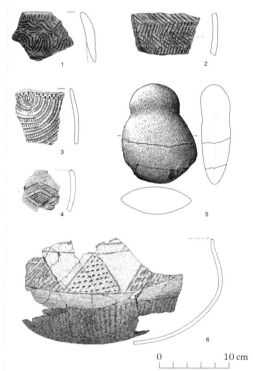

1

2

3

4

5

6

0   10 cm

the vicinity of important bodies of water (fig. 38). A dense scatter of sherds, stone tools, grinding material and bones indicates intensive long-term occupation or repeated visits over a long period. The people's livelihood was based on hunting, fishing and gathering.[7] This was still practised when domestic livestock was already well established in the Nile Valley.

A significant change occurred at the beginning of the fourth millennium BC with the onset of the Leiterband Horizon (c. 4000–2000 BC). Various Leiterband motifs (fig. 37, 3) become the most prominent decora-

tive patterns.[8] Axes appear, including the characteristic Darfur axes (fig. 37, 5),[9] and there is a marked change in the economic way of life. The people of the Leiterband Horizon were cattle keepers.[10] Ecological conditions remained favourable. The thorn savannah still persisted, offering a suitable landscape for the pastoral way of life. The dependence on animals and their need for pasture and water led to seasonality of occupation and mobility.

The Middle Wadi Howar, too swampy during Early Holocene times, now became a major centre for the prehistoric occupants.[11] The area used by the Leiterband people also included the western parts of the Lower Wadi Howar, the Ennedi Erg, Jebel Tageru and the Ennedi to the west. No Leiterband pottery has been recorded north-east of the Wadi Howar.[12] Here, different decorative patterns have been found, some of them typical of the A-Group,[13] thus proving that clear stylistic boundaries existed during that period.

Typical of Leiterband sites are concentrations of potsherds and bones which are visible in pits. These concentrations can occur in very large numbers. On the Djabarona 84/13 site in the Middle Wadi Howar over 1,000 of these features have been recorded, making this site unique (fig. 39).

The adoption of a food-producing subsistence strategy was sudden and complete.[14] Evidence for any intermediate steps is not known. The Nile Valley was possibly the origin of this pastoral subsistence strategy. The earlier stages of the Leiterband Horizon are considered a regional development of the esh-Shaheinab complex. The later stages show, however, much more affinities to areas in the west, such as the Ennedi,[15] and the link with the Nile Valley seems to have been severed.

Increasing aridity in the whole region had a great impact on settlement patterns and the way of life. During the Handessi Horizon (2200–1100 BC) sheep and goats, better adapted to a drier climate, were added to the herds, although cattle were still kept. Hunting became important again.[16] Settlement was concentrated in favourable areas such as the Middle Wadi Howar and Jebel Tageru, and north of the Wadi Howar in wadi systems with springs or wells.[17]

New decoration appears with different types of geometric patterns made by simple impression and incision. Organic temper is much more common than in the previous periods. Vessel forms are diversified to include bowls of different shapes, some with a curved profile.[18] Two phases – Handessi A (2200–1900 BC) and Handessi B (1700–1100 BC) – can be distinguished via the decorative patterns (figs 37, 4; 37, 6).[19]

Strong similarities in pottery decoration and technology can be seen on sites in the Middle Wadi Howar and

38 The Dotted Wavy
Line site, Rahib
80/87, in the western
foothills of Jebel Rahib.

39 The countless
concentrations of
potsherds and bones
at the Leiterband site
Djabarona 84/13 in
the Middle Wadi
Howar.

areas further north up to the Laqiya region. Via the
latter, contact with the C-Group and the Kerma culture
of the Nubian Nile Valley can be observed.[20] Donkeys
found at different sites of that period indicate mobility.
They were used in caravans, as described by Harkhuf,
an Old Kingdom official, in the account of his journeys
beyond the borders of Egypt.[21] Large transhumance
cycles can be supposed.

So far, the history of human settlement in the Wadi
Howar region can be traced to around 1100 BC, after
which climatic conditions became too arid for permanent use. Traces of human presence are, however, still
found, especially in the Middle Wadi Howar which
today continues to be used as pasturage by Kababish
nomads[22] and presents quite a pleasant picture of a
wadi in the desert – a green belt of Shau-bushes (*Sal-
vadora persica*) traversing the sand.[23]

1 Pachur and Kröpelin 1987.
2 For bibliographic references to the Wadi Howar see Jesse 2000;
2002a; Jesse and Keding 2002; Keding 1997a; 1997b; 1998;
2000; forth.; Kuper 1981; 1988; 1995; Richter 1989.
3 Neumann 1989; Kröpelin 1993; Berke 2001.
4 For example, Kuper 1995; Keding 1998; 2000; Keding
and Vogelsang 2001; Hoelzmann *et al.* 2001; Jesse and Keding
2002.
5 Jesse 2000; 2003.
6 Jesse 2003, 189.
7 Keding and Vogelsang 2001, 266.
8 Keding 1997a.
9 Keding 1997a, 191–5.
10 Keding 1997a; 1998, 9–10.
11 Keding and Vogelsang 2001, 271.
12 See further Richter 1989, 439–40.
13 Schuck 1989, 426.
14 Keding and Vogelsang 2001, 268.
15 Keding 1998, 8–9.
16 Berke 2001, 245.
17 Keding and Vogelsang 2001, 274; Schuck 1989; Jesse 2002a.
18 Keding 1998, 11.
19 Jesse in press a.
20 Keding 1998, 10–11; Jesse and Keding 2002, 281.
21 Berke 2001, 245.
22 Keding and Vogelsang 2001, 261.
23 Neumann 1989, 34–5.

32 Dotted Wavy Line pottery

Ceramic

Ennedi Erg S98/20

Sixth–fifth millennia BC

Th 85 mm

SNM 31239

32

34

The fragment is a typical Dotted Wavy Line sherd of the region and was part of a large vessel. The Dotted Wavy Line decoration is impressed with a rocker-stamp technique using a multiple-toothed implement to form horizontal bands. Despite the small size of the fragment it clearly indicates that the earliest pottery in the region was of good quality. The pottery of the earliest settlement phase in the Wadi Howar is well made and heavily tempered with quartz grains, suggesting that the first settlers were familiar with all aspects of pottery manufacture.

Dotted Wavy Line pottery occurs throughout the Sahara and is one of the oldest pottery design styles recorded there, with radiocarbon dates in the ninth millennium BC (Jesse 2003, 284). The presence of Dotted Wavy Line pottery indicates that the first settlers of the Wadi Howar region had contacts in all directions (Jesse 2000, 85).   BK/FJ

Hoelzman *et al.* 2001, fig. 10.1; Jesse 2002b, 86, fig. 6.6-c; 2003, 433, pl. 6.1; Keding forth., fig. 3.1

33 Triangles

Quartzite

Jebel Tageru 84/34

Fifth millennium BC (?)

H 43–57 mm, W 60–69 mm

SNM 31236

Three large triangles made of a yellowish-white quartzite were found on the settlement site of Jebel Tageru 84/34. They exhibit complete facial retouching on both sides. Similar pieces have not yet been recorded on other sites of the Southern Libyan Desert or the Nile Valley. Further west, however, in the area of the Tenerean, facial retouching is a typical feature and one of the characteristics of this cultural horizon (Tixier 1962). Radiocarbon dating places the Tenerean in the fifth to third

33

35

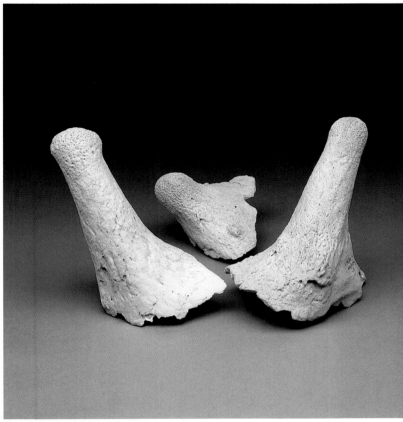

36

millennia BC (Jesse 2003, 275). The function of these large triangles remains uncertain. They were probably used as projectile points, but use as prestige objects cannot be excluded.   FJ

Jesse 2003, 255–6

34 Lunates

Quartz, quartzite, chalcedony
Rahib 80/87 and Rahib 80/73
Sixth–fifth millennia BC
L 19–26 mm, W 6–14 mm
SNM 31235

The spectrum of modified stone artefacts is rather limited on sites of the Dotted Wavy Line and Laqiya Horizons. Lunates are the most important tools found (Kuper 1981, 265). They are made of various raw materials, mostly chalcedony, quartz or quartzite. Lunates are present in large numbers at other sites of the Early Khartoum Horizon in Sudan, such as at Khartoum Hospital (Arkell 1949a), Saggai (Caneva and Zarattini 1983) and the sites of the Atbara region (Magid 1995). They can be mounted on to shafts and

formed part of the hunting toolkit. Detailed analysis of lunates found at the Atbara sites did not gave any indication of their use in harvesting and/or cutting plant material (Magid 1995, 63).   FJ

Kuper 1981, 265; Jesse 2003, 71–3

35 Harpoons

Bone
Jebel Tageru 84/34
Sixth–fifth millennia BC
L 42–70 mm
SNM 31234

Bone harpoons are rare in the Wadi Howar region. It is only at Jebel Tageru 84/34 that several fragments have been found (Jesse 2003, 255). The unilaterally and bilaterally barbed harpoons were made out of the long bones of large mammals. The harpoons present a flat oval cross section and have three or four barbs. Harpoons were used for hunting aquatic game such as hippopotamus and crocodile (Kuper 1988, 136), and for fishing. They are widespread on sites of the early pottery horizon throughout the Sahara (see

Sutton 1974), thus their rare occurrence in the Southern Libyan Desert is surprising. Harpoons found on sites of the Early Khartoum Horizon in Sudan are usually unilaterally barbed (e.g. Saggai: Zarattini 1983, 246; Khartoum Hospital: Arkell 1949a, 75; Atbara Region: Haaland 1995, 130).   FJ

Kuper 1988, 135, fig. 6.5; Jesse 2003, 255

36 Bones of a giraffe

Ennedi Erg, S98/20
Sixth millenium BC
SNM 31233

The skull elements of a giraffe are the most impressive bones discovered from Ennedi Erg, a site with Early Khartoum and Laqiya pottery situated at the shore of what was, several thousand years ago, a small lake west of El'Atrun. The other skeletal elements of this animal were intentionally broken and partly burned. They were associated with bones of hippopotamus, elephant, eland and fish.   HB

37

37 Microliths

Chalcedony, jasper

Djabarona 84/13

Fourth–second millennia BC

L 5–13 mm, W 6–19 mm

SNM 31301

The twelve microliths are transverse arrowheads. The wide range of forms includes small lunates, triangular and tanged types as well as numerous transitional forms (Keding 1993, fig. 2). The sharp sides were the cutting edges of the arrowheads, while the retouched sides guaranteed firm hafting in wooden shafts. They are made of fine-grained stone, mainly chalcedony and jasper. These raw materials are found in the adjacent mountainous areas and thus indicate middle-distance transportation or trade with people from Jebel Tageru to the south, Jebel Rahib to the east, or the Ennedi Hills to the west.

Transverse arrowheads were usually used for weapons. However, in the context of the cattle-keeping groups of the Leiterband Horizon, where remains of hunted animals are almost never found, they may also have been used to pierce the veins of the animals to extract blood. Today, the 'bleeding' of cattle is a widespread practice among cattle keepers in East Africa where blood is sometimes an important nutritional supplement (Dahl and Hjort 1976, 172 ff.; Evans-Pritchard 1937, 223 ff.; Galvin 1985, 66 ff.).   BK

Keding 1996, fig. 5.1–3; 1997a, pl. 77.1–3

38 Darfur-type axes

Trachyte

Djabarona 84/13

Fourth–second millennia BC

L 121 mm; edge: W 72 mm; neck: W 43 mm

L 71 mm; edge: W 52 mm; neck: W 45 mm

SNM 31302

The characteristic form of Darfur-type axes is dominated by a broad groove for hafting purposes and a mushroom-shaped or hemispherical neck. One axe has a sharpened and partly polished cutting edge, while the other is rounded for use as a hammer. They are made of a greenish, fine-grained, homogenous stone (trachyte). Chips on the edges and necks are the result of being used on hard material.

Ground axes of the Darfur type are a special feature of Leiterband assemblages (Kuper 1981, fig. 4.3). They were probably primarily used for woodworking, but their function as prestige items cannot be excluded. Their distribution is concentrated in the Wadi Howar region and the south-eastern Sahara (Keding 1997a, 192–5; Kuper 1981, 273).   BK

Keding 1996, figs 5.4, 5; 1997a, pls 74.1, 2

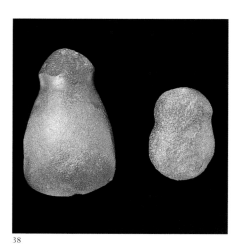

38

39 Leiterband pot

Ceramic

Djabarona 84/13

Fourth–second millennia BC

H 120 mm; rim: D 105 mm, Th 3 mm

SNM 31303

This restored spherical vessel of the Leiterband Horizon is an extraordinarily fine, carefully made piece. The red-brown colour, thin walls, sand-tempered matrix, simple rounded rim and globular shape fit well into the usual spectrum of Leiterband pottery. Decoration sometimes covers the entire body of the

vessel. The rim zone is decorated with a wavy band consisting of opposed rounded impressions that are typical of the Leiterband Horizon. Body and base are covered with narrow impressed Leiterband patterns, interrupted by two long polished triangular zones. Each triangle is embellished by a single rosette made of Leiterband ornaments. A similar rosette decorates the centre of the rounded base.

The polished surface of the vessel, as well as the more varied and complex arrangement of the decoration, suggests that the pot had more than a purely utilitarian purpose. Like most of the well-preserved pottery fragments of the Leiterband Horizon, it was found in an eroded pit together with numerous cattle bones. This unusual association, found on some sites in the Wadi Howar region, may have had a ritual significance (Keding 1997a, 204–40).   BK

Keding 1989, 35; 1997a, pl. 70.2

40 Leiterband pot

Ceramic

Djabarona 80/86

Fourth–second millennia BC

H 175 mm; rim: D 100 mm, Th 3 mm

SNM 31304

This complete, restored vessel is a typical Leiterband pot. The very homogenous thin-walled ware is of high quality. It is characterized by careful surface treatment, an almost exclusively inorganic temper consisting mainly of sand, and it was constructed using the coil technique. The round-bottomed egg-shape with no neck restriction and a non-modelled rim is a characteristic pot form of this period. As in this case, many Leiterband pots were decorated from rim to base. Typical patterns are Leiterband ornaments, impressed in the rocker-stamp technique with a gap-toothed implement and arranged in narrow horizontal bands.

While other patterns related to the Leiterband complex have also been found in the Nile Valley, the distribution of the eponymous decoration of this cultural horizon is restricted to the Wadi Howar region and adjacent areas to the west as far as Mali (Commelin 1983, pl. LIV, 3–7; Keding 1997a, fig. 74). Detailed analysis of the pottery of the Leiterband Horizon suggests a common origin with the Khartoum Neolithic of the Nile Valley, followed by a more local development which seems to have become more and more orientated towards the western areas (Keding

39, 40

1998). The people who used the Leiterband pottery were the first cattle herders in this region. They lived in an area climatically favourable for an economy based on cattle, fish and wild grains. BK

Keding 1989, 35; 1993, fig. 3.5; 1996, fig. 8.5; Kuper 1981, fig. 1; 1986, fig. 1; Richter 1989, fig. 6.2

41 Handessi A pottery

Ceramic

Djabarona 80/79

End of third millennium BC

Body sherd: Th 6 mm; rim sherd: D 220 mm, Th 6 mm

SNM 31230A–B

These two fragments belong to vessels of globular shape. Rounded quartz grains and organic material have been added as non-plastic components in the fabric. The surface is well smoothed, even slightly polished. The colour of the surface is black in one case, brown in the other. Both vessels exhibit the triangular impressions made with a single pronged implement, typical for the decoration of Handessi A pottery. Single rows of triangular impressions are combined with small bands of oblique comb impressions. The wall zone is decorated with complex geometric patterns made by incision and then filled with simple comb impressions. In one case a rhombus-shaped pattern is visible (Kuper 1981, 268–9). The pottery design style of the Handessi A

41

Horizon finds its parallels in areas further north in the Laqiya region, and in the pottery of the C-Group and the Kerma culture of the Nubian Nile Valley (Keding 1998, 10). FJ

Kuper 1981, 268, 269, fig. 39.1

42 Upper and lower grinding stone

Sandstone

Upper grinding stone

Djabarona 80/80

Date unknown

L 135 mm, W 97 mm

Lower grinding stone

Wadi Shaw 82/29

End of third millennium BC

L 490 mm, W 290 mm, Th 34 mm

SNM 31141

The upper grinding stone is made of a grey silicified sandstone. It has a triangular cross section. The large, flat lower grinding stone is of approximately oval shape and made of a yellowish silicified sandstone. Two perforations have been drilled from both sides indicating that this piece might have been transported. Grinding stones were certainly used for plant processing. The simple presence of grinding stones on archaeological sites is, however, inconclusive concerning the question of domesticated agriculture, as wild grasses can also be processed. Besides plant processing, grinding equipment can be used for various purposes, for example, to crush colour pigments or for clay processing during pottery production (Schön and Holter 1988, 159). FJ

42

43 Donkey bones

Wadi Haqriq, S97/5

Third millennium BC

SNM 31229

These hind legs, from one animal, are quite well preserved because they were sunk in a crack of drying lake sediments. They are dated to 1920 ± 200 cal BC.[1] Donkeys were the most important animals for travelling in the desert until camels were introduced. In the Wadi Hariq, some 300 km away from the Nile, they indicate connections with Sixth Dynasty Egypt.   HB

1 This date is calibrated (KN-5318).

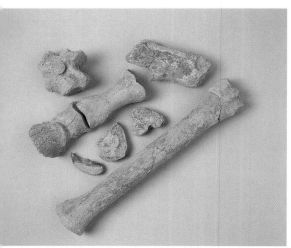

43

44

44 Handessi A pottery

Ceramic

Djabarona S98/120

Second millennium BC

Min. H 110 mm; rim: D 260 mm, Th 6 mm; wall: Th 7 mm

SNM 31144

This large vessel is a very well-made example of the ceramics of the final period of permanent occupation in the Wadi Howar region. It was found upside down near a small group of burials. The pot has a curved profile and a pronounced neck. It is thin-walled, finely smoothed, tempered with sand and fibre, and was formed by pinching and drawing. Irregularities in the ochre-brown colour of the outer surface are the result of uncontrolled firing conditions, typical of open-field firing. The outer surface has mat impressions from base to belly, a typical feature of Handessi A pottery. The clearly structured decoration is restricted to the rim and the upper part of the vessel, and underlines the composite contours of the pot. The inner rim is decorated with a narrow band of oblique comb impressions running parallel to the rim. On the outer surface, triangles are outlined by comb impressions and filled with densely dotted zig-zags produced by the rocker-stamp technique. Two rows of opposing triangles, one on either side of a group of three parallel horizontal lines, give an impression of a large rhombus.

Though following the general trend of this period towards geometric decorations on curved-profile vessels, supra-regional parallels to Handessi A pottery are found only in individual cases. They point to connections with western (Bailloud 1969) as well as northern areas (Jesse in press a).   BK

Keding 1998, pl. 6; Jesse and Keding 2002, fig. 9

45 Bowl with herringbone pattern

Ceramic

Abu Tabari S95/2

H 104 mm; rim: D 150 mm, Th 3 mm; wall: Th 6 mm

SNM 31143

This complete bowl was found in an undisturbed burial on the slope of a huge dune which had been occupied over several millennia. The simple rounded lip is decorated with dense oblique impressions. The upper part of the outer surface of the bowl is covered with

45

simple impressions forming several bands of herringbone pattern. The decoration was applied with a spatula. Two vessels, one inside the other, were placed on the pelvis of the deceased. Additional offerings including a shell, a small axe, stone artefacts, a lump of ochre; fish and burnt cattle remains were also placed in this adult male burial. The smaller of the two vessels, which is displayed here, has a brownish burnished surface and was tempered with sand.

Both the pottery and the grave are very different from the usual finds in the Middle Wadi Howar, but show some similarities with A-Group and Pre-Kerma finds in the Nubian Nile Valley (Nordström 1972, 130). This clearly points to stronger relationships with cultures to the east than to the west of the Wadi Howar region.   BK

Keding 2000, fig. 4; forth., fig. 3.3; Jesse and Keding 2002, fig. 8

3

THE PRE-KERMA PERIOD

MATTHIEU HONEGGER

While several excavations and surveys in conjunction with the building of the Aswan High Dam permitted archaeologists to acquire a good knowledge of the protohistoric periods of Lower Nubia, the same is not the case for the territory of Upper Nubia, lying between the Second and Fourth Cataracts. Recent archaeological research has revealed the presence of a population, contemporary with and later than the A-Group, the most plentiful evidence for which is currently found in the area of the Third Cataract. This population has been named Pre-Kerma because its geographic location is different from that of the A-Group and its ceramics are distinct in some respects, even though it has certain elements in common with its cousin in Lower Nubia.[1] The Pre-Kerma constitutes the cultural substratum from which the Kerma civilization developed.

The Pre-Kerma is currently known only at a few sites and its extent is yet to be defined clearly.[2] One can, however, estimate that it was located between the area to the south of the Second Cataract and the environs of Dongola (fig. 40).

40 Map showing location of the Pre-Kerma sites in Upper Nubia. The Middle Pre-Kerma is represented at Kerma and at Arduan. The late Pre-Kerma seems to correspond to the B-Group as defined by B. Gratien on the basis of the finds at Buhen (1995). It is found at Kerma, Sai, Faras, Buhen and Saras and also seems to occur in the Laqiya Oasis.

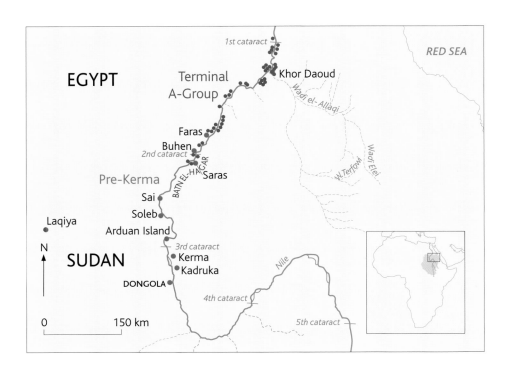

5 cm

41 A watercolour reconstruction of middle Pre-Kerma pottery (*c.* 3000 BC). Red bowls with a black mouth, decorated with a rippled band on the upper part, are characteristic of this culture.

Chronologically this culture began during the fourth millennium BC and ended with the emergence of the Kerma civilization around 2500 BC. The dating carried out so far, together with the first studies of the pottery, permit us to distinguish a middle phase around 3000 BC, and a late phase between 2900 and 2600 BC. The oldest period, which is not yet documented, probably dates to the middle of the fourth millennium BC. It follows the late Neolithic which is well known thanks to the discovery of several cemeteries and settlements in the vast alluvial plain extending south from Kerma.[3]

The Pre-Kerma pottery shares several similarities with A-Group ceramics. Many of the dishes and bowls found are red with black mouths, and their surfaces are carefully polished. A fine rippled decoration evokes a decorative technique well known in Lower Nubia, but here it is limited to the upper part of the pottery in the black-coloured area (fig. 41). Some rare pots present a more elaborate decoration composed of motifs in bands and red-coloured lines on a beige background. They are reminiscent of the eggshell pottery found at the end of the A-Group period.

The late Pre-Kerma period has a slightly different ceramic repertoire and contains some precursor elements of the *Kerma Ancien*. The most characteristic decoration is composed of combed horizontal impressions and geometric motifs made with fishbones (fig. 42). This pottery is found at Kerma and further north at Sai, Saras, Buhen and Faras. In the Kerma area it has been possible to reconstruct the evolution of pottery between 3000 and 2400 BC in detail (fig. 43). It demonstrates

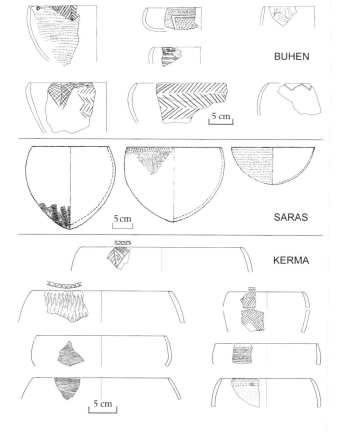

BUHEN

5 cm

SARAS

5 cm

KERMA

5 cm

42 Late Pre-Kerma pottery (*c.* 2900–2600 BC). The assemblage found at Kerma shows definite similarities with finds at Buhen (Gratien 1995) and with those from Site 11-Q-72 at Saras (Mills 1967–8).

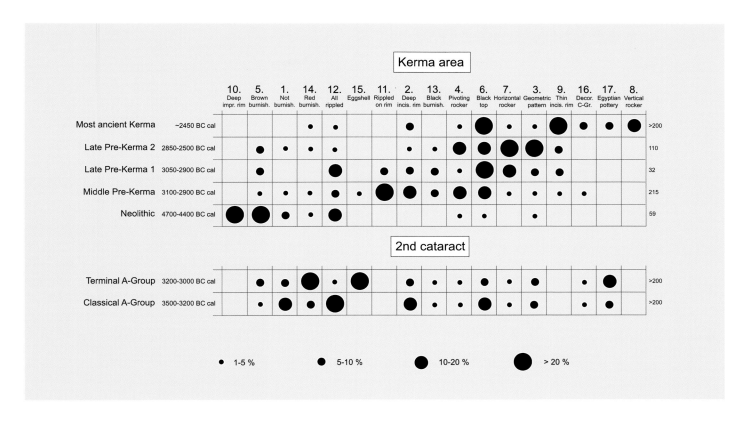

43 A typological comparison between Neolithic, Pre-Kerma, *Kerma Ancien* and A-Group, on the basis of the relative frequency of seventeen types of pottery. This typology shows a progressive transition between the middle Pre-Kerma and *Kerma Ancien*. Classic and terminal A-Group material is clearly distinct from the assemblages found in the area of Kerma.

cultural continuity between the Pre-Kerma and *Kerma Ancien*, as well as a certain degree of autonomy in relation to the A-Group. No Egyptian imported pottery has been found at Kerma amongst the settlements dated to between 3000 and 2600 BC, and thus there do not appear to have been any contacts with this civilization. Egyptian imports are on the other hand found further north on Sai Island, to the south of the Batn el-Hagar, where a settlement dating to the late Pre-Kerma phase has yielded some storage pits, of which one contained a jar dating to the earliest Egyptian dynasties.[4] Despite this discovery, the Pre-Kerma does not appear to have played an active role as a trading partner with Egypt. It was, however, involved in exchanges with the A-Group in its middle phase, the A-Group taking the role of middleman and passing the merchandise further north. Similarities in the style of the pottery and also the presence of objects characteristic of Lower Nubia, discovered in two Pre-Kerma burials, testify to these contacts.[5] The establishment of direct commercial relations between Egypt and Upper Nubia does not seem to have begun before the *Kerma Ancien* period.

1 The Pre-Kerma was first defined in 1986, on the occasion of the discovery in the Kerma region of a settlement dating to *c.* 3000 BC (Bonnet 1988).
2 Three Pre-Kerma sites are known in the Kerma region (Honegger 2002). Two other sites have been noted, one on Arduan Island (Edwards and Osman 2000), the other on Sai Island (Geus 1998).
3 Reinold 1993b; Welsby 2001d.
4 Meurillon 1997.
5 Two quartzite palettes and a copper needle with square section have been discovered in two burials of 3000 BC in the Kerma region (Honegger 1999).

THE PRE-KERMA SETTLEMENT AT KERMA

MATTHIEU HONEGGER

Research on the Pre-Kerma period at Kerma is unique in that excavation there has exposed a vast area enabling study of much of the settlement.[1] Sealed beneath the Eastern Cemetery of Kerma, the settlement plan is unique and shows the organization of a Nubian village around 3000 BC. It is composed of nearly 300 storage pits, as well as numerous wooden structures of which only post-holes remain. These structures consist of huts, palisades, rectangular buildings and cattle pens (fig. 44).

Preservation of the occupation surfaces is not always very good, erosion having caused the disappearance of the remains in several areas. Furthermore, Kerma burials dug several centuries after the abandonment of the village and the associated installations connected with their funerary ceremonies have disturbed the underlying surface. Despite these drawbacks, it has been possible to expose many architectural structures within an area of nearly 1 ha. The total extent of the agglomeration is, however, not known; it was probably in the region of 2 ha.

A total of 285 pits have been excavated (fig. 45). The construction of the later Kerma tombs has presumably destroyed a large number. However, one can estimate that originally there must have been close to 500. With the exception of two containing entire pots, the pits have not yielded more than a few fragmentary objects. They give the impression of having been emptied before the abandonment of the village and have in no instance been reused as depositories. Their function must have been for storing food stuffs as is the case with the pits on Sai Island and in Khor Daoud.[2]

Several types of construction have been recognized due to the orientation of the post-holes. The most

44 Plan of the Pre-Kerma settlement located in the same area as the Eastern Cemetery of Kerma (c. 3000 BC).

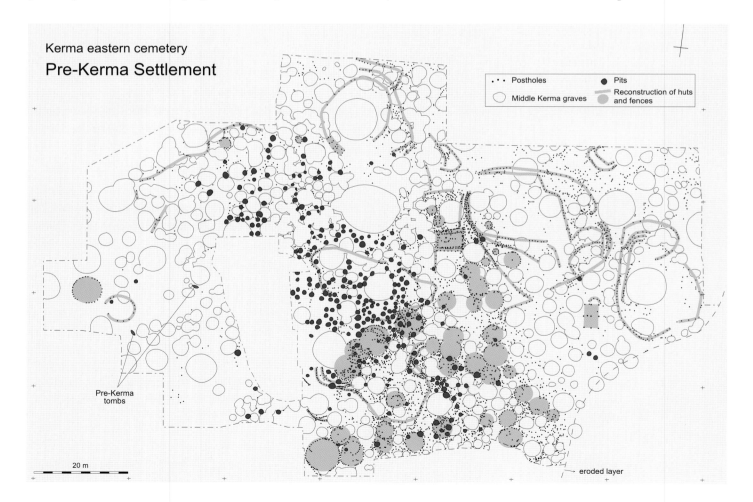

Kerma eastern cemetery
Pre-Kerma Settlement

Postholes • • •
Middle Kerma graves
Pits ●
Reconstruction of huts and fences

Pre-Kerma tombs

20 m

eroded layer

45 *Right* Storage pits during the course of excavation. In the foreground are two jars in a pit.

47 *Far right* Rectangular building rebuilt three times. In the background are three palisades. The round structures correspond to the Kerma period tombs.

46 Post-holes of huts of different diameters. The round structures correspond to the tombs of the Kerma period.

numerous are approximately fifty huts, the diameters of which vary between one and several metres (fig. 46). The majority of these huts had a diameter close to 4 m and must have been used as dwellings. The other structures, with dimensions approaching 7 m, could have had special functions, for example as dwellings of important individuals, communal meeting places, or workshops. As for the structures of about a metre in diameter, these may have been enclosures for small livestock.

Two rectangular buildings, quite different from each other, have been excavated. One follows an east–west orientation and was rebuilt three times in the same place (fig. 47). The other was orientated to the north and located on the periphery of the settlement. It was made of posts whose diameter was twice the norm. These rectangular buildings were undoubtedly intended for a specific function, which distinguishes them from the domestic huts. The successive reconstructions and unusual dimensions of the post-holes underline the important role that these buildings must have played in the community.

Certain regular alignments of posts can only correspond to palisades. These are sometimes double or triple, suggesting that they were built at different times or that they were reinforced. While some mark boundaries within the inhabited area, the majority are located on the periphery of the settlement. They form vast oval structures that resemble cattle enclosures, like those found on the outskirts of modern East African villages occupied by pastoralists.[3] It is known that raising cattle was a fundamental pursuit within Nubian society. In some well-preserved areas, hoof-prints of cattle have been found in the mud, which confirm the presence of cattle throughout the settlement. The location of the enclosures on the border of the settled area could equally fulfil a defensive function in the manner of the wooden fortifications observed in the city of Kerma.[4]

The settlement was organized in a coherent manner,

48 Reconstruction of the Pre-Kerma settlement. The reconstruction of the huts, the palisades and the rectangular buildings is inspired by modern-day villages in East Africa, as well as by ceramic scale models of mud houses found in an archaeological context.

which permits us to propose an architectural reconstruction of the whole (fig. 48).[5] The pits were grouped together and their distribution was in an area separate from the huts. As for the rectangular buildings, these were close to the cattle enclosures. The rebuilding of these structures was fairly frequent and testifies to several phases of occupation. The logic of the reconstructions and the presence of numerous storage structures underline the continuous occupation of the area. The population that lived there was sedentary and practised a mixed economy. The use of agriculture is confirmed by the importance of the storage areas, while the presence of the enclosures suggests animal husbandry.

It is possible to establish parallels between the Pre-Kerma settlement and the ancient city of Kerma, of which the oldest structures cleared must date to around 2300–2200 BC. In fact, one finds in the city certain architectural traditions inherited from the preceding period, notably the huts, storage pits and systems of palisades associated with the entrances to the city. But the similarities seem to stop there: the architecture that dominates at Kerma is in mud brick, a material that was apparently unknown in the Pre-Kerma period. The buildings were generally rectangular and had internal subdivisions. The structuring of space followed an urban scheme, with monumental buildings and a hierarchical street system. All of these elements represent novelties within Nubian architecture, of which we still lack the earliest stages and on which the influences of Egyptian civilization probably played a not inconsiderable part.

Addendum

During the recent 2003–4 field campaign an area of 1,000 m² was investigated north of the enclosures. It revealed an extremely high density of post-holes. The impressions of posts were still preserved and the remains of foundations and walls could be observed. When put together they define an entrance 8 m wide, bordered by two massive constructions from 15 to 25 m wide, which seem to correspond to bastions. It is still too early to describe in detail this imposing system of access. However, this discovery stimulates further interest in the Pre-Kerma town, which may have been more extensive and complex than previously supposed.

1 This site has been the object of excavation for a decade by the University of Geneva (Honegger 2002; 2003).
2 See further Geus 1998; Meurillon 1997; Piotrovsky 1967.
3 Denyer 1978.
4 Bonnet 1993; 1997.
5 This reconstruction depicts one phase of the village and does not take into account reconstructions and realignments of the structures. It renders a partial image of the settlement, its limits not being known except in the area where the animal enclosures developed.

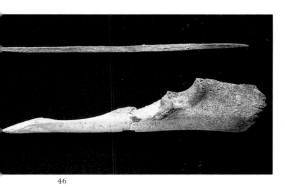

46

46 Awls

Copper alloy, bone
Kerma, Eastern Cemetery, Graves 1 and 2
Pre-Kerma
L 122 mm, W 4 mm, Th 3 mm
L 123 mm, W 26 mm, Th 21 mm
SNM 31134 (copper alloy), 31135 (bone)

The copper-alloy awl is slender, undecorated and rectangular in section. Its function was probably more decorative than utilitarian. It is an import from Lower Nubia or Egypt, as metalworking was not yet being practised in Upper Nubia around the end of the fourth millennium BC. This type recalls examples known from the A-Group and shows contacts between this culture and that of Pre-Kerma. Such awls are rare; they generally accompany burials of high rank, most usually of females (Nordström 1972, 123). The bone awl represents a more common object. Made from the ulna of a sheep or goat, its extremity has been shaped in such a way as to form a point. This will have been used to perforate soft substances such as skin or leather, which were important elements of the clothing of the pastoral populations of the period.   MH

47

mostly destroyed tomb of an adult. The smaller palette has a much finer finish. It was located in a rich, partially destroyed burial of a woman. Placed near the hands of the body, it was accompanied by two small pebbles used as grinders, and covered some fragments of malachite, used as a pigment. Make-up tablets are known from Neolithic and protohistoric Nubian burials. Examples of metamorphic rock, dating to the fifth millennium BC, have been found at Kadruka, not far from Kerma (Reinold 2000a). The quartzite examples appear to be more recent and are found in the A-Group graves of Lower Nubia (Nordström 1972, 120). Occasionally *Kerma Ancien* graves contain palettes, but these become increasingly rare in this later period (Bonnet 1990a, 200).   MH

impressing dotted motifs on the pots while the clay was still soft, hence the 'comb' appellation of this type of tool. The other comb is without teeth and must have been used to smooth the surface as well as to impress longitudinal motifs. On one side this tool has been partially perforated, perhaps to make a hole to tie a string to the object, or for some other unknown purpose.

Potters' tools are commonly found in the Kerma civilization (Bonnet 1990a, 155–6). It is probable that the manufacture of pottery was valued within society, considering the beauty of some vases. It is therefore not surprising that this activity has been marked by some objects included in funerary contexts – the time of the dead person's journey to the afterlife.   MH

47 Palettes

Quartzite
Kerma, Eastern Cemetery, Graves 1 and 2
Pre-Kerma
L 106 mm, W 50 mm, Th 18 mm
L 171 mm, W 110 mm, Th 31mm
SNM 31120, 31132

The smaller palette, from Grave 1, is roughly lozenge-shaped with convex faces and rounded edges. The other is oval with rounded edges, again with convex faces. Both taper down towards the edges and are made of quartzite. The two faces of these palettes are polished and their extremities present slight traces of percussion. They were found in graves located near the Pre-Kerma settlement. The larger one was discovered in the

48 Combs

Fine ferruginous sandstone
Kerma, Eastern Cemetery, Grave 1
Pre-Kerma
L 48 mm, W 34 mm, Th 5 mm
L 51 mm, W 39 mm, Th 5 mm
SNM 31130, 31131

These two combs of fine ferruginous sandstone come from the same female burial. They are potters' tools used to smooth and decorate ceramics. The two examples have similar dimensions. They are flat, carefully polished and their trapezoidal shape is very regular. The larger extremity on each is bevelled. One of the two tools is equipped with small incisions regularly spaced, on the bevelled part. They were intended for

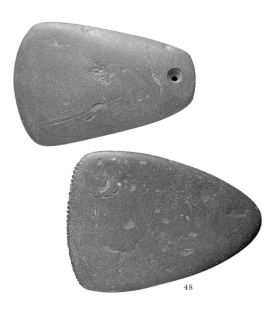

48

49 Dish

Quartzite
Kerma, Eastern Cemetery, Grave 1
Pre-Kerma
L 165 mm, W 159 mm, Th 16 mm
SNM 31262

This dish is made of grey quartzite with a very noticeable grain. Finely polished, its shape is oval and slightly concave. This object, found in a female grave, was accompanied by rich grave goods: palette, grinders, ivory cup, combs, flints and copper-alloy objects. Its function is not clear. It may simply be a dish, intended for food, unless its use is related to that of a palette and therefore was used for grinding or pounding. Such objects have also been found in A-Group graves (Nordström 1972, 121).   MH

49

50 Jar

Pottery
Kerma, Eastern Cemetery, Pit 35
Pre-Kerma
H 397 mm, max. D 385 mm; rim: Th 28 mm
SNM 31140

A sub-spherical jar with a narrowed base, its surface is not polished, but has been coarsely smoothed with the aid of a tool that has left slight striation marks. Its colour tends towards dark grey on its interior and around the rim, while it is beige on the rest of the exterior. These differences in colour are a result of the type of firing: the jar will have been placed upside down in an open-air fire. The decoration, restricted to the rim, is composed of parallel incisions, occasionally arranged in a chevron pattern. Of the 285 excavated pits in the Pre-Kerma settlement, only two contained jars. These will have been used for food storage, probably of cereals. The jar presented here was found upside down, with the opening to the bottom of the pit. This position indicates that it was probably not in use at the time the place was abandoned. This type of jar has parallels among the A-Group pottery assemblage (Nordström 1972, pl. 182).   MH

50

51

51 Beaker

Ceramic

Sai Island, Site 8-B-52.A

Pre-Kerma

H 111 mm, D 95 mm

SNM 31312

Complete pre-Kerma pottery vessels are not common. This small beaker is the only one that has been found thus far in the storage pits that are currently excavated on Sai Island. Nevertheless, being cone-shaped, undecorated and of rough workmanship, it is not really representative of the wares recovered from the site. It lay upside down at the bottom of Pit 64 where, except for large fragments of another vessel, no other remains of the original pit contents were preserved. It may have been used as a measure in the neighbouring granaries.   FG

52 Plant material

Sai Island, Site 8-B-52.A, Pit 50

Pre-Kerma

SNM 31313

This botanical material was found in Pit 50 of the Pre-Kerma storage area excavated on Sai Island. It shows the quality of preservation of the plants that were stored there some five thousand years ago. It includes chaff, stalk and grains from various species that have still to be identified. Samples from other pits analysed previously included grains and fruit stones of at least seventeen different species, particularly emmer wheat (*Triticum dicoccon*) and barley (*Hordeum vulgare*).   FG

Geus 1998, 94–5, fig. 7, pl. V, b; 2000, 127; 2003, 165–7

53 Dried Gerbil

Sai Island, Site 8-B-52.A

Pre-Kerma

L 190 mm, W 80 mm, Th 20 mm

SNM 31314

Granaries attract small rodents. This was obviously the case for the Pre-Kerma storage pits of Sai Island where their remains, including this one that was naturally mummified, have been found in quantity. It seems that once they entered the pits, they got trapped and died because of the nature of the ground: a highly carbonated sediment that they were unable to dig through. This is confirmed by burrows of 50–100 mm in length that have been found at floor level in several of the storage pits.   FG

54 Sealing

Mud

Sai Island, Site 8-B-52.A

Pre-Kerma

L 70 mm, W 40 mm, Th 20 mm

SNM 31315

The Pre-Kerma storage pits of Sai Island have yielded large mud seals displaying different types of designs. This knot-shaped one, which is deeply impressed and particularly well preserved, is evocative of some hieroglyphs of ancient Egypt. The occurrence of such sealings and the meticulous cleaning of the empty pits for further use which has been observed on the site show that the storage area, which was of great capacity, was under careful management.   FG

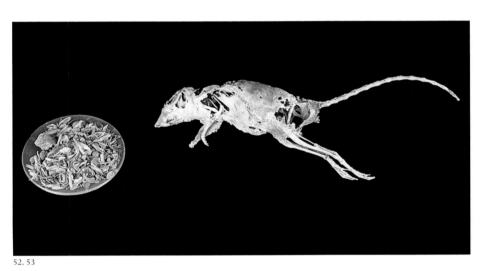

52, 53

54

4

THE KERMA CULTURE

CHARLES BONNET

Exploration of the territory of the Kingdom of Kerma has only just begun. Surveys conducted during the last few years have allowed us to find new sites that bear witness to a much larger territory than expected. If the southern boundaries can as yet not be specified, we know that these were located beyond Kurgus in the direction of the Fifth Cataract (fig. 50). On the Egyptian side, the frontier often fluctuated according to the relations, between the two countries. During the *Kerma Classique* (Classic Kerma phase), sovereignty of the Nubian kingdom seems to have extended to the First Cataract at Aswan, nearly 1,200 km along the Nile: a considerable area, even if the two banks were not densely cultivated.

The development of a complex state in Upper Nubia can be explained by its

49 Tumulus and bucrania from a *Kerma Classique* tomb.

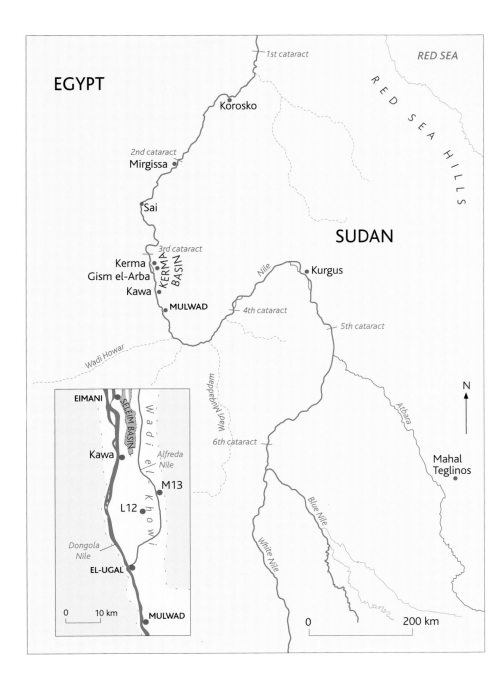

50 Map of Kerma sites mentioned in the text.

situation in an area naturally protected by the neighbouring deserts and the granite barriers of the cataracts, that was yet a meeting place between the Mediterranean world, via Egypt, and central Africa. In fact, it was to Kerma that the exotic products from the southern Sahara and the shores of the Red Sea were directed. These were of great interest to the pharaohs of the Egyptian Old Kingdom, in particular those of the 6th Dynasty. The accounts of Egyptian expeditions to the 'Country of *Iam*' inform us of these exchanges: ivory, ebony, wild animals, resin and, of course, gold were all traded. The American archaeologist George A. Reisner, the first person to undertake excavations at Kerma between 1913 and 1916, interpreted the site as a trading post run by Egyptian governors. According to his theories, these people were influenced by native customs to such an extent that they had themselves buried in large tumuli in the nearby cemetery according to Nubian rites (fig. 49).

Subsequently research carried out following the campaign to rescue the monuments of Nubia at the time of the construction of the Aswan High Dam has shown that the Kingdom of Kerma constituted one of the first African kingdoms. The population was subject to either princes or kings, independent of the Pharaonic Empire, who were able to develop a remarkable commercial network. While writing does not seem to have been used within the Kingdom of Kerma, seals and seal impressions found at control posts in the ancient town of Kerma show that there was a well-developed administrative system.[1] These peoples and chiefdoms of pastoralists seem to have united early to become a full commercial partner of Egypt, quickly becoming equipped with an impressive military force.

To follow more easily the historical development of the Kerma cultures, several chronological phases have been defined in relation to Egyptian dynastic periods.[2] *Kerma Ancien* (Ancient Kerma phase) corresponds to the end of the Old Kingdom and the First Intermediate Period, *Kerma Moyen* (Middle Kerma phase) is contemporary with the Middle Kingdom from 2050 to 1750 BC; and *Kerma Classique* corresponds to the Second Intermediate Period and the beginning of the New Kingdom (1750–1550 BC). The end of the Pre-Kerma period and the first *Kerma Ancien* tombs are thus to be placed around 2500–2450 BC. The demise of the kingdom comes about one thousand years later under pressure from the 18th-Dynasty pharaohs, who colonized the territory of Kerma. The dating takes into account carbon-14 evidence and the chronology supplied by Egyptian imports, especially pottery, as well as archaeological observations made in the cemeteries.

Funerary customs underwent significant evolution, according to the morphology or the dimensions of the graves, as well as the grave goods placed by the dead. Constants, such as the position of the bodies or of some of the offerings, the libations and the surface deposits, exist. It is from the end of the Pre-Kerma period that the ritual seems to have become more consistent. Early on there appear both in the cemeteries and the settlements signs of a hierarchy which could correspond to the move from a chiefdom to a more organized state. Some of the dead had very rich burials. From the time of the first Egyptian expeditions during the Old Kingdom an independent Nubian kingdom may already have developed.

Nubian settlements of this period are still poorly known and their remains often difficult to study. Post-holes, the branches used in wattle and daub construction, and the walls of earth leave indistinct traces whose interpretation can be problematic. Archaeological results obtained along the Nile Valley have shown that buildings constructed at the beginning of *Kerma Ancien* were made of wood and *jalous* – mud mixed with organic matter. This method of construction was widespread and current excavations allow us to reconstruct some of the architectural features.

Probably under Egyptian influence, the appearance of mud brick changed building techniques. At first the plans of new buildings were copied from those made of lighter materials. The buildings were long and narrow so as to limit the roof-span, and the walls were still quite thin (fig. 51). The dimensions of posts also represented a constraint. Defensive walls, on the other hand, became thicker and their *jalous* masonry was supported by wooden frameworks. The use of mud brick did not, however, bring about the demise of traditional architecture in wood and

51 A long, narrow building from the *Kerma Ancien* period.

earth, and one can observe that groups of huts stood alongside houses of mud brick, perhaps reserved for an elite or, in a rural setting, for the landowners.

The careful excavation of the Nubian town of Kerma offers a first view of what can be considered the capital of the kingdom.[3] Its urbanism is not comparable with that of the other known settlements and its inhabitants had important administrative, military and political responsibilities. The town appears to have been organized around different institutions of royal and religious power, including royal residences, religious buildings, storehouses, bakeries, and so on. One can suppose that the town was surrounded by ditches or a river channel. It seems, from geomorphological studies, that the metropolis was established on an irregular island that gradually joined the mainland following a change of climate.[4] This period was marked by higher temperatures that led to desertification and the disappearance of several branches of the river, whose meanderings must have characterized the plain upstream of the Third Cataract.

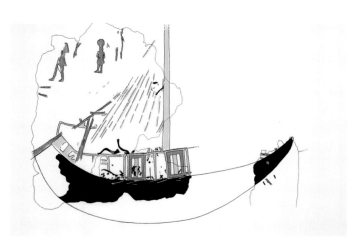

52 Painted representation of a boat from Funerary Chapel K XI.

The boat was the most common means of transportation in the Kerma basin and upriver from it, where the peaceful waters facilitated traffic (fig. 52, cats 66, 67). Everything leads us to believe that the administrative post and the nearby storehouses found to the south-west of the town were associated with a harbour quarter that developed from the beginning of the *Kerma Moyen* period, and where during the *Classique* period a temple and a chapel were added. It was in this area that the cemeteries were established after Egyptian troops took control during the New Kingdom. One wonders to what extent boats were able to reach the old necropolis 4 km further east. In the area of the rapids and cataracts, navigation seems to have been more infrequent and even today the fear is that the rocks will tear out the bottom of any kind of boat.

The land routes were often used, and Egyptian texts and animal bones indicate that donkeys were used for the transport of merchandise. Stages along these routes were marked by fortified posts, such as the one studied 17 km from Kerma, on the edge of the Eastern Desert.[5] One can assume that, when returning from the gold mines in the Red Sea hills, the king's envoys rested in the shelter of the fortified enclosure, where a garrison was stationed (its barrack blocks are still visible). A tower or room with very thick walls would have allowed for the safe storage of the more valuable goods. There are other remains elsewhere in the desert, notably stone walls built across small wadis. These could be used to retain rainwater and hold reserves of water for the flocks or for cultivated plots of land.[6]

Surveys in the interior have located agricultural sites consisting of several houses grouped on low hills.[7] These alluvial terraces used for settlements were bordered by fields where the traces of labour are still noticeable. Imprints of the hooves of cattle pulling a plough have been preserved in the damp silt. Grains of barley and other cereals, used for making bread and beer, have also been found preserved. At a short distance from these extended villages are their associated cemeteries.

While during the *Kerma Ancien* and part of the *Kerma Moyen* houses and annexed buildings were made of wood and earth, those of the following phases were built of stones bonded with lime mortar or mud bricks. It is during the later periods that regional centres like Gism el-Arba developed. These were intended to collect agricultural produce and to cope with the increased volume of trade and length of communication routes. One notes the presence of a series of storehouses of rectangular plan, raised on bases of large blocks of roughly quarried stone.[8] These, less than a metre apart, were used to support a wooden platform, so as to keep the stocks of food safe from rodents. The number of these silos, their plan, and the possible presence of external stairs, are reminiscent of examples known from Egyptian iconography and from the remains of large New Kingdom complexes; however, it is recent African constructions that offer the best comparison, the structures being almost identical. It is still necessary to locate and excavate other settlements in the territory of Kerma because they may inform us about the relationship between the town and the countryside and to what degree it was subordinate to the central power.

The construction technique using stone foundations is also found elsewhere, notably in the agglomerations of houses forming agricultural units. In these cases the blocks of ferruginous sandstone were placed next to each other so as to make a base resistant to wind erosion. Sometimes a second course is still in place; a thick layer of plaster appears to have covered the façade. In these settlements buildings made of wooden posts and woven branches are also found. In some cases remains of these structures extend over hundreds of metres. Unfortunately we do not as yet know much about the organization of these sedentary rural communities. Cattle, sheep and goats needed large pastures and agriculture could only develop in restricted areas. Traces of rounded enclosures, perhaps used for corralling stock, made with spiky acacia branches and palm trunks have been found in several places.

Data supplied by the study of the cemeteries provide much information about the wealth of the kingdom. They demonstrate extraordinary development from the small primitive tombs, which were deep and narrow, to the last tumuli of the *Kerma Classique*, nearly 100 m in diameter.[9] From the beginning, one notices the omnipresence of leather – clothes, large hides, bags, receptacles, chests – which illustrates the close relationship between the Nubian population and its animals

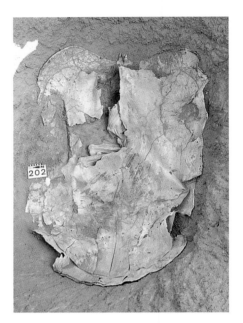

53 Leather hide covering the deceased in a *Kerma Ancien* burial.

(fig. 53). The hides, bristles shaved off, were tanned with oil. A thin border of fur has often been noticed on the oxhides lining the grave or covering the deceased. Suspension holes show that they were used before being placed in the grave. Some undisturbed, well-preserved burials have enabled us to observe that the funerary bed was made of a layer of dried grass, with the dead person being placed on top in a contracted or flexed position accompanied by grave goods and offerings. Finally, a second protective layer completely covering the whole was placed on top.

The selection of grave goods must have reflected the daily life of the individual, who could then find in the afterlife his or her domestic objects (cats 55, 59–62, 64, 246). Clothes were generally made of tanned sheepskins. Loincloths were folded or enhanced with geometric decoration made of separate pieces stitched together, on which were sewn tiny coloured beads, of faience, shell, bone or stone: the knots for tying off the stitches are sometimes preserved. In some cases, the women have their heads covered by fine leather hairnets. Quivers, bags and butter or cheese churns were very common and more or less well preserved depending on the date or state of the burial. Scrapers, awls or rubbers used to prepare the leather have been found in the cemeteries and the settlements.

54 Excavation of the bucrania of a princely tomb of the *Kerma Moyen* period.

Proof of the pastoral nature of the society is demonstrated by the large number of animals buried with the dead and by bucrania placed on the surface (cat. 71). Early on, caprines were placed in the burial, sometimes flocks of up to fifteen. Joints of sheep or goat make up part of the food offerings placed on the north side of the grave pit in ceramic containers (cat. 276). The presence of dogs, while not common, also deserves a mention. It is probable that the bucrania placed in a semi-circle to the south of the tomb super-structures were linked with remembrance ceremonies, perhaps communal feasts, to honour the memory of the dead. The number of bucrania varies from a few to several hundred. One exceptional *Kerma Moyen* tomb, almost certainly of a prince, was endowed with 4,000 bucrania, all discovered *in situ*: it has been possible to study these in detail (fig. 54). Such an extraordinary quantity makes us suppose that a number of the cattle came from far afield, perhaps brought as tribute or as offerings. The importance of the buried person can be calculated by the number of sacrificed animals, and by the dimensions of the tumulus and the richness of the grave goods.[10] The components of the latter change and increase with time, as do the offerings. Grave pits become larger and can reach more than 12 m in diameter. The mound of earth was consolidated by rings of small slabs of sandstone or basalt. The summit was covered in the centre with pebbles of white quartz, marking the location of an offering table or libation vessels.

55 A *Kerma Moyen* burial.
The deceased female was placed upon a bed.

56 The eastern *deffufa* with associated royal
tumulus in the background. The sacrificial corridor
within the tumulus is visible running from left
to right.

There is much evidence for a rite that began during the Neolithic. In several cemeteries of this period, human sacrifices were found associated with some burials. This tradition continued during the Kerma period and it is not uncommon to find double or triple burials where one can recognize the main personage, accompanied by one or two individuals whose position indicates their secondary role. All of the bodies were buried at the same time. This custom seems less common in the earlier periods, where examples are few. Beginning with the *Kerma Moyen*, the principal dead person often lies on a wooden funerary bed placed in the centre of the grave pit. Sacrifices were placed to one side or concentrated at the western end (fig. 55, cats 275–80). In the *Kerma Classique*, the rite becomes common and appears to take on new forms: whole families are placed in the burial, children or adolescents, adult males and females; undoubtedly close associates of the dead person that were following him into the afterlife.

The last rulers of Kerma pushed this custom to the limits of demographic possibility, since the human sacrifices associated with the great royal tumuli were in their hundreds (fig. 56).[11] The central tumulus alley, which led towards the funerary chamber, was used to accommodate this large number of sacrificial victims.

57 A bastioned wall designed to defend a gate.
The foundations are blocks of ferruginous sandstone.

Anthropological studies have revealed that they were not exclusively black ser-
vants as George Reisner thought, but a diverse population connected to the royal
court and its associates. The notion of submission to the royal power is reinforced
by the presence of subsidiary tombs of high dignitaries dug into the core of the
four largest tumuli. Grave goods found in these tombs are particularly impressive
and already allowed the excavators at the beginning of the twentieth century to
appreciate the quality of local workmanship.

While the conquests of the Nubian armies reached further and further afield,
the architectural achievements in the capital were of increasingly remarkable
monumentality. Temples were enlarged and their imposing silhouettes mark the
landscape. The fortifications occupied a large area, gates and bastions multiplied.
Ditches were deepened, palisades or chicanes in wood were inserted to make access
to the base of the town walls almost impossible (fig. 57). The emphasis placed on
the defences of the metropolis probably fits in with a more general policy engi-
neered to respond in an effective manner to the first attacks of the Egyptian armies.

Through a pincer action, following the river as far as Tumbus some 30 km north
of Kerma and across the desert from Korosko to Kurgus, the Nubian territory
finally fell into the hands of the pharaohs of the 18th Dynasty (1550–1295 BC).
The conquest was not easy and revolts continued for decades. However, the culture
of the *Kerma Classique* period gradually disappeared; Egyptianization obliterated
the indigenous traditions and it took several centuries before the ancient customs
manifested themselves once more.

1 Bonnet 2001a; Gratien 1993.

2 Gratien 1978.

3 For overviews of this work see Bonnet 1986;
1990a.

4 Marcolongo and Surian 1993; 1997.

5 Bonnet and Reinold 1993.

6 Osman and Edwards 1992, 58, 91/28.

7 Gratien 1999; Welsby 2001d.

8 For example, Gratien 1999, 11; Welsby 1997b, 8;
2001d, 577.

9 Bonnet 2000.

10 See further *Kerma Moyen* grave, cats 275–80
in this volume.

11 Reisner 1923a, 65–76, 141, 312, 394, 440.

KERMA

CHARLES BONNET

At the beginning of the nineteenth century the archaeological site of Kerma was often visited by European travellers curious to examine the two enormous mud-brick ruins, locally known as 'deffufas', an ancient Nubian term used to designate any imposing man-made structures (fig. 58). The one closest to the Nile, the western deffufa, stands nearly 20 m high. Excavations conducted by the American archaeologist George Reisner between 1913 and 1916 showed that the two deffufas were surrounded by cemeteries and numerous constructions whose character was not understood.[1] In 1973 research was restarted following an initiative of the Mission of the University of Geneva, and has not yet ceased! This work has revealed almost continuous occupation from prehistory to the Christian era.[2]

The Kerma period is, however, the period best represented: there is the town, of a size and organization unique in Nubia at that time, a harbour quarter that stretched along the Nile, and finally a necropolis

located 4 km to the east on the edge of the desert, containing thousands of burials (fig. 59). The evolution and development of this extraordinary ensemble began in the second half of the third millennium BC and was interrupted around 1450 BC by the Egyptian conquest. Nearby, older remains have been found in the course of the excavation: lithic material and animal bones dated to nearly a million years ago; Palaeolithic and Neolithic sites of which many are currently being studied; and protohistoric sites such as the Pre-Kerma settlement found in the large eastern necropolis, the object of several seasons of excavation.[3] Thus the Kerma cultures are the result of a very long tradition which explains their remarkable vigour. As far as later remains are concerned, of particular interest are the Egyptian town found at Dokki Gel, 1 km north of the Nubian metropolis, and a settlement and cemeteries of the Napatan, Meroitic and Christian periods.

The Nubian town is located on an alluvial terrace that formed part of the defensive system along with the

58 The western deffufa, the principal temple in the town of Kerma.

59 The archaeological site of Kerma.

ditches and the branches of the Nile that once surrounded the settlement (fig. 60). Very thick walls as well as bastions were associated with the archaic fortifications. Remains of palisades and alignments of posts form the vestiges of this primitive enclosure. At an early stage a separate quarter of the town appears to have been reserved for sacred buildings and their annexes in which hearths and ovens form part of several workshops. However, their state of preservation does not allow us to completely identify the complex: on the one hand, the layers are partially overlain by other structures; on the other, traces left by structures of earth and wood are extremely ephemeral, which makes them difficult to interpret. All the same, the hundreds of postholes and the imprints of branches used as wattle provide sufficient data to allow a reconstruction of the long but narrow plans of these buildings.

Towards 2000 BC the town was set within a rectangle measuring 200×150 m. It was protected by an enclosure wall strengthened by powerful bastions with circular bases. Several gates opened through the wall. They were flanked by two large longitudinal mounds of earth, rounded at the extremities. The actual openings were narrow, measuring no more than 1 m in width. It was during this period that the use of bricks became common.

The dwellings were often made up of two rooms placed on opposite sides of an internal courtyard. An external courtyard or a garden was usually located to the south, with kitchens, storehouses for food and workshops.

Later the town grew larger and the fortifications and the gates were transformed and enlarged. To gain land, the old ditches were filled with rubbish. The defensive system diversified; walls were faced with fired brick and stone foundations were added. The centre of the town was still occupied by a religious quarter that included the main temple and several large chapels, as well as a ceremonial palace. Outside the *temenos* in the town were the remains of successive residences of the sovereigns. The royal apartments were made of several rooms and courtyards to which were linked a series of contiguous warehouses. A large hut (fig. 61), round in plan and rebuilt several times in the same place, has been interpreted by analogy with more recent African examples as a royal audience hall. The latest residence, built over a ditch in-filled with rubbish, was of an unusual type of architecture in which can be seen influences coming both from Egypt and from more southern countries (fig. 62). A large double hall was set aside for the throne. It was preceded by a room for archives with an arrangement for sealing messages or precious produce. Huge storehouses and the royal apartments were partially preserved.

Beyond the town, passing through a deep ditch, one entered a secondary agglomeration in which the remains of several chapels were excavated. These appear to have been dedicated to an institution dealing

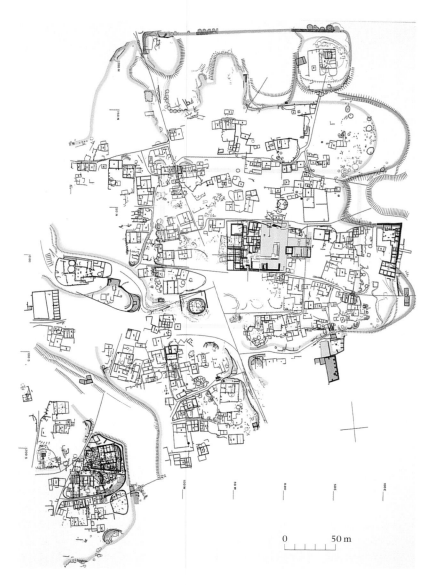

60 A topographic plan of the town of Kerma.

with the cult of the departed rulers. Ovens suggest the presence of ateliers reserved for the preparation of offerings. Impressive fortifications protected this area.

At the end of the history of the kingdom, the *deffufa*, the great temple, dominated the entire town. This building was the result of a long architectural evolution because modification and reconstruction never ceased on this venerated ground. All around one distinguishes urbanization as defined by large thoroughfares, along which were the houses of the high officials of the kingdom. In fact, the proportions of certain dwellings suggest the presence of an elite that watched

the areas where merchandise was sealed and exchanges organized. Administrative buildings were also used for this purpose. Several bakeries with batteries of ovens have been found, where bread and probably beer were prepared for use as offerings. Also deserving mention are the buildings intended for soldiers and the dwellings of the more modest townspeople, huts or small houses with a single room. The diversity of elements making up the town of Kerma makes it unique in the Nile Valley.

The associated necropolis, with more than 20,000 tombs, is also very impressive. George Reisner excavated 3,000 in the southern sector, which he called 'the Egyptian Cemetery'. This is where the *Kerma Classique* (Classic Kerma phase) burials are located. Four large tumuli are still visible, their central passageways bisecting the mounds, which were topped by conical stelae in white dolomitic marble. Two temples of some 50 m in length were used for the funerary ceremonies of the kings of Kerma, while chapels were associated with the subsidiary tombs of the dignitaries. The two temples were decorated in a sumptuous manner with blue faience tiles, some decorated with gold leaf, arranged in figurative patterns. The internal walls were ornamented with paintings. Even though these were in poor condition, it has been possible to recognize animals belonging to the African bestiary and scenes inspired by Egyptian iconography (fig. 63).

Further north, the tumuli that covered the burial pits are noticeable, covering an immense area of about 1,600×600–800 m. Vehicles and animals passing over the area have flattened the greater part of the mounds, but it is possible to find some elements of the superstructures still *in situ*. After the burial ceremonies, the tumulus was consolidated by hundreds of small black stones placed in circles. The summit of the tumulus was protected by white quartz pebbles to prevent wind erosion. Towards the middle of the cemetery are some important tombs, 30–40 m in diameter, that must undoubtedly have been associated with princes or even kings. Dates obtained for this period of development are contemporary with the Egyptian Middle Kingdom (2050–1750 BC).

The oldest section of the necropolis is found at its northern extremity. The superstructures measure about 1 m in diameter. The use of small, flat stones of black sandstone has already been mentioned. Stelae placed in a circle in the burial pit represent another type of superstructure. Bowls placed upside down on the ground, for a sharing of food between the living and the dead, clearly testify to the funerary ceremonies conducted at the time of burial (fig. 64). The participants would come together behind a windbreak made

61 The great hut,
audience hall of
the rulers.

62 Palace of the last
kings of Kerma.

out of branches, which also protected the open grave. The oldest graves, with deep and narrow pits, date to around 2500 BC. Early on wooden chapels were placed to the north-east of the burials. Later they were replaced by buildings of mud brick that were used during certain months to practise the cult of remem-

brance (fig. 65). Grave goods found in the tombs reveal workmanship of high quality, in particular the ceramics (cats 68–70, 245), and very specific customs that demonstrate the importance of the animal kingdom. Among the sheep laid next to the corpse, some carry a leather cap surmounted by a disc of ostrich feathers.

63 Painting of a herd of cattle in Temple K XI.

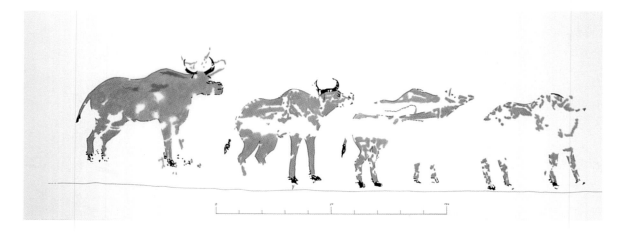

These are generally young animals, not the heads of the flocks. The headdress most likely had a religious character.

The study of the site of Kerma thus allows us to notice several architectural changes, as well as document the evolution of funerary structures. Over the course of a thousand years, the wide-ranging development of this centre shows the dynamism of the Nubian cultures.

Shortly before the fall of the kingdom at the beginning of Egyptian colonization, a circular tomb of large diameter was dug in the area of the harbour, to the south-west of the Nubian town. A truncated conical pit was constructed, using large blocks of stone. Access to the lower level, 6 m below the surrounding area, was by a large staircase on which, in a final phase, was added a funerary chapel. This unique structure was much disturbed by the Pharaonic armies.

This description of the site of Kerma relates particularly to the eponymous kingdom. However, in addition to the prehistoric settlements or Dokki Gel, one must remember that within the modern town and in the neighbouring cultivated fields are the ruins of several Napatan buildings as well as vast Napatan or Meroitic cemeteries. The Nubian town also became a vast cemetery.

1 Reisner 1923a; 1923b.
2 Reports on this work have appeared regularly in the journal *Genava* and elsewhere since 1978. See Bonnet 1978; 1982; 1986; 1988; 1990a; 1990b; 1991; 1993; 1994; 1995; 1997; 1999; 2000; 2001a; 2001b; 2003; 2004; in press; Bonnet *et al.* 1988. A monograph on the work in the cemetery has been published (Bonnet 2000).
3 See Honegger in this volume, pp. 64–9.

64 Bowls placed upside down on the ground for the division of food between the deceased and the living.

65 Remains of the religious quarter.

55 Spatula

Bone
Kerma, Eastern Cemetery, CE 7, Tomb 79
Kerma Ancien
L 265 mm, W 24 mm, Th 5 mm
SNM 25118

This spatula or spoon with a long handle carved from the diaphysis of a bone of a large mammal, perhaps a hippopotamus, was found in a man's tomb near a mirror wrapped in fabric. The piece was polished and then rubbed with red ochre. The inside surface of the head is chipped; such wear marks are not compatible with its use as a spoon. Considering the sharpened tip, it is possible that this object was used as a pin. At Sai a very similar perfectly polished object was found under the shrouds at shoulder level of the deceased in a tomb also dated to the *Kerma Ancien* period (Gratien 1986, 80–83, 362).   NF

Bonnet 1984, 15; 1990a, 140–41, 181, no. 139

56 Stopper/stamp

Ceramic
Kerma, Eastern Cemetery, CE 1, Tomb 103
Kerma Ancien
H 40 mm, D 46 mm
SNM 15300

This small biconical object made of black fired clay comes from a tomb located in the oldest sector of the necropolis. It was placed in a leather bag that contained a small bowl, also of black clay, and a pair of sandals. Its shape recalls that of a seal, particularly since one of its surfaces is incised with a few curved lines filled with white paste, like the impressions that might decorate the body of a bowl. Another small baked clay object in the shape of a mushroom, found in the same sector – albeit on the surface – resembles seals discovered at Mahal Teglinos (Fattovich 1995). Without a doubt Kerma was very early on an essential transit point on the trade routes of exotic products prized by Egypt. A seal fragment of a slightly different shape was listed among the surface finds of a Kerma site during the recent survey of P37 in the Wadi el-Khowi (Welsby 2001d, 359).   CB

Bonnet 1986, 11, fig. 13; 1990a, 172, no. 104

56

57 Vase with cover

Ceramic, paint
Kerma, Eastern Cemetery, Tumulus K III/K 315
Kerma Classique
H 106 mm (H with cover 144 mm), D 137 mm
SNM 1119

This vase with convex base and walls is equipped with a conical lid painted in red, yellow and black over a white background. Four holes are pierced under the rim of the vessel and a fifth at the top of the lid, allowing the insertion of a tie to hold the two pieces together. A series of zigzags runs along the circumference of the body, while black and red grid-like segments placed in alternation with red or yellow segments decorate the lid in a radial pattern. This vessel is part of a small series from the last two great tumuli of the eastern necropolis (K IV and K III) excavated by G.A. Reisner. The latter considered these as imitations of basketry; he had observed the remains of a basket of this same shape in a more ancient tomb (Reisner 1923b, 318 [K XX]). These vessels may however have represented huts, a prevalent type of construction as demonstrated by research in the ancient city (Bonnet 1990a, 31–3). CB

Bonnet 1990a, 211, no. 255–6; Reisner 1923a, 189, fig. 34, pl. 9; 1923b, 472–3; Wenig 1978b, 160–61, no. 68; Wildung 1997, 96, no. 95

58

58 Harpoon

Bone or ivory

Kerma, Eastern Cemetery, CE 15, Tomb 133

Kerma Moyen

L 143 mm, W 29 mm

SNM 31195

The piece illustrated is barbed; traces of the
leather thong linking the detachable head to
the shaft are visible just above the shank. It
originates from the tomb of a young man
aged between twenty and thirty years old.
Originally the harpoon head might have
been stored with other small objects, such as
a pierced lion's canine and a knife, in a small
wooden box, placed in the northern half of
the tomb. Harpoons are not numerous at
Kerma; this is not surprising considering
that hunting, just like fishing, played a secondary role within this population of stock-
breeders. The analysis of the few harpoon
fragments registered from the city shows that
they were fashioned from elephant ivory
(Bonnet 1990a 141, 159) and, considering
their size, they were most likely used for
hunting on land.   NF

Bonnet 1988, 14–15, fig. 14/3

59 Mirror

Copper alloy

Mirgissa, Kerma Cemetery, Tomb KT2

Kerma Classique

Face: L 85 mm, W 95 mm; handle: H 88 mm

SNM 14043

This mirror has a handle shaped like a
papyrus with a blooming umbel, and two falcons perched at the extremities. The almost
circular disc is inserted in the handle with a
shank fixed by a rivet in the middle of the
umbel, above the carved folioles. It was found
at the site of Mirgissa, south of the Second

Cataract, in a *Kerma Classique* tomb, richly
filled with imported objects. Placed behind
the torso, it was wrapped in thirteen layers of
fabric. This type of mirror with falcons is
attested in Nubia as in Egypt, with a few
variants: the folioles of the umbel can be
replaced with the head of Hathor or the

'stem' treated in imitation of braided leatherwork. This last variant is characteristic of
examples from the eastern necropolis at
Kerma (Reisner 1923b, 178–80, pl. 48.1).
Although the presence of mirrors among
funerary equipment dates back to the end of
the *Kerma Ancien*, it is nonetheless sporadic
and these pieces were probably imported
from Egypt (Bonnet 1990a, 180); for earlier
periods, the handles – very likely in wood or
ivory – are rarely preserved (Dunham 1982,
pl. Ib, XXXVIIa). The mirrors with braided
handles from Kerma, most of which were
found in the royal tumulus KIII, are in all
likelihood of local manufacture.   NF

Lilyquist 1979, 61, 144; Reinold 2001, 97;
Vercoutter 1970, 183, 230–40, 303

59

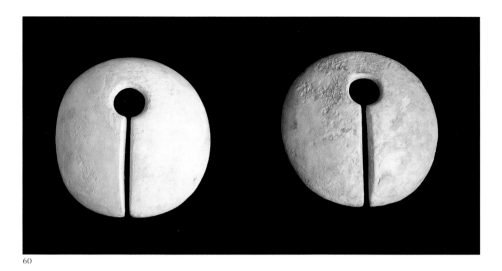

60

61

60 Hair slides

Shell

Kerma, Eastern Cemetery, CE 7, Tomb 77

Kerma Ancien

D 46–7 mm; D 45–7 mm

SNM 25115

These ovoid ornaments cut from bivalve shells are well represented at Kerma as at other Nubian sites (Reinold 1987, fig. 10a; Welsby 2001d, 365, 417). As light as they are fragile, they often show repair holes. They generally come from the backfill of tombs or were recovered on the surface; therefore, their use is not known with certainty. Their fastening system is identical to keyhole-shaped ornaments typical of the C-Group, considered by Steindorff to be hair ornaments rather than earrings, simply based on the narrowness of the slit (Steindorf 1935, 63, fig. 14). These ornaments and other finery made of mother-of-pearl appear not to have been worn during the *Kerma Classique* period.   NF

Bonnet 1990a, 180, no. 135; Dunham 1982, pls XVIIIa, XXXIIIc, XLIIb; Reisner 1923b, 318

61 Pendant

Shell

Kerma, Eastern Cemetery, CE 13, Tomb 126

Kerma Moyen

D 84–5 mm, Th 0.5 mm

SNM 25324

Pendant cut from the valve of a pearl oyster, the surface of which was worked until an iridescent polish was obtained. Two suspension holes were drilled at the top, where the thickness is greater. A fragment of the leather thong that served as a fastening remained on a similar example. The pearl oysters from which these pieces were cut came in all likelihood from the Red Sea. Like the mother-of-pearl ornaments above (cat. 60), these pierced shells are mostly found in tombs dated to the *Kerma Ancien* and *Kerma Moyen* periods. None show traces of colouring and they were probably worn for their talismanic value. In Egypt such pendants, often inscribed with the name of a 12th Dynasty pharaoh, are also well attested.   NF

Bonnet 1990a, 197, no. 204; Bourriau 1988, 154; Dunham 1982, pls XLI, XLIc, XVIIIa, XXXIIIc, XLI; Reisner 1923b, 294

62 Pendant

Rock crystal and gold

Kerma town

Kerma Classique

H 18 mm, D 11 mm

SNM 31197

This ovoid rock crystal pendant is set in two perpendicular bands of unequal width cut from a thin gold sheet and simply fashioned by pressure. The vertical band, which has a quadrangular section, was used as the shank and simply slipped under the horizontal band. Its extremities were then curved and hammered lightly. As pointed out by G.A. Reisner, the rare gold jewellery that escaped looting shows a very simple manufacturing technique and probably does not do justice to the work of the craftsmen. As for rock crystal, it appears to have been quite prized during the *Kerma Classique* period, as testified to by the deposits of crystals discovered in the western annexes of the Deffufa and the hundreds of beads recorded in the great tumuli of the eastern necropolis (Reisner 1923a, 39; 1923b, 92, 114). This pendant was also discovered in a *Kerma Classique* context, as it was unearthed in one of the rooms of the last palace built in the ancient city.   NF

Bonnet 1993, 8, fig. 12

62

63

63 Dagger

Copper alloy, ivory and wood
Kerma, Eastern Cemetery CE 20, Tomb 184A
Kerma Moyen
Blade: L 106 mm: pommel: D 32 mm
SNM 31198

This small dagger with crescent-shaped
pommel was placed on the hip of a young
child of less than two years of age, a practice
already encountered in a tomb dated to the
end of the *Kerma Ancien* (Bonnet 1990a,
183). The wooden grip that links the
pommel to the blade is very badly preserved;
originally, the three pieces were held
together by eight rivets, as shown on better
preserved examples (Dunham 1982, pl. Ia,

XXXVIII a, b). Often, the ivory pommel and
the rivets are all that is preserved of such
weapons. The crescent shape is characteristic of the *Kerma Moyen* period while daggers
of the *Kerma Classique* period have a trapezoidal pommel. The child's tomb was superimposed over that of an adult woman; both
were found intact and appear to be associated with one of the important tumuli of the
area. The child wore a large discoid gold
pendant, two earrings, also of gold, as well
as bracelets and anklets made of faience and
bone. A lamb and a few ceramic vessels
completed the funerary equipment.   NF

Bonnet 1995, 44, fig. 12

64 Razor (?)/cosmetic tool

Copper alloy
Kerma, Eastern Cemetery, CE 19, Chapel C7
Kerma Classique
L 91 mm, W 25 mm, Th 2 mm
SNM 31199

This small tool was deposited in the ground
in a chapel erected on the north-west side of
a tomb dated to the beginning of the *Kerma
Classique* period. It comprises two detachable
elements fixed by a rivet and offers the user a
sharp convex edge, tweezers and a sharp
point. Until now only five examples have
been found at Kerma, one in a *Kerma Moyen*
context. These pieces were probably imported
from Egypt where they are found in abundance (Davies 1982, 189–92; Freed 1982,
193–5). Although their use has yet to be
determined with certitude – whether razor,
tweezers, scissors, curling iron, scraper, or
surgical clamp – they are generally considered to be personal hygiene tools, often
associated with other instruments of this

category. In the *Kerma Moyen* tomb, the tool
was placed in a bag next to a big razor which
had been put in a wooden case.   NF

Bonnet 2000, 39–41; Reisner 1923b, 184–5, pl. 49

65 Relief plaque of a scorpion

Faience
Kerma, Eastern Cemetery, Tumulus K X
Kerma Classique
L 65 mm, W 54 mm, Th 17 mm
SNM 1036

This plaque, decorated with a scorpion
moulded in high relief, was placed along with
another, on the stomach of a sacrificed individual buried in tumulus K X. Other than the
suspension hole at the top, repair holes are
noted on either side of a break near the first
segment of the tail, which is curved in the
opposite direction on the second example.
These plaques, possibly sewn on clothing
facing downwards, most certainly had prophylactic properties. Scorpions may have
played a special role in relation to a cult, as
demonstrated by fragments of two extremely
large quartz sculptures discovered in the spoil
heaps of royal tumulus K III (Bonnet 1990a,
211, no. 257). These were found together
with other fragmentary animal sculptures of

65

64

quartz, including a ram's head, a crocodile and a falcon. CB

Bonnet 1990a, 211, no. 257; Reisner 1923a, 289, pl. 31.2; 1923b, 131; Wildung 1997, 101, no. 102

66 Stela with incised boat

Ferricrete sandstone
Kerma, Eastern Cemetery, K II (Eastern Deffufa)
Kerma Classique
L 420 mm, W 240 mm, Th 110 mm
SNM 31200

This stela was found reused in the flagstone pavement put in place during the partial reconstruction of the great funerary Temple KII, near the end of the *Kerma Classique* period. While the pavement consisted mostly of *Kerma Ancien* stelae, often with rounded tops and generally pockmarked, this stela is distinguished by its quadrangular shape with slightly convex sides. One of its surfaces is carved with a graffito representing a boat with a curved stern, executed with a sure hand. The craft possesses nine oars and a deck cabin. The orientation of the drawing shows that the stone was not meant to be positioned vertically. CB

Bonnet 1990a, 46; 2000, 123

67 Stela

Ferricrete sandstone
Kerma town, foundation of Chapel F (Level 13) dated to *Kerma Moyen*
End of Old Kingdom (2686–2181 BC)
H 515 mm, W 126 mm, Th 116 mm
SNM 31201

Two faces of this small and elongated block, intended to be set into the ground, were smoothed in order to be carved with an inscription in cursive hieroglyphs naming two members of an expedition: 'The captain of the boat Iymeri' and 'The captain of the boat Mereri'. This is one of the rare inscriptions written in Egyptian hieroglyphs found at Kerma itself. DV

Bonnet 1990a, 95–6

66

67: side 1

67: side 2

68 Bowl

Ceramic

Kerma, Eastern Cemetery, CE 7, Tomb 76

Kerma Ancien period III

H 112 mm, D 178 mm

SNM 25107

Lightly shouldered, hemispherical, red hand-made bowl, with a black rim. The rim, which ends with a tapered lip, is enhanced by an almost flat external fold, decorated with cross-hatching and underlined with a groove printed with a potter's comb. This groove is regularly interrupted by the decoration that covers the body, which consists of short double lines of embossed dots. The bottom is decorated with imprints made with a comb. The powdery consistency of the red slip that covers the exterior surface indicates that it was applied on the vessel after firing.   BP

Bonnet 1990a, 179, no. 131; Privati 1999, 45, 55, figs 6, 7

68

69 Bowl

Ceramic

Kerma, Eastern Cemetery, CE 21, Tomb 192/4, no. 171

Kerma Moyen period IV

H 69 mm, D 143 mm

SNM 31202

Shallow hand-made bowl with pronounced shoulder, red with a black rim, the latter being separated from the red-slipped body by a thin brown band. The vessel is polished on both surfaces. This form, which is relatively widespread at the beginning of the *Kerma Moyen*, is in the *Kerma Moyen* period IV

associated with vessels more characteristic of this horizon.   BP

Privati 1999, 47, 63, fig. 14

70 Spouted bowl

Ceramic

Kerma, Eastern Cemetery, CE 8, Tomb 81

Kerma Ancien period IV

H 47 mm, W 103 mm

SNM 25122

Hand-made spouted bowl, buff- to red-coloured clay, decorated with two crocodiles incised on either side of the body, facing the

spout. The crocodile is an animal often depicted on this type of vessel. This is most probably a representation with magic or religious properties. At Kerma crocodiles are represented in the funerary Temple K XI, and carved on ostrich eggshells or sculpted, as demonstrated by the quartz statue found in royal tumulus K III. This feeder was part of the ceramic assemblage deposited in the rich burial of a child, which contained red with black rimmed bowls polished with great care and vessels with impressed decoration.   BP

Bonnet 1984, 14–17, figs 13–17; 1990a, 182, nos 142, 143; 2000, 84–5, 135–7; Privati 1999, 45, 56, fig. 7/3–4, 57, fig. 8/2, 6

69

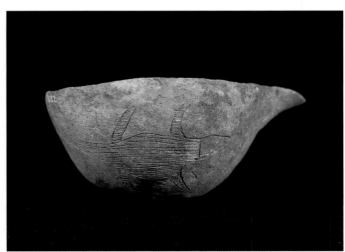

70

71a–e, clockwise from left

71 Bucrania

Bone

Kerma, Eastern Cemetery, CE 25, Tomb 253

Kerma Moyen

a Bucranium of a cow, 253/618
H 250 mm, W 555 mm

b Bucranium from an adult bull, 253/310
H 300 mm, W 870 mm

c Bucranium with parallel horns, 253/46
H 380 mm, W 265 mm

d Bucranium from a calf, 253/400a
H 200 mm, W 295 mm

e Bucranium of a young bull, 253/125
H 160 mm, W 710 mm

SNM 31109, 31111, 31113, 31112, 31110

Five different bucrania are presented here. They come from a spectacular crescent made up of 4,351 cattle skulls south of Grave 253, dated to the *Kerma Moyen* period (2050–1750 BC) (see fig. 54). Cattle skulls were carved in order to preserve only the frontal part and the horns. At the end of the *Kerma Ancien* period, the carving preserved the nasal bones, while later the skull was cut near the nasal spine. During the *Kerma Classique* period bucrania were reduced to the highest part of the frontal and the two horns. The skin was removed as attested by numerous tracks of knives or razors (Chaix 1993). Sometimes bucrania were decorated with red patches (cat. 71b) or entirely painted with red ochre.

The deposition of bucrania, always in the southern part of the tumuli, began at the end of the *Kerma Ancien* culture with an acme during the *Kerma Moyen* period, declining in the *Kerma Classique*. The number of bucrania is linked with the social importance of the deceased and the size of the grave.

The composition of an assemblage does not reflect a living herd. The proportion of the various categories (bulls, cows, calves and oxen) differs from a natural cattle herd. The disposition of the bucrania follows precise rules: in the front a row of cows, often accompanied by young calves; behind, a row of bulls, followed by a row of oxen. This arrangement may be repeated many times as shown in Grave 253 where forty rows of skulls were discovered (Chaix 1996).

In the graves of important persons there are bucrania with strong deformation of the horns that have been forced to grow parallel as illustrated by the bucranium shown here (cat. 71c; Chaix 2001). The bucranium of the calf shows a bulb at the tip of the left horn (cat. 71d). This feature can be linked with a future deformation of the horns. The bucrania with parallel horns form many rows intermixed with the normal ones. This man-made deformation is similar to those currently practised in the southern Sudan (Murle) and in the north of Ethiopia (Turkana). Saharan prehistoric rock art also presents numerous cattle with horns pointing forward. The significance of such a deformation remains unknown. LC

Chaix 1993, 175–85; 1996, 95–7; 2001, 364–70

72

72 Beaker

Ceramic

Kerma, Tumulus K III(?)

Kerma Classique

H 95 mm, D 130 mm

SNM 5282

A flat-bottomed, thin-walled beaker with flaring mouth similar to cat. 246. The body is red-polished with a black-topped rim (Reisner pottery type Bkt. Type II). A wide grey transitional stripe separates the two. The vessel has been reconstructed. Typical of the *Kerma Classique* period, this vessel type is found over a wide area in tombs and on settlement sites ranging from Kerma well into the region of the Fourth Cataract. JRA

THE NORTHERN DONGOLA REACH

DEREK A. WELSBY

Between 1993 and 1997 the Sudan Archaeological Research Society (SARS) in collaboration with the British Museum undertook a survey and limited excavations on the right bank of the Nile, covering over 80 km of the valley, between Mulwad and Eimani (fig. 50), and to the edge of the desert plateau, a maximum distance of 18 km to the east.[1] Prior to this project only the Pharaonic and Kushite town and cemetery at Kawa had been investigated. During the five-season campaign over 450 sites were recorded of which approximately 30 per cent were datable to the Kerma period (2500–1500 BC) (see cats 238–9, 244, 275–80).

Over the last fifty years the advent of diesel-powered water pumps has transformed the settlement patterns in the region allowing sedentary agriculturalists to settle over much of the area. However, for most of the last three millennia all human activity had been focused on the narrow strip of land along the main Nile channel.

In the Kerma period the geomorphology and hydrology of the region were very different.[2] At the beginning of the Kerma period, around 2500 BC, the Nile flowed along three main channels. From the diffluence in the vicinity of el-Ugal the eastern channel, the Alfreda Nile, ran north and east splitting to enclose an island 28 km in length and then running north close to, but separate from, the Seleim Basin towards Kerma. The banks of these channels and of the main (Dongola) Nile were lined with numerous settlements (fig. 67). Settlements were also found along the edge of the Seleim Basin. This low-lying area, a southern extension of the Kerma Basin, is a fertile region, especially during the period of Nile floods when the higher water table forms large, shallow lakes. Today, augmented by extensive irrigation, much of it is very rich farmland; however, even without irrigation it provides rich pasture for several months of the year.

During the Kerma period the Nile Valley to the east of the river between Mulwad and the Third Cataract, a distance of 135 km, was especially favourable for human settlement. This is documented on the ground by the presence of the large flourishing city at Kerma and well over 120 rural settlements of that period known to date. The braided channel greatly increased

66 The Kerma settlement at Site M13.

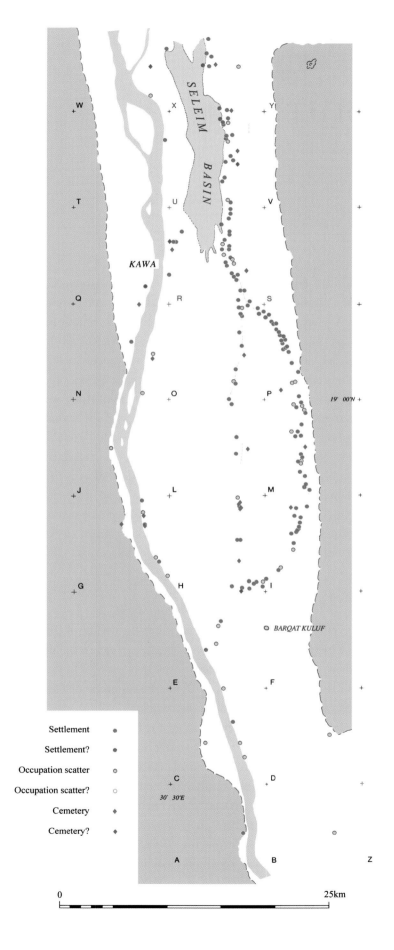

Settlement •
Settlement? •
Occupation scatter ◦
Occupation scatter? ○
Cemetery ◆
Cemetery? ◆

0   25km

the amount of *seluka* land available – land between the high and low watermarks which can be farmed without recourse to irrigation. The Seleim and Kerma Basins would also have provided extensive pasture, at least for a part of the year. This region is one of the most favoured in the Middle Nile Valley.

Kerma was set within a rich and extensive hinterland. Many of the settlements found during the SARS survey were of considerable size; M13, for example, is 13.75 ha in extent (fig. 66). Although no excavation of these sites was attempted, traces of mud-brick buildings were noted, one at Site L12 over 22.5×16 m in size. Many settlements contained large numbers of buildings of unusual form, often square or rectangular with stone walls and closely spaced rows of stone blocks within them. One isolated structure of this type, the largest noted at 11 m square, was excavated[3] but no clear evidence was found to suggest its function. The form of these buildings suggests that the rows of stones within were designed to support a raised timber floor; remains of actual timbers have been found subsequently during excavations of a similar building within Settlement 2 at Gism el-Arba.[4] The presence of a raised floor indicates that these buildings were designed for the storage of perishable goods, and served to offer protection from dampness and more importantly from rodent and insect damage. The settlement at Site M13 contains over thirty such structures.[5] The large number of store buildings may relate to a redistributive network, the local produce being collected and some of it perhaps being transported to feed the inhabitants of the metropolis at Kerma.

Within the survey area, sites of the *Kerma Classique* were abundant while those of the earlier Kerma periods may well be under-represented, their remains sealed beneath the later villages. The distribution of sites indicates extensive utilization of the region throughout the 1,000-year dominance of the Kingdom of Kush based at Kerma. Soon after, however, increasingly arid conditions coupled with the demise of the eastern Nile channels brought about a dramatic decline in the fortunes of the region.[6] Thereafter, until the mid-twentieth century, human settlement was focused on the Nile.

1 Welsby 2001d.
2 Macklin and Woodward 2001; Marcolongo and Surian 1993; 1997.
3 Welsby 1997b, 8; 2001d, 121–2, 203–5, pls 4.3–4.
4 B. Gratien pers. comm.
5 Welsby 2001d, 94, 96–7.
6 Cf. Welsby 2001d, figs 14.6, 14.7 and 14.8.

67 Sites of the Kerma period discovered in the SARS concession, 1993–7 (data on the west bank sites courtesy of S.T. Smith).

5

EGYPTIANS ON THE MIDDLE NILE

DOMINIQUE VALBELLE

Egypt's earliest contacts with Lower Nubia (fig. 68), situated between the First and Second Cataracts, began during the Early Dynastic period around 3100 BC. A plaque belonging to Aha, one of the first pharaohs of the 1st Dynasty, documents his victory over *Ta-sety* (Nubia) while one of his successors, probably Djer, left an inscription at Jebel Sheikh Suleiman near the Second Cataract, depicting slain enemies and two captives, presumably the victorious results of an Egyptian campaign into the region. However, several contemporary Nubian graves and the pits in the settlement at Khor Daoud were found to contain Egyptian goods such as pottery and copper-alloy vessels, indicating ongoing trade between the neighbours and suggesting that relations were largely peaceful. At the beginning of the Old Kingdom (2686–2181 BC) the Egyptians made forays into Lower Nubia in search of precious metals and to quarry stone, such as diorite. The remains of an Old Kingdom colony have been located at Buhen near the Second Cataract. It contained furnaces for smelting copper, workshops, and ostraca and seals with the names of several pharaohs of the period.

THE OLD KINGDOM (2686–2181 BC)

The relationship between Egypt and Upper Nubia begins towards the middle of the third millennium BC when the last kings of the 5th Dynasty begin to concern themselves with the chiefdoms above the Third Cataract and in the Red Sea hills in the land of Punt. Autobiographical accounts of the 6th-Dynasty monarchs of Elephantine refer to these regions when they discuss their own expeditions;[1] however, it is especially during the reigns of Pepi I, Merenre and Pepi II that a policy was developed towards the country of *Yam*. Nubian princes were brought to Memphis where they received an Egyptian education. Archaeological evidence in the form of ceramics and epigraphy, showing cultural and commercial exchanges, has been found at Kerma and the use of bricks in the town's buildings begins to rival the use of wood and *jalous*. Fragments of commemorative stone vases may have been gifts sent by the Egyptian rulers to the princes of Kerma, and a rough stela of sandstone, bearing the name and the title of two expedition leaders, has been found near the western *deffufa* (cat. 67).[2] This relationship seems to continue into the beginning of the Egyptian First Intermediate Period.

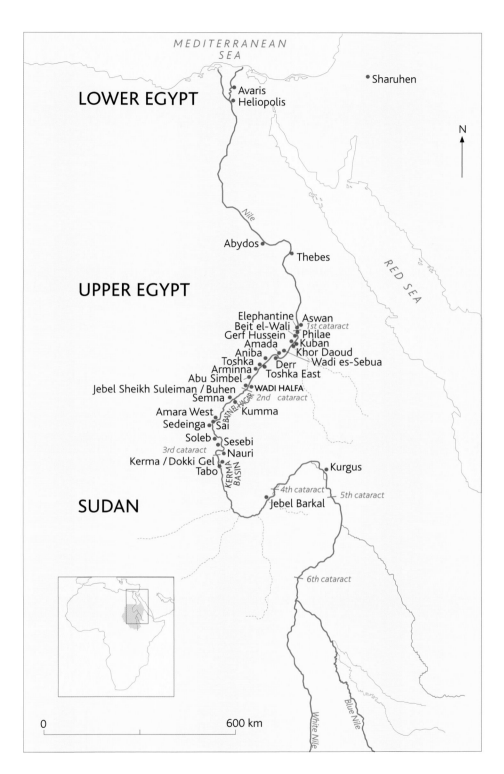

68 Map of Pharaonic sites mentioned in the text.

THE MIDDLE KINGDOM (2055–1650 BC)

It is currently more difficult to define the character of the relations between Egypt and Kerma during the Egyptian Middle Kingdom. Egyptian policy certainly became more aggressive. The border was pushed southward from the First to the Second Cataract. The impressive remains of a chain of fortresses built in several stages at the Second Cataract and in the Batn el-Hagar, and the despatches on papyrus from Semna, addressed to the high command at Thebes, reflect a defence and control system that was both powerful and rigorous. Nevertheless, evidence has been found at Kerma testifying to the existence of relations between the two powers. Vessels of stone and faience carrying the names of Amenemhat I and Senwosret I were discovered by G. Reisner, and some of the 12th- and 13th-Dynasty statues, royal and private, that were ultimately re-employed in the *Kerma Classique* tumuli, could have been brought to Kerma through the medium of Egyptian embassies.[3] Moreover, several series of imported Egyptian ceramics have been found in the necropolis and in the town.

THE SECOND INTERMEDIATE PERIOD (1650–1550 BC)

Despite the decline of Theban power during the Second Intermediate Period, relations were not interrupted between the two countries, but the balance of power was inverted and the Egyptian functionaries of the Second Cataract fortresses became vassals of the kings of Kerma (cats 73–4). Nubian armies were deployed in Egyptian territory in incursions and raids, as shown by the number of Egyptian statues and other objects buried with the last kings of Kerma (cat. 75) and by a painted inscription in the tomb of Sobeknakht, a governor of ElKab during the 17th Dynasty.[4] The liberation of Egypt began with Kamose, the last sovereign of the Theban 17th Dynasty. Two stelae and a tablet have preserved the essential historical details of this troubled period. One of these, known as the second stela of Kamose, tells of the interception of a letter sent by the Hyksos king Aauserre Apepi in Lower Egypt to his Kushite counterpart, proposing an alliance and the division of Egypt after their mutual victory over the Egyptian Theban Dynasty.[5] The letter refers to a campaign of Kamose, undoubtedly in Lower Nubia, where graffiti belonging to the first viceroy of Kush, Teti, bear his name at Toshka and Arminna. A stela from the third year of his reign commemorates the reconstruction of the fortifications at Buhen.[6] Kamose seems to have prioritized the reconquest of Lower Nubia over that of Lower Egypt, which remained occupied by the Hyksos.

THE NEW KINGDOM (1550–1069 BC)

Once the reconquest of its territory was achieved under the leadership of Ahmose, the founder of the 18th Dynasty, Egypt began to expand its empire. After retaking Heliopolis, Tjarou and Avaris, and pursuing the Hyksos as far as Sharuhen in Canaan, Ahmose followed the Nile upstream beyond the Second Cataract, built a temple inside the old fortress of Buhen and reached Sai Island where he founded a fortified town (fig. 69 and pp. 114–15 below). His son and successor, Amenhotep I (cat. 76), in his turn led a campaign into Nubia, following the Nile as far as the land of Kush according to the biography of Ahmose, son of Ibana.[7] As soon as Thutmose I was crowned king, he sent his viceroy of Kush, Turi, a decree that announced his coronation and gave the details of his protocol. Three examples of this decree have been found at Aswan, Kuban and Wadi Halfa. With Thutmose I, the limits of the empire were fixed by two inscriptions at the furthest points reached, one on the bank of the Euphrates river, the other above the Fourth Cataract, on the rock of Hagr el-Merwa at Kurgus.[8]

69 View of the southern part of the town of Sai.

It is, however, a third rock inscription, incised at Tumbus above the Third Cataract upon the return of the victorious royal expedition, which comments extensively on the course of the battles.[9] Described with an impressive realism, their violence has been confirmed at Kerma where traces of fire and destruction are evident at the main temple.[10] However, regardless of the scale of these conflicts, the Kingdom of Kerma did not yet disappear from the scene. The latest buildings at the site, contemporary with the beginning of the 18th Dynasty as documented by the archaeological material, indicate the desire of the last rulers to demonstrate a power previously unequalled.[11] A track linked the Third and the Fourth Nile Cataracts. It was, therefore, relatively easy for Thutmose I to make his way to Kurgus and to leave there a commemorative inscription without having subjugated the powerful enemy who still held the territory surrounded by the loop made by the river in this region.

Beginning with the reign of Kamose, a new administrative structure was put in place to administer Nubia.[12] A viceroy (literally 'royal son') of Kush represented the ruler in these territories. The extent of his authority naturally depended upon the advance of the armies: at first restricted to Lower Nubia, he soon covered Upper Nubia as far as Kurgus. The viceroy was assisted by two deputies (*idnw*) attached respectively to the land of *Wawat*, from the First to the Second Cataract, and to the land of Kush, south of the Second Cataract. The first task of these men was to regularly ship the products comprising the Nubian tribute, especially gold, and to carry out the architectural programmes of the pharaohs.[13]

The history of the conquest of the land of Kush by the Egyptian armies is not fully known to us. Archaeological missions currently working in the area are gradually uncovering the stages of Egyptian colonization through the remains of the monuments left by the pharaohs and their agents. Undoubtedly, we have a false idea of Egyptian occupation to the north of the Second Cataract inasmuch as the majority of the monumental Egyptian remains are temples that lack an urban context, such as the Temples of Wadi es-Sebua and Amada built by Thutmose III, Amenhotep II and Thutmose IV.[14] The construction of the second Aswan Dam and

the creation of Lake Nasser, while flooding the whole area, focused archaeological work on the stone buildings chosen to be moved to safety to the detriment of the mud-brick remains. In the Batn el-Hagar the ancient Middle Kingdom fortresses were transformed into fortified towns and adapted to a new urban model of which several examples are preserved in Upper Nubia. Hatshepsut built temples at Buhen (fig. 70), Semna and Kumma, which were later usurped by Thutmose III;[15] the latter two were completed by Amenhotep II (cat. 79) and Thutmose IV.

The town of Sai[16] was apparently the first built to serve as a base for the penetration of the Egyptian armies further south. The inscription of Thutmose I at Tumbus shows that the king built for his army a *mnnw* (fortification) named 'No-one-dares-confront-him-amongst-the-whole-Nine-Bows', but no corresponding remains have been found so far. It is undoubtedly this establishment, amongst others, of which an inscription of Thutmose II, on a rock on the route from Aswan to Philae, speaks: '*mnnw* that your father Aakheperkara – may he live for ever – has built at the time of his victories'. Another fortified town was built at Dokki Gel (fig. 71), 1 km to the north of the Nubian town of Kerma, at the beginning of the 18th Dynasty.[17] Currently, the first clearly dated attestation of the erection of an Egyptian monument in the interior of this enclosure is a lintel bearing the name of Amenhotep II (fig. 72) that may be associated with some mud-brick buildings, but some faience plaques from one of the foundation deposits of Thutmose IV (fig. 73; cat. 83) perhaps refer to Thutmose III.[18] Hopefully, future excavation campaigns will allow us to tie a specific ruler to the foundation of this town, the name of which was already *Pnubs*, the 'Jujube tree'.[19] Some 20 km to the south of Kerma, the reuse of some Thutmoside,

70 Painted relief from the Temple of Hatshepsut/Thutmose III at Buhen.

71 Aerial view of the south-west corner of the town of Dokki Gel.

72 *Below* Fragment of a lintel
of Amenhotep II at Dokki Gel.

73 *Below* Faience plaques from a foundation
deposit of Thutmose IV at Dokki Gel.

74 *Above right* 18th Dynasty block reused
in the Temple of Taharqa at Tabo.

75 *Right* The Temple of Amenhotep III at Soleb.

and Amenhotep II and Amenhotep III (fig. 74) blocks within the Temple of Taharqa
at Tabo suggests that one or more 18th-Dynasty temples existed in a settlement
whose New Kingdom dwellings were located and excavated south-west of the
temple.[20] Thutmose III confirmed the southern frontier of the Egyptian Empire by
having a commemorative inscription inscribed on the Hagr el-Merwa next to that of
Thutmose I, of which it is an exact copy; two hundred kilometres downriver, he
erected at the foot of Jebel Barkal a stela attesting to the construction of a sanctuary
to 'Amen-Ra, Lord of the Thrones of the Two Lands' in the *mnnw* called 'He-who-
massacres-foreigners'.[21] Neither the sanctuary nor any fortified structure has
survived, but blocks of Thutmose IV have been found.[22]

A second wave of building work in Nubia followed during the reigns of Amenhotep III and IV. While in Lower Nubia a *speos* was dug at Wadi es-Sebua by

Amenhotep III, in Upper Nubia he ordered the erection of a 'temple of millions of years' at Soleb (fig. 75) and built a second cult area for his spouse Tiye on the neighbouring site of Sedeinga (cat. 80). The town of Soleb has not been studied and that of Sedeinga has completely disappeared, so we do not have information on the character of these establishments. To the north of the Third Cataract, Amenhotep IV (later known as Akhenaton) built a fortified town on the site of Sesebi, as testified to by the only foundation deposits known containing the name of this king.[23] A crypt decorated with reliefs in a style similar to that of Amenhotep III could date to the very beginning of the reign of his son. The occupation continued after the changes to the royal iconography following the Amarna reform, as can be seen in the decoration of the still-standing columns (fig. 76).

Recent work has revealed that the architectural programme of Amenhotep IV in Upper Nubia was more important than was previously supposed. On the site of Dokki Gel the discovery of decorated *talatat* blocks (fig. 77; cats 84–5), re-employed in the Napatan levels of one of the temples, was followed by the exposure of the lower courses of the Aton sanctuary. These were set over the foundation of the neighbouring Temple of Thutmose IV, which served as a quarry for that of Akhenaton.[24]

The hammering-out of Amun's name on a Thutmoside relief and on the statue of a cavalry leader also testifies to the unifying policy of the king's agents. At Tabo blocks bearing the name of Amenhotep III appear in the masonry of the 25th-Dynasty temple (fig. 74), but no *talatat* has been discovered thus far, as is also the case at Kawa, despite the fact that the latter site's name remained Gematon until the Egyptian Late Period (cf. cat. 136). Finally, in the masonry of several Napatan temples at Jebel Barkal, blocks with the characteristic dimensions of *talatat* have been noted, and the hammering-out of the image and name of Amun is visible on the stela of Thutmose III.[25] It is therefore plausible that Akhenaton also built sanctuaries for the Aton cult at Kawa and Napata, but no contemporary settlement has been identified at either site so far. The Temple of Amen-Ra at Kawa, ascribed to Tutankhamun, is one of the rare architectural remains in Nubia from the end of the 18th Dynasty.[26] Nevertheless, the variety and richness of tribute brought from Nubia by his viceroy of Kush, Huy, are amply illustrated by the paintings in his Theban tomb[27] where one can see the prince Heqanefer in Nubian costume, while the burial of the latter, at Toshka East, has an Egyptian plan and decoration testifying to the phenomenon of acculturation that had developed over more than two centuries (cats 77–8).[28]

During the reigns of Seti I and Ramesses II, the architectural and urban programmes downstream of the Third Cataract seem to have been more important than those upstream.[29] The great 'temples of millions of years' built in Lower Nubia are often devoid of any urban context, as are the earlier neighbouring Thutmoside sanctuaries that are supplemented or transformed at this time. That of Abu Simbel is the most spectacular, but those of Beit el-Wali, Wadi es-Sebua, Derr and Gerf Hussein also included reliefs revealing the form that the royal cult took during the reign of Ramesses II.[30] The towns located between the Second and Third Cataracts are the object of particular interest: a new fortified town was built at Amara West[31] under Seti I (cat. 81), while the settlement and the Temple of Sesebi[32] were thoroughly restructured. The decree of Nauri, incised on a large cliff

76 Columns of the Temple of Amenhotep IV (Akhenaton) at Sesebi.

downstream of the Third Cataract, reveals the institutional ties that existed between the 'temple of millions of years' of Seti I at Abydos and the Nubian foundation destined to furnish the gold necessary for the decoration of the monument.[33] At Kerma the Ramesside testimonials (fig. 78) are limited to a few blocks, currently difficult to place in context.[34] Furthermore, at Napata, the main building datable to this period is a side chapel integrated into the Temple of Piankhi (Piye). It is extremely difficult to guess the location of the Ramesside monuments on the great sites of Upper Nubia, where later changes have completely re-fashioned the urban landscape. Only systematic dismantling of the later masonry and deep excavation may bring new answers concerning the building activity undertaken by the New Kingdom pharaohs.

The names of the immediate successors to Ramesses II and the kings of the 20th Dynasty are found on several monuments in Lower and Upper Nubia, showing the interest that the Egyptian sovereigns maintained in the land of Kush, but the time of great architectural programmes had ended in this part of the Egyptian Empire. Under the last Ramesside rulers, Nubia became an opposition stronghold of the dissident viceroy Panehesy who was buried at Aniba, north of the Second Cataract.[35] Nevertheless, the cultural mark left by the Egyptians over all of Nubia is very deep. Even with regard to funerary customs, which are always resistant to external influences, Egyptianization is considerable. It is nevertheless difficult to quantify during the Third Intermediate Period, the evidence being rare, little known and often devoid of datable criteria.[36] Despite everything, Egyptian culture became an integral part of Nubian culture and history so that, three centuries later, when one of the Kushite principalities became powerful enough to conquer an Egypt more torn apart by internal rivalries than by the greed of the Assyrians, it did so in the name of its Egyptian origins (cf. cat. 146).

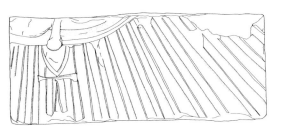

77 Amarna-style relief from Dokki Gel.

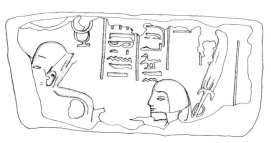

78 Ramesside relief from Dokki Gel.

1 Roccati 1982, 198–220.
2 Valbelle 1990; 1992.
3 Valbelle 1998, in press.
4 Davies 2003a, d and e.
5 Habachi 1972.
6 Smith 1976, 206–8.
7 Urk. IV, 6–8.
8 Davies 2001; 2003b and c.
9 Urk. IV, 88–90.
10 Bonnet 2004, in press.
11 Bonnet 2000, 145–56.
12 Habachi 1980.
13 Valbelle 1995; Morkot 1995a.
14 Barguet et al. 1967.
15 Emery et al. 1979, 13–17; Caminos 1974; 1998.
16 Azim 1975; Geus, this volume, p. 114 ff.
17 Bonnet 2001b, 205–14; 2003; Bonnet and Valbelle 2000; this volume, p. 109 ff.
18 Valbelle 2001, 229–31; 2002; 2003a, 295.
19 Valbelle 2003a; 2003b.

20 Jacquet-Gordon et al. 1969, 110 and pl. 23.1.
21 Davies 2001, 46–52, figs 3–4; 2003c, 24–31, figs 5–6; Reisner and Reisner 1933, 24–39, pls III–IV.
22 Reisner 1931, 76–7.
23 Blackman 1937.
24 Bonnet 1999, 74; 2001b, 205–7; Valbelle 1999, 84; 2001, 230–33; 2003a, 291 ff.
25 Kendall 2002, in press.
26 Macadam 1955, 28–44.
27 Davies and Gardiner 1926.
28 Simpson 1963.
29 Hein 1991.
30 Habachi 1969, 1–16.
31 Spencer 1997.
32 Blackman 1937.
33 Kitchen 1975, 45–58.
34 Bonnet and Valbelle 2000, 1113–15; Valbelle 2001, 232–3.
35 Steindorff 1937, 240–41, pl. 29c.
36 Morkot 2000, 145–66.

73

police the native population. The major aims were to control the rich goldmines of Nubia's Eastern Desert and the trade in African goods with lands further to the south. Towards the end of the 13th Dynasty (1795–1650 BC), Egypt underwent a great political upheaval and, among other consequences, was obliged to withdraw from Nubia. In the north a Canaanite dynasty, known as the Hyksos, took control of the Nile Delta and Lower Egypt. In the south *Wawat* and the fortresses, among them Buhen, were occupied by the forces of the powerful kingdom of Kush, based at Kerma just south of the Third Cataract. It appears that not all Egyptian personnel chose to flee. Some remained to serve the new masters.

This stela is one of a group of monuments from Buhen belonging to a single family who administered the fortress over several generations during the period of Kushite rule. A high official named Ka was the owner of the stela, which was dedicated to him by his grandson, also a high official, named Iah-user. We know from other sources that Ka was preceded in office by his father and grandfather, both named Sobekemheb. His younger brother, named Sepedhor, served as 'commandant of Buhen' and was instrumental in rebuilding the Temple of Horus at Buhen where their stelae were set up. Both proudly state that they served the ruler of Kush whose name is given on the stela of Ka as Nedjeh. There is insufficient data to decide on the precise dates of Ka and Sepedhor, and of the Kushite king in question, but the latter is perhaps to be identified as the owner of one or other of the two latest tumuli in the royal cemetery at Kerma, designated as K.IV and K.III respectively, which are roughly contemporary with the mid- to late 17th Dynasty (1650–1550 BC) in Egypt. WVD

Franke 1983, 47, 236; 1984, 411, Doss. 706; Holm-Rasmussen 1995, 55 ff.; Kubisch 2002, 37–9; Redford 1997, 5, no. 15; Säve-Söderbergh 1949, 50–54; Porter and Moss 1951, 138; Schneider 1998, 164; Smith 1976, 41; Vanderleyen 1971, 56–60; 1995, 203

73 Stela of the official, Ka

Limestone, paint

Buhen

Kerma Classique/Egyptian, 17th Dynasty

H 480 mm, W 270 mm, Th 117 mm

SNM 18

A round-topped stela, in good condition, missing only a section of the bottom left-hand corner. The body of the stela bears an incised hieroglyphic inscription, arranged in ten horizontal lines, the signs reading from right to left. The lunette is decorated, in sunk relief, with a religious motif in the form of the so-called *shen*-ring flanked by two *udjat* eyes. Both the motif and the inscription were finished in green paint, substantial traces of which remain. The text reads: '(1) A gift that the king gives (to) Osiris, Lord of Busiris, the Great God, Lord of Abydos, (2) and (to) Horus, Lord of Foreign Land[s], that they may give

an invocation offering consisting of bread and beer, oxen and fowl, and all things (3) good and pure, on which a god lives, which heaven creates and (4) earth makes, which Hapy (the Nile Indundation) brings as his perfect offering, for the spirit (5) of the nobleman Ka. It is the son of his daughter who makes his name to live, (6) namely the nobleman Iah-user. He (Ka) says: I was a valiant servant (7) of the ruler of Kush. I washed my feet (8) in the waters of Kush in the following of the (9) ruler Nedjeh. I returned (10) safe and sound (and) my family (too).'

During the Middle Kingdom, the Egyptians invaded and occupied Lower Nubia (the land of *Wawat*), establishing a new southern border upstream of the Second Cataract. Buhen was one of a chain of great fortresses which they built along the Nile in *Wawat* to consolidate and extend their economic interests and to

74 Stela with figure of a king

Sandstone, paint

Buhen

Kerma Classique/Egyptian, 17th Dynasty

H 260 mm, W 195 mm, Th 54 mm

SNM 62/8/17

A round-topped stela, quite roughly shaped, now with worn and chipped edges, especially at the bottom corners, but otherwise in good condition. It is decorated in sunk relief, with a somewhat schematic figure of a king shown as if striding to the right. He wears the white crown of Upper Egypt with a uraeus at the forehead and a short skirt with a protruding front, probably a version of the royal *shendyt*-kilt. In his rear hand he holds a mace, and in his front hand a long, double-curved bow and three arrows. The body of the figure was painted red, his kilt and crown white.

There are good grounds, both stylistic and archaeological, for identifying the figure as one of the kings of Kush, shown as having 'adopted in part at least the regalia of Pharaoh, specifically as king of Upper Egypt' (Smith 1976, 12). This was no empty aspiration on the part of the Kushites. During the *Kerma Classique* period they not only ruled the whole of Nubia but also carried out at least one substantial invasion of Upper Egypt (cat. 75). It has been suggested that the king represented here may be the Nedjeh mentioned on the Buhen stela of Ka (cat. 73).   WVD

Berenguer 2003c; Morkot 2000, 68, fig. 32; Smith 1976, 11–12, no. 691, 84, 246, pls iii, 2, lviii, 4; Soulé-Nan 2002, 161–2, fig. 31; Wildung 1997, 100, no. 100; Williams 1991b, 80, 83, fig. 8a

75 Stone vessel

Travertine
Kerma, Tumulus K.III, Grave K.334
Kerma Classique/17th Dynasty
H 135.5 mm, max. W 82.5 mm
SNM 1087

Finely polished, bag-shaped flask with a ribbed neck associated, when found, with a lid made of serpentine, now lost. It has been very skilfully worked, with a vein in the stone exploited to great effect to form a decorative central band, separating the flask's upper and lower parts which are of different hues. Inside the flask there are substantial remains of its original contents, initial analysis[1] identifying it as a now-degraded oil of plant origin.

The flask bears, incised on the exterior body, a rectangular frame enclosing a funerary inscription arranged in three columns of hieroglyphs, reading from right to left and down, identifying its contents and original owner: 'A gift which [the king] gives, that he may give incense and unguent to the spirit of the Governor, Hereditary Prince, of Nekhen (Hierakonpolis), Sobeknakht.'

This flask is one of a substantial number of Egyptian objects buried in the royal tumuli at Kerma, in this case in an elite subsidiary grave within the precincts of Tumulus K.III, the last of the great tumuli in the Eastern Cemetery. The original source of the flask would have been the Egyptian owner's tomb presumably located at Hierakonpolis (though not impossibly perhaps at ElKab), from which it was probably plundered during a Kushite raid on the region. There are several other objects originally from Hierakonpolis among the Kerma material. That such raids took place is con-

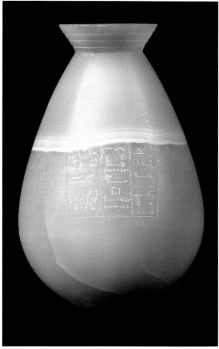

75

firmed by an inscription recently discovered (Davies 2003a, d and e) in the tomb of another Sobeknakht, a governor of ElKab, the twin-town of Hierakonpolis, during the 17th Dynasty, who may well have been related to his namesake across the river. It records the occurrence of a major Kushite attack on Upper Egypt during his governorship, one of the main aims of which was to secure booty (the aggressors are referred to in the inscription as 'looters'), much of it evidently destined for reuse and deposition at Kerma.   WVD

1 This analysis was carried out by Rebecca Stacey of The British Museum.

Davies 2003a, 53, n. 11; 2003d, 43, n. 11; 2003e, 6; Edel 1980, 42, no. 4; Hintze and Hintze 1967, 12, no. 46; Porter and Moss 1951, 178; Reisner 1923a, 169, fig. 47, 171, no. 18, pl. 11, 1; 1923b, 57, no. 6, 58, fig. 159, no. 9, 523, fig. 344, no. 46, 524, no. 46; Ryholt 1997, 162, n. 591; Williams 1975, 89–90, 94; 1992, 149–51

74

76 Statue of Amenhotep I

Sandstone, paint
Sai Island
New Kingdom, 18th Dynasty
H 1.66 m, W 563 mm, Th 1 m
SNM 63/4/5

Statue of a king, near life-size, seated on a throne with rectangular pedestal. He is identified by inscription as Amenhotep I (*c.* 1525–1504 BC), second king of the 18th Dynasty. The piece was broken into three parts and has recently been reconstructed. It now has a somewhat battered appearance, with parts of it lost and much superficial damage.

The king is shown wearing the white crown (its top missing) with uraeus at the forehead, the royal beard, now very damaged, and the *heb-sed* or jubilee dress – a cloak that envelopes most of his body from the shoulders down to just above the ankles, leaving the chest and feet exposed. His arms are held crossed (right over left) on his chest, the hands emerging from beneath the cloak. The right hand holds a crook, the left a flail. Unusually, they are not crossed over. The king's figure is thick-set with big, heavy feet and an enormous head, oval in shape, displaying full, rounded cheeks and jowls. The individual features are damaged but the mouth – thick, fleshy lips, set in a definite smile – is reasonably well preserved, as is the right eye, shown as large and wide-open, with the eyebrow rendered as a raised band. The figure was originally finished in paint. There are substantial traces of red pigment on parts of the king's body and of white sporadically elsewhere.

The royal throne has a low back-rest covered by a cloth serving as a cushion. The back of the king's figure is supported centrally by a tall, rectangular pillar which narrows slightly towards the top. It bears a finely incised inscription in large hieroglyphs, the bottom section of which is now mostly missing. It reads from top to bottom and right to left: 'He shall be foremost of the *ka*s of all the living, having arisen as king of Upper and Lower Egypt upon the throne of Horus [...] every [...].' Several hieroglyphs bear the remains of blue pigment.

The sides of the throne are both finely decorated in sunk relief with an identical motif in the form of a lotus and papyrus –

76

plants emblematic of Upper and Lower Egypt respectively – shown intertwined and flanking a large hieroglyph signifying unity, the whole symbolizing the union of the two lands. The motif is enclosed in a banded frame, done in incised work. The decoration is better preserved on the right side of the throne than on the left.

To either side of the king's legs, on the front of the throne and continuing on to the pedestal, are two neatly incised columns of inscription, enclosed in a narrow rectangular frame, the hieroglyphs facing inwards. The inscriptions, which read from top to bottom, give in each case the king's titulary, prenomen and nomen followed by an epithet and dedication to a god, one Egyptian, the other Nubian: (left) 'The good god, lord of the two lands, lord of ritual, Djeserkara, son of Ra of his body, beloved of him, Amenhotep, given life, beloved of Amen-Ra, lord [of the thrones of the two lands]'; (right) 'The good god, lord of the two lands, lord of ritual, Djeserkara, son of Ra of his body, beloved of him, Amenhotep, given life, beloved of Dedun, lord of Ta-sety (Nubia)'. In both columns the hieroglyphs reading 'Amen' show clear signs of having been erased (no doubt during the Amarna period) and subsequently recut rather clumsily. The god's epithet was also damaged.

This important statue would have been set up in the main temple of the fortified town established by Amenhotep I's predecessor Ahmose, on the island of Sai, which during this period was effectively Egypt's southern border. A statue of Ahmose is known from the same site (cf. Lindblad 1984, 20–21, C, 1a–b, pls 7 and 8a–b; Sourouzian 1994, 514, no. 23). It is also of sandstone and broken into three pieces (SNM 3828 [head] and SNM 63/4/4 [torso and throne]). It too has recently been reconstructed (fig. 79). Possibly in an act of homage, the Amenhotep I statue was closely based on that of Ahmose, being very similar in its size, style, iconography and decoration, though they are not identical and there is no reason to assume that they were made at the same time. Their overall proportions are different, the head of Ahmose being smaller in relation to the rest of the figure, and the portraits of the two kings are quite distinct. Also noteworthy is the fact that the

Ahmose statue bears a dedication only to Amen-Ra, whereas on the Amenhotep I statue, the Nubian god Dedun is included. The two statues, which originally would probably have stood near to each other, may well have been broken up and placed together in a special cache following an official clearance of the temple.

The statues were possibly products of a local workshop, which would explain some evident peculiarities, especially perhaps the disproportionately large head of Amenhotep I and his rather bulbous face, which are not found in the few other sculptures identified as his to date.

The damage and loss of colour hinder a full assessment but their original quality should not be underestimated. Far from being 'summary' and 'crude', as one commentator has suggested, both statues can be seen under the right lighting conditions to have been accomplished pieces, done in a somewhat archaizing style, but bold and imposing representations of the reigning king and decorated with well-executed motifs and inscriptions.   WVD

Lindblad 1984, 27–8 and 48, nos A2a, 2b, pls 7a–b and 12; Schmitz 1978, 133–4; Sourouzian 1994, 514, no. 24; Vandersleyen 1971, 71, 73; Vercoutter 1956, 79, no. 25; 1958, 159–60

Fig. 79 Statue of King Ahmose from Sai Island.

77 Statuette of Amenemhat

Serpentine (?)
New Kingdom, 18th Dynasty
(co-regency of Hatshepsut/Thutmose III)
Buhen
H 220 mm, W 124 mm, Th 650 mm
SNM 92

Figure of a man, identified by inscription as the 'Scribe Amenemhat', in the pose of squatting, his knees drawn up before him, on a pedestal with straight sides and a rounded front and back. The piece is finely sculpted and in very good condition.

Amenemhat is represented as wearing a long, broad, shoulder-length wig, a short beard and a tight-fitting cloak that envelops his body, except for the arms shown emerging just in front of the knees, the right crossed over the left, with the right hand clenched, the left extended palm-downwards. His face is broad and triangular in shape and his expression benign. The eyes, asymmetrically positioned, are large, wide-open and slope markedly inwards, the eyebrows and cosmetic lines rendered as raised bands. The nose is relatively narrow and pointed at the end. The mouth, with two thick lips, is small with just the hint of a smile. The ears, set high, are large and splay slightly against the wings of the headdress. The treatment overall, and particularly of the eyes, is evocative of that of royal portraiture of the period.

Incised between the knees and legs, on the front of the figure, is a hieroglyphic inscription arranged in four columns, reading from right to left and top to bottom: 'Gift that the king gives (to) Horus, Lord of Buhen, that he may give invocation offerings consisting of bread, beer, oxen, fowl, alabaster, linen, incense, unguents, all things good and pure, offerings of every vegetable, that upon which a god lives, everything which comes forth upon his offering table regularly every day, for the spirit of the scribe Amenemhat, repeating life, possessor of veneration'. Further, single columns of inscription are located towards the rear of the figure, on the right and left sides respectively and on the rear itself. The side inscriptions repeat the owner's title and name and also identify his parents. The column on the figure's right side reads (from right to left and down) 'Scribe Amenemhat, begotten of the chief of *Teh-khet* Rwiw [mis-spelt as Rwsw]', that on the left (from left to right and down) 'Scribe Amenemhat, born to the mistress of the house, Rwna'. The column on the rear reads 'Revered [before] Osiris, Scribe Amenemhat, justified'.

In form and style, this is a typical 'block-statue' of the early 18th Dynasty, a dating confirmed by the identity of the owner and his parents, who are known from other monuments of the period (cf. cat. 78). It was found buried as one of a cache of three statuettes, one of the others also belonging to the same Amenemhat (now Philadelphia E 10980). Originally placed in one of the temples of Horus at Buhen, they were probably removed and buried during the 18th Dynasty before the Amarna Period, as on both figures of Amenemhat, the name element 'Amen' has been left untouched, suggesting that the pieces were inaccessible to Akhenaton's agents.   WVD

Edel 1963, 28 ff.; Pérez Die 2003b; Porter and Moss 1951, 138; Randall-MacIver and Woolley 1911, 108, 110, pl. 37 (left); Säve-Söderbergh 1960, 25 ff., pl. 14; Säve-Söderbergh and Troy 1991, 193, fig. 48 (B1), pl. 60, 1; Schulz 1992, 337–8 (no. 192), pl. 85, b; Scott in Thomas 1996, 181; Smith 1976, 202, 208–9; Vandier 1958, 451–2, 669

78 Stela of Amenemhat

Granite (?)
New Kingdom, 18th Dynasty
(co-regency of Hatshepsut/Thutmose III)
Debeira West, Tomb of Amenemhat
H 1.07 m, W 660 mm, Th 160 mm
SNM 63/4/7

Round-topped stela of the 'chief of *Teh-khet*, Amenemhat', very finely decorated with scenes and inscriptions executed in sunk relief. It is in excellent condition, marred only by the ancient damage inflicted (three times) by Akhenaton's agents upon the hieroglyphic group reading 'Amen' in the owner's name.

At the top, within the lunette of the stela, is a large religious motif in the form of two *udjat* eyes flanking a *shen* sign surmounted by the symbol of the West. Beneath is a register containing two offering scenes, which include figures of the tomb-owner and members of his family, comprising his father, mother and wife, all of them identified in the columns of inscription above them.

The seated couple on the left, the man holding a lotus flower, are the 'chief of *Teh-khet*, Rwiw, justified', and 'his wife, mistress of the house, Rwna, justified'. The standing man, facing them and offering a libation, is 'his son, chief of *Teh-khet*, Amenemhat, repeating life'. The equivalent couple on the right are the 'chief of *Teh-khet*, Amenemhat, repeating life', accompanied by 'his wife, mistress of the house, Hatsheps[ut]'. The standing lady, extending a bowl towards them, is also 'his

77

wife, mistress of the house, Hatsheps[ut]', here standing duty for a son or daughter, probably indicating that Amenemhat died childless.

The scene surmounts a long inscription, an offering formula, arranged in ten horizontal lines, reading from right to left and down. It invokes the funerary gods to provide numerous provisions and other benefits for the spirit of the tomb-owner, who is described in the last line as 'excellent unique one, beloved of his lord, whose attention is vigilant, who sets himself against wrongdoing, chief of *Teh-khet*, Amenemhat,

justified'. The decoration was painted yellow throughout. There are also traces of the artist's original red draughting lines.

So as to control more effectively the newly conquered territories, the Egyptians sought to secure the loyalty and assistance of the surviving Nubian elite, partly through a process of deliberate acculturation (Morkot 1991, 298–9; 2000, 81–3; O'Connor 1993, 61–5; Säve-Söderbergh 1991, 188; Smith 2003, 84–6). The two monuments above (cats 77–8) exemplify the success of this policy, at least in Lower Nubia. Although Amenemhat's statue, stela and name are wholly Egyptian in appearance, he is known to have been a native Nubian. He was a member of an elite indigenous family from *Teh-khet* (covering the modern regions of Debeira and Serra), traceable over several generations, who were thoroughly 'Egyptianized' and governed their region on behalf of the imperial administration. Quite possibly educated at the Egyptian court, Amenemhat may have begun his career as a scribe based at Buhen, during the reign of King Thutmose I, eventually becoming 'chief of *Teh-khet*' at some time during the co-regency of Hatshepsut and Thutmose III, a hereditary position previously held by his elder brother, Djehutyhotep, and their father, Rwiw. Djehutyhotep, also called Paitsy, is well known for his tomb at Debeira East (situated opposite that of his brother), which was decorated with a range of painted scenes in the Egyptian mode (Säve-Söderbergh 1960; Säve-Söderbergh and Troy 1991, 197–201, figs 50–51, pl. 1). A recent discovery suggests that his duties extended beyond the Nile Valley to include the monitoring of caravan routes across the Eastern Desert (Castiglioni and Castiglioni 2003, 48, pls 1–2). The indications are that, dying childless, Amenemhat was the last 'chief of *Teh-khet*' in the family line.

Many other such officials are attested, including most famously Heqanefer, chief of *Miam* (modern Aniba) during the later 18th Dynasty. He was buried at Toshka in an Egyptian-style tomb with Egyptian funerary paraphernalia, but depicted at Thebes in the tomb of his master, Tutankhamun's viceroy Huy, as an ethnic Nubian with dark skin and dressed in traditional tribal garb (Davies and Gardiner 1926, pl. XXVII; Simpson 1963, 27).   WVD

Berenguer 2003i; Säve-Söderbergh 1963, 168–70, fig. 5, pl. xl; 1991, 187, pl. 8; Säve-Söderbergh and Troy 1991, 201–5, fig. 52 (D3), pls 48, 2, and 49–50

78

79 Statuette of Amenhotep II

Red Quartzite

Kumma, Temple

New Kingdom, 18th Dynasty (c. 1420 BC)

H 369 mm, max. W (at elbows) 155 mm; base:
L 198 mm, W 121 mm

SMN 30

Figure of a king, represented kneeling on a pedestal offering two pots (probably to be understood as containing wine), held symmetrically, one in each hand. The piece, which was finely carved and finished, is remarkably well preserved with hardly a blemish on its carefully polished surface. The king is shown wearing the *shendyt*-kilt with a broad, banded belt and the *nemes*-headdress with uraeus, its tail winding back in several loops to the crown of the king's head. The pedestal is roughly rectangular with a slightly rounded front. At the rear a narrow, rectangular pillar extends to a point about halfway up the king's back, where it meets the queue of the *nemes*.

The king's face is broadly triangular in shape, with high cheekbones and a small, delicate chin, turned up at the tip. The nose is large and long (in profile, very slightly aquiline), the mouth small and straight, the lips quite thick. The eyes, rather blandly rendered, are set a little asymmetrically. They are relatively long and wide with rounded eyeballs, the upper lids reproduced as a raised band, as are the eyebrows (which curve slightly) and the cosmetic lines that extend from the outer canthi. The ears, also asymmetrical, are splayed against the wings of the *nemes*, the right ear more than the left. The overall expression is serene if a little serious. Though it lacks an inscription, the figure can be identified on firm stylistic grounds as a representation of King Amenhotep II, an attribution fully consistent with its provenance.

Consolidating their rule, the Egyptian pharaohs of the mid-18th Dynasty embarked on a substantial programme of building throughout Nubia, which included the renovation of existing structures. The largely mud-brick temple of Kumma, a foundation of Queen Hatshepsut and Thutmose III, dedicated to the ram-headed Khnum, chief god of the cataract region, was rebuilt and enlarged by Thutmose III's successor Amenhotep II, using sandstone blocks (Hinkel 1998, 101 ff.). The Khartoum figure appears to have been one of a group of such statues of the king set up in the temple (cf., for example, Wildung 1997, 136, no. 139).   WVD

Der Manuelian 1987, 261; Porter and Moss 1951, 155; Sourouzian 1991, 70–71, fig. 25; Vercoutter 1957, 5–7, pls I–III

79

80 Stela of Amenhotep III

Sandstone

Sedeinga, sector II of the Great Necropolis, Tomb II T77, d1 and d2

New Kingdom, 18th Dynasty (1390–1352 BC)

Preserved H 490 mm, max. preserved W 1.07 m, Th c. 150 mm

SNM 31216

Upper section of the lunette of a stela reused in the construction of a Meroitic tomb in the Sedeinga Cemetery, but undoubtedly originally from the nearby Temple of Queen Tiye. Under the protective wings of Horus of Behedet, Pharaoh Amenhotep III (Tiye being his Great Royal Wife), wearing the white crown, offers incense to Amun of Soleb and his own deified

80

image. As such, he is depicted with the headdress associated with Khonsu, the child god – the disc mounted on a crescent moon. A ram's horn also curves around his ear, underlining his relationship with Amun, the ram god *par excellence* 'who resides in Soleb'. The links between the temples of Sedeinga and Soleb are thus emphasized.

The king's nomen was carefully scratched out and changed to Neb-Maat-Re, his prenomen. Similarly, the depiction of the god Amun and the two columns of hieroglyphs concerning him (located in front of him) were erased during the Amarna period (1352–1336 BC), but carved anew as early as the reign of Tutankhamun (1336–1327 BC), thus proving that the temple was still in use even after its founders had passed on.   C B-N

Labrousse 1997, 67

81 Stela of Seti I

Sandstone

New Kingdom, 19th Dynasty (*c.* 1286 BC)

Amara West, Temple

H 597 mm, W 703 mm, Th 146 mm

SNM 3063

Section of the top of a stela of Seti I (*c.* 1294–1279 BC) with remains of a scene, in fine sunk relief, showing the god Amen-Ra offering a scimitar or *khepesh*-sword (cf. cat. 82), symbolic of divine strength, to the king. The king smites, with the same sword held in his right hand, a group of Nubian captives, grasped collectively by their feathered head-dresses in his left hand, which also holds a staff. The stela was originally decorated at the top with a winged sun-disc, but only the tip of the left wing now survives.

The king, represented standing and lean-ing forward, wears a pleated knee-length kilt with a long central sporran, a short, striated wig fitted with a streamer at the back and uraeus at the forehead, a collar around the neck, a long narrow beard, and a crown consisting of a ram's horns surmounted by two large feathers, each flanked by a uraeus with a sun-disc on its head. The captives, dressed in a short skirt held up by a shoulder-strap, raise their right arms, some in obei-sance to the king, others to the god.

The king is identified by the two cartouches located above him to his right, which contain his prenomen and nomen – Men-Maat-Ra and Seti-mry-Ptah, respectively. The column of inscription at his rear reads 'Horus, mighty of arm, lord of strength, may protection and life surround him like Ra for ever and eter-nity'. The short column in front describes him as 'slaying the chiefs of vile Irem'. The god's figure is lost except for his right arm holding the *khepesh*. His speech to the king is recorded in the two columns above his arm, also now damaged and somewhat unclear: 'Words spoken by Amen-Ra, lord of the thrones of the two lands, "[Take] the *khepesh* (?). I am [your] father..."'.

The fortified town of Amara West, founded by Seti I and enlarged by his son and succes-sor Ramesses II, functioned as the adminis-

Fig. 80 *Right* Stela of Seti I with text describing a military campaign against the land of Irem. From Amara West (Brooklyn Museum of Art, 39.424).

trative capital of Kush during the Ramesside period. This stela, the bottom of which is missing, was found in the hypostyle hall of the temple built by Ramesses II. Celebrating a victory over Irem, it almost certainly commemorates the campaign of Seti's Year 8 against 'the enemies of the land of Irem' described in narrative form in two other near-duplicate stelae, one also from Amara West (now Brooklyn Mus. 39.424; see fig. 80), the other from Sai Island (MAF Sai, 1970, no. F.25.11). Indeed, it has been suggested that the Brooklyn stela is the missing bottom part of the Khartoum stela. The location of the land of Irem has been much disputed and is still uncertain, but it possibly covered a territory which included the Berber-Shendi Reach of the Nile and the northern Butana – too far south to be permanently conquered and occupied by the Egyptians, but just within reach of punitive expeditions.   WVD

Berenguer 2003h; Brand 2000, 291–2, no. 3.145; Fairman 1939a, 390; 1939b, 327; 1939c, 142–3; Hein 1991, 52; Kitchen 1975, 104, no. 50; 1993a, 87–8, no. 50; 1993b, 90, no. 50; 1999, 177; O'Connor and Quirke 2003, 8–10; Porter and Moss 1951, 161; Spencer 1997, 43, no. 111, and 23, no. 101; Wildung (ed.) 1997, 140, no. 142

82 Scimitar

Copper alloy, probably bronze
New Kingdom, possibly Ramesside period
Ez-Zuma
L 588 mm, Th (max. at back of grip) 65 mm
SNM 31316

Scimitar or sickle-sword, called by the Egyptians a *khepesh* (lit. 'foreleg of an ox' [Schoske 1980, 819]). The first such weapon to be discovered in Nubia/Sudan, it is a fine example, in good condition. It consists of three parts, cast in one piece: i) a short flanged handle with a sloping rear end, ii) an almost straight hilt, flanged on both edges, curving outwards sharply into iii) a curved blade with convex cutting edge and flanged inner edge, ending in a point at the distal end. The hilt and blade are decorated with a medial rib flanked by furrows probably executed in chased work. In the handle are the remains of metal tangs for securing ornamental inlay, now missing. There are indications of wear on the cutting edge.

This piece was, according to information supplied by Dr B. Żurawski, discovered recently, buried in sand near the so-called Anchorite Grotto in ez-Zuma, which, it is speculated, may originally have been a pharaonic tomb. Further, archaeological investigation is intended, which may shed additional light on the context. In form and size it is exactly paralleled by a scimitar excavated at the site of Tell er-Rotaba/Wadi Tumilat in the Egyptian Delta (Griffith 1890, 57, pl. XIX, 30; Muller 1987, 156, fig. 51, no. 21, and 158–9, no. 21, pl. XIXa; now British Museum EA 27490), which has been dated tentatively to the 19th Dynasty. The form is a variant, possibly developed for routine military use, of the classic *khepesh*, with deeply curved blade and squared end (Muller 1987, 150, fig. 49), a type favoured by kings and gods, as represented, for example, in the Amara West stela of Seti I (cat. 81).   WVD

Żurawski 2002b, 84, pl. 11

82

KERMA, DOKKI GEL

CHARLES BONNET AND DOMINIQUE VALBELLE

A kilometre to the north of the Nubian town of Kerma lies the site of Dokki Gel (literally the 'red hill'), previously called *Kom des Bodegas*. It has been under excavation for ten years by the archaeological mission of the University of Geneva.[1] This archaeological area, today enclosed by a wall, was mentioned by K.R. Lepsius in his *Denkmäler aus Aegypten und Aethiopien* in 1849–59. The research of G.A. Reisner also mentions it: he conducted sondages

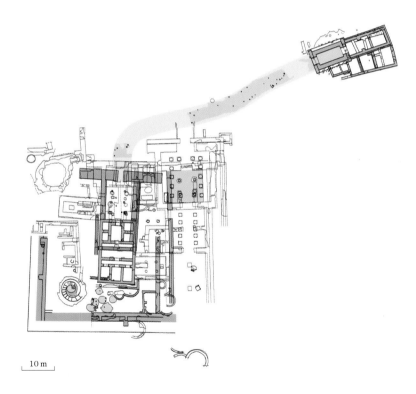

10 m

81 Schematic plan of the Temple of Thutmose IV.

that convinced him the remains were of little importance,[2] particularly those that must have belonged to a modest 'Ethiopian' temple, whose 'altar' in grey granite was preserved. He also discovered some circular storehouses and a mound of pottery sherds thought to be the refuse from a religious establishment. The local name 'Dokki Gel', in the Nubian language, evokes this mound of reddish bread moulds; their conical shape also inspired the first European travellers to use the Spanish term *bodegas*.

Recent research unearthed an enclosure wall 3–6 m thick, strengthened by rectangular/square bastions. It soon became clear that this structure was of Egyptian

origin, from the 18th Dynasty, and that its defensive system was identical to that of other fortified towns to the north of the Third Cataract. Increased land cultivation has gradually caused the disappearance of the remains and only part of the area urbanized in ancient times remains accessible. The site is thus preserved over a trapezoidal area of about 150 m per side. Today it seems clear that the remains of a religious quarter and two palaces have survived, but further excavation is still necessary to obtain a more complete picture of the area.

The main sandstone temple, undoubtedly dedicated to Amun,[3] is dated to the reign of Thutmose IV (1400–1390 BC) (figs 81, 82; cat. 83).[4] However, mudbrick walls belonging to an older monument were found under the foundation of the temple, and the cartouches of Amenhotep II (1427–1400 BC), discovered on a reused lintel, also attest to the existence of an earlier cult building. The tripartite sanctuary, preceded by a vestibule, also dates to the reign of Thutmose IV. The remains of columns belonging to a hypostyle hall, followed by a porticoed courtyard linked to a long mudbrick pylon, were found on the north side. The entrance was associated with a paved walkway of fine appearance that runs obliquely for nearly 70 m. The pavement leads to a building that is thought to be a ceremonial palace.[5] The end of the pavement is still visible at a monumental stone doorway whose foundation trenches have been studied. Around this very carefully built part are several rooms and a central hall in mud brick. A secondary southern entrance existed from the beginning. On the other side all structures have disappeared; however, traces of occupation were also found there. Numerous modifications transformed that space and can be dated to the Kushite period. It is probable that during the New Kingdom a second temple was built to the east of the main sanctuary. The occupation level of the building with its porticoed courtyard is dated by the pottery and other datable evidence found in several places beneath the later remains.

Storerooms, bakeries and a deep well, lined with sandstone blocks, were associated with the Temple of Thutmose IV. The eastern *temenos* wall and an annex near the bakeries are also noteworthy. During the reign of Akhenaton there was considerable disturbance as the temple was completely demolished and the Thutmoside

82 General view of the main temple and surroundings.
83 Schematic plan of the buildings contemporary with the 25th Dynasty.

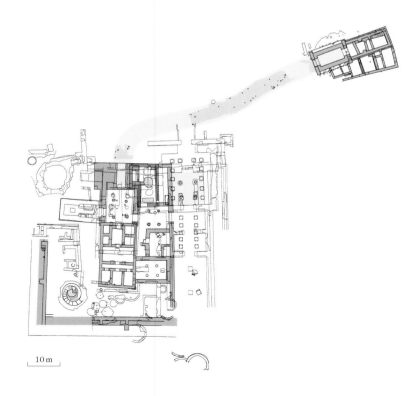

10 m

stones systematically recut. There was a clear desire to reuse the available material, but also to destroy the existing structures. The plan of the building was of necessity modified, but the three rooms of the sanctuary were retained. The proportions of the pylon changed, as did those of the porticoed courtyard, where the lateral passages suggest that the chapels on both sides were integrated within the main plan. The *talatat* blocks, inscribed or decorated, found reused in the floor of the nearby Napatan temple (cats 84–5), seem to indicate that a monument dedicated to Aton survived for several centuries, even if it underwent transformations.[6]

Two blocks with the cartouche of Shabaqo[7] were reused in the foundations of a late bench, but the structures of the 25th Dynasty are poorly preserved at Dokki Gel (fig. 83). It is possible that the great transversal chapel abutting the sanctuary belongs to this period. An L-shaped hall with an annexe was added between the courtyards of the two temples. Raised upon the mud-brick masonry, these two rooms would have had a particularly important function as, after the military campaign of Psammeticus II, a 2 m-deep hiding place was dug in the ground. The fragments of seven monumental statues of the kings Taharqo, Tanwetamani, Senkamanisken, Anlamani and Aspelta

84 View of the statue cache.

85 The head of Senkamanisken.

connects to a courtyard with a double portico that was also used for circulating between the two temples. Further bakeries were placed around the cult areas, as testified to by bread moulds of a little-known type. They were accompanied by silos for the grain reserves, which were also used for the preparation of beer. There was a bronze workshop, curiously placed between the hypostyle rooms of the two temples. Faience objects also were made there, both plaques decorated in relief as well as amulets. The cylindrical furnace was used for a long time, judging by the small statues of Osiris still made there during the Meroitic period.

The main temple was at least in part rebuilt during the Napatan period, but it is in the eastern temple that one can follow the contemporary changes. Under the remains of a Meroitic building were walls and foundations undoubtedly erected during the reign of Irike-Amanote (431–405 BC). The evidence for the last period of the building's life dates to the end of the second and first centuries BC. Unfortunately, like the later buildings, the sanctuary was destroyed down to its foundations. However, two granite bases intended for a *naos* or a bark were found very close to their original positions in the sanctuary and in a vestibule on the axis of the transverse chapel attributed to the 25th Dynasty. Two poorly preserved hypostyle halls may still be observed in the eastern temple as well as a porticoed courtyard. The small, Amarna-style blocks (*talatat*) were reused in these rooms. The pylon, like that of the neighbouring temple, was relatively narrow and elongated.

The course of the western enclosure wall of the town was changed in the Napatan period to gain more space outside the central area: a building extended over the remains of the abandoned wall. A courtyard was surrounded by several rooms and a kitchen equipped with a domestic oven. The well located to the south was still in use. Large grain silos testify to the existence of extensive bakeries. The preparation of bread for offerings required a considerable quantity of moulds that, broken *in situ*, are the origin of the hill of Dokki Gel. To the north-east of the already excavated monuments are the remains of a very large palace. The first phase of this building is poorly preserved; however, the superimposition of Meroitic structures over some of its masonry permits the attribution of some of the walls to the Napatans.

The classic Meroitic period sees an almost complete reconstruction of the religious and palatial complex (fig. 86).[9] Where the older walls and foundations are completely preserved, the new work is characterized by a widespread use of fired bricks, as facing and in the core of some walls. The plan of the eastern temple was modified with an enlarged pylon, a peristyle court and a large

were ritually placed in the pit (figs 84, 85). Forty pieces of black granite and a quantity of gold leaf that originally was placed on plaster covering some of the pecked surfaces of the statues were preserved. This burial was probably carried out during the reign of Aspelta, between 590 and 570 BC.[8]

It is interesting to note that these two rooms were created to the detriment of the pylon of the main temple and that they only were accessible independently. In fact, the door that opens on the south side

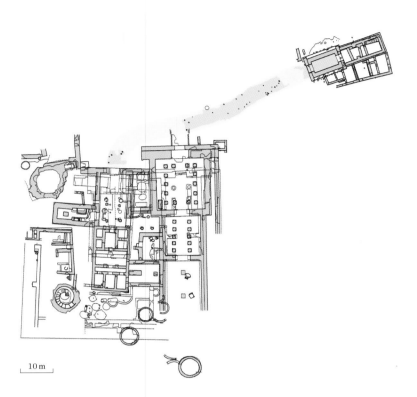

10 m

86 Schematic plan
of the site during the
Meroitic period.

hypostyle hall.[10] The main temple also was rebuilt while
respecting the restoration carried out much earlier,
during the reign of Seti I (1294–1279 BC). A chapel
abutting the structure to the west was built in *opus
africanum* masonry, and restored again during the first
and second centuries AD. Nearby, the large residential
building to the west was entirely transformed. The most
remarkable feature in this area was the presence of two
wells of exceptionally large proportions. To the south,
set over earlier stone masonry were a spiral staircase
and red-brick walls, both of excellent workmanship. To
the north, a vast circular structure more than 6 m deep
and a rectangular stone-faced arrangement show the
care devoted to the water supply. Also notable was the
work to reconstruct the north-eastern palace. The religious ensemble seems to have been abandoned at the
end of the Meroitic period, around AD 400. From then
on the site was used as a quarry.

1 Bonnet 1993, 17–18; 1997, 110–12; 1999, 70–75; 2001b,
205–14; 2003, 261–78.
2 Reisner 1923a, 36–7.
3 Valbelle 2003b.
4 Bonnet 2001b, 209–10.
5 Bonnet 2003, 270–73, figs 15–17.
6 Valbelle 1999, 84–5; 2001, 230–33.
7 Valbelle 1999, 84–5.
8 Bonnet 2003, 267–70, figs 11–14; Bonnet and Valbelle 2003,
in press; Valbelle 2003a, 295–300, figs 6–8.
9 Ahmed 1996; 1998, in press.
10 Bonnet 1999, 70–74; 2003, 276, fig. 20.

83 Foundation deposits of Thutmose IV

Faience, ceramic, bronze
Dokki Gel, nos 220, 246, 247
New Kingdom, 18th Dynasty
Plaques: L 20 mm, W 13, Th 3 mm; L 17 mm,
W 10 mm, Th 3 mm
Miniature jars: H 102 mm, D 53 mm; H 133 mm,
D 66 mm; H 127 mm, D 60 mm
Small dishes: H 35 mm D 75 mm; H 37 mm D 78 mm
Adze: L 34 mm, W 10 mm, Th 2 mm
SNM 31203

Several New Kingdom temples were rebuilt
on the same site, west of the religious complex at Dokki Gel. Foundation deposits were
found at the two exterior angles of the sanctuary. The south-western one was disturbed
during modifications dated to the Amarna
period while the south-eastern deposit was
intact. Within pits approximately 500 mm
deep below the foundations, respectively
fifteen and thirteen enamel plaques were
deposited in the sand, together with miniature ceramic vessels and beads. These
plaques, sometimes pierced with a suspension
hole, all bear the names and often the epithets
of Thutmose IV, with the exception of three
that are inscribed with the name of Thutmose
III. Approximately fifty small vessels belonging to very specific types were fashioned
using a buff-coloured clay characteristic of
the 18th Dynasty. These were preserved in
the intact pit. Small dishes and narrow-
mouthed jars remain nonetheless the preponderant types. Beads inventoried in both
deposits are tubular in shape and a miniature
bronze adze was present.   CB

Bonnet 2001b, 209, fig 10; 2003, 261–2, fig. 5

83

84

since the nineteenth century. It is adorned with typical decoration reflecting Amarna ideology: the lower section of the solar orb is adorned with a uraeus coiffed with an *ankh* sign. The rays of the sun disc stretch out to touch the members of the royal family and the offerings given to them. On its discovery, the decoration was completely covered with gypsum.   DV

85 Decorated block

Sandstone

Dokki Gel, foundation of the Napatan temple, no. DGT B84

New Kingdom, 18th Dynasty, reign of Akhenaton (1352–1336 BC)

L 526 mm, W 231 mm, Th 180 mm

SNM 31108

This *talatat* block, unearthed near cat. 84, is carved with a depiction of Queen Nefertiti's headdress. This headdress is comprised of a solar disc encircled by two long horns resting on a modius. Its lower section, like the queen's face, was chiselled out by her successors (*damnatio memoriae*) in an attempt to erase all memory of the reign of Akhenaton and Nefertiti. The rays of the sun disc were equipped with hands that presented life signs (*ankh*), as depicted on cat. 84, to the face of the queen, the king, and their daughters and towards tables laden with offerings.   DV

84 Decorated block

Sandstone

Dokki Gel, foundation of the Napatan temple, no. DGT B 186

New Kingdom, 18th Dynasty, reign of Akhenaton (1352–1336 BC)

L 530 mm, W 225 mm, Th 230 mm

SNM 31107

Belonging to the Aten Temple that Akhenaton ordered to be erected on the foundations of the Temple of Thutmose IV, which he had first razed to the ground, this block was reused in the pavement of the Napatan temple. The block was cut to the dimensions specific to this construction material, which the villagers at Karnak have called *talatat* ever

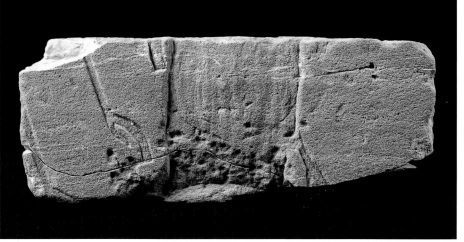

85

SAI

FRANCIS GEUS

Sai, one of the largest islands of the Nubian Nile, covers 12 km from north to south and 5.5 km from east to west (fig. 87).[1] Its core is gravelly desert; however, the river banks include extensive patches of river alluvium suitable for cultivation. Being naturally protected by the river and offering good economic opportunities, it is an attractive place for human settlement and has been inhabited since very early times. It is also located on the southern border of a vast rocky area, the Batn el-Hagar, the 'belly of rock'. This had long been the extreme limit of southern expansion for Pharaonic Egypt, hence its use as a defensive zone during the earlier second millennium BC, after which Egypt gradually extended its territorial claim over southern Nubia.

The most ancient Egyptian artefacts discovered in Sai are fragmentary pottery vessels found in storage pits dating to the late Early Dynastic period to Early Old Kingdom. At that time, Egypt controlled Lower Nubia, and Buhen, located on the northern edge of the Batn el-Hagar, either was or was about to become the main outpost of its long-distance trade with the south, where an active population centre was emerging in the Kerma Basin, upstream of the Third Cataract. It is therefore likely that, due to its location, Sai became the Nubian counterpart of Buhen and played a significant role on the trade route, a function that most likely continued if one considers the fine Egyptian artefacts found there in graves of Kerma date.

It is during this period, which witnessed increasing competition between Egypt and Kerma, that Sai also became a place of military import. Indeed, during the 12th Dynasty Senwosret I (1965–1920 BC), followed by Senwosret III (1874–1855 BC), passed the Batn el-Hagar and probably used the island, henceforth mentioned as Shaât in Egyptian inscriptions, as an outpost. The remains of a temporary camp have been interpreted as indicating a short Middle Kingdom occupation, but the discovery of undulating walls typical of that time, under New Kingdom structures, suggests that it may have been more substantial.

87 Aerial photograph of the island, from the north.

The town, made of mud brick, occupies one of the best strategic positions on the island: a sandstone outcrop that borders the eastern branch of the river and gives a view over kilometres on the eastern bank. Test excavations have shown that a 4.5 m-thick girdle wall encompasses a 238×140 m oblong area (fig. 89), of which only the southern part, where the Ottomans

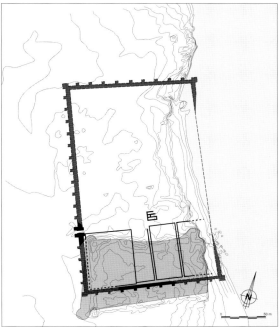

88 *Above* Fragmentary sandstone relief possibly representing Ahmose Nefertari, wife of Ahmose I.

89 *Above right* Plan of the town site.

Nevertheless, it is only at the beginning of the New Kingdom, when Egypt undertook the conquest of all Nubia, that Sai became truly Egyptian. It fell under Egyptian control during the reign of Ahmose (1550–1525 BC), the founder of the New Kingdom, whose only known lifesize statue has been found there (see p. 103, fig. 79). Ahmose established a temple of which unfortunately only fragmentary remains displaying reliefs of high quality have survived. It is possible that a female head finely carved on a sandstone fragment (fig. 88) originated from that temple and that it represents Ahmose Nefertari, his wife, whose name also appears in fragmentary inscriptions. These discoveries show the important role played by the island in supporting and legitimizing Egypt's invasion. They also suggest that the construction of the walled town began at that time.

During the five centuries that followed, Sai remained one of the major Pharaonic centres in Nubia. As stated in 1986 by Jean Vercoutter, it is 'so far ... the only site in Upper Nubia that provided documents mentioning almost all the pharaohs from the XVIIIth to the XXth dynasties'.[2] That long occupation is well documented by the walled town just mentioned, a sandstone temple, two cemeteries and several sandstone quarries.

erected a fort in the sixteenth century AD, has been excavated in detail. It is occupied by buildings and stores laid out at right angles, as is usual in Egypt's colonial foundations. It also contains numerous decorated blocks, stelae and column drums, most displaced from the temple site by the Ottomans, who used them to strengthen the walls and foundations of their fort.

The temple, located north of the fort on the river side, is the only structure of the town so far excavated outside the area just described. Only the sandstone pavement and the lower courses of the walls of the sanctuary have survived, but the reliefs carved on blocks found in the fort show that its decoration was of the highest quality. An inscription indicates that it was dedicated to Amun and built at the request of Thutmose III (1479–1425 BC) by the king's son Nehy to replace an older mud-brick temple. Excavation of the underlying layers has shown that the latter, possibly the building erected one century earlier by Ahmose, was not located there, as only remains of non-religious structures of poor quality were discovered. However, it also led to the discovery of foundation deposits that confirmed its construction date to the reign of Thutmose III, along with a block bearing the name of Nehy, and beautifully carved sandstone

90 *Top* The superstructure
of a Pharaonic grave
photographed from the east.

91 *Above* Aerial view of a Pharaonic grave
superstructure showing courtyard, chapel and
pyramid. The grave shaft and the schist slab that
covered it are visible inside the chapel area.
To the south another grave is being excavated.

lintels and door frames of Thutmose III, the latter
shaped to fit into mud-brick walls. It therefore appears
that the main religious centre of Pharaonic Sai had a
complex history that still has to be clarified.

The two cemeteries are located south of the town. In
the first, the graves dug into a layer of gravel consisted of
short shafts opening into mud-brick vaulted chambers.
In the second (figs 90, 91), deep shafts dug in the sandstone led to underground chambers, while mud-brick
structures, consisting of a courtyard, chapel and a small
pyramid, now almost completely destroyed, marked the
outside. Due to the collapse of the roof of these chambers, these deep graves have partly escaped plundering
and have consequently provided fine burial goods (cats
86–98, 247–8, 282–91), identifying them as the burials
of high officials of the period.

Stone from the sandstone quarries was used locally
and exported. Indeed, an inscription of Thutmose III
records that the beautiful 'white stone of Shaât' was
brought to Kumma in the heart of the Batn el-Hagar.

1 For references to fieldwork at Sai see Geus 1976; 1984; 1994;
1995; 1996; 1997; 1998; 2000; 2002; 2003; in press; Geus and
Lecointe 2003; Geus *et al.* 1995; Vercoutter 1958; 1979; Minault
and Thill 1974; Minault-Gout 1994; Minault-Gout and Thill
forth.; Thill in press
2 Gratien 1986, 12.

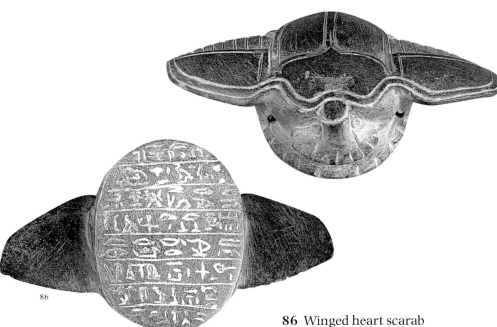

A very similar heart scarab, now in the Cairo Museum, was discovered about fifty years ago by Steindorff in a New Kingdom tomb at Aniba, the most important site in Lower Nubia at this period (Steindorff 1937, 14, 88, 240–41 and pl. 48).   FT

Geus 2002, 126, pl. VIIIc; Minault-Gout and Thill in press; Thill 2004, in press

87 Heart scarab with human head

Green stone
Sai Island, Pharaonic Cemetery, SAC5 T.8 78
New Kingdom, 18th Dynasty
L 73 mm, W 45 mm, Th 20 mm
SNM 31356

Human-headed, heart scarab in dark green hard stone. On the back the elytreas and pro-thorax are modelled in low relief. The head, sculpted in the round, represents a face with heavy features, surrounded by a short wig. The mixed form of this funerary amulet – the simple scarab and the *ba*-bird with human head – is one of the multiple aspects taken by the so-called 'heart scarab'. All of them served the same function, revealed by the presence of the text of Chapter 30B of the *Book of the Dead* on similar inscribed objects. The present item is uninscribed. It was found in a subsidiary room of the tomb, on the chest of an aged man whose funerary equipment included an inscribed shabti bearing his name, a little scarab with royal iconography (cat. 94) and a ring (cat. 88). Its position, higher than the associated bones, suggests that the amulet was placed above the coffin and not inside, as was usually the case.

Such human-headed heart scarabs are rather uncommon. A few others have been discovered in the same necropolis of Sai, as well as in the New Kingdom cemetery of Aniba in Lower Nubia (Steindorff 1937, pl. 48, no. 18; pl. 49, nos 20, 21). All of them belong to the 18th Dynasty.   FT

Minault-Gout and Thill in press; Thill 2004, in press

86 Winged heart scarab

Green stone
Sai Island, Pharaonic Cemetery, SAC5 T.8 45
New Kingdom, 18th Dynasty
L 95 mm, W 55 mm, Th 20 mm
SNM 31317

Winged heart scarab in dark green hard stone. The surface of its back is well polished. Details of the insect's body are represented by incised lines. On the flat side a hieroglyphic text runs horizontally from right to left, giving the name and title of the deceased and the beginning of Chapter 30B of the *Book of the Dead*. This object was part of the funerary equipment of an undisturbed burial, found in a secondary subterranean room of the tomb. It was located on the breast, over the position of the heart. When mummification was per-formed, the heart was generally kept inside the body. However, very often a stone amulet was added, first shaped in the form of the ancient Egyptian's conventional representa-tion of the heart in hieroglyphic writing, and from the 18th Dynasty, in the form of a large scarab, one of the forms of the god Ra, named Khepri. Several spells of the *Book of the Dead*, Chapters 26–9, were intended to prevent the heart of a man from being stolen after his death. In Chapter 30B, used here, the heart itself, regarded as a real being, is called out not to testify against its owner at the moment of the Judgement.

88 Signet ring

Electrum

Sai Island, Pharaonic Cemetery, SAC5 T.8 (94)

New Kingdom, 18th Dynasty

D 22 mm; signet: L 15 mm, W 11 mm

SNM 31327

Finger-ring made of a single piece of electrum (gold mixed with silver), with an ivory scaraboid set into it. The flat side of this scaraboid bears a design representing a palm tree topped with a terminal in the form of two spiral palm leaves. The tree is flanked by two representations of mirrors. In hieroglyphic writing the mirror is not used as a pictogram to evoke the object itself, but also to represent a prophylactic symbol, for example life, which is read *ankh*, one of the most common amulets or written symbols in Egyptian civilization. This is a good example of the constant play with words and their meanings which is characteristic of the hieroglyphic system, being at the same time pictographic, syllabic and alphabetic. More-

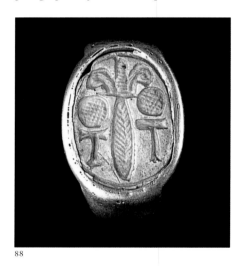

88

over, it is interesting to observe that the handles of mirrors were often made in the form of a palm-tree's trunk.

This finger-ring was discovered *in situ*, under the pelvis, when removing the skeleton of an aged man whose burial was undisturbed. In burials of this period people were laid on their backs, with their arms slightly flexed and their hands crossed over the pubis. This explains why rings, scarabs worn as rings, and bracelets are generally found between the thighs. This type of ring with a signet was rather uncommon and worn only by important people. The design of its inset is also uncommon. Only one scarab, found in

89, 90

an early 18th-Dynasty tomb at Esna, shows a design approximately similar (Downes 1974, 11, 66, 355).   FT

89 Pair of earrings

Carnelian

Sai Island, Pharaonic Cemetery, SAC5 T.8 (76 & 82)

New Kingdom, 18th Dynasty

D 14 mm, Th 2 mm and 3 mm

SNM 31328

Two penannular earrings of almost identical size cut from a semi-precious red opaque stone. This type of undecorated ring is the most common form of earring in the New Kingdom. All people wore them, whatever their sex, age and social condition may have been. These types of object of daily use were buried with the deceased in order to be reused in the Underworld. Such earrings have been found principally in their owner's tomb, sometimes near the ears of the skeleton in the case of undisturbed inhumations. The two specimens shown here were discovered in a disturbed level of the same tomb; however, due to their similar measurements, they can surely be considered a pair.   FT

90 Barrel bead

Rock crystal

Sai Island, Pharaonic Cemetery, SAC5 T.8 (70)

New Kingdom or Kushite (Napatan)

L 25 mm, D 11 mm

SNM 31329

This sort of bead, generally flanked by two cylindrical or ball beads, was usually used as part of a very common necklace considered by Aldred to be a survival of the simplest charm strung upon a cord round the neck (Aldred 1971, 114). Jewellery and amulets are some-

what difficult to distinguish functionally and a bead can have a certain amuletic value. This type of large bead was not characteristic of the New Kingdom period. Considering the context of discovery – a New Kingdom tomb reused in the Napatan period – this bead might be related to the latter period. Similar beads in carnelian or other semi-precious stone have been discovered in the Napatan cemetery of Sanam Abu Dom (Griffith 1923, pl. LXII, 4).   FT

91 Scarab

Faience

Sai Island, Pharaonic Cemetery, SAC5 T.8 (72)

New Kingdom

L 12 mm, W 9 mm, Th 6 mm

SNM 31326

On the back of this scarab the head and the legs of the beetle are sculpted in low relief, whereas the prothorax and the elytreas are incised. On the flat side several hieroglyphic signs are incised: in the centre, a probable short version of the coronation name of Thutmose III, *Men-Ra*, the missing part of the name, *kheper*, being substituted by the scarab itself, flanked by two symbols of life, *ankh*.

Among the many amulets used by the living and deceased in ancient Egypt, those of beetle form, worn as a ring or as part of a necklace or bracelet for wrists or ankles, are one of the most common at any time. A symbol of rebirth, like the sun which reappears each morning, its form was thought to protect its owner against evil and its most absolute manifestation, death. To increase the magic power of the amulet, its flat side was very often decorated with different patterns: hieroglyphic symbols, names or representations of kings or gods, wishes, real or fabulous animals, floral or geometric designs, and sometimes when they had been used as seals, the name and titles of their owners.

The three scarabs (cats 91–3), all from the same tomb, were found in a largely disturbed room and so cannot be related to any skeleton in particular. With regard to their style and inscription, two of them might be connected with the New Kingdom period (cats 91, 93) and one with the Napatan period (cat. 92).   FT

92 Scarab

Faience
Sai Island, Pharaonic Cemetery, SAC5 T.8 (73)
Kushite, Napatan period
L 13 mm, W 8 mm, Th 5 mm
SNM 31325a

Coarse scarab with still-vivid colour. Details of the body and legs are very schematically represented by incised lines. On the flat side, three hieroglyphic signs are carved, unrecognizable except for the *ankh*, on the right, and the *neb*-sign – the basket – in the lower part.

FT

93 Scarab

Faience
Sai Island, Pharaonic Cemetery, SAC5 T.8 (74)
New Kingdom
L 12 mm, W 9 mm, Th 5 mm
SNM 31325b

Faience scarab faded in colour. On the back some incised lines show the separation between thorax and prothorax. The legs are modelled in low relief. On the flat side, three vertical hieroglyphic signs give the name of Amenhotep III, *Neb-Maat-Ra*, followed by the *nefer*-sign, symbol of goodness and beauty. FT

94 Scarab

Glazed steatite
Sai Island, Pharaonic Cemetery, SAC5 T.8 (81)
New Kingdom, 18th Dynasty
L 27 mm, W 19 mm, Th 11 mm
SNM 31325c

Very well-cut scarab with some coloured pigments still remaining inside the inscribed figures. The head and elytreas are carved in low relief. On the flat side a traditional picture of royal iconography is carved: the massacre of enemies. The version represented here shows the king walking, wearing the *khepresh*-crown, his right hand holding a large mace above his head. With the other hand he grips a

91, bottom right; 92, bottom left; 93, top right; 94, top left

bound prisoner whose hands are tied behind his back. Protruding above the king's forehead, we can see the most common attribute of divine and royal figures, the rearing cobra – the uraeus – connected with the cobra-goddess *Wadjyt*. It was thought to exterminate all evil, represented here by the prisoner. A second uraeus is pictured in the space between the arm and the leg of the king.

This scarab was discovered in the same undisturbed burial as the human-headed heart scarab (cat. 87) and the signet ring (cat. 88). It had probably been hung around the neck of the deceased in the coffin.

Other scarabs bearing the same pattern, with some variants in the details of representation, have been found in certain cemeteries in Lower Nubia, such as Dakka (Firth 1915, pls 39, 41), el-Riqa (Emery and Kirwan 1935, 201, fig. 199) or another cemetery between Dakka and Qurta (Firth 1915, pls 36, 147). It seems that the first appearance of this theme might be dated to Thutmose III, a king who greatly enlarged Egyptian territory during the 18th Dynasty. During the next dynasty, this motif was reused significantly by another conquering king, Ramesses II.   FT

95, 96

95 Figure vase in the form a fish

Ceramic
Sai, Pharaonic Cemetery, SAC5 t.8 (87)
New Kingdom, 18th Dynasty
L 110 mm, W 70 mm, Th 50 mm
SNM 31319

This small vase in the shape of a fish came from a grave which contained a burial protected by the collapse of a vault; it was found together with the small, red burnished amphora (cat. 96) which seems to have been made by the same hand, some cosmetic vases in alabaster (cat. 97) and other objects dating to the first half of the 18th Dynasty. It is part of the category of pottery figure vases in moulded terracotta studied by J. Bourriau (1987, 85) and dated to the 18th Dynasty (from the beginning until Thutmose III). The fabric is fine, covered with a burnished red slip with details represented in black pigment. The body is made in two moulded parts joined manually; the dorsal and caudal fins were then added. The collar is represented by the open mouth of the fish. The vase was empty, without traces of any content. This fish is the *tilapia nilotica* that is so often represented, notably with lotuses in cups of blue faience. It has its place in a funeral context because it is a symbol of revival (Dambach and Wallert 1966, 276, 283–94; Desroches-Noblecourt 1954, 33–42). Well-known parallels offer variations in details and quality (Bourriau 1987, 89–90).

In the context of the eastern cemetery of Deir el-Medina from where vases of the same group come, it was recently proposed that they would have belonged to members of the middle class (Pierrat-Bonnefois 2003, 59). In Nubia, however, such a vase would most likely have been seen as a luxury item.   AM-G

96 Amphora

Ceramic
Sai, Pharaonic Cemetery, SAC5 t.8 (86)
New Kingdom, 18th Dynasty
H 115 mm, D 70 mm
SNM 31320

This small amphora was found together with the fish pot (cat. 95), which could be its mate, so similar are its style, material, and colour. It is also datable to the first half of the 18th Dynasty. The fabric is the same and it is covered with the same red burnished slip, partially crackled. Its decoration is applied in black lines: the frieze of triangles on the lip, the horizontal line at the base of the collar, the sheets of palm stylized on the belly of the vessel, and the grids hung as nets on the handles. The shape of the vase was perhaps inspired by contemporary Cypriot vases, but it is incontestably Egyptian from Nubia, and illustrates that which J. Bourriau (1987, 82–3) calls 'a foreign fallacy', in reference to the tendency of twentieth-century scholars to attribute to foreign (north and east) countries all that was good and original in Egyptian pottery. This shape of amphora seems to appear during the reign of Hatshepsut and lasts up to the Amarna period (Bourriau 1982b, 127).   AM-G

97 Small cup and kohl pots

a Kohl pot
Alabaster
Sai, Pharaonic Cemetery, SAC5 T.8 (90)
New Kingdom, 18th Dynasty
H 57 mm, D 56 mm
SNM 31323

b Kohl pot
Alabaster
Sai, Pharaonic Cemetery, SAC5 T.8 (91)
New Kingdom, 18th Dynasty
H 46 mm, D 53 mm
SNM 31322

c Small cup
Alabaster
Sai, Pharaonic Cemetery, SAC5 T.8 (89)
New Kingdom, 18th Dynasty
H 23 mm, D 74 mm
SNM 31321

d Kohl pot
Alabaster
Sai, Pharaonic Cemetery, SAC5 T.8 (92)
New Kingdom, 18th Dynasty
H 48 mm, D 66 mm
SNM 31324

These four vessels come from the same context as cats 95–6 and are datable to the first half of the 18th Dynasty.

Kohl pots intended as containers or for the preparation of cosmetics could, like these, be made of Egyptian alabaster (calcite), but they could also be made from other stones, or wood, faience or ivory. They are frequently part of the equipment in Egyptian tombs (Vandier d'Abbadie 1972, 85–7). Kohl was used by both men and women to protect and outline the eyes. Black kohl was made from crushed galena and green kohl from malachite. Kohl, in a funerary context, was important because of

97a–d

its use as make-up – notably, to the Eye of Horus which is referred to as early as the *Pyramid Texts*. The offering of make-up was equivalent to the offering of the Eye of Horus itself, and this was the symbol of resurrection (Troy 1991, 151). Moreover, kohl pots are often found close to the body of the deceased.

The use of kohl pots becomes frequent in the Middle Kingdom. The three examples here are of a type that was current in the New Kingdom. These small vases are of a wide and squat shape and fit well within the hand. They have not retained any traces of contents, nor of any lid, and no pestle was found with them. The small cup doubtless served as a palette for the preparation of the make-up, although no residue of colour gives evidence of its use.   AM-G

98 Mask

Terracotta

Sai, Pharaonic cemetery, SAC5 T.8 (80)

New Kingdom, 18th Dynasty

H 78 mm, W 72 mm

SNM 31318

This small funerary mask, smaller than an actual human face, was found behind the skull of the skeleton of a woman in a grave where a number of objects dated to the first part of the 18th Dynasty (cats 95–7) were also found. Another mask, in plaster, from the same cemetery is also presented here (cat. 288).

The mask is of beautiful work, and made from a well-fired fabric. The face is triangular and finely featured. The eyes are almond-shaped, with the outline incised and the interior in relief; the eyebrows are very long and extend towards the temples; the nose and the lips are in relief, with a sharp profile. The lower half of the face is damaged: the top of the nose, the lips and the chin are worn but the features are preserved as well as a sweet smile similar to that of a *kore*; the reverse is slightly concave. The mask was placed directly on the face of the deceased and fixed with linen or stucco which completely enveloped the body. Such masks were moulded, painted and often covered with a golden sheet (Troy 1991, 65).

Masks in stucco or terracotta are well known in the Nubian New Kingdom cemeteries, notably in Sai, in the cemeteries excavated by the Scandinavian expedition near the Second Cataract (Troy 1991, 64), Buhen (Randall-MacIver and Woolley 1911, 142, pl. 61) and in Aniba (Steindorff 1937, 73–4). Steindorff speculates that their small size was governed by the need of the Egyptian officials to transport them. Their latest use, in both Egypt and Nubia, dates to the end of the 18th or beginning of the 19th Dynasty (Troy 1991, 65).   AM-G

98

6

GOLD IN THE EASTERN DESERT

ANGELO AND ALFREDO CASTIGLIONI

92 Rotary quern used for grinding quartz.

The Pharaonic Egyptians called Lower Nubia and the desert to its east the 'land of *Wawat*'. The major focus of settlement in *Wawat* was at *Miam* (Aniba) and the area richest in gold was later known by the name of *Akita*. *Akita* was for the Egyptians the impenetrable mountainous area located on the eastern edge of the desert of *Wawat* (fig. 94). The majority of gold came from this region. The other important mining areas of Coptos and Kush were easier to access, but poorer in precious metal.[1] The Centro Richerche sul Deserto Orientale (CeRDO) began research on the gold mines in the Eastern Desert in 1989. To date the area explored by CeRDO covers almost 1,000 km², in which about 200 sites have been located.[2]

Diodorus Siculus mentions the brutal working conditions of those condemned to the mines.[3] Veins of gold bearing quartz were split into blocks, then crushed into small pieces 'of the size of a lentil' using stone mortars and pestles. The fragments obtained were pulverized in querns and finally the powder ('similar to flour') was 'washed' on washing tables which had sloping upper surfaces that separated the gold from the quartz powder. Diodorus's description is believed to relate to the Egyptian Ptolemaic period (305–30 BC).[4] Recent analysis of gold quartz samples has revealed the presence of 8–10 g of gold per ton of mineral. 'Washed' quartz powder, recovered from the base of the washing tables after the separation of the grains of gold from the quartz powder, still contained traces of gold, in some cases 6 g per ton of 'washed' powder. This is a high percentage, close to levels in veins mined industrially today.[5] The ancient Egyptian gold prospectors do not appear to have missed the rich veins of gold quartz that cut through the 'jebels' of the Nubian Desert and the Wadi el-Allaqi, and all of the major quartz veins discovered thus far by CeRDO were exploited in antiquity.[6]

The Wadi el-Allaqi and its tributaries are dotted with numerous mining settlements containing dwellings constructed of dry-stone walling. Frequently they were sheltered in a lateral valley next to the main wadi. The huts were usually circular in plan with a diameter that varied from 2.6 to 3 m, and could stand alone or abut one another. Some mining settlements in the Wadi el-Allaqi were composed of dozens of buildings divided into blocks that seem to suggest an organized exploitation of the gold-bearing quartz veins. Others, composed of a few huts, suggest that the gold was mined by a small number of individuals.

The querns and other lithic tools used for the pulverization of quartz were numerous in some mines, while they were lacking in others. This indicates that they were moved to other settlements after the exhaustion of the quartz veins. Rotary querns were common in the Wadi el-Allaqi (fig. 92). They are composed of a circular 'fixed part', with a diameter varying from 400 to 500 mm or greater, and a weight that can exceed 50/80 kg, and a 'mobile part', with a weight of approximately 20/35 kg that is inserted in the concave depression in the lower 'fixed part' (cat. 107). The 'mobile part' contains a groove into which a handle was inserted that enabled the rotation of the upper stone and the subsequent pulverization of the quartz. Querns of this type were certainly used in the Ptolemaic period and subsequently in the Islamic period.

Saddle querns were used during the Egyptian Pharaonic period.[7] Fragments of

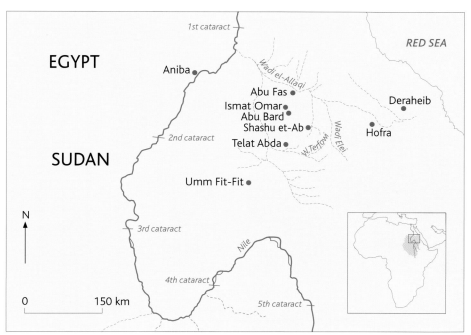

93 *Above* Washing table for separating gold from quartz powder.

94 *Above right* Map showing gold-mining sites mentioned in the text.

Pharaonic pottery[8] were found in the mines designated C13 (Wadi Terfowi) and C2[9] (Umm Fit-Fit) along with numerous saddle querns. Roughly oval and made of hard compact stone, usually basalt or dolerite, saddle querns frequently have a concave elliptical-shaped depression 450–650 mm long, 200–350 mm wide, and up to 50 mm deep. Some querns contain parallel grooves caused by abrasion made during the pulverization of the quartz.

CeRDO did not find any washing tables associated with the Wadi el-Allaqi mines, although some were found in other mines in the Eastern Desert.[10] They ranged from 2.5 to 4 m long, 800 to 900 mm wide, were built of dry stone masonry, and attained an elevation of 600–700 mm at the highest point (fig. 93). The table surface had a wooden or stone face that was marked with parallel grooves. Quartz powder would have been scattered over this surface, then rinsed with water. The quartz flowed downwards while the gold, being heavier, remained in the grooves. At the foot of the inclined plane, a rectangular pit lined with stones collected the water and the washed powder. From there, following a rudimentary channel, the water flowed into another hollow and could

95 Deraheib, possibly the town of Berenice Panchrysos, mentioned by Pliny the Elder.

be reused. The limited number of washing tables discovered at the mines suggests that they were used only as a means to estimate the amount of gold contained in the quartz before beginning intensive mining of the quartz veins. The bulk of the quartz powder produced by the mines was probably transported to other areas where water was plentiful. Presumably, large quantities of quartz powder from the mines in the Nubian Desert were brought to the Nile for processing. In some mines in the Wadi el-Allaqi blocks of quartz were extracted then abandoned. Analysis has established that these possessed a low gold content. Indirectly, this confirms Diodorus Siculus's writing concerning the presence of 'stone specialists' capable of evaluating the quantity of gold contained within the quartz.

Among the settlements of greater importance in the Wadi el-Allaqi is Deraheib.[11] It is composed of two fortresses and an extensive planned nucleated settlement that lies on the eastern side of the Wadi el-Allaqi.[12] Carbon-14 analysis of a fragment of the architrave of the main fort gave a date of AD 714, while the second fort is a classic example of a Roman *praesidium*, similar to those built along the caravan routes in the desert.

Historical research and archaeological excavations conducted between 1990 and 1999, together with the discovery of Ptolemaic objects at Deraheib, suggest that it may be the town of Berenice Panchrysos, mentioned by Pliny the Elder in his *Natural History* (fig. 95).[13] The wealth of gold located in these mountains was well known during the medieval period and is documented by Arab geographers.[14] Mines were located along the banks of the Wadi el-Allaqi and in the mountains that lie above Berenice Panchrysos on the west side of the wadi. Trenches, galleries and shafts sunk vertically to a depth of dozens of metres indicate extensive and lengthy exploitation of the quartz veins.

96 View of Wadi el-Allaqi with circular platform tombs in the foreground.

Of particular note in the region were the great tombs that consisted of a circular platform up to 1.5 m high, with diameters reaching 15 m (figs 96, 97). Circular platform tombs were found scattered over a vast territory.[15] The internal architecture of these tombs has two variants, one with a rectangular chamber and the other a vault with a corbelled dome. The significance of this difference is not yet clear. Carbon-14 analysis of cattle-hide discovered in one tomb gave a date between the seventh and eighth centuries AD.

Two tombs were excavated by CeRDO. Tomb D5.1 had an offering area in the centre of the tumulus, marked by two short stelae at the base of which was a pot, similar to those of the A-Group,[16] two animal horns, some stone pendants and a quantity of charcoal. The tomb had been robbed and among the bone fragments of the arms lay a gold bracelet, overlooked by the robbers (cat. 99).[17] Carbon-14 dating carried out on the charcoal provided a date of 5670 +/-70 BP (Pta-6214) (*c.* 4475 BC). A 5 m-deep pit found under the offering area, similar to many other pits discovered in the Nubian Desert, can be attributed to the work of a miner who had excavated a small deposit of gold-bearing quartz prior to the construction of the tumulus. One may suppose that the search for gold was practised in this area, even if in a primitive manner, during the fifth millennium BC. The extraction of gold and the ceramic finds suggest a degree of contact between the populations of

97 Circular platform tomb in the Wadi el-Allaqi.

the Wadi Elei and the contemporary Neolithic and Predynastic populations of the Egyptian and Nubian Nile Valley.[18] Wadi Elei is an important tributary of the Wadi el-Allaqi. Along its western bank were several regular circular stone structures with openings for doorways, suggesting an extensive Neolithic village. Among the hand-made pottery fragments collected from the surface were examples of pottery with a rippled surface, which in Upper Egypt is associated with the Badarian culture[19] and other fragments not dissimilar to the Butana Group of the eastern Sudan dated between the fifth and fourth millennium BC.[20]

Among our expedition's most spectacular finds is a cache of gold jewellery, from a tomb in the Wadi Terfowi (D 16.1), possibly the abandoned loot of a robber (cat. 106).

Towards the end of the twelfth century AD Nubian gold, sought after for millennia, for a variety of purposes (e.g. cats 99–106), began to lose its importance. Little gold used in Mameluk Egypt came from Nubia, but rather originated in West Africa. Gold production from the Wadi el-Allaqi and other mines was reduced and the mines were gradually abandoned after being used for over 2,000 years by the Pharaohs, Ptolemies, Romans and Arabs.

1 Vercoutter 1959; Adams 1977, 231–5.
2 For a listing of geological teams that have investigated gold-mining sites in the Eastern Desert see Klemm et al. 2002, 215–16.
3 Diodorus Siculus (III, XII.1–3) based his information upon the work of Agatharcus of Cnidus, a geographer of the mid-second century BC, whose writings are now lost.
4 Vercoutter 1959.
5 This analysis was carried out by Professor Liborio, director of the Department of Earth Sciences of the Universita degli Studi of Milan.
6 For a discussion of the geology of the region see Klemm et al. 2002, 215; and for a report on recent exploration, see Castiglioni and Castiglioni 2003.
7 A typology for the stone mortars used to process gold ore from the Predynastic through the medieval periods has been proposed by Klemm et al. 2002.
8 Pamela Rose, pers. comm.
9 Wadi Terfowi and Umm Fit-Fit are located at the following co-ordinates respectively: 20°59'05"N–34°01'81"E and 20°46'15"N–32°24'22"E.
10 Washing tables have been found at the following mines: A5 (Ismat Omar: 21°49'50"N–33°42'98"E), A7 (Abu Fas: 22°08'79"N–33°52'49"E), B11 (Abu Bard: 21°30'96"N–33°4.5'39"E), B14 (Wadi Tabak: 21°43'54"N–34°19'98"E), B24 (22°02'37"N–35°17'29"E), B32 (22°24'92"N–33°27'22"E), C52 (Telat Abda:

21°16'29"N–33°29'22"E), D5 (21°24'44"N–34°35'38"E), D7 (Shashu et Ab: 21°41'40"N–34°11'34"E). Islamic potsherds dating to the eleventh and twelfth centuries AD were found at Telat Abda, and sherds dating to between AD 850 and 1000 were found in Wadi Tabak (W.Y. Adams, pers. comm.).
11 Deraheib means 'constructions' in the Beja language.
12 It is located at 21°56'93"N–35°08'88"E at an altitude of about 550 m a.s.l.
13 '... Berenicem alteram quae Panchrysos cognomitata est ...', Einaudi 1982–8, VI, 170. In modern times, the first person who tried to find Berenice Panchrysos was the French geographer M. d'Anville (1768). Cf. Castiglioni et al. 1994; 1995; Castiglioni and Castiglioni 1999.
14 See further al-Idrisi, al-Maqrizi and al-Khuwarizmi in Vantini 1975.
15 For example, at Hofra (21°37'26"N–35°21'31"E) dozens of tombs of this type were recorded.
16 Nordström 1972.
17 Analyses of the human and faunal skeletal material was conducted by C. Simon (n.d.) and L. Chaix (n.d.) respectively.
18 Sadr 1997.
19 Brunton and Caton-Thompson 1928.
20 Fattovich et al. 1984.

99 Bracelet

Gold

Wadi Elei, Site D5.1, 21°24'44"N/ 34°35'38"E

Neolithic (associated carbon-14 date *c.* 4475 BC 5650 BP +/− 70 years (Pta 6214))

L 58 mm, W 35.9 mm, Th 2.15 mm

SNM 31352

A bracelet of gold wire, round in cross section, with one end bent upward and fashioned into a hook, while the other was flattened and pierced to enable fastening. Although the tomb from which this came had been looted, the bracelet was missed and remained *in situ* among the arm bone fragments of the skeleton. The deceased had been placed in a contracted position, on the left side, with the head facing an offering area located just to the west.

The date of this tomb was confirmed by the radiocarbon dating of associated charcoal and 'the pottery shows many similarities with characteristic wares of the Nile Valley, Upper Egypt and Lower Nubia, during the fifth millennium BC and suggests the hypothesis of a certain degree of contact between the

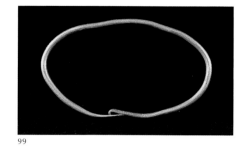

99

populations of Wadi Elei and the contemporary Neolithic and Pre-dynastic populations of the Egyptian and Nubian Nile Valley' (Sadr 1995, 167).   AC/AC/JRA

Sadr 1995, 167; 1997, 69, 73

100 Necklace

Gold, carnelian

Kerma, Eastern Cemetery, Tumulus KXIX

Kerma Classique

Gold beads: L 30–32 mm, D 29 mm

Carnelian beads: D 8–11 mm

SNM 1139

Necklace of twelve biconical gold beads and fifty spherical carnelian beads, discovered by G.A. Reisner and described by him as 'barbaric splendour'. Gold jewels were certainly more numerous than is suggested by the finds of the eastern necropolis tombs, which were systematically pillaged. The inventory mentions amulets, a few bracelets, rings and beads, of annular, spherical or tubular shape, many of which appear to have been sewn on leather clothing or belts. Although carnelian beads are present in all Kerma periods, their numbers diminish in the later royal tumuli. This necklace, which was contained in a small basket and was probably forgotten by the tomb robbers, was discovered in the spoil heap of a pillaged tomb dated to the beginning of the *Kerma Classique* period. The basket was shaped like the vase with cover (cat. 57).   NF

Berenguer 2003d; Reisner 1923a, 459–60; 1923b, 116, 109, 117–20, 283–5; Wenig 1978b, 153, no. 58; Wildung 1997, 105–6, no. 108

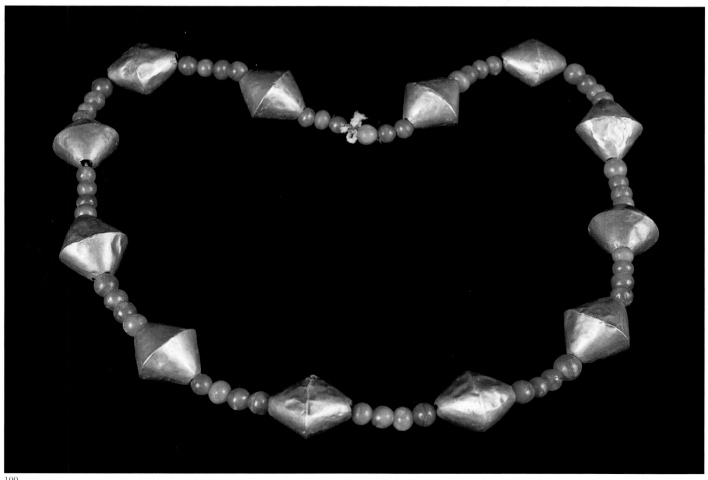

100

101 Collar

Gold

Nuri, Pyramid of Talakhamani, Nu. 16, Chamber A,
Field Number 16-12-299, Harvard University–MFA
Expedition

Kushite (Napatan), *c.* fifth century BC

H 13.5–15 mm, D 25–6 mm

SNM 1362

Fourteen blossoms, manufactured by hammering gold sheet over a form. A horizontal loop adorns the back of each flower enabling them to be linked together to form a necklace, or to be sewn to cloth. The blossoms are truncated cones displaying either seven or eight triangular petals arranged around a central convex disc. The interior of each petal is concave. Several of the elements originally belonging to this collar are now in the Museum of Fine Arts, Boston (20.310-18). These objects, once twenty-eight in number, were found in the floor debris of the first chamber in Talakhamani's tomb.   JRA

Berenguer 2003k; Dunham 1955, 206–10, fig. 159,
pl. LV.A; Vercoutter 1959, pl. XXXIIId; Wildung
1997, 234–5, no. 262

102 Statuette of a Kushite king

Copper alloy, plaster, gold leaf

Tabo, Argo Island, Court of the Great Temple

Kushite (Meroitic)

H 500 mm, W 176 mm, Th 167 mm

SNM 24705

This copper-alloy statuette of an unidentified Kushite king was discovered at Tabo on Argo Island within the court of the Great Temple in a pit. The figure has a constricted narrow waist, broad shoulders and erect carriage, and is stepping forward purposefully with arms bent as if engaged in motion. Iconographic elements of the costume indicate that this individual was a king. He is clothed in a kilt with sandals on his feet, and wears armlets and a collar over which sits a necklace of three ram-headed pendants. On his head is a Kushite cap of tight curls with diadem and double uraeus on the front signifying kingship. Streamers or ribbons from the headgear trail down his back. The armlets are similar in appearance to those worn by Natakamani in reliefs found at Naqa (Maystre 1986, fig. 38). Gold, representing the king's divine flesh, still remains on parts of the face, neck, hands, chest and kilt, and the eyes were inlaid. Gilding was applied over plaster. Small holes, visible on the legs, kilt and arms, enabled plaster to adhere to the copper-alloy surface.

He wears an archer's thumb-ring (cf. cat 214) on his right hand while two bracelets adorn his left arm. It has been suggested that his left hand once held a bow and that this statue depicts the king as an archer (Maystre 1986, 53–4; Wildung 1997, 244). These weapons also may be interpreted as insignia of the ruler and could represent his military leadership as further discussed by Lenoble in this volume (p. 186 ff.). This is the largest copper-alloy statue discovered in the Sudan thus far and currently it has no parallels. JRA

Berenguer 2003l; Leclant 1975, 234, pl. XXV, fig. 24;
Maystre 1986; Wenig 1978b, 84–5, fig. 63; Wildung
1997, 244–5, no. 270

101

102

103 Cylinder of Amaniastibarqo

Gold

Nuri, Pyramid Nu. 2, Chamber 8, Field no. 17-2-258

Kushite (Napatan), sixth to fifth centuries BC

H 42 mm, D 30 mm

SNM 1360a-b

104 Cylinder of Aspelta

Gold, silver

Nuri, Pyramid Nu. 8, Chamber A, Field no. 16-4-70i

Kushite (Napatan), c. sixth century BC

H 75 mm, D 29 mm

SNM 1372

103

ders have images of the goddess Hathor incised on the exterior, flanked on either side by cartouches bearing the name of the respective kings, Amaniastibarqo or Aspelta. Hathor wears an incised beaded shift dress on the Amaniastibarqo sheath, and lotus blossoms and a rosette adorn the base. Its upper part contains three rows of friezes: the upper decorated with a row of uraei whose heads

104

105 Earring

Gold

El-Kurru, Tumulus 2

Kushite

H 54 mm, W 31 mm, Th 20.5 mm

SNM 15171a

This hoop earring – a half circle connected to a loop – was created in three parts. The loop was made from a gold sheet formed into a tube and soldered along the join. The two halves of the pendant were also soldered together. All of the joins were carefully finished, being smoothed and polished. Although the earring is hollow, it is surpris-

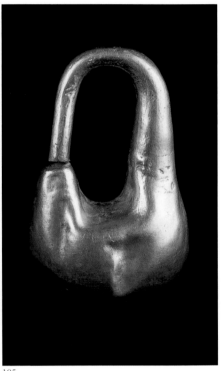

105

A total of fifteen gold or silver gilt cylindrical sheaths were discovered in the tomb of Aspelta, and nine of the royal tombs at Nuri were found to contain objects such as these. These sheaths are constructed out of three pieces: an upper cylinder which is open at both ends, a lower cylinder with a round base, and an internal liner upon which the other two pieces are fitted. Upon the silver sleeve within the cylinder of Aspelta are impressions of wood. The seam is well soldered. The cylinder of Amaniastibarqo is incomplete. The bottom halves of both cylin-

are surmounted by sun discs, the middle Amaniastibarqo's titulary, and the bottom his nomen and prenomen flanked on either side by hawk-headed Khons figures holding *ma'at*, the feather of truth. The function of these objects is uncertain. Wood impressions within the Aspelta sheath might suggest that these objects served as terminals for wooden rods or sceptres. JRA/PP

Dunham 1955, 78, 169; Gänsicke 1997, 226; Gänsicke and Kendall, forth.; Kendall 2003; Wildung 1997, 229, nos 256, 257

ingly heavy and the cleft appears too narrow to have been fitted onto the ear without great difficulty. This might suggest that it was merely a token deposited as part of the grave goods with the deceased. The tumulus from which this came had been robbed; however, the head and chest of the deceased remained intact and this earring was discovered near the head. JRA/PP

Dunham 1950, 15–16, fig. 2c, pl. LVII.B; Wildung 1997, 186, no. 184; Wilkinson 1971, 190, fig. 75

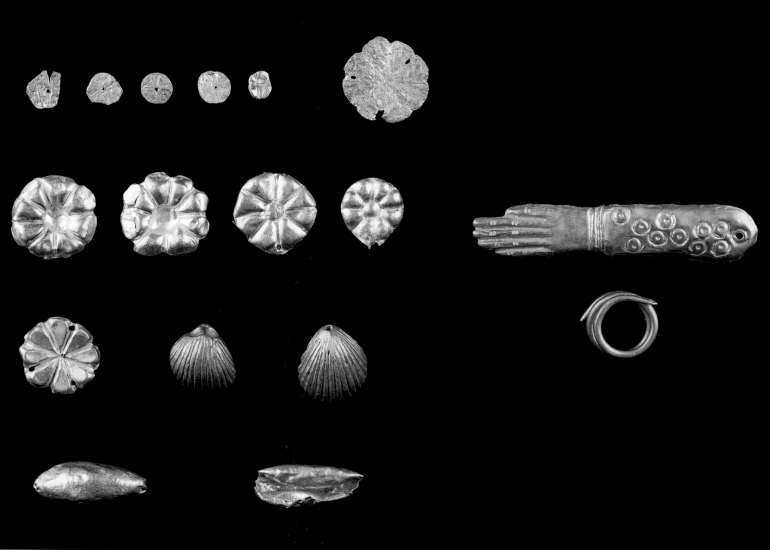

106

106 Discs (6)

Gold

Wadi Terfowi, Tomb D 16.1

Beja, late second to early first centuries BC

5 small: D 7.7 mm, Th 0.3 mm

1 large: D 18.6 mm, Th 0.4 mm

SNM 31350

Rosettes (5)

Gold

Wadi Terfowi, Tomb D 16.1

Beja, late second to early first centuries BC

D 17.1 mm, Th 0.4 mm

D 17.4 mm, Th 0.4 mm

D 19.4 mm, Th 0.3 mm

D 18.59 mm, Th 0.4 mm

D 13.5 mm, Th 0.4 mm

SNM 31355

Ring

Gold

Wadi Terfowi, Tomb D 16.1

Beja, late second to early first centuries BC

D 16.3 mm, W 4.2–8.5 mm, Th 1.9 mm

SNM 31349

Hand

Gold

Wadi Terfowi, Tomb D 16.1

Beja, late second to early first centuries BC

L 64 mm, max. W 13.5 mm, Th 0.3 mm,
D (of hole in arm) 1.3 mm

SNM 31351

Cowrie shells (2)

Gold

Wadi Terfowi, Tomb D 16.1

Beja, late second to early first centuries BC

L 23.5 mm, W 9.98 mm, Th 0.3 mm

L 24.4 mm, W 10.1 mm, Th 0.4 mm

SNM 31354

Shells (2)

Gold

Wadi Terfowi, Tomb D 16.1

Beja, late second to early first centuries BC

L 17.9 mm, max. W 15.4 mm, Th 6 mm

L 15.8 mm, max. W 14.4 mm, Th 7 mm

SNM 31348

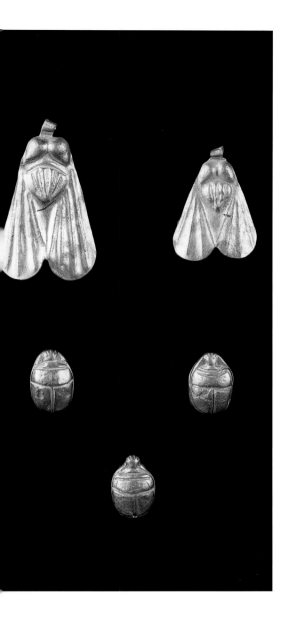

These gold objects were discovered during the excavation of a robbed circular platform tumulus in the Wadi Terfowi (Tomb D 16.1). They were manufactured in two ways. The discs, rosettes, flies, hand and possibly the cowrie shells were created by beating gold foil over a form. The stamped, often concentric ring decoration that appears on several of these items, particularly the hand, are from the form. The solid cast scalloped shells and scarabs were probably poured into an open mould. Concentric circles were marked on the underside of the scarabs: four on the first; two on the second; and traces of one on the third. One scalloped shell has a hole pierced through the top with a diameter of 1.4 mm, while the other has a loop at the top with a diameter of 1.7 mm. Each fly also has a loop on its head for suspension, suggesting that these were used as pendants or incorporated into a necklace or bracelet. Several of the discs and rosettes are also equipped with holes; however, the thinness of the gold suggests that they were probably sewn on to clothing. The ring consists of three small loops of coiled wire, round in cross-section.

Seventeen of the ornaments were contained in a cloth parcel, hidden within the tomb which had been robbed in antiquity. It is possible that an ancient looter had hidden booty that actually originated from several tombs in the area: all of the tombs in the area had been systematically robbed. The cloth wrapping was dated to *c.* 114 BC (2110 BP +/– 40 years [Pta 6216]), placing it within the Kushite, Meroitic period. The five gold rosettes stylistically belong to this period,

thus apparently further confirming the dating (Sadr 1995, 172). Gold flies were often presented as military decorations for valour in Egypt during the New Kingdom and were believed by the Egyptians to have apotropaic properties. It is uncertain what, if any, symbolism the fly held for the Kushites.   AC/AC/JRA

Sadr 1995, 172–3

107 Rotary quern

Granite

Wadi el-Allaqi

Ptolemaic/Islamic

Base: D 520 mm, Th 175 mm; top: D 350 mm, Th 111 mm

SNM 31363

The upper grinder is circular with a slightly convex, smooth working surface and a hole pierced through its centre. A second round depression that probably facilitated a shaft used for rotating the stone is situated off-centre. The upper grinder fits within the lower quern, the edges of which are unfinished. These stones were used to pulverize quartz rock in order to extract gold from within the resulting powder. After placing the quartz between the upper and lower grinders, the upper was rotated until the quartz was crushed.   AC/AC/JRA

Castiglioni *et al.* 1995, 99; Castiglioni and Castiglioni 1999, 126–9

Flies (2)

Gold

Wadi Terfowi, Tomb D 16.1

Beja, late second to early first centuries BC

L 37.4 mm, max. W 22.5 mm, Th 0.4 mm

L 26.8 mm, W 19.6 mm, Th 0.5 mm

SNM 31347

Scarabs (3)

Gold

Wadi Terfowi, Tomb D 16.1

Beja, late second to early first centuries BC

L 16.5 mm, W 10.2 mm, Th 4.9 mm

L 15.7 mm, W 10.2 mm, Th 5.3 mm

L 16.1 mm, W 10.6 mm, Th 5.4 mm

SNM 31353

107

7

THE KINGDOM OF KUSH: NAPATAN AND MEROITIC PERIODS

LÁSLÓ TÖRÖK

Internal problems forced Egypt to withdraw from Nubia at the end of the New Kingdom in the 1060s BC. The rapid emergence of Nubian successor polities after the Egyptian withdrawal may be explained as a consequence of the survival of the native elite; the continuity of 'urban' settlements which had functioned during the Egyptian rule as temple-towns, i.e., centres of territorial administration and redistribution; and with the survival of the rural communities. During the course of the three centuries following the Egyptian withdrawal, the successor polities were gradually united into the Kingdom of Kush, a vast political entity extending from the Butana region in the central Sudan – a territory which was never controlled by Egypt – to Lower Nubia (fig. 99). Kush reappeared in Egyptian history in the role of the restorer of political and national unity. Around the middle of the eighth century BC Kashta (*c.* 760–747 BC) acquired control over Upper Egypt. His successors Piankhi (Piye) (*c.* 747–716 BC), Shabaqo (*c.* 716–702 BC), Shebitqo (*c.* 702–690 BC), Taharqo (*c.* 690–664 BC) and Tanwetamani (*c.* 664–656 BC) controlled Egypt and ruled it together with their native kingdom. They constitute the Egyptian 25th Dynasty, also called Ethiopian, Kushite, or Nubian.[1]

Kushite culture was Egyptianized. The language of expression became Egyptian, literally so in the case of monumental royal inscriptions and other texts, and stylistically in the case of architecture, sculpture in the round, relief, and minor arts. The Egyptian or Egyptianized media of expression, however, articulated Kushite conceptions (fig. 98). The Amun Temples of Meroe, Sanam Abu Dom, Napata/Jebel Barkal (fig. 100), Kawa, Tabo (?) and Kerma/Dokki Gel (probably Pnubs) were erected in the centre of territories which seem to have been independent polities before they were integrated into the Kingdom of Kush. From the seventh century BC onward these settlements developed into temple-towns centered around royal residence-temple compounds.

Building activities at the Semna and Buhen forts, the fortified site of Qasr Ibrim and Philae (?), were determined by strategic considerations, while temples erected at Sedeinga, Semna West, Gezira Dabarosa (?) and Faras became nuclei of urban settlements situated in the centre of territorial units and inhabited by a population of agriculturalists. Different environments determined different subsistence and surplus-producing economies, from agriculture to seasonal shifting agriculture, from a combination of cultivation and

98 Granite sphinx of Taharqo from Temple T, Kawa. The British Museum, EA 1770.

99 Map of Kushite sites mentioned in the text.

100 Jebel Barkal with temples visible at its foot.

herding to animal husbandry. The unity of royal and temple economy, the administrative and economic role played in redistribution by the temple-towns, and the clericalization of government are attested to for the entire history of the Kushite state.

The Amun temples functioned as equal components of the central royal government. Sixth- to fourth-century BC royal inscriptions indicate that the relationship between these individual units and the king was direct. This was also expressed through the repetition of the ruler's enthronement at Napata, Kawa, Pnubs, and, later, in the Bastet sanctuary at Tare. The multiple coronation reflects the governmental practice of an ambulatory kingship in which the ruler performs certain royal duties in the course of journeys across his land. It also indicates that the memory of the pre-25th Dynasty political unification of the Middle Nile Region was elevated into the sphere of the myth of the state.

After the loss of Egypt to the Assyrians in 664/3 BC, the Kushite dynasty withdrew to the Middle Nile region. Relations with Egypt were renewed by the end of the seventh century in the mutual interest of international trade. The monuments preserved from the period following the end of the double kingdom of the 25th Dynasty, i.e., from the reigns of Atlanersa, Senkamanisken, Anlamani, Aspelta, Aramatelqo and Malonaqene, indicate considerable building activity. The high intellectual, technical and artistic standards of the previous century were maintained. In 593 BC the Egyptian pharaoh Psammetik II dispatched a military expedition to Nubia, the reasons for which remain obscure. Though Psammetik's army is supposed to have ravaged the land as far south as Napata, the monuments of Aspelta, possibly Psammetik's Kushite adversary, as well as of his successors in the sixth century BC, attest to royal control over the resources of the kingdom. The evidence of the royal burials indicates political continuity, yet, at the same time, political and cultural introversion.

A new era in Kushite history begins with the long reign of King Irike-Amanote (in the second half of the fifth century BC). The royal titulary assumed by him indicates a policy aimed at the restoration of Kushite rule in Egypt which was at that time under Persian domination. While such an ambitious policy must have been unrealistic, Egyptian revolts against Persian rule between 414/13 and 404 BC facilitated Kushite advance between the First and Second Cataracts, an area that had been lost to Egypt in the early 25th Dynasty period. Irike-Amanote's later fourth-century successors Harsiyotef and Nastasen left behind inscriptions which presented new concepts of royal legitimacy and order in the land. While these texts embedded royal legitimacy in the ideal concept of dynastic continuity from Kashta's predecessor Alara, they also convey the impression of troubled internal politics caused by dynastic conflicts (also indicated by changes in the royal burial grounds). In addition, they describe conflicts with nomadic and semi-nomadic populations living in or on the fringes of the kingdom in the south and in Lower Nubia.

Kush reacted to the news of the conquest of Egypt by Alexander the Great and the changes in Egypt during the first decades of the new rule by strengthening her position in Lower Nubia, from where incursions were now made into Egyptian territory. In return, a punitive action was directed against Nubia around 319/18 BC by Ptolemy I. A military expedition dispatched by Ptolemy II to Kushite territory around 274 BC resulted in the re-establishment of Egyptian control over Lower

Nubia between the First and Second Cataracts. Ptolemy II's expedition was destined to open the way for large-scale trade contacts and to secure for Egypt the acquisition of African elephants. The impact of trade with Egypt was decisive for it not only brought about the Hellenistic exploration of the Middle Nile region, but also promoted contacts between the Ptolemaic and the Kushite courts as well as between the literate priests of the Kushite temples and their Egyptian colleagues. The Egyptian occupation of Lower Nubia and the organization of the trade route along the Nile contributed to the development of the settlement chain in the Nile Valley north and south of the Second Cataract. The trade in exotic animals and goods originating from the southern territories of Kush, or acquired from territories south of Kush, also brought about a rapid development of the political and socio-economic structure of the southern region of Kush.

The kingdom of Kush displayed a varied ethnic, social, economic, and cultural picture. Meroitic-speakers inhabited the Butana and parts of Upper Nubia, and the aristocracy as well as the professional middle class of the kingdom was Meroitic, too. Nubian-speakers already dwelt in the Dongola Reach in the second millennium BC and were settled, from the late third century BC onwards, between the First and Second Cataracts as a consequence of the Meroitic advance into Lower Nubia. Nubian groups (Nubai) lived, furthermore, west of the Nile between Meroe and the great bend of the river. East of the Nile and south of the Egyptian frontier lived the ancestors of the modern Beja tribes. The riverine zones in Lower and Upper Nubia were settled by agriculturalists, but agriculture was also combined with sedentary animal husbandry. Sufficient rainfall rendered possible an extensive and shifting seasonal cultivation in the Butana, too, where sedentary herding as well as transhumant pastoralism played an increasingly important role. The carrying capacity of the Nubian Nile Valley was probably low. By the early centuries AD there were about fifteen to twenty-five settlements inhabited by about 1,000 individuals, and one to two hundred villages, with about fifty to a hundred individuals between Aswan and the Khartoum region. Consequently, the total population of the settlements could have been around 30,000–50,000, while we are unable to calculate the size of the semi-nomadic and nomadic populations.

One of the most conspicuous political consequences of the organization of exotic trade was the dynastic change hinted at in the frequently misunderstood Ergamenes story of the second-century BC writer Agatharchides (in Diodorus 3.6.1). The Ergamenes of the story is identical with the historical Arkamaniqo, the ruler who transferred the royal burial ground from the region of Napata to the cemetery of his aristocratic ancestors in the neighbourhood of Meroe in the first half of the third century BC. The Ergamenes story of Agatharchides hints at the violent circumstances surrounding the emergence of the new dynasty.

While the transfer of the royal burial ground to Meroe emphasizes the new dynasty's ties with the southern centre of Kush, and stands at the beginning of an archaizing cultural process in which the traditions of the Butana region seem to have played an important role, the period starting with Arkamaniqo's reign is characterized nevertheless by a proportionate development of the kingdom as a whole, and not only its southern regions. The maintenance of relations with Egypt necessitated a restructuring of contacts between the central power and the

101 Meroe, Temple of Amun.

102 Naqa, Temple of Amun.

provincial elites which, in turn, determined an increased home production of prestige goods and fostered gift exchange such as pottery and faience. It also brought about a territorial expansion through new allegiances with polities at the southern fringes of Kush.

The quantitative and qualitative development of redistribution resulted in an increase in building activity throughout the kingdom. In the third century BC the central area of Meroe, a settlement built originally on alluvial islands surrounded by temporary Nile channels and/or wadis, was enclosed by monumental *temenos* walls. The 25th-Dynasty Amun Temple standing within these walls was replaced by a new Amun Temple outside the walls (fig. 101). The palatial buildings and temples erected or rebuilt during the Meroitic period fitted into an urban structure with planned avenues and streets. Architectural complexes at Musawwarat es-Sufra and Naqa similarly indicate the existence of urban planning in which the relationships between the individual buildings were determined by ritual/ceremonial considerations (fig. 102).

The intellectual contacts with Egypt in the late fourth and early third centuries BC resulted in a last flourishing of literacy in Egyptian language and writing. The tradition of the formulation and display of royal legitimacy in monumental texts written in Egyptian language and Egyptian hieroglyphs was, however, invalidated before long by the demands of the elite from which the new dynasty originated. The creation of the Meroitic hieroglyphic and cursive scripts in the second century BC for the writing of texts in the Meroitic language may have been facilitated by the existence of everyday written (and possibly verbal?) communication in Egyptian language during the Napatan period. The Meroitic hieroglyphic writing was reserved for royal mortuary inscriptions and temple scene legends (fig. 103). The cursive script served not only for administrative communication: for the first time in Kushite history, not only non-royal mortuary inscriptions were written in it for the non-royal elite and the professional middle class but, from the very outset, it was also the vehicle of monumental royal communication. Private mortuary inscriptions in Meroitic cursive appeared in the context of a tomb type with pyramidal superstructure and miniature offering chapel: a mortuary architectural context which had been reserved previously for royal burials.

The Upper Egyptian revolt against Ptolemaic rule between 207/6–186 BC presented an opportunity for Kush to reconquer temporarily the Lower Nubian Nile Valley from Hiera Sycaminos (Maharraqa) to Aswan. After the re-establishment of Egyptian rule, the Lower Nubian population retained a twofold cultural orientation characterized by an adherence to the Egyptian cults of Philae and the maintenance of indigenous social institutions. With the gradual withdrawal of Egyptian rule, a Kushite province could be organized between the First and Second Cataracts in the latter half of the second century BC. It was governed by the *peseto* who was directly subordinate to the ruler and whose seat was first at Faras and then, from the mid-first century BC, at Karanog.

The first Roman prefect of Egypt conquered Lower Nubia in 29 BC. The ensuing Meroitic–Roman war (29–21/20 BC) ended with the establishment of a Roman frontier at Hiera Sycaminos (Maharraqa), yet the zone between Aswan and Hiera Sycaminos retained its special ethnic and social character. By the AD 220s Roman military forces were withdrawn from the frontier zone to Aswan, and Meroitic supremacy extended into the area long before the official withdrawal of the Roman frontier by Diocletian in AD 298.

The large-scale trade contacts re-established with Egypt after the Meroitic–Roman war necessitated and promoted the strengthening of centralized royal power from the southern confines of the kingdom to the Egyptian frontier. They also enabled large-scale building activity at Meroe, Naqa, Wad ban Naqa, Amara East, Karanog and Qasr Ibrim, and contributed to the creation of the superb Meroitic fine decorated pottery wares (fig. 104, cats 236, 249, 253–4).

The end of the Meroitic dynasty around AD 350–70 did not mean the end of the kingdom itself: it continued to exist as a political unit extending from the Butana to Lower Nubia until *c*. AD 400–20. While the burial place of the Post-Meroitic dynasty remains unknown, tumuli cemeteries of deputies or perhaps allies of the ruler have been identified at el-Hobagi, Firka, Gemai, Kosha, Tanqasi, ez-Zuma and Qustul. The imported objects in these tomb inventories indicate close political contacts with early Byzantine Egypt. In the early 390s a Blemmy polity conquered the Lower Nubian Nile Valley north of Hiera Sycaminos. Around AD 400–20 the Post-Meroitic kingdom disintegrated into several independent polities. It is the northernmost of these, the emerging kingdom of Nobadia, where Meroitic literacy survived for another couple of decades. The last monumental royal text in Meroitic was inscribed around AD 450 in the Temple of Kalabsha for the Nobadian ruler Kharamadoye, who drove out the Blemmyes from the Valley with the aid of Byzantine Egypt.

103 Relief from the interior of a funerary chapel of a Kushite Queen, Shanakdakhete, from Meroe, Beg. N. 11. The British Museum, EA 719.

104 Painted Meroitic jar decorated with bands of crescents, *ankhs* and rosettes. The British Museum, EA 51446.

1 For detailed analyses of the history of the Kushite Kingdom see Adams 1977; Török 1988; 1997a; 1997b; 2002. Textual sources from the Kushite Kingdom are compiled in Eide *et al.* 1994; 1996; 1998; 2000; Leclant *et al.* 2000.

HILLAT EL-ARAB

IRENE LIVERANI

Hillat el-Arab is a village situated on the sandstone terrace flanking the Nile, about 3 km south of Jebel Barkal (see fig. 99). Here the joint mission of the University of Cassino and the Sudanese National Corporation for Antiquities and Museums have uncovered a necropolis used from the Egyptian Late New Kingdom up until the period when the Kushites dominated Egypt (the 25th Dynasty).[1] Nothing remains of the superstructures which must have covered the tombs because they were destroyed before the modern village was built on top of them. As such, we do not know how the cemetery looked while it was in use. The subterranean part, on the other hand, comprising large chambers cut into the rock at varying depths, is well preserved though all the tombs have been repeatedly looted. Despite this, grave goods recovered include dishes, storage jars and imported amphorae, as well as copper-alloy objects, and occasionally scarabs and small jewels.

The overall picture which emerges is that of a rich and cultured social class which drew inspiration from the Egyptian world, without ever descending to the level of pedantic imitation. This is particularly clear from the construction of large chamber structures and from the large-scale changes in funerary rituals made to conform to those of the ruling Egyptian class.

The most ancient tombs date to the period of Egyptian colonization, when the region was formally governed by an Egyptian viceroy, but in fact probably controlled by powerful Napata families linked to Egypt through personal ties, cultural dependency and economic interests. It is probably one of these chiefs who is depicted in Tomb 1 (cats 108–9). The tomb is large and complex, and probably was used by several generations of the same family.[2] A series of chambers leads off the bottom of a rectangular shaft 2.2 m deep (figs 105–6). Elegant boats are depicted in one of the chambers on the east side. Boats are traditionally connected with Nubian funerary ritual; in this case the novelty rests in the depiction of a human figure in one of the boats. His head is represented only by a circle, but a short beard is clearly visible, lending authority to the figure (fig. 107).

105 Sections through Tomb 1.

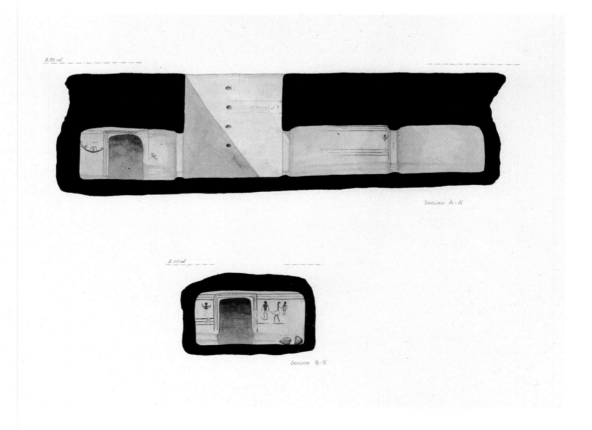

Further indications of the family's dominant role can be found in the paintings in the western chambers. A human figure is shown standing on a small boat, holding a long stick in his hand as a symbol of power. Beside him are other people and animals painted in a surprising mixture of styles which give the whole an unusually animated appearance (fig. 108). This lack of interest in the rigorous order of figures and styles is far removed from Egyptian iconography – though some elements from it are present – and is strongly reminiscent of the more casual rock-art scenes which can be found both in this region and more generally throughout Nubia.

Tomb 7 (cats 110–16) seems to be of only slightly later date, and confirms the unusual nature of the cemetery (fig. 109). The ceiling of the first chamber must have collapsed at an early date, sealing the contents of the tomb, which were found in their original positions. Six individuals were discovered lying on the floor with copper-alloy and ceramic objects next to them. Near the west wall were the remains of a horse with a man next to it. A large stone slab was used to close the door of the inner chamber where the most important person must have been buried; part of his skeleton remained. In contrast to the abundance and richness of the material contained in the chamber, the individuals buried here wore no precious objects. It is possible that these were sacrificial deaths. The scene

with which we are faced is thus that of a lord buried with his slaves or members of his household, his horse and his most precious objects.

It is worth noting that this is not the only tomb at Hillat el-Arab where horses were buried; in Tomb 12 two were found. This fact confirms the Nubians' well-known predilection for these animals which they bred, trained and sold as far afield as Assyria, and to which the Nubian pharaohs of the 25th Dynasty dedicated a cemetery at el-Kurru next to their own.

The period which follows saw the abandonment of Nubia by the Egyptians. The tombs of this period seem to reflect only the positive effects of this political situ-

ation and are, if possible, even richer. Commerce with Egypt still appears to have been flourishing, and is represented by the large containers for grain made of a whitish marl clay from the region of Thebes, pilgrim

106 *Right*
Plan of Tomb 1.

107 *Above right*
A boat depicted in one of the eastern rooms of Tomb 1.

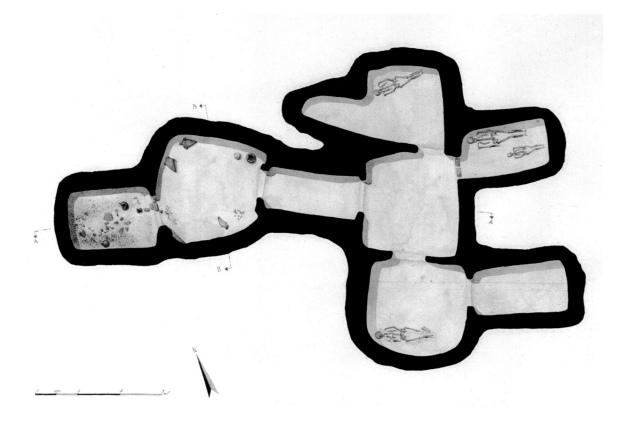

flasks, and the wine and oil amphorae found in large numbers in all the tombs. The structure of the tombs becomes more standardized with a staircase descending to one or two underground chambers on a single axis. This scheme is identical, though on a smaller scale, to that employed for the royal tombs at el-Kurru.

The upper layer of Tomb 19 contains artefacts dating to the 25th Dynasty. This tomb shows a unique stratification that is representative of the entire period during which the cemetery was in use and exemplifies its cycle of continuous use. The first deposits, found at the bottom, date to the late Ramesside period, whilst the upper strata contain progressively more and more recent materials up to the period contemporary with the 25th Dynasty.

This tomb contained an unusually rich collection of artefacts, including some perfectly preserved copper-alloy objects (cats 117–26). At the bottom lay a bowl engraved with a hieroglyphic inscription of the Ramesside period. A second bowl, belonging to the most recent layer, also has engraved hieroglyphs but these have a purely decorative function and are meaningless. Finally, a third bowl, also belonging to the most recent period during which the tomb was used, was found in the inner chamber. It was placed in the tomb wrapped in a linen cloth and put inside the small sycamore box in which it had probably arrived from Egypt as a precious gift to the deceased.

1 Vincentelli 2002.
2 Vincentelli 1999.

108 Human figures on the western wall of Tomb 1.

109 Reconstruction of Tomb 7.

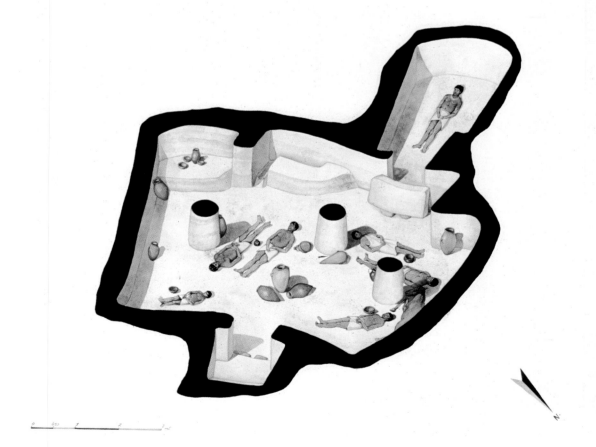

were traded under the control of the powerful families of Napata.   IV

Vincentelli 1999, 30–38, fig. 3, 10, pl. 1

109 Jar

Ceramic
Hillat el-Arab, Tomb 1, no. IB 290.96
New Kingdom, 19th Dynasty
H 425 mm, max. D 210 mm; rim: D 120 mm
SNM 31160

Ovoid jar with rounded base and flaring rim. The surface is only smoothed, not decorated. This type of pottery was among the most common in Egypt, and has also been found in many areas of Nubia (Holthoer 1977, 155–6). It was used as a container for cereals. This specimen comes from Tomb 1, one of the oldest in the cemetery.   IV

Vincentelli 1999, 30–38, fig. 3, 6, pl. 1

108

108 Canaanite Amphora

Ceramic
Hillat el-Arab, Tomb 1, no. 1B 255.96
New Kingdom, 19th Dynasty
H 535 mm, max. D 290 mm; rim: D 55 mm
SNM 31159

Large amphora with flat shoulders, tapering body and button-like base. Two round-sectioned handles are inserted at shoulder height. Amphorae of this type are of Late Bronze Age IIB Levantine production (Amiran 1969, 139), and can be found in all Mediterranean countries that traded with the Near East. In Egypt similar amphorae, either imported wares or local imitations, are found in contexts dated to the late 18th and early 19th Dynasties. They are mostly from Memphis and Quantir, but have also been found at other sites (Aston 1999, 23). In the Hillat el-Arab cemetery a total of seven were found, two of which were from Tomb 1. These amphorae provide evidence for the southernmost point reached by Levantine trade in luxury foodstuffs (oil and wine). These were exchanged for goods from sub-Saharan Africa, such as ivory, ebony, ostrich feathers, leopard skins and gum, which were greatly appreciated in Egypt and the Near East and

109

110, 112, 111

113

110 Pitcher

Copper alloy
Hillat el-Arab, Tomb 7, no. 7B 42.93
Late New Kingdom
H 230 mm; base: D 70 mm; rim: D 100 mm
SNM 31161

Copper-alloy pitcher with flat base, globular body and tall cylindrical neck. The handle, inserted between the rim and the shoulder, is in the shape of a lotus flower with a long stem. It was found in Tomb 7, on the floor, partially hidden by a burial. IV

Vincentelli 1997, 167–70

111 Bowl

Copper alloy
Hillat el-Arab, Tomb 7, no. 7B 27.93
Late New Kingdom
H 85 mm, D 270 mm.
SNM 31177

Copper-alloy bowl with a rounded base and a modelled rim. The bowl was found on the floor of Tomb 7, partially hidden by the legs of one of the burials found *in situ*. IV

Vincentelli 1997, 167–70

112 Juglet

Copper alloy
Hillat el-Arab, Tomb 7, no. 7B 28.93
Late New Kingdom
H 118 mm; base: D 50 mm; rim: D 68 mm
SNM 31178

Copper-alloy juglet with flat base, globular body and cylindrical neck. The ring-shaped handle was inserted just beneath the rim. The juglet was found in Tomb 7 on the floor next to a burial. IV

Vincentelli 1997, 167–70

113 Dish

Ceramic
Hillat el-Arab, Tomb 7, no. 7B 11.93
Late New Kingdom
H 80 mm, D 200 mm
SNM 31179

Ceramic dish with rounded base and straight rim. The surface was smoothed inside with a cloth dipped in a highly diluted clay solution (self-slip). On the outside the self-slip only appears on the upper part, while the lower part and the base are untreated and still show signs of the wheel. The decoration consists of an irregular red band on the rim, which left long drips of paint on the inside of the dish. This is the most common form of funerary offering, and in the poorest cemeteries dishes and bowls are often the only objects placed next to the deceased. In the Hillat el-Arab cemetery these objects were found in large quantities, with various shapes and decorations, but always accompanied by large pottery jars and copper-alloy objects, suggesting that the cemetery was used by a population of a higher rank. IV

Vincentelli 1997, 167–70

114

115

116

114 Pilgrim flask

Ceramic

Hillat el-Arab, Tomb 7, no. 7B 19.93

Late New Kingdom

H 135 mm, max. D 95 mm; rim: D 30 mm

SNM 31180

Small lentoid flask made up of two halves thrown separately and then joined. The slender neck with a slightly flaring rim is inserted in a hole made at the top of the two halves. The two suspension handles are inserted between the shoulder and neck. The surface of the flask is cream-coated, but the slip is only partially preserved. The halves show traces of decoration with concentric black circles. This type of flask, generally known as a 'pilgrim flask', was used to transport liquids. It was introduced to Egypt during the 18th Dynasty as an imported product and as an imitation of types from the Mycenaean and Syro-Palestinian world (Holthoer 1977, 99–100). This shape became extremely popular in Egypt where it was produced, with slight modifications, up to the Christian period. The flask shown here is an import from Egypt. It was found on the floor of Tomb 7, next to a burial under two upside-down bowls.   IV

Vincentelli 1997, 167–80

115 Amphora

Ceramic

Hillat el-Arab, Tomb 7, no. 7B 13.93

Late New Kingdom

H 480 mm, max. D 260 mm; neck: D 123 mm

SNM 31340

Large cylindrical amphora with a rounded base and two handles. The neck is broken at the base, but the edges of the fracture have been smoothed indicating that the vessel remained in use. The surface is cream-coated. The bottom was intentionally perforated with a drill. This amphora, imported from Egypt, is of a type whose production began in the 19th Dynasty and became widespread and common during the 20th Dynasty (Aston 1996, 66).   IV

Vincentelli 1997, 167–80

116 Amphora

Ceramic

Hillat el-Arab, Tomb 7, no. 7B 12.93

Late New Kingdom

H 400 mm, max. D 185 mm; rim: D 85 mm

SNM 31400

Amphora with two handles and pointed base. The surface is cream-coated but the slip is only partially preserved. The neck was broken, and the edges of the fracture smoothed. This type of amphora derives its shape from the Levantine amphorae of the Late Bronze Age I. It became extremely popular in Egypt where over time it developed a tapering body and pronounced shoulders (Hope 1989, 93). It is possible that it contained wine. This hypothesis is confirmed by the presence next to the amphora of the bronze point of a siphon which was used to filter the impurities from the wine. Such a use is well illustrated on a well-known stela from el-Amarna, showing a Syrian man drinking wine from a similar type of amphora.   IV

Vincentelli 1997, 167–80

117 Two-handled jar

Ceramic

Hillat el-Arab, Tomb 19, no. 19B 869.00

Kushite (Early Napatan)

H 400 mm, max. D 198 mm; rim: D 95 mm

SNM 31162

Ovoid two-handled jar with a slightly pointed rounded base. The surface of the jar is rippled.

A hole was drilled in the bottom. This type of container, with its characteristic two small handles of extremely crude shape, and light ripples on the body, is fairly common at all sites of the Napatan period. This jar differs, however, due to its straight rim, instead of the characteristic ridges and furrows of later types, and its much more slender body. The specimen from Tomb 19 was found about 100 mm below an intact burial whose offerings were two tall beakers of a type common in the 25th Dynasty (cat. 118). Thus, this jar should be considered slightly earlier, dating to the Early Napatan period.   IV

Vincentelli 2003, in press

118 Beaker

Ceramic

Hillat el-Arab, Tomb 19, no. 19B 881.00

Kushite (Napatan)

H 155 mm; rim: D 93 mm

SNM 31163

Beaker with a rounded base and direct or straight rim. The outer surface, although very abraded, shows traces of burnishing on a red slip. This is one of the most common vessel types from sites of the Napatan period. This beaker was found complete and was placed, together with another one of the same type, as a funerary offering next to an intact burial. This burial sealed a disturbed, but rich, layer in the eastern half the tomb, providing evidence for the different phases of use of the tomb, from the New Kingdom to the Napatan period.   IV

Vincentelli 2003, in press

117

118

119 Jar

Ceramic

Hillat el-Arab, Tomb 19, no. 19B 893.00

Kushite (Early Napatan)

H 265 mm; max. D 257 mm; rim: D 120–30 mm

SNM 31164

Hand-made globular jar with a straight neck. The surface shows traces of mat-impressed decoration with a red pigment on the upper part. The lower part is untreated.

This type of hand-made jar for domestic use is extremely common, and was produced during all the phases of Nubian culture. Thus its dating can only be inferred from the context in which it was found. Similar jars were found in the cemetery of Sanam Abu Dom (Griffith 1923, 98) and other sites of the Napatan period. Since this jar was found about 100 mm below a burial *in situ* whose offerings were two beakers of a type common in the 25th Dynasty, it should be considered to be of slightly earlier date.   IV

Vincentelli 2003, in press

120 Amphora

Ceramic

Hillat el-Arab, Tomb 19, no. 19B 904.00

Late New Kingdom/Third Intermediate Period

H 550 mm, max. D 270 mm; rim: D 95 mm

SNM 31165

An amphora with cylindrical body, prominant shoulders and a round base. The two handles are round-sectioned and the short neck has a direct rim. The surface is uncoated. A potmark was incised under one of the handles before firing. This large amphora comes from Egypt (Marl Clay A). Similar specimens, found at Deir el-Medina, date to the 20th Dynasty (Nagel 1938, 27) but their production may have continued later (Hope 1989, 94). For this specimen, found in Tomb 19, a dating to the first part of the Third Intermediate Period (1069–747 BC) seems more probable.   IV

Vincentelli 2003, in press

120

121

121 Amphora

Ceramic

Hillat el-Arab, Tomb 19, no. 19B 874.00

Late New Kingdom/Third Intermediate Period

H 520 mm, max. D 270 mm; rim: D 120 mm

SNM 31166

A large two-handled ovoid amphora with a slightly pointed base and undulating neck profile. This specimen seems to be an import from Egypt, where ovoid amphorae with rounded bases were commonly used from the 20th Dynasty onwards (Aston 1996, 66) and continued to be produced for a considerable time, including during the Third Intermediate Period (1069–747 BC) to which this jar probably belongs. Tomb 19, where this jar was found, contains artefacts mainly dating to this period.   IV

Vincentelli 2003, in press

122 Bowl

Copper alloy

Hillat el-Arab, Tomb 19, no. 19B 906.00

Kushite (Early Napatan)

H 55 mm; rim: D 140 mm

SNM 31181

Copper-alloy bowl with flat base and direct or straight rim. A small suspension hole was pierced just below the rim. The inside of the bowl has incised decoration. A band with a series of purely decorative hieroglyphs runs below the rim. The signs are repeated in groups of two or three and no complete word can be read. A rosette with six petals is incised on the bottom. It seems that the bowl was made in a place where the Egyptian writing was appreciated for its decorative value, but was not well known or commonly practised. The bowl was found about 100 mm below an *in situ* burial with two tall beakers of a type common in the 25th Dynasty (cat. 118) as offerings; it should therefore be considered slightly earlier in date.   IV

Vincentelli 2003, in press

123 Bowl

Copper alloy

Hillat el-Arab, Tomb 19, no. 19B 907.00

New Kingdom, 19th Dynasty, Ramesside

H 85 mm, D 185 mm

SNM 31182

Copper-alloy bowl with rounded base and flat, thickened rim. Copper-alloy wire has been wrapped around the ring-shaped handle. The ring was inserted into a suspension loop fixed by two rivets. The loop is asymmetrical and appears to have been repaired in the past. The outside of the bowl is decorated with an incised band just beneath the rim. A hieroglyphic inscription gives the name of the Egyptian officer for whom the bowl was made. The inscription is still under study, but the type of writing and the references to the Egyptian officer suggest a possible dating to the Ramesside period (19th Dynasty). The bowl was found upside down on the floor of the first room of Tomb 19, and thus belongs to the earliest phase of its use. However, it is earlier than the other objects found in the same layer, and therefore was possibly already old when it was placed in the tomb as a funerary offering.   IV

Vincentelli 2003, in press

124 Bowl

Copper alloy

Hillat el-Arab, Tomb 19, no. 19C 908.00

Late New Kingdom/Third Intermediate Period (?)

H 35 mm, D 170 mm

SNM 31183

Undecorated copper-alloy bowl with rounded base and modelled rim. The bowl was found on the floor of the inner chamber of Tomb 19, supposedly in the place where the deceased's head lay. The chamber had been severely looted and no other objects were found. This bowl was so shallow that it must have remained hidden from the robbers by a thick layer of mud. Remains of a linen cloth and fragments of a sycamore box were found together with the bowl. It is therefore possible that the bowl was placed in the tomb wrapped in a linen cloth and inside a box. As it was found on the floor of the room, it can therefore probably be dated to the Late New Kingdom or to the Third Intermediate Period. However, its rather common shape and lack of decoration leave some doubts as to a more precise dating.   IV

Vincentelli 2003, in press

125 Amulets

Steatite, glass

Hillat el-Arab, Tomb 19

Late New Kingdom/Kushite (Napatan)

Udjat pendant: L 12 mm, W 8 mm, Th 4 mm

Udjat pendant: L 13 mm, W 8 mm, Th 2 mm

Isis pendant: L 15 mm

Amun pendant: L 15 mm, W 25 mm, Th 5 mm

Scarab: L 15 mm, W 10 mm, Th 7 mm

SNM 31172, 31173, 31174, 31175, 31176

The glazed steatite scarab shows slight traces of green colour. A funerary formula is inscribed on the base. This is the only amulet that was found *in situ* next to the remains of a burial on the floor in the first room. It thus

123, 122, 124

125

126

belongs to the most ancient phase of use of the tomb. The green glass pendant is in the form of an *udjat* eye with a lengthwise hole. This amulet was found in the filling of the first room of the tomb, and therefore is out of context. The *udjat* eye is an extremely common type of funerary ornament, making its date uncertain. The glazed green, steatite rectangular pendant has a lengthwise hole and is decorated on both sides. The God Amun, in the shape of a sphinx wearing a crown with two tall feathers (atef-crown), is represented at the centre of one side. To the right there is a falcon-headed divinity at the bottom, and the sign of the sun Ra above. The name of the god is written in hieroglyphs on the top left. The entire scene is a figurative and graphic representation of the god Amen-Ra. The name Amun is repeated in hieroglyphs on the back. This plaque was found around 200 mm below the surface, in the tunnel that the robbers dug to reach the inner chamber of the tomb. It is possible that it belongs to the most ancient phase of use. A green glass pendant amulet in the shape of an enthroned Isis suckling Horus was found in the filling of the first chamber, in a disturbed layer, but its miniaturized form suggests a possible dating to the most recent phase of use of the tomb (25th Dynasty).

These amulets were elements of necklaces that adorned the deceased. Unfortunately these ornaments have attracted robbers since antiquity, causing disturbance to the stratigraphy of the tombs and thus making it impossible to reconstruct their context with certainty.   IV

Vincentelli 2003, in press

126 Beads

Ostrich eggshell, gilded glass, gold, shell, carnelian, faience

Hillat el-Arab, Tomb 19

Late New Kingdom/Kushite (Napatan)

Ostrich eggshell: avg. D 7 mm, avg. Th 1 mm

Glass: L 10 mm, W 8 mm, Th 0.5 mm

Gold: L 3 mm, max. D 3 mm

Shell: (A) L 18 mm, W 14mm, Th 5 mm;
(B) L 14 mm, W 9 mm, Th 3 mm

Carnelian: 10 cylindrical avg. L 14 mm, avg. D 6 mm; 23 biconical L 2–3 mm, D 3–4 mm; 11 globular max. L 6 mm, max. D 7 mm; 1 drop L 14 mm, max. D 7

Faience: approx. 800 beads, avg. D 4–5 mm, avg. Th 1–2 mm

SNM 31167, 31169, 31170, 31171

This collection of beads of various shapes and materials was found in the filling of Tomb 19, in a disturbed layer. They belong to the grave goods of the burial and must have been lost by the robbers in their hurry to loot the tomb. Considering how they were found and the fact that jewellery types change extremely slowly, they are difficult to date with certainty. The gold bead, which is in the shape of a coffee bean, is the only piece that was found in a well-defined layer – on the floor of the first room – and thus appears to have belonged to the most ancient phase of the tomb's use.

Some of these ornaments formed part of large necklaces with alternating carnelian and gold beads and pendants. Others, including the glass beads and small ostrich eggshell discs, were part of necklaces made of several strings of alternating beads and amulets. Some amulets were in the shape of *udjat* eyes or poppy seeds, such as those shown here. The two shells belong to cowries and come from the Red Sea. A badly oxidized tubular silver bead was also found.   IV

Vincentelli 2003, in press

KAWA

DEREK A. WELSBY

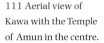
110 Head of Taharqo carved onto the north wall of the Temple of Amun.

The Egyptian town at Kawa, bearing the name Gematon, 'The Aton is Perceived' (cat. 136), was probably founded by Akhenaton (1352–1336 BC).[1] Although the earliest building so far located was constructed during the reign of Tutankhamun (1336–1327 BC), the presence of an extensive cemetery of the preceding Kerma period (2500–1500 BC) close by suggests the possibility that it occupied the site of a much earlier settlement. Little is known of the Pharaonic town; whether, like the contemporary settlement at Sesebi, it was surrounded by a defensive wall and contained extensive store buildings must await further excavations.

The fate of the town during the three centuries following the withdrawal of the Egyptian administration around 1070 BC is unknown. With the rise to power of the Kushite dynasty Kawa appears to have played a key role. An inscription of Taharqo provides evidence for one of the earliest known Kushite temples, standing within the town at the time of Alara, perhaps in the first half of the eighth century BC.[2]

Another inscription records that after Taharqo (fig. 110) visited the town on his way north to Egypt he ordered the repair of one temple and the construction of another. This new temple, dedicated to Amun, played a prominent role in the coronation ceremonies of the Kushite rulers and was one of the places visited by the king during his annual visit to the regional capitals of the realm. Epigraphic evidence indicates that the town retained its importance into the fifth century BC. Thereafter little is known of its fortunes, although archaeological discoveries indicate that occupation continued throughout the Kushite period.

The first recorded 'excavation' on the site, in 1885, was undertaken by a British Army officer, Colonel Colthorne. His soldiers uncovered a temple with hieroglyphic inscriptions and reliefs but their work was frustrated by sand-laden wind refilling their trenches.[3]

From 1929 to 1931 Francis Llewellyn Griffith, working on behalf of the Oxford Excavation Committee, uncovered the remains of four temples providing a wealth of information from which to reconstruct an outline history of the town (cf. cats 127, 136).[4] This was followed by a single season of study of temple reliefs and inscriptions by M.F.L. Macadam and of excavations outside the temples by L.P. Kirwan in the winter of 1935–6. In 1993 the Sudan Archaeological Research Society undertook an investigation of the immediate environs of the town. This has been followed by several seasons of work within the town and in the associated Eastern Cemetery.[5]

Today the town site is a prominent mound, standing to a maximum height of 11.5 m above the plain and

111 Aerial view of Kawa with the Temple of Amun in the centre.

112 *Above* Building A3 on the southern edge of the town.

113 *Above right* Wall paintings and inscriptions in the central room of the shrine, Building A1.

114 *Right* Northern part of the east wall of Room II, Building A1, shown *in situ* on right side of fig. 113.

115 *Far right* Southern part of the east wall of Room II, Building A1.

covering an area of approximately 40 ha (fig. 111). The whole site has been surveyed to produce a detailed topographical map while individual buildings are being cleaned and planned. This is providing information about urban planning of the early Kushite period for the first time. It is only possible here as the early Kushite remains are not deeply buried beneath later structures and therefore inaccessible, as it appears that the town was at its greatest extent in the early Kushite period and then rapidly contracted thereafter. Many areas seem to have had dense agglomerations of well-

built mud-brick dwellings. There were also temples, an industrial quarter with kilns, and some very large buildings including one over 85 m in length and 56 m wide. Apart from the wall delimiting the *temenos* around the temples no defences have been located.

Among the structures excavated are a group of five houses and two adjacent streets. The houses are well built, have floors of mud or sand and little in the way of internal furnishings. All houses investigated in the present campaign date to the earlier Kushite period, probably to the eighth–sixth centuries BC.

116 Stepped descendary leading to the blocked doorway of a Kushite tomb in the Eastern Cemetery.

(Piye). Clearly the building with its royal associations was of considerable importance, and was a centre for the collection, and presumably redistribution, of commodities on a large scale. Within and immediately outside the building were parts of at least four large ceramic statues, two of which are of the god Bes (cat. 143) and the goddess Beset (cat. 142).

In the main cemetery are over 1,000 monuments – tumuli, *mastabas* and possibly mud-brick and dressed stone pyramids.[6] The classic Kushite grave type consisted of a long stepped or sloping passage cut into the alluvium (fig. 116). At the end of the passage an 'arch'-shaped doorway led into the tomb. After the deceased was placed in the tomb the doorway was blocked by a wall of mud brick and the descendary was refilled with earth. The tomb monument stood above the site of the tomb on the ground surface.

Inhumations were usually placed in an extended position on their back, although one grave contained a crouched inhumation and two had bodies placed within cartonage coffins with painted decoration. Many graves were reused on several occasions. Burials were also placed in simple long, narrow pits, often dug into the fill of the descendaries of earlier tombs.

On the southern edge of the town, a group of three buildings has been investigated. The earliest building had thin buttressed walls and at least one 'D'-shaped room or courtyard (fig. 112). Although associated with Kushite pottery, the plan and construction techniques employed hark back to those well known from the Kerma period, a millennium earlier. Partly overlying this building is a small rectangular structure, 11×4.5 m in size, aligned east–west and divided into three rooms, each with a central doorway in the west wall. The eastern room had a fine floor of large white sandstone blocks, a sandstone altar or bark-stand bearing painted cartouches of Taharqo, and walls plastered with mud and painted. On the north wall was the figure of a king processing towards two gods (cat. 137). A similar scene is partly preserved on the north and south walls of the central room. On the east wall of the central room are symmetrical figures of the king striding towards the doorway which is flanked by hieroglyphic inscriptions to Amun of Gematon and Amun of Thebes (figs 113–15).

Three metres outside the building on its main axis was a mud-brick altar and a mass of pottery, faience objects (cats 128–31) and mud bungs used to seal the mouths of ceramic vessels. In this area and also in the western room were many seal impressions on mud (cf. cat. 138), one type bearing the throne name of Piankhi

1 Macadam 1955, 12–13.
2 Macadam 1949, 16.
3 Gleichen 1888, 281–2.
4 Macadam 1949; 1955.
5 For a report on the survey of the cemetery see Welsby 2001d, 148–50. For interim reports on the more recent work see Welsby 1998a; 2000; 2001a; 2001b; 2001c; 2002.
6 Welsby 2001d, 148–50.

127

127 Statue of a baboon

Granite
Kawa, Site Q3, Temple T
Kushite (Napatan), 690–664 BC
H 710 mm, W 240 mm, Th 260 mm
SNM 2689

A granite baboon depicted in an attitude of adoration with the arms raised, hands against the shoulders with the palms facing forward. On both sides of the back pillar the tail is carved in low relief while on the back are the names and titles of the Kushite king Taharqo (690–664 BC): 'king of Upper and Lower Egypt, Khunefertemra, son of Ra, Taharqo, given life eternally'.

This is one of two such statues recovered from the Temple of Amun (Temple T) erected by Taharqo at Kawa between 684 and 680 BC, and excavated by Francis Llewellyn Griffith between 1929 and 1931. It was found in Room E lying on the north-east corner of the dias. The attitude of the baboon, 'sun-ape', with arms raised, is common and represents the role of the animal in Egyptian and Kushite religion as a worshipper of the rising sun.   DAW

Berenguer 2003b; Griffith 1931, 87, pl. I; Macadam 1949, I Text, 87, I Plates pl. 35, no. XXXIII; Macadam 1955, II Text, 137, II Plates, pl. LXX, a–b

128 Ram's head amulet

Faience
Kawa, Site Q3, Building A1, Room II, SF 3852
Early Kushite (Napatan)
H 36 mm, W 14 mm, Th 6 mm
SNM 31122

A faience amulet in the form of a ram's head surmounted by a sun disc, single uraeus and a double plume with the feathering visible. Attached to the tip of the snout and the horns is an oval bead pierced horizontally. Such amulets, evoking the protective powers of ram-headed Amun, are a common find on Kushite sites.   DAW

128

129

129 Cat amulet

Lapis lazuli (?)

Kawa, Site R18, Tomb 112, SF 4019

Kushite (Napatan)

H 12 mm, W 8 mm, Th 4 mm

SNM 31127

A lapis lazuli (?) amulet in the form of a sitting cat with a suspension loop attached to its back. This is the classic portrayal of the cat goddess Bastet, local deity of the city of Bubastis in Egypt. Bastet was adored as a goddess of fertility, an attribute it was hoped extended to the wearer of her amulet. It was discovered in the Kushite cemetery at the neck of an infant buried in a crouched position.

DAW

130 Winged scarab amulet

Faience

Kawa, Site Q3, Building A1, Room II, SF 4013

Kushite (Napatan)

H 64 mm, W 67 mm, Th 10.5 mm

SNM 31121

A winged scarab moulded in low relief on its back and bearing on its front an *ankh* on each wing with two *udjat* eyes between. The front legs of the scarab and the tips of its wings, the right-hand one of which is largely missing, are attached to a horizontal bar from which three suspension loops were originally attached. Scarabs were good luck charms and worn to provide protection both in this life and the next (cf. cats 91–4, 132, 282). Winged scarabs were particularly associated with funerary ritual.   DAW

130, 131

131 *Udjat* eye amulet

Faience

Kawa, Site Q3, rubbish deposit outside Building A1, SF 2330

Kushite (Napatan)

H 53 mm, W 63 mm, Th 9 mm

SNM 31125

A rectangular amulet that is flat on the back. The front, surrounded by a narrow raised border, is divided by narrow raised ridges into three vertical registers, each bearing three representations in low relief of *udjat* eyes, one above the other. The amulet is pierced horizontally by three holes and may have formed the centre piece of a three-strand necklace. The *udjat* eye, the 'Eye of Horus', was a very popular apotropaic charm (cf. cats 283–5).

DAW

133

134

132 Scarab

Steatite

Kawa, Site R18, Tomb 1075, SF 3252

Kushite, first century BC–first century AD

H 8 mm, L 22 mm, W 15.5 mm; hole: D 2.5 mm

SNM 31126

Steatite scarab with only the front legs and the division between the head and thorax visible on the back. The face is incised with the figure of an ibex (?) above a spiked stem terminating in a floral motif. The scarab was found in the Kushite cemetery, Site R18, which lies several hundred metres to the east of the town at Kawa. It lay at the waist of an adult female, the primary burial within Tomb 1075. Also buried with the deceased were six copper-alloy toe-rings, a copper-alloy bowl and handle, gold-in-glass beads and pottery vessels (cat. 141). DAW

Welsby and Davies 2002, 26

133 Arrowheads

Chalcedony

Kawa, Site Q3, surface, SF 2918, 3028, 3073, 3089, 3316

Kushite (Napatan)

L 18–28 mm, W 10–13 mm, Th 1–4 mm

SNM 31124

Five arrowheads of chalcedony. Although copper and copper-alloy had long been used on the Middle Nile, and iron was making its appearance during the first half of the first millennium BC, the Kushites still maintained a lithic industry producing very fine-quality arrowheads. These are common finds on

132

Kushite urban sites and have also been recovered from cemeteries, including those of members of the royal family at Meroe (see Welsby 2001c, 370; Heidorn 1992, 60–62). These pieces are all surface finds from within the Kushite settlement at Kawa. DAW

134 Figurine

Mud

Kawa, Site Q3, Building B5, Room XI, SF 173

Early Kushite (Napatan) (?)

H 55+ mm, L 87 mm, W 86 mm

SNM 31137

Lower part of a seated steatopygous female figure of unfired mud, broken off at the waist. On the prominent thighs are deeply scored incisions, probably representing tattoos. Figurines of this type are well known from the Late Neolithic and particularly from the A-Group culture (for example, Wenig 1978b, 114, 116, 124, 125–7). Kushite examples are of a very different style (for example, Wenig 1978b, 220), although steatopygy is well represented on Kushite reliefs such as on the funerary chapels at Meroe. Although the Kawa piece came from a securely sealed early

Kushite context among rubbish deposits in the house, Building B5, it is possible that this is an object of much earlier date, perhaps recovered by an inhabitant of the Kushite town from one of the many Neolithic cemeteries in the vicinity.[1] DAW

1 *Kerma Classique* pottery sherds have also been found in the Kushite town.

Welsby 1998b, 19, pl. 3

135 Figurine

Ceramic

Kawa, Site Q3, Building A1, Room II, SF 3846

Kushite (Napatan)

H 43 mm, W 86 mm, L 98 mm

SNM 31138

Ceramic figure of a bird in flight with prominent bulbous eyes and a gaping mouth. It is formed of applied blobs of clay. A scar on the underside indicates where the bird had been attached to another ceramic object. The figure was sealed beneath one of the floors in the building. DAW

135

136

of Taharqo (cf. fig. 98),[1] and it almost certainly dates to his reign, 690–664 BC, as is highly likely in any event from the context. It is uncertain when the body of the statue was found: it was already in the Merowe Museum when the head was discovered.

Ptah was the chief god of Memphis, the patron deity of artists, craftsmen and builders. By the time of the construction of the Temple of Amun at Kawa, Memphis had been the *de facto* capital of Kush for a quarter of a century. The Memphite god Ptah was especially venerated by the Kushites and he is frequently depicted within the Kawa temple where he appears to have had a popular cult (for the importance of Ptah at Kawa see Török 2002, 89 ff.). The inscription includes the Pharaonic name of Kawa, Gematon 'The Aton is Perceived',[2] linking the town's foundation with Akhenaton in the mid-fourteenth century BC.   DAW/WVD

1 Cf. Russman 1974, 16–22, 47–51, 57–8, figs 8–15; Wardley and Davies 1999.

2 For a discussion of the identification of Gematon as Kawa, see Bell and Muhammad Jalal 2002.

Macadam 1955, II Text, 137, II Plates, pl. LXXI

137 Wall painting

Mud, inorganic pigments
Kawa, Site Q3, Building A1, Room I, (AB5)59g
Kushite (Napatan), 690–664 BC (?)
H 282 mm, W *c.* 460 mm, Th 12 mm
SNM 31123

Fragment of a wall painting, lime wash and inorganic pigments on a substrate of mud. On the fragment is depicted the bare lower arm of a human figure with a wide bracelet (white band) around the wrist and holding a cup-shaped receptacle, the contents of which are unclear. This fragment was recovered from the floor of the eastern

136 Statuette of Ptah

Granite
Kawa, Site Q3, Temple T
Kushite (Napatan), 690–664 BC
H 649 mm, W 376 mm, max. Th 198 mm
SNM 5216 (Merowe Museum 28)

A seated statuette of the god Ptah bearing the inscription, 'Ptah who dwells in Gematon, given all life' on the back pillar. The head was discovered by Griffith during the excavation of the Temple of Amun (Temple T) in the south-east corner of the First Court. Its facial features are consistent with the iconography

137

room of a shrine, Building A1 (Welsby 2001a). It almost certainly comes from the figure of the king on the north wall of the room, the feet of which remain *in situ*. The king is processing towards two gods, one of whom is probably Amun. Although the identification of the king is uncertain, the presence of an altar within the room bearing the cartouches of Taharqo may indicate that it is the latter who is depicted here. In a relief on the walls of Taharqo's shrine in Temple T, which is situated several hundred metres to the north, are depicted two similar objects being presented by him to a seated Amun. These contain an offering of bread and a figure of Maat (Macadam 1955, II Plates, pl. XVIIe). DAW

Welsby and Davies 2002, 26

138

138 Sealing

Mud

Kawa, Site Q3, Building Z (ZH5)85, SF 4003

Kushite (Napatan)

H 53 mm, W 75 mm, Th 60 mm

SNM 31133

A fragment from a mud sealing, perhaps originally 150 mm in diameter at the base and conical in shape. The underside is flat and smooth. In the 'centre' of the cone are impressions perhaps of the pottery vessel, with a rim diameter of approximately 80 mm, which it was designed to seal. It bears one complete and two partial seal impressions. The complete example is rectangular, 22×30 mm in size, and depicts two tall jars on jar-stands flanking a small vessel with a plant motif (palm fronds?) above. The central part of the sealing appears to have been left blank. The other two seal impressions are identical.

In the upper part of the impression is a hippopotamus facing right, standing on a ground line beneath which is a crocodile also facing right, again on a ground line. The lower part of the impression is a mirror image of the upper. The decoration is enclosed by a narrow raised oval border. Each impression was originally 68 mm high by approximately 50 mm wide and is much larger than the norm.

Many seals bearing these stamp impressions were found immediately outside the south wall of Building Z1, the function of which is unknown. Sealings of mud were attached to a wide range of objects and on occasion record information concerning the material being traded, transported or stored, its provenance, the name of the official dealing with the consignment or of the ruling king. They were also used to seal doorways. The meaning of this sealing is unknown but its presence along with many other examples probably indicates that containers were being brought to Building Z1 where their contents were used, repacked or placed in storage. Here the sealings were discarded outside the building while elsewhere at Kawa (in Building A1) and at Jebel Barkal the sealings were kept, presumably as an administrative record (for Jebel Barkal see Vincentelli 1993). DAW/JHT

139 Crocodile bowl

Ceramic

Kawa, Site Q3 (AD5) 1, pot form 3084x

Kushite (Napatan)

H 120 mm, L 288 mm, W 176 mm

SNM 31112

This is a hand-made, fragmentary coarse-ware bowl of Nile silt. It is sub-oval in shape, with an appliqué crocodile hugging the rim. Part of the bowl is missing, but there may have been another crocodile or other animal

on the opposite side. The crocodile was made separately and fixed to the rim before firing. Another much cruder and slightly later bowl was found elsewhere at Kawa with a similar animal attached to the rim and wall of the pot. Vessels with animal motifs, especially attached to the rim or body, are not uncommon in this period. IWS

140

140 Ledge-rimmed jar

Ceramic

Kawa, Site Q3, Building B, (BF2) 49A, pot form 2029x

Kushite (Napatan)

H 252 mm, D 292 mm

SNM 31115

Several jars of this type were found in domestic early Kushite contexts at Kawa. All are wheel-made, a common feature of locally made pottery in this period. The fabric is Nile silt with organic temper. An everted rim is 'buttressed' by at least six clay supports, added after the jar was thrown, but before the

139

red slip that covers the exterior and part of the interior was applied. As far as we can tell, the supports serve no purpose other than a decorative one. The jar has a foot-ring base, an uncommon feature of pottery of this period. At least one similar pot has been found at Kerma (Ahmed 1992, fig. 15, IA3c).

IWS

141 Jar

Ceramic

Kawa , Site R18, Grave 1075, pot form 2882x

Kushite (Meroitic), first century BC–first century AD

H 404 mm; max. D 306 mm; rim: D 95 mm

SNM 31106

One of four wheel-made, narrow-mouthed painted jars that were found in grave 1075 in the Kushite cemetery at Kawa. Two were complete, one had part of its rim missing, while the fourth was badly cracked. This example is one of those better preserved, although the presence of salt in the soil around the pot caused crystals to grow on the shoulder and body of two of the jars. The fabric is oxidized, and on the exterior, which is covered in a thick orange slip or paint, the neck is decorated with horizontal black bands.

IWS

Welsby 2001b, 96, pl. 6; Welsby and Davies 2002, 26

142 Statue of Beset

Ceramic

Kawa, Site Q3, Building A1, from the surface, SF 773

Kushite (Napatan)

Statue minus the base: H 962 mm, max. W 480 mm, W across the ears 432 mm

Base: L 220–65 mm, W 210 mm, Th at front 69 mm, tapering to 35 mm at back

SNM 31116

Ceramic statue in a dark grey fabric changing to orange/red at the surface. The face is broad and is dominated by the short nose, with widely flared nostrils and small nostril openings. The mouth, as wide as the nose, has markedly protruding, almost pouting, thin lips which are not quite closed, revealing a row of rectangular teeth. The large almond-shaped eyes are not clearly differentiated from the cheeks along their lower edge but the upper lids are prominent. The eyebrows are represented by four grooves over the left eye and by three grooves over the right eye. The ears, which stick out at right angles from the head, are semi-circular with a deep semi-circular depression against the side of the head and two concentric grooves towards the edge of the earlobes. The outer groove is pierced by two circular holes.

The pert breasts have prominent circular nipples with a depression in the centre, and there is a deep circular navel in the trim stomach. The pubic hair is indicated by short incised lines arranged in several horizontal rows, and with an oblique row delimiting the hair towards each thigh. A vertical groove indicates the vulva. The legs are bowed with no indication of knees and the feet are small and stubby. The arms are arranged symmetrically with the hands resting on the sides of the legs adjacent to where the knees should be. Grasped in the poorly formed right hand and held against the lower arm is a straight-bladed dagger with a pronounced median rib. The neck of a snake is held in the left hand and the sinuous body tapering into the tail extends up the arm to the neck. The snake's head is held tight against the side of the leg. Crowning the head is a large flaring feather headdress of four plumes, the median rib and the tines indicated by shallow and narrow incised grooves. The sides of the headdress round into the top which, although damaged, appears to be slightly concave towards the centre. Nine holes survive close to the top edge of the headdress. At the base of the headdress a line of short vertical grooves presumably represents the hair, the same method used to depict the pubic hair.

The whole of the front and sides of the figure is covered in whitewash, overlain in places by traces of paint in other colours. The poor preservation of the painted surface makes it difficult to reconstruct the original decoration. Fragments of yellow are visible particularly on the thighs, lower torso, shoulders, around the edge of the earlobes and at the base of the headdress above the left eyebrow. The pubic hair is picked out in black. The left shoulder has an area decorated by large black and white dots on the yellow background. This may represent a leopard skin draped over the shoulder and from the lower edge of the yellow are rectangular stripes which may represent tassels. Similar stripes are visible hanging down on the lower left leg. Some of the grooves on the headdress are filled with red paint and part of the surface is yellow. The snake along the left arm is picked out in red and the upper two grooves of the left eyebrow are filled with red paint. The rear of the statue is flat and was clearly not meant to be seen, although it is also covered in whitewash. The base, which tapers from front to back, extended 100 mm beyond the back of the statue and had presumably been set into a wall, the statue standing flush against the wall face. This may explain the absence of a tail.

141

The statue exhibits many of the characteristics of the better known representations of Bes (cf. cats 166, 285), but whereas there is often some sexual ambiguity with Bes figures, the Kawa piece is unashamedly female. A number of gods are represented in the visual form usually associated with Bes, among them Aha and Hayt (Romero 1989, 14). If a similar situation pertains to the female form the identification of the Kawa statuette with Beset may not be

strictly correct. The existence of the female form has been doubted (ibid., 16–17), but the gender of the Kawa piece calls for a reconsideration of the evidence.[1] Representations of Beset are known as early as the Middle Kingdom but only become frequent in the Ptolemaic period. Beset is regarded as the mother of Bes, sometimes depicted suckling him, but also as his consort (Altenmüller 1975).

The Kawa statue was found broken into many pieces and scattered in a number of rubbish deposits immediately outside Building A1 (see Welsby 2001a). Some of the breaks were of very recent date, probably caused when it was being dug out of the ground immediately prior to the commencement of excavations on the site in 1998. The form of the piece clearly indicates that it was designed to be set into a wall although total excavation of Building A1 failed to find any evidence for where it might have stood. DAW

1 For a discussion of representations of Beset see Bosse-Griffiths 1977.

Welsby 1998b, front cover, pl. IX; 2001b, 25

143 Statue of Bes
Ceramic
Kawa, Site Q3, Building A1, Room IV, SF 774
Kushite (Napatan)
H 450 mm, W 370 mm, max. Th 160 mm
SNM 31117

Ceramic statue of a figure of which only the head, upper chest and upper left arm are preserved. The facial features are very similar to those of cat. 142, although the eyebrows are even more prominent, with five clear almost horizontal ridges above each eye and the tongue is shown sticking out. The one surviving ear is not pierced. Only the lower part of the feather headdress survives and the tip of the dagger or sword held across the chest in the right hand.

This is clearly a representation of Bes and forms a pair with the Beset statue. Like Beset, the back is flat and was presumably affixed to a wall. Fragments of two other statues of the same type were recovered from this area and ongoing excavations may be expected to reveal more fragments, if not more figures. The Bes figure was recovered lying face-down on the sand which had begun to accumulate on the brick floor within Room IV of Building A1.   DAW

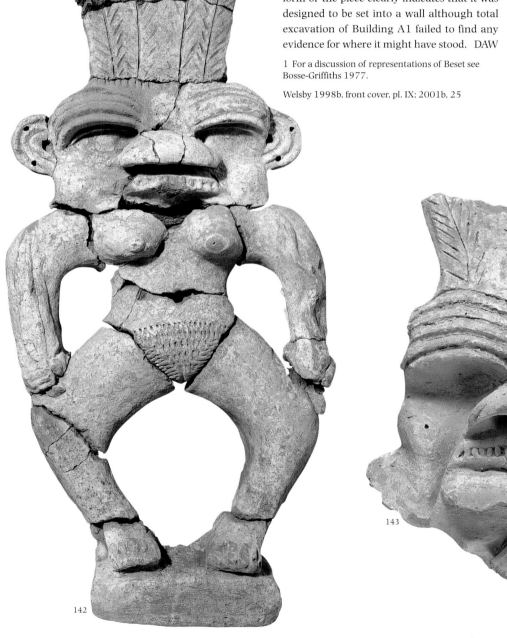

142

143

JEBEL BARKAL

TIMOTHY KENDALL

One of the most important archaeological districts in the Sudan lies on the western outskirts of the modern river town of Kareima, about 325 km north-north-east of Khartoum. This is the site of the ancient city of Napata, whose ruins, largely unexcavated, extend in three directions around the steep sides of the small table mountain known as Jebel Barkal, which stands 2 km from the right bank of the Nile (fig. 117).

The site was first noted and described by G. Waddington and B. Hanbury in 1822, and by F. Cailliaud who accompanied the Egyptian army of Muhammed Ali on its invasion of the Sudan in 1820–21. It was Cailliaud who first recognized the site as Napata.[1] To these and the few other Western explorers of the early nineteenth century, Napata was known only from classical texts as the residence of the ruling queen of Meroe, when in 24 BC it was attacked by a Roman army. In 1862, however, an Egyptian army officer stationed there found a trove of Kushite royal stelae, written in Egyptian.[2] These revealed that, from at least the eighth century BC, Napata had been the primary sanctuary and coronation centre of the Kushite kingdom. Jebel Barkal was then called the 'Pure Mountain' and was believed to be the chief southern residence of Amun, the Egyptian state god who was also the state god of Kush. Because Amun was thought to dwell inside Jebel Barkal, many temples (perhaps up to fifteen) and three palaces were built directly in front of the mountain's sheer 90 m-face (figs 100, 118). The extensive mounds of occupation debris in front of the temples suggested that the ancient town sprawled between the mountain and riverbank. During the third and first centuries BC, select rulers chose the site for their tombs and constructed small, steep-sided pyramids, identical to those at Meroe, in the desert west of the mountain. Today twelve pyramids still stand and probably mark a much larger necropolis, as yet unexplored (fig. 119).

117 Aerial view of Jebel Barkal.

No excavations were undertaken at Barkal until after the cessation of the Anglo-Egyptian war (AD 1898), although the site was briefly probed in 1897 by E.A.W. Budge for the British Museum.[3] In 1907 J.H. Breasted photographed the monuments for the University of Chicago. Then, between 1916 and 1920, George A. Reisner, representing Harvard University and the Museum of Fine Arts, Boston, conducted the first major excavations of the temples and pyramids. It was Reisner who first discovered the means of penetrating the subterranean tombs of the pyramids and excavated eighteen of them. He also cleared seven of the Barkal temples, excavated two mud-brick palaces, and recovered other inscribed monuments that carried the site's history back to the reign of Thutmose III.[4]

After Reisner no further excavation was undertaken at

118 Isometric reconstruction of the Barkal temples at the foot of the mountain.

119 Pyramid field at Jebel Barkal.

Napata until 1972, when Sergio Donadoni and a team from the University of Rome 'La Sapienza' began exploring the urban remains and exposed Meroitic house-plans and two small temples.[5] Just east of Reisner's excavation area, in 1978, the Italians found the ruins of an enormous Meroitic palace (B 1500), with brightly painted and niched walls, and doorways guarded by lion statues. The excavations have continued to the present day, and are now, since Donadoni's retirement in 1992, being directed by Alessandro Roccati.

In 1986 the Italians were joined by a renewed expedition of the Museum of Fine Arts, Boston, led by the author, who continued working in the old Reisner concession.[6] In 1996 these two teams were joined by a third, funded by the Fundacio Clos, Barcelona, under F. Berenguer, who renewed operations in the Barkal Cemetery. The Spanish team promptly discovered two unknown royal tombs of the Napatan period.[7]

Settlements existed at Jebel Barkal long before the Napata of Egyptian and Kushite historical record, for pottery of the Neolithic, Pre-Kerma, and Kerma periods has been found widely scattered about the mountain. Reisner even found two pre-Egyptian graves within the temple precinct. Although the site is best known for its Kushite architecture and monuments, and its unsurpassed religious and political importance during the

25th Dynasty (747–656 BC) and the Napatan period, archaeology has revealed that the Kushite buildings, with few exceptions, were restorations of buildings first constructed by the pharaohs of the New Kingdom (1550–1069 BC).

The earliest known architecture at Napata dates to the mid-18th Dynasty. The Barkal stele of Thutmose III is the site's earliest known document and refers to an existing native settlement and local Egyptian fort. The earliest level of the Great Temple of Amun of Napata (B 500) was apparently built by the Thutmoside pharaohs, and the small Temple (B 600) had foundation deposits of Thutmose IV. During the Amarna period, as in Egypt, the name of Amun was methodically erased from local monuments, revealing that Akhenaton (1352–1336 BC) attempted to eradicate the local Amun cult. He must have rededicated the site to the Aten, for thousands of *talatat* blocks, apparently from his dismantled temples, were found reused in later buildings. As in Egypt, the Amun cult was restored here by Tutankhamun and/or Horemheb, who rebuilt B 500 over its pre-Amarna foundations. It was then grandly enlarged by Seti I (1294–1279 BC) and Ramesses II (1279–1213 BC).

120 Hathor columns from Temple B300.

From an Abu Simbel relief depicting Jebel Barkal we know that the Egyptians conceptualized the mountain's towering pinnacle as a gigantic natural statue of a rearing uraeus wearing the white crown. This suggestive formation apparently convinced them that Jebel Barkal was an important source of Upper Egyptian kingship and the dwelling place of the patron goddesses of this kingship. The pharaohs thus built beneath the pinnacle at least two temples (B 300-sub and B 1100-first) dedicated to different goddesses (fig. 120). The lowest levels of the Napatan palace (B 1200) probably also date to the early 19th Dynasty. After Ramesses II further building at the site seems to have ceased, and five centuries elapse before we encounter evidence for new building activity.[8]

In about 780 BC, native Nubian chiefs from nearby el-Kurru commenced restoring the Barkal sanctuary with a completely new Amun Temple in mud brick (B 800), parallel to B 500. Later Piankhi (Piye) restored them both in stone and built a new palace directly over the Ramesside palace (B 1200). The two Amun Temples apparently honoured the distinct Napatan and Theban aspects of Amun, to whom Piankhi and his heirs attributed their kingship over a united Nubia and Egypt (cat. 146). Piankhi's son and third successor Taharqo made new temples for the uraeus goddesses and placed an inscription, covered with gold sheet, on the inaccessible 75 m-high summit of the pinnacle.[9]

Following their expulsion from Egypt by the Assyrians in 661 BC, the Kushites continued to develop the Barkal sanctuary. Atlanersa and Senkamanisken erected the small Temple B 700, which became a royal mortuary temple. Senkamanisken's sons, Anlamani and Aspelta, restored B 800 and Piankhi's palace late in the seventh century. Shortly afterwards the temples and palace were burned, and the royal statues, set up in B 500 and found by Reisner, were toppled and broken (cats 3, 144). This destruction can probably be attributed to the Egyptian invasion of Kush by the army of Psammetik II in 593 BC.

The Barkal sanctuary was restored in the sixth century BC and again in the fourth by Harsiyotef and Nastasen, both of whom erected stelae at the site detailing their works. Following a probable fifth or sixth restoration of B 1200 in the third century BC, a new palace, B 100, was erected 75 m in front of it in the early Meroitic period, which was probably used by the rulers buried in the Barkal pyramids. After the Roman raid of 24 BC, the sanctuary was again fully restored by Natakamani and Amanitore, who also enlarged it to the north-east. Except for their great palace, B 1500 (cat. 145), excavated by the Italian Mission, many other buildings (B 1700–2400, 3000) still remain to be excavated.[10]

With the decline of the Meroitic kingdom and the advent of Christianity, the site of Napata became a Christian village and eventually an Islamic one. Since the nineteenth century the ancient Barkal cemetery has been a Muslim cemetery. Jebel Barkal still retains its meaning as a holy place, for it is now associated with a local Muslim saint whose tomb stands beside it.

1 Cailliaud 1826–7.
2 Budge 1907, 149–50.
3 Budge 1907, 146–76.
4 Dunham 1970; Kendall 1996b; Reisner 1917; 1918; 1920; 1921; 1931.
5 Donadoni 1993.
6 Kendall 1990.
7 Berenguer 2001; 2003a.
8 Kendall 1994a.
9 Kendall 1996a.
10 Kendall 1991; 1994a.

144 Sphinx of Senkamanisken

Granite

Jebel Barkal, Great Temple of Amun, Court B 501

Kushite (Napatan), third quarter of seventh century BC

H 883 mm, L 539 mm, W 255 mm

SNM 1852

This statue depicts Senkamanisken, third successor of Taharqo, in the antique pharaonic form of a sphinx: a lion with human head, bearded and wearing the *nemes* headcloth surmounted by the double crown. The double uraeus identifies the work as Kushite. The sphinx's forelegs terminate in human arms and hands, which hold an offering jar on which are inscribed the king's names in a double cartouche: Sekheper-en-Re Senkamenisken. Two other Kushite sphinxes of the same period have forepaws terminating in hands: that of the Kushite princess and 'God's Wife of Amun' Shepenwepet II in Berlin which holds a ram-headed jar (Wildung 1997, 174–5); and the sphinx of Aspelta in Khartoum which holds an offering table.

During clearing of the first court of the Great Amun Temple at Jebel Barkal in January 1920, Reisner found this sphinx just inside the entrance, facing the temple axis. Just beside it was a small granite stand, inscribed for Atlanersa, on which rested a seated statue of Thutmose III in Heb-Sed robes (Dunham 1970, pl. IVA). The surrounding debris contained fragments of many other large and small statues, including fragments of another sphinx, revealing that B 501 had once been filled with statuary of both Egyptian and Kushite kings, and Egyptian private officials. It is doubtful that the sphinx occupied its original place, not only because the court and its statues had been so badly damaged in the Egyptian attack of 593 BC (see cat. 3), but also because the court was extensively modified in the first century AD by the Kushite rulers Natakamani and Amanitore, who erected a kiosk in its centre.   TK

Berenguer 2003e; Dunham 1970, 33, fig. 28, pl. XXXII; Reisner 1931, 83, nos 41–2; Wenig 1978b, 175, no. 186; Wildung 1997, 220–21, no. 230

144

145

145 Rondel

Ceramic

Jebel Barkal, Palace of Natakamani, GB 88.1

Kushite (Meroitic), first century AD

D 284 mm, Th 47 mm

SNM 31330

The bust of a woman depicted in Hellenistic fashion, shown *en face* holding a bunch of grapes in either hand, decorates the front of this turquoise, glazed terracotta disc. The rondel has been reconstructed. These plaques, and others of various shapes and colours, decorated the exterior of Natakamani's palace at Jebel Barkal where they had been set into the wall plaster (Donodoni 1993, 102–103, 110; 1994, 56). Similar tondi were used in the decoration of the so-called 'Royal Baths' (M 195) at Meroe where they were set in the edge above the basin alternating with statuary and other plaques (Török 1997b, 75–7, pls 28–34). There, it has been suggested that they may have depicted Maenads, the frenzied women of the Dionysian cult, and formed part of an iconographic programme relating to the use of the baths as a water sanctuary with Dionysian characteristics as derived from the Dionysian cults of Ptolemaic Egypt (Török 1997b, 76–7). The reason for the employment of such a motif on the exterior of a royal palace remains uncertain; however, it may reflect the attribution of some characteristics of the god Dionysos to the Kushite ruler or his attempt to portray himself as a Dionysiac king, as was common among the Ptolemaic pharaohs, most notably Ptolemy IV (cf. Hazzard 2000, 115–16).   JRA

146 Stela of Piankhi (Piye)

Sandstone

Kushite (Napatan) (*c.* 744 BC)

Jebel Barkal, Temple of Amun

H (surviving) 1.3 m, W 1.23 m, Th 220 mm

SNM 1851

Round-topped royal stela, carved in relief with an offering-scene and hieroglyphic inscriptions, surmounted by a religious motif

146

in the form of a winged sun-disc with pendant uraei, the workmanship being of high quality throughout. The stela is very damaged and now incomplete, with its bottom section missing and its surviving lower part much eroded, but is of great historical importance.

The scene shows on the right a standing figure of King Piankhi (Piye) (747–716 BC), identified in the cartouche above him, wearing the characteristic Kushite cap-crown with double uraei, facing left and offering a pectoral and a necklace to a triad of deities (a form of the traditional Theban triad), an enthroned Amen-Ra, followed by a standing Mut and Khons, all facing right. The deities are rendered in raised relief, as was the original (taller) figure of the king, which was removed (together with his name) at some time after the completion of the stela and

then later restored in incised work. The king's prenomen and nomen were systematically removed wherever they occurred on the stela.

Amen-Ra or Amun, shown in his Nubian, ram-headed form, presents to the king the crowns of Egypt and Kush, the red crown of Lower Egypt in his left hand, the Kushite cap-crown in his right (replacing here the traditional white crown of Upper Egypt), signifying a unified kingship and legitimate Kushite dominion over Egypt. Divine sanction of Piankhi's ascent to the throne is confirmed in the god's address 'to his son, whom he loves', inscribed in the columns of inscription above him: 'I said concerning you (even when you were still) in the womb of your mother, that you would be ruler of Egypt ... I caused you to receive the Great Crown ... It is I who decreed (the kingship) for you ... No other may decree

(who shall be) king'. The king's acknowledgement is recorded in the columns behind him, where he asserts his pre-eminence over all other rulers: 'Amun of Napata has caused me to be ruler of all foreign countries. To whomsoever I say "you are chief", he shall be chief. To whomsoever I say "You are not king", he shall not be king. Amun in Thebes has caused me to be ruler of Egypt. To whomsoever I say "Make your appearance (as king)", he shall make his appearance. To whomsoever I say "Do not make appearance", he shall not make his appearance ... Gods make a king, men make a king, (But) it is Amun who has made me'.

The main text of the stela is located directly beneath the offering scene. Arranged in horizontal lines reading right to left and downwards, it records the king's full titulary and epithets, and once continued with a historical narrative, of which only fragments of the beginning now survive. One of these fragments crucially bears the remnants of what may be a year date, possibly to be read as '(regnal-year) 3', in which case the stela is Piankhi's earliest known monument.

Piankhi's titulary was clearly inspired by that of one of his great imperial 'predecessors', King Thutmose III of the 18th Dynasty, as recorded on the latter's famous victory stela from Jebel Barkal. One especially significant difference, however, is the form of the king's so-called Horus-name. In the case of Thutmose III, the name is 'Strong Bull, Appearing (ascending to the throne) in Thebes'; in the case of Piankhi, it is 'Strong Bull, Appearing in Napata', a calculated change announcing 'a momentous reversal of history ... the place of Thebes, where the Egyptian conqueror of Kush had been crowned, was now taken by Napata, where the Kushite ruler of Egypt is crowned' (Török 1997a, 154).   WVD

Dunham 1970, 29, no. 13; Eide *et al.* 1994, 55–62, no. 8; Kendall 1997b, 163–4, fig. 27; Kitchen 1986, 359; Morkot 1995, 231–2; 2000, 169, 173, 179–80, fig. 79; Porter and Moss 1951, 217 (19); Priese 1972, 24–7; Reisner 1931, 82, no. 26, and 89–100, pls V–VI; Török 1995, 215; 1997a, 153–5, 164; 2002, 346–7, 371

147 Statuette of the god Amun with ram head

Granite

Jebel Barkal, Temple B 700, Room B 704 (sanctuary)

Kushite (Meroitic), third–first centuries BC

H 600 mm, W 157 mm, Th 205 mm

SNM 1844

This statue represents the god of Jebel Barkal as a man, wearing the royal *shendyt* kilt, with a bewigged ram's head. The drilled eyes were once inlaid. The round support on the head has a rectangular socket that would probably have supported a gilt copper-alloy crown of a pair of tall feathers and sun disc with uraeus.

The small Amun Temple B 700 at Barkal was built so close to the mountain that it was repeatedly damaged by falls of rock from the cliff. Founded by Atlanersa in the mid-seventh century BC, the temple was completed by Senkamanisken after his predecessor's premature death. Thenceforth it seems to have served the royal mortuary cult, for the ruins contained small copper-alloy Osiride figures as well as fragments of a large false door of the deceased Atlanersa.

When Reisner began clearing the ruins in March 1916, he found the second chamber (B 703) buried under huge rocks. Breaking them up, he was able to expose not only the rest of the room and the fine bark stand of Senkamanisken, now in Boston (Dunham 1970, pls XXX–XXXI), but also a tiny sanctuary (B 704) in its rear wall that still contained a small granite altar and a trove of statues. The main figures were this image of Amun, a fine standing statue of Amenhotep III (ibid., pls V–VI), and a badly decayed sandstone seated statue of a Kushite king (ibid., pl. LVII)

The reused masonry of B 703 revealed that the rear of the temple had been destroyed and rebuilt in the later Napatan or Meroitic period. The small sanctuary B 704 belonged to this later phase, which meant that all the contents had been placed there after it was built, probably after the fourth century BC. The Amun statue was perhaps made as the temple's new cult image.   TK

Berenguer 2003f; Dunham 1970, 69, pl. LVI; Reisner 1918, 101; Wenig 1978b, 177, no. 89; Wildung 1997, 272, no. 289

MEROE

KRZYSZTOF GRZYMSKI

Meroe, the main residence of the Kushite kings, is located on the east bank of the Nile, some 200 km north of Khartoum, and covers an area almost 1 km². The most impressive part of the site is a large, roughly rectangular enclosed area known as the 'Royal City' (fig. 121). On its west side there is a seasonal channel of the Nile, while on

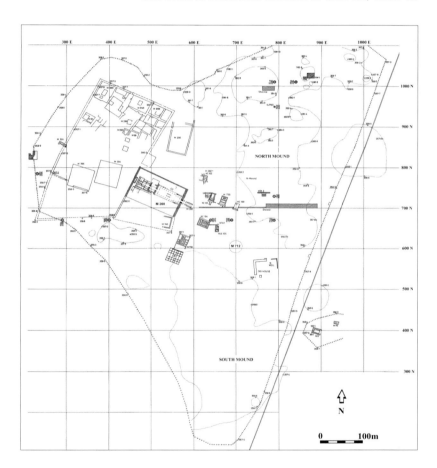

121 Map of Meroe city.

the east stands the Temple of Amun. Further east are two large mounds covered with sherds and brick fragments, known as the North and South Mounds. The mounds are separated by what seems to be a processional way, extending from the Amun Temple eastward in the direction of the so-called Sun Temple. In the desert further to the east, approximately 4 km from the Royal City, two extensive pyramid fields housing the royal tombs surmount a ridge; a third pyramid field containing the tombs of the nobles lies between the royal cemeteries and the city.

The first description of this royal capital was pro-

vided in the fifth century BC in the work of the Greek historian Herodotus. He based his description on stories told by spies sent to Meroe by the Persian king Cambyses. Over time the location of the city was lost to the West. It was only at the end of the eighteenth century that a Scottish traveller, James Bruce of Kinnaird, came across ruins which he tentatively identified as Meroe. This identification was confirmed only as a result of the excavations carried out by the University of Liverpool expedition directed by John Garstang from 1909 until 1914. Although by modern standards his excavation techniques left much to be desired, Garstang succeeded in unearthing a large part of the royal district of Meroe with its many palaces, magazines, shrines, and other buildings surrounded by a massive enclosure wall made of dressed sandstone blocks – the Royal City. Garstang numbered various components of the site by using a one- to three-digit number preceded by the letter 'M'. Garstang also discovered a large Temple of Amun (M 260) (fig. 123) and about a kilometre further east another building which he identified as the Sun Temple (M 250). He also conducted limited test excavations in other parts of the site. The results of his work were published only partially and therefore much information has been lost.[1] It was only in 1997 that the Hungarian scholar, László Török, published the final report of Garstang's excavations based on field notes and photographs kept in Liverpool.[2] Another scholar, a German architect Friedrich Hinkel, re-studied and published anew some of Garstang's sites, particularly the Sun Temple and the Royal City.[3]

A new era of field research at Meroe began with the excavations directed by Peter L. Shinnie, first under the auspices of the University of Ghana (1965), then sponsored by the University of Khartoum (1966–70), and finally as a joint mission of the University of Khartoum and the University of Calgary (1971–7, 1983–4). The emphasis was placed on the study of the domestic structures, on ascertaining the occupation history of the site, and on investigating the iron production at Meroe (cat. 149). Heaps of iron slag still visible on the surface led one early traveller to dub Meroe 'the Birmingham of ancient Africa'.[4] Shinnie found numerous iron-smelting furnaces, confirming that Meroe was not just a political and cultural capital but also an industrial centre. Another important discovery was

122 Kite photo of
Amun Temple and
the site of Meroe,
looking west.

that of several small temples on the north and south side of what was clearly a processional way leading to the Amun Temple. These were numbered in Garstang-like fashion, but prefaced by the letters KC (for Khartoum–Calgary) instead of M.[5]

In 1992 the site of Meroe was investigated by a joint mission of the University of Khartoum, the Humboldt University of Berlin and the Roemer-Pelizaeus Museum of Hildesheim.[6] Apart from surveying the site, the Meroe Joint Excavations (MJE) team also conducted small-scale excavations during which they found another temple, known as MJE 105. In 1999 the joint Sudanese–Canadian mission was revived under the co-directorship of Ali Osman M. Salih of the University of

Khartoum and the author. After the preliminary surface study, during which one of the earliest datable objects ever found at Meroe, namely a stone fragment bearing the name of King Anlamani (c. 620–600 BC), was discovered (cat. 148), the Khartoum–Toronto team carried out an excavation campaign and a geophysical survey.[7] We traced the wall outlines of the 60 m-long courtyard of the Temple of Amun, the largest building in Meroe, discovering in the process two long stairways leading up the first pylon. Excavations on mound M 712 (fig. 122), identified but not excavated by Garstang, revealed the remains of domestic occupation, dated by carbon-14 to the first–third centuries AD. A massive mud-brick wall and a bakery found immediately to the north of M712 are possibly the remains of another temple.

Although less than a third of the site has been excavated so far, we can provide a tentative reconstruction of the historical development of this, the most important urban centre of the Kushite Kingdom. The earliest remains identified to date were represented by a series of post-holes from a small, round hut found by Shinnie in the bottom layer of his North Mound trench. These are dated to approximately 1000 BC.[8] The earliest brick buildings on the North Mound appear much later, in the sixth century BC, and seem contemporary with the earliest brick and stone structures from the Royal City (M296, M298), although the discovery of objects inscribed with the names of Senkamanisken (c. 640–620 BC) and Anlamani (c. 620–600 BC) suggests an earlier Kushite occupation of the site. It has been proposed, although not proven, that in these early periods the area occupied by the Royal City

123 Meroe Mound
M712, domestic
complex, Late Meroitic,
view from the south.

was located on an island, and that the Enclosure Wall, dated to approximately the third century BC, was constructed more to protect the supposed island from the Nile floods than from enemy attacks.[9] Since the Royal City was continuously occupied until the beginning of the fourth century AD it underwent many changes and its layout is not entirely clear. Once the area was walled it became accessible only through five gates, two of which were approached along tree-lined avenues. The palace and temple architecture reflects Egyptian, Hellenistic and Roman influences. Many of the buildings were erected on platforms, perhaps to prevent the flooding of the interior during the rainy season. Among the most interesting buildings was a temple or victory shrine, M292, deco-

124 Garstang's excavation of the Royal Bath M194.

rated with wall paintings. It was under the threshold to this building that Garstang found the celebrated bronze head of the Roman Emperor Augustus, now in the British Museum (fig. 125). Another unique structure whose function remains unclear is complex M194–M195, which Garstang named the Royal Bath (fig. 124, cat. 153). Other scholars, notably Török, interpret it as a water sanctuary or a nymphaeum.[10] The red-brick structure contains a deep basin surrounded by Hellenized statuary placed in front of painted walls. Nearby there is a semi-circular exedra, whose function is also unclear: some scholars see it as a gymnasium while others a place for the cult of the ancestors. The southern part of the Royal City was never explored by Garstang, but the magnetometric survey carried out in 2002 by the Khartoum–Toronto team indicated the

125 Discovered buried beneath the threshold of a temple in the royal city of Meroe, this imperial bronze head of Caesar Augustus probably formed part of the plunder taken by the Kushites during their raids upon the Egyptian frontier in the late first century BC. The British Museum, GR 1911.9-1.1.

presence of a rectangular structure, perhaps a palace, in the south-west part of the enclosure. In the south-east corner, near the south gate, the magnetic map showed a double row of circles, probably representing round, walled tree-pits, a feature previously noticed by Garstang at the north-west gate.

The area outside the Royal City has remained largely unexplored. Our own preliminary investigations in the Amun Temple and the nearby Palace M750 revealed numerous errors and omissions in Garstang's work. The discovery by Shinnie of the processional way, flanked on each side by a series of small temples, and the results of our magnetometric survey suggest that at least in part of the city we have evidence for urban planning, with large avenues and open plazas located in selected areas. On the other hand, no single house-plan has ever been fully exposed and the ordinary domestic architecture in Meroe is poorly known. Nevertheless the discovery of numerous imported objects from Egypt, Greece, Rome and the Red Sea coast (cats 156–8) suggests a well-developed trade network of which Meroe must have been a substantial centre. Judging from the faunal remains found on the site, the 10,000 or so inhabitants of Meroe (cf. Grzymski 2003b, 85–90) consumed a substantial amount of cattle, sheep and goats as well as some African game, particularly warthogs and hartebeest.

The gradual decline of this ancient royal capital began as early as the third century AD. Although there is a Post-Meroitic cemetery nearby between the city and the Western Pyramid field, there is an apparent lack of Post-Meroitic material on the site, even in the latest occupation levels. This suggests that the site was abandoned at the latest at the time of the supposed conquest by the Axumite king Ezana in the fourth century AD (cat. 152), as may be surmised from the two Axumite inscriptions (cat. 155) found at Meroe. Afterwards the fabled capital of the Kushites was gradually covered by sand and overgrown with acacia trees and halfa grass.

1 Garstang 1910; 1911a; 1912a; 1912b; 1913; 1914; 1914–16; Garstang and George 1913; Garstang and Phythian-Adams 1914; Garstang et al. 1911; Sayce and Garstang 1910.
2 Török 1997b.
3 Hinkel 2001; Hinkel and Sievertsen 2002.
4 Sayce 1912, 55.
5 Shinnie and Bradley 1980; Shinnie and Anderson 2004; Shinnie 1974; 1984; 1987; Shinnie and Kense 1982; Ahmed 1999; Bradley 1982; 1984a; 1984b; Robertson 1992; Tylecote 1982.
6 Wenig 1994; Eigner 1996; 2000; Wolf 1996.
7 Anderson and Grzymski 2001; Grzymski 2003b.
8 Robertson 1992, 44–5.
9 Bradley 1982, 168.
10 For a complete bibliography of the nymphaeum see Wolf and Onasch 2003.

148 Inscribed jamb fragment

Sandstone

Meroe, Palace M 295

Kushite (Napatan), reign of Anlamani, *c.* 620–600 BC

H 350 mm, W 400 mm, Th 170 mm

SNM 31192

This sandstone block, broken in two fitting parts and found lying loose on the ground in the north-east corner of building M 295, is probably part of an inscribed door jamb. It was found in 2000 by the Sudanese–Canadian team conducting a surface survey at Meroe. Along both edges of the block two double lines are incised, enclosing an inscription containing a royal name written within a cartouche. Above the cartouche but below the break are two hieroglyphs, the *t* signs, presumably representing the *nsw-bity* (king of Upper and Lower Egypt) title – the prenomen. Within the cartouche the signs *Imn-in* are fully preserved, and a small depression just above the break point is clearly the head of a lion – the *l* sign. There can be little doubt that the name should be read *Imn-Inl*, that is, Anlamani, but this is a little unusual as this name normally follows the Son of Ra title. Although examples of Napatan kings using two different titles for the same name are known, this has not been documented with Anlamani thus far. At the south end of M 295 Garstang apparently found a similar architectural fragment bearing the name of the fifth-century BC king Talakhamani (Török 1997b, 167, no. 295-1 = insc. 97, fig. 125). Although the first three signs of both royal names (*Imn* = Amani) are identical, others are not, and therefore Anlamani's inscription comes from a different block, unless Garstang copied the text incorrectly and misread the name.   KG

Anderson and Grzymski 2001, 28; Grzymski 2003b, 52, pl. XXIIIb, fig. 11a

148

149

149 Tuyère and iron slag

Ceramic, iron

Meroe, Trench N80 6 (6)

Kushite (Meroitic)

Tuyère: L 270 mm, W 60–70 mm; hole: D 25 mm

SNM 31193

A typical Meroitic iron-smelting furnace consisted of a smelting chamber and six clay bowl bellows probably covered with diaphragms of animal skin or leather. Bellow nozzles, or tuyères, were used to force air into the chamber. They were cigar-shaped, hollowed inside, and tapered at both ends. They were made of the Nile silt formed round a wooden rod (Tylecote 1982, 30–32). During heating some of the slag remained on the bottom of the furnace, but most of the liquid slag was tapped away through the tap-hole.

Often solidified lumps of slag remained attached to the tuyère, as with the present example. Analysis of the iron contents in the ore and in slag suggests a yield of about 20 per cent of the iron in the ore (Tylecote 1982, 40). The presence of mounds of iron slag visible at Meroe and the nearby sites of Hamadab (Wolf 2002a, 93; 2002b, 109–10) and el-Hassa (Lenoble and Rondot 2003) suggests that this was an important industrial centre of the Kushite Meroitic kingdom. Iron used in the smelting presumably came from the sedimentary deposit of the ferruginous sandstone common in this area. Remains of iron furnaces were excavated by Shinnie at Meroe (Shinnie and Kense 1982; Tylecote 1982),[1] enabling the reconstruction of the iron-smelting process.   KG

1 See further Eigner 2000.

150 *Ka* emblem

Faience

Meroe, Palace M 294

Kushite (Napatan), *c.* 590–560 BC

L 80 mm, W 93 mm, Th 18 mm

SNM 626

This faience tablet was found together with fragments of two other similar plaques and many other artefacts in a cachette containing discarded objects of religious significance

150, nomen

(Török 1997b, 154, 157, pl. 118). The small rectangular plaque, broken off at one corner, is decorated on both sides by a pair of arms that form a *ka* sign. The *ka* was a kind of life force, a person's double that was born with them, but survived after death and could receive offerings for the deceased. Each side of the plaque bears an inscription giving the prenomen and nomen of King Aspelta

(*c.* 593–568 BC): 'King of Upper and Lower Egypt, Merikara, may he live forever' and 'Son of Ra', Aspelta, may he live forever' (Nagy 1997, 240, insc. 67a, fig. 123). The function of the object is uncertain and its possible funerary meaning may suggest that it actually post-dates the reign of Aspelta. A similarly decorated but smaller and uninscribed faience object from Sakkara was published as an amulet (Reisner 1907, 158, no. 12260, pl. XX). It is possible that the Meroe piece served as a pectoral, a decorative chest ornament, like the ones known from various Egyptian sites.[1]   KG

Berenguer 2003m

1 See examples described by Bianchi (1998a, no. 160; 1998b, no. 161).

151 Stone block with footprints

Sandstone

Meroe, Temple M 720, no. 5744

Kushite (Meroitic)

L 190 mm, W 160 mm, Th 60 mm

SNM 31194

Flat, brick-like block of red sandstone with yellow upper and lower surface, and chisel

marks visible on the bottom. Two narrow, 110 mm-long footprints are incised on top of the block parallel to each other. The left foot has all five toes incised, while the right one has only the big and second toes marked. This sandstone slab was found in front of the threshold at the entrance to Temple M 720. Another block preserving a fragment of the incised outline of one foot was found in the same temple in Room B (Näser 2004).

Depictions of outlined feet are usually associated with pilgrimages to holy sites, commemorating the devotion of the individual (Millet 1984, 112). Numerous Meroitic graffiti showing outlines of two feet and inscribed with dedicatory inscriptions have been found in the Isis sanctuary at Philae. The texts usually began with a word *štq* or *štqo* (shataqo), which Griffith translated tentatively as 'foot/feet' (Griffith 1912, 42–3, 71, pls XXXI–XXXIV). Thus, the Meroe stone block must be regarded as a sign of personal piety and devotion to the deity worshipped in Temple M 720.   KG

Näser 2004

151

152 Statue head of Sebiumeker

Sandstone, paint, gold leaf

Meroe, M 282 (KC 102), excavation no. 6420

Kushite (Meroitic)

H 620 mm, W 271 mm, Th 304 mm

SNM 24564

This bearded, sandstone head, wearing a double crown with a uraeus and a small sun disc at the forehead, was found in Temple M282.[1] The head, which is considerably over-lifesize – 620 mm in height – was found lying in sand slightly above the floor of the single room of the temple. A small fragment of gold leaf is attached to the left eye by a piece of white plaster and it is possible that considerably more of the face was so covered. Other statue fragments from the site of Meroe also have traces of gold leaf on them and it may well have been common practice to adorn statues in this way. There were also faint traces of yellow and red paint on the face of the statue, but details of a design could not be made out.

It is virtually certain that this was the head of a statue of the god Sebiumeker, which had stood to the east side of the main entrance of the temple. A sandstone base (excavator's number 6869) with a right foot and the back part of a left foot, both somewhat over-lifesize and proportional to the statue, were found at this spot. No traces were found of the remainder of such a statue nor of the figure of the god Arensnuphis which would have stood on the other (western) side of the doorway. The placing of statues of these two gods at the entrance to small single-roomed temples is known from Musawwarat es-Sufra where Temple 300 was so adorned and the two gods, known only from the Meroitic pantheon, were regarded as protectors of a certain type of temple.

It seems possible that the statues of the two gods at the entrance to this temple were destroyed at some time when Meroe was invaded, possibly by Ezana of Aksum in *c.* AD 350, and that the head of Sebiumeker was thrown into the temple by the invaders whilst

152

the rest of the body and that of the companion god Arensnuphis were further destroyed. Other evidence for some destructive act occurring at this temple is to be seen in the presence of a single wheel, perhaps of a chariot, also found lying in the sand fill of the room close to the head of the god.   PLS

1 This temple was originally numbered by the excavator (Shinnie) as KC102, until it was realized that the temple had been discovered, but not excavated, by John Garstang in 1910 and numbered in his system.

Näser 2004; Shinnie and Anderson 2004; Wildung 1997, 280–81, no. 298

153 Column Capital

Sandstone, plaster, paint

Meroe M 191 (Garstang no. 134)

Kushite (Meroitic), 100 BC–AD 100 or later (?)

Top: max. W 600 mm, max. L 830 mm; base:
D 500 mm, H 440 mm

SNM 31219

Sandstone column capital decorated with a
series of palmettes and lotus stems covered
with cream-coloured plaster. Traces of red
paint are still visible in the vertical stripes on
the capital. Part of the capital is missing.
Composite capitals of very similar shape are
known from the Ptolemaic and Roman period
temples in Egypt, particularly Philae which
might have served as a model for the present
example.

Numerous decorated column capitals were
found by Garstang in the area of the so-called
Royal Bath, particularly in Hall M 194. This
capital was described by Garstang and George
(1913) in the following way: 'A more elaborate
carved, stuccoed, and painted capital found
just outside the adjacent portion of the city
wall, probably belong[s] to the earlier period'.
The capital lying *in situ* is illustrated by Török

154

(1997b, pl. 12). The exact dating of the capital
is problematic since it was found outside the
enclosure wall and therefore may have come
either from an earlier structure in the Royal
Bath area or could have been associated with
the later building M 191.   KG

Garstang and George 1913, 17; Török 1997b, 62,
pl. 12, nos 191–2

154 Meroitic inscription

Granite

Amun Temple, Courtyard M 271

L 172 mm, W 107 mm, Th 19 mm

Kushite (Meroitic), probably reign of Amanishakheto
(10–1 BC)

SNM 31401

This small fragment of a Meroitic inscription
was found at Meroe by the Liverpool expedition. The stone is grey granite, the same material that was used for writing a long but partly
broken inscription of Queen Amanishakheto
found by Garstang in the courtyard of the
Temple of Amun (Garstang 1911a, 47).
Numerous broken fragments from the same
inscription have been found and studied by
various explorers, including Hintze (1959,
175), Haycock and Shinnie (Shinnie and
Bradley 1980, 91), but the entire text was published only recently by C. Rilly (2002). There
can be little doubt that the present fragment
was part of the same inscription, the so-called
'obelisk' of Amanishakheto (SNM 30175),
although it is given a separate number in the
catalogue of Meroitic inscriptions compiled by
French scholars, namely REM 1254C-4, the
main block bearing the number REM 1361A-D.

Thanks to the work of F. Ll. Griffith in the
early twentieth century, who established the
phonetic values of the signs, it is possible to
read Meroitic texts. The meaning of the
words, however, still eludes us. The present
fragment reads as follows:

> ...lo k...
> ...ldeyi
> ...ot:a...   KG

Rilly 2002, 137, fig. 185, no. 4 (REM 1254C-4);
Török 1997b, 126, pl. 97

153

155 Greek inscription of a king of Aksum

Ferricrete sandstone

Meroe, Royal City

Third or fourth century AD

L 328 mm, W 221 mm, Th 139 mm

SNM 508

This inscription was brought in by a villager during the first season of J. Garstang's excavations of the Royal City at Meroe. It is carved on a block of ferricrete sandstone and exhibits the remains of fourteen lines of Greek text, inscribed to a depth of 1 mm. It was first published by A.H. Sayce (1909) and has since been republished and reinterpreted several times.[1] Due to its fragmentary state of preservation, only a few facts are firmly established. The stone is part of a throne, a triumphal monument set up in Meroe by a 'king of Aksum and Himyar' (line 1) to mark his victory over the Kushites and the occupation of their capital. Similar inscribed thrones set up by Aksumite rulers recording their victorious campaigns are known from Ethiopia. In line 2, the Aksumite war god Mahrem is referred to by his Greek name Ares. Mention is made of pillaging (line 4) and hostages (line 9). We hear about another king, presumably the king of Kush (line 7), and about a tribute imposed on the defeated Kushites (line 12). The figure in line 14 probably indicates the regnal year of the king. It is uncertain whether the king who set up the throne is identical with the famous King Ezana, dating to before his conversion to Christianity (mid-fourth century), or if it was

one of his predecessors. The following is a tentative translation of the text:

1 [I, N.N., King of Aks]um and Himya[r ...]
2 [... son of the invincible god] Ares, when [the people of ...] disputed
3 [...], I conv[ey]ed from [...]
4 [...] ... and I pillaged the [...]
5 [...] ... having arrived here [...]
6 [...] (women) of noble birth, and another [...]
7 [...] with the King as far as th[e ...]
8 [...] most (things) in the ... [...]
9 [... gen]erals and [their] children [...]
10 [...] I went against [...] at once [...]
11 [...] I will [...] to you [...]
12 [...] subject to pay tribute [...]
13 [...] a bronze (statue ?) [...]
14 [...] ... 21 (?)[...]   TH

1 See FHN III, no. 285, for further references.

Eide *et al.* 1998, no. 285; Sayce 1909, 189, pl. XXIV

155

156 Elephant head lamp

Copper alloy

Meroe, West Cemetery, Tomb W. 102

First–second century AD

Total H 65 mm, W (across wick holes) 180 mm

SNM 1947

This copper-alloy lamp is decorated with two opposed elephant heads, which project from the body of the lamp with their trunks uplifted. The moulded details of eyes and wrinkles are all well observed; their oval ears with beaded rims are more stylistic. The body of the lamp is circular with lathe-turned ridges on the base. The nozzles have volute decoration on the underside with peltate wick holes surrounded at the outer edge by a bead-and-reel decorated rim, supported by a band of vertical egg-and-dart decoration. Scrolls flank the nozzles. The discus is circular and dished with shallow concentric steps. Four trefoil holes, regularly spaced, are arranged around the upstanding tubular filling hole. Parallels, such as an example from the Castellani Collection in the British Museum (GR 1873.9-20.160), suggest that this lamp is of Italian manufacture.

The number of representations of elephants at Musawwarat es-Sufra and other sites suggests that the elephant played an important part in the ceremonial and daily life of the region. This lamp, therefore, may have had more significance to its Kushite owner than could have been anticipated by the Roman smith who made it.   LAJ

Dunham 1963, 192, fig. 138d; Török 1989, no. 201; Wenig 1978b, 94, fig. 77

156

157 Porringer

Silver

Meroe, Beg. N. 18, Tomb of Queen Amanikhatashan

First–second century AD

H (at handle) 53 mm; rim: internal D 126 mm

SNM 1827

This is a very fine, straight-sided, lathe-turned silver vessel. The sides are decorated with moulded, wavy, ridge and groove motifs which run vertically from an incised line at the base to a groove just below the rolled rim. The inner surface is plain with a single deep groove running 4 mm below the rim. Two opposed flat, gilded handles project from the rim where they have been soldered into position. Each handle has a central panel which was decorated with a raised motif of ribboned vegetation; scrolls projecting on either side of this panel have stamped dots arranged as stylized flowers. The handle attachments terminate in birds' heads, possibly ducks or geese, with gilded beaks and eyes. Below each handle is an oval, penannular ring, whose open ends point towards the vessel. The base has a foot-ring containing two concentric grooves; two smaller grooves surround the lathe scar. On either side of the smaller circles are scratched Meroitic owners' marks, one depicting an acanthus leaf on a shield atop a sacrificial stand.

158

The porringer is of Italian manufacture and belongs to a common first-century AD type, but the angular profile and the low foot-ring may suggest that it is a second-century variant. Without exact dating evidence in the form of coins or scientific dating methods there will always be difficulties in being precise as to the date of individual tombs such as that of Queen Amanikhatashan (currently dated to AD 62–85); however, as further information emerges from comparative sites regarding the possible dates of the objects found in the tombs, we are slowly edging towards a clearer understanding of the chronology. LAJ

Dunham 1957, 149, pls LIV/A, B; Török 1972, no. 3; 1989, no. 198

158 Skillet handle

Copper alloy

Meroe, Beg. N. 18, Tomb of Queen Amanikhatashan

Second century AD

L 157 mm, D (of shaft) 23 mm

SNM 1825

This copper-alloy, tubular skillet handle has deep longitudinal fluting. At one end, the terminal in the form of a three-dimensional ram's head emerges from a double collar. The features, details of the horns and the curly hair on the back of its head have been incised after moulding. The opposing end also emerges from a double collar and is shaped into a flared, curved plate, the rim of which would have clipped onto the rim of the skillet while the two wings, shaped like stylized griffins' heads, lay against the walls of the skillet.

Ram's head skillets were produced in Italy in the first century AD, but the numbers found in the north-west provinces of the Roman Empire suggest that copies were manufactured elsewhere at a slightly later date. At least six similar handles were found during the excavations at Meroe, but none of the associated, very distinctive, skillets. This may suggest that the handles were valued because of the rams' head terminals. LAJ

Dunham 1957, 151, fig. 97; Török 1989, no. 196

157

KUSHITE RELIGION: ASPECTS OF THE BERLIN EXCAVATIONS AT NAGA

DIETRICH WILDUNG

Theological concepts and religious beliefs can be reflected in pictures, but first of all they find their adequate expression in texts. The basic elements of a history of ancient Egyptian religion are the *Pyramid Texts*, the *Coffin Texts*, the *Book of the Dead*, the hymns and prayers, and the mythological papyri. Without this textual evidence the meaning of the papyrus vignettes, the tomb paintings and temple reliefs would remain ambiguous and cryptic.

A history of Meroitic religion is faced with a language problem. Although the phonetic values of Meroitic hieroglyphs and cursive signs are known, the semantics of Meroitic are still one of the last problems for linguists. Except for the names of divinities and some ritual formulae, Meroitic inscriptions do not reveal their content. In consequence, textual evidence cannot help us much in outlining the structure of the religion of ancient Meroe: it is the language of art that all the more has to assume the essential role of communicating their religious ideas to us.

Funerary beliefs and practices find their highly detailed expression in the reliefs on the offering chapels of the pyramids at Begrawiya (Meroe) and Jebel Barkal, and in their offering plates and stelae. The influence of Egyptian funerary

126 Lion Temple with the lion god Apedemak and other gods receiving the Kushite king Natakamani.

iconography is obvious, but there is no proof that the meaning of a specific motif in Meroitic reliefs is exactly identical with its Egyptian prototype.

The identity of Meroitic gods cannot be simply deduced from their iconography. In the religious iconography of ancient Egypt a human figure with a lion head is normally female and represents goddesses such as Sekhmet, Bastet and Tefnut. Male lion gods – Shu and Mahes – are depicted only rarely. In Meroitic art the male lion god is one of the dominating figures. He represents Apedemak – beside Amun, the most prominent god of the Meroitic kingdom. The Egyptian transcription of his name, 'pa-ir-mek', means 'the protector', but is clearly a simple phonetic pseudo-etymology of a Meroitic name of unknown meaning.

The Lion Temple at Naga (first century AD) provides us with at least five different appearances of Apedemak. On the southern outside wall he is represented as a male human figure with a lion head (fig. 126). In several instances he takes the animal shape of a lion. On the side walls of the pylon he is a snake with a lion head, and human arms and hands, emerging from a lotus flower (fig. 127). The rear wall of the temple shows Apedemak as a male figure with four arms and three lion heads. On the inner walls of the temple he is shown in a Hellenistic style – a draped male figure with a face in front view with a full beard, similar to the iconography of Zeus or Serapis. Three levels of artistic tradition can be distinguished: the human figure with the lion head follows the typically Egyptian prototype of divine iconography; the bearded frontal face shows the influence of Hellenistic and Roman art; and the snake with the lion head is an independent, autonomous creation of Meroitic art.

The seated lion, as represented in the reliefs of the Lion Temple, seems to be the most frequent form of Apedemak: no less than five statues of seated lions have been found at Naga, one of them at a programmatic spot, outside the city proper, most probably on the road leading to Naga. The formal structure of these seated lions corresponds with the monumental lions from Basa (cats 1–2), nowadays re-erected at the entrance of the National Museum at Khartoum and with the lions in front of the first pylon of the Temple of Isis on Philae Island which, in this respect, have a Meroitic touch.

The consort of Apedemak in pure human shape is characterized by a rounded wig surmounted by a double falcon on a crescent, a composition unknown to Egyptian iconography; also unknown in Egypt is the name of this goddess, Amesemi, attested for the first time on a stela found in the hypostyle of the Temple of Amun at Naga (cat. 163).

Although of an appearance familiar in Egyptian iconography, the mummiform shape of a god on the southern outside wall of the Temple of Apedemak at Naga bears the Meroitic name Akedis. Other divinities found at Naga are still without names. The faience figures of a god in the shape of the Egyptian god Bes (cat. 166) most probably had a Meroitic identity, and the toad excavated in the easternmost part of the Temple of Amun (cat. 168) has no equivalent in Egypt, but reminds us of the frog (toad?) statues from Basa.

Animals play a predominant role in the religious iconography of Meroe. Amun – under his Meroitic name Amani – usually presents himself as a ram. The ram avenues leading to the temples of Amun at Meroe and Naga (fig. 102) recall the rams along the south avenue of Karnak and the ram-sphinxes in front of this

127 Lion Temple with Apedemak depicted as a lion-headed snake emerging from a lotus flower.

128 Lintel with the ram-headed Amun inscribed
on it, Temple of Amun.

temple; the immediate parallels can be found at Jebel Barkal, where the Kushite
kings re-erected the rams brought here from the Egyptian New Kingdom Temple of
Soleb. But there is good evidence for the Nubian origin of the ram shape of the
Egyptian Amun. The discrimination of the Egyptian and the Meroitic Amun is the
central motif above the entrance of the Temple of Amun at Naga. On the left side,
looking north, Amun is represented in pure human shape; on the right, facing
south, he has the ram's head (fig. 128).

Another source of iconographical inspiration comes from the Hellenistic and
Roman world. The most evident example at Naga is the so-called Roman Kiosk, a
small chapel in front of the Temple of Apedemak, dating to the first century AD (fig.
129). The Egyptian architectural structure of the intercolumnar walls is combined
with Hellenistic capitals and round arches over the windows; the architectural decoration stretches from uraei and winged sun discs to egg-and-dart and dental patterns.
The two doors of the chapel follow the pattern of the 'Vitruvian portal' with door
openings that narrow towards the top – a typical feature of Meroitic architecture. The
Hathor head on top of the inner door-jambs has its parallels in Meroitic minor arts.

This integration of autochthonous aspects and Hellenistic influences gives one of
the most interesting finds from Naga – a faience statue of the goddess Isis (cat. 167)
– its special importance. At first glance the figure looks purely Hellenistic, comparable to statues of Isis from Ptolemaic and Roman temples. On closer examination, Isis
reveals her Meroitic nature as expressed by her corpulence, following a Meroitic
ideal of female beauty. Is it really Isis? Or has Isis lent her appearance to a genuine
Meroitic goddess, who finally also took over the name of her Egyptian counterpart?

This ambiguity of familiar Egyptian motifs expressing non-Egyptian religious
meanings finds its analogy in the Meroitic writing system. The hieroglyphic forms are
directly borrowed from Egyptian inscriptions, but their phonetic values are different
and their orientation is opposite to the Egyptian direction of writing and reading.

Besides this masking of genuine Meroitic conceptions by Egyptian means of
representation, there is the direct, autonomous expression of Meroitic religion.

The idea of afterlife and immortality finds its visible form in the so-called *ba*-statues (cats 269, 299) – human figures with bird's wings emerging from their shoulders, quite different from the Egyptian *ba*, a bird with human face. At least one of these statues has been found in the necropolis of Naga, proving their existence not only in Lower Nubia, but all over the Meroitic Empire. Without parallel in Egypt is a small group of block statues (cat. 164), found in the Temple of Amun at Naga. Worn off at their sides, they must have been used for some ritual or magical practice. Similar traces of grinding are to be found with highly abstract small sandstone figures of animals – lion, hippopotamus, fish, turtle (?) – discovered at offering places inside the Temple of Amun.

Below the level of official theology, using Egyptian and Hellenistic means of artistic expression must have been the reality of religious practice emerging from an autochthonous tradition. It will take time to isolate the Meroitic stratum from the complex network of foreign influences and to discover behind the surface of temple reliefs the reality of religious practice and popular piety. One of the most intriguing problems of Meroitic religion will eventually find its solution: do basic aspects of Egyptian religion which have been taken over by Meroe originate from the south, from the prehistoric civilizations of Nubia and northern Sudan, thus coming back to their origins after thousands of years in a slightly Egyptianized fashion? More information is needed, to emerge from future excavations and – it is hoped – intelligible Meroitic texts.

129 The so-called Roman Kiosk with the Lion Temple in the background.

159

159 Bark stand

Sandstone

Naga, Temple of Amun, sanctuary, no. 104/1

Kushite (Meroitic), first century AD, reign of King
Natakamani and Queen Amanitore

H 1.323 m, W 855 mm, Th 860 mm

SNM 31331

The bark stand survived undamaged in its
original position in the sanctuary of the
Temple of Amun at Naga. Its shape, proportions and dimensions are almost identical to
three altars of King Natakamani and Queen
Amanitore found by Richard Lepsius in 1844
in the ruins of a temple at Wad ban Naqa.[1]
Under the cavetto cornice, the four sides of
the altar are decorated in relief. The front side
shows the falcon-headed Horus (left) and the
ibis-headed Thoth (right) binding papyrus
plants around the central hieroglyphic
emblem 'sema'. Above this sign two cartouches are placed, crowned by a sun disc
and double ostrich feather. The left (northern) cartouche contains the name of King
Natakamani, while the right (southern) one
the name of Queen Amanitore. Both are
written in Meroitic hieroglyphs.

The hieroglyphic texts in the horizontal
lines above the gods try to imitate Egyptian
texts: 'The lord of the eight, the lord of the
divine word, given life' and 'The lord of
Behedet, the great god, given life' are familiar
epithets of Thoth of Hermopolis and Horus of
Edfu; but both texts are nothing but a poor
graphic imitation of an original written in
Egyptian. This original, an altar of King
Atlanersa who lived 650 years before the
erection of the Temple of Amun at Naga,[2]
stood in Temple B700 at Jebel Barkal. The
same motif is repeated on the rear of the altar
(Wildung and Kroeper 2003), this time with
Horus on the right and Thoth on the left side;
the orientation of the cartouches follows the
pattern of the front side with the king to the
north and the queen to the south.

Reliefs on the right and left sides of the
bark stand are divided into two registers.
Below, two Nile gods are binding the papyrus
plants around the sema with the queen's
second – Egyptian – name Meri-ka-ra on the
south and the king's second – Egyptian –
cartouche Kheper-ka-ra on the north. Above,
on both sides, three kneeling male figures
with raised arm, jackal-headed and falcon-
headed, with the same Egyptian hieroglyphic
text 'the souls of Pe', are preceded by a

kneeling figure of the king and the goddess
Meret. This decoration is the standard iconography of bark stands in Egyptian temples
since the New Kingdom.

Egyptian iconography has become an
expression of Kushite royal ideology: the unification of Upper and Lower Egypt, symbolized by the sema motif (cf. motif on cat. 76), is
the emblematic sign of political and cosmic
order under the control of Kushite kingship.
A close parallel to this decoration can be
found on the altar in the Great Temple of

Amun in Meroe (M 260). In perfectly cut
relief of a strong three-dimensional effect,
these figures show a stylistic modification of
the Egyptian prototype into a clearly Meroitic
artistic expression with heavy limbs and
coarse proportions. The Egyptian and the
Meroitic elements merge in an artistic creation in its own right.   DW

1 Cf. Priese 1997a.

2 Cf. Wenig 1978b, 58, fig. 34, MFA Boston 23.728.

Wildung and Kroeper 2003, cover

159

160

160 Glazed leopard tile

Faience

Naga, interior of the Temple of Apedemak
(Lion Temple), near shrine, excav. no. 301/2

Kushite (Meroitic), first century AD

H 100 mm, W 80 mm, Th 15 mm

SNM 28045

Found near the pedestal of the shrine inside
the Temple of Apedemak (the Lion Temple),
this tile may have been an inlay of the wooden
naos. The border with its dotted line most
probably surrounded the tile on all four sides.
The pattern of the leopard's hide, yellowish
against the turquoise background, is indicated
by impressed round dots. The tail follows the
contour of the left hind leg. The upright
position of the seated animal is full of visible
tension – a masterly representation of the
feline body as a symbol of royal power.   DW

Leclant and Clerc 1997, pl. XLIX, fig. 67; Wildung
1997, 362, no. 433; 1998, 184, pl. IIb; 1999, 46
and 49, fig. 44

161 Plaque bearing the name of Queen Amanitore

Faience

Naga, Temple of Amun, Room 107, excav. no.
107/19

Kushite (Meroitic), first century AD

H 45 mm, W 40 mm, Th 6 mm

SNM 31335

The upper part of this thin rectangular faience
plaque has two round holes at its corners –
apparently for fixing or stitching it to a support. The border is decorated with a braiding of
oval dots in low relief. The vertical inscription
inside this frame is written in Egyptian hiero-

glyphs and reads 'the daughter of Isis, Meri-
[ka-]Ra'. The name, encircled by a cartouche,
is the throne-name of Queen Amanitore.

Kushite kings, queens and princes sometimes added to their personal name an Egyptian name, taken from the list of the pharaohs
of the past. Thus, King Natakamani in his
Egyptian name Kheper-ka-Ra hearkens back
to Nektanebo I (380–362 BC) or to Senwosret
I (1918–1875 BC), a name already used by
the Napatan ruler Malowiebamani (FHN I
301–2). Amanitore's throne name Meri-ka-
Ra recalls a king of the First Intermediate
Period (*c.* 2050 BC), but has its immediate
forerunner in King Aspelta's first name Meri-
ka-Ra. Although any precise historical
knowledge can be excluded, these references
to the past are part of the self-consciousness

161

of the rulers of Kush – from the 25th Dynasty
down to the Meroitic era. Their historiography included pharaonic Egypt as a part of
Kushite history.   DW

162 Stela

Sandstone

Naga, Temple of Apedemak (Lion Temple),
excav. no. 301/4

Kushite (Meroitic), first century AD

H 112 mm, W 104 mm, Th 18 mm

SNM 27499

This fragment belongs to a small stela originally
representing three figures. The woman on the
right wears a short curled wig and a diadem
with two uraei, crowned by the white and red
crown. On her head a part of the claw of a
falcon is preserved, enough to reconstruct the
headdress typical for Apedemak's consort, the
goddess Amesemi (cat. 163), a double falcon
on a crescent. A garment with fringed sleeves,
a broad collar and a bracelet complete her costume. Her raised left hand presents the *ankh*
sign to a person facing her; only the right
hand of this figure is preserved. The extremely
long fingernails of both persons are characteristic of women; therefore the figure on the left

of the fragment must be a queen. The *ankh*
sign in the uppermost left corner of the fragment is attached to a curved line descending
from above, most probably from a sceptre held
over the queen by another figure on the
extreme left, a god. The symmetrical composition showed the queen between Amesemi and
Apedemak. A stela found in the sanctuary of
the Amun Temple at Naga (Carrier 2000
(REM 1293), 5–6, 26–7, figs 17–19) presents
the same arrangement. On the reverse, seven
lines of a cursive Meroitic inscription mention
a name 'Aman[...]', either Amanitore or
Amanishakheto (cat. 163), and the epithet
'the good one in heaven'.   DW

Carrier 1999, 3 (REM 1238), 19, fig. 13; Priese
1997b, 263, no. 285; 1998, 217, 219, pl. I; Wildung
1998, 184; 1999, 48, fig. 41

163 Stela of Queen Amanishakheto and the goddess Amesemi

Sandstone

Naga, Temple of Amun, Hypostyle (101),
excav. no. 101/19

Kushite (Meroitic), late first century BC

H 255 mm, W 140 mm

SNM 31338

The front of this round-topped small stela,
found between the fallen columns of the
hypostyle hall in the Temple of Amun at
Naga, is decorated in sunk relief of high technical and artistic quality. Under the winged

162

sun-disc filling the upper fourth of the stela, two female figures are represented facing each other. Both are wearing a close-fitting dress descending to the feet, a fringed scarf over the right shoulder, a broad collar and a round curled wig. Otherwise they are represented in very different ways. The left figure has a slim, elegant body; the dress shows a fine pattern of diagonal stripes and dotted lines. A chin-band, an earring, an ornamented diadem with uraeus and a crown consisting of a pair of falcons with sun-discs sitting on a crescent contrast with the pleated dress and the simple diadem of the extremely corpulent woman on the right.

The inscriptions in Meroitic hieroglyphs identify the left figure as Amesemi, the divine consort of the lion god Apedemak (the first complete reference to this name) and the figure to the right as Amanishakheto (with-out cartouche), the well-known Meroitic queen buried in Pyramid N.6 at Begrawiya.

The goddess plays the active part: her right hand supports the elbow of the queen's right arm, raised in adoration of Amesemi; her left arm passes behind the queen, the left hand supports the neck of the queen, and a dotted line, starting at the tip of the forefinger, surrounds the head of the queen to her forehead. A chain consisting of tiny *ankh* signs extends from Amesemi's nose to the nose of Amanishakheto. This animation by the divine breath is illustrated in a similar way in the reliefs of the Lion Temple at Naga.

The rear and the sides of the stela have fifteen lines of text in cursive Meroitic, topped on the rear by a line in Egyptian hieroglyphs without specific meaning. In his still unpublished analysis of the Meroitic text Claude Rilly (letter of 8 September 2000) states the 'feeling of frustration' of the philologist in front of such a well-preserved inscription, but he succeeds at least in defining the character of the text as a religious hymn.

Not only does the text keep its secret, but an important historical question also remains open: why and how was a stela of Queen Amanishakheto, dated about sixty years before Natakamani and Amanitore, donated to the Temple of Amun at Naga, a structure not yet in existence during the lifetime of this queen? Do we have to rethink the sequence of Meroitic rulers? DW

Carrier 2000, 6 (REM 1294) 7, 28–30, figs 20–23; Leclant and Minault-Gout 2000, pl. XXXIII, no. 29; Wildung 2001, 150–51, fig. 15; 2002, fig. 10; Wildung and Kroeper 2003, 33, fig. 4

163: front

163: rear

164a–c

164 Block statues

Sandstone

Naga, Temple of Amun, Room 107, excav. nos 107/1, 107/2, 107/3

Kushite (Meroitic), first–second centuries AD

a H 185 mm, W 93 mm, Th 128 mm

b H 175 mm, W 61 mm, Th 134 mm

c H 210 mm, W 84 mm

SNM 31332a–c

No less than six small block statues and the head of a seventh have been found inside and near the Temple of Amun at Naga, some of them – like the royal statues (cat. 170) – carefully hidden in safe corners. The statue type goes back to the cube statue introduced into Egyptian sculpture at about 1950 BC (cf. cat. 77) and frequently used – mainly as temple statues – until the Ptolemaic period; besides these statues from Naga, this type is otherwise not known in Meroitic art. The style of these small sculptures is also unparalleled. Sculpted in a local workshop, they do not correspond to the stylistic expression of Meroitic art as represented in relief and sculpture of the urban centres, and are unrelated to Egyptian or Hellenistic influences. Their deeply 'African' expression relates them visually to sculptures in West Africa (Nok, Ife) and assigns them a place at the beginnings of African art.

The function of these small block statues remains unclear. All of them show traces of rubbing and have lost the original surfaces on both sides. Most probably they were used in a ritual, where ground sandstone from these statues was produced for magical practices (cf. Traunecker 1987, 221–42).   DW

Wildung 2001, 150, fig. 16; 2002, nos 17, 18, 20, pls 8.1-8, 9.1-4; Wildung and Kroeper 2003, 36, fig. 9

165 Statuette of a god

Granite

Naga, Temple of Amun, Room 103 and Sanctuary (104), excav. nos 103/6, 104/3

Kushite (Meroitic), first–second centuries AD

H 438 mm, W 161 mm, Th 219 mm

SNM 31337

Some of the statues excavated in the Amun Temple at Naga are almost purely Egyptian in structure, iconography and style. This lower part of a male striding figure, whose two parts have been found at two different points in the temple, follows in its base and back pillar, and in the position of the advanced left foot, traditional Egyptian patterns. Unusual are the disproportionately large feet and the lotus flower held in the left fist.

The *ankh* sign in the right hand identifies the figure as the representation of a god, most probably Amun. Since the feet and bases of a very similar granite statue of identical dimensions (109/1) were found in a sideroom of the same temple, one may assume they made up a pair of statues, one showing Amun in purely human form, the other with the head of a ram (cf. cat. 147).   DW

Wildung 2002, no. 1, figs 2–3, pl. 1.1-4

165

166c

166a

166b

166 Statuettes of Bes

Faience

Naga, Temple of Amun, Room 107,
excav. nos 107/12, 107/9, 107/13

Kushite (Meroitic), first–second centuries AD

a H 190 mm, W 81 mm, Th 50 mm

b H 136 mm, W 80 mm, Th 50 mm

c H 123 mm, W 80 mm, Th 50 mm

SNM 31334a–c

The dwarf-shaped god Bes, in Egyptian religion the protector of mother and child, has
his roots according to Egyptian texts on the
Upper Nile: 'Lord of Punt' and 'Ruler of
Nubia' are his epithets. These faience figures,
relief plaques rather than sculptures, show
him in frontal view with his horrifying gri-
mace combining aspects of a human face and
a lion head, surmounted by a feather-crown.
The extremely large heads with widely open
eyes distinguish these Bes figures from the
Egyptian type (cf. cats 142–3, 285). Horizontal
holes passing through the rear of the figures
served for fixing them on a support.   DW

Wildung and Kroeper 2003, 36, fig. 10

167 Statuette of Isis with Horus child

Faience

Naga, Temple of Amun, Room 107, excav. no. 107/5

Kushite (Meroitic), first–second centuries AD

H 100 mm, W 49 mm, Th 80 mm

SNM 31333

Two aspects of Meroitic art are combined in
this small statue of Isis in blue-green faience.
The Egyptian iconography of the divine
mother holding the Horus child on her lap,
presenting to him her left breast and wearing
the tripartite wig and cow horns with the sun-
disc, is integrated into the stumpy figure with
proportionally large head and short neck, and
a rough face with big ears – obviously the
product of a Meroitic workshop using its
specific means of stylistic expression.   DW

Wildung 2002, no. 6, pl. 3.1-4

167

168 Statue of a toad

Sandstone

Naga, Temple of Amun, Room 105, excav. no. 105/1

Kushite (Meroitic), first–second centuries AD

H 255 mm, W 136 mm, Th 138 mm

SNM 31336

This large-scale statue of a toad is clearly distinguished from the representation of a frog by the pattern on the back – small circles indicating the warts. The animal cranes its head and exposes between the forelegs its belly with a pattern representing the soft skin. The eyes are large globular protruberances. The position of the hindlegs indicates its readiness to jump forward. In its reduction to the basic forms this highly expressive statue is a masterpiece not only of Meroitic sculpture, but of animal sculpture in general.

The significance of this animal may be related to that of the frog in Egyptian religion, where it is connected with the primeval water, creation and birth. Frogs are a motif on painted Meroitic pottery (Wenig 1978b, 299, no. 255; Wildung 1997, 350, no. 412) and on late Meroitic bronze vessels (Wildung

1997, 384, no. 455); they take monumental dimensions in the frog statues from Basa.[1]   DW

1 Cf. Porter and Moss 1951, 262; Hinkel 1978, pl. 21

168

169 Offering basin

Sandstone

Naga, interior of Temple of Apedemak (Lion Temple), excav. no. 301/1

Kushite (Meroitic), first century AD

H 101 mm, L 722 mm, W 300 mm

SNM 27500

This oblong rectangular basin, damaged at both ends, has a central rosette, flanked by two *ankh* signs and these in turn by four-petalled blossoms. These motifs are executed in high, narrow bridges against the deeply recessed background. They are drilled through at several areas to let water flow over the basin. The flowers swimming on the water-table were – together with the *ankh* signs – an impressive symbol of life and prosperity. Similar sandstone offering basins have been found at Naga *in situ* in front of the shrine of the Lion Temple, on the altar in the open Courtyard 106 and in the sanctuary of the Temple of Amun. The shape of the *ankh* with the central circle and the triangular branches is typically Meroitic.   DW

Wildung 1997, 361, no. 432; 1999, 50, fig. 45

169

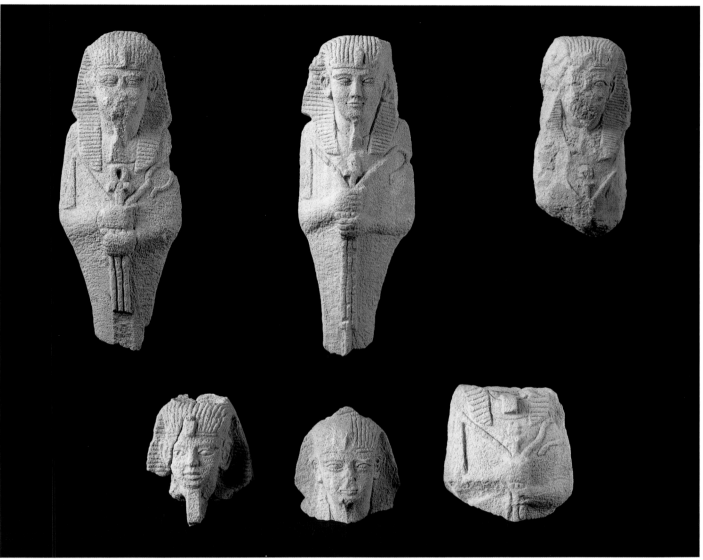

170a–c, top; 170d–f, bottom

170 Statuettes of King Natakamani

Sandstone

Naga, Temple of Amun, excav. nos 151/1, 151/2, 104/5, 146/1, 146/2, 101/25

Kushite (Meroitic), first century AD

a H 380 mm, W 133 mm, Th 138 mm

b H 140 mm, W 119 mm, Th 126 mm

c H 168 mm, W 145 mm, Th 123 mm

d H 377 mm, W 131 mm, Th 135 mm

e H 132 mm, W 121 mm, Th 109 mm

f H 165 mm, W 77 mm, Th 95 mm

SNM 30115a, 30115b, 31339b, 30116a, 30116b, 31339a

Fragments of several small royal statues in sandstone have been found at different locations inside and outside the Temple of Amun at Naga, some of them obviously deposited carefully behind altars and under fallen blocks. Originally they belonged to the ram statues, forming a monumental avenue in front of the temple. On all of these twelve statues (and on a thirteenth one behind the temple) the feet of the royal figures can still be seen between the forelegs of the rams. The prototype of these ram statues with royal figures in front can be found in Soleb, in the ram avenue of Amenhotep III. These rams, reused by King Taharko at Temple B 500 of Jebel Barkal, apparently served as direct models for the Naga rams – another case of the close connection between Naga and Napata (cat. 159).

The king is represented in mummiform shape, wearing the *nemes* headdress (the only attestation in Meroitic art) and the royal beard, and holding in his fists the *heqa*-crook, the flail and an *ankh*-sceptre descending to the feet. This iconography is the royal version of the canonical appearance of the god Khonsu, the son of Amun. The close-fitting cap and side-plait of Khonsu are replaced by the *nemes*, thus making the king the son of Amun, protected by his father in animal form.

Although all these statues belong to a uniform complex representing the same person, King Natakamani, the workmanship and style of the faces is very variable. Different artists cover the stylistic range, from idealizing faces to a clearly 'African' expression.   DW

Leclant and Clerc 1998, pl. XLVII, no. 52; Wildung 2002, nos 7–14; 1999, 60–64, figs 56–61; Wildung and Kroeper 2003, 37, fig. 12.

9

THE PRE-CHRISTIAN EMPIRE AND KINGDOMS

PATRICE LENOBLE

Past excavation of the *qore's* (kings') pyramids and the tombs of the social elite enabled the creation of a chronology for the Kushite Empire. Sovereigns' pyramids of the imperial dynasty were probably all investigated in succession on four sites. Secondary pyramids and *mastabas* were also examined on these sites and in Lower Nubia, revealing numerous lower-ranking dignitaries, viceroys in particular. There is little hope of shedding more light on this chronology without further information concerning the empire's political organization, the order and exact length of the reigns, vicissitudes caused by possible divisions and temporary extensions or successions. The chronology stops in the fourth century AD because the construction of pyramids in the southern capital ceased at this point. Victory texts found at Aksum and at Meroe (cat. 155) lead one to suppose that the Meroitic Empire was subjugated by the Aksumite Empire at this time and consequently its funerary tradition came to a halt.

The two centuries preceding the Christianization of the Middle Nile attest to the disappearance of imperial pyramid necropolises and the substitution of several cemeteries with mounds of exceptional size. One may record at least fourteen such sites along the valley (fig. 130). Five are well known in the Nubian desert following the numerous surveys and excavations upstream from Sadd el Ali (Aswan High Dam); all others in the Sahel await work with only rare and modest soundings undertaken hitherto. A royal chronology for Nubia was recently created for the fourth and fifth centuries AD.[1]

In the richest provinces one may foresee the discovery of important necropolises, either now poorly known or as yet unknown. The poverty of the southern documentation hinders any detailed description of the evolution of a unified Kushite Empire into the three kingdoms successively Christianized in the sixth century AD.

THE PROBLEMATIC IDENTIFICATION OF PRE-CHRISTIAN SOVEREIGNTY

Due to general pillaging, a funerary crown has never been found beneath a pyramid. Nevertheless, it is not difficult to recognize Kushite rulers' graves. *Qore* and dignitaries maintained royal workshops (scribes, architects, masons, sculptors, painters, bronzesmiths, etc.) for the creation of royal propaganda. Dozens of inscriptions and representations from funerary chapel reliefs and objects buried in the graves name and depict sovereigns and dignitaries, and help us to reconstruct the hierarchy and the prosopography of the Empire.

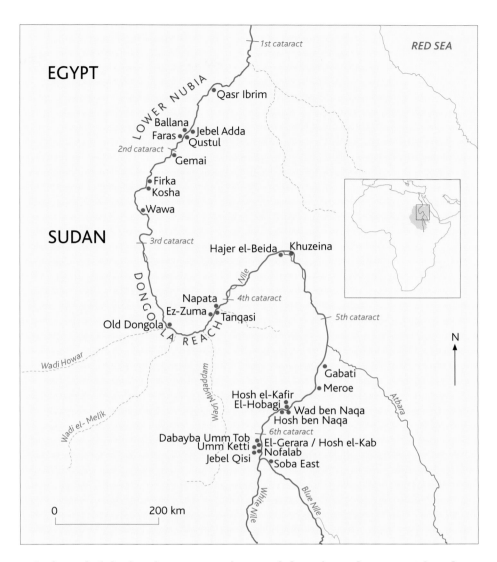

130 Map of Post-Meroitic sites mentioned in the text.

At the end of the fourth century AD these workshops focused on essential products (ceramics, bronzework, iron weapons and tools), a consequence of unknown events altering political and sacerdotal functions. Faced with the relative lack of texts and scenes, archaeologists can hardly palliate the effects of plundering and are unable to determine with any certitude the rank of the individuals buried beneath the extraordinary tumuli. Among the above-mentioned sites, only Ballana[2] yielded crowns, either due to favourable local environmental conditions or to the success of architectural features in concealing the deceased and their precious regalia.

It is thus necessary to try to determine the political meaning of important graves from the equipment of the funerary ceremonies, and to identify the insignia and symbols from among the collections of objects, animal and human skeletons buried in the *hypogea* of the social elite. The purpose is to distinguish the sovereigns, then to classify their reigns[3] so as to create a theory explaining the political evolution.[4]

THE FUNERARY IMAGE OF PRE-CHRISTIAN SOVEREIGNTY

Emblems of sovereignty may first be sought amongst the weaponry formerly depicted in Meroitic reliefs. On several sites rare weapons, such as spears with very

131 Imperial spear
with long blade (detail).

132 Tumulus el-Hobagi III:
weapons placed around the
bed of the deceased.

134 The imperial spears ruling over 'the Bows',
Meroe Pyramid N1, chapel north wall (bows).

135a Tumulus el-Hobagi VI/1,
grave (quivers of arrows).

135b Tumulus B95,
grave (archers' looses).

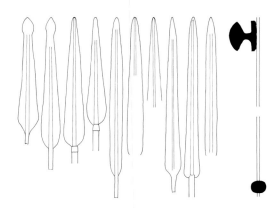

133 Tumulus el-Hobagi III: triumphal weapons
(ten iron spear-blades, one iron axe, one stone macehead).

136 Sacrifice of horses and
camels in the funerary complex
of Qustul 36.

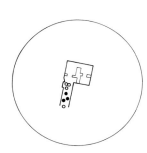

long blades (figs 131–3),[5] axes, swords and maceheads that evolved from ancient models (fig. 134),[6] signify the *imperium* and celebrate the warlike charisma of the sovereign. They also show the participation, along with other bodies, of those responsible for the arsenal in the funerary ceremony.[7] On the other hand, scattered arms, pieces of archery equipment, arrows and quivers at el-Hobagi (fig. 135a and b), and archers' rings at Meroe and Ballana symbolize the enemy 'bows' which, according to a thousand years of iconography, represent conquered or vanquished peoples.[8] The deceased, actually wearing pieces of archery equipment, ring, armband, and quiver, is dressed up as a military head of the empire.

Through anthropological analysis of the animal sacrifices one can recognize the same triumphant propaganda. The slaughter of many mounts (horses, camels and donkeys) (figs 136–7, cat. 172) is to be understood as an exaltation of the sovereign virtue, singling out the sacrifice of the victorious animals, isolated or in groups, from the dismemberment of vanquished animals.[9] This type of sacrifice developed from a sporadically practised ritual possibly initiated in the second century BC. Though more controversial,[10] the sacrifice of a dog supports this interpretation, whether it be through rarely depicted packs of hounds representing a royal war-related hunt, or the killing of one or two dogs, Kushite symbols of royal power.[11] According to the same tradition cow sacrifice, at times accompanied by a calf,[12] signifies divine tutelage, another component of royal charisma. Divine milking is illustrated by specific silver receptacles, breast-shaped cups or feeding cups.[13]

Following the same logic, funerary killings, described as human sacrifices and thus far understood as part of the domestic equipment (retainers, spouses and concubines) required for a sovereign's afterlife, now may receive a triumphal interpretation. The concept of prisoner massacre,[14] a rite with Kushite origins, has met with some objection[15] when it concerns a small number of individuals or a diadem-bearer who might be seen as an executed rebel or challenger to the throne.

Buried objects consist chiefly of vessels, with important graves including hundreds of containers. The representation of the funerary rite in the pyramid chapels suggests offerings to a deified deceased or to divinities, but its styling as a 'funerary banquet' may be misleading.[16] Analysis should decipher the details. The first results indicate a coherent series of events. Function is interpreted according to various religious gestures, purifying or sanctifying, such as censing,[17] making libations,[18] libations performed over trays of cups or goblets,[19] and divine milking (cats 171, 174).[20] Despite the lack of funerary inscriptions, a number of symbolic motifs clarify the liturgy practised.[21] Lastly, the quality of ritual vessels, either specially made or imported[22] for funerals (cat. 171), and the quantity of beverages and food, are important for assessing the rank of the deceased.

Other rare insignia may be explained as symbols of power. Folding chairs from Qustul and Ballana, along with two instances at Meroe, demonstrate the alliance with the Roman/Byzantine Empire and the status of federate sovereignty. Other interesting items recognized among the imported objects may be diplomatic gifts originating from Byzantine largesses or embassies, such as, for instance, an imperial portrait from Gemai and Christian artefacts from Ballana.

All these analyses still do not allow one to categorically distinguish the last rulers from other dignitaries of the imperial sphere or court. Weapons of significance, the immolation of animals and the slaughter of prisoners are intermingled among the tombs of the titulars and delegates of the *imperium*. Several rare weapons and animal sacrifices are found in some ordinary graves. Nevertheless, the hierarchy of the burials can be justified by the significant accumulation of emblems within a tomb and leaves opportunities for limited discussion.[23]

The meaning of the ceremonial funerals of the *qore* of the pre-Christian era becomes obvious. Equipped with insignia, publicly exposed on a funerary couch, and honoured with sacrifices, sacraments and the corresponding political propaganda, the body is the subject of an imperial *salutatio*. It is sufficient to evoke the dignitaries of the empire walking in the funerary parade, as suggested in the funerary chapels of Meroe,[24] to recognize a liturgy comparable to the Graeco-Roman *proskynesis*. Through this public salutation, the social hierarchy demonstrated its obedience to the successor, who led the burial of Osiris (the deceased ruler) and was recognized as the new Horus (legitimate successor).

THE SPREAD OF PRE-CHRISTIAN SOVEREIGNTY

Funerary propaganda rapidly evolved during the fourth century AD, stressing warlike virtues and praising triumphal charisma. This changing behaviour reflects a troubled period which was adapting the Kushite tradition of succession and founding a new imperial legitimacy based upon political values pertaining to the Mediterranean world. The spread of ostentatious warlike insignia enables the provinces of the empire to be differentiated and verifies the division of a territory formerly united.

137 El-Hobagi III, the sacrifice of a horse with harness, with iron bit and bronze bell (cat. 172).

In the south, during the fourth century AD, Meroe provides evidence for the progressive end of pyramid construction. The imperial North Cemetery for *qore* is the first to go out of use some time between AD 320 and 350, according to various authors. The West Cemetery, for secondary dignitaries, local kings[25] and victors lasts until AD 360–70.[26] The latter becomes a mound cemetery, the beginning of which is dated to the fourth century AD by ceramics,[27] and contains several triumphal tombs as determined by the presence of emblematic weapons. Exceptional tumuli appear on the left bank at el-Hobagi, similarly dated to the fourth century AD, and upstream of the Sixth Cataract at Jebel Qisi, Nofalab, and Umm Ketti, the dates and equipment of which remain unpublished (fig. 138).

In the north around AD 370–80 huge tumuli were constructed at Qustul on the right bank. These contained a great number of triumphal insignia. In AD 410–20

138 Exceptionally large burial tumuli at Jebel Qisi.

this necropolis moved to Ballana on the left bank, adding imperial crowns and secondary diadems to the regalia known at Qustul. It remained in use until AD 500, but the period following leading up to the Christianization of Nobadia is unknown. The sites of Gemai, Firka and Kosha which display elite characteristics should be inserted into the chronology built from Qustul and Ballana, while those at Wawa remain undocumented.

Between the north and south, near Jebel Barkal, nothing is known about the contents of the tombs at Tanqasi[28] and ez-Zuma. Upstream from the Fourth Cataract, the sites of Hajer el-Beida and Khuzeina have not been investigated.

In conclusion, seven sites spread between Nubia and the central Sudan have burials which exhibit the symbols of sovereignty. Due to the current state of field investigation, political development may be interpreted only in Nubia. The twin sites of Qustul and Ballana contain more than half of the imperial graves known, but as the royal capital of Meroe was still functioning when Qustul appeared, there is no need to imagine an end to Meroe or movement of the imperial throne to the Faras region, an area which served as a temporary seat of Meroitic viceroyalty and which became around AD 543 the capital of the northernmost Christian kingdom. It is enough to acknowledge the secession of Lower Nubia, dated at the latest from the appearance of funerary crowns at Ballana. If Meroe had been weakened by the Aksumites previously, this secession would be a restoration (*restitution*) in the style of contemporary Mediterranean politics, most probably inspired and triggered by a powerful neighbour. It certainly made Meroe weaker by reducing her diplomatic influence and her access to prestigious products and Mediterranean craftsmen. From this point onward, Faras controlled trade with Egypt and benefited from occasional alliances with the Roman/Byzantine Empire, whose constant policy was to protect its frontiers by federating and Christianizing bordering barbaric ethnic groups.

The evolution in other regions cannot yet receive such a detailed interpretation. Administrative continuity must be stressed. Meroe remained the capital of an empire diminished in the north but extended on the left bank, as demonstrated at least at el-Hobagi. The town retained its urban necropolis which continued to honour the elite near the city and relegated hundreds of thousands of ordinary tumuli to its distant outskirts, including the left bank of the Nile. These numerous graves do not yet provide a chronology of the pre-Christian period. The date of the transfer of the court towards Soba East, the capital of the southernmost Christian kingdom Christianized about AD 580, is unknown. The fate of Napata, situated near Jebel Barkal, a temporary seat of intermittent Kushite kinglets that are still poorly defined, is less known and the late transfer towards Old Dongola, converted to Christianity around AD 570, is not documented.

THE RISE OF ETHNIC PHENOMENA

Funerary inscriptions grow rare, but even if particular graves remain unidentified, several *qore* and other pre-Christian dignitaries are named in triumphal inscriptions or diplomatic letters that are fortunately preserved.[29] These texts, written in foreign languages such as Greek, Ge'ez and Coptic, provide ethnonyms and related territories, while texts written in Meroitic, including the latest ones, mention administrative units and functions taken from towns and religious domains.

Kasu, Beja, Blemmyes, and Noba are named in various ways. Some Roman writers report that the latter once lived in kingdoms on the left bank independent of Meroitic rule, but archaeology does not record any monument, specific tomb, or pottery which can be associated with them.[30] While the tombs at el-Hobagi and south of the Sixth Cataract might contain ethnarchs or local Noba sovereigns, just as those at Qustul are tombs of Nobades, they obviously demonstrate a lasting continuity with the Kushite culture and empire.

Since each one of the ethnic groups or nations has its own history and is in itself a singular historical object, a concept proposed by Updegraff,[31] much work still needs to be done to understand the change which, over two centuries, transformed Meroitic imperial ideology. This metamorphosis is above all due to complex social evolution, but also to the political influence of the peoples of its powerful neighbouring country. At least the archaeology of the period, as a result of the Nubian UNESCO campaign, has rewritten a cursory historiography,[32] invalidated by the facts, which characterized the Roman concept of barbarism and ethnicity in undefined 'tribalism'.

The adaptation of Mediterranean political principles by the Meroitic court during the fourth and fifth centuries AD, and the secular search for an alliance with Rome, prepared the way for the progressive abandonment of the religious foundations of the late Kushite Meroitic state in the fifth century AD and for Christianization in the sixth century. The political principles maintained the Upper Nile Empire and the succeeding kingdoms within the Mediterranean zone of influence with which they were originally linked.

1 Török 1988.
2 Török 1988, 169–73; 1987a, 55–61.
3 Török 1988, 78–81.
4 Lenoble 1999b.
5 Török 1988, 80; Lenoble 1994a, 97–9.
6 Lenoble 1994a, 99–101.
7 Lenoble in press 1.
8 Lenoble 1997; 1999b.
9 Török 1988, 79–80; 1999, 137–9; Lenoble 1994b.
10 Török 1999, 139, n. 61.
11 Lenoble 1991a.
12 Lenoble 1994c.
13 Lenoble 2003a.
14 Lenoble 1996a.
15 Török 1999, 137–9.
16 Török 1999, 137.
17 Lenoble 1998, 138–9.
18 Lenoble 1996b, 153–5.
19 Lenoble 1991b, 248–9.
20 Lenoble 2003a.
21 Lenoble 1999b, 172–80; in press 2; Dissaux et al. 1997.
22 Edwards 1996; Török 1988.
23 For instance, Williams (1991a, 4–5) adds several royal graves at Qustul and wants to modify the date of one tomb at Ballana.
24 Chapman and Dunham 1952.
25 Rilly 2001.
26 Török 1974; 1988; 1999; 2003.
27 Lenoble 1992a.
28 Shinnie 1964.
29 Eide et al. 1998.
30 Lenoble 1992a.
31 Updegraff 1978; 1988.
32 Lenoble 2003a.

EL-HOBAGI

PATRICE LENOBLE

El-Hobagi is located approximately 70 km upstream of Meroe, on the left bank, equidistant from two Meroitic urban areas located on the right bank, Wad ban Naqa and Hosh ben Naqa. Between the flood plain and the eroded relief of the sandstone hills and iron-rich outcrops, the site is situated on the gravel terrace at the Wadi Fazar confluence, one of the numerous wadis which drain the hinterland and cross large basins that retain run-off water. This sahelian savannah is today utilized for animal husbandry, as well as rain and riverine agriculture. Far removed from the massive rocks of the Fifth and Sixth Cataracts, el-Hobagi is not distinguished by geography from the abundant sites of human occupation found on the left bank of the river.

In contrast to the opposite bank, obvious ruins are lacking here, but paradoxically the ancient settlement

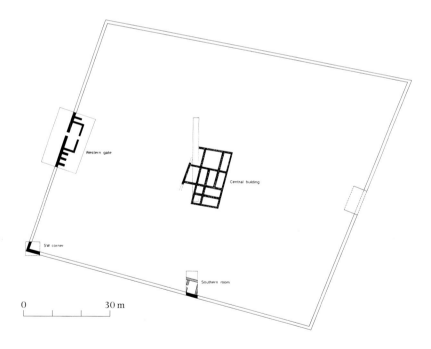

139 Plan of Hosh el-Kafir.

pattern may be detected particularly through the location of graves. The gravel terrace and the hinterland ridges are occupied by tens of thousands of tumuli, the density of which increases closer to Meroe. A large tumuli field, numbering two to three hundred structures, marks the centre of the modern village of el-Hobagi; a dozen other comparable cemeteries are

recorded in the vicinity. Most of these graves seem to date to the pre-Christian and Christian periods.

Thus far, according to survey and soundings, eight monuments draw particular attention to this locality. The first one, Hosh el-Kafir, consists of the remains of an edifice, situated in the bed of the Wadi Fazar (fig. 139). A wall roughly 1 m thick, built of unworked slabs and earth mortar, delimits a quadrilateral area 1 ha. in size. Two narrow openings in the middle of the western and eastern sides give access, each through a large rectangular room serving as a gate tower, and are built from the same materials. Contiguous habitation units, built of large-sized bricks and silt mortar, back on to the stone wall along the north and south sides. Successive work spaces along the east and west sides are delimited by small walls of bricks and slabs. In the middle of the enclosure only the stone foundation of a twelve-roomed building, formerly built of bricks or earth, remains (fig. 140).

Hosh el-Kafir is not readily comparable with known temples situated in the middle of a peribolus, and even less so with palaces. The possibility that it might be a caravanserai is hindered by the lack of stores and the narrowness of the gates. Although only 4 per cent of its interior was excavated, the edifice chiefly yielded settlement artefacts (abundant faunal remains resulting from animal husbandry and numerous grinding stone fragments) and those related to military activity (iron arrowheads and stone archers' thumb-rings, iron slag, moulds and crucibles associated with a forge belonging to the royal arsenal). The first soundings suggest an interpretation of the architectural complex as a military camp, comparable with Roman *castra*, even if the walls lack the expected bastions. By highlighting the survival of masons and smiths attached to the Meroitic sovereign power, this edifice bears witness to a persisting State in the fourth century AD.

The other archaeological monuments at el-Hobagi are funerary (fig. 141). Seven mounds, 30–40 m in diameter, are scattered across the gravel terrace, in relation to the location of ferrous conglomerate stone outcrops, over a distance of roughly 5 km. Despite rain and pillaging, these mounds still rise to a height of 4 m, and are situated inside elliptic enclosures 50–70 m in size. Walls encircling the funerary peribolus were built

140 Hosh el-Kafir,
the central building.

141 An unexcavated
tumulus.

142 Tumulus VI during excavation.

of stone blocks and slabs laid without mortar. These were dismantled in modern times.

The contents of the main burials of two of these seven exceptional tumuli were partially excavated by the National Corporation for Antiquities and Museums (fig. 142). The deceased was laid on a funerary couch around which were deposited numerous symbolic weapons: quivers containing bronze or iron-headed arrows (cf. fig. 132), archers' looses, swords, a

143 Dignitaries and musicians depicted on bronze basin HBG VI/1/21 (SNM 26313).

macehead, axes, javelins, and a dozen tall lances with long iron blades, copper-alloy heels and wooden shafts decorated with beads (cf. figs 131–5a and b). Small receptacles used for various libations and censing were deposited after the armament: they form two of the richest Meroitic collections of bronze cups, goblets and basins. Many of them were engraved (fig. 143, cat. 171). Dozens of large wheel-made or hand-made ceramic vessels, each with a capacity of around 40 litres, complete the burial equipment. Other remains, such as a horse harness and bell (cat. 172), and parts of bovid skulls with horns, suggest the possibility of animal sacrifices, but as the excavation of the tumuli and enclosures was incomplete this cannot be proven.

The disappearance of the skeleton of the deceased in one case, and its reduction to fragments in another, suggest that the bodies were stripped of ornaments by looters who left only rare fragments of precious materials, such as ivory or silver, numerous beads and a bronze shield-ring.

The walled tumulus and associated architectural remains, which ceramics and radiocarbon date to the fourth century AD, illustrate an assemblage at el-Hobagi which cannot be defined with any certainty as there has been insufficient exploration conducted thus far. Further excavation will determine whether Hosh el-Kafir is related to the performance and the renewal of funerary rites in the nearby cemetery, or whether it served to protect the seven tumuli which were plundered after it was abandoned. Complete excavation of the tumuli will determine whether or not seven generations are interred here, and whether the use of this small cemetery precedes, succeeds or coincides with the desertion of the pyramid fields at Meroe.

All of the aforementioned features find an exact Sahelian equivalent south of the Sixth Cataract, spread over several districts but again located on the left bank: the walled tumuli at Jebel Qisi (fig. 138), large tumuli at Nofalab and Umm Ketti, the military camp of Hosh el-Kab at el-Gerara, and the residence of Dabayba Umm Tob. After two decades of surveys and soundings, the National Corporation for Antiquities and Museums and the University of Khartoum has provided indispensable documentation describing the progressive move of the capital from Meroe to Soba, even though, at present, the question of the evolution of the State in the fourth century AD depends more on historiography than on archaeology.

171

171 Bowl

Copper alloy

El-Hobagi, Tumulus III, HBG III/I/135

Post-Meroitic, fourth–fifth centuries AD

H 67 mm, D 117 mm

SNM 26291

This open bowl, of a type known to have been used for libations, is inscribed with a line of text in Meroitic hieroglyphs which includes the words for 'king' and 'god'. The inscription is the latest Meroitic text known, and has been adduced as evidence for the survival of Meroitic culture into the fourth–fifth centuries AD. Important groups of metalwork were discovered in the tumuli at el-Hobagi. These included several bronze ritual vessels which were probably used for pouring libations and burning incense.   JHT

Lenoble *et al.* 1994, 60, 80, pl. 12; 1994e, 228, no. 314; Lenoble and Nigm ed-Din 1992, 634, fig. 6; Reinold 2000a, 123; Shinnie and Robertson 1993, 897; Tiradritti 1994, 13, REM 1222; Valbelle 1994, 58; Wildung 1997, 383, no. 454

172 Bell from the trappings of a horse

Copper alloy

El-Hobagi, Tumulus III, HBG III/I/174

Post-Meroitic, fourth–fifth centuries AD

H 108 mm, D 106 mm

SNM 26302

Among the contents of the tumuli at el-Hobagi were found parts of bovid skulls and horse trappings, including this bronze bell. The bell is provided with a suspension-ring and is decorated with figures of guineafowl arranged in two rows. The presence of these items in the graves might suggest that animals were sacrificed at the burial. As the excavation of the tumuli was not complete, this cannot be proved; however, the interment of horses with their trappings was a characteristic element of Meroitic royal burials, and this bell may therefore be evidence for a continuation of this tradition into the Post-Meroitic period.   JHT

172

Leclant and Clerc 1988, 389, pl. LXIII, fig. 80;
1994b, 108, pl. 1; 1994d, 227, no. 312; 1999b,
175–6, 193, fig. 16; Lenoble *et al.* 1994, 63, 79,
p. 11; Reinold 2000a, 126; 2003i; Wildung 1997,
384, no. 457

173 Bowl with embossed head

Copper alloy

El-Hobagi, Tumulus III, HBG III/I/48

Post-Meroitic, fourth–fifth centuries AD

H 49 mm, D 122 mm

SNM 26273

This simple bronze bowl has no external decoration. However, soldered to the bottom of
the interior is a bronze appliqué in the form of
a bearded male head rising from a crescent.
The general appearance of the head, and in
particular the radiate crown which it wears,
recalls Classical models. Assimilation of the
graphic styles of the Roman world is a typical
feature of Meroitic art, and this example
points to the continuation of this trend into
the Post-Meroitic period.   JHT

Wildung 1997, 386, no. 463

173

174 Statuette of a crocodile

Copper alloy

El-Hobagi, Tumulus VI, HBG VI/I/19a

Post-Meroitic, fourth–fifth centuries AD

H 14 mm, L 85 mm, W 26 mm

SNM 26311

This realistically modelled crocodile, cast by
the lost wax process, was originally attached
to the interior of a bronze libation bowl (SNM
26310) ornamented with floral designs and
images of falcons. When the bowl was filled,
the crocodile would be submerged. Its gradual appearance as the liquid was poured out
presumably carried a special ritual significance. The symbolic association of the crocodile with the Egyptian god Osiris, ruler of the
kingdom of the dead and guarantor of
renewed life, is likely to have been of key
importance in the context of the rituals in
which the bowl was used.   JHT

Leclant and Clerc 1988, 389, pl. LXIII, fig. 80;
Lenoble 1994f, 231, no. 323; 1999b, 175–6,
193, fig. 16; Reinold 2000a, 126; 2003f;
Wildung 1997, 388–9, no. 468

174

GABATI

DAVID EDWARDS

The multi-period cemetery of Gabati lies on the east bank of the Nile, some 40 km north of Meroe. The site was discovered in 1993 by a Sudan Archaeological Research Society (SARS) survey team directed by Michael Mallinson and Laurence Smith. With the encouragement of the Sudan National Corporation for Antiquities and Museums, SARS undertook a large-scale rescue excavation during the winter of 1994–5, prior to the construction of a new highway across the site.[1]

The Post-Meroitic component of this large and well-preserved cemetery was of considerable research interest. Recent work in the Shendi Reach has greatly increased our understanding of cultural transitions at the end of the Meroitic period (third–fourth centuries AD). However, Gabati has proved very interesting in having burials of the later Post-Meroitic and early medieval period (fifth–seventh centuries AD), through the period which saw the introduction of Christianity to the region. Previously very little was known of this period in the central Sudan except from excavations of the earliest levels

black stones. The majority of the tombs were constructed with large trapezoidal shafts, with a steeply sloping entrance 'ramp' with wide ledges cut along the sides. The oval or semi-circular grave chambers were accessed through narrow entrances cut in the end wall of the shaft. Similar grave forms have been found at el-Hobagi, but have not yet been found elsewhere.

In contrast to the earlier Meroitic burials, in which graves were frequently reopened and reused, the Post-Meroitic tombs only held a single burial. This appears to be a significant and widespread change in practice at the end of the Meroitic period. Most of the grave shafts were oriented along an approximately east–west axis, with the bodies in the grave chambers laid in a contracted position, oriented north–south, as was the case with the earlier Meroitic burials on the site. The bodies were usually laid on their right sides with the head to the south, facing east, apparently a relatively standard arrangement during this period (fig. 144).

The range of artefacts found with the burials was quite extensive (cats 175–8, 314–16), although there is no particular reason to believe that the people were

144 Grave 83. The burial is orientated in typical Post-Meroitic fashion.

145 Plaited hair in Grave 84.

at the medieval capital of Alwa at Soba East, near Khartoum.[2]

A total of forty-one graves of Post-Meroitic or later date were excavated, in addition to sixty-three Meroitic graves and nine burials examined during the test excavations. Most of the Post-Meroitic burials were covered by low tumuli about 5–8 m in diameter, often edged with

especially 'wealthy'. The often excellent preservation did however mean that many organic materials such as leather, textiles, wood and basketry (cat. 175) survived, rarely the case in this part of the Sudan. The pottery found in the burials was largely limited to hand-made bowls and small jars, as well as imported Egyptian oil bottles. Unusually, the larger 'beer-jars' were absent.

Only one small jar of this type, itself of an unusual form, was found. Such jars are extremely common in earlier Post-Meroitic graves throughout the central Sudan and Dongola Reach, while their wheel-made counterparts are equally common within Post-Meroitic ('X-Group') assemblages in Lower Nubia. Their absence from the Gabati burials remains difficult to explain.

Many of the other items deposited in the graves may have been the personal possessions of the deceased. Items of clothing included leather 'kilts', probably the most common form of clothing, although some also included coloured woollen cloth. Personal jewellery included bead bracelets and anklets, mainly made of glass, ostrich eggshell and stone. Faience beads, very common in the Meroitic period, were much rarer. Iron anklets, bracelets and rings were quite common. More unusual finds were a pair of silver earrings and a gold-ringed bead, mounted on horse hair, adorning the braids of a woman's hair (fig. 145).

Many of the other objects also related to personal adornment. These included kohl-pots of ivory or wood (cats 177, 316), as well as wooden combs. The Egyptian oil bottles, a type previously not found in Post-Meroitic burials, may also fall into this category, perhaps holding oil for dressing the hair or oiling the body. These were all found with burials of adult females. Examples of leather-covered baskets (cat. 175) were also found, as well as small basketry trays or covers, of a type still made in the region. Several of the bodies were laid on the remains of wooden beds (cat. 314), once strung with leather thongs and rope. These had been dismantled to get them into the small burial chambers.

Another unusual feature encountered at the site was some deposits of pottery beneath three of the tumuli, clearly deliberate deposits made at the time of burial (fig. 146). The burials with which these were associated all seem to have been of quite a late date. No parallels are known for such surface deposits in the central Sudan. It is possible that they relate to changing burial practices prior to the adoption of standard Christian burial rites in this region.

Closely dating such burials is often difficult as we still know so little about this period. Fortunately it was possible to get a series of radiocarbon dates from the site; in some cases several samples were taken from the same graves, allowing greater precision. These suggest that all the graves fall relatively late within the 'Post-Meroitic' period, the earliest probably not pre-dating the mid-fifth century AD. More interestingly, some almost certainly date to the later seventh century, possibly a century or more after Christianity was introduced to the region.

The Gabati Cemetery (fig. 147) is of considerable interest in showing burial forms which, while clearly within known Post-Meroitic traditions, have a number of new and distinctive features. For the first time we can also see that 'pagan' Post-Meroitic burial forms survived the date of the official conversion of Alwa, perhaps for a century or more. The finds from the cemetery as a whole also suggest some important continuities in mortuary culture from the Meroitic period through to the disappearance of pagan Post-Meroitic burials.

1 Edwards 1998; Mallinson *et al.* 1996.
2 Welsby 1998a.

146 Pots beneath
Tumulus T28.

147 Gabati Cemetery,
Tumulus 40 under
excavation.

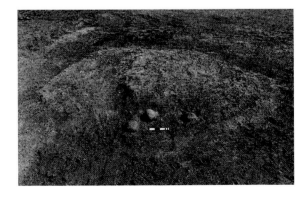

175

175 Basket

Palm, leather

Gabati, Grave 28, no. GBT2801

Medieval, late seventh century AD

H c. 52 mm, D c. 88 mm

SNM 27874

A well-preserved and essentially intact basket with a tightly woven basketry core and sewn leather exterior. Unfortunately it was impossible to open and examine the interior. Basketry and leatherwork were probably widely used during this period, although few pieces survive. A few similar examples are known from Lower Nubia.[1]   DE

1 Cf. Säve-Söderbergh et al. 1981, 38.

Edwards 1998, 124–5, fig. 5.9

176 Kohl stick

Iron

Gabati, Grave 124, no. GBT12419

Sixth–seventh centuries AD

L 163 mm, max. W (of spoon) 14 mm

SNM 27822B

Rectangular sectioned rod with 'spoon' end beaten out, which was associated with a kohl pot (cat. 177). It exhibits little corrosion.   DE

Edwards 1998, 126–7, fig. 5.11

177 Kohl pot

Ivory

Gabati, Grave 124, no. GBT12414

Post-Meroitic/Medieval, sixth–seventh centuries AD

Base: H 85 mm, D 44–5 mm; lid: H 82 mm, D 35 mm; total H 157 mm

SNM 27822A

A turned ivory vessel and lid, with a slight recess in the bottom of the lid. Few such vessels

176, 177

have been found in either Post-Meroitic or medieval Christian contexts in Nubia. One rare example was found in the late Post-Meroitic (X-Group) Cemetery 193 (Grave 122, no. 15) at Qasr Ibrim, Egyptian Nubia (Mills 1982). This was found inside a purpose-made leather pouch, complete with an iron spatula, and is now in the Royal Ontario Museum, Toronto (ROM. 963.15.26a–c). Little ivory has been found in medieval contexts in Nubia although it was probably quite abundant.   DE

Edwards 1998, 126–7, fig. 5.11

178 Jar

Faience

Gabati, Grave 94, no. GBT9402

Kushite (Meroitic), first century AD

H 133 mm, max. D 116 mm; base: D 89 mm; rim: D 68 mm

SNM 27818

A complete faience vessel, reconstructed from fragments. A decorative frieze, perhaps inspired by a pastiche of the Sa knot and djed pillar, encircles the roughly cylindrical body. The rim is straight and the neck cylindrical, joining a straight horizontal shoulder. Few

such elaborate moulded vessels have been found in Sudan. A small number of faience vessels from Meroe townsite, as well as figurines, plaques and other objects, were recovered from temple contexts (Garstang et al. 1911, 15–16). Of the vessels from the townsite, most were bowls, including one example with a moulded design of a winged ankh or Sa knot, but most other pieces are quite plain (Shinnie and Bradley 1980, no. 3091, figs 75–6), with none so elaborate as the jar from Gabati. A rare example of a more elaborately decorated faience bottle comes from Qasr Ibrim, with moulded floral decoration in panels (Mills 1982, 11, no. 193.122.15; pl. VI, LXXXVII – Cairo JE 89672). Found in an intact Post-Meroitic 'X-Group' grave, this is likely to be significantly later than the Gabati example, probably dating to the late fourth or early fifth centuries AD. It may also be of Egyptian manufacture, and the possibility that the Gabati vessel might also be from an Egyptian workshop cannot be ruled out.   DE

Edwards 1998, 67, fig. 3.3

178

179

179 Bowl

Silver

Firka, Tomb A. 14, no. A. 14/16

Post-Meroitic, late fifth century AD

H 95 mm, D 135 mm

SNM 3165

One of two silver vessels found in a large Post-Meroitic tumulus burial. Both are similarly decorated with an engraved *ankh* surmounted by Isis horns and plumes. These seem likely to be of Egyptian manufacture, along with other fine metal and stone objects in the grave, and together with cat. 180 suggest close contacts with Byzantine Egypt.   DE

Hinkel and Abdelrahman 2002, 194; Kirwan 1939, 11, pl. IX.1

180 Oil lamp and tripod

Copper alloy

Firka, Tomb A. 14, no. A. 14/7

Post-Meroitic, late fifth century AD

H 310 mm; lamp: H (preserved) 115 mm, L 157 mm, max. W 63 mm

SNM 3174

A swinging lamp hung on a column stand with tripod base, the feet of which are lion-headed. Such lamps stands are widely found in the eastern Roman world between the fifth–seventh centuries AD and several have also been found in Post-Meroitic 'royal' tombs at Ballana.   DE

Hinkel and Abdelrahman 2002, 194; Kirwan 1939, 11; Pérez Die 2003a

180

10

THE MEDIEVAL KINGDOMS OF NUBIA

JULIE R. ANDERSON

Christianity was introduced into Nubia during the mid-sixth century AD, long after Egypt and much of the Mediterranean and Near East had been evangelized. It arrived as a well-established faith. At this time there were three Nubian kingdoms: Nobadia was the northernmost with its capital at Faras, Makuria was in the centre in Upper Nubia, and Alwa was upstream in the south (fig. 148). The rulers of Makuria and Alwa resided in Old Dongola[1] and Soba East near the junction of the two Niles, respectively. Each Nubian kingdom was evangelized separately; however, the initial impetus originated in the Byzantine Empire where a great theological struggle was occurring between the Dyophysite and Monophysite Christians regarding the true nature of Christ.[2] According to literary tradition as related by John of Ephesus, in the sixth century AD the Dyophysite Emperor Justinian and his Monophysite Empress Theodora sent rival missions from Constantinople to convert the Nubians. By threatening officials in Upper Egypt,[3] Theodora ensured that her mission led by Julian, a Coptic monk, arrived in Nobadia before Justinian's emissaries. He rapidly baptized the court. By the time Justinian's mission arrived the Nobadian court had already accepted the Monophysite doctrine.[4]

Little is known of the conversion of Makuria. In AD 568 John of Biclar noted that the Byzantine Emperor Justin II received a request from Makuria 'expressing their wish to live under the peace of the Roman Empire and to embrace the Christian religion'. He later received diplomatic envoys from Makuria.[5] This is often taken to imply that Makuria initially followed the Dyophysite creed.[6] Archaeologically, the earliest ecclesiastical buildings (i.e., Building X) at Old Dongola are basilicas that appear to have been constructed after imperial Byzantine models such as the Basilica Apostolorum.[7]

In Alwa the king officially requested that the bishop who converted the Nobadians be sent to instruct his court. After a journey made difficult by opposition from the Makurians and internal church politics, Longinus arrived in Alwa and converted the court.[8] Christianity swiftly swept across the Middle Nile region as the state-sanctioned religion, and by AD 580 all the Nubian kingdoms had officially converted to Christianity. Based upon the early dates of monasteries excavated at Old Dongola,[9] it seems likely that monks played an important role in the spread of Christianity among the local population, although the archaeological and literary sources documenting Nubian monasticism are few.[10]

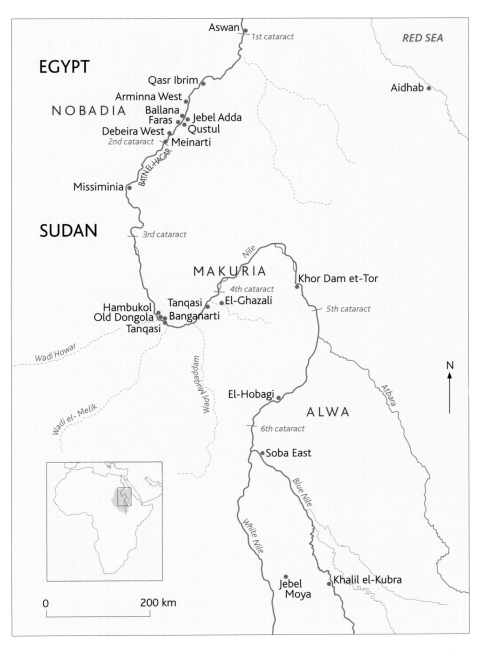

148 Map of the medieval kingdoms and sites
mentioned in the text.

Textual sources suggest that throughout the fifth–sixth centuries AD the Nobadian and Makurian kingdoms were antagonistic towards one another. King Silko of the Noubades (Nobadia) says that he 'ravaged the country ... above [upstream from] the Noubades [Nobadia], because they contended with me'.[11] Recent archaeological investigations at Kom A, Old Dongola, may confirm his statement. They indicate the presence of a large sixth-century AD settlement enclosed by a massive fortification. Furthermore, artefacts from the north such as Egyptian imports are infrequent in the region of Old Dongola after the fifth century AD.[12]

Despite their early hostility towards one another, in the mid-seventh century AD the Makurian and Nobadian kingdoms were united under the Makurian king while the Monophysite doctrine became the prevailing dogma. The king of Makuria resided in Old Dongola, perhaps because of the greater security of this location. Nobadia was governed by his deputy, the eparch, who may have initially resided in Faras, but later in Qasr Ibrim, Jebel Adda and Meinarti.[13] The exact means and date of these occurrences are uncertain, and evidence is largely literary. It has been plausibly suggested that these events were a consequence of the Muslim conquest of Egypt and the Near East, after which the Nubian Church was isolated and maintained contact only with the Monophysite Coptic see of Alexandria.[14] Certainly later in the Christian period, bishops of the thirteen recorded episcopal sees in Nubia were appointed solely by the Coptic patriarch in Egypt.[15]

The Nubians managed to hold back the flood of Arab invaders that swept the Near East and North Africa during the seventh century AD. Two attempts were made to conquer Old Dongola, the first in AD 641/2 and the second in AD 652. Both were unsuccessful even though the Muslims brought a reported 5,000 heavily armoured cavalry with them to the second attack. Nubian archers appear to have played a significant role in these battles. Arab historians recording these events described the Nubian archers as 'pupil-smiters' or 'archers of the eyes', and noted that many of the injured had been blinded.[16]

A bilateral peace treaty entitled the 'Baqt' was negotiated between the Arabs and the Makurian king. This agreement recognized the sovereignty of Makuria. Under the terms of the Baqt as related by numerous Arab sources,[17] the Makurians were to provide approximately 400 slaves in exchange for goods including grains, pulses, oil, 'drink', cloth and horses on an annual basis. This gives an idea of the commodities being traded during medieval times. Furthermore, Muslims and Nubians were free to travel between both lands, but were forbidden to settle and escaped slaves were to be returned. The Alwan kingdom was not included in the Baqt, probably due to its remote location from the Egyptian border. After the advent of this agreement, Makuria and the Muslim world largely coexisted peacefully for over six centuries with relations becoming strained occasionally due to cross-border raids or non-compliance, largely on the part of the Nubians, with the statutes of the treaty. These instances of non-compliance increased as the centuries passed.

The transition from the Post-Meroitic phase to the Christian is quite marked. The appearance of churches, monasteries, written texts and different burial customs heralds the arrival of Christianity in the archaeological record. The first state churches most likely were built within the capitals of Faras and Old Dongola as these were the first official targets of evangelization. Excavations at both sites have exposed portions of early churches, as has work at Jebel Adda and Qasr Ibrim.[18] Pagan temples were also converted.[19] Early Nubian churches at Old Dongola – 'Building X' and 'the Old Church' – have many Byzantine architectural elements, while the later Cruciform Church shows Syro-Palestinian parallels. Similarly the metrology employed in the church 'Building B' and the associated tomb at Soba East suggest Byzantine influences.[20] However, it is clear that the Nubians combined Coptic, Syro-Palestinian and Byzantine elements or models with indigenous characteristics and local materials to create a distinctive Nubian style and canon. The evolution of church architecture in Lower Nubia has been well documented by W.Y. Adams and P. Grossmann, and that of Makuria by P. Gartkiewicz.[21] Unfortunately thus far there are few ecclesiastical structures excavated within the Alwan kingdom with which to create a typology. At a generalized level, the Nubian church was rectangular, with three parallel aisles, the central one ending with the

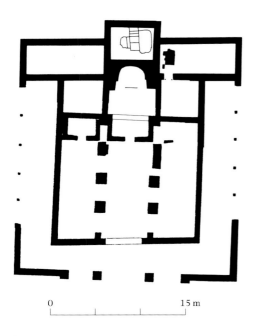

0   15 m

149 Plan of Church, Building A, at Soba East.

apse in the east (fig. 149). The baptistry was a small square chamber to the south of the apse containing a font, while the sacristy was to the north of the apse. These were linked by a narrow corridor running behind the apse.

Death served as a great social equalizer. The Post-Meroitic elite were buried with rich grave goods in large tumuli such as those found at el-Hobagi, Ballana and Qustul. Tombs at el-Hobagi were filled with beer-jars, copper bowls, bells and weapons (cats 171–4), while those at Ballana and Qustul contained silver crowns, jewellery and sacrificed horses with tack.[22] Unlike earlier burials, those of the Christian period were not provided with sumptuous grave goods or food offerings. Christian graves were sparsely endowed up until the Late and Terminal Christian phases, whereupon the role of the liturgy declines and is steadily replaced by vernacular Christianity.

Christian tombs were orientated east–west, though in some places this was done in accordance with the orientation of the Nile rather than true north. In several instances Christians continued to use older burial grounds, and Christian tombs are interspersed among Post-Meroitic tumuli, and Early and Late Kushite tombs such as at Missiminia.[23] Christian graves were most often simple tombs with a small rectangular superstructure of brick covering the narrow grave shaft. With the exception of bishops, who were buried dressed in their religious garments, the deceased was wrapped in a shroud (cat. 317), with the head often protected by a brick or stone. More elaborate superstructures were plastered white, cruciform in shape or had rounded rather than flat tops. Some were provided with small niches for lamps. Vaulted communal tombs containing many individuals were also used.[24] In Old Dongola, Kom H, there are incidences of crypt graves, notably that of the archbishop Giorgios, found beneath monastic chapels. Only rarely have crypts been found beneath cathedrals such as Building A at Soba East, Church 4 at Jebel Adda and Building X at Old Dongola. These latter tombs perhaps belong to venerated founding fathers or other such respected personages.[25]

There is little evidence for widespread literacy during the Post-Meroitic period; however, this appears to change dramatically during the Christian period with a proliferation of letters, business and legal documents, conveyance, graffiti, religious texts and tombstones. These expand our knowledge of the socio-cultural, religious and economic aspects of the period, but give little information about the history of the kingdoms themselves. This must be largely derived from records of Arab travellers and geographers. When compared with earlier phases, it appears that a greater proportion of the Christian population was literate. Coptic, Greek and the Nubian language – Old Nubian – were written and appear alongside Arabic texts. The titles of ecclesiastical and administrative officials and the liturgy were predominantly Greek (cats 181, 186, 188).[26]

The Nubian economy was largely agrarian-based. The Letti Basin to the north of the Makurian capital was described by Ibn Selim el Aswani, a tenth-century AD Arab traveller, as containing 'thirty villages with beautiful buildings, churches and monasteries, many palm trees, vines, gardens, cultivated fields and broad pastures on which one can see camels'. Further, he describes Alwa as 'more fertile and larger [than Makuria]; but palm trees and vines are less numerous ... the commonest grain among them is the white *dhurra* ... with it they make their bread [*khubz*] and their beer [*mizr*] they have plenty of meat because of the abundance of cattle

150 *Saqia* wheel at Gezeira Dabarosa.

and large plains for grazing'.[27] *Seluka* land – the land seasonally inundated by the Nile – was extensively cultivated. The agrarian base was dramatically enlarged during the Christian period by extensive adoption of the *saqia* waterwheel (fig. 150). Knobs from *saqia* pots are ubiquitous on Christian sites. Use of the *saqia* widened the available cultivatable land along the Nile and enabled large fertile basins to be irrigated year-round. *Dhurra* (sorgum), grape seeds, millet, date stones, pulses, figs, cucumber seeds, wheat and *dom* palm nuts have been recovered from several archaeological sites, thus confirming the textual evidence.[28] Tools used in food preparation such as saddle querns, grinding stones and *doka* – a flat ceramic plate used in the making of flatbreads such as the sorghum bread *kisra* – are common finds.[29] Domestic animals were an important component in the economy, providing milk, wool, meat, leather and transport. Faunal remains suggest that cattle, goats, sheep and pigs were the principal livestock kept and consumed, although finds from Kom H at Old Dongola included numerous gazelle bones.[30]

The abundance of riches together with a long period of relative peace from the eighth century AD onwards enabled Nubian artistic expression to flower. This took various forms, the most notable being ceramic production and wall painting, although crafts including woodworking, textile production, basketry and metalwork-ing all reached high technological standards. Finds from Soba East (cats 202–3) and particularly Qasr Ibrim attest to this proficiency.[31] Large urban settlements such as

151 Wall painting of the *anargyroi* saint Damianos from Banganarti.

Debeira West, Faras, Arminna West, Meinarti, Old Dongola and Soba proliferated,[32] appearing as ceramic- and detritus-covered mounds in the archaeological record. The population increased, surpassing that of earlier periods, as these numerous large mounds and cemeteries suggest. Religion becomes the dominant force in literature, iconography and art. The pious nature of decoration is apparent even in plastic arts such as terracotta window grills (cat. 183). Christian iconographic symbols such as fish, doves, crosses, palm fronds, and apotropaic graffiti are typical motifs incorporated into decorative patterns, the most numerous of which are found on pottery, either as impressed or painted designs (cats 188, 198, 230).

Traces of wall paintings have been found in over fifty churches, most of which were located in Lower Nubia.[33] This is an artificial distribution reflecting concentrations of archaeological work rather than the actual dispersal of wall paintings. These paintings show a distinct Nubian flavour though in many cases the iconography can be traced to Byzantine and/or Coptic origins.[34] Of particular note are the wall paintings that were found in the cathedral at Faras (cat. 4). In Makuria they have been discovered in private houses, such as those at Hambukol and Old Dongola, and in monasteries (cats 181–2). The most important recent finds include over seventy wall paintings discovered in the Monastery of the Holy Trinity at Old Dongola and twelve royal portraits discovered in Banganarti.[35] These paintings are religious in nature and are an expression of devotion and liturgical belief (fig. 151). Many are stained by lamp or candle soot (cf. cats 184–5). They depict Old Testament stories such as Balaam's travels to Moab (Numbers 22, 15–350), Meshack, Shadrack and Abednego in the Furnace (Daniel 3, 19–23), the baptism of Christ, the archangel Michael and the Holy Trinity, Christ and the twelve apostles, and the Virgin and Child. Christ, St Peter, the Virgin Mary and the archangels Michael and Raphael are also shown protecting members of the Nubian royal family, the Eparch of Nobadia and various ecclesiastical personages (cat. 4).[36]

The rise of secular feudalism and internal strife in the twelfth century AD signals the decline of the Nubian kingdoms. Churches shrink in size and fortified houses, known as 'castle houses',[37] and watchtowers proliferate throughout Lower Nubia. This suggests an increasing perception of external threat, a decline in the power of the clergy and Makurian king, and the corresponding rise of local authorities or kinglets. Abu el-Makarim mentions that the Old Dongola king ruled over thirteen minor rulers.[38] In Upper Nubia settlements and monasteries are abandoned or fortified. After a power struggle within the Makurian dynasty, coupled with raids and several invasions by the Mameluks and desert Arabs, Makuria likely ceased to be a Christian kingdom when in AD 1323 a Muslim, Kanz ed-Dawla, assumed the throne at Old Dongola. This was facilitated by the traditional means of succession wherein the throne passed from the king to his sister's son.[39] This was followed by a short period of Muslim rule which ended around AD 1365 as a result of internal dynastic problems, attacks by desert Arabs and interventions made by the Mameluke rulers of Egypt. Upon the disintegration of Makuria, the independent Christian kingdom of Dotawo appears in Lower Nubia in the region of Jebel Adda, as attested by several documents. Little is known about this small kingdom. Texts mention approximately ten kings of Dotawo, the last of which, a leather document, mentions King Joel and dates to AD 1484.[40]

The fall of Makuria is well documented through numerous, if confusing and contradictory, Arab sources, but the fate of Alwa is less clear. The Funj Chronicle records the sacking of Soba in AD 1504; however, archaeological research conducted there suggests that the Funj, an Islamic people from the south, were looting a city that had been in steady decline and was largely in ruins, though the reason for this is not clear.[41] The disappearance of Christianity as a state-sanctioned religion did not immediately lead to its abandonment by the local population, but it would have been difficult to receive bishops from Alexandria in the light of ongoing problems with Egypt. While Christian beliefs appear to have persisted in some regions possibly until the eighteenth century AD,[42] lacking state support and without ordained priests to lead the population, liturgical Christianity would have been replaced increasingly by vernacular Christianity. Islam was able to fill this spiritual gap and gradually the population converted.

1 The ancient Makurian capital of Dongola is now referred to as Old Dongola and will be referred to as such here.

2 The Dyophysites were also known as Melkites as they were supported by the Byzantine emperor, while the Monophysites were also called Jacobites after Jacob Baradai, a prominent Monophysite in Egypt around AD 530 (Welsby 2002, 32). Those who followed the Dyophysite doctrine, as decreed by the Council of Chalcedon in AD 451, held that Christ had distinct divine and human natures, while the Monophysites believed he had a single nature wherein God and man were united. In recent times, Pope Shenuouda has stated a preference for the term miaphysite meaning 'one as a unity, one out of two natures while "mono" implies one only', rather than Monophysite (Watson 2000, 127).

3 John of Ephesus's account of Theodora's letter to the Byzantine officials in Upper Egypt reads, 'my will is, that my ambassador should arrive at the aforesaid people before his majesty's [Justinian]; be warned, that, if you permit his ambassador to arrive there before mine, and do not hinder him by various pretexts until mine shall have reached you, and have passed through your province, and arrived at his destination, your life shall answer for it; for I will immediately send and take off your head' (Vantini 1975, 9).

4 Vantini 1975, 10–11.

5 Vantini 1975, 27.

6 Cf. Kirwan 1982.

7 Godlewski 1991b, 253.

8 John of Ephesus in Vantini 1975, 14–23.

9 Żurawski (1994b, 334) has dated phase I of the Kom H monastery at Old Dongola to the latter part of the seventh century AD, but suggests that some

parts of the monastery may be earlier in date. Cf. Dobrowolski 1991; Jakobielski 1995a; 1996; 1997; 2001a.

10 The remains of over fifty monasteries have been reported; however, most are unconfirmed (cf. Anderson 1999). In the tenth century AD, the Hudud al-'alam recorded 12,000 monks in the area of Tari, believed to be Ghazali. Abu el-Makarim further identifies six monasteries by name (Anderson 1999, 71; Vantini 1975, 174, 324–7).

11 Eide et al. 1998, 1150–51.

12 Godlewski 1999, 556–7.

13 Adams 1996, 42 ff., 217–18; Millet 1967, 59; Welsby 2002, 34–5, 94–5.

14 Adams 1977, 445–7; Welsby 2002, 34–5.

15 The Nubian Bishop Timotheos was consecrated in Old Cairo in AD 1371 (Plumley 1975).

16 Al-Balādhurī and Ibn al-Furat in Vantini 1975, 80–81, 528.

17 Al-Balādhurī, Ibn Selim al-Aswani, Ibn Al-Furat, Abu-l-Hasan Mas'udi, in Vantini 1975, 79–83, 534–5, 638–47.

18 Adams 1965, 127–9.

19 The earliest recorded temple conversion is that of the Isis Temple at Philae which was converted in c. AD 535–7 upon a decree made by the Byzantine Emperor Justinian (FHN III, 1998, 1177–81).

20 Welsby and Daniels 1991, 318–21.

21 Adams 1965; 1992; Gartkiewicz 1982; 1990; Grossmann 1990.

22 Emery and Kirwan 1938; Lenoble 1997; Lenoble et al. 1994.

23 Billy 1987, 123, fig. 2.

24 Cf. Adams 1998a.

25 Millet 1967, 59–60; Welsby and Daniels 1991, 316; Żurawski 1999.

26 Browne 1989; Jakobielski 1972; Millet 1967, 59.

27 Maqrizi in Vantini 1975, 606, 613–14.

28 For example, millet, dhurra, date pits, grape seeds, and dom nuts have been recovered from Hambukol (Grzymski and Anderson 2001, 75–6). Fig, grape, date pits, millet, and barley were found at Soba East (Cartwright 1998, 258–66).

29 For example, see Grzymski and Anderson 2001, 62–3, 127.

30 For examples of faunal remains see Grzymski and Anderson 2001, 103–7; Chaix 1998, 233–45; Shinnie and Shinnie 1978, 107; Żurawski 1994b, 323–4.

31 Preservation at Qasr Ibrim is particularly good due to its geographic situation. Cf. Welsby 1998a, 60–82, 177–85; Adams 1996, 91–212.

32 Adams 2001; 2002; Jakobielski 1995a; 1996; 1997; 2001a; Michałowski 1962; 1965; Shinnie and Shinnie 1978; Weeks 1967; Welsby 1998a; Welsby and Daniels 1991; Żurawski 1994b; 1999.

33 Adams 1978, 121.

34 Innemée 1995, 283–4, 287.

35 Cf. Godlewski 1982, 95–9; Jakobielski 2001a, 273–6; Żurawski 2002a; Grzymski and Anderson 1994, 96–7, pl. III.

36 Jakobielski 2001a, 273–4; Michałowski, 1974; Vantini 1994, 255–7.

37 Adams 1994a.

38 Evetts and Butler 1895, 272.

39 For example, in the early eleventh century AD King Solomon abdicated the throne in favour of his sister's son George (from the life of Cyril in Vantini 1975, 215).

40 Millet 1967, 62.

41 Welsby and Daniels 1991, 34; Welsby 2002, 255.

42 Welsby 2002, 257.

OLD DONGOLA

WŁODZIMIERZ GODLEWSKI

Old Dongola was one of the most important centres of the medieval kingdom of Makuria (fig. 152).[1] The town was situated on a rocky eminence overlooking the eastern bank of the Nile, halfway between the Third and Fourth Cataracts, at the southern edge of the Letti Basin, which was the city's economic hinterland. Contrary to earlier suggestions made by Egyptologists regarding the town's importance already in the Early Kushite period, it now appears that the city was not established until the end of the fifth century AD. The founder was probably one of the first kings of Makuria. He raised a huge fortress of mud brick and ferruginous sandstone at a site away from the religious centres of the earlier kingdom of Kush, but located centrally in the new kingdom. This new settlement was one of a series of newly established, heavily fortified sites that the rulers of Makuria apparently decided to build along the bank of the Nile. The purpose appears to have been more socioeconomic than military, the idea being presumably to foster a Byzantine-influenced process of urbanization. Thus, the Old Dongolan citadel became a centre of power with royal palaces and public buildings, and a place for storing economic resources.

The first rulers to reside at Old Dongola may have been buried in rock-cut *hypogea* in the desert to the

152 An aerial view of Old Dongola.

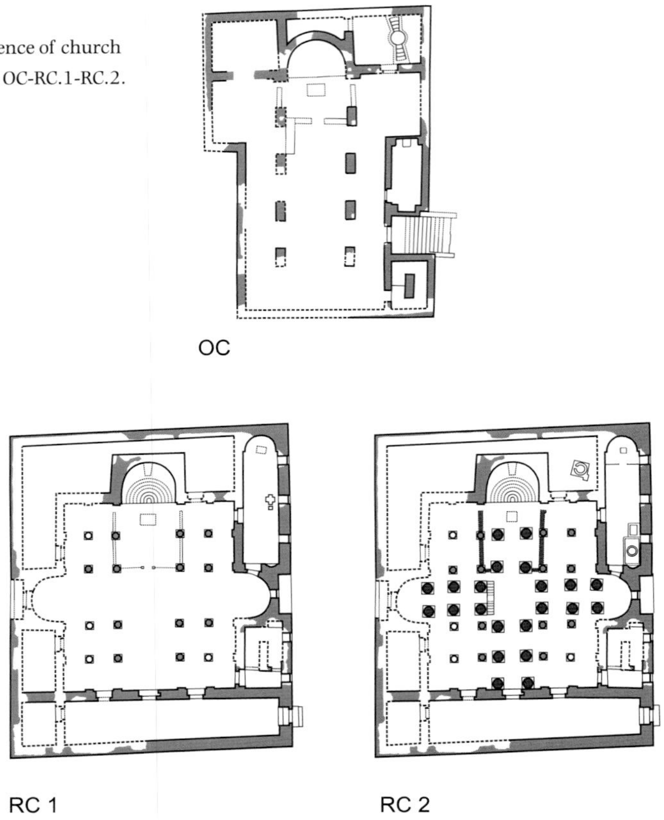

153 Sequence of church
buildings: OC-RC.1-RC.2.

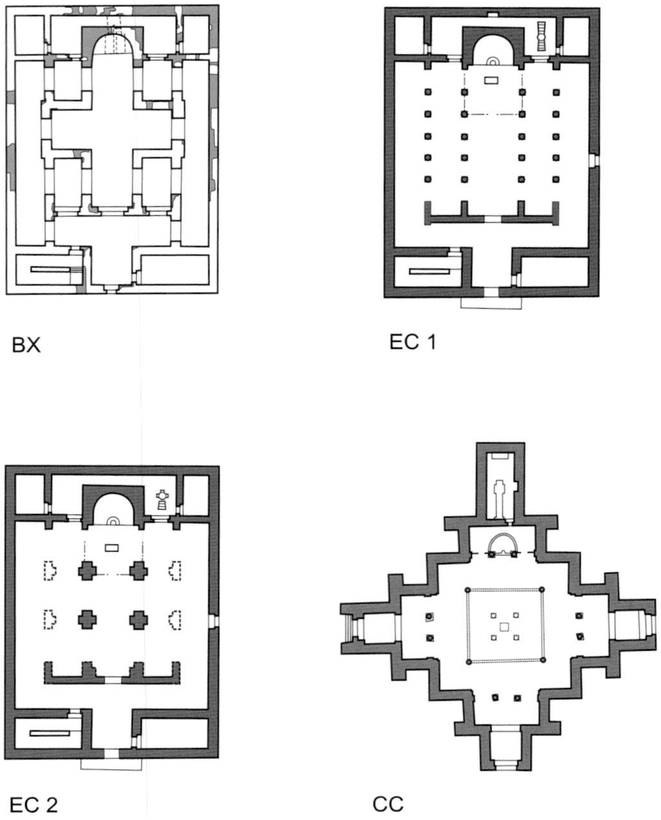

OC

RC 1

RC 2

154 Sequence of church
buildings: BX-EC.1-EC.2-CC.

BX

EC 1

EC 2

CC

north of the town, at the southern extremity of the burial ground near Jebel Ghaddar. The only parts to be preserved are the burial chambers reached by a broad staircase from the west.

With Christianity came a new challenge for urban growth. The citadel, which must have already been built up by the beginning of the sixth century AD, could not hold all the churches that the missionaries and rulers of Makuria erected. Newer buildings – the three-aisled Old Church with dwarf transept and the commemorative cruciform Building X – had to be constructed on more or less undeveloped ground to the north of the citadel. The missionaries christianizing Makuria probably came from Constantinople, and the first churches at Old Dongola shared much in common with church architecture in Palestine and Syria. By the AD 570s a bishopric had been established in Old Dongola. On the site of Building X, which was destroyed by a high Nile flood, a cathedral was erected – a five-aisled columnar basilica, dubbed by the excavators the 'Church of the Stone Pavement'. Finely worked columns of pink granite supported a wooden ceiling. The *pastophoria* and connecting corridor running behind the apse formed a block arrangement in the east end of the building, and a stone balustrade screened off the sanctuary with table altar in the eastern end of the nave; the apse had a *synthronon* built into it. The new building incorporated under the apse the two crypts which had been part of the earlier commemorative structure. Buried in these crypts were two men presumed to have been the apostles of the kingdom (fig. 153).

In the middle of the seventh century AD Arab troops laid siege to the citadel, but failed to take it. The peace treaty, or Baqt, that the reigning King Qalidurut negotiated with Egypt's governor Abdullah abu Sarh was to regulate Makuria's political and economic relations with the caliphate for the next 520 years. The city remained unconquered, but the cathedral was destroyed and other buildings north of the fortifications may have also incurred damage. Under King Qalidurut and his heir Zacharias the ruins were rebuilt and the town developed. The fortifications were enlarged with a huge tower built on a platform on top of a rocky outcrop overlooking the river. Used in the foundations of this tower were the shafts and capitals of pink granite from the ruins of the first cathedral. The cathedral itself was rebuilt as a five-aisled domed basilica, the dome and ceilings supported on piers, and the floor of the presbytery covered with a geometric mosaic made of colourful desert pebbles.

Even before the end of the seventh century AD a new complex – the Church of the Granite Columns – was built on the site of the Old Church. It was a uniquely

Old Dongolan foundation, combining elements of a central plan – two aisles ending in apses crossing in the centre of the structure – with typical features of a basilica, that is, a columnar *naos* and narthex (fig. 154). The *naos* of the new cathedral was surrounded by side annexes serving different liturgical functions. This building became a model for the cathedral that bishop Paulos founded at Pachoras (Faras) in AD 707.

Still in the reign of Qalidurut a small cruciform structure with a dome in the centre and an entrance

who ruled Makuria jointly for twenty years (AD 835–56). Upon the return of King Georgios from Baghdad in AD 836 the monumental Cruciform Church was erected on the site of the domed basilica. This was to be the largest building in the entire kingdom. The central part of the building, which was connected with the arms by porticoes, was covered with a dome that may have risen 28 m above the pavement. The eastern arm of the structure contained a chapel above the crypts. The church became a symbol of the kingdom and the

155 The citadel, churches and settlement – the locale of the churches.

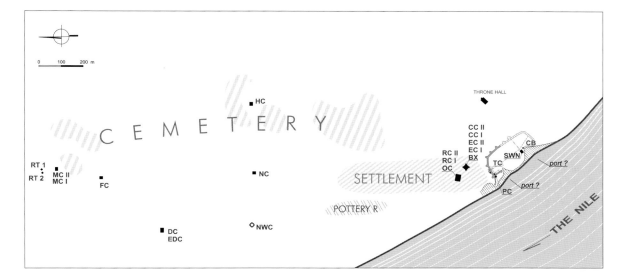

in each of the arms was erected in front of the south façade of the royal palace. Fragmentarily surviving murals evince the quality of the interior finishing of this building, which was most likely a monument raised in commemoration of the defenders of Old Dongola.

Beside the citadel and complex of cathedrals to the north, Old Dongola in the seventh and eighth centuries AD included a vast urban district with regular villa-type architecture spreading for more than a kilometre north of the citadel (fig. 155). The houses measured some 100–120 m² in ground area and were multi-storeyed. The plans were functional: there were toilet facilities in the buildings and living quarters on the upper floor, where the standard of interior finishing clearly surpassed that of the domestic rooms on the ground floor (fig. 156). In House A there was a bathroom on the ground floor with a furnace for heating water which was then piped through to two pools; hot air from the furnace was circulated through flues in the walls to heat the building. Murals on the bathroom walls depicted Victorious Christ next to archangels, warrior saints, symbols and floral motifs.

The most representative buildings in Old Dongola – symbols of the kingdom – were established in the ninth century AD, in the reign of Zacharias and Georgios,

156 Window grille from the House of the Ecclesiastics (A.106).

157 The Citadel,
southern façade of
the Palace, SWN.

pride of its rulers until it was destroyed during the
Mamluk wars in the late thirteenth century AD.

In the ninth century AD a new royal palace was
built on a rocky outcrop east of the citadel (fig. 157).
The throne room was situated on the upper floor and
there was a terrace approached by a monumental
flight of steps, affording a breathtaking view of the
town and river. Murals decorated the walls of the
staircase and throne hall. This Byzantine concept of
architecture expressed most fully the aspirations of
the rulers of Makuria.

On the riverbank just below the western line of the
fortifications a small but very important church, the
Pillar Church (fig. 158), was constructed, also in the
ninth century AD. Its central plan of a cross circum-
scribed within a rectangle highlighted once again the
creativity of the Old Dongolan architectural milieu.

Old Dongola in the ninth–eleventh centuries AD
reached the apogee of its development. Writing around
AD 1200, the Egyptian monk Abu el-Makarim
described the town in the following terms: 'Here is the
throne of the king. It is a large city on the bank of the
blessed Nile, and contains many churches and large

houses and wide streets. The King's house is lofty, with
several domes built of red brick.' But Old Dongola also
featured important architectural complexes situated
outside the city. In the desert, some 1,500 m to the
north-east of the citadel, there lay a vast monastery,
the origins of which are tentatively ascribed to the first
bishops of Old Dongola. Currently under excavation is
mainly the North-west Annexe erected next to the
monastic compound some time in the eleventh–twelfth
centuries AD. This building still defies interpretation,
though it is now clear is that it was altered and reno-
vated repeatedly. It was both sacral and residential, and
its walls were painted prolifically, the repertory today
constituting the fullest testimony to Old Dongolan
painting in the Late Period. Evident is a curious new
trend of representing the dignitaries of the kingdom,
presumably members of the royal family, inside small
chapels, depicted under the protection of an archangel
and the apostles. This new type of official representation is evidenced for the first time in the second half of
the eleventh century and is connected with Georgios
(AD 1031–1113), archimandrite and archistylite, later
archbishop of Old Dongola. Archbishop Georgios built

158 The Pillar
Church.

his tomb with a chapel above a funerary crypt inside the monastery annexe. The walls of the crypt were covered with a unique selection of Greek and Coptic texts of a religious and magic nature. The next bishops of Old Dongola after Georgios were also buried in the crypt. After the conflict with the Ayyubids in AD 1172 and the abandonment of the Baqt treaty, Makuria faced new economic and military challenges. The fortifications of the capital city, not unlike those of other Makurian towns, were rebuilt and enlarged. But new churches were also constructed on the northern edges of the urban agglomeration and on the fortifications of the citadel.

The final stages of the drama were played out in the last quarter of the thirteenth century AD. King David's adventurous and unwise expedition against Aidhab, a port on the Red Sea, and Aswan provoked Mamluk retribution. The sultan Baybars attacked and took Old Dongola. Later Egypt continued to meddle in Makurian affairs, backing various pretenders to the throne in Old Dongola. The main buildings of Old Dongola – the Cathedral and Cruciform Building – were destroyed at the turn of the thirteenth century, but the small

churches remained in use. In AD 1317 the throne hall of the royal palace was turned into a mosque. The royal court abandoned Old Dongola in AD 1364, the rulers of Makuria being unable to cope with the desert tribes and prevent their taking the entire southern part of the kingdom up to the Batn el-Hagar. Even so, Old Dongola remained a centre of importance. Over time new residential architecture mushroomed in the citadel area and on the ruins of the Cathedral and Cruciform Church.

1 For a full bibliographic reference and listing of annual work at Old Dongola see Jakobielski 2001b, 1–48.

181

181 Wall painting of Christ Victor trampling evil powers

Mud plaster, paint

Old Dongola, House PCH A, Room 3 (Bathroom), 6/A-3

Medieval, late eighth–early ninth centuries AD

H 1.9 m, W 900 mm

SNM 31260

This painting represents a standing, beardless figure of Christ, blessing with his right hand and holding a codex in his left. He tramples under his feet a dragon (usually in Nubia represented in the form of a snake), a viper and a lion, according to the Greek text of Psalm 91.13 which is written on both sides of the figure. It reads in literal translation: 'You will tread upon the serpent and the basilisk and you will trample the lion and the dragon'. The Christ figure is described on both sides of the cruciform nimbus as 'The Son of Righteousness'. It was painted on the dividing wall in Room 3, facing east. The lower part was found *in situ*. The upper, composed of loose fragments of plaster, was found in the sand.

This type of representation of Christ points to ancient sources of inspiration as this theme is rare: it is found only in the early Christian art of Italy, North Africa and Coptic Egypt. The painting is of great iconographic value as it is thus far unique in Nubia. The place where the mural was painted – the bathroom in a private house – is also unique, as is the iconographic context which strongly suggests a liturgical use. It was associated with a tondo of the bust of St John (the Baptist?), the text of the Gospel of John (the beginning and the end written, in order to symbolize the whole), and God's hand appearing from heaven, which were on the same wall as this painting. On the other walls were figures of archangels and saints: Mercurius killing Julian the Apostate, and Theodore fighting the dragon. The special, perhaps therapeutic, character of the room is moreover stressed by two basins in the interior, with an installation to provide hot water by means of pottery pipes.   SJ

Godlewski 1982, 95–9; 1992, 302–3; Jakobielski 1979, 238–43; 1982, 117, 125; Łaptaś 1999, 230–35; Martens-Czarnecka 1990a, 233–46; 1990b, 224–37; 2001a, 254–9; Partyka 1984, 115–22

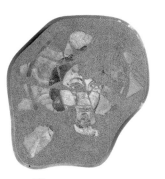
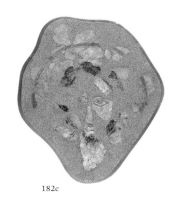

182a   182b   182c

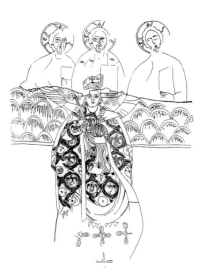

Fig. 159 Reconstruction of cat. 182.

182 The Holy Trinity: fragments of a wall painting of a Nubian king in the coronation scene

Mud plaster, paint

Old Dongola, Kom H, Monastery of the Holy Trinity, the North-western Annexe, Room 12, P.18a/NW12.S

Medieval, twelfth century AD

H 484 mm, W 405 mm; H 570 mm, W 450 mm; H 400 mm, W 439 mm

Estimated H of the whole composition c. 2.2 m

SNM 30303a, b, c

This piece was composed of several fragments of painted plaster found in rubble. They belong to the destroyed upper part of the painting extant on the south wall of Room 12.

The Holy Trinity in Nubian art was always represented in the form of three identical figures (or busts) of Christ, characterized by a cross in a nimbus with individual letters of the expression, 'That, who is' (verify!), displayed on the arms. Traditionally the place in the centre was occupied by the Son of God.

The scheme of the whole composition from which these fragments originate is as follows (fig. 159): the central place was occupied by the huge, standing figure of a Nubian king of light brown complexion, dressed in a long tunic and a large scarlet cloak decorated with yellow (golden) eagles within medallions, which were no doubt of a Byzantine inspiration. In his left hand, against his chest, he supported a golden crown, while in his right hand he held a cross on the long stick. To the left of the figure a long, fragmentary and not fully understood text in Old Nubian mentioning the king and Holy Trinity was written in ink. In the upper part of the representation, the three members of the Holy Trinity appear from within a band of clouds. The right hand

of the outermost figures rested on the king's shoulders. A small, loose fragment of plaster depicted the right hand of the central figure, holding a crown topped with a cross. This helps to decipher the symbolic meaning of this composition as a coronation scene with the 'heavenly' crown.   SJ

Godlewski 1996, 40, 51, fig. 3; Jakobielski 1995b, 44, figs 6, 7; Martens-Czarnecka 1998, 96–100; 2001a, 272, pl. L; 2001b; 2001c, 296–9, fig. 10; Żurawski 1998, 125, fig. 2

183 Window grille or partition screen

Ceramic

Old Dongola, Kom H, Monastery of the Holy Trinity, the North-western Annexe, D.15/91-2

Medieval, second half of eleventh century AD

Fr. I: H 140 mm, W 504 mm; fr. II: H 150 mm, W 150 mm, Th 50 mm

SNM 30304

Terracotta grille with figural decoration of similar design on both sides, situated within a rectangular frame. The scene on one side is sculptured and painted. On the other side it is only painted in brown-red, red, black, white, yellow and pink. A figure is partly preserved on two pieces. One piece depicts the head of a Nubian warrior wearing a type of turban. The other shows part of the body with the right arm, part of the galligaskins and a fragment of a sword in a decorated sheath. The person is

either in reclining position or sitting in a Turkish fashion with sword on the knees and the head bent forward.

The grille fragments were found in rubble scattered over several rooms of the Annexe as a result of levelling made during its latest phase in the Terminal Christian period, after a serious destruction. Originally they were probably used in the upper storey of the Annexe. Fragments of at least three other grilles (or parts of neighbouring screen panels), with similar decoration differing only in ornamentation patterns, were found in the Annexe amongst numerous fragments of grilles of different designs and shapes. All were sculptured and painted in the same manner, proving that this kind of object was quite common in ecclessiastic architecture of the Late Christian Period.   SJ

Jakobielski 1995a, 90, 92; Ryl-Preibisz 1997, 229–30, pls 30A, B; 2001, 381–2, pl. LXI

183

184

184 Oil lamp

Ceramic

Old Dongola, Kom E, the 'Mosaic Church', D.75/93-4

Medieval, Late or Terminal Christian Period
(thirteenth or fourteenth centuries AD)

H 47 mm, L 80 mm, W 77 mm

SNM 31261

Square pottery oil lamp on a round plain base, complete and heavily blackened by soot. Originally wheel-made, but the body was shaped by hand before firing to accomodate four wicks. The form is typical for the latest period of Christianity.   SJ

185 Starburst lamp

Schist

Old Dongola, Kom H, Monastery of the Holy Trinity, the North-western Annexe, Room 39, D.26/00

Medieval, Christian

H 40 mm, D 202 mm

SNM 31358

An oil lamp made of schist, designed to form a twelve-petal rosette. Each of the sculptured petals was intended for use as a wick, the end of which was soaked in oil and stored in the round container in the centre of the lamp. It bears traces of an intensive use. The lamp was

discovered amongst rubble and extracted from within a matrix of burnt oil that originated from another lamp. This object is unique in Nubia and is possibly an import.   SJ

Jakobielski 2001a, 270–71; Jakobielski and Scholz 2001, pl. LXIV,2–3

186 Tombstone of Petros, the Eparch of Nobadia

Sandstone

Old Dongola, found reused in the Yard of House PCH-1, D.22/89

Medieval, AD 798

H 400 mm, W 260 mm, Th 120 mm

SNM 27595

Grave stela inscribed in Greek on a rectangular grey sandstone slab. It is complete except for part of the missing bottom right corner and some superficial breaks. The surface is covered with single incised lines containing fifteen lines of the text carved within a simple 20 mm-wide border. The stela was composed for Petros, a previously unknown eparch of Nobadia (i.e. the governor of the northern province of the Makurian kingdom who usually resided in either Faras or Qasr Ibrim), who apparently died in Old Dongola on 7 January AD 798. The stela reads:

'By the will and order of the Lord who created all things, the blessed Petros, Eparch of the land of Nobades fell asleep in

185

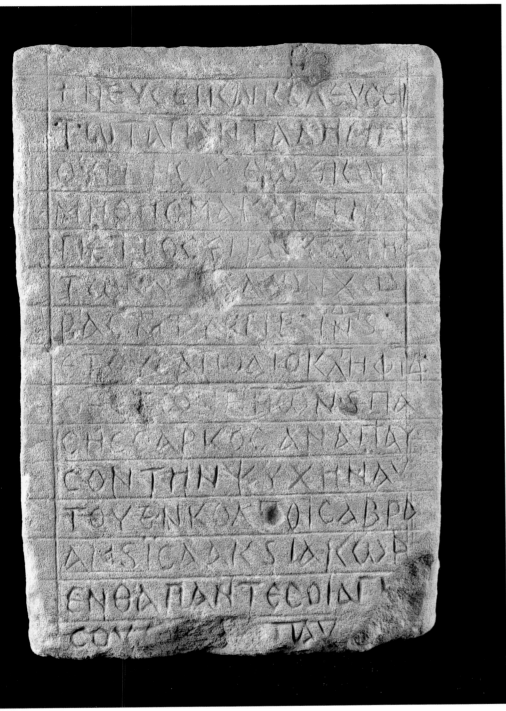

186

the month Tybi [day] 13, in the sixth indiction, in the year after Diocletian 514. God of spirits and of all flesh, rest his soul in the bosom of Abraham, Isaac and Jacob, where all your saints went to rest before.'
(Łajtar 2003, no. 23)   SJ

Ann. 1995, 1618; Godlewski 1989, 3; 1990a, 15–16; 1991a, 85–6; Jakobielski 2001b, 40 (note); Łajtar 1991, 157–9; 1997, 122–3; 2003, no. 23

187 Key

Copper alloy, iron

Old Dongola, Kom H, Monastery of the Holy Trinity, North-western Annexe, Room 28B, D.3/97

Medieval, eleventh century AD (possibly earlier)

L 205 mm, W 82 mm, Th 57 mm

SNM 31357

This large iron key with copper-alloy handle was found in a cellar, accessible from above through the upper storey, which had been used as a midden during the Terminal Christian Period. The cylindrical handle was cast in wax, then placed on the iron key shank. Two decorative beaded or twisted bands ring both the top and bottom ends of the handle, and a hole pierces the upper part to allow for the attachment of a cord. There are two short cylinders in the middle of the handle that are arranged perpendicular to it to faciliate the turning of the key. Another iron key was discovered in the north-east service area in Room 7 (D. 318/89; Żurawski 1994b, 331, fig. 9). The presence of these keys suggests that there were several places or containers within the monastery accessible only to a privileged few.   SJ/JRA/PP

Jakobielski 1998, 161–2; 2001c, 161, no. 43, 407, pl. LXIV,1

187

188 Bowl of Lazaros

Ceramic

Old Dongola, Kom H, Monastery of the Holy Trinity, North-western Annexe, Room 21, no. D.38/93-4

Medieval, late Christian, thirteenth century AD

H 85 mm; rim: D 285 mm

SNM 31359

A large, footed ceramic bowl with ledge rim, painted before firing and later inscribed with the owner's name which is deeply scratched into the fabric. A dark orange band runs around the rim while the body of the vessel is

188

painted a lighter orange. A decorative brown band with a zig-zag motif runs around the interior of the bowl just under the rim, and a flower rosette is painted in the centre. The inscription reads: 'Lazaros the archimandrite'. It is preceded by the name Michael written five times in a cryptographic form, '689', this being the sum of the numerical

value of the individual Greek letters in the name Michael. This type of cryptography is often used in texts from medieval Nubia.

The bowl comes from Room 21 in the North-western Annexe. This space was used as a midden during the Terminal Christian Period. The bowl belongs to a table set of Lazaros, an abbot of the Monastery of the Holy Trinity. Fragments of sixteen other pieces were found in the area of the monastery, including a large bowl, six smaller footed bowls or deep plates, three saucers, five cups of different forms and one storage jar. On some vessels the text refers to Lazaros along with his title of archimandrites (abbot) and contains the monastery denomination, the Holy Trinity, and his other title arch(i)styl(ites). The meaning of the latter is a matter of debate, but most probably it is the title of the person in the monastery who takes care of the spiritual life of monks (cf. Łajtar and Pluskota 2001, 347–9).   SJ

Łajtar and Pluskota 2001, 342–3, no. 13, 347; Pluskota 1997, 236, 242, no. 6

189 Cross

Sandstone

Old Dongola, Kom H, Monastery of the Holy Trinity, the North-western Annexe, Rooms 2 and 5, D.48/93

Medieval, early Christian (?), reused in the twelfth century AD

H 397 mm, D 312 mm, Th 124 mm; base: H 108 mm, max. W 136 mm

SNM 31360

An open-work sandstone Maltese cross carved in a circle. The cross is incised on both sides of the stone. A stone shaft shaped like a truncated cone extends from the base of the cross and is now broken. It was evidently used to fix the cross into a stand or screen wall in order to make both sides visible. The cross was discovered broken into three pieces on the floor of the mortuary chapel over the top of the crypt of Archbishop Georgios (deceased in AD 1113). Crosses of similar design have been discovered in the Church of the Stone Pavement and on column capitals at Old Dongola, and in various carvings from Philae and Faras (Ryl-Preibisz 2001, 377).   SJ

Jakobielski 2001b, 42; 2001c, 166; Ryl-Preibisz 2001, 378, pl. LX,2

190 Plaque with a representation of a warrior saint

Wood

Old Dongola, Kom H, Monastery of the Holy Trinity, Staircase 40, North-western Annexe, D. 1/98

Medieval, late Christian, twelfth century AD

H 164 mm, W 65 mm, Th 20 mm

SNM 31364

A wooden relief representing the standing figure of a warrior saint. It is incomplete, with the right side missing, and its surface has been charred. The figure is clad in a tunic onto which a shorter cloak is tied with a strip around the waist and the other one crossed at the breast. A nimbus surrounds his head. In his right hand he holds a javelin pointing downwards, perhaps piercing a snake-like dragon. The area around his left arm is partly preserved. There he either holds an oval shield or, as on the plaque found in the church at Attiri (SNM 20719; Wenig 1978b, 324, no. 290), part of a horse accompanying the saint was depicted. Only a few objects of this kind have been found in Nubia. Judging

190

from the somewhat similar figure of an angel found in a grave in Qasr Ibrim, lying on the body as a pectoral (Plumley 1970, 133, fig. 81), it seems likely that they were worn suspended from the neck. A hole pierced through the plaque near the elbow of the raised arm and a groove, perhaps left by a cord, below the mouth may indicate such a use.   JRA

Jakobielski 1999, 144–5; 2001b, 46, pl. LXIV,4

189

BANGANARTI

BOGDAN ŻURAWSKI

Banganarti,[1] the 'Island of the Locusts'[2] in Old Nubian, is situated on the right bank of the Nile about 10 km upriver from Old Dongola. The *kom* (mound) that covers two superimposed churches (subsequently labelled the 'Lower' and 'Upper Churches') is located in the sandy area separating the village and the riverbank fields. The Southern Dongola Reach Survey team began fieldwork there in 1998 with a series of aerial (kite) photographs taken above the central *kom* (fig. 160). Three campaigns in 2001, 2002, and 2003 duly followed and a magnetic survey conducted in 2001 traced the outer girdle walls beyond the point where they are visible on the surface.

Only a small portion of the Lower Church has been unearthed so far. Two layers of painted decoration with figures of saints were found accompanied by Greek inscriptions in ink. The biblical majuscule used suggests a date between the sixth and eighth centuries AD. A pattern imitating stonework rendered with white

and red paint, found on the eastern wall of the nave, also belongs to the first layer of painted decoration. The Lower Church was constructed of well-fired red bricks and squared sandstone blocks. Ceramics found in the fill above the Lower Church flooring consisted of sherds dated to the seventh–tenth centuries AD. A dense layer of broken early Christian amphorae that had accumulated above and below the pavement was a diagnostic feature of the pottery assemblage.

While the Lower Church was still in use, a row of tombs was dug along its eastern wall. Sondages were conducted into two of them (T.2 and T.3) in 2002 and one (T.1) was excavated *in toto* in 2003. The sepulchres were provided with solid *mastabas* made of red brick bonded with mud and plastered with very hard, slightly yellow, lime plaster. The superstructures were either flat or semi-cylindrical in shape. In Grave T.1, two adult male skeletons were found. Water had entered the crypt destroying the vault and damaging

160 Aerial view of Banganarti.

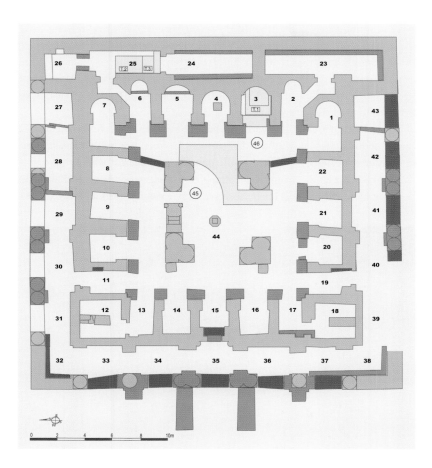

161 Plan of the church.

162 Isometric reconstruction of the church.

Another stela was found in the fill of the Lower Church's apse, a metre or so below the Upper Church pavement. It contained the epitaph of a woman (her name not preserved) who died sometime between AD 783 and 884. However, the most important epigraphic testimony from the Lower Church was a long prayer to the archangel Raphael for the benefit of King Zacharias. It was written in black ink, on the second layer of plaster on the stone wall to the right of the apse. It reads:

'... who accompanied your servant ... who lived abroad together with your servant ... accompany the King Zacharias to Christ ... of life ... and also is to ... for yours is ... Archangel, guide of God, Raphael, guide, guard, protect and save him from the traps of the enemy, our King Zacharias, amen, so be it, amen.'[3]

The inscription provides little data that would allow for the identification of the King Zacharias mentioned with one of the known Nubian kings bearing that name; however, the tenor of the text speaks in favour of Zacharias I as it refers to a trip made to a foreign country, perhaps the trip to Baghdad undertaken by Zacharias's son Georgios. If so, the inscription should be dated to the period shortly after AD 836.[4]

The reasons for the destruction of the Lower Church are unknown. High Nile floods in the mid-tenth century may have raised the water level in the foundations and caused the walls to subside.[5] After the Lower Church walls were purposely levelled off to a height of about 2.8 m above the original pavement, another church was constructed. The pavement of this new church, designated the 'Upper Church', was laid directly on the levelled walls of its predecessor. The disaster that befell the Lower Church must have been well remembered as the foundations of the new church were soundly built. All of the foundations of the outer walls were laid on a layer of well-worked stones and the most vulnerable parts, such as the north-west corner, were abutted with solidly built *mastabas* made of red bricks and stone.

The Upper Church was constructed following a most unusual plan (figs 161, 162). It consisted of a square, perfectly symmetrical edifice, topped by a huge dome surrounded on the southern, western and northern sides with porticoes. It was planned and executed with a significant consideration for the set of graves located along the eastern wall of the Lower Church.[6] These were overbuilt with a huge mud-brick *mastaba* into which the church's foundation trench was sunk. The new church building was raised in such a way that a row of seven chapels was constructed directly above the sepulchres. It is on the walls of these chapels that

the bones, which were found in a most fragile condition. In the fill above Graves T.2. and T.3, the sepulchral stela of *hegemon* Markos (deceased AD 798) (cat. 191) was found. Apparently it had once belonged to one of the eastern tombs.

the portraits of Nubian kings and high dignitaries (*hegemones?*) were painted.

All of the eastern chapels in the Upper Church had apses that were painted with a uniform composition: a king dressed in robes of honour, crowned, holding a sceptre in the right hand and another crown in the left hand. The king was painted among the apostles under the holy patronage of an archangel, possibly Raphael, who stood behind. The central chapel was constructed according to a different plan. The wall curvature was divided into seven spaces by six pillars provided with

dignitaries are neither protected by an archangel nor accompanied by apostles. Instead of carrying elaborate columnar sceptres, they are painted holding plain sticks that have no religious emblems. They wear horned headgear both with and without religious symbols (fig. 164).

In its first phase the Upper Church was furnished with a pulpit situated between the two northern piers. Inserted in the pavement in front of the pulpit was a sandstone epitaph of a king whose name is difficult to decipher; however, the surviving letters strongly suggest

163 *Left* One of the apostles flanking the Nubian ruler.

164 *Right* Portrait of a Nubian dignitary.

capitals and bases, all covered with various painted designs. The central *intercolumnium* contained a portrait of a ruler under the patronage of an archangel (fig. 163).

The Banganarti royal portraits have been found only in the eastern chapels thus far; however, another portrait group was discovered in the side chapels. As a rule, these portraits were situated on the eastern walls of the southern chapels. They differ significantly from the royal portraits in the church's presbytery. The

the name David. It is dated on palaeographical grounds between the eleventh and thirteenth centuries AD.

The octagon was one of the principles used in the church's decoration and octagonal pillars flank the main western entrance to the church. In the central part of the nave, the focal point of the church as a whole, was a curious octagonal object constructed of red brick and plastered with lime render. It contained a subterranean cache plastered on the interior. It was possibly for relics, although it could also have served as a socket for a standing wooden (?) object such as a cross.

The Upper Church was first entered through an elaborate portal placed in the middle of the western wall. It was provided with a stone threshold, stone jambs and probably a stone arch that has not survived. It was blocked during the first reconstruction of the church interior and two entrances were used instead in the southern and northern walls. Both were made of well-dressed sandstone blocks. It was on the voussoirs of the northern archway where the inscription of 'Durere, deacon of the church of Great Jesus, epirshil of the king Siti' was found.

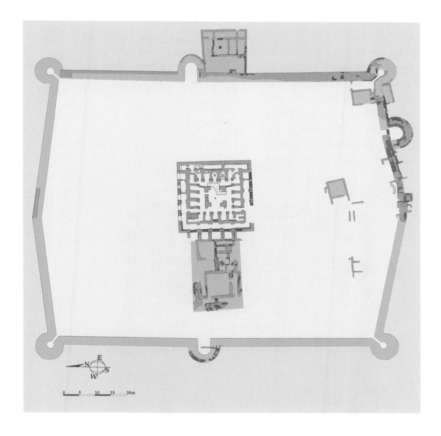

165 Plan of the church, additional buildings and enclosure.

Surface evidence suggests the Banganarti church stood unaccompanied by any building until the very end of the eleventh century AD. Raising the defensive walls gave impetus to the building activity within the enclosure. First a huge building was added to the church's western wall. Other structures were then built but on a very limited scale when compared with the 'Western Building' (fig. 165).

The enormous number of inscriptions left by visitors strongly suggests that Banganarti was one of the most important pilgrimage centres in the Middle Nile. Thus far, 650 inscriptions have been documented. They are composed in Greek and Old Nubian, or in a mixture of these two languages. Banganarti, as with other pilgrimage centres in the Nile Valley, was also visited by people who expected miraculous healing. The faith-healing idiom is to some extent suggested by a splendid mural found in the northern staircase vestibule. It depicts two standing figures of the *anargyroi* saints, Cosmas and Damianos.

The Upper Church underwent at least one major reconstruction. This did not affect the general layout, but new walls, piers and partitions were introduced. The general purpose was to narrow the spaces spanned by the arches and vaults. This was achieved by doubling the wall thicknesses and extending the pillars. It was on these new additions that most of the graffiti were found. The church was re-plastered as a result of these modifications and repainted. The last murals in Banganarti, painted in the late twelfth and thirteenth centuries AD, bear all the characteristics indicative of a decline in Nubian visual art.

The unique layout of the Banganarti Upper Church has raised several questions about the sources and inspirations for Makurian architecture. The design of its eastern part bears analogy to the church of St George in Dayr Mari Girgis near Akhmim,[7] nevertheless its general layout is paralleled by church, Building A at Soba East.[8] The apparent similarity between the Banganarti and Soba churches not only suggests trans-Bayuda contacts between Makuria and Alwa but might also shed new light on a tenth-century AD unification of the two kingdoms, so far evidenced only by literary testimony.

1 The site is located at 18°10′00.4″ N longitude, 30°47′04.8″ E latitude. It is known also as Jebel En-Nassara (Mountain of the Christians), or simply Kenissa (The Church), and was surveyed and registered by the Royal Ontario Museum Expedition to Nubia in 1985 as ROM 53 (Grzymski 1989, 11).
2 Armbruster 1965, 29.
3 The translations of all Greek inscriptions found in Banganarti, together with commentaries, were done by Adam Łajtar.
4 Vantini 1975, 420–21.
5 Welsby 2002, 75, after Adams 1968, 189, n. 16.
6 It must be stressed that its archetype, Buildings A and B at Soba, also had associated graves on their eastern side. Both buildings, according to Derek Welsby (Welsby and Daniels 1991, 316–17), had a commemorative character.
7 Grossmann 2002, 543–4, fig. 160,
8 Welsby and Daniels 1991, 33–80, fig. 2. I owe this reference to Derek Welsby, director of the Soba excavations.

191 Epitaph of Markos, a *Hegemon*

Marble

Banganarti, 'Upper Church', Room 24,
no. SDRS 21/03

Medieval, AD 786

H 378 mm, W 235 mm, Th 48 mm

SNM 31225

This roughly rectangular, blue-grey marble funerary stela, inscribed in Greek, was found inserted, the script upside down, in the brick pavement of Room 24 of the Upper Church. The text, but for some minor surface damage, is entirely preserved. Faint guidelines indicating both the bottom and top of the letters are visible in lines 1–4 and 7 of the inscription. The hand may be described as round epigraphic majuscles.[1] The stonemason used *nomina sacra* in lines 2 and 7. He abbreviates words through shifting the last written letter as in line 5, or by crossing the last written letter by an oblique stroke. Numerals are marked by a horizontal dash above, and β in line 5 also has points on both of its sides. The initial *iota* in the names Ἰσαάκ and Ἰακώβ has a trema. Letter heights range between 11 and 25 mm. The text reads:

> 'Through the inclination and order of the living God, Markos, a Hegemon, fell asleep in the month of Phamenoth [day] 2nd, in the 9th indiction, in the year from Diocletian 502. God of spirits and of all flesh, rest his soul in the bosom of Abraham and Isaac and Jacob, in a shining place, in a place of refreshment, from which pain and grief and lamentation have fled away.'

The formula νεύσει καί κελεύσει, found in the first three lines, is rare. It is found in the epitaph of Petros, Eparch of Nobadia (died AD 798), recovered at Old Dongola (cat. 186).[2] It also occurs in a fragmentarily preserved epitaph from Khor Dam Et-Tor near Bageri (Łajtar 2003, 73). The office of *Hegemon* is attested here for the second time so far in Christian Nubia. The other attestation is yielded by an epitaph, now in the Sudan National Museum, commemorating a *Hegemon* with the name Theodorou (Theodoros).[3] The Theodorou epitaph may be dated on palaeographic grounds to the eighth–tenth centuries. According to the Museum register, it came to light in Tangasi. There are two villages of this name between the Third and Fourth Cataracts: one on the right bank immediately south-east of Banganarti,[4] and the other on the left bank several kilometres west of Merowe. The discovery of the epitaph of the *Hegemon* Markos at Banganarti argues strongly for the former of these two villages as the provenance of the epitaph of the *Hegemon* Theodorou. It can be hypothesized that both *Hegemones* were originally buried not far from each other, in the cemetery surrounding the 'Lower Church' at Banganarti.

The exact meaning of the term *Hegemon* relative to Christian Nubia remains unknown.[5] Since in the Eastern Roman Empire of the fifth–sixth centuries, the word *Hegemon* was a quasi-technical term for the governor of a province (Lat. *praefectus, praeses*), we may suppose that the same or similar meaning may also be applied to it in Nubia. The *Hegemones* Markos and Theodorou living in the eighth–tenth centuries may have been governors of some administrative units within the Kingdom of Makuria.

Indiction and the Era of Diocletian are the standard systems used to indicate a year in early epitaphs from Nubia until the first half of the tenth century. Both indications agree with each other here, which is not always the case in Nubian inscriptions. The present epitaph is the second oldest dated funerary inscription from the Dongola area, the oldest being the epitaph of a woman, Kel, discovered at Old Dongola and dated to AD 785.[6]

The prayer for the dead contained in lines 7–16, is clearly modelled on the prayer of the Euchologion Mega-type characteristic of Nubian funerary inscriptions. It preserves from this prayer the initial invocation to God and the list of places of eternal rest for the deceased's soul. The prayer from Markos's epitaph seems to have no exact parallel in Nubian epitaphs written in Greek, but more or less similar prayers do occur; the differences consist in the kind of invocation and the choice of names for the places of rest. The epitaph of Christina originating from Merowe is one such example.[7]   AŁ

1 Note the alpha '*á barres brisées*' while the sigma is both square and lunar.

2 See the commentary in Łajtar 2003, 23, where similar formulae in Greek and Coptic are cited.

3 See further ibid., 29.

4 Some local people say that Banganarti *kom* is part of Tangasi village.

5 Ibid., 29.

6 Ibid., 20.

7 Ibid., 30.

191

192 Buckle (?)

Copper alloy

Banganarti, Church, south entrance,
no. SDRS 34/03

Medieval

L 27–8 mm; wire: D 1.5 mm; terminals: L 12 mm,
Th 5 mm; loop: D 15 mm

SNM 31228A–B

The thick copper-alloy wire of this pair of
identical elements is shaped into an omega
(Ω), with thicker hexagonal (in section) rod
terminals. Incised zigzags run around the
circumference of the terminals. The identification is problematic since no analogies exist.
They could possibly be a pair of earrings. The
diagnostic feature is that the diameters of the
wire loops are slightly different, thus allowing
one to be hooked to the other and, in fact, the

194, 193

192

wires were found looped together. Thus, the
most plausible solution is that they functioned as a pair of clasps attached, for example, to either end of a leather belt similar to
the specimen seen on the Dongolese murals
and found in a monk's grave from *Kom* H in
Old Dongola (Żurawski 1999, 243, fig. 42;
1995, 353, fig. 28). Ω-shaped buckles were
well known in Nubia and in neighbouring
countries, both in medieval and earlier
times.[1]   BŻ

1 See further, Dunham 1955, 67 (Nu.21, 17-1-550
Br. 1:2); Munro-Hay 1989, 217, figs 15.73–4.

193 Chalice

Ceramic

Banganarti, Church, niche in Room 26, east wall, no.
SDRS 5/02

Medieval, thirteenth–fourteenth centuries AD

H 180 mm; bowl: D 123 mm; foot: D 85 mm

SNM 31224

Found inverted inside the paten (cat. 194) in
a niche in the eastern wall of Room 26 in the
Banganarti Church, this is a typical Nubian
liturgical chalice. Throughout the Christian
period in Nubia, this shape of vessel was
reserved for liturgical use only.[1] It is made of
well-fired clay with a reddish brown (10R
5/8) slip. A black stripe runs around the
upper rim and the foot edge. The upper bowl
sits on a high neck that is hollow inside. The
splash, which looks like a drop of black paint
from the rim band, seems to be intentional – a
convention also found on other objects of this
kind.[2] Objects like patens (cat. 194) were
modelled on metal and glass objects such as
the superb Faras chalice (SNM 24395).

Earthenware chalices are not an uncommon find in Nubian churches. In the eastern
rooms of the Banganarti church at least four
other chalices were found, although fragmentarily preserved. The latest, dating to the
second half of the fourteenth century, of
pinkish ware, was identified by its Old Nubian
inscription as belonging to *Diakon* Mesi.[3]   BŻ

1 See, however, the Soba Ware chalice (cat. 198) and
Khider and Welsby 1996; Welsby 1998a, 113.

2 See further a paten from the Faras cathedral
in Seipel 2002, 137, no. 70.

3 See also Mileham 1910, 35, 53 fig. 6, pl. 19a;
Godlewski 1990b, 53, fig. 14 a.b.c; Van Moorsel *et al.*
1975, 24, no. 27.

Żurawski 2002b, 79, pl. L

194 Paten

Banganarti, Church, niche in Room 26, east wall,
no. SDRS 4/03

Medieval, twelfth–thirteenth centuries AD

H 67 mm, D 196 mm

SNM 31227

Found together with a chalice (cat. 193), this
saucer-shaped earthenware paten was well
fired and matt-slipped reddish brown, with a
black rim band and circular splash in the
middle body section (upper surface). The
black band was precisely painted while the
vessel was revolving on a wheel. Fragments of
four other patens were found in the eastern
rooms of the Banganarti Church; characteristically enough they were made in matching
pairs with the chalices, the latest examples of
which were of pinkish ware. Contrary to the
chalices, the paten shape was common in the
Nubian ceramic repertory and frequently
employed in everyday usage.[1]   BŻ

1 For published analogies, cf. Godlewski 1990a, 54,
fig. 15; Mileham 1910, 36, no. 28, 53, fig. 7; Seipel
2002, 137, 70.

Żurawski 2002b, 79, pl. L

195 Jar

Ceramic

Banganarti, Church, Room 23, no. SDRS 6/03

Medieval, thirteenth–fourteenth centuries

H 233 mm, D 105 mm; base: D 88 mm

SNM 31223

A wheel-made necked jar with a convex base, slipped to matt orange (10R5/8) with the upper shoulders painted white. The upper body is divided into four equal parts by four vertical white bands bordered with black vertical lines. The lower, horizontal terminations of the white bands lack this black line border. The uppermost white painted section is separated from the orange slipped body by a black double line. This was probably a product of a local kiln; however, no exact parallels are known among the rich repertoire from Old Dongola and the Southern Dongola Reach. It may have played some role in the liturgy as a holy water, milk[1] or wine container, as may be suggested by its find spot (in the so-called southern *pastoforium*) among the lamps, chalice and paten fragments. The ceramic debris in the eastern part of Banganarti church was also strongly mixed with broken wine amphorae.   BŻ

1 See further the inscribed altar from Banganarti (cat. 196).

Żurawski 2002b, 79, pl. LI

196 Inscribed altar top (?)

Baked brick, mud and lime mortar

Banganarti, Church, Room 26, no. SDRS 9/02

Medieval, eleventh–thirteenth centuries

H 213 mm, L (upper) 270 mm, L (lower) 220 mm, W (upper) 220 mm, W (lower) 75 mm

SNM 31226

Altar top in the form of a truncated, inverted pyramid made of three baked bricks (the fourth brick is missing), bonded with mud mortar and covered by a thick layer of lime mortar. It was inserted into the late pavement in front of the altar niche.

It is inscribed, with a corrupted Greek text, in black ink with thick *kalamos*. The hand is rather hasty Old Nubian majuscles. Numerous phonetic notations and a number of syntactic mistakes suggest that the scribe did not understand what he wrote or that his understanding was very superficial. The text reads:

I. 'You have said to your pupil apostles these words: 'If someone will not be born again he would not have been able to enter[?] the kingdom of God' and 'If you do not change

yourself and will not be like children, you will not enter the Kingdom of God' [...]. Save us through your only begotten son [...].'

II. '[...] the Saviour, You who [...], You who [have ...] the esteemed [...] of the table, You, God, who have fed with five [scil. breads] five thousand men, without counting women and children, and there was an overabundance, now, feed us with this food of Yours, the food which is of heaven, through His [*sic*! it should be Your] pupils, for You are blessed.'

III. (The fourth brick that contained the beginning of the third prayer, about ten lines long, is lost.)
'[...] of the nature [...] we beseech You [...] to make the Holy Spirit appear [...] according to the power [... on] this milk, change [...] and transform [it] in order that [it ...], O Lord, [...] that [...] for the remission [of sins ...].'

Most probably the above prayers are closely interconnected and together formed a framework for the liturgy. The sequence of prayers is apparently I-II-III. In prayers I and II (*anamnesis*) the author makes use of the sayings of Jesus as given in Jh. 3.3 (Prayer I, ll. 2–5) and Matt. 18.3 (Prayer I, ll. 6–10), as well as the description of the miraculous multiplication of bread as contained in Matt. 14.20–21 (Prayer II, ll. 5–7). Prayer III (*epiclesis*) invites the Holy Spirit to come and transform the offerings put on the altar. Here, the offering under consideration is 'milk'. Milk plays a prominent role in only one known liturgy, namely baptismal liturgy. The distribution of milk and honey to

195

the newly baptized is well attested in the Latin Church. In the East, it was apparently restricted to the Alexandrian Patriarchate. It is mentioned in the *Traditio Apostolica* of Pseudo-Hippolytus, a text that probably came into existence in the fifth century describing liturgical practices of the then Patriarchate of Alexandria. A late attestation is mentioned by E. Renaudot with reference to the Coptic liturgist Abu'l-Barakat Ibn Kabar (died AD 1324). The inscription on the altar-like object from Banganarti must also refer to the baptismal liturgy. It testifies to the fact that the custom of distributing milk (and honey) among those newly baptized also existed in the Nubian Church, which in this respect presents itself as a true part of the Alexandrian Patriarchate.   AŁ

196

SOBA EAST

DEREK A. WELSBY

Covering an area of at least 2.75 km², Soba is one of Sudan's largest archaeological sites. The ruins at Soba were brought to the attention of the modern Western world when they were visited by the Frenchman Frederick Cailliaud in 1821.[1] Throughout the nineteenth century there are reports of the site being extensively quarried to supply building materials for the construction of Khartoum, some 22 km downstream. Most of the buildings constructed of red brick have been reduced to piles of rubble, the mud-brick buildings being preserved to a greater degree under the remains of their collapsed superstructures.

The first 'archaeological' work was conducted by Wallis Budge of the British Museum in 1903. Unfortunately he published only one short note on his discoveries.[2] The excavations of Somers Clark in 1910 are a little better known,[3] while the work of Peter Shinnie, between 1950 and 1952, was on a small scale.[4] Between 1981 and 1992 the British Institute in Eastern Africa conducted a detailed survey of the medieval town followed by seven seasons of excavation in a number of areas within it.[5] This work dramatically altered our perception of Soba and has done much to support the impression of its richness given by the medieval historians.

The earliest literary evidence for the town dates to the ninth century AD but archaeological evidence indicates that the site was of much greater antiquity. Although a number of Kushite stone sculptures have been recovered,[6] the earliest structural evidence dates from the transitional period, between the decline of the Kushite state and the rise of the Nubian kingdoms, which were converted to Christianity in the sixth century AD. One building (Building G), excavated between 1990 and 1992, began its life as a masonry structure approximately 5 m². Only the foundations remained, but what little was found led to the suggestion that it may have been a funerary monument of pyramidal form (fig. 166).[7] However, no associated tomb could be found. It was succeeded by a building of red brick set within a rectangular enclosure bounded by a wall of mud brick. The plan of the building has much more in common with temples of Kushite date than with structures of any later period.

166 The stone foundations under Building G.

167 The remains of
timber structures,
presumably fences,
adjacent to Building G.

168 Granite columns
of the church on
Mound C.

The missionary Longinus, according to the sixth-century Byzantine ecclesiastical historian John of Ephesus, converted the King of Alwa to Christianity in AD 580.[8] How quickly the new religious ideology percolated down through Alwan society is unclear, but its ultimate and profound effect on art and architecture can readily be seen. The earliest evidence for the spread of Christianity can be observed in the style of decoration employed on the abundant local fine pottery, the so-called Soba Ware (cats 198, 259) which has been found associated with pottery generally recognized as of pre-Christian date. At this time the inhabitants of the town were living in circular huts of timber construction. This type of building soon gave way to the construction of rectilinear buildings, firstly of timber (fig. 167) and thereafter of mud brick, which was to become the ubiquitous building material for domestic structures.

The earliest known church may be that close to the river (fig. 168). The use of granite columns and the forms of the granite capitals suggest that, on analogy with the better-known church architecture in northern Nubia, it pre-dates the other churches so far uncovered at Soba.

Towards the centre of the town, excavations revealed an ecclesiastical complex of considerable size. Here, at the western end of the largest complex of monumental buildings on the site, are three churches. Although constructed over a period of time, they were certainly in use contemporaneously. Two of these churches are five-aisled basilicas (fig. 169) and are among the largest churches known in Nubia, being only surpassed in size by churches at Old Dongola. In the northern church three main building phases were observable. One of the earliest features was a barrel-vaulted crypt lying immediately to the east of the apsidal sanctuary chamber. In its second phase the church was entered through a 12.5 m-wide, probably three-portalled entrance to the west and by two 14.8 m-wide five-portalled entrances to north and south. In the final phase the *haikal* was paved in white and dolomitic marble (fig. 170), coinciding with the provision of massive brick piers presumably to support a vaulted and domed roof. It was built throughout of well-laid red brick and was presumably decorated with fine wall paintings.

Immediately adjacent to this complex is a very large mud-brick structure almost certainly originally at least two storeys high. It appears to have been palatial in character and may have been the residence of the metropolitan of the city. Reused within the structure was one of the few royal tombstones known from Christian Nubia (cat. 197), a slab of marble inscribed in Greek recording a hitherto unknown king called David.[9]

At Soba, graves are generally associated with red-brick structures, all of which were presumably churches. Most inhumations were placed in long, narrow graves aligned east–west, with the body placed on its back with

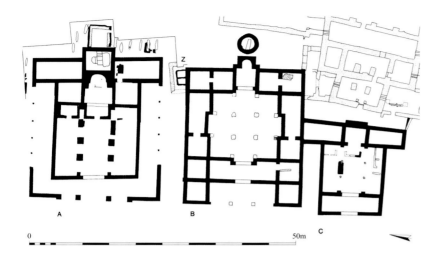

169 The churches at the western end of Mound B.

as reported by medieval travellers and historians, can now be appreciated. As well as the remains of impressive buildings, the artefacts recovered testify to this wealth and to the existence of wide-ranging trade links. Among the imported items is glassware of types familiar from sites around the Arabian peninsular and the western littoral of the Indian Ocean and Islamic pottery. The most exotic items are pieces of Chinese porcelain.

By the thirteenth century there is evidence that squatters were living within the largest of the Soba churches. At this time also, a number of rich burials to the east of the churches on mound B were pillaged, and the bodies dumped into the crypt. Clearly the city was in decline, although we know nothing of how this process came about. The kingdom may have been infiltrated by Muslims over a long period, leading to its gradual collapse. A late source, the Funj Chronicle, records that Soba was destroyed in AD 1504. By that date much of the city may already have been in ruins.

the head to the west. There is some variation, particularly in the burials of children where some are placed in a crouched position and one is laid with its head to the east. More elaborate graves have a vaulted burial chamber (fig. 171) covered by a rectangular *mastaba*. The most elaborate tomb was found immediately to the east of the central church on mound B. Here the individual was placed in a mud-brick vaulted chamber which was marked on the surface by a cylindrical red-brick tomb, the only one of this Byzantine type known in the Nile Valley. To the east of the presumed church on Mound UA 3 are two contemporary red-brick vaulted tombs, the

1 Cailliaud 1826–7, II, 203 ff.
2 Budge 1907, I, 324–5.
3 Clarke 1912, 34–8.
4 Shinnie 1955.
5 Welsby 1998a; Welsby and Daniels 1991.
6 Welsby 1999b.
7 Welsby 1998a, 40–42.
8 Vantini 1975, 17 ff.
9 Jakobielski 1991, 274–6.
10 Welsby 1998a, 56–9.

170 The marble floor in the *haikal* of Church A.

171 Red-brick vaulted burial chamber with remains of a wooden coffin.

northern of which contained the bodies of sixteen adults and one unborn child.[10] Later burials intruding into Christian cemeteries have the bodies placed in a crouched attitude with a wide range of orientations. The identity of this group is unknown, but they are clearly neither Christian nor Muslim.

Although badly destroyed, the importance and wealth of the capital of the medieval kingdom of Alwa at Soba,

197 Stela of King David

Marble
Soba East, Building D, Room m 18
Medieval, AD 1015 (?)
L 460 mm, W 360 mm
SNM 31251

This roughly rectangular marble funerary stela belongs to an Alwan king named David. It is one of the few royal tombstones known and the only one of a king of Alwa. It is inscribed with twenty lines of Greek, below which three crosses are incised. The first three lines of the text are slightly larger in size than the following registers. It may have been set into the floor of a church in a fashion similar to the stela of Mariankouda (cat. 318). This may account for

mourning hath fled. Pardon [every sin committed] by him in word or deed [or thought; remit and annul,] because [there is no man who will live] and will not sin. For [Thou only, O God, art without] sin, and thy justice [is justice for]ever.

O Lord, thy word [is truth,] for Thou art the rest and resurrection of thy servant and to thee we sing The glory of the father and the Son and the Holy Ghost, now and always and forever. Amen.

The years from his birth when he was not a king [were] [...], whereas he was king sixteen years three months. After the Martyrs 732 he completed [his life] in the month of Hathor the 2nd; Thursday.'

The dating of the King's death at AD 1015 has recently been questioned (Łajtar 1999, pers. comm.).   JRA/DAW

Jakobielski 1991, 274–6, fig. 153, pl. 47

198 Chalice

Ceramic
Khalil el-Kubra
Medieval, Early Christian
H 310 mm; rim: D 85 mm; base: D 173 mm
SNM 26941

One of the few complete Soba Ware vessels discovered thus far, this chalice was uncovered at Khalil el-Kubra by a resident digging for fertile soil. Both its decoration and form

197

198

the illegible, worn text in the centre of the stone. The edges are also worn. The text contains a Nubian version of a common Byzantine prayer for the dead known as the Εὐχολογίον μεγα. The humble nature of this stone may be contrasted with the more opulent, finer stela of Mariankouda. This may be a reflection of King David's personal piety or an indication of the type of raw materials and the level of skilled artisans available in Makuria as opposed to Alwa. The inscription reads as follows:

'O God of the spirits and all flesh, Thou who hast rendered death ineffectual and has trodden down Hades, and hast given life to the world, rest the soul of [Thy] servant David, the King, in the bosom of Abraham and Isaac and Jacob, in a place of light, in a place of verdure, in a place of refreshment, whence grief and pain and are analogous to the numerous Soba Ware fragments (cf. cat. 259) discovered at Soba East, the site where these vessels were most likely manufactured. The entire chalice was first covered with a cream slip over which various colours were applied. The stem and interior were covered with brown slip. The primary exterior decoration on the base and cup is a wide band containing a horizontal repeating diamond pattern sandwiched between two smaller red-painted registers containing a repeating cross motif. Roundels containing the most common decorative motif found on Soba Ware – a small cream four-petal flower or cross – were placed at the junction point where the diamonds overlap. The diamonds and the triangular spaces in between are filled with a black crosshatch pattern. Two cream bands and two black bands separate the base and cup from the stem. The colour sequence on the base and cup are reversed, making them mirror images. This vessel probably originated in a

grave, which in itself is unusual, as Christian graves usually lack accompanying goods; thus a pagan may have been buried accompanied by a ware typical of the Early Christian period in Alwa. The find site, located about 250 km to the south of Soba, gives an insight into the southern limits of the Alwan kingdom.   JRA/DAW

Khider and Welsby 1996

199 Baptismal basin

Ceramic
Soba East, Building F, fill of pit (Z6)119
Medieval
H 356 mm, L 1054 mm, W 642 mm
SNM 31204

This oval basin was discovered in a pit smashed into several pieces, rather than in the baptistery of a church as might be expected. It has a smooth matt finish and is of brick-red fabric. The basin walls are straight

and four long ridges run parallel along the bottom in the interior. The underside is smooth. Each ridge stands approximately 10 mm high and is 32 mm wide. At one end, a spout level with the bottom of the basin protrudes 82 mm beyond the vessel's wall, above which is a raised Greek cross with all four splayed arms of roughly equal length. Over the cross, the rim is perforated by three holes that angle downwards at 53 degrees. The function of these holes is uncertain. A similar basin, inscribed with a painted invocation to John the Baptist, was discovered at Hambukol, Kom H, in the church baptistery (Anderson and Blitz 1998, 47), and a second basin was discovered set in the ground in trench D9 at Soba suggesting that it might have been reused as a coffin (Welsby and Daniels 1991, 17, pl. 4).   JRA/DAW

Welsby 1998a, 174–5

199

200 Cross

Shell

Soba East, (B3)1, Building A, no. SF 325

Medieval, tenth–eleventh centuries AD

L 20 mm, W 20 mm, Th 1 mm

SNM 31252

This freshwater oyster-shell cross has arms of equal length that gradually widen towards the ends and terminate in points. Circular holes, 1 and 2 mm in diameter, pierce two opposing arms so that it might be sewn on to a garment or other cloth item. It was dis-

200

covered in the vicinity of Building A, the North Church at Soba, and is of such high quality that it perhaps comes from a liturgical vestment.   JRA/DAW

Allason-Jones 1991, 141

201 Cross

Iron

Soba East, (B7)23, no. SF 1396

Medieval

H (of arms) 55 mm, L 386 mm, W 243 mm

SNM 31253

This Greek cross is made of a single piece of iron, and is the largest cross excavated at Soba. Its arms are of equal length, the ends of

which are rounded and have been hammered flat to create a splayed appearance. A 130 mm-long spike, rectangular in cross-section, tapers downward from the bottom arm. This spike suggests that the cross was fitted into a wooden handle enabling it to be carried by hand, or was mounted in a staff or inserted into the back of a chair or throne. All three alternatives are depicted in the wall paintings discovered at Faras (Michałowski 1974, nos 19, 30, 35, 39). The numerous crosses, particularly of iron, discovered at Soba indicate the widespread nature of Christianity among the population and might indicate preferential usage of this metal. Iron was a valued commodity and it has been suggested that it was credited with apotropaic properties, particularly during phases or ceremonies of transition such as initiation, births and deaths (Żurawski 1994a, 211–12).

JRA/DAW

Allason-Jones 1991, 132–3, 160

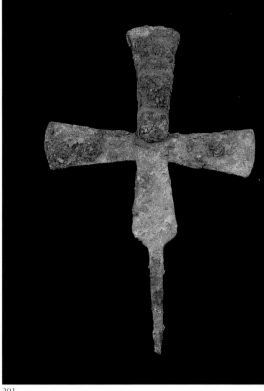

201

202

202 Cross

Iron

Soba East, (B3)1, Building A, no. SF 310

Medieval, tenth–eleventh centuries AD

L 139 mm, W 97 mm, Th 4 mm

SNM 31254

Two rectangular iron bands are set perpendicular to one another with the horizontal arm being hammered into a groove in the vertical shaft. The ends of the cross's arms were flattened and widened by hammering, and the horizontal arm is slightly shorter than the vertical arm. The arms of most iron crosses found at Soba are finished in this fashion. There is no indication as to how this cross was attached or mounted.   JRA/DAW

Allason-Jones 1991, 132–3

203

203 Earring

Silver, amber (?)
Soba East, (Z4)81, no. SF 2008
Medieval
L 23 m, D 10.5 mm, Th 4 m
SNM 31255

An incised six-pointed star decorates the obverse and reverse faces of the amber (?) disc element of this earring. An incised band runs around the edge of the disc enclosing the star. A hole pierces the disc through the side, and a silver wire 4 mm thick was threaded through this perforation and bent to form an 'S'-shape to facilitate the addition of other segments. Numerous objects of personal adornment were discovered at Soba. The majority are of modest materials that were available locally.   JRA/DAW

Allason-Jones 1998, 60–61

204 Beads

Clay
Soba East, no. SF 2291
Medieval
Avg. D 25 mm, Th 20 mm
SNM 31250

These globular beads form a selection from over 350 pottery beads discovered at Soba. No decoration or paint was evident on any of them. The beads vary slightly in shape from globular to ovoid as production practices were not consistent and little care was taken when rolling the wet clay during their manufacture. As the number of beads used in different pieces of jewellery varies dramatically, it is difficult to determine how many items of adornment these represent. Beads were not associated with any specific feature and were scattered randomly across the site of Soba. The large quantity of clay beads discovered might suggest that they were employed for a specific purpose such as for rosaries, similar to those used in the Coptic Church in Egypt.   JRA/DAW

Allason-Jones 1991, 151; 1998, 74

205 Finger-ring

Sandstone
Soba East, (B16)2, Building D, no. SF 829
Medieval, eleventh–twelfth centuries AD
L 30 mm, W 25 mm, Th 20 mm
SNM 31249

A decorative asterisk was incised on the oval face of this yellow sandstone finger-ring fragment. The decoration is roughly applied, contrasting with the high technical skill used in the actual carving of the ring. This suggests that the decoration was applied by a second artisan or perhaps an apprentice. Similar rings have previously been found at Soba (SNM 11223 A and B) and at Jebel Moya (ROM 947.52.457), and appear to have been manufactured from local materials.   JRA/DAW

Allason-Jones 1991, 147

204, 205

206 Jewellery mould

Slate

Soba East, (B13)5, Building D, no. SF 1285

Medieval, tenth–twelfth centuries AD

L 65 mm, W 44 mm, Th 10 mm

SNM 31248

206

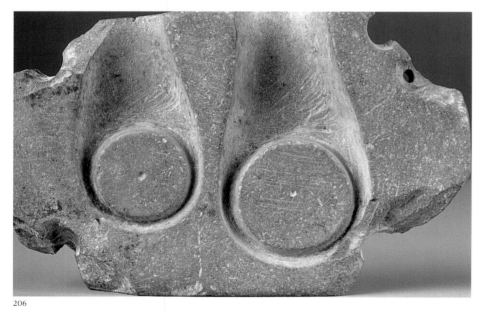

206

Two moulds for finger-rings are found on one side of this rectangular slate mould, while a delicately incised, inscribed, circular medallion is found on the other face. Each side forms one half of a rectangular slate mould, which would have been held together with wooden pins inserted through holes in the corners. Lead was discovered in three of the pin-holes. These moulds could not have been used at the same time, as the conical channels for pouring the lead are orientated perpendicular to one another. The rings produced would have been similar in appearance to cat. 205, also discovered at Soba. As the interior of the mould is rough, the rings would have been finished by hand. A dot incised in the centre of each ring indicates that a compass was used to create the circular shape. The medallion on the other side has an Arabic inscription in the centre, surrounded by a circle of dots. A horizontal groove runs above it, which may have functioned as an air vent or mould for a chain. Similar moulds for finger-rings and earrings have been discovered in Egypt, but moulds for medallions are rare (Ogden 1982, fig. 4; Jenkins and Keen 1982, 147). The medallion may have served as a talisman for young women as the first line refers to safeguarding the chastity of a virgin, while the second comes from Surah 25 of the Koran. The mould's presence suggests that these items were being manufactured on site, rather than imported, and indicates the movement of the producer rather than of the finished product. Ibn Selim records the presence of a large Muslim colony at Soba (el-Maqrizi in Vantini 1975, 613, 615), and it is possible that the medallion was produced for this community.

The inscription reads:

'Glory [or power] and might are protected [or fortified] through thee, And I place my reliance on the Ever-Living who dies not.'

JRA/DAW

Allason-Jones 1991, 145, 147, pl. 39

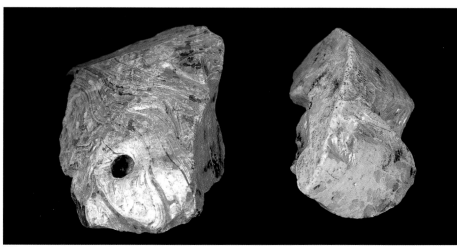

207

207 Raw glass

Glass
Soba East, (Z4)250, no. SF 2148
Medieval
L 30 mm, W 25 mm, Th 30 mm
L 75 mm, W 36 mm, Th 33 mm
SNM 31247A–B

These two amorphous, unworked blue glass lumps were the raw material used in the manufacture of glass objects. Areas of silver and brown weathering are visible on their surfaces. Despite the presence of raw material suggesting the manufacture of glass objects on site, no glass-making equipment was discovered at Soba. Apart from numerous glass beads, glass objects remain uncommon finds; however, crucibles for glass bead production have been identified at other medieval sites (Adams 1977, 373). This raw material may have been part of a bead workshop that manufactured blue glass beads at Soba. Certainly a wide range of manufacturing was occurring at Soba, as cats 208–10 can attest. A kiln for the manufacture of *qawadis* was also discovered (Welsby and Daniels 1991, 105, 245)   JRA/DAW

Ward 1998, 83–4

208 Crucible

Ceramic
Soba East, (MN13)76, no. SF 503
Medieval, sixth–ninth centuries AD
H 48 mm, D 50 mm
SNM 31246

This hand-made vessel was manufactured by inserting a thumb into a lump of clay and pinching the sides up, resulting in a small

208

circular pot with a round bottom. The exterior is rough and coated with slag. The vitrification of the vessel fabric indicates exposure to extreme heat. Over one hundred crucible fragments were discovered at Soba. Within this collection traces of precious metals, including gold and silver, as well as copper alloy, lead, tin, zinc and a small amount of iron, were detected, suggesting that a wide range of metallurgy was being practised in Alwa. Small ingots or metal blanks may have been created for object production or trade.

There is no evidence, either artefactual or textual, to suggest that coins were produced or widely in use in the Alwan kingdom, though they may have been used (but not produced) in a limited way in Nobadia.

JRA/DAW

Allason-Jones 1998, 74; Freestone and Stapleton 1998, 81–3

209 Nails

Iron
Soba East, nos SF 1286, 1200, 1226
Medieval, seventh–thirteenth centuries AD
L 35–137 mm, W 5–30 mm
SNM 31245A–F

These nails have disc- or square-shaped heads and their shafts are rectangular in cross-section. The shaft tapers to a point. Most nails found at Soba were highly corroded masonry nails. Brads, usually used for affixing floorboards, were also discovered in several Soba churches. These may have been used in staircase construction or in an upper floor or choir, as the ground levels of these buildings do not appear to have had wooden floors. Timber was more widely used at Soba than in medieval sites further north in Makuria. Long timber fences, huts and enclosures are evident, particularly in the Early Christian period (Welsby 1998a, 21–7).   JRA/DAW

Allason-Jones 1991, 141

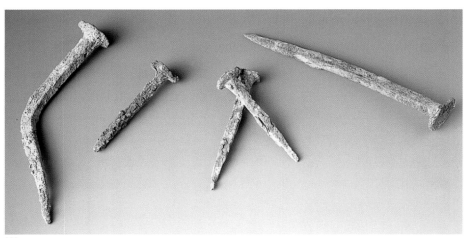

209

210

211 Sandals

Leather

Soba East, Grave (Z3)284, (Z3)316, nos SF 2422, 2249

Medieval

L 160 mm, W 60 mm

SNM 31243A–B

Reconstructed from almost one hundred small fragments of goat leather, ranging in size from 2 x 2 mm to 30 x 40 mm, these finely-made sandals were found *in situ* in the grave of an adult woman. The leather appears to have been tanned with a vegetal agent. The bottom of the sandals is constructed from four thin layers of leather, the uppermost being decorated with a series of impressed and stitched disc-shaped patterns. Impressed or punched leather decoration is present in Nubia from the C-Group onwards and geometric patterns are most commonly

210 Spindle whorls

Ceramic

Soba East, no. SF 2357; 2349; 2543; 2580

Medieval, seventh–thirteenth centuries AD

D 24–75 mm, Th 4–8 mm

SNM 31244A–D

These ceramic discs have a round hole that approximately perforates the disc centre and are made of reused potsherds. They vary in thickness, diameter and quality of manufacture, and may be flat or slightly convex. These are one of the most common finds on medieval sites. Many may have functioned as spindle whorls for spinning wool, indicating a thriving cloth industry; however, in cases where the hole is too small to accommodate a spindle other functions such as gaming pieces, loom weights, buttons or lids must be considered.   JRA/DAW

Allason-Jones 1991, 149; 1998, 69

211

depicted. Four roundels containing a cross-shaped pattern are orientated along the axis of the sandal from the heel towards the toe. This pattern is also found on the strap supports, which were made separately from the sole and later attached between the midsoles with leather thongs. Across the ball of the foot two partial roundels were added perpendicular to the sandal axis. These are decorated with flower petal patterns. The sandals were certainly utilized as the sole of one is thinning and its decorative stitching worn away. Stitching runs around the edge of the sole and serves to attach the different layers of leather and a thin strip of leather binding together. The lower edge of this binding runs beneath the two midsoles and above the sole, while its upper edge is fringed and woven into the stitching on the insole. Decorative stitching is still present on the straps. A double strap, partially concealed within a leather cylinder, ran between the first and second toes, connecting to a single leather band that ran through the strap supports and around the ankle and heel. JRA/DAW

Wills 1998, 182–5, fig. 113

212 Axe

Chlorite

Soba East, (B4)149, Building A, no. SF 765

Medieval, post-ninth century AD

L 150 mm, W 62 mm, Th 37 mm

SNM 31242

A circular hole for the attachment of a wooden handle pierces this polished diamond-shaped chlorite schist axehead through its centre. Evidence suggests that this hole was drilled from both faces. A slight ridge runs along the central axis across the hole and wear marks appear on the axe's surface. Similar axes have been discovered at Jebel Moya (Addison 1949, fig. 100). JRA/DAW

Allason-Jones 1991, 147

213 Macehead

Chlorite (?)

Soba East, no. SF 450

Medieval

D 57 mm, Th 14 mm

SNM 31241

Round stone macehead with convex upper surface that tapers downward to the flat lower surface. The cross-section is semi-circular. This biconical shape is extremely unusual. The edges are rounded and the faces well polished. The centre of the disc is pierced by a hole for a wooden shaft. The presence of maceheads at Soba hearkens back to earlier periods when they were symbols of power and prestige. It is

possible that cats 212–14 actually date to an earlier period and were reused at Soba during the medieval period. JRA/DAW

214 Archer's loose

Claystone

Soba East, (B4)76, Buildig A, no. SF 764

Medieval, post-ninth century AD

H 24 mm, D 48 mm, Th 15 mm

SNM 31240

This white claystone ring was designed to fit securely over the thumb, allowing the first joint enough flexibility to hold the ring in place while drawing a bowstring against it. The edges are rounded and the external face of the ring is slightly convex. This particular style of loose is depicted in the Kushite reliefs at Musawwarat es-Sufra in association with archery equipment and is usually dated between 120 BC and AD 180 (Hayes 1973). Its appearance in a medieval context at Soba, along with other thumb-rings, suggests either reuse or continued production at a later date. The presence of Nubian archers is documented at Old Dongola in the seventh century AD, where they fought against Arab invaders (Al-Balādhurī and Ibn al-Furat in Vantini 1975, 80–81, 528); however, it is unknown whether archers were primarily engaged in warfare or hunting. JRA/DAW

Allason-Jones 1991, 147, 149

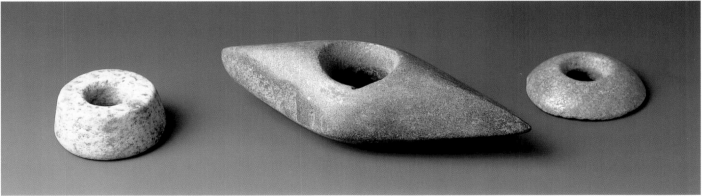

214, 212, 213

11

ISLAMIC ARCHAEOLOGY IN SUDAN

INTISAR SOGHAYROUN EL-ZEIN

Sudan, the largest country in Africa, is highly differentiated both geographically and ecologically, and possesses a considerable diversity of ethnic and cultural traditions. Prior to the arrival of the Arabs, the inhabitants of the Nile Valley had experienced some 3,500 years of urban and literate civilization. This influenced cultural development as Arabic-speaking nomads entered the country from the seventh century AD onwards via Sinai, the Eastern Desert and the Red Sea. Sudan with its vast area, varied geographical zones and peoples presents a unique pattern of Islamic archaeology in Africa (fig. 172). By the time the process of Islamization was well underway, regional resistance stemming from popular beliefs was strong and had to be overcome.

Islamization was carried out to some extent by Muslims who immigrated to Sudan during the earliest Islamic period; however, the majority of this process was accomplished by indigenous individuals and/or groups who had previously converted to Islam, probably through the mediation of the aforementioned immigrants.[1] The country as we know it was never part of an Islamic Caliphate except for a narrow strip of the Nile stretching downstream from the Third Cataract towards Egypt and the port of Suakin on the Red Sea coast. Both were part of the Ottoman Empire, so one would not expect Islam's cultural manifestations in Sudan to have been modelled after those of Egypt, Iraq or Iran.

The rise of the al-'Umari state in the Eastern Desert, the Tunjur and the Keira Sultanates in the west, and the Funj Kingdom in central Sudan was only the culmination of a slow process of Arab migration. Three distinct phases in this lengthy and complex process can be recognized:

Phase I – AD 640–1300 (AH 20–680)
Phase II – AD 1300–1500 (AH 680–920)
Phase III – AD 1500–1800 (AH 920–1480)

PHASE I

Islamization began gradually in AD 641 through contact with the first Muslims in Egypt, who signed a treaty with the kingdom of Makuria. This treaty, known as the Baqt, was primarily commercial but allowed for the slow infiltration of the nomadic tribes of Arabia into Sudan. Evidence for Islamization includes a mosque which is mentioned in the Baqt Treaty. A mosque is later referred to by al-Aswani in the late

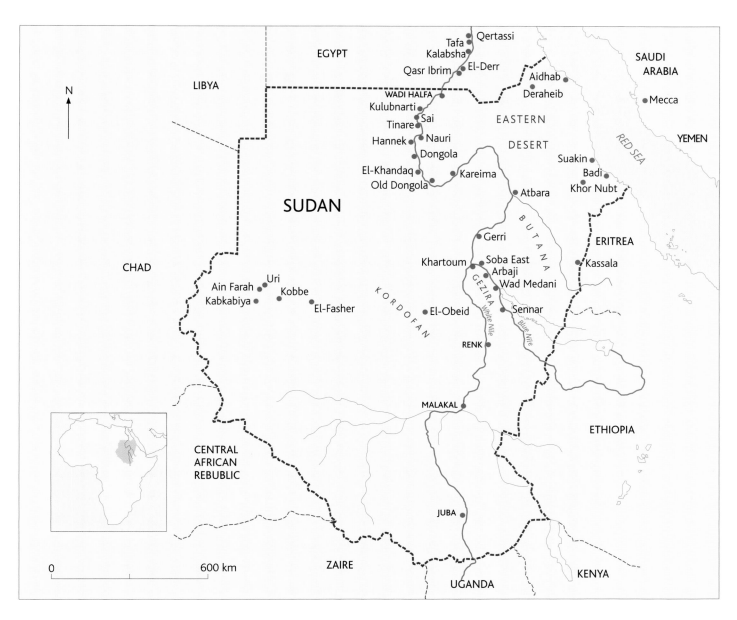

172 Map of Islamic sites mentioned in the text.

tenth century AD, where he is said to have performed the Qurban Bayram prayer at Old Dongola. Fatimid documents from Qasr Ibrim indicate the existence of Muslim settlement in lower Nubia as early as the ninth century AD, and tomb-stones (cf. cat. 215) from Nubia and the Eastern Desert show the gradual spread of Muslims.[2] Imported Islamic objects, especially pottery, textiles (particularly Fatimid silk) and glass were among the traded commodities which have been found in excavations conducted at Kulubnarti,[3] Qasr Ibrim,[4] Soba East,[5] Badi' and 'Aidhab[6] and Deraheib.[7]

PHASE II

The 200 years that elapsed between the fall of Makuria in AD 1323 and that of Alwa in AD 1504 was not a dark period in the northern Sudan. The era witnessed the arrival of *'Ulama* (scholars) from Arabia who established *khalwas* (Koranic schools) and mosques.[8] Some churches and parts of palaces were also converted into mosques, such as those found at Old Dongola and elsewhere in the Middle Nile region. In AD 1323 a Muslim member of the ruling class became king of Makuria. This was the result of a long period of intervention by the Mameluke rulers of Egypt in the internal affairs of the Makurian kingdom. With the removal of the political barrier, Arab migration into the Middle Nile Valley and the Eastern Desert increased, penetrating southwards into the Butana (the area between the Blue Nile, the Nile and the River Atbara), the Suakin hinterland and the Gezira (between the Blue and White Niles). The destruction of the Christian kingdom of Alwa took place in the late fifteenth century AD when Arab tribes of the Abdallab confederation overran the Gezira and subjugated its population. The period witnessed the decline of the port of 'Aidhab which had flourished since the tenth century AD after the decline of Badi'. Both events are evidence for the growing number of Muslim residents resulting from an increase in trade by Muslim merchants from the second half of the tenth century AD onward.

In most of northern Sudan the people became bilingual, particularly the Beja, Nubians and Fur, who today still use indigenous languages in a domestic context and Arabic as their international and religious language. There is archaeological evidence from the west, where the Tunjur kingdom was in its heyday during the thirteenth–fourteenth centuries AD. Palaces and mosques have been reported in different capitals of the Tunjur sultans. Imported objects have been found at many sites such as Qasr Ibrim, where Ayyubid and Mameluke metalwork was discovered.[9] Thai ceramics of the fourteenth–sixteenth centuries AD, white porcelain and celadon of the fourteenth century AD have been recovered at 'Aidhab,[10] while Fustat and Fayyumi pottery from Egypt have been found at Kulubnarti,[11] Soba East,[12] and in the Eastern Desert.[13]

PHASE III

The beginning of the sixteenth century AD witnessed the rise of the first powerful Islamic state in the Middle Nile Valley, the Funj or the Black Sultanate that marked the supremacy of Islam in the present Republic of the Sudan. At the end of the century the Ottomans, who conquered Egypt in AD 1517, extended their territories along the Nile Valley to Hannek, 10 km south of the Third Cataract, after a battle with the Funj army. They rehabilitated the fortress of Sai to house a garrison, as at Qasr Ibrim, and many small forts were located upstream as far as Hannek, such as Tinare and Nauri.

During the same period and in the early seventeenth century, Darfur witnessed the rise of an Islamic state under the Keira dynasty. At this time trade flourished with Egypt via the *Darb al Arba'in* (the Forty Days Road) and across the savannah of central Sudan to West Africa, following the pilgrimage route to Mecca.[14] With the establishment of these regimes the stage of proselytization came to an end. A new era of reform and of Koranic teaching began in central, western and eastern Sudan except at the port of Suakin on the Red Sea, which had been annexed by the Ottomans in AD 1523 and on the narrow strip of the Nile from Hannek to the Egyptian boarder. The Funj and the Fur invited *'Ulama* from abroad as well as those from within Sudan.

The form of Islam that prevailed in the seventeenth century AD reflected the duality that was widespread at that time throughout the *Dar al-Islam*. Islam in the Funj Kingdom bore two faces: the orthodox and the ecstatic. Each brought with it a distinctive set of institutions; the orthodox emphasized the mosque while the Sufi emphasized the *khalwa* in which the teacher was a holy man who possessed *baraka* (blessing). Several towns including el-Derr, Old Dongola, el-Khandaq, Wad Nimeiri, Gerri, Arbaji, Sennar (fig. 173) and Suakin, and to the west Uri, Kobbe, Kabkabiya and el-Fashir were occupied in this period. *Qubba* (tombs of holy Sheikhs) are found in numerous cemeteries and fortresses such as Sai, and smaller forts are found along the Nile in the regions of the Third, Fourth and Fifth Cataracts (figs 174, 176). Artefactual evidence includes textiles, ceramics, skin water bags, basketry, glass vessels, household equipment such as bridles, straps, pads and querns, and farming equipment such as *saqia* parts and tethering pegs; there is also documentary evidence from Qasr Ibrim.

There were no Christian or Islamic missionaries before the end of the nineteenth century AD south of latitude 10°N. Prior to that, Muslim traders penetrated south of the Sudd and some settled there with no intention of propagating Islam. Archaeological work conducted in that region thus far has revealed the existence of Stone and Iron Age cultures[15] and ethnoarchaeological and ethnohistorical studies have been carried out on the local pottery traditions.[16] Archaeological work conducted on Debbas near Renk and at Malakal revealed the presence of Funj potsherds and smoking pipes.[17] The Shilluk people in this area are known to use ceremonial stools and to have a tradition of regicide: ethnographic details which through analogy might help clarify Funj cultural characteristics.[18]

173 Remains of the mosque at Sennar as seen in February 1910.

CONCLUSIONS

It is evident from the historical and archaeological evidence that Islam entered Sudan as early as the seventh century AD and co-existed with Christianity until the end of the Christian Kingdom of Makuria. A new era of reforms began with the arrival of *'Ulama* from Arabia who settled in the Dongola region. From there, their descendants moved southwards to the Shaiqiya area where they established more *khalwas* for teaching the Koran and religious theology. When the Funj kingdom came into existence, there were already Muslims in the Gezira and Butana areas, the domain of the Funj. The first Islamic state in Sudan came into being without a *jihad* (holy war), which serves to emphasize the prior existence of a large Muslim community in the area.

The nature of Islamic evidence in the Sudan shows that considerable differences in regional material culture are to be expected both chronologically and geographically. Evidence derives from archaeological, ethnoarchaeological, historical and ethnohistorical sources. It is also likely that great differences will be found

174 The *qubba* of the holy man Sheikh Idris at Koyekka.

between the sedentary population of the Nile Valley and the savannah belt population as well as the nomads, except in religious matters.

The study of settlement sites has revealed four building traditions in Islamic Sudan: the mud or mud-brick rectangular house with flat roof, the rectangular stone or mud-brick house with barrel vaults, Red Sea coral buildings, and the round conical roof hut; however, the extensive use of mud as the main building material and the abandonment or rebuilding of most earlier structures have led to few buildings being available for study today. When conducting excavations the following objects tend to be found:

- Objects connected with administration – the Kakar (stool of authority), sceptres, seals, documents and coins (cat. 220).
- Military equipment – firearms, swords, spears, kettle drums, saddles, chainmail and helmets (cats 217–19).
- Household equipment – furniture, doors, locks, keys, mats, beds, spinning and weaving equipment, perfume containers and leather skirts (*rahat*).
- Religious objects – prayer mats, rosaries, ablution pitchers, *hijab* (an amulet usually containing a Koran verse or prayer) and *loah* (wooden slate) (cat. 215).
- Agricultural and animal husbandry equipment – *saqia* parts, adzes, sickles, ropes, baskets, tethering pegs and harnesses.
- Personal belongings, including clothing, jewellery (glass and metal), shoes, smoking pipes, daggers and sheathes (cat. 216).
- Food debris which includes plant and animal remains.
- From nomad campsites – knee hobbles, herdsmen pipes, bullets, water skin, daggers and sheathes.

Islamic military architecture in the Sudan is a field that requires urgent work; many of these structures – castles and forts – are still visible. The military artefacts mentioned above came from Phase III. With the exception of some cannons and armour, all were of iron and include firearms, spears, swords, chainmail, stirrups, slings and shields. Few objects of earlier date have been reported.

1 El-Zein 1982.

2 For example, tombstones have been found in northern Sudan: Tafa AD 822 (AH 207), Kalabsha AD 929 (AH 317), Qertassi AD 933 (AH 321), and Derheib AD 1027 (AH 418); eastern Sudan: Badi' AD 977, AD 1014, AD 1017, AD 1045 (AH 367, AH 405, AH 408, AH 446); Khor Nubt AD 877, AD 980, AD 927, AD 945 (AH 264, AH 277, AH 315, AH 329); towns and ports of the east such as

Deraheib and Badi', and 'Ain Farah and Uri in the west.

3 Adams 1998b.

4 Adams 1996.

5 Welsby and Daniels 1991.

6 Kawatoko 1993.

7 Castiglioni *et al.* 1994.

8 Dayf Allah 1992, 10.

9 Plumley 1983, 163.

10 Kawatoko 1993b, 206.

11 Adams 1998b, 80.

12 Welsby and Daniels 1991, 323.

13 Castiglioni *et al.* 1994, 22.

14 Insoll 1996, 456.

15 El-Zein 2000, forth.

16 David 1982; Siiriainen 1984.

17 Kleppe 1982.

18 Ibid.

SENNAR

INTISAR SOGHAYROUN EL-ZEIN

Sennar, the capital of the Funj kingdom, was a royal, administrative, military and trade centre (fig. 175). It lies in the Gezira, on the banks of the Blue Nile, about 250 km south of Khartoum. It was founded in AD 1504 (AH 910) and continued to be the capital until AD 1821. The reasons behind the choice of Sennar as the capital are still a matter of controversy;[1] however, it was probably in order to control the east–west pilgrimage and trade route from Kordofan to Suakin.

There are several reports about Sennar during the sixteenth–nineteenth centuries from travellers such as Reubeni, Poncet, Bruce, Krump, and Cailliaud.[2] It was a large unfortified town with a circumference of about 4.8 km. The main features of the site were the palace, mosque, marketplaces and cemeteries (fig. 176). In the early twentieth century AD the mosque walls were still standing with its elaborate entrance, mihrab and red-brick columns. By 1982 the walls were in ruins which made the taking of reliable measurements a difficult task.[3] It was situated near the royal residential area towards the southern limit of the town, about 250 m to the south-east of the identified marketplace, as expected. Generally in Islamic towns, the mosque is built next to the ruler's palace. The mosque was built of large red bricks and measured approximately 10 x 15 m. This seems too small for a Friday mosque in a town of this size.

Sennar was known to have had a daily market, which shows its commercial significance, as markets in other towns were restricted to certain days of the week. According to el-Sayed,[4] there were two market-places, one of which occupied a wide area in the centre of the city, and there were three markets there during the nineteenth century.[5] The main market, including the slave market, was an essential part of the town. When surveyed in 1982, the market interior yielded no finds; however, the surface collection from the entire site included Funj tobacco pipes (16 fragments), Chinese ceramics (46 fragments), other potsherds (399), metal implements (11 fragments) and glass-ware of recent date (14 fragments).[6]

There were two cemeteries – the *Fuqara* (sheikhs/holy men) and the Commoners' Cemetery. The first one is the most prominent Islamic feature of Sennar. The names of these sheikhs are well known to the local inhabitants, whereas no one knows the burial places of any famous kings. This shows the degree of importance of these sheikhs in the past and present. The *Fuqara* were buried under substantial superstructures (*qubba*) and their followers were buried around them in simple oval graves. The Commoners' Cemetery was an extension of the *Fuqara* Cemetery and lies to its east.

The most famous palace in Sudan was that of the Funj sultans of Sennar (cf. cat. 217). The palace was already in ruins in AD 1833, as it was demolished after the conquest of Mohammed Ali Pasha (AD 1821). In 1982 only the foundations survived. It is said to have been built by Badi II in the middle of the seventeenth century. According to one manuscript, the palace had a five-storey-high tower with council hall inside it and the whole was surrounded by a high wall with nine gates.[7] However, a contemporary description of the palace by Poncet (in AD 1699) described it as a confused heap of buildings, without symmetry or beauty, surrounded by high walls of mud brick, inside which was a large court paved with small square tiles of different colours. Nearby was an open hall where the kings usually gave audience to ambassadors.[8] Krump (AD 1701) described the palace as composed of a single-storeyed room which, though high, was dark and bare of furniture. Floors were covered with mats and the buildings were surrounded for the most part by a *zareeba* (barricade) of thorns in place of walls, which had presumably collapsed. It had a slightly inclined roof covered with

175 The palace of the Funj sultans of Sennar. A lithograph taken from a drawing made by F. Cailliaud and published in *Voyage à Meroé, au Fleuve Blanc* (1826–7).

176 Remains of a *qubba* at Sennar as seen in 1910.

earth.[9] In 1772 Bruce found buildings of one storey built of clay with floors of earth. The king's room was small, less than 6 m long, and was reached by ascending two short flights of narrow steps, so that it must have been in the tower which was still standing in AD 1821. The floor was covered with broad square tiles over which was placed a Persian carpet, and the walls were hung with tapestry.[10]

Drawings by Cailliaud and Linant de Bellefonds both show the palace as having a tower with four storeys (fig. 175). Crawford's analysis suggests that the palace must have first been built in the sixteenth century and was enlarged or modified from time to time by later kings.[11]

The site has been badly damaged by erosion, heavy rainfall, Arab nomads who settled on the mounds, agricultural schemes and above all negligence. When Crawford visited the site in the 1950s, he noticed great changes in the landscape from the town that he had known in the 1930s. Our knowledge of the archaeology of this region is scanty, as limited archaeological work has been conducted there, and there is little to be seen there today.

1 Crawford 1951, 77.
2 Adams 1977, 594–5.
3 El-Zein 1982, 26.
4 El-Sayed 1971, 66.
5 Crawford 1951, 79.
6 El-Zein 1982, 25.
7 MacMichael 1967, 363.
8 Crawford 1951, 189.
9 Ibid.
10 Bruce 1805, IV, 352.
11 Crawford 1951, 189.

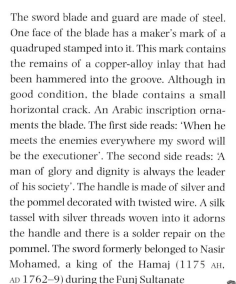

215

215 Stela

Felsite

Al-Rih Island, Badi'

Islamic, AD 1015

H 430 mm, W 360 mm, Th 168 mm

SNM 24379

This funerary stela, broken across the top, is written in Kufic Arabic. The text relates that Mohamed ibn Mahmoud ibn Ahmed ibn al-Walid died on a Tuesday during the month of Sha'ban in 405 AH (AD 1015). The beginning of the inscription is missing, but likely began with 'In the Name of God, the Merciful and the Compassionate'. It is followed by four Koranic verses from sura 112 (sura Ikhlas): 'He is Allah, the one and only. Allah, the Eternal, Absolute. He begetteth not, nor is He begotten. And there is none like unto Him.' Islamization was a gradual process in the Sudan and the presence of this early Arabic tombstone attests to the spread of

216

Muslims into the region. This began during the seventh century AD, and Muslims coexisted with Christians, particularly in Lower Nubia, until the end of the medieval Christian kingdom of Makuria (AD 1323).   JRA

Kawatoko 1993a, 191–2, 200–2; Sijpesteijn and Zozaya 2003, 141, no. 44

216 Bowl

Copper alloy

Provenance unknown

Islamic

H 125 mm, D 463 mm

SNM 5714

A shallow, open, copper-alloy bowl with a flattened rim and a repair on the base. The rim is decorated with incised geometric patterns among which are three Arabic words which read: 'owned by Othman Digna'. It apparently also includes the number 1,050 written in Arabic. These are enclosed within ovals that are evenly distributed around the edge. If the number is a date, 1050 AH (1640 AD), then the Othman Digna referred to in the inscription is not the well-known Beja leader of the Mahdiya period, but must be another individual of the same name. The vessel's shape is not unlike wooden bowls used for sharing food, known as *gada*, and it probably served a similar function.   JRA

Pérez Die 2003c

217 Sword

Steel, copper alloy, silk, silver

Provenance unknown

Islamic, Funj (AD 1762–69)

Blade: L 884 mm, max. W 48 mm, max. Th 3 mm; guard: L 170 mm, max. W 30 mm, max. Th 20 mm; handle: L 157 mm, min. D 30.6 mm, max. D 54.5 mm

KH.394

The sword blade and guard are made of steel. One face of the blade has a maker's mark of a quadruped stamped into it. This mark contains the remains of a copper-alloy inlay that had been hammered into the groove. Although in good condition, the blade contains a small horizontal crack. An Arabic inscription ornaments the blade. The first side reads: 'When he meets the enemies everywhere my sword will be the executioner'. The second side reads: 'A man of glory and dignity is always the leader of his society'. The handle is made of silver and the pommel decorated with twisted wire. A silk tassel with silver threads woven into it adorns the handle and there is a solder repair on the pommel. The sword formerly belonged to Nasir Mohamed, a king of the Hamaj (1175 AH, AD 1762–9) during the Funj Sultanate (cf. Holt 1999, 19–20, 183, 185; Holt and Daly 1989, 38–9; O'Fahey and Spaulding 1974, 98–100). PP/JRA/AR

217

218 Chainmail

Iron

Provenance unknown

Islamic, Turkiya (AD 1820–81), reused during the Mahdiya (AD 1881–98)

L 1.46 m, W (across shoulders) 1.13 m, Th 2 mm; ring: D 10 mm

SNM 31212

This is a horseman's chainmail with long sleeves and a long skirt slit in front and back to allow the wearer to sit astride a horse. It has a scoop neck joining a vertical slit on the front to allow the head access. The chainmail consists of butt-joined rings and there is no sign of any organic lining. The mail is in good condition with no dents visible. Armour, such as this chainmail and helmet (cat. 219), were maintained and in continuous use for long periods, particularly during the seventeenth to nineteenth centuries.   PP/JRA

219 Helmet

Iron, silk, cotton, gilding

Provenance unknown

Islamic, Turkiya (AD 1820–81), reused during the Mahdiya (AD 1881–98)

Helmet: max. H (with silk padding) 550 mm, H (of iron helmet) 300 mm, max. D 210 mm, min. D 23 mm; chainmail curtain: L 160 mm; noseguard: L 262 mm

KH.409

A conical-shaped iron helmet with iron curtain and soft padding to protect the neck when worn. The helmet was painted black then gilded with gold leaf. It was fabricated with brass solder. It is decorated with Arabic writing on the gilding around the rim and bands of gold gilding swirl up the helmet. It reads:

> In the name of Allah, the compassionate, the merciful, I will follow the will of God as he will bestow upon you other blessings which you desire: help from Allah and speedy victory. Proclaim the good tiding to the faithful.

The chainmail curtain around the rim is made of butt-joined rings with the exception of a small 60 x 45 mm patch on the lower edge of the right side. This portion is made of riveted rings. These rings are of finer wire than the others, though the ring diameter and linking pattern remains the same. The padding under the mail is filled with cotton wadding and is quilted on the exterior with blue cotton fabric. The inner lining, which would have been in contact with the head and neck, consists of red, black and yellow or white silk threads.   PP/JRA/AR

218

220 Coins

Copper alloy, silver

Provenance unknown

Islamic, Turkiya and Mahdiya periods

Turkiya: D 29–36 mm, Th 1–2.5 mm; Mahdiya:
D 35–7 mm, Th 2 mm

SNM 31362

This collection of ten Islamic coins dates to the Turkiya and Mahdiya periods. Among the group are eight Egyptian copper coins of 10, 20 and 40 gurush (piastre) denominations. The obverse has the Ottoman sultan's *tughra* (his seal or cipher with his name and titles in monogram form), and the coin denomination. The reverse face gives the place of minting, 'Struck in Misr' (Cairo); the sultan's regnal year, here between years five and ten; and the Islamic date of 1277 Hijri, the first year of his reign. These coins date from between AD 1864 and 1869. The Egyptian silver coin is a 10-gurush (piastre) denomination and contains information similar to that found on the copper coins. The obverse shows the Ottoman sultan's *tughra* in a wreath with crossed quivers and floral ornament, the denomination and a mint mark H (Birmingham, Heaton mint); the reverse reads 'Struck in Misr' (Cairo), 10 (regnal year) and 1327 (Hijri year of start of the sultan's reign) within a wreath.

220

219

The Mahdiya coin is in base silver and has irregular edges. The obverse contains the Khalifa's *tughra* with stars, wreath and floral motif, the denomination and the *maqbul* (meaning 'legal' or 'acceptable'). The reverse side reads 'Struck in Omdurman', 12 (regnal year) and 1312 (Hijri year) within a wreath and stars. It dates to AD 1894. The Mahdiya coins were based upon the Ottoman coins in circulation in Egypt. The Mahdi was the first Sudanese ruler to mint his own coinage, though while these coins were in use, foreign coins remained in circulation (Holt and Daly 1988, 97–8). During the earlier medieval period, coinage circulated only north of the Batn el-Hajar in Lower Nubia and was closely linked with Arab trading. It was only with the advent of the Islamic period that its use became widespread.   JC/JRA

12

POTTERY PRODUCTION

HANS-ÅKE NORDSTRÖM

The potter's craft has a long history in Sudan, indeed one of the longest in the world, beginning at least 10,000 years ago. It is not difficult to find a district in this country where traditions of pottery-making have been practically unbroken over this enormous span of time. An archaeologist could select, for example, the Dongola Reach on the Middle Nile, where lines of development may be discerned through millennia up to modern times, related to technology, to the choice of decorative methods and motifs, or to the shapes and functions of the pots.

Remains of pottery are usually the most common artefact category on most ancient sites in the Sudan (fig. 177). While most vessels were broken, their sherds did not perish. They appear to be ubiquitous along the Nile Valley but are also present in the vast regions to the east and west of the river basin. There are tens of thousands of potsherds on town sites and other settlements, and in temple areas. There are numerous vessels placed as funerary offerings in the tombs, and a number of sites have preserved kilns and other structures related to large-scale pottery production.

Ceramic products have a great number of qualities that are fairly easy to record and analyse systematically: clay, temper, surface treatment, decoration, vessel shape and size. It is quite natural, therefore, that archaeologists use pottery in many ways that the ancient potters themselves could not have anticipated. Above all, pottery is used as a cultural and chronological marker. However, there is a growing interest in the craft itself and the setting of the potters, and also in the socio-economic function of the pottery, the contents of the vessels, the extent of trade and large-scale production, and the flow of ideas and technological knowledge between different cultural groups. A useful tool of modern ceramological research is called the *chaînes opératoires*, an analytical approach following the different steps of, for example, lithic industries and potters' work, and the lifespan of the finished product.[1]

Apart from this specialist approach we may look at the Sudanese ceramic heritage from an aesthetic viewpoint. There are not only vast amounts of utility vessels but also numerous objects with expressive shapes and decorations of high artistic standard. Pot-making was not always considered to be low-status dirty work. Like modern artists, the ancient potters and their customers must have been fascinated by the transformation of the grey amorphous clay into appealing and colourful objects. Highlights include the slender beakers of the Neolithic period (cat. 240),

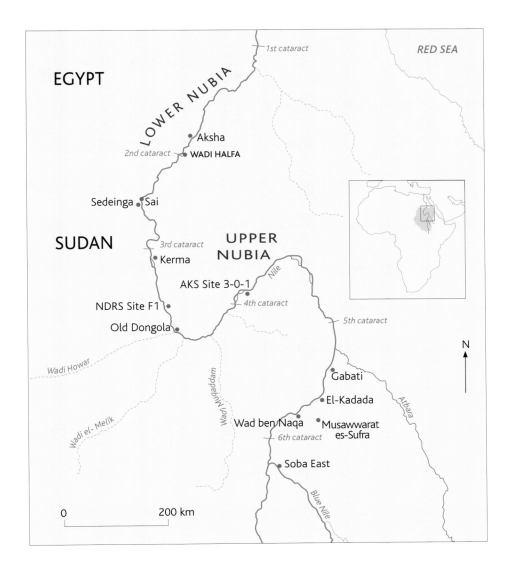

177 Map showing the sites mentioned in this chapter.

the fanciful products of the Kerma culture (cat. 235), and the artistic achievements of the potters in the realm of Meroe (cats 226–9, 249–50, 253–4).

THE FUNDAMENTALS OF ANCIENT POTTERY PRODUCTION

Pottery industries are divided into two large categories, the hand-made and the wheel-made. The raw materials consisted of plastic clays and some non-plastic components. These were cheap and easily available in various formations along the Nile and its tributaries, and in lacustrine deposits. Clay content was carefully estimated by the ancient potters. Today it is known that clay minerals – hydrated silicates of aluminium, magnesium and iron – are essential ingredients of a clay, accounting for its plasticity and the ceramic properties brought about by firing. The chosen clay was tempered with finely crushed rock, sand or organic materials, such as chaff or dung, and sometimes also with other clays.[2] The temper improved the quality and workability of the paste, reduced the shrinkage and, in some cases, increased the porosity of the vessel. The skilled assessment of these properties and the careful preparation of the potting clay, crucial as they were for the durability and function of the final product, were, therefore, important starting points in the pottery production of ancient times. The accumulated knowledge, through trial and error, of the raw materials probably formed strong traditions that were carried from generation to generation, from the beginning usually on the matrilineal side.

After shaping, surface treatment and careful drying of the vessels came the moment of truth for the potter: the firing. Usually a fairly large number of vessels were fired at the same time and some ritual probably surrounded this. The clay transforms into a resistant ceramic material only when the clay minerals lose the water chemically tied up in the crystals. For this, temperatures between 550 and 600°C are required, and could be achieved in ancient times in simple pits or bonfires. Fuel consisted of wood, grass or dung. Hard, dense fabrics or a porous strong fabric, of a water jar, for example, were produced at higher temperatures, up to 1,000°C, in specially built kilns which permitted prolonged firing. The alluvial clays in the Sudan generally sinter and melt in temperatures approaching 1,150–1,200°C.[3]

HAND-MADE POTTERY

Ethnographic evidence implies that women were generally responsible for the manufacture of hand-made pottery. We have, however, no indications confirming this during prehistoric times. Hand-made vessels were fashioned using different methods: direct shaping, coiling, paddle-and-anvil, or shaping over a mould. The surfaces were treated in different ways: scraped, smoothed or burnished with a pebble or a piece of bone, preferably when the paste had dried for some hours and the consistency was leather-hard. Many vessels were decorated before the firing with impressed, incised or painted designs, or using a combination of these techniques (fig. 178, cats 240–42). Sometimes impressed patterns were filled in with white or light-coloured pigments.

Firing took place in simple bonfires or pits. Hand-made pottery was usually baked at temperatures of between 600 and 800°C, and the effective firing time was short, frequently less than one hour. The atmosphere could be controlled only to a limited extent. Often it was neutral or sooty in the initial phase. Oxidizing set in during the peak of the firing producing a drab, pale brown or reddish colour due to the presence of finely disseminated iron hydroxide and organic material in the paste.

Inventive people in the central and eastern Sahara produced the earliest hand-made pots during the ninth millennium BC.[4] The vessels produced were large bowls made of carefully selected clay tempered mainly with quartz grains. They were remarkably well fired in temperatures near to 800°C. Some variants had a conspicuous amount of mica in the paste, visible on the surface as tiny glistening plates. Coiling was the principal shaping method. The characteristic decoration, covering the major part of the exterior, consisted of incised or impressed wavy-line patterns made with serrated tools of bone, shell, or potsherds. Eight thousand years ago, the impressed Dotted Wavy Line (DWL) pottery (fig. 178, cat. 32), as it is known among archaeologists, was spread over most of the present Sahara, from Mali to the Red Sea.[5] The desert was then a savannah

178 Dotted Wavy Line pottery. This characteristic decorative motif occurs across the entire Sahara and is among the oldest pottery designs, appearing 8,000 years ago from the Wadi Howar, Rahib 80/87.

inhabited by mobile groups of hunters and gatherers. It has been suggested that the remarkable continuity of the development of DWL can be attributed to a rather free flow of ideas and people between different groups.[6] Wave-like patterns have been attested for a period of seven millennia in the desert and the Sahel belt; the latest date of the first millennium BC is recorded in Senegal.[7]

Later, during the Neolithic period, wolf's tooth decoration made with a rocker stamp with a serrated edge became common, and this tradition continued up to Christian times (cats 233–4). There were also designs made with a double-pronged tool or a stylus. The most remarkable of the vessels produced by these Neolithic potters were caliciform beakers, decorated with structured patterns of polished bands alternated with intricate geometric fields of parallel lines of impressed dots (cats 22, 240).[8]

Another tradition with a long history was the production of red-polished, black-topped cups and bowls. The potter brought out the red colour of the vessel by covering the exterior surface with a wash of red ochre before firing. A certain clay content in this coating allowed for careful polishing, creating a lustrous surface. Sometimes this surface was further emphasized with ripple-like marks made by the polishing tool. The pots were fired in simple pits in the usual way. When still hot they were placed mouth downwards on organic material which carbonized and smoked so that the interior was blackened, and a characteristic black band on the exterior rim was formed.[9] The black-topped technique was developed about 6,000 years ago in Egypt. It dominated the pottery of the Early and Middle Nubian cultures, notably the A-Group, the C-Group, Pan Grave and the Kerma, and also is attested in the Sudanese Neolithic.[10]

The ceramic production at Kerma represents the peak of the potters' hand-made art in the Sudan. The famous Kerma beakers of the Classic period (1750–1500 BC) (fig. 179, cats 72, 246), thin-walled and well fired, with a highly lustrous red exterior and a broad black top with an almost metallic feel, were in all probability the products of specialized craftsmen working at the king's court. However, they are found on even the most humble rural settlements. A characteristic feature of these beakers was the so-called secondary stripe, an irregular, greyish-white band of vitrified clay underneath the black top. This band may have occurred initially by accident, but was later deliberately brought about by skilful firing. Several workshops have been excavated in the town site of Kerma dated to the Classic Kerma period, including some circular or oval kilns between 2.7 and 4 m in size.[11]

179 A well-fired, black-topped red ware Kerma beaker from the *Kerma Classique* period. The British Museum, EA 55423.

WHEEL-MADE POTTERY

The potter's wheel (cf. cat. 224), originally a Mesopotamian invention, was introduced into Egypt during the Old Kingdom. In Lower Nubia it was first in use during the Egyptian New Kingdom (*c.* 1500 BC) in the Egyptian administrative centres. Large cemeteries connected with these displayed a wide range of funerary pottery where some common types probably were made locally, perhaps under the direction of Egyptian craftsmen.[12] Further south, wheel-made pottery was produced in the Napatan centres and this tradition continued during the Meroitic period (fig. 180, cats 226–9, 249–50, 253–4).[13]

From the outset, the production of wheel-made pottery was in the hands of part-time or full-time specialists. Representations in Pharaonic Egypt show the activities at numerous pottery workshops where only men were working.[14] It is highly likely that this was also the rule in Nubia. Wheel-made pottery was market sensitive, produced particularly during periods of prosperity, in workshops near villages or population centres where the demand was consistent. During periods of poverty, for example, after the end of the Christian era in Nubia, the wheel-made industry disappeared altogether.[15]

Our knowledge of the ceramic production during the Kushite and medieval periods has improved greatly since the 1960s. An important recent discovery has been that of a Meroitic pottery workshop at Musawwarat es-Sufra (cats 224–9). The elegant vessels of the later part of the Meroitic culture represent a peak in wheel-made production in the Sudan. It has been suggested that when Lower Nubia was resettled from the south around AD 200, professional potters – Egyptians or more likely Graeco-Egyptians – moved down from the north and started to produce the famous vessels of fine eggshell ware decorated with various Hellenistic motifs. A second influx of craftsmen working in the Roman tradition may have taken place during the Post-Meroitic period.[16]

Numerous potteries, large and small, have been recorded from the medieval period.[17] At a few centres the workshops were substantial, perhaps employing twenty to twenty-five individuals. One representative example is the Faras factory, excavated in 1960.[18] On this site twenty-two kilns were recorded, surrounded by enormous amounts of ash and waste. The kilns were cylindrical, built of brick, open at the top and had a double-chamber structure with a vault that separated the furnace from the firing chamber where the pots were stacked (fig. 181). Each chamber averaged 1.35 m in height. Experimental re-firing has shown that the normal peak temperature achieved was around 850°C.

This workshop was located on a site believed to be an old monastery in the Christian capital of Nobadia. In all probability, the development of high-quality pottery industries in the Christian kingdoms of northern Sudan, especially at Faras, Old Dongola and el-Ghazali further south, was initially the work of specialized monks. At a later stage most of the manufacture had been taken over by indigenous potters. Still, foreign specialists inspired by the illuminations of Coptic manuscripts carried out the decoration of the finer vessels of the Classic Christian period.[19]

180 Wheel-made painted pottery of later Kushite (Meroitic) date. The British Museum, EA 51448 and EA 51449.

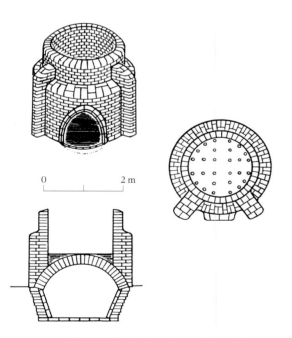

181 A double-chambered pottery kiln with firing chamber above and furnace below.

1 Garcea in press.
2 Nordström 1972, 35 ff.
3 Nordström and Bourriau 1993, 160 ff; Nicholson 1993, 103 ff.
4 Jesse 2003, 301 ff.
5 Ibid., fig. 52.
6 Caneva 1993, 410.
7 Jesse 2003, 301.
8 Welsby 1997a, 29–31.
9 Nordström 1972, 45.
10 Gatto in press.
11 Privati 1990, 120–23.
12 Holthoer 1977; Holthoer et al. 1991, 17.
13 Ahmed 1994; Edwards 1999.
14 Arnold 1993, 39 ff.
15 Adams 1986, 38.
16 Ibid., 41.
17 Pluskota 2001; Adams 1986, 42.
18 Adams 1986, 16 ff.
19 Ibid., 42.

222

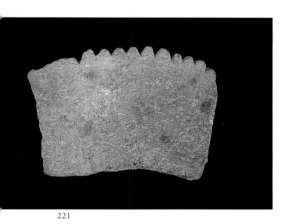

221

221 Pottery comb

Ferruginous sandstone

Sai Island, Site 8-B-52.A

Pre-Kerma

L 57 mm, W 38 mm, Th 9 mm

SNM 31342

This fragment was used as a comb to decorate pottery vessels. The thicker of its edges was partially abraded to make a thinner section. A series of ten teeth approximately 2 mm thick were engraved on it forming a working edge of 41 mm in length. This comb could be applied singularly on the pot surface (called simple impression) forming lines of dots, or with a rocker stamp motion forming dotted zig-zag patterns. Simple impressed dotted horizontal lines are typical of the Pre-Kerma period. They are particularly common on some red-polished, black-mouthed bowls. MCG

222 Pottery comb

Ferruginous sandstone

Sai Island, Kerma Habitation Site SKP1

Kerma

L c. 52 mm, W 39 mm, Th 4 mm

SNM 28767

This tool, possibly made of fine-grained ferruginous sandstone, was used to decorate pottery vessels leaving dotted impressions when applied singly or with a rocker stamp motion. To make it, a very well-polished flat natural pebble was used. One side was engraved to create a working edge of 67 mm in length. The comb was found on Sai Island in a Kerma habitation site. Many similar combs are known from this period.   MCG

Gratien 1986, 74, fig. 289d; Gratien and Olive 1981, 69–130; Reinold 2000a, 139, no. 68

223 Pottery comb/burnisher

Fine ferruginous sandstone

Kerma town

Kerma Moyen

L 74 mm, W 29 mm, Th 6 mm

SNM 25088

Although potters' combs made of ferricrete sandstone are quite widespread at the site of Kerma, this particular example is distin-

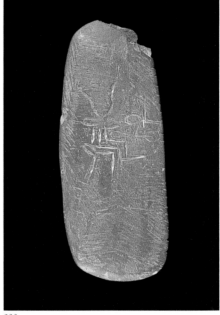

223

guished by the presence of an incised decoration as well as by the theme of this decoration: a small bucephalic deity seated on a throne with two *ankh* signs located in front of her face, one right side up, the other upside down. The horizontal grooves observed on the toothed side show that the piece was primarily used to smooth the surface of ceramic vessels rather than to impress motifs. The depiction of the goddess is sketchy and probably denotes the end of the piece's use as a comb.   CB

Bonnet 1990a, 155, no. 34

224 Slow potter's wheel

Sandstone

Musawwarat es-Sufra, Room 225, find no. I A/54

Kushite, Meroitic

H (of top and bottom) 157 mm; H (of top) 45 mm, H (of base) 112 mm, D 210 mm

SNM 19367

Within Courtyard 224 of the Great Enclosure at Musawwarat es-Sufra is a small room designated 225. It was excavated by F. Hintze in 1965–6 and was considered by him to have been a kitchen or living room. Here he found a stone object, consisting of two parts, which was described as a 'handmill'. When conducting excavations in this area in 1997 D. Edwards, upon seeing a drawing of this object, made the proposal that it was not a 'handmill' but rather 'a potter's wheel, the first example of such an object of Kushite date' (Edwards 1999, 42). Later, in 1999, many pigments and clay lumps were found in Room 225. This was not a kitchen but a potters' and/or draughts-men's workshop; the pigments were used for painting the Meroitic fine pottery wares.   SW

Edwards 1999, pls 6.32, 6.33, 6.34; Hintze 1973

225 Potters' stamps

Ceramic

Musawwarat es-Sufra, Great Enclosure, Courtyard 224

Kushite, Meroitic

a *Ankh*

IA 224.12-0-2; find 1997-8

L 25 mm; stamp end: H 8 mm, W 5 mm

SNM 31153

b Four-lobed rosette

I A-224.8-0-0, find 1999-162

L 10 mm; stamp end: H 19 mm, W 10 mm

SNM 31151

c Shell (?)

IA 224.12-616-2; find 1997-80

L 25 mm; stamp end: H 12 mm, W 8 mm

SNM 31152

d Double diamond

Find 1999-61

L 9.5 mm; stamp end: H 24.6 mm, W 7.2 mm

SNM 31150

e Double diamond

I A-224-13-675, find 1999

L 11 mm; stamp end: H 24 mm, W 8 mm

SNM 31154

About sixty-five different motifs of stamps were found at Musawwarat es-Sufra. Some of the potters' tools, including several hard-fired stamps for impressing designs on wet clay, were found among a garbage deposit of minerals, sherds and ashes. At the flat ends is a raised design in bold relief. The shell stamp (SNM 31152) fits the stamped impressions on bowl SNM 31158 (cat. 226).   SW

Edwards 1999, pls 1.5, 1.6, 2.7

224

225a–e, clockwise from top left

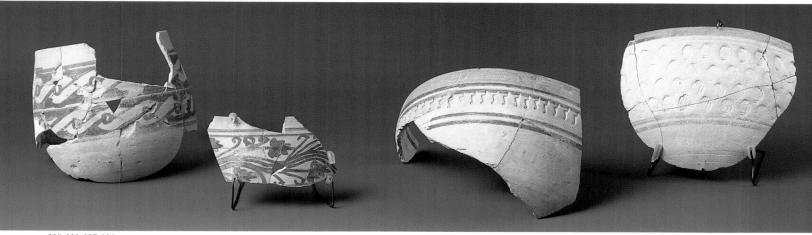

228, 229, 227, 226

226 Bowl

Ceramic

Musawwarat es-Sufra, Great Enclosure, Courtyard
224, ZN 857

Kushite (Meroitic), first century BC to first century AD

Max. H 97 mm, D 142 mm; rim: Th 5 mm

SNM 31158

A fragment of a bowl with a small red polished rim. Within two dark bands the body shows a rare impressed (shell?) design. The motif of this impression is thus far unique. Luckily enough, the corresponding stamp (cat. 225c) was also found in this deposit.

While excavating test trenches in 1996 for a new architectural plan in the northern Courtyard 224 of the Great Enclosure at Musawwarat es-Sufra many sherds of Meroitic fine wares, both painted and/or stamped, were found. Although a few samples of Meroitic fine wares had come to light during the 1960s when F. Hintze excavated in this location, this find was unexpected.

Subsequently, in 1997, a 5 x 5-m trench was opened and approximately 22,500 sherds were excavated. Among the masses of household wares mixed with ashes, almost 15 per cent consisted of beautiful pottery – an extremely high percentage. All of these sherds originate from a pottery workshop that flourished between the first century BC and the first century AD. Similar pottery of this quality has been found, but only in a royal context (i.e., in pyramids or the palaces of the Royal City of Meroe). That these high-quality vessels were produced at Musawwarat es-Sufra indicates that the royal court visited from time to time.

Because no traces of a kiln were found, it soon became clear that this pottery was pro-

duced in an open bonfire. Traces of the fire are still visible on the inside walls of the north-eastern corner of courtyard 224. As a result of the poor firing process, many vessels collapsed during firing.

These fine wares were made of local clay, with some of the vessels made of kaolin clay. Primarily three colours were used (purple, black and red). Among the refuse were minerals, but also some of the potters' tools: hard-fired stamps for impressing designs on wet clay (cat. 225) and a slow potter's wheel (cat. 224). This is the first time that ancient potters' tools were identified in the Sudan.

Motifs, both painted and stamped, are typically Meroitic: some are religious (Hathor, *sa*-knot) and royal (uraei: cat. 227), while others show plants (vine leaves: cat. 229) or common designs (guilloche, stars: cat. 228). Although similar pottery has been found in the Royal City of Meroe and at Hamadab, there is no exact parallel to that found at Musawwarat, which suggests that the potters at Musawwarat had their own 'hand-writing' and artistic traditions.   SW

Edwards 1998, 67, fig. 7; 1999, 28, pl. 3.14

227 Bowl

Ceramic

Musawwarat es-Sufra, Great Enclosure, Courtyard
224, ZN 334B

Kushite (Meroitic), first century BC to first century AD

Max. H 97 mm, D 148 mm; rim: Th 5 mm

SNM 31155

Fragments of a wide thin bowl with red polished rim. Two dark bands enclose a row of impressed cobras. This royal design is repre-

sented many times among the Musawwarat material and indicates that the royal court visited this place to participate in religious ceremonies.   SW

Edwards 1999, 28, pl. 3.13

228 Bowl

Ceramic

Musawwarat es-Sufra, Great Enclosure, Courtyard
224, ZN 902

Kushite (Meroitic), first century BC to first century AD

Preserved H 95 mm, D 90 mm; rim: Th 3 mm

SNM 31157

Fragment of a bowl with two dark bands of guilloche design. The guilloche design is also found on pottery from Meroe, but there is no exact parallel.   SW

Edwards 1999, 32 and pl. XII

229 Cup

Ceramic

Musawwarat es-Sufra, Great Enclosure, Courtyard
224, ZN 911

Kushite (Meroitic), first century BC to first century AD

Preserved H 44 mm, D 100 mm; rim: Th 2 mm

SNM 31156

Fragments of a thin cup with vine-leaf design. This very elegant design is also known from Meroe, both the Royal City and the Pyramids; however, as in other cases, there are significant stylistic differences.   SW

Edwards 1999, 33, pl. XII

230

231

impressed (238168 MN; 238169 MN). The stamp, however, could also have been used to decorate eucharistic loaves before baking (cf. Galey 1980, fig. 177)   KP

231 Pot separators

Ceramic
Old Dongola, Kilns R1C, R1F
Medieval
L *c.* 150 mm, W *c.* 100 mm, Th *c.* 50 mm
SNM 31214

Pot separators, or 'kiln pads'(Corder 1957, pl. VD), were made of ceramic. Their crescent-like form with wedge-shaped cross section and slightly concave upper surface made them useful for stabilizing pots with rounded bottoms on the flat surfaces of the kiln's firing chamber. Another potential function was the separation of large vessels that were stacked in piles, in order to improve the circulation of hot gases and to promote the even oxidation of their surfaces during the firing process. At Old Dongola separators were found in the rubble of Kilns R1C and R1F.   KP

232 Kiln-wasters

Ceramic
Old Dongola
Medieval
SNM 31211

Medieval pottery production was on a massive scale, generating large quantities of waste such as ash, slag, brick rubble and potsherds from failed products – 'wasters'.

230 Pottery stamp

Ceramic
Old Dongola, no. D.11/91-2
Medieval
H 60 mm, D 67 mm
SNM 31213

The conical object is ceramic covered with a cream slip. In the upper part a hole through the cone for a string or a leather strap would allow the stamp to be hung. On the circular base the concave stamp is impressed and incised. It represents the Holy Lamb, which stands in front of a chalice with the eucharistic bread. Identification of the animal, which resembles an antelope, is stressed by the inscription in Greek (mirror image) above the

spine of the lamb: *O AMNOΣ TOY ΘY*, 'The Lamb of God'. The lamb's head is embellished with the cross. The cross with pendants between its arms appears also on the eucharistic bread. The scene is surrounded by two concentric circles and by a circle of satellite dots which allows us to date the stamp to the Classic Christian period (Adams 1986, 222). The stamp was found among the rubble of Room 2 of the service area of the Monastery of the Holy Trinity (Żurawski 1994b, 340, fig. 15).

The most probable use of the stamp was to decorate pottery. In the collection of Nubian pottery in the National Museum in Warsaw there are two examples of centrepieces from small bowls with almost identical scenes

232

233, 234

Layers of waste covered the area surrounding the kilns, finally creating artificial hills, *koms*, on which other kilns were built. In Old Dongola, at *Kom* R1, the thickest rubble of such layers reached 4.6 m (Pluskota 2001, 360). The high percentage of potsherds in the debris indicates that either 'Nubian potters were not careful enough' (Adams 1986, I, 32) or that the speed of mass production resulted in numerous breakages. Some of the vessels were smashed during the removal from the kilns, but most of them broke in the kilns during firing or the subsequent stage of cooling. KP

233 Wolf's-tooth decorated sherd

Ceramic

Soba East (CE2),1

Medieval

H 240 mm, W 215 mm, Th 25 mm, D *c.* 160 mm

SNM 31263

The wolf's-tooth decoration on this hand-made medieval sherd is a monument to the continuity of traditions in Nubian pottery manufacture. This particular decorative technique has a long history of usage harkening back to the Neolithic and A-Group (cat. 234) and is also present at Soba throughout the medieval period. The wolf's-tooth pattern is incised on the vessel prior to firing. JRA/DAW

Welsby 1998a, 119, 128, 129

234 Bowl

Ceramic

Halfa Degheim, Scandanavian Joint Expedition Site 277, Tomb 16A, 16A:5

A-Group

Rim: D 165 mm, max. H 191 mm

SNM 14009

This mottled brown, coarse-ware, deep bowl with a pointed base was discovered in an undisturbed A-Group adult burial. It is hand-made and the exterior is decorated with wolf's-tooth decoration, incised prior to firing. Wolf's-tooth decoration was used over a long period of time, appearing even in the medieval period (cat. 233). JRA

Nordström 1972, Bd 3:1, 195; Bd 3:2, pls 4, 102

235

235 Ostrich-shaped vessel

Ceramic

Kerma, Eastern Cemetery, Tumulus K XIV or K XV, east of Chapel A

Kerma Classique

H 155 mm, W 190 mm

SNM 1134

Only two examples of this peculiar red black-rimmed tripod vessel were inventoried by G.A. Reisner during his excavations between 1913 and 1916. Discovered in the spoil heaps near chapels associated with tumuli K XIV and K XV, these are dated to the end of the *Kerma Classique* period. The curve of the spout, the small wings and the tail are reminiscent of an ostrich. Although ostriches are rarely depicted in the bestiary of mica ornaments, ivory inlays or wall paintings of the great funerary temples, they are present in funerary equipment in the form of feather fans from the *Kerma Ancien* period onwards. Ostrich eggs are also present, used as vessels or as raw material for bead-making.   NF

Berenguer 2003n; Reisner 1923a, 108–9; 1923b, 374, 354, 315–17; Wenig 1978b, 156, no. 63; Wildung 1997, 99–100, no. 98

236

236 Aquamanile

Ceramic

Wad ban Naqa, Kom B, Palace

Kushite (Meroitic), first century AD

H 137 mm, L 220 mm; rim: D 43 mm, max.
D 103 mm

SNM 62/9/71

This vessel was reconstructed after being
found in sherds above the floor level in the
palace of Amanishakheto. It is an unusual
shape: roughly cylindrical, tapering at each
end into a flat disc. There is a spout at one end
beside which is an opening for the addition of
fluids; the spout has a flaring rim and is

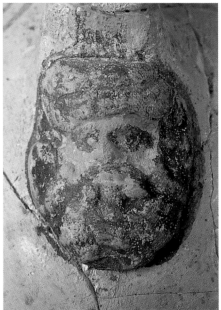

236 (detail)

placed off-centre. A strap handle is attached
to the neck and runs parallel to the vessel
body. The exterior is slipped in orange and
decorated with a naturalistic motif of four
parallel vines painted in a dark reddish-
brown colour. This is a common type of
Meroitic design. The base of the handle is
decorated with a boss bearing the Hellenistic
image of a man whose hair and beard are
painted a dark reddish-brown. This may have
been intended as a representation of Serapis
or Zeus.   JRA

Reinold 2000a, 122; Vercoutter 1962, 292, fig. 27

237 Aquamanile

Ceramic

Soba East, Building D, Rooms m23, m24, (B25)20,
31, 34

Medieval

H 344 mm, L 258 mm, D 206 mm

SNM 31205

The body of this vessel is cylindrical with
convex ends. A spout protrudes from one end,
while there is an opening for the addition of
liquids on top. Often these vessels are given
zoomorphic attributes: including those of
bulls, rabbits and elephants, and have an
animal head at the spout end, hollow stubby
legs on the underside and a tail at the opposing end. Frequently a round or strap handle
joins the body at the back of the animal head.
This vessel has a spout in the shape of an elephant head. A small wrapped or hooded
figure stands atop its head.

Aquamanile form a distinctive class of
green-glazed, wheel-made vessels at Soba. The
glaze on most aquamanile found at Soba
remains a powdery yellow-lime slip as they
were not fired at a temperature high enough
to vitrify the glaze. The fabric of these vessels
is fine and ranges in colour from brick-red to
pale orange. This is the only known production of glazed ware in Nubia. Though no
closely analogous vessels are present from
Egypt, aquamanile are found throughout the
Near East. Close parallels to the Soba vessels
may be found in twelfth- to thirteenth-century
AD Persia (Watson 1985, figs 97, 98); however, unlike their counterparts, the Soba
vessels are non-functional and appear to be
rudimentary local imitations. The local manu-
facturer was clearly unaware of the functional
aspects of these vessels. The handles are weak
and would have difficulty supporting the
weight of the vessel when filled, and often the
spouts do not perforate the body.   JRA/DAW

Welsby and Daniels 1991, 174–6

237

238

238 Bowl

Ceramic
NDRS, Site F1, pot form B10.2
Neolithic
H 124 mm, D 128 mm
SNM 30584

Found at the Neolithic cemetery F1 in the Northern Dongola Reach Survey (NDRS) concession, this pale brown bowl with burnished exterior is covered with bands of incised decoration in horizontal registers, probably made with a fish bone or potter's comb. The fabric is typical of the Neolithic period, containing a great deal of fine clear quartz sand and little or no organic temper. The bowl is hand-made and has a pronounced in-turned rim and a gently pointed base.　　IWS

Welsby Sjöström 2001a, 300, fig. 5.31

239 Jar

Ceramic
NDRS, Site L14, pot form J6.5
Neolithic
H 256 mm, D 168 mm
SNM 31210

This 'bag'-shaped, hand-made jar, of Neolithic date, was unique within the NDRS. The exterior is brown in colour and burnished, decorated with rouletted decoration over the whole of the body, which is relatively unusual. The fabric is the most common of the period, with a high proportion of fine quartz sand and no organic temper. It was found in a cemetery context.　　IWS

Welsby Sjöström 2001a, 281, fig. 5.12

239

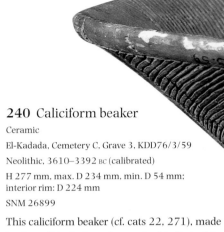

240 Caliciform beaker

Ceramic

El-Kadada, Cemetery C, Grave 3, KDD76/3/59

Neolithic, 3610–3392 BC (calibrated)

H 277 mm, max. D 234 mm, min. D 54 mm;
interior rim: D 224 mm

SNM 26899

This caliciform beaker (cf. cats 22, 271), made by the coil technique, has undoubtedly had its lower part shaped by means of modelling. Both external and internal surfaces were slipped and burnished. On the interior this treatment does not reach further than the waist. It is decorated by the incision technique. The opening is very wide and carries an internal decoration made up of a series of five incised triangles, joined together and facing five others whose surfaces have only been burnished and present a 'rippled ware' appearance. The body is divided into three bands, the middle one having been left without decoration. The other two are divided into panels by thin vertical bands, themselves divided into two by a thin band that runs vertically, forming angular motifs of the chevron kind. The compartments thus marked out are filled with incised parallel and oblique lines that are encrusted with a white substance in order to highlight the decoration. It should be emphasized that this decoration exactly matches that on the bowl found in the same grave and so must have been made by the same person. Placed on the edge of the grave cut together with a pestle and ten bivalve shells, it belonged to a man whose burial was rich in grave goods. He was the principal burial in a grave containing three bodies, one of whom had been sacrificed. The mollusc shells allowed for carbon-14 dating.   JR

Geus 1984, fig. 4, pl. VII; Reinold 1994a, 60, no. 63; 1998, fig. 1; 2000a, 61, 138, no. 27; 2000b, 15, no. 27; 2002, 107, fig. 4; 2003j, 274, no. 248; Welsby 1995, 105, no. 1.75; Wildung 1997, 23, no. 10

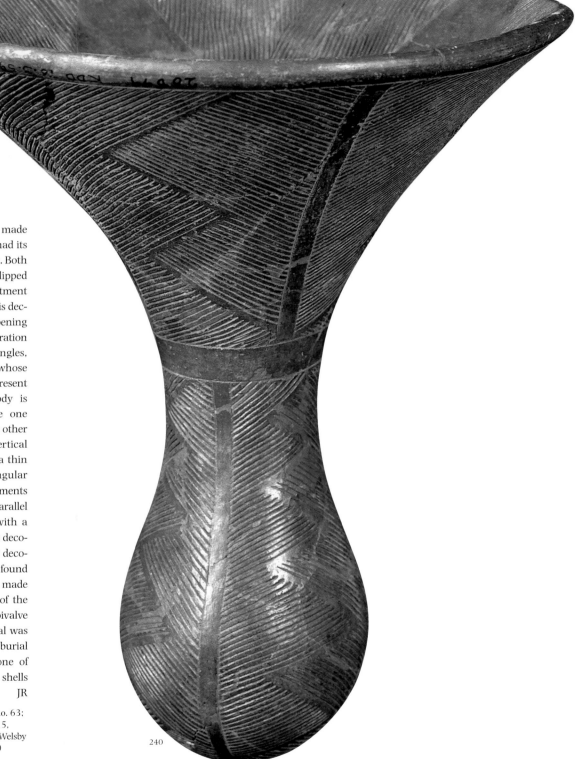

240

241

241 Basin-jar

Ceramic with gypsum infill

El-Kadada, Cemetery A, Grave 2, KDD12/2/5

Neolithic, second quarter of fourth millennium BC

H 168 mm, max. D 182 mm; rim: D 164 mm

SNM 26905

This pot is morphologically on the borderline between two categories: that of receptacles with not very wide mouths, and that of receptacles with slightly narrowing rim, of medium size (PE-M and PR-M), which places it in the class of basins or jars. These two forms are very common at el-Kadada. Its decoration, however, is of a very rare kind. The motifs are made up of encased rectangular lines. The few examples found always have encrustations of a white substance (gypsum) in the incised lines to make the decoration stand out.

Pottery is a form of expression in which the 'Sudanese' craftsmen have always excelled. It allows us to find strands that attest to links between successive civilizations. This vessel comes from a grave that has been destroyed by a bulldozer. It was found in a rich deposit (also partially destroyed) that contained five other pots, a quern and grinder, three palettes, a lithic scatter, a polished axe and 141 beads – the majority still linked together – probably belonging to a necklace.   JR

242 Jar

Ceramic

Aksha, Mission Archéologique Franco-Argentine 1963, Acs IX Tx/25-3

A-Group (3500–2800 BC)

H 567 mm, max. D 437 mm; rim: D 125–8 mm

SNM 14028

This large, pale red jar with a broad shoulder, narrow neck and pointed base originated from the Gerzean phase of Predynastic Egypt (Naqada IIIa–b, 3500–3100 BC). It was found in a rich burial of Terminal A-Group date. It is strong and well fired, and made of marl clay probably in a workshop in Upper Egypt. A turning device was used for the shaping of the neck. It is decorated with groups of wavy lines painted with dark red ochre and has a fine, incised drawing of a bull or a cow with long legs.

242

Jars of this type and more slender shapes were made in various sizes. In the older archaeological literature they were called 'wine jars', but a more differentiated function for transport and storage is probable. Many were exported to Nubia filled with miscellaneous commodities, and during the Terminal A-Group phase much of this trade was concentrated in the southern parts of Lower Nubia. Potmarks, probably related to exchange and ownership, were common. These precious jars had a long life. They were often reused and mended, having repair holes along old cracks. A few whole specimens of smaller size were even placed as offerings in C-Group burials 1,000 years later.　　H-ÅN

Reinold 2000a, 87, 138; 2003g; Wildung 1997, 45, no. 38

243 Dish

Ceramic

Aksha, Mission Archéologique Franco-Argentine (AA XXX AA-3)

A-Group (3500–2800 BC)

H 58 mm, D 317 mm

SNM 14026

This large, shallow dish was found in a burial of Terminal A-Group date at Aksha on the west bank of the Wadi Halfa reach. It is made of a local Nubian clay tempered with finely divided organic material. The original surface is pale brown. The exterior is enhanced with a red wash and is well polished. The polished interior is decorated with brownish red lines, one band around the rim and several sets of three wavy lines that extend downward from the rim to the centre of the bowl. This is marked with a circle of a light red colour. The dish has been reconstructed and a small piece of the rim is missing.

Shallow dishes with a diameter exceeding 300 mm were common in burials of Terminal A-Group date, especially in rich village cemeteries in the southern part of Lower Nubia. They were usually plain, red-polished on both exterior and interior, and undecorated, unlike this fine specimen. The wavy lines were probably inspired by the decoration common on Late Predynastic vessels of Egyptian origin. The dishes were part of the finer household paraphernalia of the A-Group. They were probably used for display and for serving food during feasts.　　H-ÅN

Reinold 2000a, 86, 138; 2003h

243

244 Bowl

Ceramic

NDRS, Site P37, (G4)49, pot form B15.2

Kerma Moyen

H 100 mm, D 150 mm

SNM 30022

The decoration on this hand-made bowl places it within the C-Group ceramic tradition, although it was found in a cemetery of the *Kerma Moyen*. The exterior is black-burnished, while the interior has been roughly smoothed. The whole of the exterior surface of the bowl is covered in quasi-geometric impressed decoration, possibly made with a fishbone. The sides gently curve inwards while the base has been pushed in, giving it an omphalos shape. Running around the rim immediately below it is a register of holes, pierced before firing from the exterior towards the interior. Traces of red ochre suggest that a coloured red strip of leather (?) was once threaded through the holes. Alternatively, because traces of colour were not found in the holes, the effect of a strip may have been simply painted on. It has been suggested that the holes were for hanging the bowl, but the traces of colour and the close spacing of the holes suggest that they were more likely to have been for additional decoration in the form of a trim. Two sets of holes further down the body were possibly intended as 'suspension holes', although their location does not seem suitable for this purpose. Another almost identical but smaller bowl was found in the same grave.   IWS

Welsby Sjöström 2001a, 302, fig. 5.33

245 Bowl

Ceramic

Kerma, Tumulus KN 168, North Cemetery, 168/X-N.XIV.5

Kerma Ancien

H 137 mm, D 220 mm

SNM 3907

A black-topped, red-polished, hand-made bowl with a round bottom discovered in a large tumulus. A decorative band of finely incised cross-hatching runs around the rim on the exterior. The highly polished surface of the vessel was created by burnishing the surface with a pebble; the red colour results from the application of red ochre. Both were done before firing in an oxidizing (oxygen-rich) atmosphere. The black top was created by upending the vessel into a reducing atmosphere during firing (Gratien 1978, 220–28). The *Kerma Ancien* period does not display a wide variety of vessel forms. Those shapes that are found have an affinity with C-Group pottery from Lower Nubia, and it has been suggested that the two pottery traditions may have developed from a common origin (Bonnet 1990a, 126–31; Gratien 1978, 307–13).   JRA

Dunham 1982, 208; Reisner 1923a, 120

246 Beaker

Ceramic

Sai, SKC2, Tomb 13/16, inv. S. 763

Kerma Classique

H 116 mm, D 150 mm

SNM 24406

Black-topped, red-polished, tulip-shaped beaker with thin walls, an open flaring rim and round base. The black band reaches almost halfway down the body and a shimmering grey band runs around the middle of the body. This is a beautiful example of a typical hand-made beaker of the *Kerma Classique* period and is found widely distributed throughout cemeteries and settlements. The dimensions of these beakers are quite standardized, suggesting that they may have been manufactured using a mould (Gratien 1986, 432).   JRA

Gratien 1986, 303, fig. 246g, 304, p. 431, fig. 321

244

245

246

247 Double pilgrim flask

Ceramic

Sai, Pharaonic Cemetery, SAC5, Grave 20

New Kingdom, 18th Dynasty

H 124 mm, D 93–5 mm

SNM 28740

This vase made of two New Year or 'pilgrim' flasks stuck together was found in Grave 20, with many other objects mixed with fragments of bones that had been disturbed during the plundering.

It is made of two small, flat flasks and belongs to the same group as the double vase (cat. 248). The two bottles, which in profile appear flat, were made separately then joined together after drying. The fabric, fine and with mica inclusion, is of chamois (yellowish-brown) colour and the exterior is covered with a scaly slip that is orange-coloured. According to J. Bourriau, this type of double vase, like the one made of a flask and a jar conjoined (cat. 248), appears from the time of Amenhotep III until the beginning of the 19th Dynasty (Bourriau 1982a, 83). Parallels are known from the cemeteries of this time in both Egypt and Nubia. Their use is doubtless cosmetic, as is the case for a lot of vases of small dimensions made of terracotta, stone or faience.   AM-G

248 Double pot: pilgrim flask and small jar

Ceramic

Sai, Pharaonic Cemetery, SAC5, Grave 2

New Kingdom, 18th Dynasty

Flask: H 10 mm, D 72 mm; jar: H 77 mm, D 59 mm

SNM 28741

This double pot was found in Grave 2 which notably yielded objects with names of persons from the end of the 18th Dynasty such as Userhat (cf. cat. 284) and Huy. The vessel is made up of two miniature vases separately fashioned, then attached after drying: a New Year or pilgrim flask and a jar connected to the belly of the vase by a pottery cylinder and to the collar by a sort of stirrup-handle. The fabric is fine and well fired, the surface covered with a smooth white-beige slip. According to J. Bourriau, this type of vase, as well as that made of two pilgrim bottles attached to each other (cat. 247), appears from the time of Amenhotep III until the beginning of the 19th Dynasty, if we consider the examples that come from securely datable contexts (Bourriau 1982a, 83). Parallels were found in the cemeteries of this time not only in Egypt but also in Nubia, such as in Aniba (Steindorff 1937, 136, pl. 85, no. 44a). This vase was doubtless intended for cosmetic use: an analysis carried out in 1900 on the contents of a similar vase from Gurob (Quibell 1901, 142–3 and pl. I) revealed the presence of gum resin.   AM-G

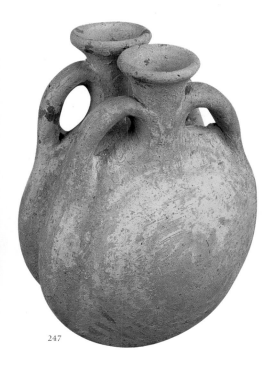

247

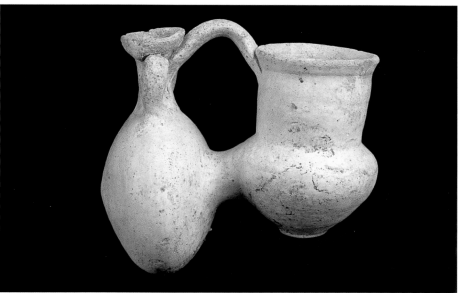

248

249

250

249 Jar

Ceramic

Kerma, Western Necropolis, surface find

Kushite (Meroitic)

H 192 mm, D 187 mm

SNM 31209

Wheel-made jar of fine clay with light orange slip. The decoration painted in red and black on the upper half of the spherical body is organized in several registers divided by a double line traced on the wheel. The largest register comprises *ankh* signs in diamonds and triangles of a lattice motif. It is bordered by a chain of trefoil motifs. The cleanness and the regularity of the lines, as well as the frieze of large beads running along the rim, ascribe this vessel to the 'severe pharaonic style' (Török 1987b, 199–202).

The Meroitic cemetery at Kerma is much larger than G.A. Reisner's excavation originally led one to suspect: it developed from the centre of the ancient Nubian city to the district of Dokki Gel, where the ruins of the New Kingdom city and the subsequent Kushite period are found (see p. 109 ff.). The cultiva-tion of certain areas caused disturbances in loci that destroyed or disturbed numerous burials; therefore it is not rare for ceramics to appear on the surface.   NF

Bonnet 1988, 19

250 Goblet

Ceramic

Kerma, Western Necropolis, surface find

Kushite (Meroitic)

H 81 mm, D 83 mm

SNM 31208

This wheel-made goblet of red clay and slip, found in the same cemetery as the large jar above (cat. 249), is characterized by a stamped decoration that covers three-quar-ters of the body, starting at the rim, which is in itself rare. Two grooves incised on the turning wheel and filled with black complete the decoration. The diamond motifs, which include trefoil elements, were stamped very closely together.   NF

Bonnet 1988, 19, fig. 20; Zach 1988

251 Jar with incised Meroitic graffito

Ceramic

Gabati, Grave 11A, GBT1103

Kushite (Meroitic), first century BC

H 328 mm, max. D 322 mm; rim: D 98 mm

SNM 27849

A complete wheel-made jar, probably Gabati fabric G1. The exterior is coated with a cream slip which shades to pale orange in some areas. The rim, neck and top of the shoulder are coated in red. On the shoulder a single motif is painted three times and there are a post-firing inscription and 'owner's mark'. DE

Rose 1998, 142–3, fig. 6.6

252 Jar

Ceramic

Gabati, Grave 74, GBT7401

Kushite (Meroitic), second–first centuries BC (?)

H 367 mm, max. D 276 mm; rim: D 109 mm

SNM 27806

Hand-made jar, probably Gabati fabric G5. The base is worn from use. The exterior is bur-nished over the naturally mottled grey-black-brown surface, horizontally on the body and vertically on the neck. The neck, shoulder and upper body are decorated with complex comb-impressed designs, including paired short- and long-necked animals, probably giraffes. Such designs are common on Meroitic hand-made pottery of the last centuries BC.   DE

Rose 1998, 165, fig. 6.21

253 Vase

Pottery

Sedeinga, Sector I of the large necropolis, Grave I T16 c5

Kushite (Meroitic), first century AD

H 330 mm, max. D 152 mm

SNM 27368

Vase of painted ceramic with globular body and a long cylindrical neck. The black mono-chrome decoration stands out against the beige background. All around the body, between two double horizontal lines, four

252

253

frogs face an *ankh* emerging like a flower from a stalk. At the shoulder is a kind of necklace, a geometric frieze of alternate circles and triangles, while at the rim runs a very stylized floral frieze.

These globular bottles with a long neck have been found in large numbers at Sedeinga. In general, they are found at the entrance of the funerary chamber, often sealed by a small upside-down ceramic bowl. They probably belonged to a rite practised at the end of the funeral: a meal was shared with the departed and a toast was drunk in his/her honour before the tomb was sealed. Throughout the Graeco-Roman world and in neighbouring Egypt the frog, which seems to have been born from the mud of the Nile and the humidity of the flood, was a symbol of renaissance and eternal life.   CB-N

Berenguer *et al.* 2003o, 230, no. 189; Leclant 1982, fig. 49; 1985, figs 1a–b; Reinold 2000b, 143, no. 186 ; Török 1987c, 84, fig. 58

255

254

254 Beaker

Ceramic

Sai Island, Site 8-B-5.SAS2

Kushite (Meroitic)

H 100 mm, D 91 mm

SNM 28779

Beakers decorated with painted designs are common among the finest Meroitic pottery wares. This light cream-coloured piece displays a frieze of large stylized frogs painted in brown and placed between two double horizontal lines of the same colour. Because of its

close association with water, this animal was related to life and rebirth. This explains its occurrence on numerous Meroitic pottery vessels found in a funerary context, where it is often associated with the *ankh* (cf. cat. 253), the well-known sign of life found in ancient Egyptian hieroglyphic writing.   FG

Geus 1994, 27; Reinold 2000a, 143, no. 182; Vercoutter 1979, 221, 223, 233, no. 13, fig. 8

255 Eastern Desert Ware bowl

Ceramic

AKS, Site 3-O-1 (A), Tumulus 11, Grave 37, 42c, pot form 49x

Post-Meroitic

H 127 mm, D 230 mm

SNM 31220

This hand-made bowl formed part of the grave goods of a Post-Meroitic burial. Together with two other vessels from the same cemetery, it presents clear similarities with Eastern Desert Ware, which is widely distributed from the Red Sea coast in southern Egypt into the Nile Valley. The top of the rim is decorated with seven impressed groups of dots; the exterior is slipped and decorated with incised wavy lines and triangles infilled with wavy lines. The interior is bisected by four lines painted with a thinned-out slip, each running from side to side across the centre of the bowl.   IWS

256 Bowl

Ceramic

Dabbat el-Tor

c. 100 BC, possibly earlier (Jebel Moya, Phase III)

H 154 mm, max. D 190 mm; rim: D 117 mm

SNM 23367

This is a heavily manufactured, plain-rimmed globular bowl with thick walls and a narrow mouth. The exterior is red-burnished and decorated with incised bands enclosing rocker-stamp impressions. This hand-made vessel has previously been described as 'dry-scratched' ware and has been discovered at other sites such as Jebel Moya and Abu Geili. The exact dating of this vessel type is uncertain and it appears at Abu Geili after Jebel Moya was abandoned (cf. Crawford and Addison 1951, 44–50, pls XXXVIIIA, XLIV 11; Gerharz 1994, 134–6).   JRA

256

257

257 Beer jar

Ceramic

AKS, Site 3-O-1 (B), Tumulus 5, Grave 34, 62e,
pot form 59x

Post-Meroitic

H 524 mm, max. D 432 mm; rim: D 60 mm

SNM 31184

This hand-made vessel was discovered intact,
forming part of the grave goods of a Post-
Meroitic burial. A so-called 'beer jar' with
narrow neck and large bulbous body, it has
raised decoration on the shoulder and neck.
The decoration consists of three trident
shapes on the shoulder, while at the base of
the neck are three circular bosses.   IWS

258 Spouted jar

Ceramic

Gabati, no. GBT T5/93c

Early medieval, late sixth century AD (?)

H 184 mm, max. D 207 mm; rim: D 102 mm

SNM 31267

Wheel-made spouted jar with a burnished red
slip and black painted decoration on a white
background, Gabati fabric G19. This is a
common Post-Meroitic and early medieval
form; the decoration seems likely to date to
the beginning of the Christian period. Parallels for such vessels with similar decoration
can be found both at Soba East and Old
Dongola.   DE

Smith 1998, 186, fig. 6.32

259 Soba Ware sherds

Ceramic

Soba East, (MN10)15, 51, 79, Dec. 434.8; 388.2;
433.1; pot form 230N

Medieval, Transitional to Classic Christian

L 3.7–9 mm, W 3–8 mm, Th 2–6 mm

SNM 31266

Soba Ware forms a distinctive assemblage of
finely painted and slipped, wheel-made
ceramics that date from the Post-Meroitic
transitional period to the Classic Christian
period. It has little affinity with the ceramics
of the earlier Kushite period or with other
medieval Nubian wares. It was produced in
the vicinity of Soba, suggesting the presence
of a thriving local ceramic industry there
during the early medieval period. Imported
wares are rare at this time at Soba. Many
characteristic styles are present, with painted
designs applied on the exterior and occasionally the interior overtop of brown, red or

cream slipped surfaces. Usually the interior and exterior are slipped with the same colour; however, when differing colours are used sometimes the darker slip is extended over the rim to form a band around the rim on the interior or exterior. Bowls, basins, jars, cups, chalices (cats 193, 198) and lids are the primary vessel forms used. The painted decoration appears to be strongly influenced by Christian decorative artistic traditions as seen in contemporary Nubian wall paintings. A wide range of distinctive designs are present, with the decoration commonly situated within horizontal or vertical registers. Decorative motifs include human faces, roundels, animals such as lions, birds, frogs and gazelle, backgrounds filled with dots, ovals or crosses, repeating friezes and geometric patterns. Crosses are among the most common motifs. Bosses may also be painted and modelled in the shape of animal heads. Some of these motifs are quite distinct and might suggest the hand of one artist, or of a school or group following a set pattern.   JRA/DAW

Welsby and Daniels 1991, 214, 227–8, 324–34; Welsby 1998a, 113, 136–72

258

260 Black and White Decorated Ware

Ceramic

Soba East, (Z3)38

Medieval, Early Christian

H 160 mm, L 120 mm, W 85 mm, Th 50 mm, D *c.* 132 mm

SNM 31265

Painted pottery at Soba during the early medieval period falls into two categories: the first is Soba Ware and the second Black and White Decorated Ware. Black and White Decorated Ware is distinct and seems to be associated only with certain forms and fabrics, primarily jars of the narrow-mouthed, thin-walled or enclosed varieties such as pilgrim flasks. It is much rarer than Soba Ware, suggesting that it might have been imported to the Soba region. Analogous examples have been discovered at Old Dongola and Gabati (cat. 258), and there may have been a kiln producing this ware in the vicinity of Old Dongola. The exterior surface of these vessels is usually covered with orange or red slip on to which the design is applied in black paint. Spaces within the pattern are then filled in white; however, in certain instances the positions of the red/orange slip and the white are

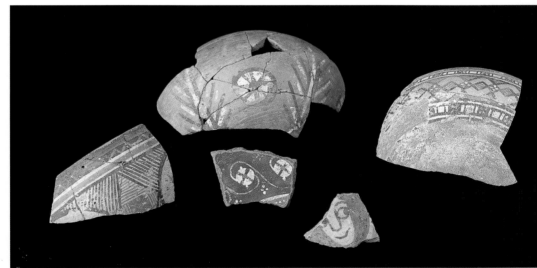

259, 260 (top centre)

reversed. Common decorations include boxes or discs filled with cross-hatching, horizontal bands containing crosses, triangles or diamonds, horizontal or vertical arrangements of ovals and decorative motifs that cover the pot body but are not restricted to registers or linear arrangements.   JRA/DAW

Welsby 1998a, 119, 136–9, 170

261 Black-burnished sherd

Ceramic

Soba East, (M14)445, pot form 48L

Medieval

L 198 mm, W 23 mm, Th 148 mm, D *c.* 165 mm

SNM 31264

261

Red- and black-burnished wares have been among the most common found at Soba and in the Kingdom of Alwa, encompassing most forms and fabrics. This decoration technique was also found further north, though not in any great quantity, thus suggesting a Soba-influenced local tradition or a tradition originating further to the south. It may be contrasted with ceramics from Old Dongola (cat. 188). Burnishing is produced by rubbing the pot surface after firing with a rounded stone or other smooth object, thus making the surface shiny and less porous. This pot is also decorated with incised motifs and bears a graffito – a monogram in the shape of a cross, made after firing. JRA/DAW

Welsby 1998a, 91

262 Pilgrim flask

Ceramic

Meinarti, reg. no. 151

Medieval, late Christian

D *c.* 163 mm, Th *c.* 131 mm; rim: D *c.* 53 mm

SNM 15309

A distinctively shaped vessel with two pre-formed, wheel-made, convex discoid faces joined together. On the top, loop handles emerge from the base of the neck on either side

262

263

of a spout. The shape of late Christian pilgrim flasks appears to be of Nubian design (Adams 2002, 66). A wide reddish-orange band with black geometric and guilloche designs adorns the sides, while two knotted serpents decorate the exterior faces. This is an extremely unusual decoration as snakes are not normally depicted in this fashion: they are usually shown being trampled underfoot as a symbol of evil. It is uncertain what these vessels carried, though the slender neck suggests liquids. The handles on such vessels found at Soba East were extremely worn, and a cord was found tied to the handles and neck of one suggesting that it may have been attached to a pack animal (Welsby and Daniels 1991, 172).　　JRA

Adams 2002, 52, 66, col. pl. IIe, f, pl. 12e, f, back cover

263 Bowl

Ceramic
Abu Geili, field no. 400/9/2
Islamic, Funj
H 113 mm, D 315 mm
SNM 9286

An open, hand-made, black-burnished bowl with a flat base. The colour is not uniform and some brown areas are visible. The interior is decorated with a band of impressed dots around the rim, while the exterior is adorned with a wide incised band of 'X's, beneath which is another of impressed dots. The bowl was broken and repaired in antiquity. Two repairs, consisting of three pairs of holes each, straddle the breaks and would have allowed the bowl to be repaired with a thong or cord, though not to hold liquids following the repair. Although this bowl is circular in form, others of this type were purposefully shaped into squares or ovals, and no two bowls appear to share the same decorative motifs, though all are incised with geometric patterns. These vessels have been found predominantly in graves, and virtually all bowls of this type discovered thus far appear to have been repaired, possibly an indication of their value or importance.　　JRA

Crawford and Addison 1951, 53, 59, pls XXXII, XLVI 3

13

FUNERARY CULTURE

FRANCIS GEUS

The most ancient burials ever found in Sudan belong to three cemeteries located in Lower Nubia north of the Second Cataract that date to the end of the Palaeolithic (13000–8000 BC). The most significant are found at Jebel Sahaba (fig. 182). These tombs are the forerunners of traditions that developed subsequently in Nubia: the graves are concentrated in an area that is exclusively funerary; the burials occupy pits protected by thin sandstone slabs; some pits include two to four individuals; all the skeletons display the same position and orientation, contracted on their left side, with heads to the east, and hands in front of their faces in a foetal posture. This probably showed that death was viewed as a passage towards another form of existence.[1] At Toshka the bucrania of wild cattle found over several graves possibly indicated their location. None of those early burials contained grave goods.

These initial mortuary traditions do not seem to have continued in Lower Nubia, where no Neolithic grave has ever been found, in contrast with Upper Nubia and the central Sudan where a wealth of evidence has been collected for that period. The most ancient tombs excavated there, dating from the Khartoum Mesolithic (8000–5000 BC), contrast with those just described. They were not located in specialized areas, but were within settlements. No precise rules governed the orientation and position of the dead, though most were contracted, and no covering protected them. So far, apart from a very few exceptions, none ever contained burial goods. A recent discovery at Kerma has shown that the custom of burying the dead with personal belongings appeared during the final stages of the Mesolithic period, initiating more elaborate mortuary behaviour which was to develop considerably during the two following millennia in the Kerma Basin and the central Sudan, where large cemeteries were characterized by contracted burials displaying an increasing amount of personal adornments and belongings. This may have resulted from the fact that kinsmen, ignorant of what the passage towards the other existence involved and perhaps inclined to see it as a final initiation rite, tried to assist their deceased individuals by providing elements of their prior existence.

At el-Ghaba small rounded pits contained a single occupant lying in the contracted position with no particular orientation. The skeleton, occasionally with personal adornments, was generally at the centre of the pit, which also contained pottery vessels, stone and bone tools, mollusc shells and malachite fragments.

Green traces were occasionally present on teeth and skulls; red traces appeared on the bones and on the surrounding sediment. Thick white-coloured regions were found underneath the skulls and the feet. In the more recent tombs, one or two bucrania occasionally were laid near the skull. The ornaments found on the deceased were undoubtedly those that adorned them during their lifetime and to which they probably attributed prophylactic powers. The colours are remains of ochred clothes and wraps (red), headrests and footrests (white), and facial painting possibly of magical significance (green). All features show that considerable attention was given to the bodies. The pottery vessels, usually found upturned, might have been used during rituals leading up to the sealing of the tomb, while the other objects certainly refer to the individual's lifetime activities or social rank. Finally the bucrania, whose precise function remains unknown, indicate the importance of cattle for the society, hence their inclusion in funeral rituals. Recent fieldwork at el-Multaga has shown that such complex burial customs may be specific to settlers of the Nile Valley. At el-Multaga, poorly furnished scattered graves seem to document a nomadic population related to both the Nile environment and the hinterland.

While appearing to be the perfect illustration of the burial modes that were to

182 Map of sites discussed in this chapter.

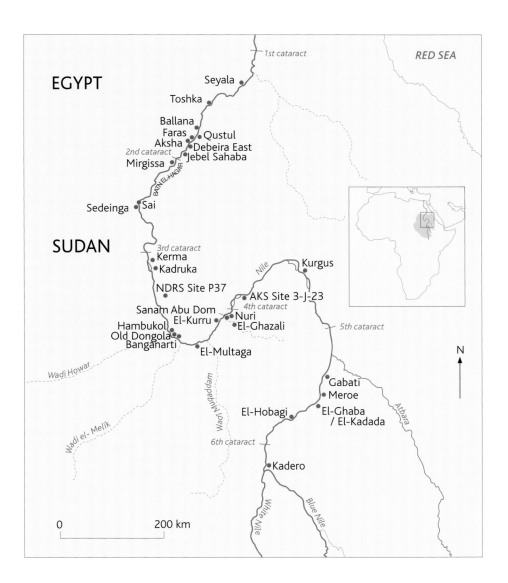

remain until the advent of Christianity, el-Ghaba is much less revealing of other mortuary customs. No external marking of the graves has been identified and the whole cemetery seems to have developed along topographical lines, a likely indication of an egalitarian society. Although contemporary with el-Ghaba, Kadero exhibits more complex development since its tombs were organized into clusters and contained differentiated equipment, presumably indicating family or social units. This is even more obvious at Kadruka, where cemeteries of medium size included wealthy graves that have been interpreted as those of local chieftains and as the starting point of the burial field itself. Other features such as stone grave-markers, dog burials, animal sacrifices, anthropomorphic figurines and the possible building of tumuli over graves indicate considerable progress in mortuary conceptions.[2]

Even so, it was at el-Kadada, near el-Ghaba, that Neolithic customs flourished (fig. 183). There the graves are circular or sub-circular pits where the body lies contracted on its side with no particular orientation. Coloured areas indicate that clothes, cloth, pillows and mats were present, but no facial painting was identified, though fragments of malachite were found among the offerings. While more varied and numerous, the funerary assemblages were of the same

183 El-Kadada, Grave 86/16.

nature, but the pottery vessels were in an upright position. Female ceramic figurines, whose precise function remains a matter of discussion, were usual.[3] Dog and goat skeletons were present in the graves alongside bucrania. Several pits contained superimposed burials that seem to document the practice of human sacrifice, the first occurrence of a custom destined subsequently to become widespread, particularly at Kerma.[4]

It is Lower Nubia, where the end of the Neolithic is marked by important cultural developments, labelled by archaeologists A-Group, C-Group, Pre-Kerma and Kerma, that has provided the bulk of our information for the subsequent two millennia (c. 3500–1500 BC) so far. The mortuary assemblages are comparable with those just described but the graves show spectacular developments that reached their peak at Kerma in the final stage of the period, around 1600 BC.

In A-Group graves (*c.* 3500–3000 BC) the deceased were usually placed in sub-rectangular or oval pits, contracted on their left side, head in the south, with a large range of goods. The choice of a precise orientation, obviously borrowed from Egypt, reflected religious beliefs probably related to the rising and setting of the sun. From then on, it became a well-established custom in Nubia. The goods, which display affinities with those of the earlier southerly cemeteries, include numerous imports from Egypt. Superimposed burials are present but, contrary to el-Kadada, they do not include human sacrifices. Being relatively homogeneous and of small size, the A-Group cemeteries have long been viewed as reflecting an egalitarian society. But a few sites included graves of amazing wealth that have led scholars to revise their opinions and to conclude that the last stages of the culture evidenced a more complex society. Two of them, located at Qustul and Seyala, are now considered elite cemeteries, possibly of royal rank, the first of their kind in Nubia.

During the C-Group (*c.* 2200–1500 BC) a change in funerary ideology is attested by the orientation of the bodies, the absence of superimposed burials, the building of mud-brick burial chambers, the generalization of surface monuments and, in

184 C-Group cemetery, SJE Site 35.

its latest stage, the presence of animal offerings in the shafts. Moreover that culture, rooted in Lower Nubia for about eight centuries, experienced through time particularly significant changes in burial structures.

The stone monuments covering the shafts (fig. 184) consisted of circles of dry stones, filled with rubble and sand. Initially 2–3 m in diameter, they increased in size, progressively reaching 16 m in diameter. At the beginning pottery vessels and occasionally oblong stelae and bucrania were placed along their edges where, later, a mud-brick chapel or an offering place was sometimes erected. The early graves had small, deep rounded or oval shafts, but these gradually became oblong with stone slabs sometimes lining and covering them. In the more elaborate graves of the final stages, they were transformed into mud-brick rooms that were occasionally vaulted. The deceased lay contracted following an east–west orientation, head to the east facing north. This was altered during the Egyptian Middle Kingdom (2055–1650 BC) to become north–south, head to the north facing west: a change most likely of religious significance. In the best graves, the deceased was adorned with ornaments, wore a loincloth, cap and sandals, and was provided with a blanket and a pillow. Other goods included pottery vessels, various artefacts and numerous figurines representing women and cattle. In the latest stage the deceased lay on a bed. In most cemeteries, grave size and distribution seem to indicate an egalitarian society, but in the latest stages larger and richer graves reveal an incipient social stratification. This, together with such innovations as funerary chapels, bucrania and bed burials, demonstrates influences coming from the Kerma culture which flourished south of the Batn el-Hagar during the same period.

Indeed, it is in southern Nubia that the most impressive development of mortuary traditions of that period have been recorded, particularly at Kerma, where a cemetery of approximately 30,000 graves has been extensively sounded, providing information about their evolution through three successive stages labelled *Kerma Ancien*, *Moyen* and *Classique* (*c.* 2500–1500 BC). The grave shafts of the non-royal burials changed through time in shape and size. Their shape, oval or circular during *Kerma Ancien*, became circular during *Kerma Moyen* (fig. 185) and rectangular during *Kerma Classique*. Their size, small at the beginning, grew to considerable proportions through *Kerma Ancien* and *Moyen*, then became smaller again during *Kerma Classique*. The position and orientation of the tomb occupants were and remained those of the C-Group but, from the end of *Kerma Ancien*, it became usual to bury the corpse on a bed. Cloth, loin-cloths, sandals, caps, fans of ostrich feathers and personal adornments were regular features, while pottery vessels and artefacts, including weapons, were common and diversified. Animal sacrifices, mainly small bovids, were usual while human sacrifices, which first appeared during *Kerma Ancien*, increased in frequency during *Kerma Classique*, particularly in the rulers' tombs. One contained 322 sacrificed individuals, of which many had apparently been buried alive. If these below-ground developments attest to the emergence of a highly stratified society and a powerful ruler, a significant evolution in funerary beliefs and rituals is also indicated above ground. Indeed, all Kerma graves seem to have been covered with tumuli, of which the best preserved are on Sai Island, where circular mounds covered with white pebbles were surrounded by black stones in a remarkable contrast (fig. 186). Size soon became an indicator of social rank, a trend that reached its peak at Kerma in the latest phase, when royal tumuli reaching 90 m in diameter were built over mud-brick corridors and rooms, apart from the main burial that contained furnishings, sacrificial bodies and subsidiary graves. Oblong stelae, bucrania of large bovids and upturned vessels are commonly found around *Kerma Ancien* tumuli. Judging by their inverted position, the vessels were probably used during burial ceremonies. Later, such rituals were

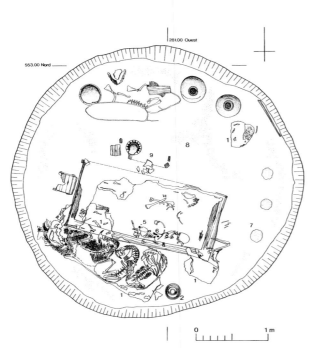

185 *Kerma Moyen* burial, Kerma, Eastern Cemetery, Grave 9.

186 Aerial photograph of the Kerma period tumuli at Sai.

associated with the burial itself, but placing bucrania around the edge of the tumulus, which reached spectacular proportions during *Kerma Moyen* (cat. 71), became unusual during *Kerma Classique*. During *Kerma Moyen* some tumuli were associated with chapels, of which the most remarkable is the so-called Eastern Deffufa. It is likely that this idea came from Egypt, as the painted internal decoration of the latter appears to confirm.

The size, contents and distribution of the graves excavated at Kerma reflect the development of a stratified and centralized society. Throughout different areas of the cemetery, clusters of graves surround larger ones, a custom that reached its peak during *Kerma Classique* when smaller tumuli were built around the royal ones. Moreover, the latter contained numerous burials that had no tumuli of their own but included goods and sacrifices, and were most likely those of ranking officials who chose to be buried close to their sovereign.

The Egyptian conquest of Nubia at the beginning of the New Kingdom (1550–1069 BC) marked a partial end of local traditions. Many Nubian graves became indistinguishable from those of the Egyptians, the most striking change being the shift from the contracted to the extended position, usual in Egypt since the Old Kingdom. In Lower Nubia decorated tombs of local princes illustrate the deep Egyptianization of the elite (cf. cats 77–8).

Unfortunately, information is scarce for the period from Egypt's withdrawal to the emergence of the Kushite kingdom several centuries later (*c.* 850 BC; cf. Hillat el-Arab, p. 138 ff.). Henceforth the archaeological record shows a revival or the survival of the old burial styles competing with Egyptian influence, of which the most notable are in cemeteries reserved for the rulers. The most ancient of these cemeteries, el-Kurru (fig. 187), includes the graves of the Napatan kings' ancestors that evi-

187 Aerial photograph of el-Kurru.

188 Aerial photograph of Meroe, North pyramid field.

dence a strong revival of Nubian traditions. The deceased lay on a bed, contracted on the right side, in a shaft covered by a tumulus. The orientation, head to the north facing west, was the one adopted by the C-Group during the Middle Kingdom. Soon tumuli were reinforced by circular walls of stones and associated with eastern chapels. The entire tumulus structure was then surrounded by a wall forming a horseshoe-shaped enclosure. Later, the wall and the structure became rectangular, the latter being henceforth a *mastaba* which, in turn, gave way to a pyramid; a change that introduced a tradition that was to last for centuries in the royal cemeteries of Nuri and Meroe (fig. 188, cat. 267). Meanwhile, the burial pit was replaced by rock-cut rooms reached by a long eastern stairway. Increasing Egyptian influence led to drastic changes: during the eighth century BC the royal bodies were mummified, placed extended in coffins orientated east–west, and provided with canopic jars, shabtis and amulets of Egyptian manufacture. In the chambers of Tanwetamani's tomb part of the painted decoration of Pharaonic tradition is preserved. Later, chapels of the Meroitic royal pyramids were decorated with reliefs commemorating the king's funeral (fig. 189). Burial goods that survived plundering confirm the strong influence of Egypt on the royal family which continued later at Meroe, where royal graves included artefacts from Graeco-Roman Egypt and beyond (cats 156–8).

The private graves of the Napatan period exhibit a great variety in tomb types, burial styles and mortuary assemblages, which resulted from both Pharaonic and local traditions. This found its most significant expression at Sanam Abu Dom where,

189 Relief decoration on the north wall
of the chapel of Beg N.5 at Meroe.
Photograph © 2004 Museum of Fine Arts, Boston.

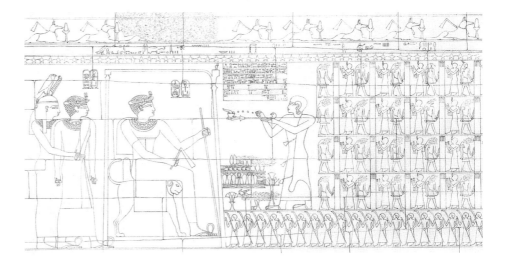

unfortunately, the superstructures did not survive. There, four main types of sub-structures appear, forerunners of all later grave forms of Kushite and Post-Meroitic age: sloping shafts leading to caves or mud-brick vaulted chambers; rectangular pits lined with mud bricks; simple rectangular or oval pits; and narrow pits with lateral niches. In the first type, the body was extended, goods were mostly Egyptian and mummification, coffins and cartonnage were common. In the others, those features were less common and pottery vessels included wheel-made wares of Egyptian man-ufacture and hand-made wares reminiscent of the earlier local tradition.[5] Animal offerings, so common in Kerma graves, did not occur, but three lions and two fish were buried within the cemetery. Most skeletons were east–west orientated, skulls to the west. Personal ornaments included numerous amulets of Egyptian manufacture. Most remarkable was the occurrence, side by side, of extended and contracted burials displaying similar assemblages that were interpreted as evidence for two contempo-rary elements in the population, one Egyptianized and the other conservative.

Meroitic burials followed the same tradition as those just described. In Nubia, the frequency of cave graves and extended burials, and the favoured east–west orientation with the head to the west reveal the strong influence of Egyptian and royal models (fig. 190). In the central Sudan, where Egypt's influence was limited and restricted to the capital city and its surroundings, burial patterns were less codified. Extended burials prevailed only around Meroe, where they appeared at a much later date, then vanished towards the end of the period, while the orienta-tion of the corpses displayed variation. Even in Nubia, Egypt's influence began to weaken as mummies and cartonnages were absent and coffins rather rare. How-ever, recent excavations on Sai Island have revealed that wooden coffins were very common there and a few sites yielded evidence of bed-burials.[6] Many graves were richly furnished, contrary to those of contemporary Egypt, which included at most a coffin and a cartonnage. The first centuries AD witnessed an increasing frequency of painted and stamped ceramics displaying motifs reminiscent of former amulets, whose scarcity at that time is striking. However, the most typical features of the Meroitic cemeteries in Nubia are quadrangular structures of stone or mud brick usually identified as the remains of pyramids and *mastabas* indicat-ing Egyptian and royal influence (fig. 191). On their eastern side, chapels were

190 Meroitic burial 2923 at Faras.

191 Meroitic tomb superstructure at Sai.

192 Magical and religious texts on the walls
of the crypt of Archbishop Georgios.

obviously connected to the stelae, offering tables (cats 300–304) and statues that were used in the rituals. Human-headed winged statues (cats 269, 299) have been interpreted as representing the *ba* of the Egyptian religion while offering tables (cat. 303) yield formulae and iconographic data indicating the deep influence of Osirian beliefs.

The decline, then end of Meroe's political leadership in the fourth century AD led to major changes involving a gradual revival of local customs.[7] The use of tumuli as tomb superstructures is a major feature of Post-Meroitic cemeteries, where bed-burials, contracted bodies and north–south orientations reappear alongside previous customs. As formerly at Kerma, the royal tombs of Lower Nubia contained human sacrifices and were surrounded by smaller private burials. Significantly, stone objects and associated inscriptions became exceptional. Continuity with the preceding period is striking in private tombs, where the change involves mostly the style and quality of the furnishing which, as before, included pottery vessels, personal adornments, weapons, tools and toilet articles. The most impressive burials of the period are undoubtedly those of the northern kings at Ballana and Qustul. Their large tumuli, the largest being 77 m in diameter and 13 m high, had long been mistaken for natural hills and therefore partly escaped plundering. Consequently, their excavation provided numerous objects, many originating from Byzantine Egypt. As with other graves of similar status excavated further to the south, they represent the ultimate point that deeply rooted traditions were to reach before their extinction with the adoption of Christianity.

Henceforth burial customs underwent a major transformation. Tomb superstructures occasionally with funerary stelae still occurred but, in most instances, the substructures contained only the deceased wrapped in a shroud or laid in a coffin. Recent research in Old Dongola has nevertheless shown that graves of ecclesiastics could also include wall inscriptions (fig. 192) and objects related to burial rituals. Most amazing is the recent discovery at Banganarti of a vast mausoleum with painted chapels that may have contained the burials of the kings of Christian Makuria, whose residence was at Old Dongola.[8]

So far, there has been little interest in post-Christian funerary customs. One of the most impressive features in Muslim cemeteries is the *qubba*, a domed structure covering the graves of holy men, the shape of which may have originated with the Meroitic pyramids.[9] It is also possible that the tradition of laying palm branches on the graves during feast days relates to an ancient custom now lost to archaeology.

1 See Garcea, this volume, p. 20 ff.
2 See Reinold and Krzyzaniak, this volume, pp. 42–5, 49–52.
3 See cats 20, 23, 25, 271.
4 See Bonnet's discussion of the Kerma Period, this volume, p. 70 ff.
5 See further this volume, pp. 138–47.

6 See Geus, this volume, pp. 114–16.
7 See Grzymski and Lenoble, this volume, pp. 165–7, 186–92.
8 See Anderson, Godlewski and Żurawski, this volume, pp. 202–13, 220–23.
9 See Intisar el-Zein, this volume, fig. 174.

264 Chisel

Copper alloy

Meroe, Southern Cemetery, Beg S 32,
Harvard–Boston Mus. no. 21-2-156.a, A.M.S.
no. NE-36-O/03-J-0002.032

Kushite, Napatan, mid-sixth century BC (Gen. 11–12)

L 104 mm, W 12 mm, Th 7 mm

SNM 2455

This chisel, along with cats 265–6, is described by D. Dunham as one of the three chisels and two bronze adzes found as grave goods, along with a bronze mirror, during the excavation in 1921 'outside head end of coffin' in the burial chamber of *mastaba* or pyramid Beg S 32 belonging to a male. The chisel has a square-sectioned shank that widens out into a lozenge shape. The cutting edge is flat and slightly rounded.

It was originally registered as coming from Beg S 22, but the excavator G. Reisner listed the provenance as S XXXII. This is confirmed in his excavation diary where he wrote on 2 February 1921: 'Cleared thieves' hole in Pyr. Beg S XXXII. They came down at head-end of a coffin burial, broke away the end of the coffin and plundered the head of the mummy. Just outside the coffin, apparently shoved aside by the thieves, is a small group of objects – a bronze mirror, two adzes, etc. The tomb is a simple pit burial covered by a *mastaba* or pyramid of sandstone, and a chapel, after burial.' Few mason's tools, particularly chisels, have been found. Within the Sudan National Museum the tools in the collection come from many different periods and sites, for example, from the A-Group cemetery in Faras, from Aksha (C-Group), Mirgissa (New Kingdom), Attiri (Meroitic), and Debeira East (Post-Meroitic), as well as one of iron from el-Ghazali (Christian). Chisels of this type would have been used for carving soft materials such as sandstone and were presumably also used in pyramid construction.   FWH

Dunham 1963, 374, figs 203, 204.A.3 [S 32, 21-2-156.a]; Hinkel and Abdelrahman 2002, 143; Reisner n.d., XXXII

266, 264, 265

265 Chisel

Copper alloy

Meroe, Southern Cemetery, Beg S 32,
Harvard–Boston Mus. no. 21-2-156.c, A.M.S.
no. NE-36-O/03-J-0002.032

Kushite, Napatan, mid-sixth century BC (Gen. 11–12)

L 104 mm, W 12 mm, Th 8 mm

SNM 2455A

The chisel belongs to the same group as cats 264 and 266. It has a round-sectioned shank that widens out into a lozenge-shape. As with cat. 264, its cutting edge is flat and rounded. The chisel slightly tapers outward from the shank to the cutting edge.   FWH

Dunham 1963, 374, figs 203, 204.A.5 [S 32, 21-2-156.c]; Hinkel and Abdelrahman 2002, 143; Reisner n.d., XXXII

266 Adze

Copper alloy

Meroe, Southern Cemetery, Beg S 32,
Harvard–Boston Mus. no. 21-2-157, A.M.S.
no. NE-36-O/03-J-0002.032

Kushite, Napatan, mid-sixth century BC (Gen. 11–12)

L 123 mm, W 44 mm, Th 3 mm

SNM 2456

Flat, with a clearly defined square butt end, this adze tapers outward from the shaft to the cutting edge. The cutting edge was broken in antiquity and was formerly rounded. It belongs to the same group of grave goods as cats 264–5.   FWH

Dunham 1963, 374, figs 203, 204.A.2; Hinkel and Abdelrahman 2002, 143; Reisner n.d., XXXII

267 Pyramid capstone

Sandstone

Meroe, Northern Cemetery, probably pyramid Beg
N 27, A.M.S. no. NE-36-O/03-J-0001/0029

Kushite, Meroitic, AD 270–300

H (incl. remains of column) 330 mm; base:
560 x 560 mm; top: 400 x 400 mm

SNM 31222

This object was found in the sand about 8 m
south-east of the south-eastern corner of
pyramid Beg N 27, which is the pyramid of a
king. According to the situation on the site, a
connection between the ruined pyramid and
the object is highly likely. The object is the
uppermost stone of a Meroitic truncated
pyramid, the so-called 'capstone'. In shape it
represents a truncated pyramid and thereby
repeats the truncated form of the pyramid
below it. The extension in the form of a
column is only preserved at its base and
shows that the column was not centred
exactly on top of the sandstone block. The
part of the block forming the column might
have been broken and destroyed when,
during the collapse of the pyramid, the block
fell about 7.5 m to the ground. Two square
holes through the block show that the cap-

stone was originally fixed with long metal
dowels to the centre of the truncated pyramid
into the wooden pole, which was the vertical
part of the lifting device – the *shaduf* – used in
its construction. The column as the highest
point of the structure might have been
intended to represent the continuation of the
trunk of the *shaduf* inside the pyramid. So far,
there is no proof that the upper end of the
two metal (copper/iron?) dowels bore decoration, for example, perhaps in the form of a
sun disc made of copper which would catch
the first sun rays in the morning.   FWH

Hinkel 1982, 129–31, pl. V.b (type PS)

268 'Pyramidion'

Sandstone

Sai Island, Site 8-B-52.B

Kushite, Meroitic

H 485 mm, D 190 mm

SNM 31346

This piece of sculpture, made out of whitish,
coarse-grained sandstone, is composed of a
roughly carved cylindrical base topped with a
stylized representation of a lotus flower. The

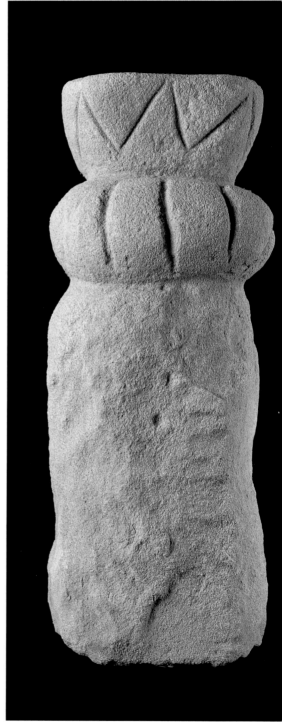

268

267

latter has been shaped as a flattened sphere covered by a truncated cone, both decorated with deep incisions. According to C. Berger (1994b), who found comparable objects in the nearby necropolis of Sedeinga, they must have been placed at the top of Meroitic pyramids, hence her decision to call them 'pyramidions'. Few have been recovered from previously excavated Meroitic cemeteries (Geus 1989, 172), but they may have been a regular feature on Sai Island and at Sedeinga.   RP

Geus 2002, 111, pl. XIVa

269 Statue of a *ba*-bird

Sandstone

Sedeinga, sector I of the large necropolis, Grave I T41, p2

Kushite, Meroitic, 50 BC–AD 50

Total H 680 mm, H (of the tenon) 275 mm, W (of the front of the socle) 140 mm

SNM 31215

This beautiful sandstone statue, whose head has unfortunately disappeared, is probably that of a *ba*-bird (cf. cat. 299): a bird with a human head well known in Egypt where it was deemed to represent the soul leaving the body of the deceased. Early on the Kushites seem to have adopted this representation. It was gradually transformed into that of a man or woman standing upright on a socle, a long pair of wings falling from their shoulders to the ground behind them. The perch, cut from the same block as the bird, has a 100 mm vertical hole drilled in its base, possibly to allow it to be mounted on a tenon of wood or metal and assuring its stability.

This statue was found together with other decorated blocks, blocking the access to a grave that was reused at a later date, in one of the oldest sectors of the cemetery. For a statue of the same type see Schiff-Giorgini *et al.* 1971, 391, fig. 769.   CB-N

Berger 1994a, fig. 34; Leclant 1984a, pl. XXXII, figs 39, 41; 1984b, 1116, fig. 2a

270

270 Bottle

Ceramic

Kadruka, Cemetery 1, Grave 106, KDK1/106/4

Neolithic, first quarter of fifth millennium BC

H 230 mm, max. D 176 mm; rim: D 58 mm

SNM 26880

This vessel belongs morphologically to the category of medium-sized (TR-M) containers with the sides narrowing markedly towards the mouth, which classifies it in the bottle series. This type of receptacle is found in the central Sudan, but in those cases the opening is simply the extension of the body. Here, the neck is marked by an inflexion of the wall of the pot. In a Neolithic context the 'bottle forms' indicate a late date. The body is undecorated, but has been slipped, and its exterior has been lightly burnished, the interior smoothed. The decoration is limited to the rim, as is common, with a series of incised lines forming a lozenge-shaped pattern. The diversity of the forms in this cemetery is characteristic of the final phases of the Neolithic. In Upper Nubia it is accompanied by an impoverishment of the traditional decoration repertory (based on incised and/or impressed lines), and the appearance of painted decoration. This bottle comes from the grave of an adult male, which also yielded another pot, a bucranium, an oblong sandstone palette and a deposit of seven large pebbles of carnelian.

JR

Leclant and Clerc 1988, fig. 74; Reinold 1994b, 84–5, no. 91; 2000a, 138, no. 32; 2000b, 15, no. 32; 2002, 207, fig. 3; Wildung 1997, 28, no. 17

271 Caliciform beaker

Ceramic with gypsum infill

Kadruka, Cemetery 1, Grave 121, KDK1/121/1

Neolithic, first quarter of fifth millennium BC

H 336 mm, max. D 230 mm, min. D 69 mm; interior rim: D 215 mm

SNM 29000

This receptacle belongs morphologically to the group of pots of medium-sized (ER-M) composite form – the category called 'calici-form'. The surfaces are burnished. The decoration is made by the process of rocker-stamping. It is similar to that already seen on vessels cats 22 and 240. Although not very common, this form is however found in different Neolithic periods, both in the central Sudan and in Nubia. These caliciform beakers are perhaps older than their Egyptian equivalents, dated to the Badarian period (5500–4000 BC; cf. Friedman 1999, 9; Friedman and

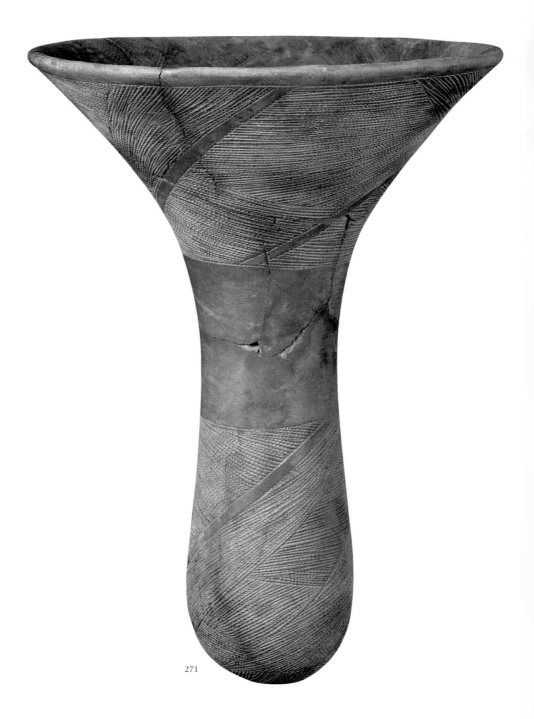

271

Hobbs 2002, 189). They are always found in the graves of important people. As with cemetery KDK18 at Kadruka, they are found in female graves. The main grave of this cemetery is of a woman. On the other hand, at cemetery KDK1 where the main burial is of a man, they are found in male burials. Their style of decoration, made with a rocker stamp (cats 221–3), came into use practically with the invention of pottery. It is significant in this respect that the caliciform beaker, with its religious connotations, was used for funerary libations, maintaining this tradition at a period when incised or dotted decoration is limited to decorating the rims of other types of vessels, whose bodies no longer are given any treatment other than polishing or burnishing.   JR

Reinold 2000b, 15, no. 35; 2002, 107, fig. 4

272 Female anthropomorphic figurine

Veined Nubian sandstone

Kadruka, Cemetery 21, Grave 200, KDK 21/200/1

Neolithic, second half of fifth millennium BC

H 199 mm, W 46 mm, Th 61 mm

SNM 28731

This piece is made of a veined sandstone that is not found in the area: the nearest source is over 150 km to the west, on the other bank of the Nile. This exceptional figurine is a form of geometric expressionist art. Its shape was roughed out before being finally polished. The extreme stylization of the body, which has been reduced to a simple silhouette, skilfully uses the vein of the stone with (as the sole anatomical detail) the representation of a roll of fat at the level of the abdomen. Together with figurine cat. 273, it is an important testament, both in terms of its characteristics as well as its meaning. If the first Neolithic figurines found in the Near East since the eighth millennium BC have a religious significance (as the mother goddess), and are habitually described as fertility symbols, it seems that in a Nilotic context the interpretation must be different. The purpose of these figurines, so stylized that the sexual attributes are not shown, still remains to be deciphered. Furthermore, the discovery of such a statuette in the grave of an adolescent, in which it was the sole grave good, restricts its potential meaning.   JR

Reinold 1998, fig. 15; 2000a, 84, fig. 138, no. 42; 2000b, 15, no. 42; 2001, pl. XIII; 2002, 216, fig. 21; 2003b (no. 212)

272, 273

273 Female anthropomorphic figurine

Veined Nubian sandstone

Kadruka, Cemetery 1, Grave 131, KDK1/131/8

Neolithic, second half of fifth millennium BC

H 196 mm, W 58 mm, Th 42 mm

SNM 26861

The material of this figurine comes from the same source as that used for cat. 272. Of exceptional quality, its production required all the technical skills for the treatment of stone known at the time. Cutting, roughening, and pecking (of which it retains the points of impact) were used to obtain the rough shape before the final polish.

It is an oblong figurine with a swelling at the level of the shoulders, which are only hinted at. It succeeds, without showing any actual anatomical detail or sexual attributes, in indicating that it is a female representation. This statuette is of the same special style as cat. 272, where the process of stylization of the forms seeks accuracy of proportion, a phenomenon that is accentuated by the way the veining of the rock has been made use of. The treatment of the face is particularly characteristic of this style, with only a few lines incised with a burin, showing sight rather than the eyes. Its stylization connects it not only to figurine cat. 272, but also to a figurine of terracotta (cat. 25) found in a grave at another cemetery at Kadruka. These three pieces are of a hitherto unknown type that distinguishes itself from all other anthropomorphic statuettes found in the Nile Valley. This example comes from the grave of the head of the community of cattle farmers.   JR

Reinold 1991, 28, fig. 6; 1994b, 76, no. 72, fig. p. 70; 1994c, 96–7, fig. 71; 2000a, 67, 138, no. 41; 2000b, 16, no. 41; 2002, 216, fig. 20; 2003b (no. 211); Welsby 1995, 104, no. 1.72; Wildung 1997, 16, no. 1

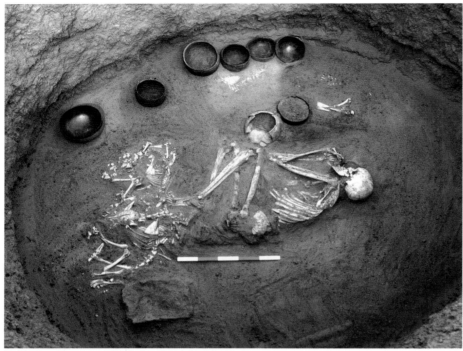

Fig. 193 *Kerma Moyen* grave at P37, Northern Dongola Reach Survey.

Northern Dongola Reach Cemetery P37

The graves at this cemetery (fig. 193) vary in richness, but it is clear that open-mouthed bowls were the principal requirement in terms of receptacles, followed by jars and bottles (closed forms). The latter were occasionally imported from Egypt. The repertoire clearly reflects the kind of goods that would have been placed in the grave to sustain the dead in the afterlife (Welsby Sjöström 2001b, 349–54).

274 Human skeleton

Bone
Northern Dongola Reach Survey, Site P37 (G4)8-36
Kerma Moyen
Est. H of individual 1.75 m

The skeleton in Grave 8 was identified as a thirty-five- to fifty-year-old male who was about 1.75 m tall, one of the larger individuals from this cemetery (Judd 2001, 505). Osteoarthritis was endemic, but most severe at the shoulder, elbow and knee joints, as well as along the spinal column, particularly the left side. While osteoarthritis is to be expected as one ages, the cumulative effects of a person's lifestyle are also contributing factors to decreasing flexibility. The ageing process is also evident in dental wear, and the condition of an individual's teeth reflect health, hygiene and diet. This man's teeth show heavy dental

wear, cupping, an abscess, slight calculus build-up and osteoarthritic lesions of the jaw, all of which characterize the shift to a mixed economy during the *Kerma Moyen* period (Iacumin *et al.* 1998; Judd 2001, 482–4).

Both large toes had injuries typical of stubbing one's toe, while the left tibia sustained an injury typical of 'jarring' the foot against the lower leg when landing on one's feet from a fall. The most serious injury was to the midshaft of the right ulna, typical of an injury sustained when warding off a blow to the head and commonly referred to as a 'parry' fracture. While it is impossible to determine the specific behavioural circumstances that led up to the incident when these injuries were sustained, it has been shown that individuals (known as 'injury recidivists') bearing at least one major bone with a violence-related injury supplemented by other minor bone injuries most often lead a more active or hazardous lifestyle – by analogy we should expect that a similar trend existed in the past (Judd 2002).

The burials of the *Kerma Moyen* period followed a strict regime which was adhered to in this grave. The grave was a roundish unlined pit measuring 2.55 x 2.2 m and 1.09 m deep. The skeleton was laid in a flexed position on its right side facing north, with the head to the east. Pottery vessels were placed on the north side of the grave, a meat cut laid in the north-east quadrant and a sacrificial sheep was in the lower leg

and foot region. Remnants of a leather cord were found under the individual's left ankle and left tibia, suggesting that binding may been used to sustain the flexed burial position; red and brown leather scraps, possibly the remains of a cloth cover, were north of the forearms. Aside from pottery, the grave goods were relatively simple. In this case, a pebble tool lay against the anterior left tibia, and blue faience beads were found around the neck and left wrist. However, it is possible that more intrinsically valuable artefacts originally accompanied this individual, but were removed when the burial was robbed in antiquity.　　MAJ

Judd 2001, 505; Welsby 2001d, 222–4, fig. 4.41

275 Sheep skeleton

Bone
Northern Dongola Reach Survey, Site P37 (G4)8-43
Kerma Moyen
L 620 mm, W 340 mm

The sacrificial animal included in Grave 8 was identified as a young male sheep, likely thirteen to sixteen months of age (Grant 2001, 547, 553). These animals were intended as companions to the deceased and were killed just prior to the interment; however, the method of slaughter remains unknown as no evidence of perimortem trauma was visible on any of the animals. Particularly poignant were the scraps of a rope lead located just under the neck and a leather cord that bound the femora, tibiae and right foot.

Sacrificial animals were common in *Kerma Moyen* burials and universally placed in the west end of the grave near the feet or lower legs of the human. Like the humans, the animals were laid on their right side with the forelegs flexed so that the head rested upon them. Among the graves of elite individuals, the sheep or goat may have worn a headdress of ostrich feathers and earrings.　　MAJ

Grant 2001, 547, 553

276 Meat cut

Bone
Northern Dongola Reach Survey, Site P37 (G4)8-37
Kerma Moyen
L 120 mm, W 30 mm

In order that the individual might be nourished after death, cuts of meat, usually of sheep or goats, were often placed north of the body amongst the pots or above the head during the *Kerma Moyen* period. The cuts were typically those of young male animals but never included the skulls or feet. In Grave 8 a sternum was the cut of choice, which is unusual as it offers little meat; however, it is likely that some of the internal organs, such as the heart which lies below the sternum, were still attached (Grant 2001, 547).   MAJ

Grant 2001, 547

277 Jar

Ceramic

Northern Dongola Reach Survey, Site P37 (G4) 49D, pot form J35.4

Kerma Moyen

H 180 mm, D 130 mm, max. W 216 mm

SNM 30028

This jar has a beaded rim, a bulbous body and a rounded, plain base. Decoration is present in the form of registers of impressed triangles on the shoulder of the vessel, with a zig-zag pattern of incised dots below. Both the form and decoration of this hand-made jar are typical of the *Kerma Moyen* period.[1] The vessel forms part of the characteristic grave goods of a burial of this period.   IWS

1 For close parallels, cf. Privati 1999 fig. 17.1-2.4.

Welsby Sjöström 2001a, 241; 2001b, 353, figs 5.22, 6.8

277

body is coloured with red ochre and burnished. Typical of the fine wares of the Kerma period, the fabric is made of Nile silt, reduced to a dark grey in the firing process. This is one of two identical hand-made bowls found in a grave of the *Kerma Moyen* period at Site P37 in the Northern Dongola Reach.   IWS

Welsby Sjöström 2001a, 242; 2001b, 350, figs 5.39, 6.3

278 Bowl

Ceramic

Northern Dongola Reach Survey, Site P37 (G3) 63B, pot form BU5.4

Kerma Moyen

H 80 mm, D 180 mm

SNM 30001

Bowl with a slightly outward-curving rim and a rounded base, whose surfaces are burnished a glossy black on the interior and at the top of the rim on the exterior, while the rest of the

279 Bowl

Ceramic

Northern Dongola Reach Survey, Site P37 (G4) 35a, pot form BU5.5

Kerma Moyen

H 112 mm, D 190 mm

SNM 30017

Hand-made bowl with a rounded base, found in one of the burials at Site P37. The interior is black-burnished, while the exterior below the rim has been left unburnished, but coloured red with ochre and decorated with a wide band of roughly incised cross-hatched lines. Of a less common type than the black-topped burnished but otherwise undecorated bowls, this style of decoration shows some similarities with Pan-Grave type decoration. It was nonetheless common for both decorated and undecorated vessels, closed as well as open forms, to be placed in burials of the period. The exact nature of the food stuffs that the vessels may have contained is not known.   IWS

Welsby Sjöström 2001a, 242; 2001b, 354, figs 5.39, 6.9

278

279

280

mification was aimed at transforming the lifeless corpse into a new and perfect body, an eternal image which would accommodate the spirit of the deceased in the Afterlife. The mask was crucial in fulfilling this purpose. It was not a reflection of the owner's appearance in life, but represented him or her in the transfigured state: eternally youthful, physically perfect and endowed with the attributes of a divine being. Hence masks such as this, though vivid, are not likenesses of specific individuals but iconic images of those who have become immortal.   JHT

Reinold 2003c, 279, no. 258; Vila 1975, 134–7; 1976, 217, 219, fig. 24 (82), pl. H-T III, 17 (3)

281

280 Jar

Ceramic

Northern Dongola Reach Survey, Site P37 (G3) 63P, pot form J32.6

Kerma Moyen

H 340 mm, max. D 260 mm; rim: D 120 mm

SNM 30027

Ovoid hand-made jar with a wide mouth and a beaded rim. The vessel has buff-coloured surfaces and fabric, with signs of the interior having been smoothed with a grooved tool, a common technique of the period. It is of an uncommon shape and fabric colour in the context of contemporary ceramics, suggesting that it may have been an import, although the fabric is not unusual for the area. The decoration on the shoulder and upper body of the vessel is presented in lozenge-shaped registers, formed of impressed registers of dots, probably made with a fishbone. The decoration on the rim is common on other jar types of the period.

IWS

Welsby Sjöström 2001a, 240; 2001b, 350, figs 5.21, 6.3

281 Mummy mask

Plaster, textile, paint

Mirgissa, Cemetery M X, T.112-3

Second Intermediate Period (*c.* 1700 BC)

H 106 mm, W 87 mm, Th 62 mm

SNM 18683

Cemetery M X at Mirgissa contained many graves of members of the Egyptian community that occupied the site in the Second Intermediate Period. The burials were in Egyptian style, distinguished by the use of mummification and the adornment of the corpse with a mask. This face, one of eight found in Tomb 112, is a typical example. It is made of painted plaster, with a textile base. The majority of these masks were probably fashioned over a mould, with details such as ears made separately and attached afterwards. The masks were placed over the linen wrappings of the body and most of them originally had headdresses decorated with the feathered *rishi* motif, commonly found on anthropoid coffins made in Egypt in the late Second Intermediate Period.

The lengthy and complex process of mum-

282 Heart scarab

Green stone

Sai Island, Pharaonic Cemetery

New Kingdom

L 86 mm, W 37 mm

SNM 23381

Large scarab in dark green hard stone. Its back is very well polished and sculpted in the form of a beetle with details indicated by double incised lines. In spite of its uninscribed flat side, this object undoubtedly belongs to the heart scarab category. It is thought that these funerary amulets were manufactured in advance and inscribed later, at the moment of their utilization or when a man was preparing his own funerary equipment. While the existence of the name of the deceased and Chapter 30B of the *Book of the*

Dead enhanced the magic power of the talisman, this power was also present in the form of the object itself, bearing the concept of renewal connected with the scarab. Moreover the heart scarab function of the specimen exhibited here is beyond doubt, since it was discovered next to another heart scarab, a shabti and other pieces of funerary equipment.   FT

Minault and Thill 1974, 99, pl. IVb

282

283 Heart pendant with human head

Green stone
Sai Island, Pharaonic Cemetery
New Kingdom
H 50 mm, W 30 mm, Th 5–25 mm
SNM 28748

Large pendant in the form of a human-headed heart carved in a hard dark green stone. Around the face, which is sculpted in the round, a tripartite wig falls on the shoulders and back. On the chest some beads represent the *ousekh*-collar. A hole through the head shows that the object was intended to be hung around the neck. This hybrid object is a good illustration of an important Egyptian idea regarding the heart. It was not only the main organ in the body – the place where all the vital functions converged in life as well as in the afterlife, mainly at the crucial moment of the Judgement – but it was also thought to be a real being, here indicated by its personification through a human head. The pendant shown here is uninscribed and undecorated. Sometimes similar items give the name of the deceased or representations of the *benou*-bird, the purple heron or phoenix, thought to be the soul of the sun god Ra.

This human-headed version of the object is not known before the 19th Dynasty. Some examples have been found in New Kingdom

Egyptian or Nubian cemeteries such as Gurob (Petrie 1890, pl. XXIV, 8), Abydos (Randall-Maciver and Mace 1902, pl. XLV, D.28) and Aniba (Steindorff 1937, pl. 50, no. 27).   FT

Minault-Gout and Thill in press

284 Funerary *tyet*-amulet

Faience
Sai Island, Pharaonic Cemetery
New Kingdom
L 72 mm, W 33, Th 8 mm
SNM 23407

The form of this amulet is somewhat mysterious. It looks like a a twisted and knotted piece of cloth, and so has been named 'Isis knot' by Egyptologists. It has been modelled in dark red faience and the upper ties painted in black. The verso is flat. The front side bears the name of the deceased, inscribed between two vertical lines, the whole painted in black. He is the 'Osiris' Userhat.

One of the most frequently found in a funerary context, either in pictorial form as represented in the vignettes of the *Book of the Dead*, or as a real prophylactic ornament, this amulet symbolized protection by the blood of the goddess Isis. It was frequently associated with another amulet, the *djed*-pillar, symbol of the Ruler of the Realm of the Dead, Osiris. A special spell of the *Book of the Dead* is dedicated to the *tyet*-amulet, prescribing that it must be made of red jasper, hung on a cord made of sycamore fibre and placed around the neck of the deceased on his burial day. By this means, the deceased could get the magic power of Isis and have

his body protected in the Underworld. Another proof that the present object was intended to be used in a funerary context is the inscription which specifies that its owner has become 'an Osiris'. This means he is now united with this god in the 'Field of Offerings', having passed the test of the weighing of his heart against the feather of truth (*ma'at*), in the presence of the divine tribunal presided over by Osiris.   FT

Minault-Gout 1994, 31; Reinold 2000a, 109

285 Bes-amulet

Carnelian
Sai Island, Pharaonic Cemetery
New Kingdom
H 20 mm, W 13 mm, Th 6 mm
SNM 28761

Ornament in the form of a stylized *Bes*-god. This deity, very popular in Egypt, was generally represented as an old dwarf with a curly beard, stylized lion's mane, protruding tongue and squashed nose (cf. cats 142–3, 166). It was believed that because of his strange and terrifying appearance *Bes* could ward off evil and catastrophe. Thus he was the special protector of expectant mothers. As a domestic deity, his image was commonly used to decorate pieces of furniture or toilet objects. His image was also worn as an amulet around the neck or tattooed on the body. The example shown here has been cut in a semi-precious stone and the face's features only roughly indicated by short incised lines. It was probably used as a component unit of a necklace made of several beads and amulets.   FT

283   284   285

286

this period, and it is interesting to note that, in Sai island, another complete group as well as four lids and elements of other groups were brought to light in that particular cemetery. Nonetheless, a parallel piece and fragments that were a little larger have been found in Soleb (Schiff-Giorgini *et al.* 1971, 193, 247–8). AM-G

286 Inlaid eyes

Faience, stone

Sai, Pharaonic Cemetery SAC5, Grave 21, S. 1334 a, b

New Kingdom

H 20 mm, L 51 and 61 mm, Th 14 mm

SNM 31344

These two eyes found in Grave 21 were originally set in the face of the lid of a wooden anthropomorphic sarcophagus. Each eye consists of a shape in faience, lengthened by a cosmetic line towards the temple. The form is hollow and contains the remains of a paste forming the cornea in which the pupil, a hard black stone, polished and brilliant, was inserted. The colours of these two eyes have certainly been altered, due either to some combustion or to some contact with another type of material: the faience is grey and the white paste is in some places bluish. One of the pupils has become red.

It is very often the case that these eyes are the only evidence for the presence of a wooden sarcophagus. Many examples have been found in copper, instead of faience. Numerous pairs of inlaid eyes of this type have been found, for example, in the cemeteries excavated by the Scandinavian expedition near the Second Cataract (Troy 1991, 55–6), in Soleb (Schiff-Giorgini *et al.* 1971, 230, 304), and in Sai. AM-G

287 Miniature canopic jars

Ceramic

Sai, Pharaonic Cemetery, SAC5

New Kingdom, 18th Dynasty

Jars: H 93–103 mm, D 70–80 mm; lids: H 40–47 mm, D 40–48 mm

SNM 28742, 28743, 28744, 28745

This group of four models of canopic jars with human-headed lids was found in Grave 14, where numerous individuals had been buried and which yielded rich material, namely pottery pieces that were small in size, models or cosmetic vases.

The vases have the usual shape of canopic jars, with a high rounded shoulder closing on a narrow collar and with a narrow flat base; the fabric is fine, the colour of chamois (yellowish-brown), and it is covered with a bright burnished red slip. The rather conical lid has a concave base to match the profile of the vase. It is provided with a small extension and is surmounted with a human head moulded in the round; the features, of which the eyes, nose and mouth are indicated by light relief work, are framed by a wide wig. This shape imitates that of the human-headed canopic jars of the 18th Dynasty. These miniature vases had a magical role and did not contain any organic remains. Models of canopic jars such as these, with well-known context, are not so common in Egypt and Nubia during

288 Funerary mask

Plaster

Sai, Pharaonic Cemetery, SAC5

New Kingdom, 18th Dynasty

H 94 mm, W 80 mm

SNM 28750

This small funerary plaster mask was found on the surface near the pit of Grave 16; two fragments of other masks of the same type come from the pit of this grave which had been plundered. Several others were discovered in this site, for example cat. 98. Made in a mould, of small size – smaller than that of a face – the general shape of the mask is oval.

288

287

289

The features are full, the eye is recessed and almond-shaped, the nose is wide; the smiling mouth has full lips; only the right corner of the mouth is preserved, marked by a line which falls gradually. The back is flat. There are remains of an impression made by very fine linen in several places, evidence of the attachment of the enveloping mask which had covered the head of the deceased. The surface is quite worn, particularly the left-hand side. The plaster was covered with a binder which could have been painted and, possibly, covered with a gold foil. Smaller than the face and integrated into the wrapping covering the body, this mask did not reproduce the features of the living person. This type of mask in plaster or in clay is well attested during the 18th Dynasty in Nubian cemeteries, for example at Soleb (Schiff-Giorgini *et al.* 1971, 167), Buhen (Randall-MacIver and Woolley 1911, 142 and pl. 61) and Aniba (Steindorff 1937, 73–4).   AM-G

289 Miniature sarcophagus

Sandstone

Sai, Pharaonic Cemetery, SAC5, Grave 5

New Kingdom, 18th Dynasty

Lid: L 268 mm, W 99 mm, Th 61 mm; trough: L 271 mm, W 102 mm, Th 73 mm

SNM 23428

This model of a sarcophagus comes from Grave 5 of Sai's Cemetery SAC5. It was found with the beautiful shabti of 'Count' Neby for whom it was intended. The sandstone sarcophagus consists of a coffer with an anthropomorphic lid and imitates the type of coffin in use in the 18th Dynasty. The lid, whose decoration is almost completely erased, was originally painted in black. It contained four white columns – a vertical median band and three horizontal columns – reserved for a text which had not been inscribed. The columns continue on the coffer which is also black, and on the bottom of the lid. On the lid the human head wears a wide, originally black tripartite wig, which leaves the ears free. The features of the face, the eyes, nose and mouth, are sculpted in relief; one of the pupils retains its black colour. This evokes in miniature the bitumen-coated sarcophagi with inscribed bands on a black ground. The four holes for mortises correspond to each other, on opposite sides, on the box and on the lid. Remains of a red colour are preserved inside the coffer which must have been repaired in the ancient past, because on the base three wide grooves have been hollowed out to receive the bonding medium.   AM-G

290 Shabti

Serpentine

Sai, Pharaonic Cemetery, SAC5, Grave 1

New Kingdom, 18th Dynasty

H 143 mm, W 48 mm

SNM 23424

This shabti was found in the plundered Tomb 1 of Cemetery SAC5 in Sai. The funerary figurine, made of black serpentine, is mummiform in shape. The features of the face, very carefully sculpted, are framed by a smooth tripartite wig which leaves the ears free; a wide necklace is present between the two lappets of the wig. The text of Chapter 6 of the *Book of the Dead* is carefully incised in five horizontal rows on the body of the shabti; on the shoulders are two short formulae introducing the text: on one side 'He says' and on the other 'May he be enlightened'. The name of the owner is missing in the

space which was reserved for it in the first row of text, but it is possible that it was written in ink and has vanished.

The figurine belongs to a type dating to the beginning of the 18th Dynasty, heir to the first shabtis which were intended as substitutes for the mummy. In the appeal written on the figurine, workers like this one were meant to replace the deceased in his duties in the Underworld. This statuette is in every respect comparable (almost identical), in its design and in the form of the hieroglyphic signs, to that of a certain Nebmehyt who was a 'child of the royal harem' (Aubert and Aubert 1974, 44 and fig. 4, pl. 2). This parallel is particularly interesting because it concerns someone who was buried in Nubia, and this title can apply to a foreigner educated in the Egyptian court with the royal children, as was Heqanefer at the end of the 18th Dynasty (Simpson 1963, 5).   AM-G

290

291 Shabtis

Faience (3 blue, 1 white)

Sai, Pharaonic cemetery

New Kingdom, Ramesside period

H 108–15 mm, W 29–33 mm

SNM 28736, 28737, 28738, 28739

These shabtis come from a tomb in SAC5 Cemetery in Sai, where a total number of forty-seven of these moulded figurines, many in faience but also in terracotta, were found. They are of the usual mummiform type from the Ramesside period, made of both turquoise blue and white faience, the details and text added in black pigment before firing. The face, framed by a tripartite wig, has been rapidly sketched, as has the wide necklace. The two hands are crossed on the breast and hold two large hoes, while on the back of the shabti, a basket and flail holding two pots were drawn. All these instruments were intended for the shabti's use in the Afterlife, where he would carry out those duties asked of him and those that he would perform in the place of his owner. A brief and almost erased text is written in a vertical column: 'Words to be said for the justified Osiris Pb'. The name begins with the two signs *Pb* [*h*]?... and ends clearly (on SNM 28738) with the determinative of a seated man. The white shabti (SNM 28739) is the same as the three others, but the vertical column was not inscribed with the name of its owner. This kind of shabti is very common and was found for example in the Nubian cemetery of Aniba (Steindorff 1937, 80 and pl. 44, 2).   AM-G

292

292 Two canopic jar lids of Shabaqo

Calcite

El-Kurru [Ku. 15], Tomb of Shabaqo

Kushite (Napatan), *c.* 716–702 BC

H 185 mm, L 200 mm, D 160 mm

SNM 1894 a, b

These two lids are all that remain of the set of jars provided for Shabaqo, the successor of Piankhi (Piye). Carved in calcite (alabaster), they represent two of the sons of Horus – the human-headed Imsety, who guarded the liver, and the baboon-headed Hapy, who protected the lungs. Stylistically, the lids are indistinguishable from Egyptian examples, and they were almost certainly made by experienced Egyptian craftsmen. Differences in scale and technique suggest that two different sculptors may have produced them, a circumstance seen in other sets of visceral containers from Egypt.

A set of four jars, made of stone, pottery or wood, formed an important element of the traditional Egyptian elite burial. These vessels, known to Egyptologists as canopic jars, were the receptacles for the viscera that were removed from the corpse during mummification. Liver, lungs, stomach and intestines were each placed in a separate jar, the lid of which was carved to represent the head of a deity. These gods, the Sons of Horus, were responsible for the protection of the various body parts. The jars were introduced in the Old Kingdom around 2500 BC. With changes in mummification procedures, in about 1100 BC, the preserved viscera began to be replaced inside the body, but empty or dummy canopic jars continued to be deposited in the tomb, out of respect for tradition (cf. cat. 287).

Beginning with Piankhi (Piye), the Kushite kings gradually adopted more and more features of Egyptian funerary practice. They were buried beneath pyramids, and their bodies were mummified and enclosed in anthropoid coffins. Canopic jars, *shabti* figures and amulets of Egyptian type were placed in their tombs.

The two missing lids and the jars to which they belonged had been plundered from Shabaqo's tomb; it is likely, however, that they were either solid 'dummies' or contained only

291

a rudimentary cavity, since it was not until the reign of Taharqo that canopic jars began once more to fulfil their practical purpose of holding the viscera.   JHT

Berenguer 2003j; Dodson 1994, 99, 139, pl. XLVb (cat. 54/1-2); Dunham 1950, 56, pl. XXXVII, B, C, H

293 Shabti of Taharqo

Ankerite
Nuri, Pyramid Nu. 1
Kushite (Napatan), 690–664 BC
H 314 mm, W 116 mm, Th 59 mm
SNM 1415

When Taharqo died he was placed in his tomb at Nuri with at least 1,070 stone shabtis. According to Egyptian custom these were small figures that took the form of the mummy of the deceased (cf. cats 290–91) and were thought to be his magical alter egos. Just as, in life, the king could call upon his subjects to perform such hard labour as dredging canals and hauling sand, it was also feared that in the afterlife even the king might be called to work by the great god. Shabtis, it was believed, made it possible to avoid this work.

Taharqo's shabtis are individually inscribed with a standard text that explains their purpose:

> If anyone summons King Taharqo to his
> work [in the City of the Dead?] indeed,
> there is a good reason why he should not
> do it! [?] for you, Shabti, shall say: 'Anyone
> may summon at any time and I shall act
> according to orders, whether it be planting
> fields, irrigating river banks, or even if it be
> conveying the sands of the west bank to
> the east and vice versa. If anyone orders
> forth King Taharqo, the justified, to do any
> of the work which is customarily done in
> the City of the Dead, then verily I shall do
> it, and I shall speak up in the City of the
> Dead, saying: I am he!'

Taharqo's shabtis range in height from 180 to 600 mm and are carved of speckled granite, green ankerite, or white calcite. They were placed standing around the walls of the tomb's chambers and corridors, sometimes two and three rows deep. They wear either the *khat* headdress or the *nemes* royal crown (with one uraeus rather than two), and they hold the royal crook and flail, or hoes and baskets (slung over the shoulders), or in some cases *djed* amulets symbolizing eternity. Certain repetitive details and facial features reveal the hands of different sculptors. The

293

fact that calcite is only found in Egypt suggests that some or all of the shabtis were carved there and shipped south in preparation for the king's burial.   TK

Dunham 1955, 6–16, figs 197, 200, pl. IVD; Kendall 1982, 35

294 Shabti of Senkamanisken

Steatite ('serpentine')
Nuri, Pyramid Nu. 3
Kushite (Napatan), 643–623 BC
H 180 mm, W 55 mm
SNM 1581

Although the shabtis of Senkamanisken are smaller than those of Taharqo, they are more numerous, numbering 1,277, and some are of even finer workmanship. They were made

of two materials: 867 were of faience (individually carved), and 410 were of carved green steatite. The faience examples have no crown or uraeus and wear only a black-painted wig, but the stone examples wear the *nemes* (like this one) or, more rarely, the *khat* headdress, each with the double uraeus. Most hold a pair of hoes and carry baskets over their shoulders, but this one carries the royal crook and flail. Most of the figures were

294

strewn over the floors of the tomb chambers, as they had been left by the ancient tomb robbers, but two small groups remained *in situ*, showing that they had been originally arranged standing, shoulder to shoulder, against the walls. The steatite shabtis of Senkamanisken are so similar in workmanship and material to those of the Theban officials of the late 25th Dynasty and early 26th Dynasty one would suppose that most or all of them were made in Thebes in the early 26th Dynasty and shipped south to Kush. At that time most of the high priestly offices were still held by members of the Kushite royal family.   TK

Berenguer 2003g; Dunham 1955, 43, fig. 29, pls XII A–B, CXI; Kendall 1982, 36

295

295 Cup of Penamon

Copper alloy

Kerma, Western Cemetery, Tomb 1

Kushite (Napatan)

H 50 mm, D 138 mm

SNM 24745

This cup was found together with a second cup, two bowls, a plate and two bronze bowls with handles, all skilfully manufactured. The inscription on the circumference is dedicated to Amun for the *ka* of the *wab*-priest of Amun of Pnubs, Penamon. Discovered almost twenty-five years ago, this cup is the first clue to the localization of Pnubs at Kerma. The excavations at Dokki Gel have since confirmed that the toponym is to be equated with the city founded by the Egyptians at the beginning of 18th Dynasty and occupied until the Meroitic period.   DV

Bonnet 1990a, 236, no. 344; Bonnet and Valbelle 1980, 1–12; Valbelle 2003b, 201

296 Amulet

Glazed composition

Sai Island, Site 8-B-5.SAP1

Kushite (Napatan)

H 68 mm, W 18 mm, Th 12 mm

SNM 28770

Glazed amulets were very popular in Egypt and Nubia during the Late Period. This piece, made in the round in white and yellow glaze, is in the shape of a naked boy, arms at his sides, wearing a side-lock of hair. It undoubtedly represents 'Horus-the-Child', often men-

296

tioned in later literature as Harpocrates, then a very popular deity, who was frequently shown with a finger to his mouth. According to the legend, the young god had escaped the forces of evil, represented by the murderer of his father Osiris, his uncle Seth, when he was hidden by his mother Isis in the swamps of the Nile Delta. The object was therefore supposed to have strong prophylactic power. It was found on Sai Island with other amulets and beads in a Napatan grave which was unfortunately plundered.   FG

Geus 1976, 67–8, 74 (bottom left), pl. IV; Reinold 2000a, 141, no. 129

297 Bottle

Blue faience

Kerma, Western Necropolis, COT 112

Kushite (Napatan)

H 175 mm; rim: D 43 mm

SNM 31206

This little ovoid bottle with flared mouth was discovered *in situ* in the tomb of a woman buried in a fœtal position, with her left arm bent towards the face. The bottle appears to have been placed in her hand and against her forehead, near a New Year's flask. The skilled manufacture together with the elegant lines accentuated by the fluted decoration make

297

this a remarkable piece. Similar faience bottles, albeit without the fluted decoration, have been attested at Sanam (Griffith 1923, 163, pl. XVI [t. 1011]) and in the Western Cemetery at Qustul (Williams 1994, 59, pl. 13).   NF

Bonnet 1995, 52

298

299 Head of a *ba*-statue

Sandstone, wood

Sedeinga, sector II of the large necropolis, Grave II
T84, s2

Kushite (Meroitic), second–third centuries AD

H 157 mm, W 126.8 mm, Th 93.4 mm

SNM 31118

This superb head of a *ba*-statue with distinctive traits is characteristic of Kushite art, where accentuated brachycephalia, for example, is well known in the statuary and monumental decoration from the Napatan period onwards. This is seen in the short and tight hairstyle over the cranium, with small, detailed curls and the geometric cut at the temple in front of the ears. The beautiful smiling face, with a dimpled chin, the large eyes bordered by a listel, is that of a serene man in his prime. Traces of red ochre prove that the statue was painted. At the top of the cranium a hole was cut to receive a disc that crowned the statue. A wooden one (cat. 299b) was found nearby, whose tenon would fit perfectly; it was possibly once gilded.   CB-N

298 Lotus cup

Copper alloy

Kerma, Western Cemetery, Girls' School

Kushite (Napatan)

H 81 mm, D 102 mm

SNM 24746

Cup in the shape of a lotus flower, with a knob soldered with tin at the base. The ribbed foliole decoration was chiselled and so was the band filled with ovoid motifs divided by a series of small vertical and horizontal lines. This cup and the cup of Penamon (cat. 295) belong to the same group of objects, and the former's manufacture is as skilled as the latter. In fact, the alloy used is identical (85.5 per cent copper and 14.5 per cent tin, with traces of iron and lead). The interior of the cup has a golden colour.   CB

Bonnet 1990a, 236, no. 11; Bonnet and Valbelle 1980, 1–12

299b

299a

300

300 Chapel lintel

Sandstone

Sedeinga, western sector of the large necropolis

Kushite (Meroitic), second half of second century AD

H 400 mm, W 1100 mm, Th 150 mm

SNM 20434

The door jambs of the Meroitic chapels at Sedeinga supported a lintel of sandstone with a cavetto cornice decorated with a solar disc and a winged uraeus above a horizontal torus moulding. This lintel comes from the chapel of Netemkhor (cf. cats 301–4) and carries on the cornice a text of five lines in cursive Meroitic that continues with two lines below the torus; the inscription is continued on the threshold of the chapel (cat. 302). The whole repeats, with some slight variants, the litany of the stela (cat. 304) and the offering table (cat. 303): after an invocation to Isis and Osiris, gods of mercy whose aura (or essence) had arrived from Graeco-Roman Egypt at the

beginning of our era, the epitaph specifies the ancestry of the dead person and his titles before the customary formula of benedictions and prayers.   CB-N

FHN II, 670; III, 1014; Heyler 1965, 192; Leclant 1966a, 162, pl. XXXI, fig. 54; 1970, 257, 276, figs 7A, 7B; Reinold 2000a, 112, 141, no. 143; *REM* 1091; Schiff-Giorgini 1966a, 255, pls XXX, XXXII; 1966b, 10, fig. 13

301 Door jamb of chapel

Sandstone

Sedeinga, western sector of the large necropolis, near Grave W T2

Kushite (Meroitic), second half of second century AD

H 880 mm, W 280 mm, Th 140 mm

SNM 23060

A small chapel stood on the east side of Meroitic pyramids, sealing the sloping passage that led to the subterranean funerary chamber. The dimensions of the chapels were often so small

that it would have been impossible to carry out the ceremonies within. On each side of the door, the door jambs that supported the entablature could be decorated with deities in the act of adoration (raised arms in front of the face) or pouring water for the funerary libation, as here on the superbly preserved northern jamb of the chapel of Netemkhor, a man of note at Sedeinga in the second century AD. Anubis, with a jackal's head, wearing a long fringed skirt tied with a sash, wears rich jewellery on his arms, wrists and ankles; in honour of the dead person, he pours water from a *situla* (a breast-shaped vessel frequently used in the cult of Isis). On the other door jamb, now lost, a female deity would have faced him in the same attitude as can be seen on the offering table from the same chapel (cat. 303).

The whole of the monument was probably painted, to judge by the traces of yellow and red colour found on the relief. On the under-

side of the door jamb, a lateral tenon allowed it to be set into the threshold (cat. 302) of the doorway into the chapel.   CB-N

Leclant 1972, 276, pl. XXX, fig. 36; Reinold 2000a, 115, 142, no. 146; 2003d, 262, no. 235; Schiff-Giorgini 1971, 9, fig. 2; Wildung 1997, 285, no. 303; Yellin 1978, 226, fig. 1

302 Threshold of chapel

Sandstone

Sedeinga, western sector of the large cemetery

Kushite (Meroitic), second half of second century AD

H 280 mm, W 640 mm, Th 140 mm

SNM 23059

An exceptional object, this sandstone threshold is well preserved and includes rectangular cuts on each side into which were inserted the door jambs of the chapel of Netemkhor (cat. 301). Seven well-preserved lines of a cursive Meroitic inscription were inscribed here, completing the text on the lintel (cat. 300) which crowned the doorway of the chapel.

CB-N

FHN III, 1014; Leclant 1966a, 162; 1970, 257, 258, 276, fig. 6; Priese 1997b; Reinold 2000a, 142, no. 145; REM 1116; Schiff-Giorgini 1966a, 255, pl. XXXIII

301

302

303

303 Offering table

Sandstone

Sedeinga, western sector of the large necropolis

Kushite (Meroitic), second half of second century AD

H 500 mm, W 440 mm, Th 100 mm

SNM 23058

Placed at the entrance of the chapels that lay to the east of Meroitic pyramids, offering tables, generally of sandstone but sometimes of terracotta, must have been used during the funeral ceremonies; a libation, probably of water, would have been poured while prayers were recited invoking the mercy of Isis and Osiris. The representation on this table, in the name of Netemkhor (cf. cat. 304), identifies the ceremony: in the centre is Isis holding a small round vase, while facing her is Anubis with a jackal head, pouring for the dead person the libation over loaves of bread and trussed ducks piled up over an altar-chapel. An inscription in cursive Meroitic runs around the spouted offering table, with the verses of traditional prayers.   CB-N

Heyler *et al.* 1975, 29–31; Hofmann 1991, 26, 29, 109, 174, 185, 189; Leclant 1972, 275, pl. XXIX, fig. 35; Reinold 2000a, 115, 141, no. 144; *REM* 1144; Schiff-Giorgini 1971, 12, fig. 4

304 Funerary stela

Sandstone

Sedeinga, western sector of the large necropolis, W2

Kushite (Meroitic), second half of second century AD

H 600 mm, W 360 mm, Th 100 mm

REM 1090

Probably originally placed in the eastern chapel of the pyramid of Netemkhor (cf. cats 300–303), this round-topped stela was found in several fragments. Cut in a local sandstone of poor quality and very friable, it was partially reconstructed by Clément Robichon. Decorated with a winged disc with uraei, it is inscribed in cursive Meroitic with fifteen lines that are almost identical to those on the lintel (cat. 300), associated threshold (cat. 302) and the offering table (cat. 303); thanks to these texts, it is possible to reconstruct the career of Netemkhor, a person of note in the Kushite Empire particularly between the Second and Third Cataracts, at the end of the second century AD. The text records the toponym of the island of Sai – *Art Syet*, 'Horus of Sai' – and gives Netemkhor's title as *arbtke* ('corn measurer'?).[1] CB-N

1 See further Török 1997c, 3 ff., 147 ff.

FHN II, 670; III, 1014; Heyler 1965, 192; Leclant 1966a, 162, pl. XXIX, fig. 52; 1970, 257, fig. 19, 276; Reinold 2000a, 142, no. 147; *REM* 1090; Schiff-Giorgini 1966a, 255, pl. XXXIII

305 Cup

Copper alloy

Kerma, Western Cemetery, Girls' School, Tomb 3B

Kushite (Meroitic)

H 60 mm, D 138 mm

SNM 24744

This small hammered bronze cup, thinned on a wheel, covered the mouth of one of the four large jars placed in the tomb of a presumably male individual, who was buried in a rectangular coffin (Bonnet 1990a, 239, nos 355–9). The cup is a classic element of Meroitic funerary equipment. This tomb was coupled with another (no. 3A), in which the individual, presumably female, lay in an anthropomorphic coffin. The equipment deposited in this second tomb comprised two large jars, a jug, a strainer and a small pouch containing various personal hygiene tools. CB

Bonnet 1978, 122, fig. 7

306 Bowl with handle

Copper alloy

Kerma, Western Cemetery, Girls' School, Tomb 10

Kushite (Meroitic)

H 90 mm, D 176 mm

SNM 24903

Bowl with a slightly flattened base and fitted with one small rounded handle. The extremities of the handle socket riveted to the body are cut in the shape of flowers. Traces of fabric are still visible on the body. This bowl comes from a tomb in which three individuals were successively buried. It was found in the fill layer above the four large jars associated with the latest burial, the jars being dated to the first century BC. The funerary chamber was accessible by a sloping shaft more than 2.5 m in length. CB

Bonnet 1978, 123–6; 1990a, 240, nos 360–61

306

305

307

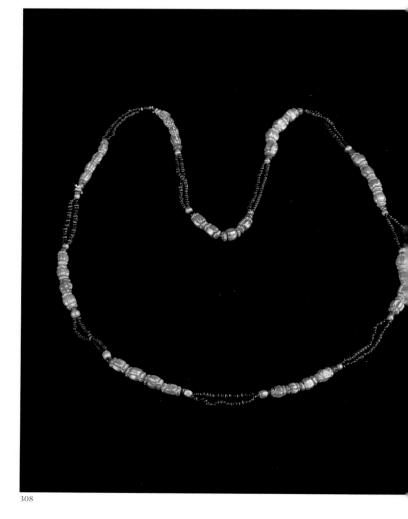

308

307 Bucket

Bronze, iron

Kerma, Western Cemetery, Girls' School, Tomb 72

Kushite (Meroitic)

H 162 mm, H (with handle) 180 mm, D 162 mm

SNM 25371

This bucket was discovered in a tomb that accommodated at least three successive burials, the latest inside an anthropomorphic coffin. The vessel, which has a carinated shoulder and a slightly flared base, is fitted with an iron handle that is curved at the top to form a loop. The five blocked holes observed under the rim were, without a doubt, part of an ancient suspension system. A long bronze strainer with a tubular handle and ovoid tip, similar to those discovered at Meroe (Dunham 1963, 93), was still in place inside the vessel.   CB

Bonnet 1990a, 248, no. 391

308 Necklace

Glass, carnelian

Sai Island, Site 8-B-5.SAS2

Kushite (Meroitic)

L 754 mm, beads of various sizes

SNM 28780

In Meroitic graves the deceased often wear personal decoration, more particularly necklaces and armlets made of beads of various types. According to J. Vercoutter, the excavator, this string of beads was found in its original place, strung as it is shown here. On both sides of the groups of four golden glass beads, smaller beads made of glass and carnelian are separated by series of tiny brown glass beads.   FG

Reinold 2000a, 142, no. 153; Vercoutter 1979, 222, 225–7, 234, no. 20, fig. 9b

309 Necklace

Quartz, glass, carnelian

Sai Island, Site 8-B-5.SAS2

Kushite (Meroitic)

L 500 mm, avg. L of pendants 20 mm

SNM 28779

According to J. Vercoutter, the excavator, this string of beads was also found *in situ*, strung as shown here. It is made of milky quartz pendants separated by two or three tiny beads made of glass or carnelian. Quartz pendants of this type were widely distributed in all areas under Meroitic influence.   FG

Reinold 2000a, 142, no. 152; Vercoutter 1979, 222, 227, 234, no. 21

310, 311

310 Vessel with unguent

Glass
Sai Island, Site 8-B-5.SAS2
Kushite (Meroitic)
H 150 mm, D 155 mm
SNM 28775

Up to now, glass vessels have been found in Meroitic graves dating to the first centuries AD. This round-bellied two-handled one belongs to a type known in Greek literature as an *aryballos*. It is made of pale green, heavy glass and is decorated with incisions and round spots. It contained an unguent that has partly survived dehydration, though an analysis failed to identify it with precision. Such vessels, produced between the first and the fourth centuries AD, were distributed widely over the Roman world. Those found in Nubia were probably manufactured in Alexandria and distributed once filled with their contents. Like other objects found in the same graves, they document long-distance trade between Roman Egypt and the Kushite Meroitic kingdom. A number of them have been found in Sai, but most were broken and incomplete. This example was found in a grave near the feet of the deceased.   FG

Reinold 2000a, 143, no. 176; Vercoutter 1979, 225–6, 233, no. 16, fig. 11e

311 Vessel with unguent

Glass
Sai Island, Site 8-B-5.SN
Kushite (Meroitic)
H 134 mm, D 114 mm
SNM 31345

This glass vessel is an *aryballos* similar to cat. 310, though it is slightly smaller and displays a different decoration. It also contains an unguent that has partly survived dehydration. It was found north of a wooden coffin that contained the disturbed remains of a young woman lying with her head to the south.   FG

Geus 1995, 88, fig. 8; 1996, 78, 80 (photograph upper right); 1997, 102, 107, fig. 3b; Geus *et al.* 1995, 113, fig. 13, pl. VIIa

312 Kohl container with lid

Wood
Sai Island, Site 8-B-5.SAS2
Kushite (Meroitic)
H 163 mm, D 28 mm
SNM 28777

Cylindrical containers made of hard, dark red wood have been found in many Meroitic graves. This one and its lid display a simple decoration of incised parallel lines. It contains remains of galena, a black powder used to paint the eyelids and known as 'kohl' in Arabic. An analysis has shown that the wood is a kind of palisander, *Dalbargia sp.*, which does not grow in the Nile Valley. As several species occur in different places in Asia and one type in Oman, it is likely that the wood was imported from one of those areas.   FG

Reinold 2000a, 142, no. 165; Vercoutter 1979, 224–5, 233, no. 17, fig. 10d

313 Funerary stela

Sandstone
Sai Island, Site 8-B-52.B
Kushite (Meroitic)
H 500 mm, W 335 mm, Th 50 mm
SNM 28782

Round-topped stelae are a regular feature in Meroitic cemeteries. None has ever been found in its original place, but they were certainly set up in the small chapels built against the eastern walls of the pyramids (cf. cat. 304) or the *mastabas* that covered the graves. This piece, carved out of fine sandstone, was found mixed with disturbed material in the descendary of a grave. It belongs to the most usual type, on which a winged disc flanked by two uraei is carved over a long cursive inscription arranged in horizontal lines. Although the Meroitic language has not been deciphered yet, funerary inscriptions which include an invocation to Isis and Osiris, the name and parentage of the deceased and formulae of benediction are repetitive and may be confidently translated. According to C. Rilly (in press), the stela dates from around AD 150 and belongs to Waleye, son or daughter of Kadite and 'the chief' (?), niece or

312

nephew of the *athmo* Warebali, of the *asidi* Shatameterura and of the *asidi* Shateqala. The title *athmo* apparently indicates an important function which has been documented previously on inscriptions from Sedeinga, while the title *asidi*, which appears here for the first time, probably indicates a local function. Such details make funerary inscriptions a precious source of information on the society of that period. FG

Carrier 1999, 11 (*REM* 1273); Geus 2002, 111, 131, pl. XIIIa, pl. XV; Leclant *et al.* 2000, 1934–5; Reinold 2000a, 36, 142, no. 148; Rilly forth.

314 Bed leg

Wood

Gabati, Grave 27, no. GBT12401

Early medieval, late seventh century AD

L 420 mm, W 100 mm, Th 100 mm

SNM 27868

This leg belongs to a set of four carved wooden legs that came from a dismantled bed. All were quite similar, nearly square in section with a simple carved decorative design. Wear-marks on the bottom of the legs suggests that they had seen much use and fresh chips on the lower part of two reflect

damage incurred when the bed was dismantled, perhaps at the grave-side. While dating to after the introduction of Christianity to the central Sudan, this burial followed earlier pre-Christian practices. Elements of beds were found in several Post-Meroitic burials in the cemetery. The bodies were often laid in the grave on the bed frame after the removal of the bed legs, which were then either placed in the grave or dumped in the shaft. Complete beds have been found in some large Post-Meroitic graves at Meroe and el-Hobagi. DE

Edwards 1998, 124, fig. 5.7

313

314

315

Bone, textile
Et-Tereif, Site 3-J-23 (B), Grave 92
Medieval
L 850 mm, W 180 mm
SNM 31268

The medieval Christian burials at et-Tereif were very spartan in contrast to the earlier Kerma and Kushite graves, and Grave 92 was no exception (Welsby 2003, 27–8). Medieval graves were orientated east–west, with the head usually to the west. The grave monuments were built of irregularly-shaped stones infilled with small pebbles and soil, forming a 'box' over the actual burial. Grave 92, however, did not have an associated superstructure. If such a monument had been provided it must have been demolished during the later use of the cemetery. This rectangular grave measured 1.4 x 0.35 m and was 0.98 m deep. A series of flat stones spanned the ledges on either side of the body so that it was protected from the grave infill. This is a common occurrence in burials of this period. Usually the body was laid on its back in an extended position, but this skeleton was either too large for the grave or had been deliberately placed in a flexed position. The body was wrapped in a coarsely woven brown shroud which was held in place by a cord around the head, neck, waist, knees and feet. In order to preserve the

316

315 Incense burner/pot-stand

Ceramic
Gabati, Grave 5, no. GBT T5/92c
Post-Meroitic/early medieval, sixth century AD (?)
H 193 mm, max. D 147 mm
SNM 31217

Hand-made incense burner or pot-stand in Gabati fabric G5, with a rather dark purplish-red slip on all surfaces. It is decorated with a white design of vertical wavy lines and vertical rows of heart-shaped motifs. Similar vessels have been found in several Post-Meroitic cemeteries in the central Sudan, mainly in the area between Berber and Shendi.   DE

Smith 1998, 180, fig. 6.28

316 Kohl pot

Ivory
Gabati, Grave 5, no. GBT T5/5
Post-Meroitic/early Medieval, sixth century AD (?)
Base: H 95 mm, D 64 mm; lid: H 86 mm, max. D 57 mm
SNM 31218

Complete turned ivory kohl pot with drilled centre. Very few such vessels have been found in either Post-Meroitic or medieval Christian contexts in Nubia. Found in the grave of an adult female, these pots were used to contain kohl, a green or black paint primarily of malachite or galena that was applied to the eyes with a wooden or metal spoon or stick (cf. cat. 312).   DE

Edwards 1998, 115, fig. 5.5

317

integrity of the burial, the body has remained unwrapped and therefore any demographic or pathological analysis must await radiographic examination. MAJ

Welsby 2003, 27–8

318 Stela of Mariankouda

Marble

Hambukol, North Kom

Medieval, 5 June AD 887

D 660 mm, Th 40 mm

SNM 30149

This well-finished white marble funerary stela was set in the pavement of the *haikal* in the North Kom church and later broken *in situ*. Ten fragments were preserved. Part of the bottom of the inscription and edge are missing. A raised rim, 40 mm wide, encloses the inscription and the face is polished while the back is smoothed. Three small crosses are incised above the inscription and one incised cross is preserved below the text. Prior to carving the inscription, several register lines were lightly engraved and remain visible. The text contains twenty-eight lines of incised Greek. It bears a late ninth-century date, the name of the Makurian king, Georgios, and mentions the name of Mariankouda and his administrative title, *Tetrarchos* – the only reference to this office discovered thus far. Mariankouda was probably buried in a crypt close to the inscription. The Mariankouda stela is similar to the circular inscription of King Georgios discovered in Egypt in the Wadi Natrun (Griffith 1928, 124). Another similar stela was discovered in the Cathedral of the Brick Pillars at Old Dongola embedded in the floor in a comparable manner (Gartkiewicz 1990, 302, pl. 177a), and two fragments from a different round stela were recently found in excavations at Kom H, Old Dongola (Łajtar 2003,

pers. comm.). This extremely fine stela, of a high-ranking Makurian official, contrasts dramatically with the poor quality stela of the Alwan king David (cat. 197), both in the sophistication of the Greek text and quality of material utilized.

The inscription reads as follows:

'O patient, compassionate, very merciful, true God, You, at the beginning, have created man according to Your likeness and resemblance and then, when he, through the trick of the snake, has fallen out from the paradise of joy and, as a consequence of his disobedience, was subjected to death and became different from You, the one that you have held in esteem, [and You], in Your unspeakable glory, did not overlook [his] troublesome life and wearisome living but in Your mercy have shown compassion on him and were willing to look for and to save the sheep that was led astray and have sent Your only-begotten son that having been born of woman was subjected to law in order that he would redeem those who were subjected to law, for which reason he directly has come (and), after receiving a human body and becoming man and through ascending onto the wood [= cross] has saved all those who were subjected to death, [and] on the account of what God said to Adam 'you are earth and into earth you will turn again', through the inclination and will of God the blessed Mariankouda, son of T[.]ophena, Tetrarch of the land of

Makouria, has fallen asleep in the month of Payni [day] 11th, in the year from the Martyrs 603, from his birth until his destiny he lived 72 years receiving all his authority from the order of our blessed and orthodox King Georgios. Wherefore we beseech you, o Lord, rest this very Caesar in the apartments of the illuminated ones, as well as this very servant of him [i.e. Mariankouda]. Rest their souls in the bosom of Abraham and Isaac and Jacob, in the shining place, in the place of refreshment, from which pain and grief and lamentation have fled away. Pardon every sin committed by him in word or in deed or in thought, forgive [it] and redeem, because there is no man who would live and not sin. For You alone are without sin and Your justice is justice for ever, O Lord, and Your word is truth. For You are [unidentified words].' (Łajtar 2003)

JRA/AŁ

Anderson 1999, 74, pl. XXXVI; Grzymski 2000, 35; Łajtar 2003

318

14

THE MEROWE DAM ARCHAEOLOGICAL SALVAGE PROJECT

SALAH ELDIN MOHAMED AHMED

Building a dam at the Fourth Cataract of the Nile is not a new idea; this project dates back to 1943, the period of the Anglo-Egyptian administration in the Sudan. Previously known as the Hamdab Dam, it has recently been renamed 'Merowe' after a small island, the northern part of which will be cut through by the structure of the dam itself. Most of the local inhabitants pronounce the name of this island *Mirowy*.

For various reasons this project was not realized for sixty years. Ever since it came to power in 1989 the present government has considered the dam a project of top priority because it will create enough hydroelectric power (1250 mg/w) to develop many sectors of the national economy. After many studies made by expert international institutions and companies, the government of the Sudan decided to build a single dam, crossing the island of Merowe, located about 26 km upstream from the pyramids of Nuri. The completion of the project is scheduled for August 2008.

The highest water level (reached during flood season) will be about 300 m above sea level. This will result in the inundation of a strip of land, about 170 km upstream of the dam. A lake approximately 4 km wide will be formed immediately behind the dam. This will necessitate the relocation of more than 48,000 people from their homes.

The aim of the Merowe Dam Archaeological Salvage Project (MDASP) is to rescue archaeological sites endangered by the construction of this dam (figs 194–5).[1] A considerable number of archaeological sites will be affected to varying degrees:

- Sites which will either be destroyed by the engineering activities at the dam site or covered by the waters of the lake upstream. This will include a strip of land of about 170 km on both banks of the Nile, together with many islands.
- Sites which will be destroyed by the building of houses and digging of irrigation canals in the resettlement areas.
- Sites which will be affected by the construction of power transmission lines.
- Although the monumental sites of the Napatan Region will not be directly affected by these activities, the National Corporation for Antiquities and Museums (NCAM) is concerned about the expected environmental changes. These sites include the famous Pharaonic and Kushite towns and cemeteries at Jebel Barkal, Nuri, Sanam, el-Kurru, Hillat el-Arab, the Post-Meroitic tumuli of ez-Zuma and Tanqasi, the Christian monastery of el-Ghazali, and the later strongholds at Merowe East, Kagabi, el-Datti, and possibly other sites located further downstream.

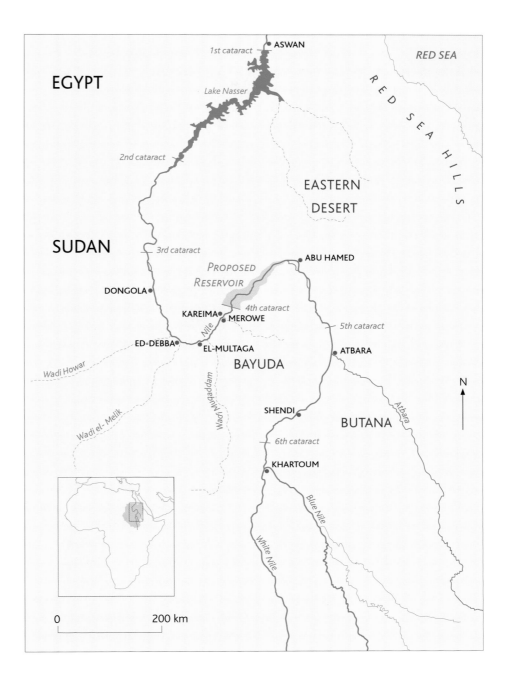

194 Map showing the location of the new dam and reservoir.

Recent archaeological work

Many campaigns to the region have been organized during the last thirteen years. These are principally:

- Campaigns by NCAM on both banks of the Nile and on some islands. One of these campaigns was directed by a UNESCO expert (Prof. Jean Leclant).
- Campaigns by the University of Rome in the downstream portions of the region.
- An assessment of the impact of the dam on archaeological sites made by Dr K. Grzymski for Monenco, the Canadian Company responsible for the feasibility study of the project.
- Surveys and test excavations conducted by the Sudan Archaeological Research Society (SARS) in collaboration with the British Museum on the left bank of the Nile and on the islands (Dar el-Arab to Kerbikan) (fig. 196).[2]

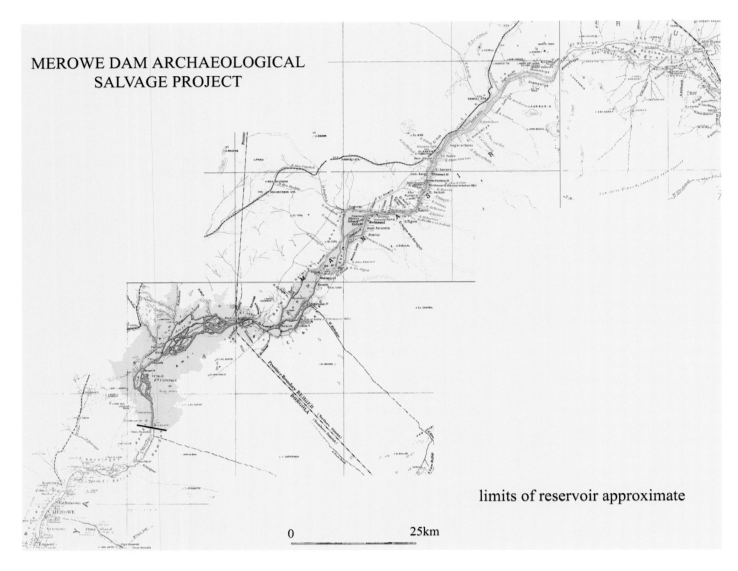

MEROWE DAM ARCHAEOLOGICAL SALVAGE PROJECT

limits of reservoir approximate

0   25km

195 Map of the reservoir area.

196 Excavations in progress of the early Kushite pyramid at AKS Site 4-F-71 near et-Tereif (February 2003).

- Surveys by the Mission of the Archaeological Museum of Gdańsk (Poland) on the right bank; they also conducted test and rescue excavations.

These activities have thrown more light on the archaeological potential of the region and resulted in the recording of hundreds of sites. These consist of cemeteries and isolated tombs, rock drawings of various periods, remains of settlements, mainly of later periods (Christian) and monumental fortresses of the medieval period (fig. 197). The various surveys have shown a high density of Post-Meroitic and Christian remains; however, the discovery of vast sites of the Kerma period on the right bank and important Kushite cemeteries on the left bank of the Nile indicate that future investigations may be very fruitful in finding considerable remains of all the periods of the country's history.

THE CURRENT SITUATION

Preliminary preparation for the construction of the Dam has started.

The first resettlement area, el-Multaga, is located about 40 km to the south-east of ed-Debba. The resettlement programme here consists of the construction of two villages and a complex of administrative premises to run a vast agricultural scheme. This area is reserved for the resettlement of about 8 per cent of the relocated population – the inhabitants of the villages which are going to be directly affected by the engineering activities at the dam site. A large number of people have already moved to their new homes.

A campaign (2001–2002) was organized by NCAM in collaboration with the French Archaeological Section (SFDAS) to rescue antiquities in the el-Multaga region (13,000 feddans: about 30,940 ha).[3] The operation resulted in the recording of over one hundred concentrations of prehistoric sites, together with a Christian settlement near the Nile, in a location which had been chosen by the Ministry of Irrigation for the installation of the new pumping station for the resettlement project.

197 Aerial view of the fortress of El-Kab.

Further upstream, roads on both banks of the Nile leading to the dam site from Kareima and Merowe, together with a railway linking the dam with the existing line on the right bank, have been built. A small township for the engineers and later for the administration of the dam and the power station has been completed. Engineering work for the dam itself began at the end of 2003.

NCAM organized a six-month campaign (2001–2002) to rescue sites endangered by the engineering activities on the left bank, over a distance of about 8 km. The result of this campaign was the recording and testing of many sites including prehistoric settlements, graves of the pre-Napatan, Post-Meroitic, and Christian periods, and others of undetermined dates. Many rock drawings of various periods have also been recorded. These are mainly drawings of animals (camels, donkeys and horses), boats and crosses.

198 Rugged terrain above the Fourth Cataract. Aerial view looking upstream.

Special attention was paid to a vast Post-Meroitic cemetery containing 318 mounds. These were classified into different types based on the criteria of their size, material of construction and the location of the small projection linked to the mounds. A selection of graves of each type was excavated. Although almost all of the burials were robbed in antiquity, they produced an abundance of ceramics and other archaeological material. The investigation of this cemetery will be continued during the coming seasons. It is expected that this site will throw considerable light on the history of the region during the Post-Meroitic period and, in particular, on the transition between the Meroitic and Post-Meroitic phases. The campaign also included the excavation of a big *kom* on the island of Mirowy which contains ten Christian graves on the surface and an earlier Post-Meroitic burial at a lower level, in addition to houses of the Christian period. The surface of this island has also yielded rare prehistoric tools.

The Mission of the Archaeological Museum of Gdańsk covered the equivalent area on the right bank.[4] Sites of all periods have been recorded and tested. The main achievement of this mission is the discovery for the first time of dozens of Kerma sites in this region. Hence the previously known geographical boundaries of this culture have been extended more than 200 km further upstream. On the left bank, in the area between Dar el-Arab and Kirbekan, SARS with the British Museum has conducted extensive surveys and excavations of sites representing all phases of the country's history. The discovery of the remains of a Kushite pyramid in this concession (fig. 196) is a real surprise.

At the time of writing this essay NCAM is conducting rescue work in the second resettlement area at Wadi Muqaddam (New Amri) in collaboration with the French Archaeological Unit (SFDAS). The project is located to the east of the town of Korti and covers an area of about 35,000 feddans (83,300 ha). Dozens of prehistoric sites have been recorded and an intact, rich Post-Meroitic tomb is being excavated.

FUTURE WORK

During the next five years intensive archaeological work is needed in the lake area upstream from the dam site, along the power transmission lines, in the new resettlement areas and on the sites in the Napata region. The Director of NCAM has issued an appeal to the international scientific community to contribute to the salvage of archaeological sites in the region. A session of the last annual meeting of SARS, held in the British Museum, London, in May 2003, was devoted to the discussion of this problem. The response was very encouraging and immediate: many archaeological missions will take part in the work. On the left bank of the Nile the following is currently planned:

- NCAM will continue its work between the dam site and Dar el-Arab. This will be directed by the author of this article.
- Bogdan Żurawski, from the Polish Centre of Mediterranean Archaeology of the University of Warsaw in Cairo, will direct the Polish team on the islands of Uli and Saffi.
- SARS and the British Museum will organize three campaigns directed respectively by Derek Welsby, Dorian Fuller and Pawel Wolf. The last one is partly supported by the British Institute in Eastern Africa. The Egypt Exploration Society has also undertaken to participate. This operation will cover a strip of about 40 km between Dar el-Arab and Wadi Kirbekan.
- Further upstream the Humboldt University, Berlin, will begin survey and salvage excavations. These activities will be directed by Frank Kammerzell.
- Claudia Näser, from the same institution, will be active on the corresponding islands in this region. The work of this German mission will cover the islands Us, Sur, Sherari, Kidir and Shirri.
- A mission from the Heinrich Barth Institute, University of Cologne, will rescue the antiquities of the island of Boni. This will be directed by Hans-Peter Wotzka.
- Another Polish mission from the Centre of Mediterranean Archaeology of the University of Warsaw in Cairo, directed by Lech Krzyzaniak, will be working at the upstream end of the projected reservoir.

The right bank will be covered by the following missions:
- The Mission of the Archaeological Museum of Gdańsk, directed by Henryk Paner, will continue its activities from the dam site to Khor Daghfeli.
- A combined Italian mission will work in the middle region on the same bank, directed by Donatella Usai, Sandro Salvatori and Mauro Cremaschi.
- The upstream part of the region will be rescued by the Archaeological Mission of the University of California, Santa Barbara (USA), directed by Stuart T. Smith.

Five power transmission lines are going to be installed:
- Dam site – Omdurman
- Dam site – Atbara
- Dam site – Dongola
- Atbara – Khartoum North (through the Butana)
- Atbara – Port Sudan

NCAM has agreed with the dam administration to undertake the survey of these lines as soon as they are demarcated on the ground (2003). Using this method the contractors can avoid the destruction of ancient remains and less rescue excavation will be needed. This has already been practised in 'road' and 'pipeline' archaeology.

THE RESETTLEMENT PROGRAM

In addition to el-Multaga and Wadi Muqaddam (New Amri), two other resettlement areas will be prepared for the relocated population of the region:
- Wadi el-Mukabrab (24 km south of Atbara) will accommodate some of the Manasir people. The project covers an area of 42,000 feddans (about 99,960 ha). The realization of this project is planned for 2004.
- Some of the Manasir will be resettled on the banks of the new lake, probably in the region of El-Kab-Station No. 10 (about 40 km downstream from Abu Hamad). This project has not yet been precisely defined.

THE NAPATA REGION

Although the sites of the Napata region are not going to be affected directly by the construction of the dam, expert advice concerning the expected environmental changes (i.e. the level of the water table and humidity) is needed. NCAM submitted a nomination file for the inclusion of Jebel Barkal, el-Kurru, ez-Zuma, Nuri and Sanam on the World Heritage List. A Unesco expert visited these sites in September 2002 to evaluate their state of preservation and the integrity of their landscape. The nomination of the aforemented sites was accepted by the World Heritage Center on 3 July 2003. Furthermore, NCAM and the Merowe Dam Implementation Unit are planning to create a museum at the first resettlement area (el-Multaga) for the preservation and exhibition of the archaeological and ethnographical wealth of the Fourth Cataract.

1 Ahmed 2003, 11–14.
2 Welsby 2003, 26–32.
3 Geus and Lecointe 2003, 33–9.
4 Kołsowska 2003, 21–5; Paner 2003, 15–20.

UPPER EGYPT | LOWER NUBIA | UPPER NUBIA | CENTRAL SUDAN

Timescale (years): 300,000 · 70,000 · 34,000 · 17,000 · 13,000 · 8500 · 5500 · 5000 · 4500 · 4000 · 3500 · 3000 · 2500 · 2000 · 1500 · 1000 · 500 · 0 · 500 · 1000 · 1500

UPPER EGYPT

Predynastic period: 5500–3100 BC

Tasian

Badarian

Nagada I/Amratian

Nagada II/Gerzean

Nagada III

Early Dynastic period: 3100–2686 BC

Old Kingdom: 2686–2181 BC

First Intermediate period: 2181–2055 BC

Middle Kingdom: 2055–1650 BC

Second Intermediate period: 1650–1550 BC

New Kingdom: 1550–1069 BC *

Third Intermediate period: 1069–747 BC

25th Dynasty: 747–656 BC

Late period: 747–332 BC

Ptolemaic period: 332–30 BC

Roman period: 30 BC–AD 395

Byzantine period: AD 395–640

Islamic period: AD 640–present

Ottoman Period: AD 1517–1917

LOWER NUBIA

Lower Palaeolithic
Acheulian
c.120 000 BC

Middle Palaeolithic

Upper Palaeolithic
Khormusan

Halfan

Qadan

Mesolithic

Khartoum Variant

Abkan

A-Group:
c. 3700–2800 BC

C-Group:
2300–1600 BC

X-Group: Ballana culture:
fourth–sixth centuries AD **

Nobadia:
sixth–end of seventh centuries AD

Dotawo: AD 1323–c. 1500

UPPER NUBIA

Lower Palaeolithic
Sangoan

Mesolithic

Khartoum Mesolithic

Post-Shamarkian

Neolithic

Pre-Kerma:
c. fourth millennium BC–c. 2600 BC

KINGDOM OF KUSH

Kerma Ancien: 2500–2050 BC

Kerma Moyen: 2050–1750 BC

Kerma Classique: 1750–1500 BC

KINGDOM OF KUSH

Napatan phase: ninth–fourth centuries BC

Meroitic phase: fourth century BC–fourth century AD

Post-Meroitic: fourth–sixth centuries AD ***

MEDIEVAL PERIOD

Makuria: sixth century AD– 1323/1365

ISLAMIC PERIOD
AD 1323–present

Turkiya: AD 1820–81

Mahdiya: AD 1881–98

CENTRAL SUDAN

Pre-Saroba

Early Neolithic/
Saroba

Khartoum Neolithic

Neolithic

Kassala

Taka

Alwa: sixth century AD–1504

Funj Sultanate: AD 1504/5–1820

---

* (to the Fourth Cataract) ** (First to Third Cataracts) *** (upstream of the Third Cataract)

GLOSSARY

anargyro (sing. anargyros) Faith-healing, healing by prayer. Often associated with incubation.

ankh The Egyptian symbol of life, shaped like a 'T' with a loop on the top.

archimandrite The head of a convent or monastery.

archistylite A religious title for the bearer of the *stylos*, possibly one of the Bishop of Makuria's titles; also attributed to Makurian kings depicted at Banganarti.

ba One of the manifestations of the human spirit, usually depicted as a human-headed bird, free to travel outside the tomb.

bark stand An altar or plinth upon which the sacred boat of the god rested. The cult image of the god was often placed in a *naos* or shrine on the boat.

bucranium (pl. bucrania); also bucrane An ox or cattle skull.

castra (sing. castrum) A protected encampment or military camp.

cataract A region of rapids and waterfalls in a river.

chiton A tunic, the earliest form of which lacked sleeves (origin: Ancient Greece).

debbas Habitation mounds found in southern Sudan on natural ridges running parallel to rivers. Referred to as *otong* in Shilluk.

deffufa Nubian term used to describe an imposing man-made structure.

djed pillar A symbol representing the resurrection of the god Osiris, thought to represent his backbone and the concept of stability.

exedra A portico used for conversation and dispute.

Euchologion A comprehensive Christian liturgical prayerbook including prayers for the administration of sacraments, Eucharistic rites and unchanging portions of the Divine Office.

facial retouching Secondary working or shaping of a stone tool.

Fuqara (Arabic sing. Feqi) Holy men, Sheikhs.

hafir A man-made earthen enclosure for storing water.

haikal The sanctuary of a church.

hypogea A vault or chamber located underground.

intercolumnium The space between two columns.

jalous Mud laid in horizontal courses, one atop the other, to form walls.

jebel Arabic for mountain.

kalamos A writing pen made of reed.

khepesh Lit. 'foreleg of an ox'. The Egyptian name for a scimitar.

kom A mound made up of strata of archaeological deposits.

maphorion Veil or shawl that covers the head and shoulders.

mastaba Arabic word for bench. It is used to describe a tomb whose shape resembles the shape of mud-brick benches found outside many modern Egyptian and Nubian houses.

metropolitan A bishop who oversees the other bishops in a province.

mnnw A transcription of the ancient Egyptian word for 'fortress'.

naos The inner sanctuary of a temple.

Naga/Naqa Alternate spellings used for a Kushite site located in Central Sudan.

nemes Royal regalia. A striped headcloth pulled tight across the brow and tied at the back. A strip of cloth hangs down on either side of the face. A uraeus, or snake, adorns the brow.

New Years flask An Egyptian vessel, similar in shape to a pilgrim flask, with an inscription running around the edge.

nymphaeum A building or room designed as a shrine for nymphs, usually associated with water.

parallel A geographical term to indicate a line of latitude.

pastophoria (sing. pastophorium) Cells or rooms where priests are housed.

peribolus A wall enclosing a court and temple.

potamoi Decoration of plain bands.

praesidium A Roman military station or outpost fort.

proskynesis An ancient Greek public salutation.

qadus (Arabic pl. qawadis) A ceramic jar used to lift water in a *saqia*.

qore A Meroitic title for the Kushite ruler.

queue A long braided strand of hair hanging down from the back of a headdress.

rotulus A tube-shaped document scroll.

salutatio The formal morning greeting or welcome given to a Roman *patronus* (patron) by his supporters or clients.

saqia A waterwheel powered by animals, used for irrigation.

Serapis A composite god dating to the Egyptian Ptolemaic period. He combines attributes of the Egyptian god Osorapis (Osiris and Apis) and several Greek gods, among them Zeus and Dionysos.

shendyt kilt An Egyptian apron style of short skirt worn by men, with ties at the front.

speos A temple in a cave.

steatopygous Characterized by large thighs and buttocks.

stylos A column-shaped sceptre.

synthronon A semi-circular arrangement of seats in the apse of a church with the throne or seat of the bishop in the centre.

talatat Small architectural stone blocks dating to the Egyptian 18th Dynasty, Amarna period. They could be carried by one man and were used for the rapid construction of buildings.

temenos A sacred area around a temple usually enclosed by a wall.

tetrarchos A high official of unknown function in the Makurian kingdom.

tughra A monogram into which the name and title of the ruler (esp. sultan) are incorporated.

udjat The eye of the Egyptian falcon-god Horus, used to symbolize protection, strength and healing.

wadi A valley that becomes a water channel during the rainy season.

BIBLIOGRAPHY

ÄA   *Ägyptologische Abhandlungen.* Wiesbaden.

ADAIK   *Abhandlungen des Deutschen Archäologischen Instituts Kairo. Ägyptologische Reihe.* Berlin, Glückstadt, Hamburg, New York.

ANM   *Archéologie du Nil Moyen.* Lille.

Ann.Épigr. *L'Année Épigraphique.* Paris.

AMS   Archaeological Map of the Sudan. Berlin.

ANRW   *Aufstieg und Niedergang der Römischen Welt.* Berlin–New York.

ASAE   *Annales du Service des Antiquités Égyptiennes.* Cairo.

ASE   *Archaeological Survey of Egypt.* London.

BMOP   *British Museum Occasional Paper.* London.

BSFE   *Bulletin de la Société Française d'Égyptologie.* Paris.

BzS   *Beiträge zur Sudanforschung.* Vienna–Mödling.

CdE   *Chronique d'Égypte.* Brussels.

CDEAE   *Centre de Documentation et d'Études sur l'Ancienne Égypte.* Cairo.

CRAIBL   *Comptes Rendus à l'Académie des Inscriptions et Belles-Lettres.* Paris.

CRIPEL   *Cahier de Recherches de l'Institut de Papyrologie et d'Égyptologie de Lille.* Lille.

ET   *Études et Travaux.* Warsaw.

FHN I–IV See Eide *et al.* 1994; 1996; 1998; 2000.

GM   *Göttinger Miszellen.* Göttinger.

HÄB   *Hildesheimer Ägyptologische Beiträge.* Hildesheim.

JARCE   *Journal of the American Research Center in Egypt.* Cairo.

JEA   *Journal of Egyptian Archaeology.* London.

JWP   *Journal of World Prehistory.* New York.

LAAA   *Annals of Anthropology and Archaeology.* University of Liverpool.

LdÄ   *Lexicon der Ägyptologie.* Wiesbaden.

MÄS   *Münchner Ägyptologische Studien.* Berlin, Mainz, Munich.

MittSAG   *Mitteilungen der Sudanarchäologischen Gesellschaft zu Berlin.* Berlin.

MNL   *Meroitic Newsletter.* Paris.

OINE   *Oriental Institute Nubian Expedition.* Chicago.

PÄ   *Probleme der Ägyptologie.* Leiden, Boston, Cologne.

PAM   *Polish Archaeology in the Mediterranean.* Warsaw.

REM   See Leclant *et al.* 2000.

RdE   *Revue d'Égyptologie.* Cairo, Paris.

SAGA   *Studien zur Archäologie und Geschiche Altägyptens.* Heidelberg.

SDAIK   *Deutsches Archäologisches Institut. Abteilung Kairo. Sonderschrift.* Mainz.

SNR   *Sudan Notes and Records.* Khartoum.

Urk. IV   Sethe K. 1905–1907. *Urkunden der 18. Dynastie.* Leipzig.

ZÄS   *Zeitschrift für Ägyptische Sprache.* Berlin.

Adams, W.Y. 1965. 'Architectural Evolution of the Nubian Church, 500–1400 AD', *JARCE* IV, 87–140.

Adams, W.Y. 1968. 'Settlement Pattern in Microcosmos: The Changing Aspect of a Nubian Village during Twelve Centuries', in K.C. Chang (ed.), *Settlement Archaeology.* Palo Alto, 174–207.

Adams, W.Y. 1977. *Nubia Corridor to Africa.* London.

Adams, W.Y. 1978. 'Medieval Nubia', in Wenig (ed.) 1978a, 121–5.

Adams, W.Y. 1986. *Ceramic Industries of Medieval Nubia,* Parts I, II. Lexington.

Adams, W.Y. 1991. 'The United Kingdom of Makouria and Nobadia. A Medieval Nubian Anomaly', in Davies (ed.), 257–63.

Adams, W.Y. 1992. 'Nubian Church Architecture and Nubian Church Decoration', Bonnet (ed.), 317–26.

Adams, W.Y. 1994a. 'Castle Houses of Late Medieval Nubia', *ANM* 6, 11–46.

Adams, W.Y. 1994b. *Kulubnarti 1: The Architectural Remains.* Lexington.

Adams, W.Y. 1996. *Qasr Ibrim. The Late Mediaeval Period.* London.

Adams, W.Y. 1998a. 'Toward a Comparative Study of Christian Nubian Burial Practice', *ANM* 8, 13–41.

Adams, W.Y. 1998b. *Kulubnarti II: The Artefactual Remains.* London.

Adams, W.Y. 2001. *Meinarti II. The Early and Classic Christian Phases.* London.

Adams, W.Y. 2002. *Meinarti III. The Late and Terminal Christian Phases.* London.

Addison, F. 1949. *Jebel Moya. Wellcome Excavations in the Sudan.* London.

Ahmed, K.A. 1999. 'The island of Meroe?', *Meroitica* 15, 457–8.

Ahmed, M.A. el Hakim 1979. 'University of Khartoum excavations at Sururab and Bauda, North of Omdurman', *Meroitica* 5, 151–5.

Ahmed, Salah M. 1992. *L'agglomeration napateene de Kerma. Enquete archéologique et ethnographique en milieu urbain.* Paris.

Ahmed, Salah M. 1994. 'A Napatan Pottery Workshop at Kerma', in Bonnet (ed.), 127–30.

Ahmed, Salah M. 1998, in press. 'A Meroitic Temple on the site of Dokki Gel (Kerma)'. *XIᵉ Conférence Internationale des Études Nubiennes.* Boston.

Ahmed, Salah M. 2003. 'Merowe Dam Archaeological Salvage Project (MDASP)', *Sudan & Nubia* 7, 11–14.

Ahmed, Salah M. and C. Bonnet 1999. 'Excavations at Dokki Gel (Kerma)', *Recent Research in Kushite History and Archaeology. Proceedings of the 8th International Conference for Meroitic Studies.* London, 251–6.

Aldred, C. 1971. *Jewels of the Pharaohs.* London.

Allason-Jones, L. 1991. 'The Finds', in Welsby and Daniels, 126–245.

Allason-Jones, L. 1998. 'The Finds', in Welsby, 60–81.

Altenmüller, H. 1975. 'Beset', in *LdÄ* 1, 731.

Amiran, R. 1969. *Ancient Pottery from the Holy Land.* Jerusalem.

Anderson, J.R. 1999. 'Monastic Lifestyles of the Nubian Desert: Seeking the Mysterious Monks of Makuria', *Sudan & Nubia* 3, 71–83.

Anderson, J.R. and S.J. Blitz 1998. 'Recent Excavations at the North Kom Monastery, Hambukol Sudan (Upper Nubia)', in T. Kendall and P. Der Manuelian (eds), *Ninth International Conference of Nubian Studies. Abstracts of Papers.* Boston, 47.

Anderson, J. and K. Grzymski 2001. 'Sudan: Land of the Hidden Temples', *Rotunda* 34 (1), 22–9.

Arkell, A.J. 1949a. *Early Khartoum.* Oxford.

Arkell, A.J. 1949b. *The Old Stone Age of the Anglo-Egyptian Sudan.* Sudan Antiquities Service, Occasional Papers 1. Khartoum.

Arkell, A.J. 1953. *Shaheinab.* London.

Armbruster, C. 1965. *Dongolese Nubia. A Lexicon.* Cambridge.

Arnold, D. 1993. 'Techniques and Traditions of Manufacture in the Pottery of Ancient Egypt', in Arnold and Bourriau (eds), fasc. 1, 11–102.

Arnold, D. and J. Bourriau (eds) 1993. *An Introduction to Ancient Egyptian Pottery,* fascs 1, 2, *SDAIK* 17.

Aston, D.A. 1996. *Egyptian Pottery of the Late New Kingdom and Third Intermediate Period (Twelfth–Seventh Centuries BC). SAGA* 13.

Aston, D.A. 1999. *Elephantine XIX. Pottery from the Late New Kingdom to the Early Ptolemaic Period.* Mainz am Rhein.

Aubert J.-F. and L. Aubert 1974. *Statuettes égyptiennes. Chaouabtis, ouchebti.* Paris.

Azim, M. 1975. 'Quatre campagnes de fouilles sur la forteresse de Saï, 1970–1973. 1ᵉʳᵉ partie: l'installation pharaonique', *CRIPEL* 3, 91–125.

Bács, T.A. (ed.) 2002. *A Tribute to Excellence. Studies Offered in Honour of Erno Gaal, Ulrich Luft, Lásló Török*. Budapest.

Bailloud, G. 1969. 'L'évolution des styles céramiques en Ennedi (République du Tchad)', in *Mémoires I, Actes du Premier Colloque International d'Archéologie Africaine, Fort Lamy (Rép. du Tchad) 1966*, 31–45.

Barguet, P., Dewachter, M. *et al.* 1967. *Le temple d'Amada*. CDEAE. Cairo.

Bate, D.M.A. 1951. 'The mammals from Singa and Abu Hugar', in *The Pleistocene Fauna of Two Blue Nile Sites. Fossil Mammals of Africa* 2. London.

Bates, O. and D. Dunham 1927, 'Excavations at Gammai', *Varia Africana IV, Harvard African Studies* 8, Cambridge, Massachusetts, 1–121.

Bell, H. and Muhammed Jalal Hashim 2002. 'Does Aten Live On in Kawa (Kówwa)?', *Sudan & Nubia* 6, 42–6.

Berenguer, F. 2001. *En busca de los faraones negros. Misión de la Fundación Arqueológica Clos en Sudán Memoria de las Excavations en el Yacimiento de Djebel Barkal (Kareima Sudan)*. Barcelona.

Berenguer, F. 2003a. 'La antique Nubia (el Yacimiento de Djebel Barkal-Napata)', in Berenguer *et al.* (eds), 104–7.

Berenguer, F. 2003b. 'Estatua De Babuino', in Berenguer *et al.* (eds), 256, no. 228.

Berenguer, F. 2003c. 'Estela', in Berenguer *et al.* (eds), 172, no. 85.

Berenguer, F. 2003d. 'Collar', in Berenguer *et al.* (eds), 205, no. 136.

Berenguer, F. 2003e. 'Esfinge del rey Senkamanisken', in Berenguer *et al.* (eds), 174–5, no. 89.

Berenguer, F. 2003f. 'Estatua del dios Amón', in Berenguer *et al.* (eds), 252–3, no. 221.

Berenguer, F. 2003g. 'Ushebti de Senkamanisken', in Berenguer *et al.* (eds), 296, no. 290.

Berenguer, F. 2003h. 'Fragmento de relieve', in Berenguer *et al.* (eds), 188, no. 107.

Berenguer, F. 2003i. 'Estela del principe Amenemhet', in Berenguer *et al.* (eds), 153, no. 59.

Berenguer, F. 2003j. 'Dos tapaderas de vasos canopos de Shabaqo', in Berenguer *et al.* (eds), 282, no. 265.

Berenguer, F. 2003k. 'Coll con ornamentos florales', in Berenguer *et al.* (eds), 207, no. 140.

Berenguer, F. 2003l. 'Estatua de rey', in Berenguer *et al.* (eds), 179, no. 94.

Berenguer, F. 2003m 'Ka con cartucho de Aspelta', in Berenguer *et al.* (eds), 287, no. 272.

Berenguer, F. 2003n 'Recipiente globular (con patas) en forma de animal', in Berenguer *et al.* (eds), 127, no. 18.

Berenguer, F. 2003o 'Vaso globular de cuello alto', in Berenguer *et al.* (eds), 230, no. 189.

Berenguer, F., C. Pérez Die, S. Sauquet and S. Vilalta (eds) 2003. *Nubia, Los reinos del Nilo en Sudán*. Barcelona.

Berger, C. 1994a. 'Sedeinga', in Gratien and Le Saout (eds), 209–15.

Berger, C. 1994b. 'Les couronnements des pyramides méroïtiques de Sedeinga', in Bonnet (ed.), 135–7.

Berke, H. 2001. 'Gunsträume und Grenzbereiche. Archäozoologische Beobachtungen in der Libyschen Wüste im Sudan und Ägypten', in Gehlen *et al.*, 237–56.

Bianchi, R. 1998a. 'Pectoral inscribed for Panhesi', in Friedman, 160.

Bianchi, R. 1998b. 'Pectoral with Anubis', in Friedman, 161.

Billy, G. 1987. 'La Population de la Necropole D'Abri – Missiminia', *ANM* 2, 121–40.

Blackman, A.M. 1937. 'Preliminary Report on the Excavations at Sesebi', *JEA* 23, 145–51.

Bonnet, C. 1978. 'Les fouilles archéologiques de Kerma (Soudan). Rapport préliminaire sur les campagnes de 1977–1978', *Genava*, n.s., XXVI, 107–27.

Bonnet, C. 1982. 'Les fouilles archéologiques de Kerma (Soudan). Rapport préliminaire sur les campagnes de 1980–81 et de 1981–82', *Genava*, n.s., XXX, 29–53.

Bonnet, C. 1984. 'Les fouilles archéologiques de Kerma (Soudan). Rapport préliminaire sur les campagnes de 1982–1983 à 1983–1984', *Genava*, n.s., XXXII, 5–20.

Bonnet, C. 1986. *Kerma. Territoire et métropole. Quatre leçons au Collège de France*. Bibliothèque Générale, vol. 9. Paris.

Bonnet, C. 1988. 'Les fouilles archéologiques de Kerma (Soudan). Rapport préliminaire sur les campagnes de 1986–87 et 1987–88', *Genava*, n.s., XXXVI, 5–20.

Bonnet, C. (ed.) 1990a. *Kerma, Royaume De Nubie*. Geneva.

Bonnet, C. (ed.) 1990b. *Seventh International Conference for Nubian Studies*. Geneva.

Bonnet, C. 1991. 'Les fouilles archéologiques de Kerma (Soudan). Rapport préliminaire sur les campagnes de 1988–1989, de 1989–1990 et de 1990–1991', *Genava*, n.s., XXXIX, 5–20.

Bonnet, C. (ed.) 1992. *Études nubiennes: Conférence de Genève. Actes du VIIᵉ Congrès international d'études nubiennes 3–8 septembre 1990, vol. 1*, Geneva.

Bonnet, C. 1993. 'Les fouilles archéologiques de Kerma (Soudan). Rapport préliminaire sur les campagnes de 1991–1992 et de 1992–1993', *Genava*, n.s., XLI, 1–18.

Bonnet, C. (ed.) 1994. *Études nubiennes: Conférence de Genève. Actes du VIIe Congrès international d'études nubiennes 3–8 septembre 1990, vol. 2*, Geneva.

Bonnet, C. 1995. 'Les fouilles archéologiques de Kerma (Soudan). Rapport préliminaire sur les campagnes de 1993–94 et de 1994–95', *Genava*, n.s., XLIII, 31–52.

Bonnet, C. 1997. 'Les fouilles archéologiques de Kerma (Soudan). Rapport préliminaire sur les campagnes de 1995–1996 et de 1996–1997', *Genava*, n.s., XLV, 97–112.

Bonnet, C. 1999. 'Les fouilles archéologiques de Kerma (Soudan). Rapport préliminaire sur les campagnes de 1997–1998 et 1998–1999', *Genava*, n.s., XLVII, 57–76.

Bonnet, C. 2000. *Edifices et rites funéraires de la nécropole de Kerma*. Paris.

Bonnet, C. 2001a. 'Les empreintes de sceaux et les sceaux de Kerma: Localisation des découvertes', *CRIPEL* 22, 27–32.

Bonnet, C. 2001b. 'Les fouilles archéologiques de Kerma (Soudan). Rapport préliminaire sur les campagnes de 1999–2000 et 2000–2001', *Genava*, n.s., XLIX, 197–234.

Bonnet, C. 2003. 'Kerma. Rapport préliminaire sur les campagnes de 2001–2002 et 2002–2003', *Genava*, n.s., LI, 257–80.

Bonnet, C. 2004. *Le temple principal de la ville de Kerma et son quartier religieux*. Paris.

Bonnet, C. 2004, in press. *Kerma: Die Entwicklung einer Stadt im Niltal während des 3. und 2. Jahrtausends v. Chr.* Berlin.

Bonnet, C. and J. Reinold 1993. 'Deux rapports de prospection dans le désert oriental', *Genava*, n.s., XLI, 19–26.

Bonnet, C., B. Privati, C. Simon, L. Chaix and P. De Paepe 1988. 'Les fouilles archéologiques de Kerma (Soudan). Rapport préliminaire sur les campagnes de 1986–1987 et de 1987–1988', *Genava*, n.s., XXXVI, 5–35.

Bonnet, C. and D. Valbelle 1980. 'Un prêtre d'Amon de Pnoubs enterré à Kerma', *BIFAO* 80, 1–12.

Bonnet, C. and D. Valbelle 2000. 'Les sanctuaires de Kerma du Nouvel Empire à l'époque méroïtique', *CRAIBL* July–October 2000, 1099–120.

Bonnet, C. and D. Valbelle 2003, in press. 'Un dépôt de statues royales du début du VIᵉ siècle av. J.-C. à Kerma', *CRAIBL*.

Bosse-Griffiths, K. 1977. 'A Beset Amulet from the Amarna Period', *JEA* 63, 98–106.

Bourriau, J. 1982a. 'Double vase', in *Bulletin of the Museum of Fine Arts, Boston*, 83, no. 64.

Bourriau, J. 1982b. 'Amphora', in *Bulletin of the Museum of Fine Arts, Boston*, 127, no. 114.

Bourriau, J. 1987. 'Pottery figure vases of the New Kingdom', *Cahiers de la Céramique Égyptiennes* I, 81–96.

Bourriau, J. 1988. *Pharaohs and Mortals. Egyptian art in the Middle Kingdom*. Cambridge.

Bradley, R.J. 1982. 'Varia from the City of Meroe', *Meroitica* 6, 163–70.

Bradley, R.J. 1984a. 'Meroitic Chronology', *Meroitica* 7, 195–211.

Bradley, R.J. 1984b. 'Wall Paintings from Meroe Townsite', *Meroitica* 7, 421–3.

Brand, P.J. 2000. *The Monuments of Seti I. PÄ* 16.

Browne, G. 1989. *Old Nubian Texts from Qasr Ibrim II*. London.

Bruce, J. 1805. *Travels to discover the source of the Nile*. 2nd edition. Edinburgh.

Brunton, G. and G. Caton-Thompson 1928. *The Badarian Civilisation and Predynastic Remains near Badari*. London.

Budge, E.A.W. 1907. *The Egyptian Sudan*, vols I, II. London.

Bushra-al, S. 1971. 'Towns in the Sudan in the 18th and early 19th centuries', *SNR* LII, 63–70.

Cailliaud, F. 1826–7. *Voyage à Meroé, au Fleuve Blanc, au-delà de Fazoql dans Le Midi du Royaume de Sennar, à Syouah et dans cinq autres oasis; fait dans les années 1819, 1820, 1821 et 1822*. Paris.

Caminos, R.A. 1974. *The New Kingdom Temples of Buhen. ASE* 33.

Caminos, R.A. 1998. *Semna-Kumma*, vols I, II. *ASE* 37, 38.

Caneva, I. (ed.) 1983. 'Pottery using gatherers and hunters at Saggai 1 (Sudan): preconditions for food-production', *Origini* 12, 7–278.

Caneva, I., 1985. 'The prehistory of Central Sudan: Hints for an overview', in M. Liverani, A. Palmieri and R. Peroni (eds), *Studi di Paletnologia in onore di Salvatore M. Puglisi*. Rome, 425–32.

Caneva, I. (ed.) 1988. *El Geili. The history of a middle Nile environment 7000 B.C.–A.D. 1500*. BAR International Series 424, Oxford.

Caneva, I. 1991. 'Jebel Moya revisited: a settlement of the 5th millennium BC in the Middle Nile Basin', *Antiquity* 65, 262–8.

Caneva, I. 1993. 'Pre-Pastoral Middle Nile: Local Developments and Saharan Contacts', in Krzyżaniak *et al.* (eds), 405–11.

Caneva, I. 1996. 'Post-Shaheinab Neolithic remains at Geili', in Krzyżaniak *et al.* (eds), 315–20.

Caneva, I., E.A.A. Garcea, A. Gautier and W. Van Neer 1993. 'Pre-pastoral Cultures along the Central Sudanese Nile', *Quaternaria Nova* 3, 177–252.

Caneva, I. and A.E. Marks 1990. 'Early pottery from Shaqadud: the Sahara and the Nile', *ANM* 4, 11–35.

Caneva, I. and A. Zarattini 1983. 'Microlithism and functionality in the Saggai 1 Industry', in Caneva (ed.), 209–33.

Carlson, R.L. and J.S. Sigsted 1967/8. 'Paleolithic and Late Neolithic Sites Excavated by the Fourth Colorado Expedition', *Kush* 15, 51–8.

Carrier, C. 1999. 'Pour suite de la Constitution d'un Répertoire d'épigraphie Méroïtique (*REM*)', *MNL* 26, 1–46.

Carrier, C. 2000. 'Pour suite de la Constitution d'un Répertoire d'épigraphie Méroïtique (*REM*)', *MNL* 27, 1–30.

Cartwright, C. 1998. 'The Wood, Charcoal, Plant Remains and other Organic Material', in Welsby, 255–68.

Castiglioni A., A. Castiglioni and K. Sadr 1994. 'Discovering Berenice Panchrysos. Interium Report on the Eastern Desert', MSS.

Castiglioni A., A. Castiglioni and J. Vercoutter 1995. *L'Eldorado dei Faraoni alla Scoperta di Berenice Pancrisia*. Novara.

Castiglioni, A. and A. Castiglioni 1999. 'Berenice Pancrysos', in A. Roccati (ed.), *Napata E Meroe Templi D'Oro Sul Nilo*. Milan, 126–9.

Castigloni, A. and A. Castiglioni 2003. 'Pharaonic Inscriptions along the Eastern Desert Routes in Sudan', *Sudan & Nubia* 7, 47–51.

Chaix, L. 1993. 'The archaeozoology of Kerma (Sudan)', in W.V. Davies and R. Walker (eds), *Biological anthropology and the study of Ancient Egypt*. London, 175–85.

Chaix, L. 1996. 'Les boeufs à cornes parallèles: archéologie et ethnographie', *Sahara* 8, 95–7.

Chaix, L. 1998. 'The Fauna', in Welsby, 233–55.

Chaix, L. 2001. 'Animals as symbols: The bucrania of the grave KN 24 (Kerma, Northern Sudan)', in H. Buitenhuis and W. Prummel (eds), *Animals and man in the past*. Essays in honour of Dr A.T. Clason, Emeritus Professor of Archaeozoology, Rijksuniversiteit Groningen, The Netherlands. ARC Publicatie 41, Groningen, 364–70.

Chaix, L. n.d. 'Preliminary report on animal remains from the CeRDO Excavation of 1993', in K. Sadr, A. Castiglioni, A. Castiglioni and G. Negro, *Interim Report on the Eastern Desert Research Centre's (CeRDO) Archaeological Activities 1989–1993*, 165–6.

Chapman, S.E. and D. Dunham 1952. *The royal cemeteries of Kush, Vol. III, Decorated chapels of the Meroitic pyramids at Meroe and Barkal*. Boston.

Chłodnicki, M. 1984. 'Pottery from the Neolithic settlement at Kadero (Central Sudan)', in Krzyżaniak and Kobusiewicz (eds), 337–42.

Chmielewski, W. 1968. 'Early and Middle Palaeolithic sites near Arkin, Sudan', in Wendorf (ed.), 110–47.

Clark, J.D. 1984. 'Prehistoric Cultural continuity and economic change in the Central Sudan in the Early Holocene', in J.D. Clark and S. Brandt (eds), *From Hunters to Farmers. The causes and Consequences of food production in Africa*. Berkeley, 113–26.

Clark, J.D. 1989. 'Shabona: an Early Khartoum settlement in the White Nile', in Krzyzaniak and Kobusiewicz (eds), 387–410.

Clarke, S. 1912. *Christian Antiquities in the Nile Valley*. Oxford.

Commelin, D. 1983. 'Céramique', in N. Petit-Maire and J. Riser (eds), *Sahara ou Sahel? Quaternaire recent du Bassin de Taoudenni (Mali)*. Paris, 343–66.

Corder, P. 1957. 'The Structure of Romano-British Pottery Kilns', *The Archaeological Journal*, CXIV, 10–27.

Crawford, O.G.S. 1951. *The Funj kingdom of Sennar*. Gloucester.

Crawford, O.G.S. and F. Addison 1951. *Abu Geili. The Wellcome Excavations in the Sudan. Vol. III*. London–New York–Toronto.

Crowfoot, J.W. 1911. *The Island of Meroë*. London.

D'Anville, J.B.B. 1768. *Géographie ancienne abrégée*. Paris.

Dahl, G. and A. Hjort 1976. *Having Herds. Pastoral Herd Growth and Household Economy*. Stockholm Studies in Social Anthropology 2. Stockholm.

Dambach, M. and I. Wallert 1966. 'Das Tilapia-Motiv in der altägyptischen Kunst', *CdE* 41, 273–94.

David, N. 1982. 'The BIEA Southern Sudan Expedition: Interpretation of the Archaeological Data', in J. Mack and P. Robertshaw (eds), *Culture and History in the Southern Sudan: Archaeology, Linguistics and Ethnohistory*. Memoir no. 8 of BIEA, Nairobi, 49–57.

Davies, N. de G. and A.H. Gardiner 1926. *The Tomb of Huy, Viceroy of Nubia in the Reign of Tut'ankhamun (No. 40)*. London.

Davies, W.V. (ed.) 1991. *Egypt and Africa. Nubia from Prehistory to Islam*. London.

Davies, W.V. (ed.) 1999. *Studies in Egyptian Antiquities. A Tribute to T.G.H. James. BMOP* 123.

Davies, W.V. 2001. 'Kurgus 2000: The Egyptian Inscriptions', *Sudan & Nubia* 5, 46–58.

Davies, W.V. 2003a. 'Kush in Egypt. A new historical inscription', *Sudan & Nubia* 7, 52–4.

Davies, W.V. 2003b. 'Kurgus 2002: the inscriptions and rock-drawings', *Sudan & Nubia* 7, 55–7.

Davies, W.V. 2003c. 'La frontière méridionale de l'Empire: Les Égyptiens à Kurgus', *BSFE* 157, 23–37.

Davies, W.V. 2003d. 'Kouch en Égypte: Une nouvelle inscription historique à El-Kab', *BSFE* 157, 38–44.

Davies, W.V. 2003e. 'Sobeknakht of Elkab and the coming of Kush', *Egyptian Archaeology* 23, 3–6.

Dayf Allah, A. 1992. *The Tabaqat of Saints, Scholars and Poets of the Sudan*. Hassan, Y.F. (ed.) Khartoum.

Denyer, S. 1978. *African traditional architecture*. London.

Desroches-Noblecourt, C. 1954. 'Poissons, tabous et transformations du mort', *Kêmi* 13, 33–42.

Der Manuelian, P. 1987. *Studies in the Reign of Amenophis II. HÄB* 26.

Dinkler, E. (ed.) 1970. *Kunst und Geschichte Nubiens in Christlicher Zeit*. Recklinghausen.

Diodorus Siculus 1737. *Histoire Universelle*, De Bure. Lib. III. Paris.

Dissaux, R-P., J. Reinold and P. Lenoble 1997. 'A Funerary Dance of Political Meaning at Meroe', in E.A. Dagan (ed.), *The Spirit's Dance in Africa. Evolution, Transformation and Continuity in Sub-Sahara*. Montreal, 36–41.

Dobrowolski, J. 1991. 'The First Church at Site "D" in Old Dongola (Sudan)', *ANM* 5, 29–40.

Dodson, A. 1994. *The Canopic Equipment of the Kings of Egypt*. London and New York.

Donadoni, F.S. 1993. 'Preliminary Report: Excavations of the University of Rome at "Natakamani Palace", Jebel Barkal', *Kush* 16, 101–15.

Donodoni, S. 1994. 'Le palais de Natakamani au Djebel Barkal', *Les Dossiers d'Archéologie* 196, 54–7.

Downes, D. 1974. *The excavations at Esna 1905–1906*. Warminster.

Dunham, D. 1950. *El Kurru. The Royal Cemeteries of Kush*, vol. I. Cambridge.

Dunham, D. 1955. *Nuri. The Royal Cemeteries of Kush*, vol. II. Boston.

Dunham, D. 1963. *The West and South Cemeteries at Meroe. The Royal Cemeteries of Kush*, vol. V. Boston.

Dunham, D. 1970. *The Barkal Temples*. Boston.

Dunham, D. 1982. *Excavations at Kerma*, Part VI. Boston.

Edel, E. 1963. 'Zur Familie des *Sn-msjj* nach seinen Grabinschriften auf der Qubbet el Hawa bei Assuan', *ZÄS* 90, 28–31.

Edel, E. 1980. 'Der alteste [*sic*] Beleg für den Title *h3tj-p't* und sein Weiterleben bis in die römische Zeit hinein', *Serapis* 6, 41–6.

Edwards, D.N. 1996. *The Archaeology of the Meroitic State, New perspectives on its social and political organisation*, BAR International Series 640, Oxford.

Edwards, D.N. 1998. *Gabati. A Meroitic, Post-Meroitic and Medieval Cemetery in Central Sudan*, vol. 1. London.

Edwards, D.N. 1999. *A Meroitic Pottery Workshop at Musawwarat Es Sufra. Meroitica* 17.2. Wiesbaden.

Edwards, D.N. 2000. 'A Meroitic Inscription and some Pot Graffiti from central Sudan', *BzS* 7, 37–47.

Edwards, D.N. 2004. *The Nubian Past. An Archaeology of Sudan*. London.

Edwards, D.N. and A. Osman 2000. 'The archaeology of Arduan Island – The Mahas project', *Sudan & Nubia* 4, 58–70.

Eide, T., T. Hägg, R.H. Pierce and L. Török (eds) 1994. *Fontes Historiae Nubiorum. Textual Sources for the History of the Middle Nile Region Between the Eighth Century BC and the Sixth Century AD*, I. *From the Eighth to the Mid-Fifth Century BC*. Bergen.

Eide, T., T. Hägg, R.H. Pierce and L. Török (eds) 1996. *Fontes Historiae Nubiorum. Textual Sources for the History of the Middle Nile Region Between the Eighth Century BC and the Sixth Century AD*, II. *From the Mid-Fifth to the First Century BC*. Bergen.

Eide, T., T. Hägg, R.H. Pierce, and L. Török (eds) 1998. *Fontes Historiae Nubiorum. Textual Sources for the History of the Middle Nile Region Between the Eighth Century BC and the Sixth Century AD*, III. *From the First to the Sixth Century AD*. Bergen.

Eide, T., T. Hägg, R.H. Pierce and L. Török (eds) 2000. *Fontes Historiae Nubiorum. Textual Sources for the History of the Middle Nile Region Between the Eighth Century BC and the Sixth Century AD*, IV. *Corrigenda and Indices*. Bergen.

Eigner, D. 1996. 'Die Grabung am Schlackenhügel NW1', *MittSAG* 4, 23–7.

Eigner, D. 2000. 'Meroe Joint Excavations: Excavation at Slag Heap NW1', *MittSAG* 10, 74–6.

Einaudi, G. (ed.) 1982–8. *Pliny the Elder. Storia Naturale 1982–88*. Vol. 1, libri II, VI; vol. 5, libro XXXVII. Turin.

Emery, W. and L.P. Kirwan. 1935. *The excavations and survey between Ouadi es-Sebua and Adindan (1929–1931)*. Cairo.

Emery, W. and L.P. Kirwan 1938. *The Royal Tombs of Ballana and Qustul*, vols 1, 2. Cairo.

Emery, W.B., H.S. Smith, and A. Milliard 1979. *The Fortress of Buhen. The archaeological report*. London.

Evans-Pritchard, E.E. 1937. 'Economic life of the Nuer: cattle', *SNR* 20, 207–45.

Evetts, B.T.A. and A.J. Butler 1895. *The Churches and Monasteries of Egypt and Some Neighbouring Countries, Attributed to Abu Salih, the Armenian*. Oxford.

Fairman, H.W. 1939a. 'An Ancient Egyptian Frontier Town', *Discovery NS*, 39, 385–92.

Fairman, H.W. 1939b. 'The Recent Excavations at Amarah West', *The Connoisseur* 103, 322–8.

Fairman, H.W. 1939c. 'Preliminary Report on the Excavations at 'Amārah West, Anglo-Egyptian Sudan 1938–39', *JEA* 25, 139–44.

Fattovich, R. 1989. 'The late Prehistory of the Gash Delta (eastern Sudan)', in Krzyżaniak and Kobusiewicz (eds), 481–90.

Fattovich, R. 1993. 'The Gash Group of the Eastern Sudan: an outline', in Krzyżaniak *et al.* (eds), 439–48.

Fattovich, R. 1995. 'The Gash Group. A complex society in the lowlands to the east of the Nile', *CRIPEL* 17, 191–200.

Fattovich, R., A.E. Marks and A. Mohammed-Ali 1984. 'The archaeology of the Eastern Sahel, Sudan: preliminary results', *African Archaeological Review* 2, 173–88.

Fernandez, V.M., A. Jimeno, M. Menendez and G. Trancho 1989. 'The neolithic site of Haj Yusif (Central Sudan)', *Trabajos de Prehistoria* 46, 261–9.

Firth, C.M. 1915. *The Archaeological survey of Nubia. Report for 1909–1910*. Cairo.

Fischer, A. 1998. *Africa adorned* (re-edition). New York.

Franke, D. 1983. *Altägyptische Verwandtschaftsbezeichnungen im Mittleren Reich*. HÄS 3.

Franke, D. 1984. *Personendaten aus dem Mittlern Reich (20.-16. Jahrhundert v. Chr.) Dossiers 1–796. ÄA* 41. Wiesbaden.

Freed, R. 1982. 'Toilet Implements', in Museum of Fine Arts, Boston, 193–5.

Freestone, I. and C. Stapleton 1998. 'The Metalworking Debris', in Welsby (ed.), 81–3.

Friedman, F.D. 1998. *Gifts of the Nile. Ancient Egyptian Faience*. London.

Friedman, R.F. 1999. 'Badari Grave Group 569', in Davies (ed.), 1–11.

Friedman, R. (ed.) 2002. *Egypt and Nubia: Gifts of the Desert*. London.

Friedman, R. and J.J. Hobbs 2002. 'A "Tasian" Tomb in Egypt's Eastern Desert', in Friedman (ed.), 178–91.

Galey, J. 1980. *Sinai and the monastery of St. Catherine*. Givatayim.

Galvin, K. 1985. *Food procurement, diet, activities and nutrition of Ngisonyoka, Turkana. Pastoralists in ecological and social context*. PhD Thesis, State University of New York. Binghamton.

Gänsicke, S. 1997. 'Cylinder Sheaths', in Wildung (ed.), 226–7.

Gänsicke, S. and T. Kendall forthcoming. 'A Fresh Look at the Cylinder Sheaths from Nuri, Sudan', in Kendall (ed.)

Garcea, E.A.A. 2003. 'Palaeolithic sites at El-Multaga, Sudan', *Nyame Akuma* 59.

Garcea, E.A.A. in press. 'Comparing *Chaînes Opératoires*: Technological, Cultural and Chronological Features of Pre-Pastoral and Pastoral Ceramic and Lithic productions', *The Proceedings of the UISPP Congress*.

Garstang, J. 1910. 'Preliminary Note on an Expedition to Meroe in Ethiopia', *LAAA* 3, 57–70.

Garstang, J. 1911. *Excavations at Meroe, Sudan. Second Season, 1910. Guide to the Ninth Annual Exhibition of Antiquities Discovered*. London.

Garstang, J. 1912a. 'Second Interim Report on the Excavations at Meroe in Ethiopia', *LAAA* 4, 45–52.

Garstang, J. 1912b. *Excavations at Meroe, Sudan, 1912. Guide to the Eleventh Annual Exhibition of Antiquities Discovered*. London.

Garstang, J. 1913. 'Third Interim Report on the Excavations at Meroe in Ethiopia', *LAAA* 5, 73–83.

Garstang, J. 1914. 'Fourth Interim Report on the Excavations at Meroe in Ethiopia', *LAAA* 6, 1–21.

Garstang, J. 1914–16. 'Fifth Interim Report on the Excavations at Meroe in Ethiopia', *LAAA* 7, 1–24.

Garstang, J. and W.S. George 1913. *Excavations at Meroe, Sudan, 1913. Fourth Season. Guide to the Twelfth Annual Exhibition of Antiquities Discovered*. London.

Garstang, J. and W.J. Phythian-Adams 1914. *Excavations at Meroe, Sudan, 1914. Fifth Season. Guide to the Thirteenth Annual Exhibition of Antiquities Discovered*. London.

Garstang, J, A.J. Sayce and F. Ll. Griffith 1911. *Meroe – City of the Ethiopians*. Oxford.

Gartkiewicz, P. 1982. 'An Introduction to the History of Nubian Church Architecture', in Jakobielski (ed.), 43–105.

Gartkiewicz, P. 1990. *The Cathedral in Old Dongola and its Antecedents*. Warsaw.

Gatto, M.C. in press. 'Prehistoric Nubian Ceramic Traditions: Origin, Development and Spreading Trajectories', *The Proceedings of the 10th International Conference of Nubian Studies, 9–14 September, 2002, Rome*.

Gautier, A. 1986. 'La faune de l'occupation néolithique d'El Kadada (Secteurs 12-22-32) au Soudan Central', *ANM* 1, 59–111.

Gautier, A. 1989. 'A general review of the known prehistoric faunas of the Central Sudanese Nile Valley', in Krzyżaniak and Kobusiewicz (eds), 353–7.

Gehlen, B., M. Heinen and A. Tillmann (eds) 2001. *Zeit-Räume. Gedenkschrift für Wolfgang Taute. Archäologische Berichte* 14. Bonn.

Gerharz, R. 1994. *Jebel Moya. Meroitica* 14. Berlin.

Geus, F. 1976. 'Sondages à Saï près du Fort Adu', *CRIPEL* 4, 61–74.

Geus, F. 1984. *Rescuing Sudan ancient cultures. A cooperation between France and the Sudan in the field of archaeology.* Khartoum.

Geus, F. 1986. 'La section française de la Direction des Antiquités du Soudan. Travaux de terrain et de laboratoire en 1982–1983', *ANM* 1, 13–58.

Geus, F. 1989. 'Enquête sur les pratiques et coutumes funéraires méroïtiques. La contribution des cimetières non royaux, approche préliminaire', *RdE* 40, 163–85.

Geus, F. 1992a. 'Sites et cultures à céramique de la préhistoire tardive du Soudan du Nord; rétrospective des travaux de terrain', in Bonnet (ed.), 239–66.

Geus, F. 1992b. 'The Neolithic in Lower Nubia', in Klees and Kuper (eds), 219–37.

Geus, F. 1994. 'L'île de Saï à travers l'histoire du Soudan', *La Nubie, L'archéologie au Soudan, Les Dossiers d'Archéologie* 196, 22–7.

Geus, F. 1995. 'Saï 1993–1995', *ANM* 7, 79–98.

Geus, F. 1996. 'Cimetières méroïtiques de l'île de Saï', *Soudan 5000 ans d'Histoire, Les Dossiers d'Archéologie, Hors-Série* no. 6, 78–81.

Geus, F. 1997. 'Two Seasons in Sai Island (1993–1995), a Preliminary Report', *Kush* 17, 95–107.

Geus, F. 1998. 'Sai 1996–1997', *ANM* 8, 85–126.

Geus, F. 2000 'Geomorphology and prehistory of Sai Island (Nubia): Report on a current research project', in Krzyżaniak *et al.* (eds), 119–28.

Geus, F. 2002. 'Sai 1998–1999', *ANM* 9, 95–134.

Geus, F. 2003. 'Two Seasons in Sai Island (1996–1997), A Preliminary Report', *Kush* 18, 61–80.

Geus, F. in press. 'Pre-Kerma storage pits in Sai Island', in Kendall (ed.) forthcoming.

Geus, F. and Y. Lecointe. 2003. 'Survey and Excavation at el-Multaga, a Resettlement Area related to the Construction of the Merowe Dam: preliminary results', *Sudan & Nubia* 7, 33–9.

Geus, F., Y. Lecointe and B. Maureille 1995. 'Tombes napatéennes, méroïtiques et médiévales de la nécropole Nord de l'île de Saï. Rapport préliminaire de la campagne 1994–1995 (archéologie et anthropologie)', *ANM* 7, 99–141.

Gleichen, A.E.W. 1888. *With the Camel Corps up the Nile.* London.

Godlewski, W. 1982. 'Some comments on the wall painting of Christ from Old Dongola', in Plumley (ed.), 95–9.

Godlewski, W. 1989. 'Old Dongola. The House PCH.1', *Nubian Letters* 13, 1–3.

Godlewski, W. 1990a. 'Old Dongola 1988–1989. House PCH.1', *PAM* I, 14–16.

Godlewski, W. (ed.) 1990b. *Coptic Studies.* Acts of the Third International Congress of Coptic Studies, Warsaw, 20–25 August, 1984.

Godlewski, W. 1991a. 'Old Dongola 1988–1989. The House PCH.1', *ANM* 5, 79–101.

Godlewski, W. 1991b. 'The Birth of Nubian Art: Some Remarks', in Davies (ed.), 253–6.

Godlewski, W. 1992. 'The Early Period of Nubian Art, Middle of 6th–Beginning of 9th Centuries', in Bonnet (ed.), 277–305.

Godlewski, W. 1996. 'The Late Period in Nubian Art – from the middle of 13th to the end of 14th centuries', in Gundlach *et al.* (eds), 37–63.

Godlewski, W. 1999. 'The Earliest Evidence of the Settlement at Old Dongola', *Meroitica* 15, 554–9.

Grant, A. 2001. 'The Animal Remains', in Welsby 2001d, 544–55.

Gratien, B. 1978. *Les Cultures Kerma. Essai De Classification.* Publications de l'Université de Lille III Lille.

Gratien, B. 1986. *Saï I. La nécropole Kerma.* Paris.

Gratien, B. 1993. 'Nouvelles empreintes de sceaux à Kerma: Aperçus sur l'administration de Kouch au milieu du 2e millénaire Av. J.-C.', *Genava* n.s. XLI, 27–32.

Gratien, B. 1995. 'La Basse Nubie à l'Ancien Empire: égyptiens et autochtones', *JEA* 81, 43–56.

Gratien, B. 1999. 'Some Rural Settlements at Gism El-Arba in the Northern Dongola Reach', *Sudan & Nubia* 3, 10–12.

Gratien, B. and M. Olive 1981. 'Fouilles à Saï: 1977–1979', *CRIPEL* 6, 69–169.

Gratien, B. and F. Le Saout (eds) 1994. *Nubie – Les Cultures Antiques du Soudan à travers les explorations et les fouilles françaises et franco-soudanaises.* Exposition organisée à la Fondation Prouvost, Marcq en Baroeul, 16 September–27 November 1994. Lille.

Gratien, B., S. Marchi, O. Thuriot and J.M. Willot 2003. 'Gism el-Arba, habitat 2. Rapport préliminaire sur un centre de stockage Kerma au bord du Nil', *CRIPEL* 23, 29–43.

Griffith, F.Ll. 1890. *The Antiquities of the Tell el-Yahudiyah.* London.

Griffith, F.Ll. 1911. *Meroitic Inscriptions.* London.

Griffith, F.Ll. 1912. *Meroitic Inscriptions, Part II – Napata to Philae and Miscellaneous*, Archaeological Survey of Egypt, 20th Memoir, London.

Griffith, F.Ll. 1923. 'Oxford excavations in Nubia. The cemetery of Sanam', *LAAA* 10, 73–171.

Griffith, F.Ll. 1928. 'Christian Documents from Nubia', *Proceedings of the British Academy* 14, 117–46.

Griffith, F.Ll. 1931. 'Excavations at Kawa', *SNR* 14, 87–9.

Grossmann, P. 1990. 'Typologische Probleme der Nubischen Vierstützenbauten', in Godlewski (ed.), 151–60.

Grossmann, P. 2002. *Christliche Architektur in Ägypten.* Leiden.

Grzymski, K. 1989. *Archaeological Reconnaissance in Upper Nubia.* Toronto.

Grzymski, K. 2000. 'Nubia Before the Pyramids', *Rotunda* 32(2), 30–35.

Grzymski, K. 2003a. 'In Search of a fabled City: Meroe in the Sudan', *ROM Archaeological Newsletter*, Series III (14), 1–4.

Grzymski, K. 2003b. *Meroe Reports I.* Mississauga.

Grzymski, K. and J. Anderson 1994. 'Three Excavation Seasons at Hambukol (Dongola Reach):1998, 1990 and 1991–92', *ANM* 6, 93–105.

Grzymski, K. and J. Anderson 2001. *Hambukol Excavations 1986–1989.* Mississauga.

Guichard, J. and G. Guichard 1968. 'Contributions to the study of the Early and Middle Paleolithic of Nubia', in Wendorf (ed.), 148–93.

Gundlach, R., M. Kropp and A. Leibundgut (eds) 1996. *Der Sudan in Vergangenheit und Gegenwart.* Nordostafrikanische/Westasiatische Studien 1, Frankfurt.

Haaland, R. 1987. *Socio-economic differentiation in the Neolithic Sudan.* BAR International Series 350, Oxford.

Haaland, R. 1995. 'Bone artifacts: production technique and function', in Haaland and Magid (eds), 123–36.

Haaland, R. and A.A. Magid (eds) 1995. *Aqualithic sites along the rivers Nile and Atbara, Sudan.* Bergen.

Habachi, L. 1969. *Features of Deification of Ramesses II.* ADAIK 5. Glückstadt.

Habachi, L. 1972. *The second stela of Kamose and his struggle against the Hyksos ruler and his capital.* ADAIK 8. Glückstadt.

Habachi, L. 1980. 'Königssohn von Kusch', *LdÄ* 3, 630–40.

Hägg, T. (ed.) 1987. *Nubian Culture Past and Present Sixth International Conference for Nubian Studies in Uppsala.* Uppsala.

Hayes, R. 1973. 'The Distribution of Meroitic Archers' Rings: An Outline of Political Borders', *Meroitica* 1, 113–22.

Hazzard, R.H. 2000. *Imagination of a Monarchy: Studies in Ptolemaic Propaganda.* Toronto–Buffalo–London.

Heidorn, L.A. 1992. *The Fortress of Dorginarti and Lower Nubia during the Seventh to Fifth Centuries BC.* PhD Dissertation, University of Chicago, Chicago.

Hein, I. 1991. *Die ramessidische Bautätigkeit in Nubien.* Wiesbaden.

Hendrickx, S., B. Midant-Reynes and W. Van Neer 2001. *Mahgar Dendera 2 (Haute Egypte), un site d'occupation Badarien.* Leuven.

Heyler, A. 1965. 'Cinq nouvelles "invocations solennelles" méroïtiques', *RdE* 17, 192.

Heyler, A., J. Leclant and M. Hainsworth 1975. 'Préliminaires à un Répertoire d'Épigraphie Méroïtique (*REM*) (following)', *MNL* 16, 29–33.

Hinkel, F.W. 1978. *Auszug aus Nubien*. Berlin.

Hinkel, F.W. 1982. 'Pyramide oder Pyramidenstumpf? Ein Beitrag zu Fragen der Planung, konstruktiven Baudurchführung und Architektur der Pyramiden von Meroe (Teil C und d)', *ZÄS* 109.2, 127–48.

Hinkel, F.W. 1998. 'Appendix', in Caminos, vol. II, 101 ff.

Hinkel, F.W. 2001. *Der Tempelkomplex Meroe 250*. AMS 1.1. Berlin.

Hinkel, F.W. and Abdelrahman Ali Mohamed 2002. *Catalogue of Objects in the Sudan National Museum, I. Accession Nos. 00001–04000*, AMS, suppl. 3. Berlin.

Hinkel F.W. and U. Sievertsen 2002. *Die Royal City von Meroe und die Repräsentative Profanarchitektur in Kusch*. AMS, suppl. 4. Berlin.

Hintze, F. 1959. 'Preliminary Report of the Butana Expedition 1958', *Kush* 7, 171–96.

Hintze, F. 1973. 'Preliminary Report on the Excavations of the Institute of Egyptology, Humboldt University, Berlin. 1963–66. (Fourth–Sixth Seasons)', *Kush* 15, 283–98.

Hintze, F. and U. Hintze 1967. *Alte Kulturen im Sudan*. Munich.

Hoelzmann, P., B. Keding, H. Berke, S. Kröpelin and H.-J. Kruse 2001. 'Environmental change and archaeology: lake evolution and human occupation in the Eastern Sahara during the Holocene', *Palaeogeography Palaeoclimatology Palaeoecology* 169, 193–217.

Hofmann, I. 1988. 'Überlegungen zur "Venus von Meroe" ÄS 1334', *BzS* 3, 25–38.

Hofmann, I. 1991. '*Steine für Ewigkeite. Meroitische Opfertafeln und Totenstelen*', *BzS* 6. Vienna–Mödling.

Holm-Rasmussen, T. 1995. 'The Original Meaning of *ḥr mw*', *GM* 148, 53–61.

Holt, P.M. 1999. *The Sudan of the Three Niles. The Funj Chronicle 910-1288/1504-1871*. Leiden.

Holt, P.M. and M.W. Daly 1988. *A History of the Sudan from the Coming of Islam to the Present Day*. New York.

Holthoer, R. 1977. *New Kingdom Pharaonic Sites. The Pottery*. The Scandinavian Joint Expedition to Sudanese Nubia, Publications, vol. 5:1. Lund.

Holthoer, R., T. Säve-Söderbergh and L. Troy 1991. 'Wheel-made Pharaonic Pottery', in Säve-Söderbergh and Troy (eds), 17–49.

Honegger, M. 1999. 'Kerma: les occupations néolithiques et Pré-Kerma de la nécropole orientale', *Genava*, n.s., XLVII, 77–82.

Honegger, M. 2001. 'Evolution de la société dans le bassin de Kerma (Soudan) des derniers chasseurs-cueilleurs au premier royaume de Nubie', *BSFE* 152, 12–27.

Honegger, M. 2003. 'Peuplement Préhistorique

dans la région de Kerma', *Genava*, n.s., LI, 281–90.

Honegger, M. forthcoming. 'The Pre-Kerma settlement at Kerma: new elements throw light on the rise of the first Nubian Kingdom', in Kendall (ed.)

Hope, C.A. 1989. *Pottery of Egyptian New Kingdom. Three Studies*. Burwood.

Iacumin, P., H. Bocherens, L. Chaix and A. Marioth 1998. 'Stable carbon and nitrogen isotopes as dietary indicators of ancient Nubian populations (Northern Sudan)', *Journal of Archaeological Science* 25, 293–301.

Innemée, K. 1995. 'Observations on the System of Nubian Church Decoration', *CRIPEL* 17/1, 279–88.

Insoll, T. 1996. 'The Archaeology of Islam in Sub-Saharan Africa: A review', *JWP* 10(4), 439–504.

Jacquet-Gordon, H., C. Bonnet and J. Jacquet 1969. 'Pnubs and the temple of Tabo on Argo Island', *JEA* 55, 103–11.

Jakobielski, S. 1972. *Faras III. A History of the Bishopric of Pahoras*. Warsaw.

Jakobielski, S. 1979. 'Dongola 1976 ', *ET* 11, 229–44.

Jakobielski, S. 1982a. 'Polish Excavations in Old Dongola in 1976 and 1978', in Plumley (ed.), 116–26.

Jakobielski, S. (ed.) 1982b. *Nubia Christiana*. Warsaw.

Jakobielski, S. 1991. 'The inscriptions, ostraca and graffiti', in Welsby and Daniels, 274–96.

Jakobielski, S. 1995a. 'Old Dongola 1993/94', *PAM* VI, 84–92.

Jakobielski, S. 1995b. 'Monastery of the Holy Trinity at Old Dongola – A short archaeological report', in M. Starowieyski (ed.), *The Spirituality of Ancient Monasticsn*. Acts of the internatonal collolquium held in Cracow-Tyniec 16–19 November 1994. Carcow, 35–45.

Jakobielski, S. 1996. 'Monastery 1995', *PAM* VII, 103–13.

Jakobielski, S. 1997. 'Kom H, Site NW', *PAM* VIII, 161–8.

Jakobielski, S. 1998. 'Old Dongola. Kom H', *PAM* IX, 160–69.

Jakobielski, S. 1999. 'Old Dongola Excavations, 1998', *PAM* X, 137–47.

Jakobielski, S. 2000. 'Old Dongola Documentation Work in the Monastery, 1999', *PAM* XI, 207–8.

Jakobielski, S. 2001a. 'Old Dongola, Season 2000', *PAM* XII, 265–79.

Jakobielski, S. 2001b. '35 Years of Polish Excavations at Old Dongola. A Factfile', in Jakobielski and Scholz (eds), 1–48.

Jakobielski, S. 2001c. 'Das Kloster der Heiligen Dreifaltigkeit. Bauphasen des nordwestlichen Anbaus', in Jakobielski and Scholz (eds), 141–68.

Jakobielski, S. and P. Scholz (eds) 2001. *Dongola-Studien. 35 Jahre polnischer Forschungen im Zentrum des makuritischen Reiches*. Warsaw.

Jenkins, M. and M. Keene 1982. *Islamic Jewelry in the Metropolitan Museum of Art, New York*. New York.

Jesse, F. 2000. 'Early Khartoum Ceramics in the Wadi Howar, Northwest Sudan', in Krzyżaniak *et al.* (eds), 77–87.

Jesse, F. 2002a. 'Excavations in the Wadi Hariq, Northwestern Sudan – A preliminary report on the field season 2001', *Nyame Akuma* 57, 33–7.

Jesse, F. 2002b. 'Wavy Line Ceramics: Evidence from Northeastern Africa', in K. Nelson (ed.), *Holocene Settlement of te Egyptian Sahara. Volume 2: The Pottery of Nabta Playa*. New York, 79–96.

Jesse, F. 2003. *Rahib 80/87. Ein Wavy-Line-Fundplatz im Wadi Howar und die früheste Keramik in Nordafrika. Africa Praehistorica* 16. Cologne.

Jesse, F. in press a. 'The development of pottery design styles in the Wadi Howar Region, Northern Sudan', *Préhistoire Anthropologie Méditerranéenes*.

Jesse, F. in press b. 'No link between the central Sahara and the Nile Valley? (Dotted) Wavy Line ceramics in the Wadi Howar, Sudan', in Kendall (ed.) forthcoming.

Jesse, F. and B. Keding 2002. 'Death in the Desert – Burials in the Wadi Howar Region (Eastern Sahara)', in *Tides of the Desert – Gezeiten der Wüste. Contributions to the Archaeology and Environmental History of Africa in Honour of Rudolph Kuper. Africa Praehistorica* 14, 277–93.

Jimeno, A., V.M. Fernandez, M. Menendez and J. Lario 1996. 'The Mesolithic/Neolithic of the Blue Nile (East bank)', in Krzyżaniak *et al.* (eds), 335–45.

Judd, M.A. 2001. 'The Human Remains', in Welsby 2001d, 458–543.

Judd, M.A. 2002. 'Ancient injury recidivism: an example from the Kerma Period of Ancient Nubia', *International Journal of Osteoarchaeology* 12, 89–106.

Judd, M. 2003. 'Jebel Sahaba revisited'. Paper presented at the *International Symposium Archaeology of the Earliest Northwestern Africa*, Poznan, 2003.

Kawatoko, M. 1993a. 'On the tombstones found at Badi', the al-Rih island', *Kush* 16, 186–202.

Kawatoko, M. 1993b. 'Preliminary Survey of 'Aydhab and Badi Sites', *Kush* 16, 203–24.

Keding, B. 1989. 'Vom Uferstrand zum Wüstensand. Siedlungs- und Landschaftswandel im Wadi Howar', *Archäologie in Deutschland* 2, 32–5.

Keding, B. 1993. 'Leiterband sites in the Wadi Howar, North Sudan', in Krzyżaniak *et al.* (eds), 371–80.

Keding, B. 1996. 'Leiterbandkeramik aus dem Wadi Howar – ein Spiegel kultureller Verbindungen zwischen Niltal und Tschadbecken im dritten und zweiten vorchristlichen Jahrtausend', in Gundlach *et al.* (eds), 81–101.

Keding, B. 1997a. *Djabarona 84/13. Untersuchungen zur Besiedlungsgeschichte des Wadi Howar anhand der Keramik des 3. und 2. Jahrtausends v. Chr. Africa Praehistorica* 9. Cologne.

Keding, B. 1997b. 'Prehistoric investigations in the Wadi Howar region: A preliminary report on the 1995–1996 Season', *Kush* 17, 33–46.

Keding, B. 1998. 'The Yellow Nile: new data on settlement and the environment in the Sudanese Eastern Sahara', *Sudan & Nubia* 2, 2–12.

Keding, B. 2000. 'New data on the Holocene occupation of the Wadi Howar region (Eastern Sahara/Sudan)', in Krzyżaniak *et al.* (eds), 89–104.

Keding, B. 2003. 'Two Seasons in the Wadi Howar Region (1996–1998): A preliminary report', *Kush* 18, 89–96.

Keding, B. forthcoming. 'The Yellow Nile – Settlement Shifts in the Wadi Howar region (Sudanese Eastern Sahara) and adjacent areas from between the sixth to the first millennium BC', in Kendall (ed.).

Keding, B. and R. Vogelsang 2001. 'Vom Jäger-Sammler zum Hirten – Wirtschaftswandel im nordöstlichen und südwestlichen Afrika', in Gehlen *et al.*, 257–82.

Kendall, T. 1982. *Kush: Lost Kingdom of the Nile*. Brockton.

Kendall, T. 1990. 'The Gebel Barkal Temples 1989–90: A Progress Report on the Work of the Museum of Fine Arts, Boston, Sudan Mission', *Seventh International Conference for Nubian Studies. Geneva, Sept. 3–8, 1990* (privately distributed).

Kendall, T. 1991. 'The Napatan Palace at Gebel Barkal: A First Look at B 1200', in Davies (ed.), 302–13.

Kendall, T. 1994a. 'A New Map of the Gebel Barkal Temples', in Bonnet (ed.), 139–45.

Kendall, T. 1994b. 'Le Djebel Barkal: Le Karnak de Koush', in *La Nubie. Les Dossiers d'Archéologie* 196, 46–53.

Kendall, T. 1996a. 'Die Könige vom Heiligen Berg: Napata und die Kuschiten-Dynastie', in Wildung (ed.), 161–71.

Kendall, T. 1996b. 'The American Discovery of Meroitic Nubia and the Sudan', in Thomas (ed.), 151–67.

Kendall, T. 1996c. 'Fragments Lost and Found: Two Kushite Objects Augmented', in P. Der Manuelian (ed.), *Studies in Honor of William Kelly Simpson*, vol. 2. Boston, 468–76.

Kendall, T. 1997a. 'Excavations at Gebel Barkal, 1996: Report of the Museum of Fine Arts, Boston, Sudan Mission', *Kush* 17, 320–54.

Kendall, T. 1997b. 'Kings of the Sacred Mountain: Napata and the Kushite Twenty-Fifth Dynasty of Egypt', in Wildung (ed.), 161–71.

Kendall, T. 2002, in press. 'Napatan Temples: A case study from Gebel Barkal'. 10th International Conference for Nubian Studies. La Sapienza University, Rome (September 2002).

Kendall, T. 2003. 'Cinco "fundas cilindricas" (¿mangos para penachos ceremoniales de plumas de avestruz?)', in Berenguer *et al.*, 260, no. 233.

Kendall T. (ed.) forthcoming. *Nubian Studies 1998: Proceedings of the Ninth International Conference of Nubian Studies*. Boston.

Khider A. Eisa and D. Welsby 1996. 'A Soba Ware Vessel from the Upper Blue Nile', *BzS* 6, 133–6.

Kirwan, L.P. 1939. *The Oxford University Excavations at Firka*. London.

Kirwan, L.P. 1982. 'Some Thoughts on the Conversion of Nubia to Christianity', in Plumley (ed.), 142–5.

Kitchen, K.A. 1975. *Ramesside Inscriptions. Historical and Biographical* I. Oxford.

Kitchen, K.A. 1986. *The Third Intermediate Period in Egypt (1100–650 BC)*. 2nd edition. Warminster.

Kitchen, K.A. 1993a. *Ramesside Inscriptions Translated and Annotated: Translations. I Ramesses I, Sethos I and Contemporaries*. Oxford.

Kitchen, K.A. 1993b. *Ramesside Inscriptions Translated and Annotated: Notes and Comments I Ramesses I, Sethos I, and Contemporaries*. Oxford.

Kitchen, K.A. 1999. 'Further Thoughts on Punt and its Neighbours', in A. Leahy and J. Tait (eds), *Studies on Ancient Egypt in Honour of H.S. Smith*. London, 173–8.

Klees, F. and R. Kuper (eds) 1992. *New Light on the Northeast African Past. Current Prehistoric Research. Africa Praehistorica* 5. Cologne.

Klemm, D., R. Klemm and A. Murr 2002. 'Ancient Gold Mining in the Eastern Desert of Egypt and the Nubian desert of Sudan', in R. Friedman (ed.), 215–31.

Kleppe, E. 1982. 'Research on Debbas, Upper Nile Province, Southern Sudan'. MSS.

Kobusiewicz, M. 1996. 'Technology, goals and efficiency of quartz exploitation in the Khartoum, Neolithic: the case of Kadero', in Krzyżaniak *et al.* (eds), 347–54.

Kołsowska, E., Mahmoud el-Tayeb and H. Paner 2003. 'Old Kush in the Fourth Cataract Region', *Sudan & Nubia* 7, 21–5.

Kröpelin, S., 1993. Zur *Rekonstruktion der spätquartären Umwelt am Unteren Wadi Howar (Südöstliche Sahara/NW-Sudan)*. Berlin.

Krzyżaniak, L. 1984. 'The neolithic habitation at Kadero (Central Sudan)', in Krzyżaniak and Kobusiewicz (eds), 309–15.

Krzyżaniak, L. 1991. 'Early farming in the Middle Nile Basin: recent discoveries at Kadero (Central Sudan)', *Antiquity* 65, 515–32.

Krzyżaniak, L. 1992a. 'Some Aspects of the Later Prehistoric Development in the Sudan as seen from the Point of View of the Current Research on the Neolithic', in Bonnet (ed.), 267–73.

Krzyżaniak, L. 1992b. 'The Later Prehistory of the Upper (main) Nile: Comments on the Current State of the Research', in Klees and Kuper (eds), 239–48.

Krzyżaniak, L. 1995. 'Late prehistory of the Central Sudan: a summary of the results of the last thirty years', *CRIPEL* 17.1, 117–22.

Krzyżaniak L. and M. Kobusiewicz (eds) 1984. *Origin and early development of food-producing cultures in north-eastern Africa*. Poznan.

Krzyżaniak, L. and M. Kobusiewicz (eds) 1989. *Late Prehistory of the Nile Basin and the Sahara*. Poznan.

Krzyżaniak, L., M. Kobusiewicz and J. Alexander (eds) 1993. *Environmental Change and Human Culture in the Nile Basin and Northern Africa until the Second Millennium BC*. Poznan.

Krzyżaniak., L., K. Kroeper and M. Kobusiewicz (eds) 1996. *Interregional Contacts in the Later Prehistory of Northeastern Africa*. Poznan.

Krzyżaniak, L., K. Kroeper, and M. Kobusiewicz (eds) 2000. *Recent Research into the Stone Age of Northeastern Africa*. Poznan.

Kubisch, S. 2002. *Lebensbilder der 2. Zwischenzeit. Biographische Inschriften der 13.–17. Dynastie*. Doctoral dissertation. Heidelberg.

Kuper, R. 1981. 'Untersuchungen zur Besiedlungsgeschichte der östlichen Sahara. Vorbericht über die Expedition 1980', *Beiträge zur allgemeinen und vergleichenden Archäologie* 3, 215–75.

Kuper, R. 1986. 'Wadi Howar and Laqiya – Recent Field studies into the Early Settlement of Northern Sudan', in M. Krause (ed.), *Nubische Studien*. Mainz, 129–36.

Kuper, R. 1988. 'Neuere Forschungen zur Besiedlungsgeschichte der Ost-Sahara', *Archäologisches Korrespondenzblatt* 18, 127–42.

Kuper, R. (ed.) 1989. *Forschungen zur Umweltgeschichte der Ostsahara. Africa Praehistorica* 2. Cologne.

Kuper, R. 1995. 'Prehistoric research in the Southern Libyan Desert. A brief account and some conclusions of the B.O.S. project', *CRIPEL* 17.1, 123–40.

Labrousse, A. 1997. 'Récentes recherches au Temple de la Reine Tiy a Sedeinga', *Dossiers d'Archéologie* 6, 66–7.

Lacaille, A.D. 1951. *The stone industry of Singa-Abu Hugar. The Pleistocene Fauna of Two Blue Nile Sites. Fossil Mammals of Africa* 2. London, 43–50.

Łajtar, A. 1991. 'Two Greek Funerary Stelae from Polish Excavations at Old Dongola', *ANM* 5, 157–66.

Łajtar, A. 1997. 'Greek Funerary Inscriptions from Old Dongola, General Note', *Oriens Christianus, Hefte für die Kunde des christlichen Orients* 81, 107–26.

Łajtar, A. 2003. *Catalogue of Greek Inscriptions in the Sudan National Museum, Khartoum*. Leuven.

Łajtar A. and K. Pluskota 2001. 'Inscribed vessels from the Monastery of the Holy Trinity at Old Dongola', in Jakobielski and Scholz (eds), 335–55.

Łaptaś, M. 1999. 'Comments on wall paintings from "House A" in Old Dongola', in S. Emmel, M. Krause, S.G. Richter and S. Schaten (eds), *Ägypten und Nubien in spätantiker und christlicher Zeit*. Akten des 6. Internationalen Koptologenkongresses Münster, 20–26 July 1996. Wiesbaden, 230–37.

Leclant, J. 1966a. 'Fouilles et travaux en Égypte et au Soudan, 1964–1965', *Orientalia* 35, 126–78.

Leclant, J. 1970. 'La nécropole à l'ouest de Sedeinga en Nubie soudanaise', *Comptes rendus de l'Académie des Inscriptions et Belles-Lettres*, 246–76.

Leclant, J. 1972. 'Fouilles et travaux en Égypte et au Soudan, 1970–1971', *Orientalia* 41, 249–91.

Leclant, J. 1975. 'Fouilles et travaux en Égypte et au Soudan, 1973–1974', *Orientalia* 44, 200–44.

Leclant, J. 1982. 'Fouilles et travaux en Égypte et au Soudan, 1980–1981', *Orientalia* 51, 411–92.

Leclant, J. 1984a. 'Fouilles et travaux en Égypte et au Soudan, 1982–1983', *Orientalia* 53, 350–416.

Leclant, J. 1984b. 'Taharqa à Sedeinga', in Westendorf, W. (ed.), *Studien zu Sprache und Religion Ägyptens*, Göttingen, 1113–17.

Leclant, J. 1985. 'Bouteilles globulaires à long col de Moyenne Nubie', in Geus, F. and F. Thill (eds), *Mélanges offerts à Jean Vercoutter*. Paris, 185–204.

Leclant, J. and G. Clerc 1988. 'Fouilles et travaux en Egypte et au Soudan 1986–1987', *Orientalia* 57, 307–404.

Leclant, J. and G. Clerc 1997. 'Fouilles et travaux en Egypte et au Soudan 1995–1996, Naga', *Orientalia* 66, pl. XLIX, fig. 67.

Leclant, J. and G. Clerc 1998. 'Fouilles et travaux en Egypte et au Soudan 1995–1996, Naga', *Orientalia* 67, pl. XLVII, fig. 52.

Leclant, J. and A. Minault-Gout 2000. 'Fouilles et travaux en Egypte et au Soudan 1995–1996, Naga', *Orientalia*, 69, pl. XXXIII, fig. 29.

Leclant, J., A. Heyler, C. Berger-el Naggar, C. Carrier, and C. Rilly 2000. *Répertoire d'Épigraphie Méroïtique. Corpus des inscriptions publiées* I–III. Paris.

Lecointe, Y. 1987. 'Le site néolithique d'el Ghaba: deux années d'activité (1985–1986)', *ANM* 2, 69–87.

Lenoble, P. 1989. '"A new type of mound grave" (continued): le Tumulus à enceinte d'umm Makharoqa, près d'El Hobagi (AMS NE-36-O/7-O-3)', *ANM* 3, 93–120.

Lenoble, P. 1991a. 'Chiens de païens. Une tombe postpyramidale à double descenderie hors de Méroé', *ANM* 5, 167–83.

Lenoble, P. 1991b. 'Plateaux de gobelets dans les sépultures de Méroé. Un équipement liturgique de la libation isiaque éthiopienne', in Davies (ed.), 246–52.

Lenoble, P. 1992. 'Documentation tumulaire et céramique entre 5e et 6e Cataractes. Un exemple de prospection orientée visant à renseigner la Fin de Méroé dans la région de Méroé', in Bonnet (ed.), 79–97.

Lenoble, P. 1994a. 'Le rang des inhumés sous tertre à enceinte à el Hobagi', *MNL* 25, 89–124.

Lenoble, P. 1994b. 'Une monture pour mon royaume. Sacrifices triomphaux de chevaux et de méhara, d'el Kurru à Ballana', *ANM* 6, 107–30.

Lenoble, P. 1994c. 'Le sacrifice funéraire de bovinés, de Méroé à Qustul et Ballana', in Berger,

C., G. Clerc and N. Grimal (eds), *Mélanges Leclant*, Bibliothèque d' Étude 106, fasc. 2, Cairo, IFAO, vol. 2, 269–83.

Lenoble, P. 1994d. 'Cloche', in Gratien and Le Saout, 227, no. 312.

Lenoble, P. 1994e. 'Coupe', in Gratien and Le Saout, 228, no. 314.

Lenoble, P. 1994f. 'Bassin au crocodile', in Gratien and Le Saout, 231, nos 322–3.

Lenoble, P. 1996a. 'Les "sacrifices humains" de Méroé, Qustul et Ballana. I, Le massacre de nombreux prisonniers', *BzS* 6, 39–67.

Lenoble, P. 1996b. 'La petite bouteille noire: un récipient méroéen de la libation funéraire', *ANM* 7, 143–62.

Lenoble, P. 1997. 'Enterrer les flèches, enterrer l'empire. I, Flèches et carquois des tombes impériales d'el Hobagi', *CRIPEL* 17/2, 137–52.

Lenoble, P. 1998. 'Le vase à parfum et le brûleur d'encens, des récipients de la purification funéraire méroéenne', *ANM* 8, 127–43.

Lenoble, P. 1999a. 'Enterrer les flèches, enterrer l'Empire. II, Les archers d'El-Kadada et l'administration de l'imperium méroïtique', *CRIPEL* 20, 125–44.

Lenoble, P. 1999b. 'The division of the Meroitic Empire and the end of the pyramid building in the 4th century AD: an introduction to further excavations of imperial mounds in the Sudan', in Welsby (ed.) 1999, 157–97.

Lenoble, P. 2002. 'Mystérieux recipients royaux de l'allaitement divin dans les tombes de Ballana?', in Bács (ed.), 331–8.

Lenoble, P. 2003, 'El periodo precristiano en el desierto y el Sahel nubios', in Carmen Pérez Die (ed.), *Nubia, Los reinos del Nilo en Sudan*, Barcelona, 80–85.

Lenoble, P. in press 1. 'L'arsenal de Méroé et le monopole royal du fer dans l'Empire méroïtique', *Mediterranean Archaeology*.

Lenoble, P. in press 2. 'Satyres extravagants', in Kendall (ed.).

Lenoble, P. and Nigm ed-Din Sharif 1992. 'Barbarians at the Gates? The Royal Mounds of el Hobagi and the End of Meroe', *Antiquity* 66, 626–35.

Lenoble, P. and V. Rondot 2003. 'À la rédecouverte d'El-Hassa temple à Amon, palais royal et ville de l'Empire Meroitique', *CRIPEL* 23, 101–15.

Lenoble, P., R.-P Disseaus, A. Ali Mohammed, B. Ronce and J. Bialais 1994. 'La fouille du tumulus à enciente el Hobagi III. AMS NE-36-O/7-N-3', *MNL* 25, 53–88.

Lepsius, C.R. 1849–59. *Denkmaler aus Aegypten und Äthiopien* (plates). Berlin.

Lepius, C.R. 1897–1913. *Denkmaler aus Aegyptien und Äthiopien* (text). Berlin.

Lilyquist, C. 1979. *Ancient Egypt Mirrors from the Earlier Times throught the Middle Kingdom*, *MÄS* 27.

Lindblad, I. 1984. *Royal Sculpture of the Early Eighteenth Dynasty in Egypt*. Medelhavsmuseet, Memoir 5. Stockholm.

Macadam, M.F.L. 1949. *The Temples of Kawa I: The Inscriptions*. London.

Macadam, M.F.L. 1955. *The Temples of Kawa II. History and Archaeology of the Site*. Oxford.

Macklin, M.G. and J.C. Woodward 2001. 'Holocene Alluvial History and the Palaeochannels of the River Nile in the Northern Dongola Reach', in Welsby 2001d, vol. I, 7–13.

MacMichael, H.A. 1967. *The History of the Arabs in the Sudan*, vols I, II. Cambridge.

Magid, A.A. 1995. 'The lithic material from the sites of Aneibis, Abu Darbein and El Damer', in Haaland and Magid (eds), 52–83.

Mallinson, M., L.M.V. Smith, S. Ikram, C. Le Quesne and P. Sheehan 1996. *Road Archaeology in the Middle Nile*, vol. I. London.

Marcolongo, B. and N. Surian 1993. 'Observations préliminaires du contexts géomorphologique de la plain alluviale Du Nil en amont de la IIIe cataracte en rapport avec les sites archéologiques', *Genava*, n.s., XLI, 33.

Marcolongo, B. and N. Surian 1997. 'Kerma: les sites archéologiques de Kerma et de Kadruka dans leur contexte géomorphologique', *Genava*, n.s., XLV, 119–23.

Marks, A.E. 1968a. 'The Halfan industry', in Wendorf (ed.), 392–460.

Marks, A.E. 1968b. 'The Khormusan: An Upper Pleistocene industry in Sudanese Nubia', in Wendorf (ed.), 315–91.

Marks, A.E. 1968c. 'The Mousterian industries of Nubia', in Wendorf (ed.), 194–314.

Marks, A.E. 1993. 'Climatic and cultural changes in the Southern Atbai, Sudan, from the fifth through the third millennium B.C.', in Krzyżaniak *et al.* (eds), 431–8.

Marks, A.E. and A. Mohammed-Ali (eds) 1991. *The Late Prehistory of the Eastern Sahel. The Mesolithic and Neolithic of Shaqadud, Sudan*. Dallas.

Marks, A.E. and K. Sadr 1988. 'Holocene environments and occupations in the Southern Atbai, Sudan: A preliminary formulation', in J. Bower and D. Lubell (eds), *Prehistoric cultures and environments in the Late Quaternary of Africa*. BAR International Series 405. Oxford, 69–90.

Marks, A.E., J.L. Shiner, and T.R. Hayes 1968. 'Survey and Excavations in the Dongola Reach, Sudan', *Current Anthropology* 9, 319–23.

Marks, A.E., J.L. Shiner, F. Servello and F. Munday 1971. 'Flake assemblages with Levallois technique from the Dongola Reach', in Shiner *et al.* 1971a, 36–83.

Martens, M. 1972. 'Observations sur la composition du visage dans les peintures de Faras (VIIIe–IXe siècles)', *ET* 6, 207–50.

Martens-Czarnecka, M. 1982. *Les éléments décoratifs sur les peintures de Faras. Faras VII*. Warsaw.

Martens-Czarnecka, M. 1990a. 'Some known and some new features of Nubian painting on the murals from House "A" in Old Dongola', in Godlewski (ed.), 233–46.

Martens-Czarnecka, M. 1990b. 'Caractéristiques du style "violet" dans les peintures à Dongola', *ET* 14, 223–37.

Martens-Czarnecka, M. 1992. 'Late Christian Painting in Nubia', in Bonnet (ed.), 307–16.

Martens-Czarnecka, M. 1998. 'Mural Paintings from Old Dongola', *Gdańsk Archaeological Museum African Reports* I, 95–113.

Martens-Czarnecka, M. 2001a. 'Wall Paintings discovered in Old Dongola', in Jakobielski and Scholz (eds), 253–84.

Martens-Czarnecka, M. 2001b. 'Nubian King – a painting from the Monastery in Dongola', in Jakobielski and Scholz (eds), 285–300.

Martens-Czarnecka, M. 2001c. 'Dongola share in Nubian painting', in E. Papuci-Władyka and J. Sliwa (eds), *Studia Archaeologica Liber Amicarum Ianussio A. Ostrowski*. Krakow, 287–302.

Maystre, Ch. 1986. *Tabo I: Statue en bronze d'un roi mérotique*. Geneva.

Meurillon, L. 1997. *Les greniers Pré-Kerma de l'île de Saï*. Lille.

Michałowski, K. 1962. *Faras. Fouilles Polonaises 1961*. Warsaw.

Michałowski, K. 1964. 'Die wichtigsten Entwicklungsetappen der Wandmalerei in Faras', *Christentum am Nil*. Recklinghausen, 79–94.

Michałowski, K. 1965. *Faras. Fouilles Polonaises 1961–1962*. Warsaw.

Michałowski, K. 1966. *Faras. Centre Artistique de la Nubie Chretienne*. Leiden.

Michałowski, K. 1967. *Faras. Die Kathedrale aus dem Wüstensand*. Zürich–Cologne.

Michałowski, K. 1972. 'Classification générale des peintures murales de Faras', *Revue Archéologique* 2, 373–80.

Michałowski, K. 1974. *Faras*. Warsaw.

Mileham, G.S. 1910. *Churches in Lower Nubia*. Philadelphia.

Millet, N.B. 1967. 'Gebel Adda Preliminary Report 1965–66', *JARCE* 6, 53–63.

Millet, N.B. 1984. 'Meroitic Religion', *Meroitica* 7, 111–21.

Mills, A.J. 1967–8. 'The archaeological survey from Gemai to Dal: Report on the 1965–1966 season', *Kush* 15, 200–10.

Mills, A.J. 1982. *The Cemeteries of Qasr Ibrim*. London.

Minault, A. and F. Thill 1974. 'Tombes du Nouvel Empire à Saï (SAC5)', *CRIPEL* 2, 75–102.

Minault-Gout, A. 1994. 'Une nécropole du Nouvel Empire', *Les Dossiers d'Archéologie*, no. 196.

Minault-Gout, A. and F. Thill forthcoming. *Saï II. La nécropole SAC5 à hypogées du Nouvel Empire*. Cairo.

Mohammed-Ali, A. 1982. *The Neolithic Period in the Sudan, c. 6000–2500 BC*. BAR International Series 139. Oxford.

Mohamed-Ali, A.S. and A.R.M. Khabir 2003. 'The wavy line and the dotted wavy line pottery pottery in the prehistory of the central Nile and the Sahara-Sahel belt', *African Archaeological Review* 20, 1, 25–58.

Monneret De Villard, U. 1935. *La Nubia Medioevale*, vols 1, 2. Cairo.

Monneret De Villard, U. 1938. *Storia Della Nubia Cristiana*. Rome.

Monneret De Villard, U. 1957. *La Nubia Medioevale*, vols 3, 4. Cairo.

Morkot, R.G. 1991. 'Nubia in the New Kingdom: The Limits of Egyptian Control', in Davies (ed.), 294–301.

Morkot, R.G. 1995a. 'The economy of Nubia in the New Kingdom'. *CRIPEL* 17/1, 175–89.

Morkot, R.G. 1995b. 'The Foundations of the Kushite State', *CRIPEL* 17/1, 229–42.

Morkot, R.G. 2000. *The Black Pharaohs. Egypt's Nubian Rulers*. London.

Müller, H.W. 1987. *Die Waffenfund von Balâta-Sichem und die Sichelschwerter*. Abhandlungen/ Bayerische Akademie de Wissenschafte, Philosoplischistorische Klasse, n.F. Hft 97. Munich.

Munroe-Hay, S. 1989. *Excavations at Axum. An Account of the Research at the Ancient Ethiopian Capital Directed in 1972–1974 by the Late Dr N. Chittick*. London.

Murray, G.W. 1923. *An English-Nubian Comparative Dictionary*. Harvard African Series. vol. 4. London.

Musa, I. 1986. *The Archaeology of Central Darfur in the 1st Millennium AD*, Cambridge Monographs in African Archaeology 14, BAR International Series 285. Oxford.

Museum of Fine Arts, Boston 1982. *Egypt's Golden Age. The Art of Living in the New Kingdom (1558–1085 BC)*. Boston.

Nagel, G. 1938. *La céramique du Nouvel Empire à Deir el Médineh*. Cairo.

Nagy, I. 1997. 'Transcriptions and translations in "The textual finds"', in Török 1997b, 233–43.

Näser, C. 2004. 'The Small Finds', in Shinnie and Anderson (eds), 215–311.

Neumann, K. 1989. 'Zur Vegetationsgeschichte der Ostsahara im Holozän. Holzkohlen aus prähistorischen Fundstellen', in Kuper (ed.), 13–181.

Nicholson, P. 1993. 'The Firing of Pottery', in Arnold and Bourriau (eds), 103–27.

Nordström, H.-Å. 1972. *Neolithic and A-Group sites*. The Scandinavian Joint Expedition to Nubia. Bd. 3, 1–2. Stockholm.

Nordström, H-Å. and J. Bourriau 1993. 'Ceramic Technology: Clays and Fabrics', in Arnold and Bourriau (eds), fasc. II.

O'Connor, D. 1993. *Ancient Nubia. Egypt's Rival in Africa*. Philadelphia.

O'Connor, D. and S. Quirke (eds) 2003. *Mysterious Lands*. London.

O'Fahey, R.S. and J.L. Spaulding 1974. *Kingdoms of the Sudan*. London.

Ogden, J. 1982. *Jewellery of the Ancient World*. London.

Osman, A. and D. Edwards 1992. *The Mahas Survey 1991*. Cambridge.

Pachur, H.-J. and S. Kröpelin 1987. 'Wadi Howar: Paleoclimatic evidence from an extinct river system in the Southeastern Sahara', *Science* 237, 298–300.

Paner, H. 2003. 'Archaeological Survey on the Right Bank of the Nile between Karima and Abu Hamed: a brief overview', *Sudan & Nubia* 7, 15–20.

Partyka, J. 1984. 'La représentation disparue du Christ d'Alexandrie et la nouvelle peinture nubienne du "Christus Sol et Victor"', *Rivista di archeologia cristiana* 60, 109–22.

Pérez Die, C. 2003a. 'Suporte de lucerna', in Berenguer *et al.*, 218, no. 161.

Pérez Die, C. 2003b. 'Estatua-cubo de Amenemhat', in Berenguer *et al.*, 149, no. 53.

Pérez Die, C. 2003c. 'Recipiente de bronce', in Berenguer *et al.*, 219, no. 165.

Petit-Marie, N. and J. Riser (eds) 1983. *Sahara ou Sahel? Quaternaire Récent du Bassin de Taoudenni (Mali)*. Paris.

Petrie, W.M.F. 1890. *Kahun, Gurob and Hawara*. London.

Phillips, T. (ed.) 1995. *Africa – The Art of a Continent*. London.

Pierrat-Bonnefois, G. 2002. 'Cimetière est du village ou cimetière à l'est de Deir el-Médineh', in G. Andreu (ed.) 2002, *Les Artists de Pharaon Deir el-Médinet et la Vallée des Rois*. Paris, 49–65.

Piotrovsky, B. 1967. 'The Early Dynasty Settlement of Khor-Daoud and Wadi-Allaki: The Ancient Route to the Gold Mines', *Fouilles en Nubie (1961–1963)*. Cairo, 97–118.

Piponnier, D., F. Bechtel, M. Schvoerer and J. Reinold 1996. 'Concrétionnement ou application volontaire de minéraux sur des céramiques néolithiques de la vallée du Nil soudanais', *ANM* 7, 191–201.

Plumley, J. 1970. 'Some Examples of Christian Nubian Art. from the Excavations at Qasr Ibrim', in Dinkler (ed.), 129–40.

Plumley, J. 1975. *The Scrolls of Bishop Timotheos*. London.

Plumley, J. (ed.) 1982. *Nubian Studies*. Warminster.

Plumley, J. 1983. 'Qasr Ibrim and Islam', *ET* XII, 158–70.

Pluskota, K. 1997. 'Old Dongola recent pottery finds', *CRIPEL* 17/II, 235–45.

Pluskota, K. 2001. 'The Kiln Sites of Old Dongola', in Jakobielski and Scholz (eds), 357–66.

Porter, B. and R. Moss 1951. *Topographical Bibliography of Ancient Egyptian Hieroglyphic Texts, Reliefs, and Paintings. VII: Nubia, the Deserts, and Outside Egypt*. Oxford.

Priese, K.-H. 1972. 'Der Beginn der kuschitischen Herrschaft in Ägypten', *ZÄS* 98, 16–32.

Priese, K.-H. 1996. 'Meroitische Schrift und Sprache', in Wildung (ed.), 252–5.

Priese, K.-H. 1997a. 'Bark stand of King Natakamani', in Wildung (ed.) 1997, 256–7, no. 279.

Priese, K.-H. 1997b. 'Door threshold', in Wildung (ed.) 1997, 263, no. 285.

Priese, K.-H. 1998. 'Naga Project (Sudan) Egyptian Museum Berlin. Epigraphic Documentation 1996', ANM 8, 217–19.

Privati, B. 1990. 'Les ateliers de potiers et leur production', in Bonnet (ed.) 1990a, 121–31.

Privati, B. 1999. 'La céramique de la nécropole orientale de Kerma (Soudan): essai de classification', CRIPEL 20, 41–69.

Quibell, M.J.E. 1901. 'A Tomb at Hawaret El Gurob', ASAE II, 141–3.

Radja, I. 2003. 'Le réveil des étranges pharaons noirs', Le Monde, Sunday 16 February 2003, 27.

Randall-MacIver, D. and A.C. Mace 1902. El-Amrah and Abydos 1899–1901. London.

Randall-MacIver, D. and C.L. Woolley 1911. Buhen. Philadelphia.

Rassart-Debergh, M. 1972. 'Visages de Faras', ET 6, 251–75.

Redford, D. 1997. 'Textual Sources for the Hyksos Period', in E. Oren (ed.), The Hyksos: New Historical and Archaeological Perspectives. Philadelphia, 1–44.

Reinold, J. 1987. 'Les fouilles pré- et proto-historiques des la Section Française de la Direction des Antiquités due Soudan: Les campagnes 1984–85 et 1985–86', ANM 2, 17–67.

Reinold, J. 1991. 'Néolithique soudanais: Les coutumes funéraires', in Davies (ed.), 6–29.

Reinold, J. 1992. 'Conservation et préservation des sites archéologiques', in Bonnet (ed.), 187–92.

Reinold, J. 1993a. 'Section Française de la Direction des Antiquités du Soudan: Preliminary Report on the 1991/92 and 1992/93 Seasons in the Northern Province', SARS Newsletter no. 5, 33–43.

Reinold, J. 1993b. 'SFDAS: rapport préliminaire de la campagne 1991/1992', Kush 16, 142–68.

Reinold, J. 1994a. 'Les fouilles franco-françaises – el-Kadada (Soudan central)', in Gratien and Le Saout (eds), 51–66.

Reinold, J. 1994b. 'Les fouilles franco-françaises – Kadruka' (Nubie)', in Gratien and Le Saout (eds), 70–86.

Reinold, J. 1994c. 'Le cimetière néolithique KDK.1 de Kadruka (Nubie soudanaise); premiers résultats et essai de corrélation avec les sites du Soudan central', in Bonnet (ed.), 93–100.

Reinold J. 1997. 'SFDAS: un quart de siècle de coopération archéologique', Kush 17, 197–230.

Reinold J. 1998. 'Le Néolithique de Haute Nubie – Traditions funéraires et structures sociales', BSFE 143, 19–40.

Reinold, J. (ed.) with the collaboration of C. Berger-El Naggar, F. Geus, B. Gratien, P. Lenoble, A. Minault-Gout, A. Sacko-Autissier

and F. Thill 2000a. Archéologie au Soudan – Les civilisations de Nubie. Paris.

Reinold, J. 2000b. Fouilles françaises et franco-soudanaises – contribution à l'histoire du Soudan, (catalogue de l'exposition). Khartoum.

Reinold J. 2001. 'Kadruka and the Neolithic in the Northern Dongola Reach', Sudan & Nubia 5, 2–10.

Reinold, J. 2002. 'Néolithique du Soudan central et de Haute Nubie – données sur le matériel céramique', in Tides of the Desert – Gezeiten der Wüste. Contributions to the Archaeology and Environmental History of Africa in Honour of Rudolph Kuper. Africa Praehistorica 14, 203–18.

Reinold, J. 2003a. 'El Neolitico en Sudan', in Berenguer et al. (eds), 28–34.

Reinold, J. 2003b. 'Estatuilla antropomorfa femenina', in Berenguer et al. (eds), 246, nos 211, 212

Reinold, J. 2003c. 'Máscara funeraria', in Berenguer et al. (eds), 279, no. 258.

Reinold, J. 2003d. 'Jamba de "puerto falsa"', in Berenguer et al. (eds), 262, no. 235.

Reinold, J. 2003e. 'Campanilla de arreos de caballo', in Berenguer et al. (eds), 298, no. 296.

Reinold, J. 2003f. 'Figurilla de cocodrilo', in Berenguer et al. (eds), 293, no. 285.

Reinold, J. 2003g. 'Recipiente de almacenaje, con decoración pintada e inscripciones incisas', in Berenguer et al. (eds), 144, no. 47.

Reinold, J. 2003h 'Fuente con decoración pintada', in Berenguer et al. (eds), 222, no. 170.

Reinold, J. 2003i. 'Cuenco litúrgico grabado', in Berenguer et al. (eds), 293, no. 284.

Reinold, J. 2003j. 'Vaso de libaciones funerario', in Berenguer et al. 2003, 274, no. 248.

Reinold, J. 2003k. 'Vaso de libaciones funerario', in Berenguer et al. 2003, 220, no. 166.

Reisner, G.A. 1907. Amulets. Catalogue Général. Cairo.

Reisner, G.A. 1917. 'The Barkal Temples in 1916 (Part I)', JEA 4, 213–27.

Reisner, G.A. 1918. 'The Barkal Temples in 1916 (Part II)', JEA 5, 99–112.

Reisner, G.A. 1920. 'The Barkal Temples in 1916 (Part III)', JEA 6, 247–64.

Reisner, G.A. 1921. 'Historical Inscriptions from Gebel Barkal', SNR 4, 59–75

Reisner, G.A. 1923a. Excavations at Kerma, Parts I–III, Harvard African Studies 5. Cambridge.

Reisner, G.A. 1923b. Excavations at Kerma, Parts IV–V, Harvard African Studies 6. Cambridge.

Reisner, G.A. 1931. 'Inscribed Monuments from Gebel Barkal', ZÄS 66, 76–100.

Reisner, G.A. n.d. Begarawiyah. Diary 1920–1922. South Cem. Pyramids S XVI to XLVII. (Typescript.)

Reisner, G.A. and M.B. Reisner 1933. 'Inscribed monuments from Gebel Barkal', ZÄS 69, 24–39.

Richter, J. 1989. 'Neolithic sites in the Wadi Howar (Western Sudan)', in Krzyżaniak et al. (eds), 431–42.

Rilly, C. 2001. 'Approche comparative de la paléographie et de la chronologie royale de Méroé', MNL 28, 71–89.

Rilly, C. 2002. 'L'Obélisque de Méroé', MNL 29, 95–190.

Rilly, C. forthcoming. 'Les textes méroïtiques de l'île de Saï', ANM 10.

Robertson, J.H. 1992. 'History and Archaeology at Meroe', in Sterner and David (eds), 35–50.

Robisek, C. 1989. Das Bildprogramm des Mut-Tempels am Gebel Barkal. Veröffentlichungen der Institute für Afrikanistik und Ägyptologie der Universität Wien 52. Beiträge zur Ägyptologie 8. Vienna.

Roccati, A. 1982. La littérature historique sous l'Ancien Empire égyptien. Paris.

Romero, J. 1989. The Bes-image in Pharaonic Egypt. Ann Arbor, Michigan.

Rose, P. 1998. 'Part I: The Meroitic Pottery', in Edwards, 142–77.

Rostkowska, B. 1972. 'Iconographie des personnages historiques sur les peintures de Faras', ET 6, 197–205.

Russmann, E. 1974. The Representation of the King in the XXVth Dynasty. Monographies Reine Elizabeth 3. Brussels–Brooklyn.

Ryholt, K. 1997. The Political Situation in Egypt during the Second Intermediate Period c. 1800–1550 B.C. Copenhagen.

Ryl-Preibisz, I. 1997. 'Architectural Decorative Elements recently discovered at Old Dongola', CRIPEL 17/II, 227–33, pls 28–31.

Ryl-Preibisz, I. 2001. 'Elements of architectural decoration from Old Dongola', in Jakobielski and Scholz (eds), 367–85.

Sadr, K. 1995. 'Barlumi di Archeologia nel Deserto Nubiano', in Castiglioni et al., 146–76.

Sadr, K. 1997. 'The Wadi Elei Finds', CRIPEL 17/2, 67–76.

Salvatori S. and D. Usai 2001. 'First Season of Excavation at the R12 Late Neolithic Cemetery in the Northern Dongola Reach (Kawa, Sudan): Preliminary Report', Rivista Di Archeologia XXV, 12–65.

Salvatori, S. and D. Usai 2002. 'The second excavation season at R12, a Late Neolithic Cemetery in the Northern Dongola Reach', Sudan & Nubia 6, 2–7.

Sausse, F. 1975. 'Etude de quelques restes humains trouvé à Soleb (Soudan)', West African Journal of Archaeology 5, 41–51.

Säve-Söderbergh, T. 1949. 'A Buhen Stela from the Second Intermediate Period (Khartūm no. 18)', JEA 35, 50–54.

Säve-Söderbergh, T. 1960. 'The Paintings in the Tomb of Djehuty-hetep at Debeira', Kush 8, 25–44.

Säve-Söderbergh, T. 1963. 'The Tomb of the Prince of Teh-Khet, Amenemhet', Kush 11, 159–74.

Säve-Söderbergh, T. 1991. 'Teh-khet, the Cultural and Sociopolitical Structure of a Nubian Princedom in Tuthmoside Times', in Davies (ed.), 186–94.

Säve-Söderbergh, T. and L. Troy (eds) 1991. *New Kingdom Pharaonic Sites. The Finds and the Sites*. The Scandinavian Joint Expedition to Sudanese Nubia, vol. 5:2 and 3. Uppsala.

Säve-Söderbergh, T., G. Englund and H.-Å. Nordström 1981. *Late Nubian Cemeteries*. The Scandinavian Joint Expedition, vol. 6. Solna.

Sayce, A.H. 1909. 'A Greek inscription of a King (?) of Axum found at Meroe', *Proceedings of the Society of Biblical Archaeology* 31, 189–203, pl. XXIV.

Sayce, A.H. 1912. 'Second Interim Report on the Excavations at Meroe in Ethiopia. Part II – The Historical Results', *LAAA* 4, 53–65.

Sayce, A.H. and J. Garstang 1910. *Excavations at Meroe, Sudan, 1910. Guide to the Ninth Annual Exhibition of Antiquities Discovered*. London.

El-Sayed el-Bushra. 1971. 'Towns in the Sudan in the 18th and early 19th centuries', *SNR* LII, 63–70.

Schiff-Giorgini, M. 1966a. 'Sedeinga 1963–1965', *Kush* 14, 244–61.

Schiff-Giorgini, M. 1966b. 'Scavi di Sedeinga', *Levante* 12, 1–31 (and 1–19 in Arabic).

Schiff-Giorgini, M. 1971. 'Novita archeologiche a Soleb e Sedeinga', *Levante* 18, 5–29 (and 1–28 in Arabic).

Schiff-Giorgini, M., C. Robichon, and J. Leclant 1971. *Soleb II. Les nécropoles*. Florence.

Schmitz, F-J. 1978. *Amenophis I. Versuch einer Darstellung der Regierungszeit eines ägyptischen Herrschers der frühen 18. Dynastie. HÄB 6*.

Schneider, T. 1998. *Ausländer in Ägypten während des Mittleren Reiches und der Hyksoszeit. Teil 1, Die ausländischen Könige. Ägypten und altes Testament 42*. Wiesbaden.

Schön, W. and W. Holter 1988. 'Zum Gebrauch von Reib- und Mahlsteinen in der Ostsahara', *Archäologische Informationen* 11, 156–60.

Schoske, S. 1980, 'Krummschwert', *LdÄ* 3, 819–21.

Schuck, W. 1989. 'From lake to well: 5,000 years of settlement in Wadi Shaw (Northern Sudan)', in Krzyżaniak and Kobusiewicz (eds), 421–9.

Schulz, R. 1992. *Die Entwicklung und Bedeutung des kuboiden Statuentypus*, vols 1, 2. *HÄB*.

Scott, G. 1995. 'Go Down into Egypt: The Dawn of American Egyptology', in N. Thomas (ed.), *The American Discovery of Ancient Egypt*. Los Angeles, 37–48.

Seipel, W. (ed.) 2002. *Faras. Die Kathedrale aus dem Wüstensand*. Vienna.

Shaw, W.B.K. 1936. 'An expedition in the southern Libyan Desert', *Geographical Journal* 87, 193–221.

Shiner, J.L. 1968. 'The Khartoum Variant Industry', in Wendorf (ed.), 768–90.

Shiner, J.L. (ed.) 1971a. *The prehistory and geology of northern Sudan*. Report to the National Science Foundation. Grant GS 1192.

Shiner, J.L. 1971b. 'Pre-Ceramic sites', in Shiner *et al.* (eds) 1971b, 306–16.

Shiner, J.L., A.E. Marks and V. Chmielewsky (eds) 1971a. *The Prehistory and Geology of Northern Sudan, Part I*. Report to the National Science Foundation.

Shiner, J.L., A.E. Marks and V. Chmielewsky (eds) 1971b. *The Prehistory and Geology of Northern Sudan, Part II*. Report to the National Science Foundation.

Shinnie, P.L. 1955. *Excavations at Soba*. Sudan Antiquities Service Occasional Papers 3, Khartoum.

Shinnie, P.L. 1964. 'Excavations at Tanqasi, 1953', *Kush* 2, 66–85.

Shinnie, P.L. 1967. *Meroe: A Civilisation of the Sudan*. London.

Shinnie, P.L. 1974. 'Meroe in the Sudan', in G.R. Willey (ed.), *Archaeological Researches in Retrospect*. Cambridge, 237–65.

Shinnie, P.L. 1984. 'Excavations at Meroe 1974–1976', *Meroitica* 7, 498–504.

Shinnie, P.L. 1987. 'Meroe 1984/1985', *Nyame Akuma* 28, 48–9.

Shinnie, P.L. 1996. *Ancient Nubia*. London.

Shinnie, P.L. and J.R. Anderson (eds) 2004. 'The Capital of Kush 2.' *Meroitica* 20.

Shinnie, P.L. and R.J. Bradley 1980. 'The Capital of Kush 1', *Meroitica* 4.

Shinnie, P.L. and F.J. Kense 1982. 'Meroitic iron working', *Meroitica* 6, 17–28.

Shinnie, P.L. and J.H. Robertson 1993. 'The end of Meroe – a comment on the paper by Patrice Lenoble and Nigm el Din Mohamed Sharif', *Antiquity* 67, 895–8.

Shinnie, P.L and M. Shinnie 1978. *Debeira West. A Mediaeval Nubian Town*. Warminster.

Siiriäinen, A. 1984. 'Two Southern Sudanese Pottery traditions', *Norwegian Archaeological Review* 17 (1), 11–18.

Sijpesteijn, P and J. Zozaya 2003. 'Estela con inscripción islámica', in Berenguer *et al.*, 141, no. 44.

Simon, C. n.d. 'Etudes des ossements humains provenant des fouilles du Centre de Recherche sur le désert oriental en 1993', in K. Sadr, A. Castiglioni and G. Negro, *Interim Report on the Eastern Desert Research Centre's (CeRDO) Archaeological Activities 1989–1993*, 161–5.

Simpson, W.K. 1963. *Heka-nefer and the Dynastic Material from Toshka and Arminna*. New Haven–Philadelphia.

Smith, A.B. 1968. 'Adrar Bous and Karkarichinkat: Examples of Post-Palaeolithic Human Adaptation in the Saharan and Sahel Zones of West Africa', unpublished PhD Thesis, Berkeley.

Smith, H.S. 1976. *The Fortress of Buhen. The Inscriptions*. London.

Smith, L. 1998. 'Part II: The Post-Meroitic and Medieval Pottery', in Edwards, 178–93.

Smith, S.T. 2003. *Wretched Kush. Ethnic Identities in Egypt's Nubian Empire*. London–New York.

Soulé-Nan, J. 2002. *La Nubie des Pyramides*. Paris.

Sourouzian, H. 1991. 'A Bust of Amenophis II at the Kimbell Art Museum', *JARCE* 28, 55–74.

Sourouzian, H. 1994. 'Inventaire iconographique des statues en manteau jubilaire de l'époque thinite jusqu'à leur disparition sous Amenhotep III', in C. Berger, G. Clerc and N. Grimal (eds), *Hommages à Jean Leclant*. Vol. 1. *Études Pharaoniques*. Cairo, 499–530.

Spencer, P. 1997. *Amara West. I. The architectural report*. London.

Steindorff, G. 1935. *Aniba I*. Glückstadt–Hamburg.

Steindorff, G. 1937. *Aniba II*. Glückstadt–Hamburg.

Stemler, A. 1990. 'A scanning electron microscopic analysis of plant impressions in pottery from the sites of Kadero, El Zakiab, Um Direiwa and El Kadada', *ANM* 4, 87–105.

Sterner, J. and N. David (eds) 1992. *An African Commitment: Papers in honour of Peter Lewis Shinnie*. Calgary.

Stringer, C.B. 1979. 'A re-evaluation of the fossil human calvaria from Singa, Sudan', *Bulletin of the British Museum of Natural History (Geology)* 32, 77–83.

Sutton, J.E.G. 1974. 'The Aquatic Civilization of Middle Africa', *Journal of African History* 15, 527–46.

Thill, F. 2004, in press. 'La tombe 8 de la nécropole pharaonique de Sai', Acts of the 10th International Conference for Nubian Studies. La Sapienza University, Rome (September 2002).

Thomas, N. (ed.) 1995. *The American Discovery of Ancient Egypt*. Los Angeles.

Tiradritti, F. 1994. 'Préliminaires à un répertoire d'épigraphie Méroïtique (*REM*) suite (*)', *MNL* 25, 3–19.

Tixier, J. 1962. 'Le "Ténéréen" de l'Adrar Bous III', in H.-J. Hugot (ed.), *Missions Berliet Ténéré-Tchad*. Paris, 333–48.

Török, L. 1972. 'A special group of Meroitic property marks from the 1st to the 2nd centuries AD', *MNL* 10, 35–44.

Török, L. 1974. 'An archaeological note on the connections between the Meroitic and Ballana cultures', *Mélanges Wessetsky, Studia Aegyptiaca* I, 361–78.

Török, L. 1987a. *The Royal Crowns of Kush, A study in Middle Nile Valley regalia and iconography in the 1st millenia B.C. and A.D.*, BAR International Series 338. Oxford.

Török, L. 1987b. 'The Historical Background: Meroe, North and South', in T. Hägg (ed.), *Nubian Culture Past and Present. Sixth International Conference for Nubian Studies in Uppsala*. Uppsala, 139–229.

Török, L.1987c. 'Meroitic Painted Pottery: Problems of Chronology and Style', *BzS* 2, 75–106.

Török, L. 1988. *Late Antique Nubia. History and Archaeology of the Southern Neighbour of Egypt in the 4th–6th c. A.D. With a Preface by Sir Laurence Kirwan*. Antaeus 16. Budapest.

Török, L. 1989. 'Kush and the External World', *Meroitica* 10, 49–215.

Török, L. 1990. 'The Costume of the Ruler in Meroë. Remarks on its Origins and Significance', *ANM* 4, 151–202.

Török, L. 1995. 'The emergence of the Kingdom of Kush and her myth of the state in the first millennium BC', *CRIPEL* 17(1), 203–28.

Török, L. 1997a. *The Kingdom of Kush. Handbook of the Napatan–Meroitic Civilization*. Leiden–New York–Cologne.

Török, L. 1997b. *Meroe City, An Ancient African Capital. John Garstang's Excavations in the Sudan*. London.

Török, L. 1997c. *Economic Offices and Officials in Meroitic Nubia (A Study in Territorial Administration of the Late Meroitic Kingdom.). Studia Aegyptiaca* 5. Budapest.

Török, L. 1999. 'The End of Meroe', in Welsby (ed.), 133–56.

Török, L. 2002. *The Image of the Ordered World in Ancient Nubian Art. The construction of the Kushite Mind (800 BC– 300 AD). PÄ* 18.

Török, L. 2003. 'El reino de Meroe, 300 a.C.–350 d.C.', in Berenguer *et al.* (eds), 69–75.

Traunecker, C. 1987. 'Une pratique de magie populaire dans les temples de Karnak', in A. Roccati (ed.), *La magia in Egitto ai tempi dei faraoni*. Verona, 221–42.

Trigger, B.G. 1969a. 'The royal tombs at Qustul and Ballana and their Meroitic antecedents', *JEA* 55, 117–28.

Trigger, B.G. 1969b. 'The social significance of the diadems in the royal tombs at Ballana', *Journal of Near Eastern Studies* 28, 255–61.

Trigger, B. 1976. *Nubia under the Pharaohs*. London.

Troy, L. 1991. 'Other finds', in Säve-Söderbergh and Troy (eds), 51–181.

Tylecote, R.F. 1982. 'Metal working at Meroe, Sudan', *Meroitica* 6, 29–42.

Udal, J.O. 1998. *The Nile in Darkness. Conquest and Exploration 1505–1862*. Norwich.

Updegraff, R.T. 1978. *A study of the Blemmyes*. PhD thesis. Brandeis University.

Updegraff, R.T. 1988. 'The Blemmyes I: The Rise of the Blemmyes and the Roman Withdrawal from Nubia under Diocletian' (with additional remarks by L. Török), *ANRW* II, 10.1, 44–106.

Valbelle, D. 1990. 'L'égyptien à Kerma sous l'Ancien Empire', in Bonnet (ed.), 1990a, 95–7.

Valbelle, D. 1992. 'L'égyptien en Nubie', in Bonnet (ed.), 359–62.

Valbelle, D. 1994. 'La Restauration des Bronzes d'El-Hobagi', *Les Dossiers d'Archéologie* 196, 58.

Valbelle, D. 1995. 'Formes et expressions de l'Etat égyptien en Nubie au Nouvel Empire', VIIIe Conférence Internationale des Études Nubiennes, Lille (September 1994), *CRIPEL* 17/1, 167–74

Valbelle, D. 1998, in press. 'The cultural significance of iconographic and epigraphic data found in the kingdom of Kerma', in Kendall (ed.) forthcoming.

Valbelle, D. 1999. 'Kerma: les inscriptions', *Genava*, n.s., XLVII, 83–86.

Valbelle, D. 2001. 'Kerma: les inscriptions', *Genava*, n.s., XLIX, 229–34.

Valbelle, D. 2002, in press. 'Les temples du Nouvel Empire à Doukki Gel. Témoignages épigraphiques'. 10th International Conference for Nubian Studies. La Sapienza University, Rome (September 2002).

Valbelle, D. 2003a. 'Kerma, les inscriptions et la statuaire', *Genava*, n.s., LI, 291–300.

Valbelle, D. 2003b. 'L'Amon de Pnoubs', *RdE* 54, 191–217.

Vandersleyen, C. 1971. *Les Guerres D'Amosis*. Brussells.

Vandersleyen, C. 1995. *L'Égypte et la Vallée du Nil. Tome II: De la fin de l'Ancien Empire à la fin du Nouvel Empire*. Paris.

Vandier, J. 1958. *Manuel d'Archéologie Égyptienne*, III. Paris.

Vandier d'Abbadie, J. 1972. *Catalogue des objets de toilette égyptiens au Musée du Louvre*. Paris.

Van Moorsel, P., J. Jacquet and H. Schneider, 1975. *The Central Church of Adbullah Nirqi*. Leiden.

Van Neer, W. and H.-P. Uerpmann 1989. 'Palaeoecological significance of the Holocene Faunal Remains of the B.O.S.– Missions', in Kuper (ed.), 307–41.

Van Peer, P., R. Fullagar, S. Stokes, R. Bailey, F. Steenhoudt, A. Geerts, T. Vanderbeken, M. De Dapper and F. Geus 2003. 'The Early to Middle Stone Age Transition and the Emergence of Modern Human Behaviour at site 8-B-11, Sai Island, Sudan', *Journal of Human Evolution* 45, 187–93.

Vantini, G. 1975. *Oriental Sources Concerning Nubia*. Heidelberg–Warsaw.

Vantini, G. 1994. 'The Faras Mural of the Three Youths in the Fiery Furnace – Some Observations', in Bonnet (ed.), 255–7.

Vercoutter, J. 1956. 'New Egyptian Texts from the Sudan', *Kush* 4, 66–82.

Vercoutter, J. 1957. 'Hatshepsut, Tuthmosis III or Amenophis II? (Khartoum Museum statue no. 30)', *Kush* 5, 5–7

Vercoutter, J. 1958. 'Excavations at Sai 1955–7. A Preliminary Report', *Kush* 6, 144–69.

Vercoutter, J. 1959. 'The Gold of Kush', *Kush* 7, 120–53.

Vercoutter, J. 1962. 'Un palais des "candaces" contemporain d'Auguste (Fouilles à Wad-Ban-Naga, 1958–1960)', *Syria* 39, fasc. 3/4, 263–99.

Vercoutter, J. 1970. *Mirgissa I*. Paris.

Vercoutter, J. 1975. *Mirgissa II. Les Necropoles i*. Paris.

Vercoutter, J. 1976. *Mirgissa III. Les Necropoles ii*. Paris.

Vercoutter, J. 1979. 'La tombe méroïtique SA.S.2.T.1. (1) de Sai', *CRIPEL* 5, 210–36.

Vila, A. 1975. 'La necropole du plateau occidental (M X)', in Vercoutter, 134–7.

Vila, A. 1976. 'Les masques funeraires', in Vercoutter, 217, 219, fig. 24 (82), pl. H-T III, 17 (3).

Vila, A. 1980. *La nécropole de Missiminia. I. Les sépultures napatéennes. La prospection archéologique de la Vallée du Nil, au sud de la cataracte de Dal (Nubie Soudanaise), fasc. 12*. Paris.

Vincentelli, I. 1993. 'A discharge of clay sealings from the Natakamani Palace', *Kush* 16, 116–41.

Vincentelli, I. 1997. 'Two Field Seasons in the Napata Region', *Kush* 17, 162–85.

Vincentelli, I. 1999. 'Two New Kingdom Tombs at Napata', *Sudan & Nubia* 3, 30–38.

Vincentelli, I. 2002. 'An Early Napatan Cemetery in the Jebel Barkal Region', in Bács (ed.), 487–92.

Vincentelli, I. 2003, in press. 'Tomb 19 in the Cemetery of Hillat el-Arab', *ANM* 10.

Waddington G. and B. Hanbury 1822. *Journal of a Visit to Some Parts of Ethiopia*. London.

Ward, R. 1998. 'The Glass Vessels', in Welsby, 83–4.

Wardley, K and V. Davies, 1999. 'A new statue of the Kushite Period', *Sudan & Nubia* 3, 28–9, pls 14–17.

Watson, J. 2000. *Among the Copts*. Brighton.

Watson, O. 1985. *Persian Lustre Ware*. London–Boston.

Weeks, K. 1967. *The Classic Christian Townsite at Arminna West*. Newhaven–Philadelphia.

Wells, L.H. 1951. 'The fossil human skull from Singa', *The Pleistocene Fauna of Two Blue Nile Sites. Fossil Mammals of Africa* 2. London, 29–42.

Welsby, D.A. 1995. 'Catalogue of objects', in Phillips (ed.), 104–7, 111–12, 114–15.

Welsby, D.A. 1996. *The Kingdom of Kush. The Napatan and Meroitic Empires*. London.

Welsby, D.A. 1997a. 'Early Pottery in the Middle Nile Valley', in I. Freestone and D. Gaimster (eds), *Pottery in the Making*. London, 26–31.

Welsby, D.A. 1997b. 'The Northern Dongola Reach Survey: Excavations of Site O16, P1, P4, and P37', *Sudan & Nubia* 1, 2–10.

Welsby, D.A. 1998a. *Soba II. Renewed Excavations within the Metropolis of the Kingdom of Alwa in Central Sudan*. British Institute in Eastern Africa Memoir 15. London.

Welsby, D.A. 1998b. 'Survey and Excavations at Kawa, the 1997/8 Season', *Sudan & Nubia* 2, 15–20.

Welsby, D.A. (ed.) 1999a. *Recent Research in Kushite History and Archaeology*, BMOP 131.

Welsby, D.A. 1999b. 'Meroitic Soba', *Meroitica* 15, 663–77.

Welsby, D.A. 2000. 'The Kawa Excavation Project', *Sudan & Nubia* 4, 5–10.

Welsby, D.A. 2001a. 'An Early Kushite Shrine at Kawa in Northern Sudan', *Egyptian Archaeology* 19, 25–7.

Welsby, D.A. 2001b. 'Excavations within the Pharaonic and Kushite Site at Kawa and in its Hinterland, 2000–2001', *Sudan & Nubia* 5, 64–70.

Welsby, D.A. 2001c. 'Kushite Buildings at Kawa', *British Museum Studies in Ancient Egypt and Sudan* 1, 32–45. http://www.thebritish museum.ac.uk/BMSAES/issues.html#is1.

Welsby, D.A. 2001d. *Life on the Desert Edge.* Vols I, II. London.

Welsby, D.A. 2002. *The Medieval Kingdoms of Nubia. Pagans, Christians and Muslims along the Middle Nile.* London.

Welsby, D.A. 2003. 'The Amri to Kirbekan Survey: the 2002–2003 Season', *Sudan & Nubia* 7, 26–32.

Welsby, D.A. and C. Daniels 1991. *Soba Archaeological Research at a Medieval Capital on the Blue Nile.* British Institute in Eastern Africa Memoir 12. London.

Welsby, D. and V. Davies (eds) 2002. *Uncovering Ancient Sudan. A Decade of Discovery by the Sudan Archaeological Research Society.* London.

Welsby Sjoström, I. 2001a. 'The Pottery from the survey', in Welsby 2001d, vol. I, 230–348.

Welsby Sjoström, I. 2001b. 'Pottery from the Kerma Moyen graves at Site P37', in Welsby 2001d, vol. II, 349–54.

Wendorf, F. (ed.) 1968. *The Prehistory of Nubia.* Dallas.

Wendorf, F. and R. Schild 2001. *Holocene settlement of the Egyptian Sahara. The archaeology of Nabta Playa*, vol. 1. New York.

Wendorf, F., J.L. Shiner, A.E. Marks, J. De Heizelin, W. Chmielewski and R. Schild 1966. 'The 1965 Field Season of the Southern Methodist University', *Kush* 14, 16–24.

Wenig, S. (ed.) 1978a. *Africa in Antiquity. The Essays I.* New York.

Wenig, S. (ed.) 1978b. *Africa in Antiquity. The Exhibition II.* New York.

Wenig, S. 1994. 'Meroe Joint Excavations – Bericht über die Vorkampagne 1992', *MittSAG* 1, 15–18.

Wildung, D. (ed.) 1996. *Sudan: Antike Königreiche am Nil.* Munich.

Wildung, D. (ed.) 1997. *Sudan, Ancient Kingdoms of the Nile.* Paris–Munich. (*see also* French translation, *Soudan Royaumes sur le Nil.* Paris, 1997)

Wildung, D. 1998. 'Naga Project (Sudan) Egyptian Museum Berlin Preliminary Report 1995–1996, Seasons 1 and 2', *ANM* 8, 183–90.

Wildung, D. 1999. *Die Stadt in der Steppe – Grabungen des Ägyptischen Museums Berlin in Naga. Sudan.* Berlin.

Wildung, D. 2001. *Jahrbuch Preussischer Kulturbesitz* XXXVII.2000. Berlin, 150–51, igs 15, 16.

Wildung, D. 2002. *Jahrbuch der Berliner Museum. Neue Folge* 44, 1, 6–20, figs 3.2, 10, pls 1, 3, 8, 9.

Wildung, D. and K. Kroeper 2003. *Common aims. Sudanese–German co-operation in Archaeology.* Berlin.

Wilkinson, A. 1971. *Ancient Egyptian Jewellery.* London.

Williams, B. 1975. *Archaeology and Historical Problems of the Second Intermediate Period.* Dissertation, University of Chicgo. http:www-oi.uchicago.edu/OI/DEPT/RA/BBWIntro.html.

Williams, B.B. 1991a. *Noubadian X-Group remains from royal complexes in cemeteries Q and 219 and from private cemeteries, Q, R, V, W, B, J and M at Qustul and Ballana.* OINE 9. Chicago.

Williams, B.B. 1991b. 'A prospectus for exploring the historical essence of ancient Nubia', in Davies (ed.), 74–91.

Williams, B.B. 1992. *New Kingdom Remains from Cemeteries R, V, S, and W at Qustul and Cemetery K at Adindan.* OINE 6. Chicago.

Williams, B.B. 1994. *25th Dynasty and Napatan Remains at Qustul, Cemeteries W and V.* OINE 7. Chicago.

Wills, B. 1998. 'The Leather Sandals and Shoes', in Welsby, 182–5.

Wolf, P. 1996. 'Vorbericht über die Ausgrabungen am Tempel MJE 105', *MittSAG* 4, 28–43.

Wolf, P. 2002a. 'Ausgrabungen in Hamadab bei Meroe – Erste Kampagne 2001', *MittSAG* 13, 92–104.

Wolf, P. 2002b. 'Ausgrabungen in Hamadab bei Meroe – Zweite Kampagne 2002', *MittSAG* 13, 105–11.

Wolf, S. and H.-U. Onasch. 2003. 'Investigations in the so-called Royal Baths at Meroe, 1999', *Kush* 18, 191–203.

Yellin, J. 1978. *The Role and Iconography of Anubis in Meroitic Religion.* PhD thesis, Brandeis University.

Zach, M. 1988. 'Die gestempelte meroitische Keramik', *BzS* 3, 121–50.

Zäid, N. 2003. 'Pharaons noirs, La fin du mystère', *Le Figaro* magazine, Saturday 8 March, 44–9.

Zarattini, A. 1983. 'Bone tools and their cultural-economic implications', in Caneva (ed.), 243–51.

El-Zein, I.S. 1982. 'The Site of Sennar'. BA Honours dissertation (unpublished), Department of Archaeology, University of Khartoum.

El-Zein, I.S. 2000, forthcoming. *Islamic archaeology in the Sudan.* PhD dissertation, Department of Archaeology, University of Khartoum.

Żurawski, B. 1994a. 'Some Christian Foundation Deposits from the Region of Old Dongola', in Bonnet (ed.), 211–17.

Żurawski, B. 1994b. 'The Service Area on Kom H in Old Dongola', *Nubica* III/I, 318–60.

Żurawski, B. 1995. 'Old Dongola 1984–1993. The mortuary complex. A preliminary report. *ET* XVII, 327–64.

Żurawski, B. 1998. 'A Study of the Origins of Nubian and Ethiopian Horned Headgears of the Medieval Period', in *Äthiopien und seine Nachbarn, 3. wissenschaftliche Tagung des Orbis Æthiopicus, 25–29 September 1997*, Gdańsk, 121–35.

Żurawski, B. 1999. 'The Monastery on Kom H in Old Dongola. The monks' graves', *Nubica* IV/V, 201–53.

Żurawski, B. 2002a. 'Nubian Mortuary Complex of the Christian Period'. Paper presented at the 10th International Conference for Nubian Studies. La Sapienza University, Rome (September 2002).

Żurawski, B. 2002b. 'Survey and Excavations between Old Dongola and ez-Zuma', *Sudan & Nubia* 6, 73–85.

INDEX

ACKNOWLEDGEMENTS

The editors gratefully acknowledge the support of the many people, too numerous to name individually here, museums, institutions and authorities who contributed to the creation of the exhibition and catalogues and without whom they could not have been achieved.

The Embassy of the Republic of the Sudan in London
The British Embassy, Khartoum
Our colleagues from the National Corporation
 for Antiquities and Museums, Sudan
Our colleagues from the University of Khartoum
 and University of Dongola
Our many colleagues who supported and collaborated
 with us and who contributed text and photographs
 to the catalogues and exhibition
Our colleagues from many departments in the British
 Museum, and Laura Brockbank and staff of the
 British Museum Press, London
Rocco Ricci
Francoise Morasso
Harry Green
Johanna Stephenson
The Pagoulatos family and staff of the Acropole Hotel,
 Khartoum
Fundación 'la Caixa', Madrid
The Sudan Archaeological Research Society
The British Council, Khartoum
Pentagram Design Limited

Translations
Okasha el Daly
Fathi Khider
Caroline Rocheleau
Isabella Welsby Sjöström

PHOTOGRAPHIC ACKNOWLEDGEMENTS

All catalogue photography by Rocco Ricci © The British Museum, apart from the following cat. entries:
7 Photographer J.-F. Gout, Mission la Section Française de la Direction des Antiquités du Soudan (SFDAS), Sai 8-11-B
12–15 Courtesy of I. Caneva
32–41, 43–4 Photographer S. Marshall © The British Museum
20–23, 57, 59, 74, 77, 78, 81, 100–103, 127, 144, 147, 150, 152, 171, 172, 174, 179, 180, 182b, 183, 215, 216, 235, 240, 242, 243, 253, 272, 273, 281, 292, 294, 301 Photographer Rocco Ricci © The Sudan National Museum
110–16, 122–24 Courtesy of I. Vincentelli
166b–c Courtesy of D. Wildung, K. Kroeper
208, 279 © D.A. Welsby
304 Courtesy of C. Berger-el Naggar

Chronology by Harry Green © The British Museum
Maps by Claire Thorne © The British Museum
Title page photo of Nuri pyramids by W.V. Davies

Figure credits:
1 Philippa Pearce
3 Courtesy of F. Geus, SFDAS
4 © The Natural History Museum, London
6 F. Wendorf, courtesy of the Wendorf Collection, The British Museum
7 Courtesy of F. Geus, SFDAS
8–9 Courtesy of P. van Peer, Mission SFDAS, Sai 8-11-B

10–14 M. Honegger, courtesy of the Mission archéologique de l'Université de Genève à Kerma au Soudan
15 W.V. Davies
16 Arkell 1953, pl. 1.1-2
17 After Arkell 1953, pls 7, 9, 14, 30–31
19 ACACIA project, University of Cologne
20 D.A. Welsby
21–2 ACACIA project, University of Cologne
23 After Honegger 2001, 19, fig. 4
24 After Haaland 1987, 36, diagram 3
25–30 J. Reinold
31–4 L. Krzyżaniak
35–9 ACACIA project, University of Cologne
41 Watercolour by Alain Honegger
42–4 M. Honegger, courtesy of the Mission archéologique de l'Université de Genève à Kerma au Soudan
45–6 D. Berti, courtesy of the Mission archéologique de l'Université de Genève à Kerma au Soudan
47 M. Honegger, courtesy of the Mission archéologique de l'Université de Genève à Kerma au Soudan
48 Drawing by Alain Honegger
49, 51–3 D. Berti, courtesy of the Mission archéologique de l'Université de Genève à Kerma au Soudan
54 P. Kohler-Rummler, courtesy of the Mission archéologique de l'Université de Genève à Kerma au Soudan
55–8 D. Berti, courtesy of the Mission archéologique de l'Université de Genève à Kerma au Soudan
59 D. Bunand, courtesy of the Mission archéologique de l'Université de Genève à Kerma au Soudan
60 T. Kohler, M. Berti, courtesy of the Mission archéologique de l'Université de Genève à Kerma au Soudan
61–5 D. Berti, courtesy of the Mission archéologique de l'Université de Genève à Kerma au Soudan
66 D.A. Welsby
67. Welsby 2001d, 4, fig. 1.2
69–71 D. Valbelle
72–3 P. Rumhler
74–6 D. Valbelle
77 Drawing by M. Bundi, N. Favry
78 Drawing by F. Plojoux, N. Favry
79 Photograph Rocco Ricci © The British Museum
80 Lower portion of large stela from Amara West, Nubia. New Kingdom, early XIX Dynasty, reign of Sety I, year 4 (?). Brooklyn Museum of Art 39.424. Gift of the Egypt Exploration Society.
81 M. Berti, G. Deuber, A. Peillex, F. Plojoux
82 Courtesy of the Mission archéologique de l'Université de Genève à Kerma au Soudan
83 M. Berti, G. Deuber, A. Peillex, F. Pojoux
84–5 Courtesy of the Mission archéologique de l'Université de Genève à Kerma au Soudan
86 M. Berti, G. Deuber, A. Peillex, F. Plojoux
87 J. Vercoutter
88 J.-F. Gout
89 Drawing Azim 1975, 94
90 J. Vercoutter
91 Kite photography by B.N. Chagny, Mission SFDAS
92–3, 95–7 Angelo and Alfredo Castiglioni, courtesy of the Centro Richerche sul Deserto Orientale
98 EA 1770 © The British Museum
100–102 D.A. Welsby
103 EA 719 © The British Museum
104 EA 51446. © The British Museum
105–9 Courtesy of I. Vincentelli

110–13 D.A. Welsby
114–15 S. Roundtree, C. Thorne
116–17 D.A. Welsby
118 T. Kendall
119 D.A. Welsby
120 T. Kendall
121 After Shinnie and Bradley 1980 and the Meroe Joint Expedition, with additions by K. Grzymski
122 Kite photography by B.N. Chagny, Mission SFDAS 2001
123 K. Grzymski
124 Negative M.175 (Meroe excavations 1912 season, Site 194). © School of Archaeology, Classics & Egyptology, University of Liverpool
125 GR 1911.9-1.1 © The British Museum
126–9 D.A. Welsby
131–8 P. Lenoble
139–42 P. Lenoble
143 Drawing by R.-P. Dissaux
144–7 Courtesy of the Sudan Archaeological Research Society, Gabati Archive
149 After Welsby and Daniels 1991, 2, fig. 2
150 W.Y. Adams
151–2 B. Żurawski
153–8 Courtesy of W. Godlewski
159 Courtesy of S. Jakobielski
160–65 B. Żurawski
166–71 D.A. Welsby
173 Courtesy of the University of Durham, Sudan Archive, S.C. Dunn collection
174 D.A. Welsby
175 F. Caillaud, 1821, pl. 6
176 Courtesy of the University of Durham, Sudan Archive, S.C. Dunn collection
178 ACACIA project, University of Cologne
179 EA 55423 © The British Museum
180 EA 51449 © The British Museum
181 W.Y. Adams
183 F. Geus
184 Courtesy of H.-Å. Nördström, Scandinavian Joint Expedition to Sudanese Nubia, 1961
185 Courtesy of the Mission archéologique de l'Université de Genève à Kerma au Soudan
186–8 Kite photography by B.N. Chagny, Mission SFDAS
189 *The Royal Cemeteries of Kush, Volume III. Decorated Chapels of the Meroitic Pyramids at Meroë and Barkal.* By Suzanne E. Chapman, Department of Egyptian Art, Museum of Fine Arts with text by Dows Dunham, curator of Egyptian Art, Museum of Fine Arts. Letterpress printed by Harvard University Printing Office, Cambridge, MA, USA. Reproductions reprinted by Meriden Gravure Co., Meriden, Connecticut, USA. Bound by Arno Werner, Pittsfield, Mass, USA. © Museum of Fine Arts, Boston, Massachusettes, 1952. Library of Congress Catalogue Card number 51-9344. Photograph © 2004 Museum of Fine Arts, Boston
190 F.Ll. Griffith MSS. Faras negative 641. Faras, Grave 2923 © Griffith Institute, Oxford
191 F. Geus
192 B. Żurawski
193 D.A. Welsby
195 D.A. Welsby
196 D.A. Welsby
197 Elżbieta Kołosowska, courtesy of the Gdańsk Archaeological Mission
198 D.A. Welsby